32-Bit Windows Programming

Ben Ezzell

SAMS PUBLISHING

201 West 103rd Street
Indianapolis, Indiana 46290

Copyright © 1996 by Sams Publishing

FIRST EDITION

All rights reserved. No part of this book shall be reproduced, stored in a retrieval system, or transmitted by any means, electronic, mechanical, photocopying, recording, or otherwise, without written permission from the publisher. No patent liability is assumed with respect to the use of the information contained herein. Although every precaution has been taken in the preparation of this book, the publisher and author assume no responsibility for errors or omissions. Neither is any liability assumed for damages resulting from the use of the information contained herein. For information, address Sams Publishing, 201 W. 103rd St., Indianapolis, IN 46290.

International Standard Book Number: 0-672-30762-6

Library of Congress Catalog Card Number: 95-70102

99 98 97 96   4 3 2 1

Interpretation of the printing code: the rightmost double-digit number is the year of the book's printing; the rightmost single-digit, the number of the book's printing. For example, a printing code of 96-1 shows that the first printing of the book occurred in 1996.

Composed in AGaramond and MCPdigital by Macmillan Computer Publishing

Printed in the United States of America

All terms mentioned in this book that are known to be trademarks or service marks have been appropriately capitalized. Sams Publishing cannot attest to the accuracy of this information. Use of a term in this book should not be regarded as affecting the validity of any trademark or service mark.

Publisher	*Richard K. Swadley*
Acquisitions Manager	*Greg Wiegand*
Development Manager	*Dean Miller*
Managing Editor	*Cindy Morrow*
Marketing Manager	*Gregg Bushyeager*

Acquisitions Editor
Bradley L. Jones

Development Editor
Anthony Amico

Software Development Specialist
Cari Skaggs

Production Editor
Alice Martina Smith

Copy Editors
Susan Christophersen
Elaine Sands
Angie Trzepacz

Technical Reviewer
Ricardo Birmele
Greg Guntle

Editorial Coordinator
Bill Whitmer

Technical Edit Coordinator
Lynette Quinn

Formatter
Frank Sinclair

Editorial Assistants
Sharon Cox
Andi Richter
Rhonda Tinch-Mize

Cover Designer
Tim Amrhein

Book Designer
Alyssa Yesh

Production Team Supervisor
Brad Chinn

Production
*Mary Ann Abramson,
Mona Brown, Terrie Deemer,
Jason Hand, Mike Henry,
Louisa Kluznik, Casey Price
Brian-Kent Proffitt, Bobbi
Satterfield, Susan Van Ness,
Andrew Stone, Colleen
Williams*

Indexer
Cheryl Dietsch

Overview

		Introduction 1
Part I		Operating in a 32-Bit Environment 7
	1	Understanding the 32-Bit Environment 9
	2	Creating an MFC Application 27
	3	Moving from Windows 3.1 to WinNT/Win95 51
Part II		The User Interface 75
	4	Using Message Boxes 77
	5	Introducing AppStudio and Application Resources 107
	6	Using Menus, Toolbars, and Status Bars 121
	7	Designing Custom Dialog Boxes 141
	8	Customizing Dialog Boxes with Additional Controls 171
	9	Using Customized Controls 189
	10	Using Common Dialog Boxes, Fonts, and Colors 229
Part III		Graphics Operations 259
	11	Understanding Device Capabilities and Mapping Modes 261
	12	Working with Mapping Modes 275
	13	Working with Colors, Palettes, and Drawing Modes 297
	14	Using Drawing Tools 323
	15	Using Bitmaps and Screen Images 347
Part IV		Other Elements in Visual C++ 375
	16	Interfacing Data with Object Classes 377
	17	Understanding the ODBC Connection 397
	18	Using Simple OLE Operations 411
	19	More about MFC Classes 447
	20	Understanding DLLs and Derived Descendent Classes 497
	21	Tracing and Debugging Classes 517
		Index 525

Contents

Introduction 1
    A Change of Perspective 3
    How This Book Is Organized 3
    Conventions Used in This Book 4

Part I   Operating in a 32-Bit Environment   7

  1 Understanding the 32-Bit Environment 9
      Differences and Similarities 10
        The Hardware Environment 10
        The Software Environment 11
        Other Features in Win95/WinNT 17
      Tools for 32-Bit Application Development 17
        The Build Process 18
        Microsoft Developer Studio 20
      Summary 25

  2 Creating an MFC Application 27
      Selecting a File Type 28
      The New Project Dialog Box 30
        Step 1: Architecture 32
        Step 2: Database Support 33
        Step 3: OLE Support 35
        Step 4: Application Features 36
        Step 5: Source Code Options 39
        Step 6: Class Name Options 41
        New Project Information 42
      The Project Skeleton 42
      The ReadMe.TXT File 45
      The Skeletal Application 47
      Summary 50

  3 Moving from Windows 3.1 to WinNT/Win95 51
      Windows Programming Conventions 52
        Hungarian Notation 52
        Other Prefix Conventions 53
        Windows Data Types 54
        Windows Macros 55

        Windows Types and MFC Classes 55
            AFX and AppWizard Prefixes 57
        Changes in Message Handling with MFC 57
        Windows NT versus Windows 95 60
        Thunking 62
            Generic Thunks versus Universal Thunks 64
        From Clipboard to DDE to OLE2 65
        MFC Database Classes in OLE Controls 68
        INI Files versus the Registry 68
        Registry for OLE2 70
        Other New Features 70
            New User Interface Classes for Win95 71
            MAPI Support 71
            Networking Protocols: Windows Sockets 71
            MFC Migration Kit 72
        Summary 72

Part II   The User Interface   75

    4   **Using Message Boxes** **77**
        MessageBox Displays 78
            MessageBox Icons 80
            MessageBox Buttons 81
            MessageBox Responses 83
            MessageBox Modality 83
            AfxMessageBox Displays 85
        Dialog_1: A Message Box Demo 85
            Linking Menu Items to Class Methods 86
            Implementing a Member Function 89
            Reporting Button Selections 92
            The *CString* Class 95
            Creating a Custom Exit 98
        Source Code 100
        Summary 105

    5   **Introducing AppStudio and Application Resources** **107**
        Application Resource Types 108
            Accelerator Keys 109
            Dialog Boxes 109
            Font Resources 110

Image Resources 110
Menu Resources 110
String Tables 111
Version Information 111
Application Files and File Types 111
Resource File Types 112
Compiling and Linking Resources 113
Dynamic Link Libraries 114
Header Files 114
AppStudio 115
Managing Resources 116
Creating a New Resource 116
Editing a Resource as Binary Data 117
Importing and Exporting Resource Items 117
Using the Symbol Browser Dialog Box 118
Using the Set Includes Dialog Box 118
Summary 119

6 Using Menus, Toolbars, and Status Bars 121
A Starting Point 122
Menus and Menu Structures 122
Creating a Menu 123
Structured Menus 124
Menu Conventions and Formatting 126
Menu Limits 127
Toolbars 127
Creating Toolbar Bitmaps 127
Linking Messages and IDs to Toolbars 129
Tool Tips 134
Switching Toolbars 134
Switching Menus 136
Summary 139

7 Designing Custom Dialog Boxes 141
Dialog Box Design 141
Creating a Dialog Box 142
The Standard Controls Dialog Box 145
Assigning Member Variables 146
Initializing Member Variables 147

Retrieving Values from Dialog Box Controls 148
Closing the Dialog Box.. 148
Initializing Dialog Box Elements 150
Retrieving Dialog Box Results 150
Other Response Provisions 151
The Special Controls Dialog Box—WinNT Version 152
Scrollbar Event Messages 153
Closing the Special Controls Dialog Box 155
The Special Controls Dialog Box—Win95 Version 155
The Hotkey Control 156
The Progress Control 157
The Slider Control 159
The Spin Button Control 160
The Tree View Control 162
Summary 170

8 Customizing Dialog Boxes with Additional Controls 171
The Tab Control 171
Creating a Tab Control 172
Using Child Dialog Boxes 176
Using Additional *CTabCtrl* Methods 179
The Animation Control 181
Requirements for Animation Control AVIs 181
Creating a *CAnimateCtrl* Dialog Box 182
Notifying Parent Windows 185
Constructing AVI Files 185
A Useful AVI Control Class 186
Summary 187

9 Using Customized OCX Controls 189
Introducing OLE Custom Controls (OCX) 190
OCX Properties 190
OCX Methods 191
OCX Events 191
The *COleControl* Class... 191
Constructing an OLE 2 Custom Control (OCX) Using Visual C++
Version 2.x 191
Selecting Options 192
Modifying the Controls 194
Accepting Control Information 195

Constructing an OLE 2 Custom Control (OCX) Using Visual C++
  Version 4.0 196
    ControlWizard Files 199
    Optional ControlWizard Files 201
  Initializing the OCX Control 203
  Drawing the OCX Control 204
    The OCX *OnDraw* Function 204
  Mouse Messages in the OCX Control 208
  OCX Control Properties 210
    Adding a Property to an OCX Control 211
    Adding A New Property 212
  Defining the Property Page Dialog Box 217
    Using the Test Container Utility 219
  Testing the OCX Control 219
    Registering an OCX Control 219
    Testing an OCX Control 220
  Source Code 222
  Summary 226

10 Using Common Dialog Boxes, Fonts, and Colors 229
  Understanding Common Dialog Boxes and Data Types 230
  Selecting Fonts and Colors 230
    The *LOGFONT* Structure 232
    Initializing the *LOGFONT* Structure 235
  Choosing a Font 236
  Selecting Colors 241
  Using the File Open, Save, and Save As Dialog Boxes 244
    The *OPENFILENAME* Structure 245
    Filter Strings 249
    Multiple File Selection 250
  Using the Print Dialog Box 250
  Using the Find and Find/Replace Dialog Boxes 252
  Summary 256

Part III   Graphics Operations   259

11 Understanding Device Capabilities and Mapping Modes 261
  The *GetDeviceCaps* Function 262
  The *CreateIC* Function 262
  Driver Versions and Hardware Types 264

Video and Printer Resolutions 264
RASTERCAPS 268
TEXTCAPS 269
LINECAPS 271
CURVECAPS 271
POLYGONALCAPS 272
Summary 273

12 Working with Mapping Modes 275

Standard Mapping Modes 276
    The *SetMapMode* Function 277
Origins, Windows, and Viewports 283
The *SetWindowExt* and *SetViewportExt* Functions 285
Related Mode, Viewport, and Window Functions 286
    The *GetMapMode* Function 286
    Additional Window and Viewport Extent Functions 287
Window and Viewport Origins 288
The WinModes Demo 288
The Life Demo 292
    The Game of Life 293
    Forest Life 294
Summary 295

13 Working with Colors, Palettes, and Drawing Modes 297

Windows Palettes 298
Color Definitions 300
Standard Color Palettes 302
Color Composition 303
The Color1 Program 305
Three Formats for COLORREF Values 306
    Absolute RGB COLORREF Values 307
    Palette-Index COLORREF Values 307
    Palette-Relative COLORREF Values 307
Dithered Colors 308
Custom Colors 309
Trapping Keyboard Events 311
Other Keyboard Events 313
Trapping Mouse Events 314

	Mouse Messages in the Color2 Demo	316
	Colors to Grays	316
	Raster Drawing Operations (ROP2)	318
	The Color3 Demo Program	320
	Summary	322
14	**Using Drawing Tools**	**323**
	Shape and Line Tools	323
	Logical Pens	324
	Logical Brushes	327
	Standard Drawing Shapes	331
	The *LineTo* Function	332
	The *Rectangle* Function	333
	The *RoundRect* Function	334
	The *Ellipse* Function	334
	Arcs, Chords, and Pie Sections	335
	The Draw1 Demo Program	337
	Creating Pie Graphs	338
	The *Polygon* and *PolyPolygon* Functions	339
	Polygon Fill Modes	340
	PolyPolygon with Errors	341
	Other Drawing Functions	342
	The *PolyPolyline* Function	342
	The *PolyBezier* Function	343
	The *PolyDraw* Function	344
	Summary	345
15	**Using Bitmaps and Screen Images**	**347**
	BMP versus DIB	348
	DIB Image Files	348
	The *BITMAPINFOHEADER*	349
	BITMAPINFO versus *BITMAPCOREINFO*	350
	The DIB Bitmap Color Table	351
	DIB Image Data	351
	OS/2 versus Windows Images	351
	The Capture and Display of Screen Images	352
	The Capture Utility	352
	Setup and Cleanup Provisions	353

Further Initialization 354
The *OnImageDisplay* Procedure 354
Capturing Screen Information 355
Displaying the Clipboard 357
Writing a Bitmap File 358
Bitmap Compression Formats 362
BI_RLE4 for 16-Color Images 362
BI_RLE8 for 256-Color Images 364
Reading and Displaying Images 365
The *ReadDIBFile* API 365
The *SaveDIBFile* API 366
The *PaintDIB* API 367
Other Utility Functions in ImageAPI 370
The BmpImage Demo 371
Clipboard Operations in BmpImage 372
Summary 374

Part IV Other Elements in Visual C++ 375

16 Interfacing Data with Object Classes 377

File Access Methods 378
MFC File Capabilities 378
Opening a File Using *CFile* 380
Access and Share Flags 381
Serialization 382
Customizing Serialization 383
Implementing a Custom Serialization Method 384
The Insertion and Extraction Operators 385
The *CArchive* Class 386
Random File Access 388
The *CStdioFile* Class 389
CStdioFile Text Input 389
CStdioFile Text Output 390
The AARL_HAM Demo 390
Reading and Writing *CArchive* Records 392
Overloaded Operators 393
The *GetEntry* Function 394
The *UpdateData* Function 396
Summary 396

17 Understanding the ODBC Connection 397
Creating an ODBC Application 399
The Default Database 405
A Quick Review 405
The AARL3 Demo 405
Indirect Editing—An Idiosyncrasy 408
Summary 410

18 Using Simple OLE Operations 411
Integrating Applications 411
Clipboard Services 411
Dynamic Data Exchange 412
Metafiles 412
Object Linking and Embedding 412
Compound Documents 414
Linked versus Embedded Objects 414
Packages 415
OLE Verbs 416
OLE Containers versus OLE Servers 418
Creating an OLE Container 418
The *COle_cntrView* Class 420
The *COle_cntrCntrItem (COleClientItem)* Class 422
OLE Server Registration and Selection 423
The RegEdit Utility 423
Selecting a Server: *COleInsertDialog* 425
Registering an OLE Server 426
Creating an OLE Server 427
OLE Server Types 427
Using AppWizard to Create an OLE Server 429
The *COle_srvrSrvrItem* Class 431
The *CInPlaceFrame* Class 433
The *COle_srvrApp* Class 436
The *InitInstance* Method 436
The *COle_srvrView* Class 438
Server Application Menus 443
The OLE2View Utility 444
Summary 445

19 More about MFC Classes 447
MFC General Purpose Classes 448
CObject 449
File Classes 451
Coordinate Classes 451
CString 452
Time Classes 452
Debug and Utility Classes 453
MFC Visual Object Classes 454
CDC and *CDC*-Derived Classes 455
CGdiObject and *CGdiObject*-Derived Classes 456
CWnd and *CWnd*-Derived Classes 457
Associated Object Classes 466
MFC Application Architecture Classes 467
Associated Object Classes 470
Array Collections 471
MFC Collection Classes 471
List Collections 472
Map Collections 473
Wrapper Classes 474
User-Specified Base Class 475
Collection Class Helpers 475
MFC OLE2 Classes 476
User Client Items 482
User Server Items 483
Associated OLE Classes 484
MFC Database Classes 485
User Record Sets 486
MFC Windows Common Control Classes 487
MFC Windows Socket Classes 490
MFC DAO Classes 491
Summary 495

20 Understanding DLLs and Derived Descendant Classes 497
Dynamic Link Libraries 498
The Dynamic Linking Process 498
Creating a Dynamic Link Library 501
Calling a DLL 507
Testing a DLL During Development 509

	Deriving Descendant Classes 510
	Beginnings 510
	Reverting to Ancestral Methods 513
	Summary 515
21	**Tracing and Debugging Classes** **517**
	The Developer Studio Tool Set 517
	The Quick Watch Window 519
	The Call Stack Window 521
	Other Debug Options 522
	The Memory Window 523
	The Registers Window 523
	Summary 524
	Index **525**

Acknowledgments

Since, on the whole, books are not written by committees, the author remains the single person responsible for any and all errors that appear between the covers of his or her books. But it is only the responsibility for error that belongs solely to the author—any good book is written only with the assistance of at least one and usually several editors. Further, although editors as a group are long-suffering individuals entirely too accustomed to hearing screams of outrage from the authors whom they are attempting to present in the best possible form, a good editor is and always will be absolutely essential to the author's craft.

Having offered this convoluted caveat—and my peripatetically expressed gratitude—it seems appropriate to mention several of these sometimes maligned individuals by name. Ergo, my thanks to Tony Amico, Alice Martina Smith, Elaine Sands, Angie Trzepacz, and Susan Christophersen for their efforts and assistance in preparing this volume.

About the Author

An experienced programmer since the days when PCs were built at home with a soldering iron in hand, **Ben Ezzell** has written 17 computer books under a variety of operating systems ranging from DOS to OS/2 to Windows 3.1 and finally, WinNT and Win95. Ben is also completing his first non-technical book (publishers take note), a mystery entitled *Buddy, Can You Spare A Crime*, in which computers play a very minor role. When not writing or programming, Ben enjoys traveling—he speaks several languages very badly—international cuisine, and interesting people. Ben can be reached at `ezzell@sonic.net`. Criticisms, flames, and letter bombs, however, should be directed to `gatekeeper@anon.com`.

INTRODUCTION

For many (if not most) computer users, it may seem that the 16-bit environment has been around forever—or at least, ever since personal computers were invented. In many ways, this is not an inaccurate perspective because the earlier 8-bit (and 4-bit) operating systems were the parvenu of hobbyists and were obsolete long before the explosion in personal computer sales made PCs almost as common as TVs.

From a historical perspective, however (if you will permit a short two decades to be called *historical*), PCs have passed through several evolutionary stages. The current change from 16-bit to 32-bit environments is hardly unique—and not even particularly new. As a matter of fact, for many of us, this change is not only not new but long overdue.

Sixteen-bit operating systems took advantage of the capabilities of the 80286 CPUs and replaced earlier 8-bit OSes which, to put it bluntly, were slow, restricted, and cumbersome—but were also all that the earliest PC CPUs (8080s/8088s/Z80s) could handle. To be perfectly honest, these 8-bit systems weren't quite as restricted as their bus size would imply, but they were pretty limited and it didn't take much incentive for people to upgrade.

However, when the 80386 CPUs appeared (CPUs that could, potentially at least, handle 32-bit operations), there was no corresponding change in operating systems. Even though there was an immediate demand for these newer, faster chips (as well as a corresponding demand for memory beyond the 1M limit and for XMS and EMS drivers to access this memory), there was no new OS waiting in the wings to step in and allow the 386 systems to be used to their fullest potential.

Several new versions of DOS were released during the interim—by Microsoft, by Digital Research, and by IBM—but all of these, even after the 80486 CPU appeared, were 16-bit operating systems. For that matter, even OS/2 version 1.*x*, which was jointly developed by Microsoft and IBM, was a 16-bit OS (although OS/2 did support extended memory somewhat better than DOS).

Why this reluctance to change?

Because developers like Microsoft, Digital Research, and IBM considered compatibility with older PCs (meaning 8080/8088s as well as 80286 systems) more important than a totally new system that satisfied the relatively few individuals who could purchase the newest CPUs.

Of course, this is an oversimplification; during this period, a great deal of work was going into the development of several new operating system that would not maintain backward compatibility with earlier CPUs. These new OSes, however, were considerably more complex than earlier OSes. The complexity was not caused by 32-bit addressing and 32-bit instructions but because the new OSes were intended to be completely different in appearance, not just in function.

These differences in appearance, of course, are so familiar today that it is almost easier for us to ignore them than to recognize them. The most obvious difference is the change from a principally text-oriented environment to a graphics-oriented environment. The more important difference, however, is the less-visible but more pervasive change from a single-tasking environment to a multitasking system. We take for granted the existence of background processes—such as e-mail programs, print spoolers, and screen savers—as well as multiple primary processes—such as an editor, a compiler, and a net browser—opened and active simultaneously. Although some limited multitasking was possible (in a *very* limited sense) with DOS by using TSRs, these were always more notable for their conflicts and kludges than for their successes. Today, in true multitasking environments, we not only expect flawless performance of multiple processes, we become downright irate if any process interferes with another.

If creating a 32-bit OS had only been a matter of producing a new version of MS-DOS or PC DOS, the 16-bit world would have disappeared long ago.

The first real departure from the archaic 16-bit scene came about with the appearance of OS/2 version 2.0. For the first time, an operating system appeared that was not designed for backward compatibility At this time, however, OS/2 was no longer a joint project between IBM and Microsoft but was being developed and marketed by IBM alone.

Not that Microsoft was leaving the 32-bit market to IBM; Microsoft was readying their own entry in the form of Windows NT (version 3.1). Like OS/2, Windows NT no longer supported the older CPUs and was designed to execute only on 80386/80486 CPUs. Windows NT also required a minimum of 12M of RAM (16M or more was preferred).

Unfortunately, when Windows NT was released, RAM was still relatively expensive. In addition (perhaps partially because of marketing), Windows NT was viewed more as a server platform than an OS for the average user. This was a pity, because Windows NT—despite a few shortcomings—was vastly superior to the existing DOS/Windows 3.1 combination. Still, for most users, the differences between Windows 3.1 and Windows NT were a matter of perception: WinNT was perceived as expensive, with a demand for more elaborate equipment, and did not offer any real gain in performance.

At the same time, OS/2 version 2.0 found itself with a tough market to satisfy. In general, developers were satisfied with Windows 3.1 because their market was also happy with Windows 3.1. Developing separate product versions for OS/2 required more resources than most software developers could afford to allocate for what was viewed as a minor market. Although this may have been a matter of a self-fulfilling prophecy, OS/2 could not gain the major market share necessary to attract the application developers who would help to attract the major market share that would attract the developers...*ad infinitum*.

A Change of Perspective

Some observers see the 80586 (a.k.a. the Pentium) chip as responsible for the change in the market's perception; others credit Microsoft's marketing efforts to introduce the Windows 95 OS; still others hold that 16-bit OSes are dying because their inherent limitations cannot support the performance expectations of modern users; a few even suggest that the performance demands of video and CDs are driving the change to more responsive systems. Whatever the reasons—no single reason is sufficient explanation—a 32-bit operating system is no longer regarded as something needed by only a few, specialized users.

Today, general users are demanding more responsive systems and are looking to the new 32-bit operating systems to support faster, more powerful, larger, feature-bloated applications.

Whatever the reasons (and it may be simply that 32-bit is an idea whose time is finally now), 32-bit operating systems are the new standard. Therefore, the principal topic of this book is developing applications in a 32-bit environment.

How This Book Is Organized

In this book, we look at how 32-bit applications are written, how 32-bit applications differ from 16-bit applications, how services provided by 32-bit compilers can be used to simplify application development, and, not least, how the Microsoft Foundation Classes (MFCs) in their 32-bit versions can be used to develop applications.

In the first part of the book, we look at the characteristics of the 32-bit environment. We begin by comparing the Windows NT and Windows 95 environments, including the hardware and software requirements, the file and directory formats, and other options of these OS formats. Next, we look briefly at executing DOS applications (16-bit) in a 32-bit environment and then consider the problems of moving applications from the 16-bit Windows 3.1 environment to the 32-bit WinNT/Win95 environment, paying attention to obsolete functions, portable APIs, and the differences between these environments.

In Part II of this book, we look at designing the user interface. You begin by learning to create message boxes and other application resources; you also learn to use WinNT and Win95 common dialog resources. Second only to the concept behind your application, the user interface is probably the most important aspect of any application. The user interface is of paramount importance because it is the "face" your application presents to the user and is the basis on which your program is first judged.

In Part III, the topic turns to graphics operations. Working with graphics covers a range of topics from handling the device context and paint operations; to colors, palettes, and drawing tools; to metafiles; to typefaces; and also includes the Clipboard and ClipBook. Although perfectly sound applications have been and will continue to be written without relying on elaborate graphics, even a simple application can profit from the designer's understanding of how graphics work and how they can be incorporated to best advantage in application design.

Part IV examines the Microsoft Foundation Classes and how object-oriented programming practices and MFC classes can be used to create applications and to create custom classes. Although object-oriented programming (OOP) is not essential (and is certainly not the end-all and be-all of application development), OOP is a useful tool—if it is used well. When used badly, OOP can be a trial for both the programmer and the unfortunate individuals who later try to use the application.

This is a brief outline of the topics and the territory covered by this book. Of course, you are not required to proceed linearly though this book; you can skip around as you like, selecting topics and examples according to your interests and whims. Regardless of your path, you will find the contents of this book to be of value.

Conventions Used in This Book

A series of formatting conventions have been used in this book to clarify the presentation of material. Look for the following conventions in this book:

Tips indicate the author's simple and direct advice. Tips are formatted in the following manner:

> Tip: If you use Generic Thunks, you can isolate them in platform-specific DLLs. Alternatively, you can incorporate provisions that detect the platform at run time and call the APIs appropriate to the active platform.

Notes are pertinent comments about the text. Notes are formatted in the following manner:

> Note: There is no single, standard, version of Hungarian notation. Several versions have been published at different times and different groups have adopted different variations for different circumstances. However, because the "standards" are, first and foremost, intended as mnemonic devices, you can follow, alter, or modify the standards as you need.

Cautions let you know that something is very important to observe or do. Cautions are formatted in the following manner:

> Caution: The registry database can be accessed with the RegEdt32 (Registry Editor) utility in WinNT. It can be accessed with the RegEdit utility in Win95. Make modifications only with extreme care because errors or accidental changes can seriously disrupt system operations.

Sidebars are lengthier asides you can choose to read or skip. Although sidebars contain useful information, this information is not necessary to your understanding of the chapter. Sidebars have headings that give you an idea of what is discussed.

Program code, function and method names, flags, variables, and other pieces of special text are presented in a special monoface type: the `GetClientRect()` method. Lengthy samples of code are set apart from the rest of the text as they would appear on-screen in an editor. Code that has been generated by a Wizard is shown in a shaded box within the listing. For example, in the following listing, the first nine lines and the last line have been generated by the AppWizard; the middle eight lines were added manually:

```
/////////////////////////////////////////////////////////////////////////
// CHellowinView drawing

void CHellowinView::OnDraw(CDC* pDC)
{
    CHellowinDoc* pDoc = GetDocument();
    ASSERT_VALID(pDoc);

    // TODO: add draw code for native data here
    CString    csHello = "hello, world";
    CRect      cRect;

    GetClientRect( cRect );
    pDC->SetTextAlign( TA_BASELINE | TA_CENTER );
    pDC->SetTextColor( ::GetSysColor( COLOR_WINDOWTEXT ) );
    pDC->SetBkMode( TRANSPARENT );
    pDC->TextOut( ( cRect.right / 2 ), ( cRect.bottom / 2 ), csHello );
}
```

Hotkeys used by Visual C++ are made bold and underlined in this text. When you see menu commands or dialog box fields presented this way, you know you can press the Alt key and the bold, underlined letter to access that command or field without using the mouse. For example, when you see the **F**ile, **N**ew command in the text, you know you can press Alt+F, release the F key, and then press the N key to access that menu command. Of course, you can also use the mouse to access any menu command or dialog box option.

PART I

Operating in a 32-Bit Environment

Part I • Operating in a 32-Bit Environment

They say that all things come to he (or she) who waits—but sometimes it helps to scream and kick and raise Cain while you're waiting. At any rate, whether you're ready for this or not, 32-bit environments are here in the forms of WinNT and Win95. Many of us programmers feel this change has been long overdue. Of course, some of us have been so impatient for the change that we've switched to OS/2; others of us happily embraced WinNT way back when WinNT 3.1 was still in Beta releases. And more than a few of us have been running multiboot systems and switching back and forth between OSes at the drop of a bit—or byte.

Regardless of your existing preferences, the 16-bit OS is as much history as the earlier 8-bit (and even the 4-bit) OSes. And happily, the old limitations of 640K of addressable memory (and segment-offset addressing) can be forgotten along with 64K memory and data block limits and other burdensome restrictions imposed by archaic address limits.

Granted, changing from 16 bits to 32 bits means abandoning old habits and practices. But if you think of it as abandoning shackles and chains, maybe it won't be so hard to take.

Whatever your attitude, we begin by looking at what comprises a 32-bit environment—and particularly, how a 32-bit environment differs from a 16-bit system.

After looking at differences and similarities, we then turn to the topic of creating a 32-bit Windows application using Visual C++. (Both versions 2.*x* and 4.0 are used in this book, but we concentrate on the latter.) Because there are two 32-bit systems to consider—both Windows NT and Windows 95—we look at both and how the same application appears in each.

To conclude the first part of the book, Chapter 3 turns to moving applications from 16-bit Windows 3.1 to the 32-bit WinNT/Win95 systems. After all, odds are that you have existing applications written for Windows 3.1 that would benefit from conversion—and the conversions will probably be easier than you expect.

CHAPTER 1

Understanding the 32-Bit Environment

Until now, Windows has been an overlay, working on top of a DOS environment and extending the capabilities of DOS but also limited by DOS. Because no 32-bit versions of DOS have appeared, previous versions of Windows have been limited to 16-bit operations.

Both the Windows NT and Windows 95 systems, however, are operating systems in their own right. They replace DOS instead of relying on DOS and being limited by DOS. As such, both are true 32-bit operating systems...right?

Unfortunately, however much Microsoft wants you to believe this, the preceding statement is only three-quarters true for Windows 95.

The truth is that Windows NT is, indeed, a 32-bit operating system. WinNT contains support for older 16-bit applications and provides DOS boxes (virtual machines) in which 16-bit DOS applications can execute as if each were present on its own individual machine. Still, underlying everything, the system itself uses 32-bit instructions and handles 32-bit data, not 16-bit data. The old-style virtual machines are a convenient illusion but not the reality.

Windows 95 is a hybrid operating system. Although it appears to be a 32-bit system, it also contains and uses a great deal of old 16-bit code. Like WinNT, Win95 supports DOS boxes for DOS applications and also supports execution of older 16-bit Windows 3.1 applications. One difference, however, is that the virtual 16-bit machines provided by Win95 are not as secure as those provided by WinNT. For Win95, a second difference is that 32-bit applications are supported by 16-bit code in the operating system—exactly the reverse of WinNT, where 16-bit applications are executed by a full 32-bit operating system.

Still, for our purposes, we treat Windows 95 as if it were a true 32-bit OS.

Differences and Similarities

Although the 32-bit WinNT looks and acts essentially the same as the 16-bit Windows 3.*x* systems, Windows 95 has an entirely different appearance. WinNT's GUI environment (its desktop) follows the older, application-oriented format. Under WinNT, applications are opened and then used to load documents or other work files.

In contrast, Win95 is a document-oriented desktop. In Win95, you open documents, called *work files*, and expect the document to call the appropriate application. At least, this is the rational presented for the new look and feel incorporated in Windows 95.

Underneath both OSes, however, are more similarities than differences. These similarities are far more important—particularly from the programmer's viewpoint—than the cosmetic differences between the two graphic desktop formats.

The Hardware Environment

Both WinNT and Win95 require an 80386, 80486, or Pentium processor. Computers employing the older 8080/8086/80286 CPUs simply cannot execute either OS. According to specs, both systems are capable of operating with a minimum of 8M of RAM. However, using either OS on a 386 with 8M of memory is about the same as removing several spark plugs from your car: it may still run, but....

A more realistic minimum configuration is 12M of RAM; the faster and more powerful CPUs are strongly recommended over the 80386.

A second requirement is hard disk space. For either system, you need at least 100M of hard disk space for the WinNT or Win95 operating system, the SDK tools, examples, and a 20M paging (swap) file.

> **Note:** Windows NT is not limited to the Intel platform (that is, to Intel and Intel-compatible CPUs). WinNT also operates on the MIPS R4000 RISC and ALPHA CPUs. Aside from this acknowledgment, however, this book ignores the question of which platform the OS is operating on and concentrates on the code itself.

Disk Compression

If, after reading about disk-space requirements, your first instinct is to reach for a disk compression utility, *stop*. In the case of WinNT, few—if any—disk compression utilities work. The problem is simple: existing disk compression utilities are 16-bit drivers written to work with DOS; they are not compatible with non-DOS 32-bit operating systems. And neither WinNT nor Win95 are DOS dependent, even though both provide emulation to support DOS applications.

If you are using WinNT, keep in mind that WinNT supports two quite different file systems: the DOS-derived FAT file system and its own, newer NTFS file system. The NTFS file system, however, is not compatible with either DOS or Win95 and, in essence, is invisible to both. The Win95 version of the FAT file system—which supports long filenames—is compatible with WinNT's recognition of the FAT system.

On the other hand, Windows 95 (unlike WinNT) provides built-in support for DriveSpace and DoubleSpace disk compression and maintains compatibility with the corresponding DOS compression utilities.

> Caution: Some documentation suggests that Win95—but not WinNT—may be able to load 16-bit resident drivers such as screen savers, virus utilities, and 16-bit disk compression utilities during boot. This author, however, has not experimented in this area and does not plan such investigations. If you want to try this approach, proceed with caution.

> ### The Author's System
> Because you may be wondering, I used two development platforms while I wrote this book and the example programs. One has a 33/66 MHz 80486 CPU with 16M of RAM, two 540M IDE hard drives, and a Cirrus Logic graphics accelerator card. The second system uses a 90 MHz Pentium CPU with 32M of RAM, two 1-gigabyte hard drives, and a 2M Hercules graphics card.
>
> Performance was acceptable on both systems and showed little distinction between the two platforms.

The Software Environment

As you are probably already aware, the single biggest advantage of WinNT/Win95 over Windows 3.*x*—and the real reason why you are either changing or considering moving to these new OSes—is the change from a 16-bit to a 32-bit environment. As mentioned earlier in this chapter, neither Windows NT nor Windows 95 requires or uses the DOS operating system. Instead, each provides its own, new, 32-bit operating system. How you work with this 32-bit environment is the principle topic of this book and is far too extensive to cover in a few paragraphs.

Of course, the biggest change in moving from a 16-bit to a 32-bit system is simply the available address space: a whopping 4 (2^{32}) gigabyte upper limit on the size of addressable memory and also a limit on the size of an application. More immediately, this change means that all the memory in your system (as well as all the memory you are likely to be capable of installing in the foreseeable future) is addressable and accessible by a single 32-bit address.

> Note: The next step—to a 64-bit system—would raise the theoretical limit to 1.84×10^{19} bytes—a number that not only lacks a name but boggles the imagination.

Booting Multiple Systems

When you install it, Windows NT offers a dual-boot option you can use to select which operating system (DOS or WinNT) you want to load at boot time. You can also use the WinNT Flexboot utility with Win95 for a two-way or three-way boot selection. A few third-party boot loaders have appeared as well, some of which are compatible with OS/2 and with the Microsoft OS versions.

> Note: To use dual boot capabilities, WinNT must be installed before installing Win95. Refer to Win95's installation notes for further details.

The WinNT File Systems

DOS and Windows 3.*x* have always relied on the FAT (File Allocation Table) system; Win95 continues to use the 16-bit FAT system. But Windows NT offers a choice between the 16-bit file system and two new 32-bit file systems: NTFS (NT File System) and HPFS (Hewlett-Packard File System).

Both the NTFS and HPFS file structures are different from the traditional FAT system. Both offer several advantages but also have one major disadvantage.

The disadvantage (let's get the bad news over first) is that the NTFS and HPFS file systems are not compatible with DOS, Windows 3.*x*, or Windows 95. If you use the NTFS or HPFS formats—for a single drive or partition or for your entire system—these volumes are not accessible by any other operating systems. On the other hand, Windows NT does recognize and support FAT file structures without penalty.

NTFS Penalties

Using the NTFS file system has several drawbacks you should be aware of before you create an NTFS volume:

- If your boot drive (that is, the C drive) is an NTFS file system, you cannot use the Flexboot option because DOS systems boot only from the C drive and cannot boot from an NTFS drive. WinNT, on the other hand, is less restricted and can be booted from any partition; the NT boot partition may be FAT, NTFS, or HPFS.
- If you boot from a floppy disk, any NTFS drives are invisible. (No, you cannot boot WinNT from a floppy disk except for installation.)
- Many backup utilities continue to have problems with NTFS drives, even when WinNT drivers are used.

NTFS Advantages

In view of the problems listed in the preceding section, why use the 32-bit NTFS structure? Because there are advantages in using a 32-bit file system as well as problems:

- The NTFS file system provides support for long filenames, liberating you from the old 8-character-name/3-character-extension format. Long filenames permit you to assign descriptive names to files.
- NTFS supports backward compatibility and even generates old-style filenames from the new, long filenames.
- When files are written to removable media (such as floppy disks), FAT filenames (and the FAT file system) are automatically used.
- NTFS files are, reputedly, less susceptible to corruption by viruses and system bombs. This resistance to infection stems directly from the highly protected nature of the WinNT OS but, unfortunately, the same does not apply to the Win95 OS. However, because NTFS files can be recognized only by WinNT—unless some brighter-than-average virus hacker finds a workaround—NTFS files should remain relatively secure even if you are running both WinNT and the less-secure Win95.

The Win95 File System

Although it does not recognize the NTFS file system, Win95 does provide an extended version of the DOS FAT file system that simultaneously supports both the old 8-character-name/3-character-extension (8.3) filenames and the new, extended filenames. The Win95 file system also supports additional file date and time attributes.

In the Win95 file system, extended filenames can be up to 255 characters in length. Listing 1.1 shows a sample disk directory with both long filenames and their corresponding, old-style 8.3 filenames.

Listing 1.1. Volume in drive C is NEWFORMAT.

```
Volume Serial Number is 1F45-34B7
Directory of C:\NEWFORMAT

.            <DIR>         04-09-95  10:23p  .
..           <DIR>         04-09-95  10:23p  .
1995BA~1 WP1        5678   04-10-95  08:15a  1995 bank accounts.wp1
NEWSTY~1 TXT       78901   04-10-95  08:19a  newstyle long format filename.doc
DOC1     DOC      123456   04-10-95  08:19a  DOC1.DOC
         3 file(s)    208,035 bytes
         2 dir(s)  79,234,587 bytes free
```

> **Note:** The old-style 8.3 filenames appear at the left of this listing; on the right, the new, long filenames resemble comments and may contain punctuation and spaces. Each long filename, however, ends with the same dot-plus-three-character extension as the short filename. The third file in this listing, where no long filename was supplied, shows the 8.3 filename in both locations. Where a long filename has been used, the short 8.3 format name has been automatically generated by taking the first eight characters (excluding punctuation and spaces) from the long name.

If a drive or floppy disk containing long filenames is viewed outside of Win95 (using the DOS DIR command or something similar), only the old-style 8.3 filenames are visible. Also, when a file has been imported with only an 8.3-format filename, the old 8.3 filename is also the long filename. If you call the Win95 Explorer from the Start menu or click the My Computer button at the upper-left corner of your desktop, you open a directory window that offers a choice of four views (see Figure 1.1).

The first four views that are selected from the **V**iew menu are shown from top to bottom in Figure 1.1: Large Icons, Small Icons, List, and Details. In each of these views, the long filename format is shown; Details view also shows the file size, file type, and the date and time the file was last modified.

Alternatively, you can use the old, familiar WinFile.EXE (File Manager) utility (as shown at the bottom in Figure 1.1). This view does not display long filenames; only the conventional 8.3 DOS format filenames are visible although the file type icons are included both in the tree and in the file list.

In the File Manager view, also notice that, as is not true with DOS, some punctuation is permitted. However, when the filename is longer than eight characters, the filename is displayed as six characters followed by a tilde and a number (for example, *keepit~1.doc* is the short form for the original *Keep it simple, stupid.doc*).

Figure 1.1. *Five views of a Win95 directory.*

Large Icons view

Small Icons view

List view

Details view

File Manager view

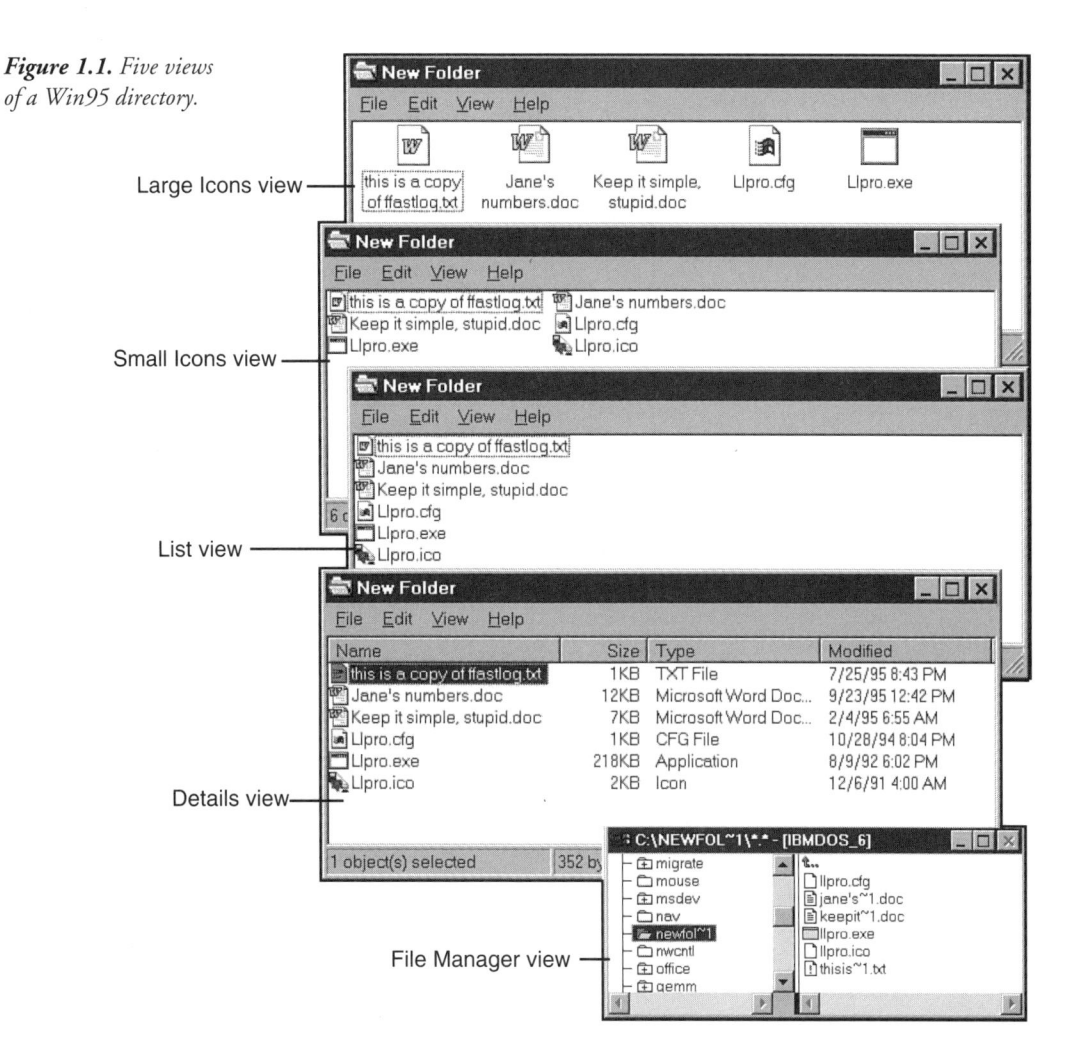

In addition to long filenames, Win95 maintains the following three date/time stamps for each file:

- ◆ The file creation date/time stamp
- ◆ The date/time the file was last modified
- ◆ The date/time the file was last opened

Figure 1.2 shows the Win95 Properties dialog box, with the new file attributes. (Display the Properties dialog box by right-clicking a file entry in the Explorer or desktop window and then select **P**roperties from the menu list.) In Figure 1.2, the complete (long format) filename appears at the top of the dialog box, followed by type, location, and size properties. Under this information are the DOS filename and the three time stamps: the creation time/date, the last time the file was modified, and the last time/date the file was accessed. The file attributes appear at the bottom of the dialog box.

Figure 1.2. The Properties dialog box shows the three time/date stamps maintained by Windows 95.

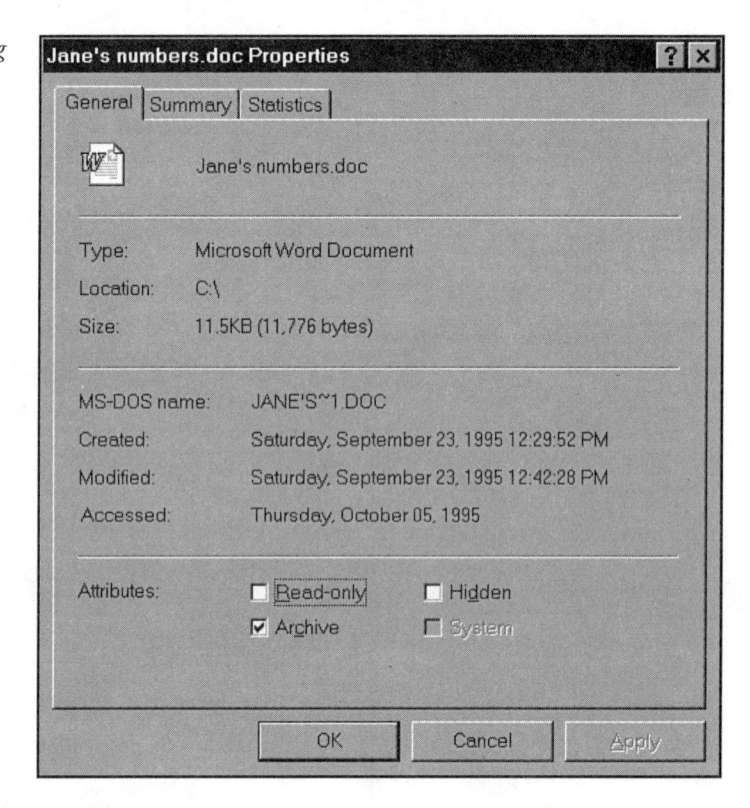

> **Note:** Existing DOS-based disk management utilities (such as disk defragmenters, disk bit editors, and some tape backup software) that manipulate the FAT table entries may destroy any long filename entries in the FAT. The corresponding old-style 8.3 filenames, however, are not affected.

32-Bit File Access

Thirty-two-bit file (disk) access should not be confused with the 32-bit NTFS file structure. Thirty-two-bit file operations work with both 16-bit FAT and 32-bit NTFS volumes when supported by a 32-bit disk controller card. Disk access is a measure of the rate of access to the drive, not the way the disk files are organized. The 32-bit disk access and file system used by Windows 95 are adapted directly from Windows for Workgroups 3.11.

Summary of NTFS and FAT

Unless you use WinNT exclusively, there is little point considering the NTFS format. NTFS is not supported by Windows 95, NTFS volumes are invisible to other operating systems, and NTFS offers no special advantages in most circumstances.

Chapter 1 • Understanding the 32-Bit Environment

Other Features in Win95/WinNT

Following is a list of some of the other features available in Windows NT and Windows 95:

- **Plug-and-Play.** As the new Plug-and-Play standards are implemented by peripheral (hardware) vendors, users should be able to install expansion cards, hard drives, modems, printers, video cards, and other components without having to reconfigure their computers.
- **Preemptive multitasking.** Both Win95 and WinNT support preemptive multitasking. This feature ensures that processes or threads cannot monopolize the CPU. In preemptive multitasking, individual applications, processes, and threads are summarily tabled to pass control and resources to other tasks for execution.
- **Multithreading.** Multithreading is a process designed primarily for multiprocessors, in which individual threads are allocated among the separate processors for execution. On a single-processor system, however, multithreading can still be used to execute separate threads (tasks) in a pseudo-simultaneous manner by using preemptive multitasking.
- **Graphical User Interface.** Although Windows NT continues to use the familiar Windows 3.*x* GUI design, Windows 95 has taken a new approach organized around hierarchical folders rather than directory structures (although directories and subdirectories are still used). The hierarchical folders are similar to the program groups used in earlier versions of Windows. Like directories, hierarchical folders can contain other folders as well as individual documents or applications.

  Note: A future release of WinNT is expected to implement the same GUI used by today's Win95.

- **Networking.** WinNT and Win95 both support peer-to-peer networking by using the facilities first made available in Windows 3.11 (Windows for Workgroups).
- **OLE (Object Linking and Embedding).** OLE 2.0 support allows applications to control embedded objects from the client application without actually launching the server application.

Tools for 32-Bit Application Development

Quite a variety of programming tools have been created for developing 32-bit applications, ranging from prototype generators (many of which purport to create source code as well) to the popular Visual Basic to various C/C++ compilers and object libraries. Each of these have their advocates and their critics. However, this book does not review or compare these several and separate development paths.

Instead, this book uses Microsoft's Visual C compiler and the Microsoft Foundation Classes (MFC), not because Visual C/C++ is inherently superior or otherwise exceptionally versatile but because Visual C/C++ is a recognized and popular choice used by many professional programmers.

The Visual C++ compiler package (a.k.a. the Visual Workbench or Developer Studio) is an integrated development environment that operates under Windows (Windows 3.*x*, Windows 95, or Windows NT). It combines into a single package the variety of tools necessary to develop Windows applications. The concept of an integrated development environment is nothing new: A decade or more past, Borland's Turbo Pascal, under DOS, featured an integrated editor/compiler; since that time, other integrated examples have been found in QuickC for Windows, Borland's C/C++, and the Programmer's Workbench. If, however, you're new to integrated development environments, a word of explanation may be in order.

An *integrated development environment* (IDE) is a compendium of interrelated development tools that make up a complete suite of services required to create an application project. For example, to create a Windows application—without an IDE—you need (at a minimum) a text editor to prepare source files; a paint utility to create icons, bitmaps, and cursor images; a compiler to process the source files and create OBJ files; a resource compiler to process the image and resource (RC) scripts; and a linker to combine all the preceding product files into an executable. Oh, yes—you'd also want something like an nmake manager to execute the compiler and linker instructions.

The Build Process

The build process is shown in Figure 1.3. Beginning at the top, the Visual Workbench editor (along with other tools) is used to create the C, CPP, and H source files. At the same time, the AppStudio is used to create various image and resource files as well as the RC resource script. (Because the resource script is an ASCII file, you can use the Visual Workbench editor, but this is not recommended as a general practice.)

> Note: The principle reason for editing an RC file directly (that is, as an ASCII file) occurs when an error prevents the AppStudio from loading the resource file. You may also want to use an ASCII editor to modify values or reorder elements in a dialog box. However, these and most other tasks are more easily accomplished using AppStudio—and with less chance of an operator error.

> Note: The DEF project definition file used with earlier versions of Visual C++ is no longer required and does not appear as an element in the compile/link process.

Once the source files are prepared, the compiler is invoked to use the application source files and the Windows runtime and class library include files to create OBJ object files.

Figure 1.3. *The complete build process.*

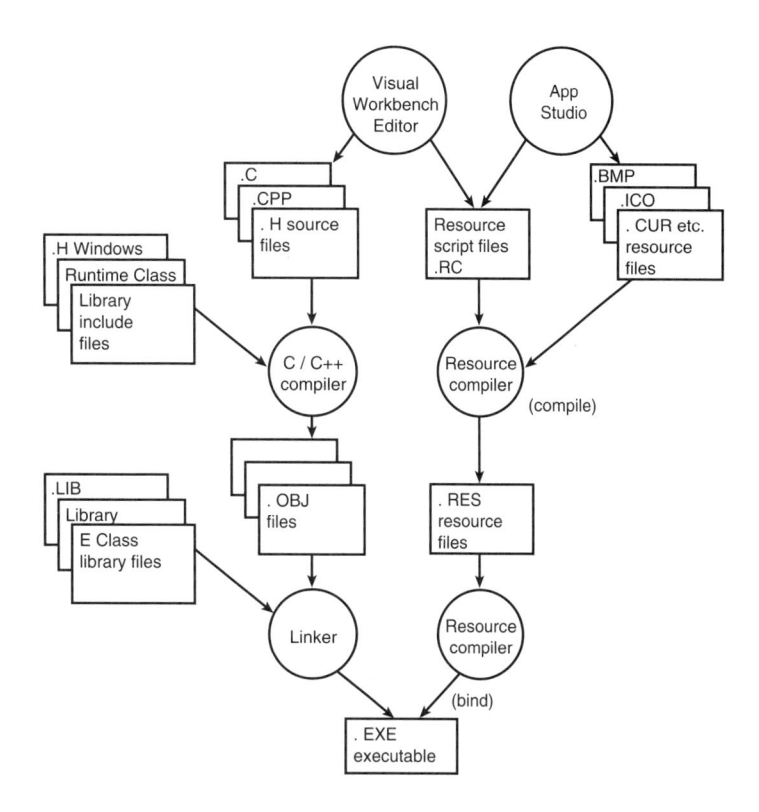

The resource script and source files must also be compiled, using the resource compiler, to produce a RES resource file. Although the Visual C++ resource compiler is an integral part of the IDE, it is also possible to use other resource editors or compilers external to the Visual Workbench. However, even if an application's resources are compiled externally, Visual C++ may—depending on the source file date/time stamps—still recompile the RES file during a build.

Next, the linker is invoked to link the OBJ files with the Windows runtime and class LIB library files. The result is the EXE executable.

However, the EXE executable is not ready to execute until the resource compiler is invoked a second time, this time to bind the RES resource file to the EXE. The result is a ready-to-execute EXE application (or, perhaps, a DLL dynamic link library).

Doing all this by hand from the command line, or by using a MAK script file and the nmake facility, is a lot of trouble (in addition, it's a time-consuming, tedious, and error-prone process). But if you have nothing better to do with your time, you can take this route.

Or you can use an IDE package such as the Microsoft Developer Studio.

Microsoft Developer Studio

The Developer Studio (or Visual Workbench) gathers all the tools and utilities mentioned in the preceding section—plus several others not mentioned—into a single package. As important, using an IDE such as the Developer Studio allows you to define a *project* and its interdependencies rather than on individual files; it also keeps you from spending much of your time trying to keep all the files straight.

The Developer Studio not only provides an editor you can use to write source code, it provides a smart editor that recognizes C/C++ keywords, handles alignment and block indentation, tracks matching braces, and offers online documentation for API and C/C++ functions. The Studio also handles a host of other useful tasks, including compiling and interactively debugging the application.

The Developer Studio also connects with the AppStudio to create, test, and maintain application resources; it connects with the AppWizard to create application skeletons; it connects to the ClassWizard to maintain object classes; it also connects to the Source Browser to assist in locating objects or functions across multiple source files.

Figure 1.4 shows the Microsoft Developer Studio. The menu bar across the top of the screen and the toolbar immediately below the menu offer options for most of the functions you need when creating an application. Below the toolbar, the Target box shows the application name and the type of executable currently selected for creation. (In this example, the application shown is BmpImage and the type of executable is a 32-bit debug version. Other options include a 16-bit debug or release version, a 16-bit or 32-bit dynamic link library for either debug or release, or a 32-bit release version of the executable.) The Target pull-down list, however, offers only two choices: Debug or Release; the selection of 16 or 32 bits and the choice between a dynamic link library and an executable are made elsewhere.

Figure 1.4. *The Microsoft Developer Studio.*

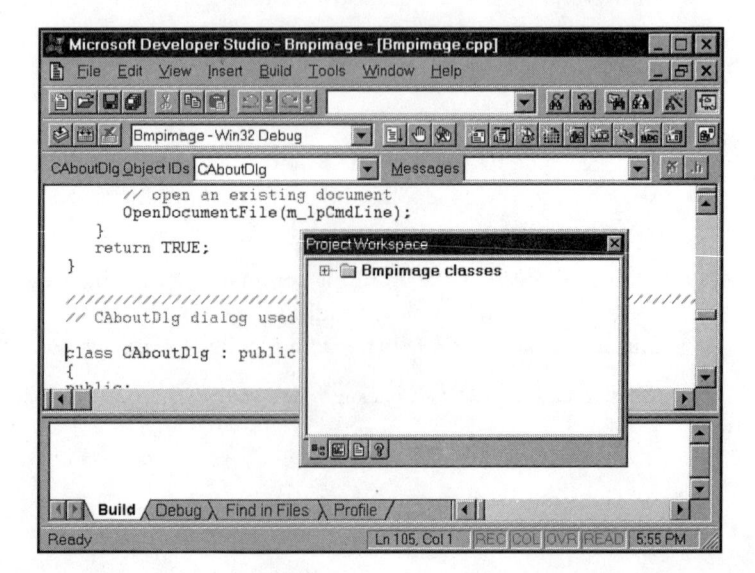

> Note: The selection of a 16-bit or 32-bit target is made when you create a project. If, however, you have installed only the 32-bit compiler, the 16-bit option does not appear. Likewise, if you have installed only the 16-bit compiler, the 32-bit option is not offered.
>
> When creating a project, you're offered a choice of three options: using the MFC AppWizard to create an executable or a dynamic link library; using the OLE ControlWizard to create an OLE custom control; or creating a conventional application, dynamic link library, console application, or static library.

The output window at the bottom of the Visual Workbench screen shows four tabs: Build, Debug, Find in Files, and Profile. These tabs offer four different views from output buffers maintained by the Developer Studio. Select the desired output buffer by clicking the appropriate tab.

During compiling and linking, the Build tab displays the compile/link progress. Too frequently, it also shows error or warning messages caused by flaws in the source files. Both errors and warnings are listed by filename, line number, and error number/error message. For compiler errors—but not link errors—clicking, or selecting, a warning or error message displays the corresponding line in the source file; double-clicking moves the focus from the Build pane to the edit window.

The Debug tab displays any output information generated during a debug execution of the application.

The Find in Files tab displays the results of the last Find in Files search (executed from the **F**ile menu).

The Profile tab displays profile information (performance measurements) generated during execution of the application.

Of these four tabs, the Build and Debug tabs are probably the most important; the Find in Files and Profile tabs are used relatively infrequently. Many other features in the Developer Studio are discussed later in this book.

The next section takes a look at the major components of the Developer Studio, beginning with the Project Workspace dialog box.

The Project Workspace Dialog Box

In earlier versions of Visual C++, the project files were displayed as a tree in a single window in the main display. With Visual C++ version 4.0, the previous display is replaced with the tabbed Project Workspace dialog box that displays the four trees (see Figure 1.5). The four windows are selected by the tabs at the bottom of the dialog window.

Figure 1.5. The Project Workspace tabbed dialog box.

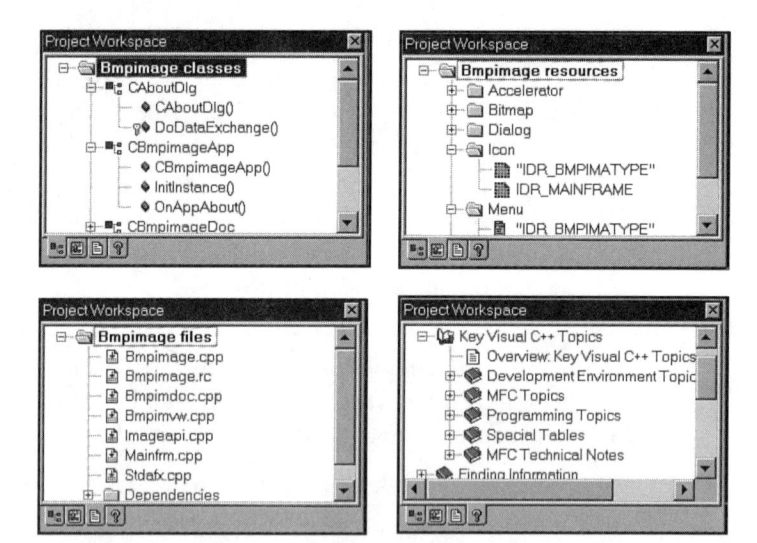

Beginning at the top-left corner of Figure 1.5, the first display shows the project classes. As with other tree lists, individual classes can be expanded to show member functions and member variables. The key icon next to a member function identifies a message mapped function. Click any individual function or variable to open the source file in which the member is defined and position the cursor on the member definition. You can also right-click an item to display an options menu with additional selections, including a Properties option that lists a function member's calling parameters or a variable member's type.

The second display at the top-right corner of Figure 1.5 shows the application resources in much the same format used to display the RC file under earlier versions of Microsoft Visual C++. Again, the resource tree can be expanded to show individual resource elements such as dialog boxes and menus; double-click an individual element to open the resource editor for the selected item. Right-click an element to display a menu with additional selections, including a Properties option that (where practical) shows a preview of the resource object.

The third display at the lower-left corner of Figure 1.5 lists the source files and dependencies for the project. Open individual files for editing by double-clicking the desired file. Right-click the file to see options to open or compile the source file. The Properties option displays information about the source file, a list of input sources, an output list, and a list of dependencies.

The last display at the lower-right corner of Figure 1.5 shows Help files and information sources for Visual C++ and the Microsoft Developer Studio. From here, you can access a wide variety of information and examples from the distribution CD-ROM.

> Note: Because these documentation files are located on the distribution CD-ROM instead of on your hard drive, Beta versions of Microsoft Visual C++ version 4.0 have exhibited aberrant behavior if you try to open projects without having the source CD in the CD player. Although these aberrations have been more annoying than serious and were limited to destroying existing MDP project files, it might be a good idea to back up your MDP project files—or to use a separate CD player to listen to Douglas's *Circle of Moons* while you're working. Hopefully, this problem will be corrected before the release of Microsoft Visual C++ version 4.0.

Instead of relying on printed and bound documentation, Visual C++ online help offers complete documentation not only for C/C++ functions but also for Windows API functions and Microsoft Foundation Classes. Additional help is also available in the AppStudio, AppWizard, and ClassWizard utilities.

Of all the features in Visual C++ and the Developer Studio, online help may be the most useful; give it a try.

The AppWizard

The AppWizard is a useful feature that generates a skeletal framework for a Windows application. This framework consists of minimalist application code and resources and also includes the basic classes and features you specify for the application. AppWizard is not, however, an application generator in the sense that Caseworks, WindowsMaker, or PowerBuilder are. The AppWizard-generated application is minimalist, even though the application code generated is fully functional and compiles and links as a complete executable.

On the other hand, the AppWizard skeleton is a good starting point and framework for building your own application. The AppWizard can save you a good deal of otherwise routine drudgery.

The ClassWizard

The ClassWizard utility operates both in the Visual Workbench and the AppStudio. The ClassWizard is convenient for managing application classes and creating prototypes, function bodies, message maps, member variables, and other links between the various source files.

The C/C++ Compiler

The Visual C++ compiler can handle both conventional C and object-oriented C++ source files. It uses the source file extension (C or CPP/CXX) to determine which form of compilation is appropriate. The compiler is ANSI-compliant but has extensions supporting the Microsoft Foundation Classes, templates, and exception processing.

The Linker

The linker is used to process OBJ files produced by the compiler, converting the OBJ files into executable code and linking library routines into the executable file.

The AppStudio Resource Editor

The AppStudio resource editor, discussed in detail in Chapter 5, "Introducing AppStudio and Application Resources," is used for all types of application resources. You can use the resource editor to edit bitmaps, icons, and cursor images; design dialog boxes; create menus and string tables; design toolbars; and connect resource elements to source code or class definitions. The AppStudio also supports VBX (Visual Basic) controls in dialog boxes.

The Resource Compiler

The resource compiler is invoked during the build process to compile RC resource scripts and individual resource image files to produce a binary RES resource. After an application has been linked, the resource compiler is invoked a second time to bind the compiled resources to the executable. If an application's resources are modified after building, they must be recompiled and a second bind must be performed to update the executable. The RES file may be re-bound to the EXE file without relinking the executable.

The Source Browser

In general, object-oriented applications can be very confusing to trace; Visual C++ applications are no exception. As you build your applications, you'll find that member variables and functions seem to take on a life of their own: You can't always remember where a function was defined or how many places a member variable is used. To help clear the confusion, enter the Source Browser (or just Browser, for short) from the **T**ools menu to locate functions and variables across multiple source files.

The Browser offers three views:

- **Definitions and References.** This view shows where a class, function, macro, type, or variable is defined and where it is used within a project.
- **Call Graph/Caller Graph.** This view shows a graphic map of all functions called by a selected function or all functions calling the selected function.
- **Derived Class/Base Class.** This view shows a graphic class hierarchy that displays the ancestor class for a selected class or the descendent classes derived from a selected class.

Summary

This opening chapter has taken a look at the two principal 32-bit environments: Windows 95 and Windows NT. The environments were contrasted with the 16-bit DOS environment and with each other. You looked at what a 32-bit OS is and received quick overviews of the NTFS file system (in WinNT) and the extended FAT file system (in Win95). The chapter also looked at the necessary hardware requirements and touched briefly on the use of disk compression utilities.

On the development side, the Visual C++ compiler and the Visual Workbench (version 2.*x*) or Developer Studio (version 4.0) were introduced—not as the only compiler available but as the compiler used throughout this book.

After discussing the major elements of the build process, a number of key features in the Visual Workbench and Developer Studio were introduced. Many of these features are covered in greater depth in later chapters.

Chapter 2, "Creating an MFC Application," continues with the creation of applications using Visual Workbench and the Developer Studio.

CHAPTER 2

Creating an MFC Application

The simplest way to explain how to create an application is simply to create one. Instead of presenting you with a finished creation—a *file accompli*, so to speak—this chapter begins with an application program that is simple in design. The purpose of the application in this chapter is to show how the application is created with the AppWizard rather than to use the application to demonstrate programming topics. If you prefer, the subject of this chapter is the compiler—the Visual Workbench or Developer Studio—rather than the program itself.

> ### Terminology
> Unfortunately, TLAs (Three Letter Acronyms) are unavoidable in today's programming world. In this book, TLAs are defined as they are introduced or in explanatory notes like this one.
>
> One TLA used extensively throughout this book is MFC—short for Microsoft Foundation Classes.

The first step, if you will forgive the obvious, is to load Visual C++—assuming, of course, that you have already installed Windows 95 or Windows NT and have also installed either version 2.*x* or 4.0 of Visual C++.

After loading Visual C++, you create a new project by clicking the **F**ile menu and selecting **N**ew (alternatively, press Ctrl+N)—do not use the New Source File button on the toolbar. The New dialog box appears (see Figure 2.1).

Figure 2.1. *Selecting a file type.*

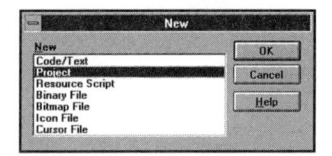

At the bottom of the **F**ile menu, notice the two blocks of files listed, numbered 1 through 8. The first four items are recently opened *source files*; the second four items (numbers 5 through 8) are the four most recently used *project files*. If this is your first project, you obviously won't see entries for previous projects or for previous source files. Also, once you have opened a project file, the source file names listed will reflect files opened for the active project.

> Note: The term *source file* refers to any ASCII file containing source code used by an application. This includes C, CPP, H, and RC program files and may also include files with other extensions.
>
> The term *project file* refers to a single file that contains a list of the source files required for a project and instructions for the compiler about how to compile and link these files.
>
> For Visual C++ version 2.*x*, the project file is normally a MAK (make) file (an ASCII file). Although a MAK file can be edited and revised using a text editor, it is certainly simpler in most cases to use the IDE to change compiler conditions and set compiler and linker flags.
>
> For Visual C++ version 4.0, the project file is normally an MDP (Microsoft Development Project) file; unlike a MAK file, the MDP file is not ASCII text and cannot be edited directly. Existing MAK project files can be opened by Visual C++ 4.0 and converted to MDP project files.

Selecting a File Type

The Visual C++ 2.0 New dialog box offers a selection of common file types used in Windows C++ applications. File types include those in the following chart.

File Type	Description
Code/Text (version 2.*x*) Text File (version 4.0)	Creates an ASCII text file; may be used for source code, header, script, and so on.
Project (version 2.*x*) Project Workspace (version 4.0)	Displays the New Project dialog box from which you select specifications before building a file that defines options for the new project.
Resource Script (version 2.*x*) Resource Template (version 4.0)	Creates a new resource script file. Application resources are discussed in Part II, "The User Interface," in Chapters 5, 6, and 7.
Binary File	Creates an empty binary data file with a raw-data editor. Can be used to create a new or edit an existing custom resource (at the binary level) in either hexadecimal or ASCII format.
Bitmap File	Calls the AppStudio bitmap resource editor.
Icon File	Calls the AppStudio icon resource editor.
Cursor File	Calls the AppStudio cursor resource editor.

Because our purpose is to create a new application project, select the Project option from the New dialog box. The New Project dialog box appears (see Figures 2.2 and 2.3).

Figure 2.2. *The New Project dialog box (version 2.x).*

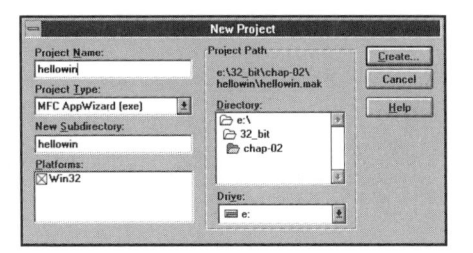

Figure 2.3. *The New Project Workspace dialog box (version 4.0).*

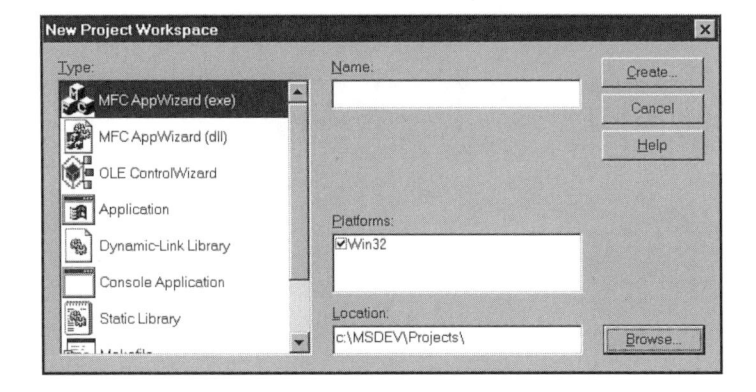

The New Project Dialog Box

The New Project dialog box is used to specify a drive, directory, and project name as well as the project type and the platform on which the application will execute.

Project options available on the New Project dialog box include the following:

Option	Description		
Project **N**ame	Project names can be up to eight characters long. The name you enter is automatically repeated as the directory name in the New **S**ubdirectory box as well as in the Project Path. This entry is also used to derive default names for application files and classes.		
Project **T**ype	Specifies the type of program built by the project. Click the arrow to see a list of the following choices:		
		MFC AppWizard (exe)	Default; an executable application
		MFC AppWizard (dll)	An MFC-based dynamic link library
		OLE ControlWizard (4.0 only)	An OLE custom control
		Application	A non-MFC application (executable)
		Dynamic Link Library	A non-MFC dynamic link library
		Console Application	A console (DOS-based or text-based) application
		Static Library	A static function library
		Makefile	Creates a conventional MAK (make) file

Option	Description	
	Custom AppWizard	Creates an AppWizard application using custom-defined steps and provisions
	When you select a non-AppWizard project type and click **C**reate in the New Project dialog box, the Project Files dialog box appears.	
Dri**v**e (version 2.*x*)	Specifies the drive on which the project directory will be created.	
Directory (version 2.*x*)	Specifies the directory in which the project directory will be created.	
	Use the Directory and Drives list boxes to select the drive and root directory in which the new project directory will be located.	
New **S**ubdirectory (version 2.*x*)	By default, a new subdirectory is created, using the project name, under the directory shown in the **D**irectory pane. You can specify a different subdirectory name if you want.	
	Note: If you select a non-AppWizard project type (such as Application or Static Library), the New **S**ubdirectory field remains blank and the existing directory is used for the project source files. You may, however, enter further directory specifications if you want.	
Location (version 4.0)	Replaces the Drive and Directory list boxes from version 2.0. Use the Browse button to display a Directory Selection dialog box from which you can choose a drive and directory on a local drive or select a network drive.	
Platforms	Shows the type of application to be created by the project. In this case, only the default Win32 target platform is available. To see additional target selections, you must install the cross-development edition of Visual C++.	

After you have specified the particulars of the project you want to create, select **C**reate to continue.

If you select an AppWizard executable project or a dynamic link library, the MFC AppWizard uses a series of six dialog boxes to guide you in setting up further conditions and options for your project skeleton. As you use these dialog boxes, you can select < **B**ack to return to the previous step, **N**ext > to move forward, or **F**inish to skip over the remaining dialog boxes (accepting the default settings) to complete the project initialization.

The six dialog boxes, or steps, are detailed in the following sections.

Step 1: Architecture

In Step 1, the MFC AppWizard prompts you for the architecture your application requires. After you select **C**reate from the New Project dialog box, the Step 1 (Architecture) dialog box appears (see Figure 2.4).

Figure 2.4. Use the MFC AppWizard—Step 1 dialog box to specify the architecture of your project.

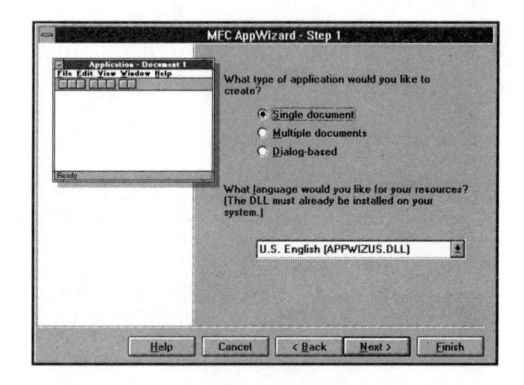

> **Note:** Both Visual C++ 2.x and 4.0 use the same AppWizard dialog boxes and steps to create an application skeleton.

From the Step 1 dialog box, select one of the following architecture options:

Option	Description
Single Document	The new application will use a single document interface, allowing the user to work with one document at a time. For an example, see the Notepad or Paint utility.
Multiple Documents (default)	The new application will use a multidocument interface, allowing the user to open one or more documents (each document has a separate window). For an example, see the File Manager, in which multiple file directories can be cascaded, tiled, iconized, or otherwise arranged independently.

Chapter 2 • Creating an MFC Application

Option	Description
Dialog-Based	The new application will be based on a dialog template from the application resources.
Language	The drop-down list displays all languages whose DLLs are installed on your system. Regardless of which type of application you select from the top part of the dialog box, you can specify the language of your resources with this option.

Select **N**ext > to continue or **F**inish to accept the remaining default selections and skip the next five dialog boxes.

Step 2: Database Support

In Step 2, the AppWizard allows you to select database support options for your application. When you select **N**ext > from the Step 1 dialog box, the Step 2 (Database Options) dialog box appears (see Figure 2.5).

Figure 2.5. *Use the MFC AppWizard—Step 2 dialog box to specify database options.*

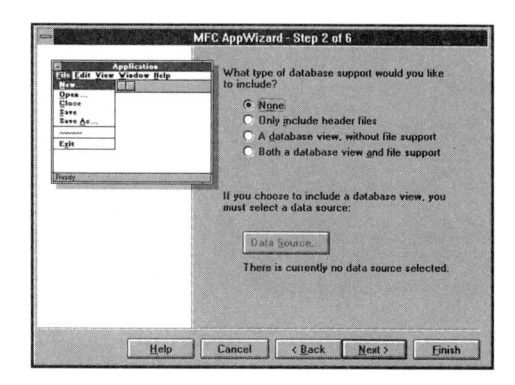

Select one of the following database options:

Option	Description
N**o**ne (default)	No database support is included.
Only **I**nclude Header Files	The new application includes the AFXDB.H header file, which offers basic database support. This header file allows the application to create recordsets and to examine and update records.

continues

Option	Description
A **D**atabase View, Without File Support	The new application includes a `CRecordView`-derived class as the view class and an associated `CRecordSet`-derived class. These classes provide the basis for a form-based application in which the record view is used to view and update recordsets through the provisions in the `CRecordSet`-derived class. Because most database applications operate on a record rather than file basis, the application does not support document serialization.
Both a Database View **a**nd File Support	The new application includes a `CRecordView`-derived class as the view class and an associated `CRecordSet`-derived class. These classes provide the basis for a form-based application in which the record view is used to view and update recordsets through the provisions in the `CRecordSet`-derived class. The new application also supports document serialization. *Note:* If you use a database view, you must specify the data source.
Data **S**ource	This command button displays the SQL Data Sources dialog box, from which you select the database files and tables to be used by the application. After you select a database and table, the AppWizard binds all columns of the table to the member variables of a `CRecordSet`-derived class. (SQL Data Sources are discussed further in Chapter 17, "Understanding the ODBC Connection.")

> Note: *View classes* in an AppWizard-developed application refer to the class (or classes) that handle the application's client window display (the visual portion of the application).
>
> The record view classes provide the functional interface between data records on the disk or network and their display and edit fields, commonly in a dialog box or a dialog-based view.

Select **N**ext > to continue or **F**inish to accept the remaining default selections and skip the next four dialog boxes.

Step 3: OLE Support

The MFC AppWizard then displays the Step 3 dialog box (OLE Support), shown in Figure 2.6. In Step 3, you are offered options to provide support for object linking and embedding in the new application.

Figure 2.6. Use the MFC AppWizard—Step 3 dialog box to specify OLE options.

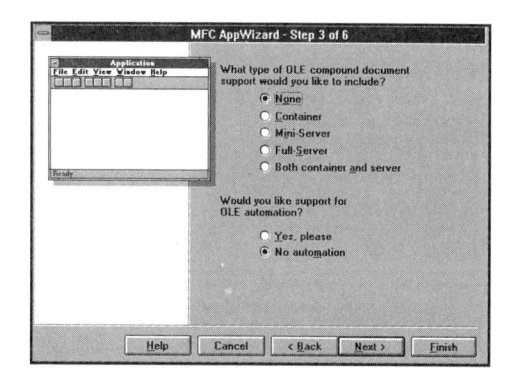

Select from the following OLE options:

Option	Description
None (default)	The new application will not support Object Linking and Embedding.
Container	The new application may contain linked and embedded objects.
M**i**ni-Server	The new application will have the capability of creating and managing compound document objects. A mini-server cannot run standalone; it only supports embedded items.
Full-**S**erver	The new application will have the capability of creating and managing compound document objects. A full server can run standalone and supports both linked and embedded items.
Both Container **a**nd Server	The new application will have both container and server capabilities.

In the second part of the Step 3 dialog box, select from the following OLE automation support options:

Option	Description
Yes, please	Allows the application to be accessed by other automation clients such as Excel.
No Auto**m**ation (default)	The application will not be accessible by other automation clients.

Select **N**ext > to continue or **F**inish to accept the remaining default selections and skip the next three dialog boxes.

Step 4: Application Features

The Step 4 AppWizard dialog box, shown in Figure 2.7, provides application feature options. You can include toolbar, status bar, and print options as well as context-sensitive help and 3D controls.

Figure 2.7. Use the MFC AppWizard—Step 4 dialog box to include special features in the new application.

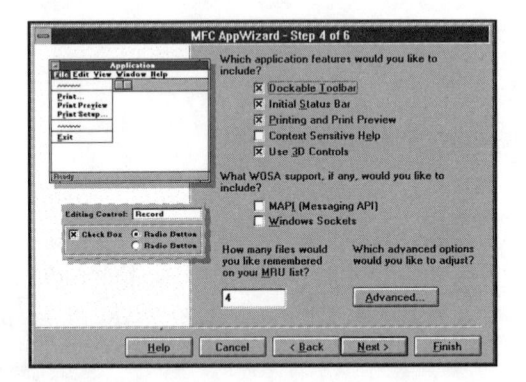

Select from the following application features:

Option	Description
Dockable **T**oolbar (default)	The toolbar generated by AppWizard will be dockable and can be placed along the application window's border. The toolbar contains buttons for creating a new document, opening and saving files, cutting, copying, pasting, and printing, as well as displaying the About dialog box and invoking Help.
Initial **S**tatus Bar (default)	The application will contain a status bar with automatic indicators for CAPS LOCK, NUM LOCK, and SCROLL LOCK; the status bar will also include a message line that displays help strings for menu commands and toolbar buttons. Options are also added to the **V**iew menu to display or hide the toolbar and status bar.

Option	Description
Printing and Print Preview (default)	AppWizard generates code to handle print, print setup, and print preview by calling member functions from the MFC CView class library. Options for these functions are also provided on the **F**ile menu.
Context Sensitive H**e**lp	AppWizard generates a set of help files used to provide context-sensitive help. ***Note:*** Help support also requires a help compiler such as RoboHELP from BlueSky or Microsoft's Help Author to prepare interactive hypertext document files.
Use **3**D Controls (default)	Visual interface controls in the application and dialog boxes will use 3D shading.
MAP**I** (Messaging API)	Adds provisions that allow an application to create, manipulate, transfer, and store mail messages.
Windows Sockets	Adds provisions that allow an application to communicate using TPC/IP networks. How Many Files Would You Like Remembered on Your **M**RU List specifies the number of files to be listed on the application's "most recently used" list. The default is 4.
Which Advanced Options Would You Like To Adjust	The **A**dvanced button opens the Advanced Options dialog box, which offers options for document template strings and frame characteristics. The Advanced Options dialog box is described in the following two sections.

Select **N**ext > to continue or **F**inish to accept the remaining default selections and skip the next two dialog boxes.

Advanced Options: Document Template Strings Tab

When you click the **A**dvanced button from the AppWizard Step 4 dialog box, you see the Advanced Options dialog box (see Figure 2.8). Use the Document Template Strings tab to specify identifying filenames and extensions for the application.

Figure 2.8. *Use the Document Template Strings tab from the Advanced Options dialog box to specify filenames and extensions.*

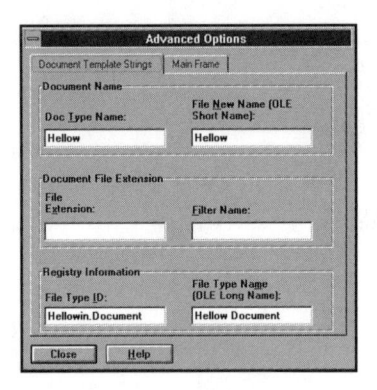

Use the text boxes to specify the following template string options:

Option	Description
Doc **T**ype Name	Filename associated with a class derived from the `CDocument` class. The default is the same as the application name.
File **N**ew Name	If multiple document templates are used, this is the name (OLE Short Name) that appears in the File New dialog box. For OLE server applications, this is the short name for the OLE object. The default is the same as the application name.
File E**x**tension	The file extension associated with a class derived from the `CDocument` class. This is any three-letter extension used for application-specific files (such as TXT for text files).
Filter Name	The filter string used in the Type list box in the Open and Save As dialog boxes. This consists of an identifying label for the application-specific file type such as text file or AppName Document.
File Type **I**D	The ID used to label the application document type in the system registry. By default, this takes the form AppName Document.
File Type Na**m**e	The name of the file type in system registry and used as the long (OLE Long Name) name for OLE objects if the application is an OLE server. By default, this takes the form AppName Document.

Select the Main Frame tab in the Advanced Options dialog box for further options; select Close to return to the AppWizard Step 5 dialog box.

Advanced Options: Main Frame Tab

The Main Frame tab in the Advanced Options dialog box is used to set the *caption string* (the title string that appears at the top of the application's frame) and styles for the application's main frame window (see Figure 2.9).

Figure 2.9. Use the Main Frame tab of the Advanced Options dialog box to specify the caption for the application's main frame window.

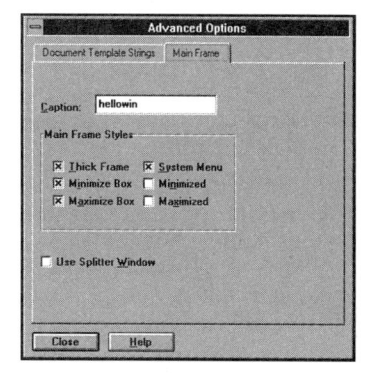

The frame options you can select are listed here:

Option	Description
Caption	The name appearing on the application's title bar. The default is the project name.
Thick Frame (default)	The window has a resizable border.
Minimize Box (default)	The application includes a minimize control.
Maximize Box (default)	The application includes a maximize control.
System Menu (default)	The application includes a system menu. This is the standard menu normally used by all applications; it includes File, Edit, View, and Help pull-down menus.
Minimized	The application opens as an icon (minimized).
Maximized	The application opens maximized (full screen).

Select the Document Template Strings tab for further options; select Close to return to the AppWizard Step 5 dialog box.

Step 5: Source Code Options

The AppWizard Step 5 dialog box lists source code options you can specify to control source code comments, makefile formats, and how the MFC library is linked. The Step 5 dialog box is shown in Figure 2.10.

Figure 2.10. *Use the MFC AppWizard—Step 5 dialog box to select the functionality you want to include in your application.*

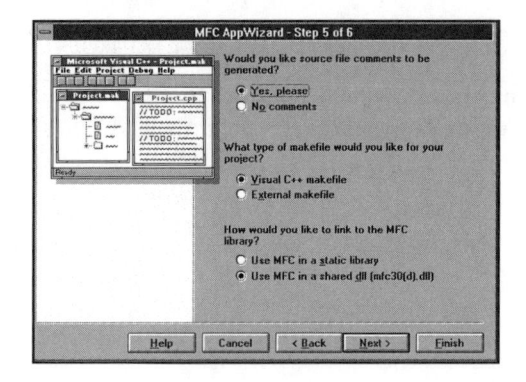

Following is a list of the source code comment options from which you can select:

Option	Description
Yes, Please (default)	AppWizard inserts comments in the generated source files, offering guidelines on adding functional code to the program.
N**o** Comments	No comments are added by AppWizard to the generated source files.

Following is a list of the available makefile options. These are provided only for Visual C++ 2.*x*; they do not appear in version 4.0, which uses a project file (MDP) instead of a make file (MAK).

Option (version 2.*x* only)	Description
Visual C++ makefile (default)	The AppWizard-generated project file is Visual C++ and NMAKE compatible.
E**x**ternal makefile	The AppWizard-generated NMAKE makefile uses the external project format but can be edited directly (that is, it is in ASCII text format).

The available MFC options are listed here:

Option	Description
Use MFC in a **S**tatic Library	Microsoft Foundation Classes are linked as a static library.
Use MFC in a Shared **D**LL (mfc30(d).dll) (default)	Microsoft Foundation Classes are linked as a shared DLL.

Select **N**ext > to continue or **F**inish to accept the remaining default selections and skip the next dialog box.

Step 6: Class Name Options

The AppWizard Step 6 dialog box allows you to change the new or base class names of the application. The Step 6 dialog box is shown in Figure 2.11.

Figure 2.11. Use the MFC AppWizard—Step 6 dialog box to change the class names of the application.

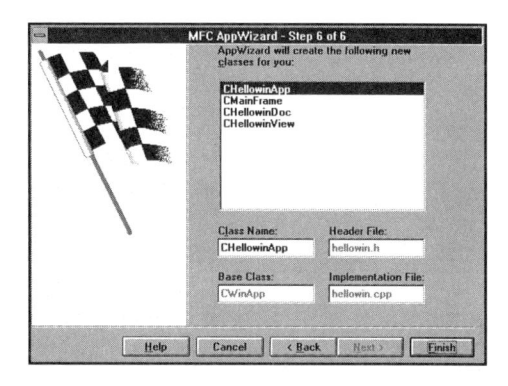

The class name options you can change are listed here:

Option	Description
New Classes	This list box lists the new classes that AppWizard will generate. There are commonly five classes: C*Name*App, CMainFrame, CChildFrame, C*Name*Doc, and C*Name*View (where *Name* is the name you have given the application).
Class Name	Shows the name of the class selected in the New Classes list box. Edit the class name here.
Base Class	The source class from which the selected class will be derived. The C*Name*View class offers a pull-down list with a choice of six view base classes with the CView class as the default. Other choices are CEditView, CListView, CRichEditView, CScrollView, and CTreeView. The base classes for other project classes cannot be changed.
Header File	The name of the header file for the selected class.
Implementation File	The name of the source file for the selected class.

Note: AppWizard does not allow the C*Name*App class header and implementation filenames to be edited. However, for the CMainFrame, CChildFrame, C*Name*Doc and C*Name*View classes, the header and implementation filenames can be revised as desired; by default, these filenames are derived from the class names.

Select Finish to continue. The New Project Information dialog box appears.

New Project Information

The New Project Information dialog box (see Figure 2.12) shows a summary of the selections you made in the six AppWizard dialog boxes.

Figure 2.12. The New Project Information dialog box summarizes the specifications you made in the six steps of the AppWizard.

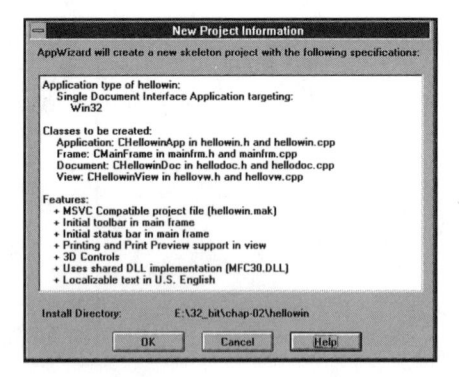

Select OK to continue and build the basic MFC application using the selections shown.

If you want to make modifications to the information shown in the New Project Information dialog box, select Cancel to return to the Step 6 dialog box. Then select < **B**ack until you see the dialog box that contains the options you want to change.

> Note: You cannot step back through AppWizard dialog boxes you skipped. When you click Cancel, you return to the last options dialog box you used.

The Project Skeleton

After you complete the six steps used by AppWizard (or even if you skipped one or more steps and accepted the default settings) and accept the summary shown in the New Project Information dialog box, the AppWizard actually creates the requested application *skeleton*. Up until now, if you backed out, canceled the AppWizard, or simply shut down Visual C++, nothing happened because all work has been done in memory: nothing has yet been written to the disk, no directories or files have been created, and all is transitory.

But once you accept the summarized specifications, AppWizard begins building the skeletal application framework, creates a subdirectory (if necessary), builds a series of source files, and defines application classes. When the AppWizard is done, it returns you to the Visual Workshop.

Figure 2.13 shows the HelloWin project—or project skeleton—created by AppWizard. The HelloWin project uses as its target the default, Win32 Debug, meaning that the application as it now stands would be complied with complete debug information so that you can step through the project and test and examine how the code actually operates.

Figure 2.13. *The project skeleton (in Developer Studio).*

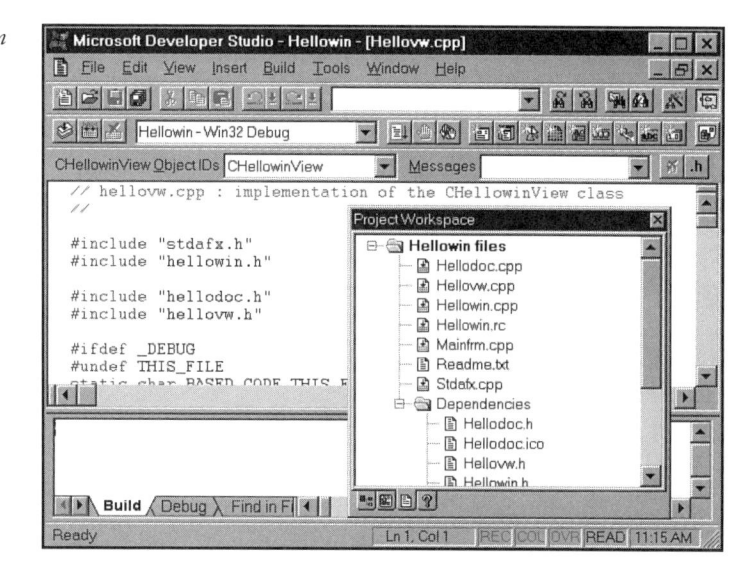

If you select a Win32 Release target (the only other target applicable to the current project), the application is compiled and linked without debug information; this option creates a more compact version of the executable.

Other Target Options		
The targets available for a build are determined in part by the compiler version(s) selected during installation. Target options can include the following:		
Target	*Description*
Win32 Debug	Debug build for WinNT/Win95 Intel platform, without Unicode support.
Win32 Release	Release build for WinNT/Win95 Intel platform, without Unicode support.
Win32 Unicode Debug	Debug build for WinNT Intel platform, with Unicode support.
Win32 Unicode Release	Release build for WinNT Intel platform, with Unicode support.
Win32 (MIPS) Debug	Debug build for WinNT MIPS platform, without Unicode support.
Win32 (MIPS) Release	Release build for WinNT MIPS platform, without Unicode support.

> Which options appear on your system depend on whether you're executing on WinNT or Win95, and also on which Visual C++ options have been installed. For example, if the Apple cross-compiler has been installed, the Apple Macintosh platform appears as an option. Under Win95, however, only the Win32 Debug and Win32 Release options appear.
>
> To change your configuration or to create a new configuration, select the **C**onfiguration option from the **B**uild menu.

As a general rule, all the example programs in this book are compiled as Win32 Debug targets. You may, however, use the source code and project files included on the disc that accompanies this book to recompile release versions as desired.

Figure 2.13 shows a tree structure for the application. Under the first branch are the principal CPP source files, the RC resource script, and a TXT ReadMe file. If you expand the Dependencies branch, you find the H header files, the ICO application icon image, the ToolBar.BMP image file (for the toolbar bitmaps), and HelloWin.RC2 (a second resource script used by AppWizard, ClassWizard, and AppStudio).

If, instead of using the Project Workspace window to view the project skeleton, you use File Manager to examine the disk directory, you see quite a different directory structure (see Figure 2.14).

Figure 2.14. *The application directory structure, seen from File Manager.*

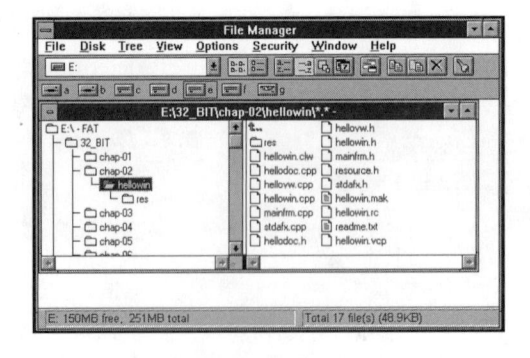

In the disk directory shown in Figure 2.14, most files are found in the ..\hellowin directory; however, you also find three image files (two ICO and one BMP file) and the RC2 script file in the ..\hellowin\res directory. The point is that the tree structure shown by Visual C++ is a logical tree; the structure shown by File Manager is a directory tree. The two do not necessarily match, nor are they required to match.

The ReadMe.TXT File

The ReadMe.TXT file was prepared by AppWizard and contains a list of all the source files and notes on the function of each. Although the ReadMe file may not answer all your questions about the skeleton application, it is worth reading for an overview of the files—and classes—provided by AppWizard.

The ReadMe.TXT file generated for HelloWin is shown in Listing 2.1.

Listing 2.1. The ReadMe.TXT file generated by AppWizard for the HelloWin sample application.

```
==============================================================================
        MICROSOFT FOUNDATION CLASS LIBRARY : HELLOWIN
==============================================================================


AppWizard has created this HELLOWIN application for you.  This application
not only demonstrates the basics of using the Microsoft Foundation Classes
but is also a starting point for writing your application.

This file contains a summary of what you will find in each of the files that
make up your HELLOWIN application.

HELLOWIN.MAK
    This project file is compatible with the Visual C++ development
        environment.
    It is also compatible with the NMAKE program provided with Visual C++.

    To build a debug version of the program from the MS-DOS prompt, type
nmake /f HELLOWIN.MAK CFG="Win32 Debug"
    or to build a release version of the program, type
nmake /f HELLOWIN.MAK CFG="Win32 Release"

Since we will be using the IDE - the Visual Workshop - instead of a command line
compiler, the preceding instructions are superfluous but do give you an idea of what
is happening within the IDE.

HELLOWIN.H
    This is the main header file for the application.  It includes other
        project specific headers (including RESOURCE.H) and declares the
        CHellowinApp application class.

HELLOWIN.CPP
    This is the main application source file that contains the application
        class CHellowinApp.

HELLOWIN.RC
    This is a listing of all of the Microsoft Windows resources that the
        program uses.  It includes the icons, bitmaps, and cursors that are stored
        in the RES subdirectory.  This file can be directly edited in the
        Visual C++ development environment.

RES\HELLOWIN.ICO
    This is an icon file, which is used as the application's icon.  This
        icon is included by the main resource file HELLOWIN.RC.
```

continues

Listing 2.1. continued

```
    RES\HELLOWIN.RC2
        This file contains resources that are not edited by the Visual C++
            development environment.  You should place all resources not
            editable by the resource editor in this file.

    HELLOWIN.CLW
        This file contains information used by ClassWizard to edit existing
            classes or add new classes.  ClassWizard also uses this file to store
            information needed to create and edit message maps and dialog data
            maps and to create prototype member functions.

/////////////////////////////////////////////////////////////////////////////

For the main frame window:

mainfrm.H, mainfrm.CPP
    These files contain the frame class CMainFrame, which is derived from
    CFrameWnd and controls all SDI frame features.

RES\TOOLBAR.BMP
    This bitmap file is used to create tiled images for the toolbar.
    The initial toolbar and status bar are constructed in the
    CMainFrame class.  Edit this toolbar bitmap along with the
    array in mainfrm.CPP to add more toolbar buttons.

/////////////////////////////////////////////////////////////////////////////

AppWizard creates one document type and one view:

hellodoc.H, hellodoc.CPP - the document
    These files contain your CHellowinDoc class.  Edit these files to
    add your special document data and to implement file saving and loading
    (via CHellowinDoc::Serialize).

hellovw.H, hellovw.CPP - the view of the document
    These files contain your CHellowinView class.
    CHellowinView objects are used to view CHellowinDoc objects.

/////////////////////////////////////////////////////////////////////////////
Other standard files:

STDAFX.H, STDAFX.CPP
    These files are used to build a precompiled header (PCH) file
    named HELLOWIN.PCH and a precompiled types file named STDAFX.OBJ.

RESOURCE.H
    This is the standard header file, which defines new resource IDs.
    Visual C++ reads and updates this file.

/////////////////////////////////////////////////////////////////////////////
Other notes:

AppWizard uses "TODO:" to indicate parts of the source code you
should add to or customize.

    /////////////////////////////////////////////////////////////////////////////
```

The Skeletal Application

The skeletal application generated by AppWizard is a complete set of source files; it will compile and run as-is. It requires no further changes to produce an executable application. Of course, the resulting application doesn't do much aside from appearing on-screen with a full menu, toolbar, status bar, and client window—but it does provide a good entry point for adding your own functional code without having to slog through all the background preparation common to most Windows applications.

In addition, because the purpose of HelloWin was to demonstrate how to create an application using AppWizard, the current application comes very close to satisfying our design requirements (creating a simple application that executes, displays a standard frame and window, and offers the default menu options). Still, simple elegance demands that the HelloWin application *do* something. You should add your own direct touch to the application, however simple it might be.

To give HelloWin a bit of substance, add the few lines of code shown in Listing 2.2 to the file HelloVW.CPP. The lines shown with a gray background were generated by AppWizard and have not been changed. The remaining lines (those without the gray background) were added to generate a simple message and to position the message in the center of the application's client window.

Listing 2.2. Changes made to the HelloVW.CPP file.

```
/////////////////////////////////////////////////////////////////////////////
// CHellowinView drawing

void CHellowinView::OnDraw(CDC* pDC)
{
   CHellowinDoc* pDoc = GetDocument();
   ASSERT_VALID(pDoc);

   // TODO: add draw code for native data here
   CString    csHello = "hello, world";
   CRect      cRect;

   GetClientRect( cRect );
   pDC->SetTextAlign( TA_BASELINE | TA_CENTER );
   pDC->SetTextColor( ::GetSysColor( COLOR_WINDOWTEXT ) );
   pDC->SetBkMode( TRANSPARENT );
   pDC->TextOut( ( cRect.right / 2 ), ( cRect.bottom / 2 ), csHello );
}
```

All that remains to do for the present example is to compile it—click the Build or Build All button in the Visual C++ toolbar—and to run it—click the Run button after the compile and link is finished. The resulting screen generated by HelloWin is shown in Figure 2.15.

Figure 2.15. *The screen displayed by the HelloWin application.*

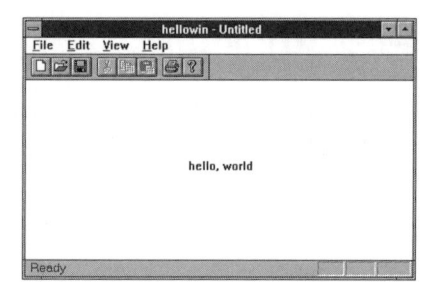

Although the example code may seem quite strange to those unfamiliar with object classes in general (or those unfamiliar with MFC classes in specific), a discussion of the whys and wherefores, of Hungarian notation, and of class instances is left for the following chapters.

And there you have it. A simple application built using the Microsoft Foundation Classes and the AppWizard to provide the skeleton for a complete Windows executable.

Toolbar Buttons in Visual C++

Visual C++ versions 2.*x* and 4.0 share similar toolbars with similar buttons but differ in the arrangement. Version 4.0 has added a number of buttons not found on the version 2.*x* toolbar.

Beginning at the top left of the toolbar, the New, Open, and Save file buttons appear on both versions of the toolbar; version 4.0 adds a fourth button for Save All files.

Continuing to the right, the Cut, Copy, and Paste buttons handle Clipboard operations.

Both versions of the toolbar provide Undo and Redo buttons, but version 4.0 adds multiple undo and multiple redo capabilities: the two down-arrow buttons display lists of actions for undo and redo.

In the version 2.*x* toolbar, the Find Next and Search buttons offer convenient search capabilities in your source files. Version 4.0, however, expands these features to include Find Next and Find Previous plus Find In Files and Search functions.

Chapter 2 • Creating an MFC Application   49

In the version 2.x toolbar, the Compile, Build, and Build All buttons are used to compile individual source files or to build or rebuild entire applications. The fourth Stop Build button is enabled only during a compile or build and is used to interrupt the operation.

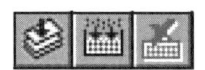

In the version 4.0 toolbar, the Compile and Build buttons are followed by the Stop Build button; the Build All button from version 2.0 has been dropped.

In the version 2.0 toolbar, the Run button is used to execute an application after it is compiled and linked. The Breakpoint button sets a breakpoint in the source file—at the instruction where the text cursor is positioned—to interrupt execution when this instruction is reached during execution. Clicking the Breakpoint button a second time clears a breakpoint on the selected instruction.

In the version 4.0 toolbar, the Run and Breakpoint buttons are supplemented by a third Clear All Breakpoints button, which removes all breakpoints in the current source file but does not affect breakpoints in other source files.

The ClassWizard button in the toolbars for both version 2.x and 4.0 is used to display the MFC ClassWizard dialog box.

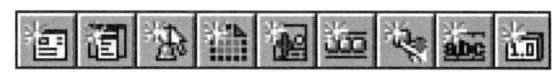

The remaining toolbar buttons are found only in Visual C++ version 4.0's Developer Platform. The block of nine buttons are used to add new resource elements to an application. These buttons are, from left to right, the Dialog, Menu, Cursor, Icon, Bitmap, Toolbar, Accelerator, String Table, and Version buttons.

The Component Gallery button calls the Component Gallery dialog box (new in version 4.0), which is used to organize reusable components such as OLE controls and other tools.

The Project Workspace button is used to show or hide the Project Workspace dialog box (new in version 4.0). Because the Project Workspace dialog box remains on top of other open windows, this button provides a convenient method of moving the dialog box out of the way when it isn't needed.

Summary

In this chapter, you've taken a walk through with AppWizard to set up a simple application. In the process, you've gained a bit of familiarity with Visual C++'s Visual Workbench or Developer Studio. As you have seen, AppWizard offers template creation for a wide variety of application features, including creating project MAK files and a project directory, selecting a single or multiple document interface, choosing database and OLE support, selecting default menu settings, and specifying support for status bars and toolbars. You've also had the opportunity to set the style characteristics for your Windows application, to register document types and default extensions, and to decide how the application source files are to be generated.

All in all, you've accomplished quite a lot—particularly when you consider that you did it all with a few clicks of the mouse. Granted, the finished application is only a skeleton (fleshing it out remains for you to do), but think about how much work you've already been saved.

Chapter 3 looks a bit further into how the Visual Workbench can simplify application design; it also looks at names, naming conventions, Hungarian notation, and how 32-bit applications differ from 16-bit applications. You also consider the differences between the current Windows APIs and the APIs from earlier versions.

CHAPTER 3

Moving from Windows 3.1 to WinNT/Win95

If this is not your first foray into the world of 32-bit programming—if, for example, you've already worked with WinNT—you're probably familiar with many (but not necessarily all) the topics discussed in this chapter. However, if you're new to 32-bit programming, there are a few surprises in store for you. And, if you're new to Windows programming entirely—well, look at it this way: there's a lot you won't have to unlearn.

Before returning to creating application examples, in this chapter, you look at the differences between 16-bit and 32-bit programming, at some of the conventions used in Windows programs, and at differences between conventional Windows programming and creating applications using the Microsoft Foundation Classes, the AppWizard, and the ClassWizard. And, last but not least, you look at a few of the differences between Windows NT and Windows 95.

None of these are brief topics (we will not attempt to cover all of these in detail in a single chapter). We will, however, give you a brief overview, or introduction, for each before later chapters return to these subjects in greater detail.

Perhaps you wonder whether it would make more sense to wait and introduce these topics individually when they can be covered in detail. If the topics could be isolated from one another, separate coverage *would* make more sense. But that is not the case. These topics are interrelated and entwined and cannot be conveniently separated for individual treatment. Some topics apply to both 16-bit and 32-bit programs, but there are also topics that separate 16-bit and 32-bit applications. And even though Windows NT and Windows 95 are both 32-bit systems, there are differences between them as well.

In the face of such conflicts, this chapter starts with one bit of common ground and looks at a few conventions that apply to both 16-bit and 32-bit programs.

Windows Programming Conventions

Over the years, many systems for naming variables have been tried. The common standard did not emerge because it was markedly superior to another. Popular consensus has made the variable-naming convention commonly referred to as *Hungarian notation*—so named for its developer, Microsoft programmer Charles Simonyi—the *de facto* standard.

> Note: There is no single, standard version of Hungarian notation. Several versions have been published at different times and different groups have adopted different variations for different circumstances. However, because the "standards" are, first and foremost, intended as mnemonic devices, you can follow, alter, or modify the standards as you need.

Hungarian Notation

Hungarian notation suggests that variable names should begin with one or more lowercase letters that identify the variable type. The next letter following the type identifier is commonly capitalized.

As a variation, type definitions use the same prefix as type identifiers except that type definition names commonly appear in all capitals.

For example, a variable `iNum` is self-identified as an integer; the variable `hWnd` identifies itself as a handle to (we can assume) an application window; the variable `lpszString` is read as a long pointer to a NULL-terminated string. Table 3.1 lists the more common Hungarian notation conventions.

Table 3.1. Hungarian notation conventions.

Prefix	Data Type	Example
b	Boolean	bIsPresent, bValid
by	byte, unsigned char	byFlag, byBlock
ch	char	chArray, chText

Prefix	Data Type	Example
c	class	`cString`, `cMain` (object class instances)
cs	CString	`csName`, `csLabel` (CString object instances)
cx/cy	short	`cxWnd`, `cyPos` (commonly used for coordinates)
dw	DWORD	`dwFlags` (double word or unsigned long)
fn	function	`fnCallback`
h	handle	`hWnd`, `hDlg`, `hBrush`
i	int	`iCount`, `iNum`
lp	far pointer	`lpPtr` (obsolete, with 32 bits, all pointers are near)
n	unsigned int	`nMax`, `nLimit`
p	pointer	`pszString` (pointer to NULL-terminated string)
s	string	`sName` (not commonly used)
sz	ASCIIZ string	`szName` (NULL-terminated string array—ASCII Zero terminated)
v	void	`vPointer`
w	WORD	`wVal`, `wArrVal` (same as unsigned int)
x/y	coordinates	`xPos`, `ySize` (usually short, may be signed or unsigned)

Other Prefix Conventions

In addition to the prefixes used in Hungarian notation, several prefixes are used by the Windows Application Frameworks (AFX) and the MFC object classes. These prefixes are listed in Table 3.2.

Table 3.2. AFX and MFC prefixes.

Prefix	Type	Example
C	class or structure	`CDocument`, `CString`
m_	class member variable	`m_nVal`, `m_bFlag`
Afx	application framework public function	`AfxGetMainWnd()`
afx	application framework public variable	`afxDump`
_Afx	application framework internal function	`_AfxGetPtrFromFarPtr()`
_afx	application framework internal variable	`_afxExLink`
AFX_	application framework internal structure	`AFX_CMDHANDLER`
AFX_ID	application framework internal identifier	`AFX_ID_PREVIEW_PRINT`

Of this group of prefixes, only two—the C class prefix and the m_ member variable—will see much use in your own code. The rest are principally used within MFC/Windows libraries. But even if you don't use them directly, you should still be able to recognize them when you find yourself tracing class ancestry into an MFC library.

Windows Data Types

All systems, at some level or another, define basic data types used to create data elements, to define structures, to determine how data is exchanged between procedures, and, of course, to determine how data is stored, retrieved, and displayed. Of course, you know all this. After all, you've been using data elements and data types since you wrote your first program, right?

Well...there are changes. For one, although Windows defines a number of data types, several of these are quite different from their original, 16-bit counterparts—and the differences are more than minor. Table 3.3 lists the changes among data types in the different versions of Windows.

Table 3.3. Windows data types and how they differ.

Data Type	Windows 3.x	WinNT/Win 95	Notes
BOOL	16-bit int	32-bit int	changed
BYTE	8-bits	8-bits	unchanged
WORD	16-bits	16-bits	unchanged
DWORD	32-bits	32-bits	unchanged
int	16-bits	32-bits	changed
UINT	16-bits, unsigned	32-bits, unsigned	changed
HANDLE	16-bits	32-bits	changed
WPARAM	16-bits	32-bits	changed
LPARAM	32-bits	32-bits	unchanged

Where an old-style 16-bit int is required—or anywhere you need a specific sized variable—a good practice has always been to declare custom data types rather than to rely on system-dependent types. Three byte-specific integer types are defined in Windows for 1-byte, 2-byte, and 4-byte values (see Table 3.4).

Table 3.4. Sized integers.

int Type	Bytes	Common Examples	Range
__int8	1	char, signed char	–128 to 127
__int16	2	short, short int, signed short int	–32,768 to 32,767
__int32	4	signed, signed int	–2,147,483,648 to 2,147,483,647

You may prefer to declare your own types; for example, you can use INT2 and INT4 for 2-byte and 4-byte integers and define other custom types with clearly identifiable labels.

Windows Macros

In addition to data types, Windows defines a variety of macros for various purposes. Many of these macros are so widely used that they seem almost like inherent features of the language, steadfast and unchanging elements in an ever-changing world.

Unfortunately, although comforting, this stability is more illusion than fact. Today, many of the old macros have been redefined as NULL macros and are retained only for compatibility; others have changed their definitions in various fashions. A few macros are listed in Table 3.5 to show representative differences.

Table 3.5. Windows macros and their changes.

Macro	Defined As	Comments
VOID	((void *) 0)	Under Win 3.x, VOID was defined simply as 0
FAR	NULL macro	Defined as a NULL macro and retained only for backwards compatibility
NEAR	NULL macro	Defined as a NULL macro and retained only for backwards compatibility
PASCAL	__stdcall	Was _pascal under Windows 3.x
WINAPI	__stdcall	was _far _pascal under Windows 3.x
CALLBACK	__stdcall	was _far _pascal under Windows 3.x
FALSE	0	Commonly, all Boolean operations return TRUE for any non-zero result regardless of magnitude or sign
TRUE	1	

Other macros such as LOBYTE, HIWORD, and MAKELONG remain essentially unchanged from their earlier functions. Because of differences in how applications pass parameters when they are written using MFC, these macros are not as commonly used as previously.

In any case, if you depend on macros carried over from a previous version of Windows, they will probably function essentially the same as before; but it is still a good idea to check rather than assume.

Windows Types and MFC Classes

Earlier versions of Windows and Windows compilers have defined a variety of data types for everything from bitmap handles to windows. Although these Windows data types still exist and still serve their old purposes, the Microsoft Foundation Classes replace many of these common variable types with object classes. Table 3.6 lists the common variable types and their equivalent class definitions.

Table 3.6. Common Windows types and MFC class equivalents.

Type	Sample Variable	Class	Sample Object	Notes
HBITMAP	hBitmap	CBitmap	pBitmap	1
HBRUSH	hBrush	CBrush	pBrush	1
HDC	hDC	CDC	pDC	
HDLG	hDlg	CDialog	pDlg	
HFONT	hFont	CFont	pFont	1
HGDIOBJ	hGdiObj	CGdiObject	pGdiObj	
HMENU	hMenu	CMenu	pMenu	1
HPALETTE	hPalette	CPalette	pPalette	1
HPEN	hPen	CPen	pPen	1
HRGN	hRgn	CRgn	pRgn	1
HWND	hButton	CButton	pButton	2
HWND	hComboBox	CComboBox	pComboBox	2
HWND	hEditBox	CEdit	pEdit	2
HWND	hListBox	CListBox	pListBox	2
HWND	hScrollBar	CScrollBar	pScrollBar	2
HWND	hStatic	CStatic	pStatic	2
HWND	hWnd	CWnd	pWnd	
POINT	pt	CPoint	pt	
RECT	rect	CRect	rect	
SIZE	size	CSize	size	

[1] GDI object instances are commonly allocated as local variables and should be named using the c prefix convention (for example, cRgn, cPen, cMenu).

[2] Controls are normally allocated as member variables within another object class and should be named using the m_ prefix (for example, m_cFileListBox, m_cEditName).

In subsequent chapters, most, if not all applications use class objects instead of the old-style handles. In a few cases, a mixture of the two are used—partially for convenience and partially to cover gaps in some object-class definitions. In those chapters, you'll see how handles can be derived from class instances (but not necessarily vice versa).

AFX and AppWizard Prefixes

Along with generating a lot of utility code for your application that helps to link dialog and resource elements with existing code, the Visual C++ AppWizard and ClassWizard also generate identifiers using standard symbol prefixes. Although you are not bound to observe these conventions, you will find it useful to recognize them. Table 3.7 lists most of the common AFX prefixes.

Table 3.7. Application framework symbol prefixes.

Prefix	Symbol Type	Example
ID_	menu item or toolbar button	ID_TOOL_SEARCH
IDB_	bitmap resource	IDB_LOGO
IDC_	cursor resource	IDC_TARGET_CURSOR
IDC_	dialog box control	IDC_REPORT
IDD_	dialog resource identifier	IDD_SEARCH
IDI_	icon resource	IDI_APP_ICON
IDP_	message box prompt	IDP_SEARCH_FOR
IDR_	resource ID shared by multiple types	IDR_MAINFRAME
IDS_	resource string	IDS_CAUTION
HID_	help context command	HID_TOOL_SEARCH
HIDD_	help context dialog box resource ID	HIDD_SEARCH
HIDP_	message box help context	HIDP_SEARCH_HELP

Changes in Message Handling with MFC

In conventional DOS applications, the core of an application has always been the main procedure, which controls program execution. With Windows, the focus changed to the WinMain procedure, which provides an entry message-handling loop that passes messages to other procedures—generally the WndProc procedure—for response and parcels tasks out to other routines or subprocedures.

When you use the Microsoft Foundation Classes, however, one of the first things you notice is that there are no WinMain or WndProc procedures—or at least, none that are readily visible.

Because there is no WinMain procedure—and, therefore, no visible code to initiate either the application or the application instance—there is no opportunity for such utilitarian tasks as defining the window class, the application icon, installing a custom cursor, setting the window background color, or loading a menu. Likewise, in the case of application instance, there is also no opportunity for setting the initial window caption, position, and size.

The odds are you haven't been concerning yourself with these details anyway (most programmers accept the default settings for all these elements or make minimal provisions if necessary), but you're probably not ready to totally give up control either.

Is there an alternative?

For most of these elements, yes, there is an alternative (as you see later when we introduce methods to substitute for the missing initialization settings).

The missing WndProc procedure, however, is a more serious story. Without WndProc and the old familiar switch(msg){...} case statement, how can you control your application? The answer is a device provided by MFC and the AppWizard; the device is called *message mapping*.

You've already seen one example of message mapping in Chapter 2, "Creating an MFC Application"; in that chapter, the HelloWin example uses the HelloWin.CPP source file, which has the one message map shown in Listing 3.1.

Listing 3.1. The message map used by the HelloWin.CPP file in the HelloWin example.

```
/////////////////////////////////////////////////////////////////////
// CHellowinApp

BEGIN_MESSAGE_MAP(CHellowinApp, CWinApp)
    //{{AFX_MSG_MAP(CHellowinApp)
    ON_COMMAND(ID_APP_ABOUT, OnAppAbout)
        // NOTE - the ClassWizard will add and remove mapping macros here.
        //    DO NOT EDIT what you see in these blocks of generated code!
    //}}AFX_MSG_MAP
    // Standard file based document commands
    ON_COMMAND(ID_FILE_NEW, CWinApp::OnFileNew)
    ON_COMMAND(ID_FILE_OPEN, CWinApp::OnFileOpen)
    // Standard print setup command
    ON_COMMAND(ID_FILE_PRINT_SETUP, CWinApp::OnFilePrintSetup)
END_MESSAGE_MAP()
```

This message map block is a series of macros that functionally duplicate the customary switch..case structure. In this example, four menu messages (About, File New, File Open, and Print Setup) are mapped to methods defined in the CHellowinApp class. With this mapping, whenever the application receives an ID_APP_ABOUT message, for example, the CHelloWinApp::OnAppAbout method is invoked. And, of course, the OnAppAbout method is where you should place any special responses.

In the end, this format is only partially a departure from conventional programming practices. Previously, the conventional switch..case structure has been a mixture of case statements that call subroutines and other case statements that contain direct instruction blocks—and, some case statements that did both. In contrast, the MFC format and its the macro structure that uses messages to call class methods parallels the first type (in which subroutines are called) and does away with the second type (in which instructions appear directly in the case statement).

In some cases, the ClassWizard does more than simply provide links to a class method. In the case of the File New, File Open, and Print Setup messages, the ClassWizard, at AppWizard's behest, also provides default handling for these messages. But the ClassWizard also leaves you the option of providing your own special handling for each of these messages.

As you see later, you can use the ClassWizard to modify the message map so that you can define your own methods of responding to additional menu messages or to customize responses to other application condition messages. In any case, these methods are the heart of your application, and replace the old familiar `switch..case` message tree.

Incidentally, if you've already looked through the source code for the HelloWin example in Chapter 2, you may have noticed that other message maps appear in the HelloVW.CPP, HelloDoc.CPP, and MainFrm.CPP source files because different tasks are allocated to different application classes for handling. In the HelloWin example, the `CHellowinApp` class handles the About, File New, File Open, and Print Setup commands; the `CHelloWinView` class (in HelloVW.CPP) handles the Print and Print Preview commands; and the `CMainFrame` class (in MainFrm.CPP) receives and responds to `WM_CREATE` messages. The `CHelloWinDoc` class (in HelloDoc.CPP) also has a message-handling block but does not yet have any messages assigned for response.

Later in this chapter, you see how these message maps are used and how additional message maps are created using the ClassWizard. You also learn how some methods are called indirectly, without a message map (or perhaps more accurately, without a visible connection).

In any case, the important point is that MFC-based applications are constructed differently than conventional Windows applications. Instead of building a single `switch..case` statement to serve as the heart of the application and handle all messages responses—even if they are subsequently directed to other subprocedures—AppWizard/ClassWizard applications begin by distributing tasks among the various classes according to their areas of responsibility.

This also means that you, the programmer, have to recognize which classes are responsible for which parts of the application. Some, of course, are self-explanatory.

First, a **frame class**, `CMainFrame`, receives the `WM_CREATE` message and is responsible for setup. If, for example, you want to control the initial position and size of the application window, you can issue a `MoveWindow` instruction on receipt of the `WM_CREATE` message to provide this service.

Next, the **view class**, `CHelloWinView`, is your entry point not only for drawing and display operations, but also for retrieving device context information.

The **document class**, `CHelloWinDoc`, is often ignored, particularly in the case of single-document applications. In other examples (particularly in the case of multiple-document applications in which two or more document views are maintained as separate windows), multiple-document classes or multiple instances of a single document class are used to maintain the various views.

Last, the **application class**, `CHelloWinApp`, is the catch-all and takes responsibility for everything not handled by another object class. In the HelloWin example, this includes everything from the About and Print Setup dialog boxes to the File New and File Open operations.

In future examples in this book, other object classes may be defined in addition to these basic four. If, for example, you create a dialog-based application, the dialog box must have its own object class for internal operations.

Windows NT versus Windows 95

This chapter has spent quite a bit of time talking about differences between 16-bit and 32-bit systems and about differences between conventional and MFC-based programs. As you may know, there are also differences between the WinNT and Win95 applications.

The most obvious differences you encounter between WinNT and Win95 are in appearance; the same application looks quite different depending on the operating system. Figure 3.1 shows two views of the HelloWin application—the one on the left is under Windows NT; the one on the right is the same application under Windows 95.

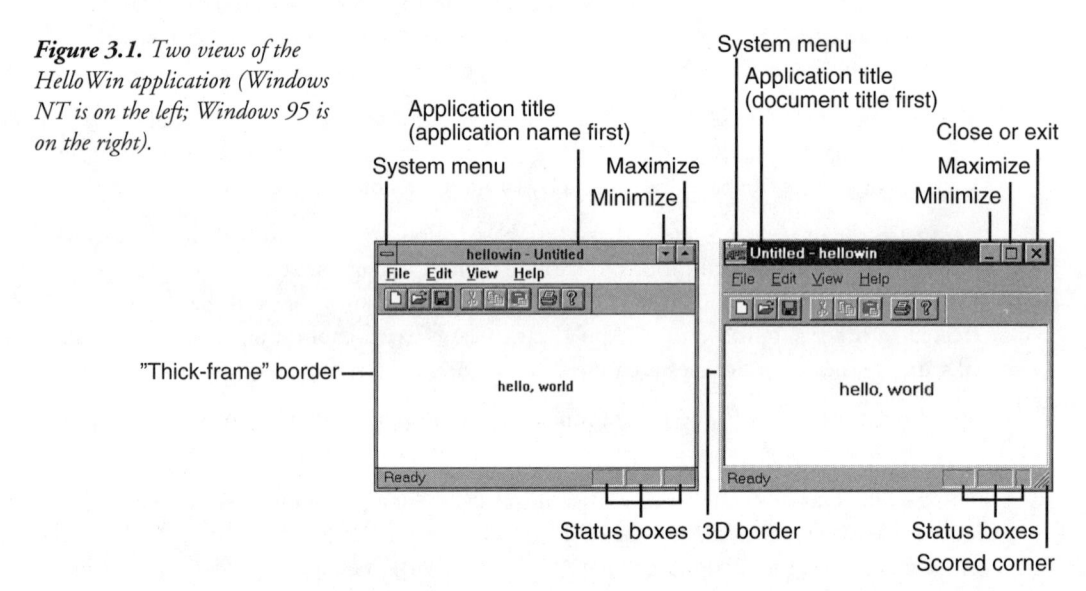

Figure 3.1. Two views of the HelloWin application (Windows NT is on the left; Windows 95 is on the right).

Note: The HelloWin application shown in Figure 3.1 was not recompiled to move between operating systems; the differences in appearance are inherent in the operating systems themselves.

Between these two images, a variety of differences are worth noting. First, the application frame (the outline) in the Windows 95 version on the right is quite different from the familiar "thick frame" Windows NT version on the left. In Windows 95, the default appearance for an application is the 3D look. Functionally, however, both are the same; in both cases, positioning the mouse on an edge or corner produces a double-headed arrow you can use to drag the application border and resize the application window.

Now look at the system menu (in the upper-left corner in both images); the Windows NT version shows the usual "box button"; the Windows 95 version uses the application icon. In both cases, clicking the system menu (the box button or the application icon) results in the display of identical system menus.

Next look at the title bar: in the WinNT version, the application title is centered; in the Win95 version, the title displays to the left. In addition, the title ordering changes between the two operating systems. In the WinNT version, the application name appears first, followed by the name of an application document (if any). In the Win95 version, in-keeping with the document-centric design of Windows 95, the document name appears first, followed by the application name.

Then notice that the WinNT version shows the familiar up and down arrow buttons for minimize and maximize. In the Win95 version, however, there are three buttons: minimize, maximize, and (at the far right) a close or exit button lacking in the WinNT version.

Below the title bar in both examples (except for differences in system fonts), the menu and toolbars are identical both in appearance and in function.

Next is the application client window, in which the words *hello, world* are centered in the display. Again, aside from font differences, the two versions are identical.

At the bottoms of the application frames are some additional differences. In the WinNT version, notice the prompt, Ready, and three blank status boxes. In the Win95 version—on the right—the third status box is slightly truncated with a triangular corner overlaying part of the field. If you enlarge the application, you still see the scored corner (although it no longer lays over the third status box). This scored corner provides a thumbpad for resizing the window—supplementing the still-present but less-visible frame borders.

These differences in the appearance of the application (the differences in typefaces aside) have little or no affect on the application itself. Within the application framework, the rest of the program functions pretty much independently of the operating system because both Windows NT and Windows 95 supply the same services.

Other differences you will see, however, appear when calling some of these supplied services. For example, when you call the File Open or File Save dialog boxes, the WinNT and Win95 versions are quite different in appearance and in arrangement—even though they both supply the same elements and same functionality. As will be discussed in Chapter 10, "Using Common Dialog

Boxes, Fonts, and Colors," both versions can be modified, so that you can link the system-supplied functionality to your own custom dialog box designs.

You will also find that other common dialog services differ drastically between Windows NT and Windows 95—but only in appearance, not in functionality.

Obviously, there are some differences between the two systems on a more primitive and functional level. In the interests of portability, however, these more fundamentally incompatible elements are avoided—except, of course, to point out their presence and reasons for incompatibility.

Thunking

When Windows NT was introduced as a 32-bit operating system, the sheer size of the installed 16-bit application base necessitated a means of allow existing, 16-bit applications to run under the new OS. To accomplish this, the concept of *thunking* was introduced. In brief, thunking is the process of translating between 16-bit and 32-bit code. When a 16-bit application calls an API function under WinNT, the function call and its parameters are converted to their 32-bit equivalents. In like fashion, when the 32-bit API returns a result, the result must be converted back to a form the 16-bit application can understand.

With the development of Windows 95, new constraints were introduced. Where WinNT was aimed at advanced users such as businesses with serious applications, Win95 has been positioned as the operating system for everyone. Therefore, Win95 has to be able to run existing 16-bit applications—and has to be able to run them at least as well as Windows 3.1.

In many respects, this has meant retaining many of the original 16-bit capabilities of Windows 3.1—both 16-bit and 32-bit architectures have been integrated within a single system. The problem, of course, is that 16-bit operations simply are not directly compatible with 32-bit operations. Which means more thunking.

Table 3.8 shows most of the principle 32-bit DLLs used in Win95 (in WinNT, of course, these DLLs are replaced by full 32-bit services with some support from the 16-bit application up to the 32-bit service layer).

Table 3.8. Windows 95 32-bit DLLs and 16-bit services.

32-Bit DLL	*Services Supplied*	*Implementation*	*16-Bit Equivalent*
ADVAPI32.DLL	Windows registry	Full 32-bit implementation	None
COMDLG32.DLL	Common Windows dialogs	Thunks to 16-bit code	COMMDLG.DLL
GDI32.DLL	Graphics device interface	Mixed 32-bit code with 16-bit thunks and calls to GDI.EXE	GDI.EXE

32-Bit DLL	Services Supplied	Implementation	16-Bit Equivalent
KERNEL32.DLL	Win95 kernel services	Full 32-bit implementation	KRNL386.EXE
OLE32.DLL	OLE 2.0 basic services	Full 32-bit implementation	None
OLEAUT32.DLL	OLE 2.0 automation	Full 32-bit implementation	None
OLECLI32.DLL	OLE client services	Thunks to 16-bit code	
OLESVR32.DLL	OLE server services	Thunks to 16-bit code	
SHELL32.DLL	Win95 Explorer services, desktop services	Mixed 32-bit code with some thunks to the 16-bit SHELL.DLL (WinNT uses a 32-bit SHELL.DLL)	SHELL.DLL
USER32.DLL	Windows Manager services	Thunks to 16-bit code	USER.EXE
WINMM.DLL	Multimedia services	Thunks to 16-bit code	

You can get a better explanation of the nature of mixed 16-bit and 32-bit operations by looking at how a 32-bit application under Win95 interacts with the 32-bit and 16-bit components (see Figure 3.2).

Figure 3.2. A 32-bit application under Win95.

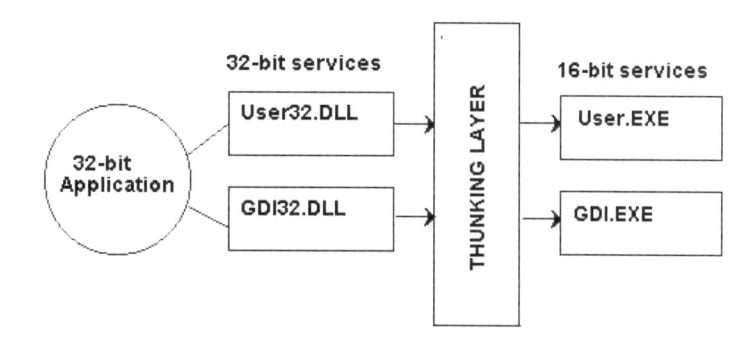

In this arrangement, the USER32.DLL and GDI32.DLL functions are thunked—largely or in part—to their 16-bit equivalents to supply the basic Windows Manager and graphics interface functions.

On the flip side, a 16-bit application operating under Win95 is a slightly different picture (see Figure 3.3).

Figure 3.3. A 16-bit application under Win95.

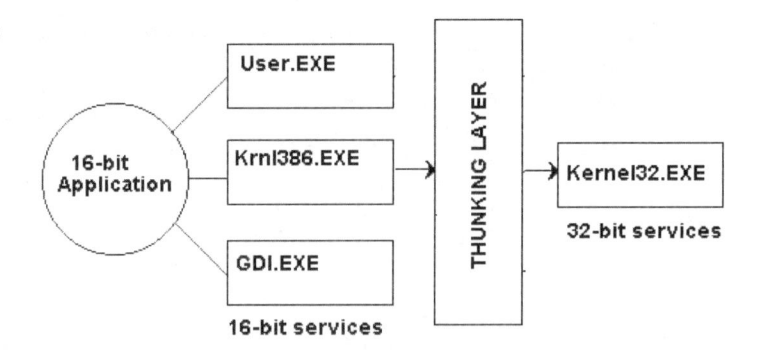

In this scenario, the 16-bit application calls the 16-bit GDI and user services directly but requires the thunking layer to process the KRNL386 calls to the KERNEL32.EXE services to handle 32-bit memory management.

A number of other thunking operations can also be pointed out. Here's another example: the ComDlg32.DLL services supply all the features previously provided by the CommDlg.DLL services—as well as some newer common dialog features. Although 16-bit applications cannot access the new services, they can—through the thunking layer—rely on the 32-bit analogs of the original 16-bit features.

Generic Thunks versus Universal Thunks

WinNT provides support for 16-bit applications through a technology known as WOW (an acronym for Windows On Windows) NT. WOW under NT offers several ways for 16-bit applications to execute. A 16-bit application can execute in a shared address space along with other 16-bit applications (the default); alternatively, each 16-bit application can be provided with its own address space in the form of a virtual machine (VDM). In either situation, 16-bit API calls are mapped to 32-bit APIs in the WOW thunking layer.

Because WinNT does not allow 16-bit and 32-bit code to be combined in a single process, WOW provides support for the standard IPC mechanisms including DDE, named pipes, OLE, and RPC. There remain, however, situations in which calls are made to 32-bit DLLs (including 32-bit APIs in system DLLs) from 16-bit applications. For this purpose, the WOW Generic Thunks are supplied.

Generic Thunks operate on the assumption that the 16-bit code is executing in a VDM that will not be relocated in linear (32-bit) memory. Under Win95, however, a mixture of 16-bit and 32-bit operations are supported; the VDMs of WinNT are not supported. Generic Thunks are unique to Windows NT.

However, any application that relies on Generic Thunks is not transportable to other 32-bit Windows platforms such as Win95 (which relies on the alternative Universal Thunks).

> Tip: If you use Generic Thunks, you can isolate them in platform-specific DLLs. Alternatively, you can incorporate provisions that detect the platform at run time and call the APIs appropriate to the active platform.

The Universal Thunk permits Win32-based applications to call routines from 16-bit DLLs and also permits 16-bit routines to call 32-bit functions. This task is accomplished by translating data pointers to shared memory from flat (32-bit) to segmented (16-bit) form and vice-versa.

The Universal Thunk also allows a Win32-based application to isolate driver-specific routines in a 16-bit DLL for Windows 3.1, and for WinNT or Win95 to replace the 16-bit DLL with a 32-bit version.

From Clipboard to DDE to OLE2

The question of transferring information between applications, particularly applications of different types and different formats, has long been both a problem and an opportunity. Under DOS, where—nominally—only one application could execute at any time, data transfers relied either on one application writing information to a temporary holding file until the data could be retrieved by another application or on some form of TSR utility that acted as the transferring agency.

Under Windows, a common transfer method was introduced in the form of the Clipboard. The Windows Clipboard actually consists of two quite different features. One is the Clipboard service itself: a utility within Windows that provides the holding facility for information being transferred as well as the services for capturing and pasting information in several different formats.

The second Clipboard, however, can more accurately be called the *clipboard viewer*. In Win95 and WinNT, this utility is now referred to as the *ClipBook utility*. It allows the user to look at the contents of the Clipboard. The real Clipboard, however, is independent of the ClipBook.

Simple transfers of blocks of information (text, raw data, images, or what have you) was supplemented several versions past by the introduction of the Dynamic Data Exchange (DDE).

DDE is a protocol allowing applications to exchange messages in a mutually defined format and to exchange information in response to requests. In this fashion, a DDE server can supply data to several DDE clients in response to the clients' requests; the client applications are responsible for displaying or otherwise using the provided information.

Of course, a single DDE client can also query and request information from several servers; both clients and servers can also be interchangeable.

The drawbacks, however, were multifold. DDE exchanges were complicated, applications had to agree on protocols, servers had to register their formats before clients could query them, clients were still responsible for presenting the data (which meant formatting or drawing as appropriate), and the overall result was complicated, cumbersome and, unfortunately, error prone.

Which brings us to OLE2. Okay, there was an OLE1 (or just plain OLE—object linking and embedding), but it was never very popular. The reasons were several: OLE was extremely complex, difficult to program, impossible to understand, and didn't work worth a hill of beans.

On the other hand, OLE2 is complex, difficult to understand, almost impossible to program—but it has the single saving grace of working. And more important, OLE2 supplies everything that the Clipboard and DDE did not.

With OLE2, instead of transferring information or messages, a client application simply makes itself available—essentially as a Device Context—to the OLE server application. OLE2 allows the server to "draw" its own display within the client application's display space.

For example, consider a word processor application in which you want to embed a section from a spreadsheet. Most word processors have some simple math capabilities and allow you to set up a table and run totals (or other operations) on figures in the table. If, instead, you pass the data through the word processor to a cooperating spreadsheet, you can have the spreadsheet not only perform the operations but also draw the results within the document. This arrangement relieves the word processor of having to duplicate all the functions of the spreadsheet.

Taking this one step further, suppose that you are deriving the original data from a database. Again, instead of building database capabilities into the word processor, you can have the spreadsheet call a database application and ask it to supply the raw data which, after processing, is drawn in the document. On the other hand, the figures can originate in the word processor and be passed to the spreadsheet, but a database certainly seems like a more reasonable source.

Of course, instead of simply presenting columns of figures, you may want to display a graph. Because the spreadsheet already has graph capabilities, you can allow it to provide this service as well. *Presto!* You have raw data from a database transformed into a bar graph in your report to the board.

More important, this is not necessarily a static presentation. If *linked objects* are used and the figures in the database change, the spreadsheet can recalculate the results and redraw the graph without you having to recreate the letter (at least, not until you've printed it).

In this example, the word processor becomes an OLE *container*—that is, it contains the results of operations carried out by other applications. The database and spreadsheet applications become OLE *servers*.

Note the definition of the OLE acronym: object linking and embedding. There are several implications here, beginning with the terms *linking* and *embedding*, because OLE applications actually function in two different fashions.

The first term, *embedding*, defines a static process that isn't too different from using the Clipboard to cut (or copy) and paste information from another application. In this form, OLE is a one-time operation; returning to the word processor/spreadsheet/database example, once the graph has been calculated and drawn, the supplied image is fixed.

On the other hand, if the operations are *linked*, any changes to the data source are immediately reflected in the document, both in columnar text and in any graphs based on these figures.

In both cases, however, the process is not entirely automatic. First, the container application (the word processor in the example) remains the responsible party in several respects. The container is responsible for requesting a "chart" object and passing the request to OLE. The container knows nothing about the server application and does not request a specific server; it only requests a server capable of providing a specific type of object identified by the moniker *chart*.

In response, OLE processes the request and decides to launch, in the background, a spreadsheet program registered with Windows (NT or 95) as being capable of handling a request of this type.

At the same time, OLE passes information to the container application about the server's interface requirements. In turn, the container is responsible for positioning and sizing the object in the container's user interface. The container is not responsible for the calculations or drawing operations.

When the server is asked to serve the object, the *object window* (the chart presented in the word processor's document window) is also a link from the word processor to the spreadsheet. The link allows the user to access the spreadsheet just as if it had been loaded as a regular application. In addition, even though the spreadsheet has been opened as a server application, it can also function as a container, making its own OLE request (this time to a database application) to retrieve the figures needed to create the graph requested by the document.

Of course, the word processor can also be a server, called, perhaps, by a database application to provide formatted text for its display. A vicious circle, yes?

The Object of the OLE Object

To a programmer, the term *object* has several meanings. When we're talking about OLE, the usual meaning of the term is not the correct meaning. An *OLE object* has only a cursory resemblance to a *C++ object*, even though a C++ object can be used by your application's code to represent an OLE object. The principle difference is that an OLE object is an object registered with the Windows NT or 95 system; C++ objects have no relevance outside the compiler source code.

In OLE, an *object* is what you embed in an application. This can be many things: a group of cells from a spreadsheet, an image, a block of text, a graph, an AVI file, a sound bite, or something uniquely different from any of these things.

Further, from a programmer's viewpoint, a single OLE object is probably composed of any number of C++ objects, or Pascal objects, and so on.

In like fashion, the term *method* also has overloaded meanings. To a programmer, a method is a member function from a C++ class. In OLE, a method is an interface function. An OLE object can have multiple interfaces, each with multiple methods.

MFC Database Classes in OLE Controls

The `CDatabase` and `CRecordSet` classes can be used to create OLE data access controls. These are designed to provide access to any database supporting ODBC (Open DataBase Connectivity). ODBC allows a control to access data in a variety of formats and configurations; it also relieves your application of having to include provisions to handle multiple database management systems.

INI Files versus the Registry

Having introduced the topic of OLE applications, it seems appropriate to follow this topic by discussing the Windows registry.

Originally, applications—and Windows itself—relied on initialization (or INI) files to contain a wide variety of information concerning application states, drivers, protocols, locations, and virtually anything else you can image (including running totals for games or the names of the last half-dozen files used by an application).

> Note: In addition to replacing INI files, including the venerable WIN.INI, the registry database also replaces the old AUTOEXEC.BAT and CONFIG.SYS files. The AUTOEXEC.BAT and CONFIG.SYS files that remain are intended to provide compatibility with DOS and Windows 3.1 applications, many of which continue to rely on INI files for application data.

Beginning with WinNT and continuing with Win95, INI files have been replaced, or at least supplanted, by the Windows registry. The purpose of the registry is essentially the same as the older INI files. The difference, however, is that instead of storing information as ASCII text, the registry stores information in a more direct, often binary, format. The Win95 RegEdit utility is shown in Figure 3.4.

> Caution: The registry database can be accessed with the RegEdt32 (Registry Editor) utility in WinNT. It can be accessed with the RegEdit utility in Win95. Make modifications only with extreme care because errors or accidental changes can seriously disrupt system operations.

> Note: Exactly which folders and registry entries appear on your computer depend on the installed software and configuration of your system.

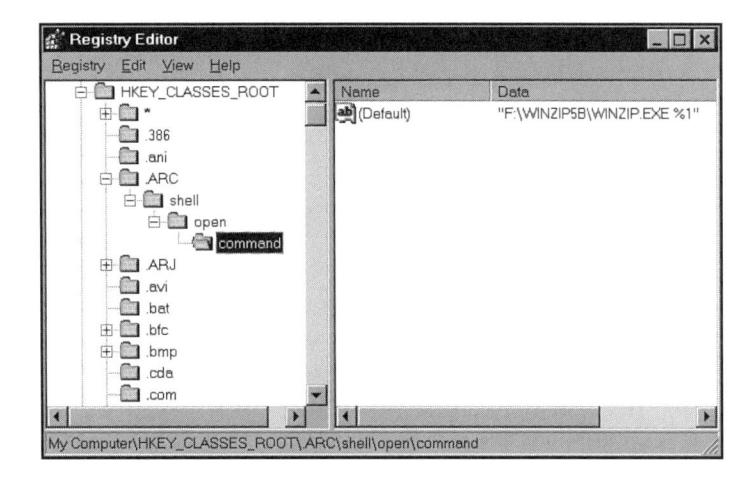

Figure 3.4. *The RegEdit utility and the Win95 registry.*

In this figure, the Registry Editor shows the HKEY_CLASSES_ROOT registry. If you drill down through the ARC extension, through the shell, open, and command keys, you finally find a command-line prompt that identifies the location of the WinZip utility. The upshot of the instruction in this entry is that, when you open a document with the extension ARC, the WinZip utility is called with a fully qualified pathname; it uses the %1 argument to supply the name of the file to open.

If you search a bit further, you can find similar entries for the ZIP and LZH file extensions.

The information encoded in this way is not particularly different from the data stored in the WIN.INI and other INI files under earlier versions of Windows. The principle differences are that, in the registry, the information is stored in a structured database rather than in a flat ASCII file, retrieval is faster than searching through a text file, and the database provides a greater degree of protection over the ASCII file format.

The registry is not, however, limited to storing information for the File Manager and the Win95 Explorer. Instead, the registry is used to register virtually everything the system may need to know—ranging from which video driver and screen resolution you use to private message values to operational statistics as well as (and not least of all) OLE server and container formats. For applications, however, a host of API functions provides access to registry information without you having to navigate the registry structure.

> Tip: Using the RegEdit utility, check under My Computer\HKEY_LOCAL_MACHINE\SOFTWARE\Microsoft\Windows\CurrentVersion and skim through a few of the registry keys assigned for Win95. You should find a wealth of information including your name and the Win95 version number as well as other, more cryptic entries.

As an example, the `RegCreateKeyEx` function creates a registry key (if the key already exists in the registry, the function opens the key). More commonly, the `RegOpenKeyEx` function is called to open a registry key before the `RegEnumKeyEx`, `RegQueryValueEx`, or `RegQueryInfoKey` functions are called to retrieve registry values.

Other registry functions include those in the following list:

`RegCloseKey`	`RegConnectRegistry`	`RegCreateKey`	`RegDeleteKey`
`RegDeleteValue`	`RegEnumKey`	`RegEnumValue`	`RegFlushKey`
`RegGetKeySecurity`	`RegLoadKey`	`RegOpenKey`	`RegQueryValue`
`RegReplaceKey`	`RegRestoreKey`	`RegSaveKey`	`RegSetKeySecurity`
`RegSetValue`	`RegSetValueEx`	`RegUnLoadKey`	

Registry for OLE2

For OLE2 registrations, look under HKEY_CLASSES_ROOT\CLSID and HKEY_CLASSES_ROOT\Interface; chances are, a rather impressive list of OLE2 objects and methods will appear. Unfortunately, these entries are not designed for casual reading.

Although OLE registrations are included in the registry, instead of using the `Reg...` APIs, the `IRunningObjectTable` interface offers access to the Running Object Table (ROT). The Running Object Table is a globally accessible lookup table that resides on each workstation. The ROT tracks objects identified by monikers and presently executing on a workstation. When a client application attempts to bind a moniker to an OLE object, if the object is registered in the ROT, the moniker binds to the current instance rather than loading a new instance of the application.

Perhaps the most common type of moniker is the compound-document link source. This moniker includes OLE server applications that support linking to their documents (or portions of a document) and OLE containers that support linking to embeddings within a document.

> Note: OLE objects that can be named must be registered with the ROT on loading; their registration must be revoked when execution terminates. Refer to `IRunableObject` in the Visual C++ help system for details.

Other New Features

A few other features in Win95 and WinNT are worth your attention. These include new user interface classes, MAPI support, new Windows Sockets classes, and (last but not least for conventional C programmers) the MFC Migration Kit.

New User Interface Classes for Win95

In addition to the common dialog boxes, Windows 95 has also introduced a number of new user interface classes. Given the demands of designers and the expectations of users, the continuing introduction of additional graphics control innovations is not difficult to predict.

When Visual Basic was introduced, one of the more popular aspects of this modern version of the much maligned language was the VBX (Visual Basic eXtension) controls that were quickly adapted to work with languages other than Visual Basic.

Windows 95 and Microsoft Foundation Classes (MFC) 3.1 have added a variety of graphics extensions (including the toolbar, the status bar, and tabbed dialog boxes); they have also introduced OCX controls, which offer C++ users the functional equivalent of VBX controls.

Extensions to the existing GDI and new user interface idioms appear both within and without the MFC as independent developers create and package new controls. Both the new MFC classes and original OCX controls are introduced later in this book.

> Note: Although these new user interface objects are currently available only in Win95, future releases of WinNT are expected to include similar support.

MAPI Support

Simple MAPI support is provided in both MFC 3.1 and 4.0 and in Visual C++ 2.1 and 4.0 through the CDocument and COleDocument classes. The CDocument class offers applications the ability to send documents using the resident electronic mail host; the COleDocument class is used for OLE compound documents.

MAPI (Messaging API) is a series of functions used by applications to create, manipulate, transfer, and store mail messages. Using MAPI, developers have the tools to manage mail-aware applications, to manage stored mail messages, and to define the purpose and content of mail messages. Further, MAPI offers a common interface for use by mail-enabled and mail-aware applications; it operates independently of the actual messaging system.

Networking Protocols: Windows Sockets

New Windows Sockets classes have been added for network programming. Both Visual C++ 1.52 (16-bit) and Visual C++ 2.1 and 4.0 (32-bit versions) provide MFC support for Windows Sockets, the network-independent API for network communications programming under Microsoft Windows and Microsoft Windows NT.

The new classes include `CAsyncSocket`, `CSocket`, and `CSocketFile`. Class `CAsyncSocket` encapsulates the Windows Sockets API. Class `CSocket`, derived from `CAsyncSocket`, additionally provides a simple programming model that lets you serialize data from one socket application to another with a `CArchive` object, using a `CSocketFile` object.

MFC Migration Kit

The MFC Migration Kit (included with Visual C++ 2.1 and 4.0) provides facilities and assistance to move existing Windows applications written in C to Visual C++. Migration can be accomplished with or without using the Microsoft Foundation Classes. The MFC Migration Kit consists of the following elements:

- The MFC Migration Guide that illustrates the conversion process for both 16-bit and 32-bit applications using the Microsoft Foundation Classes and supplied example programs.
- A migration tool in both 16-bit and 32-bit versions used to scan your C source files; the tool then offers suggestions on how to convert the application.
- Example applications in both 16-bit and 32-bit versions. These Windows examples are supplied in both conventional C and C++ forms.

Before you advance too many plans that rely on the MFC Migration Kit, a bit of experimentation is in order. Although the Migration Kit is certainly a great idea and has many interesting capabilities, it is not a cure-all or a magic carpet ride.

On the other hand, the Migration Kit can be a good starting point: it *does* offer useful suggestions on conversion.

But don't expect it to do everything—or even to do it efficiently. Just be grateful for what it can do.

> Note: The MFC Migration Kit is located in the \MFCKIT\DISK1 directory on your Visual C++ CD-ROM disc. Run the Setup program from this directory to install the Migration Kit on your system. Installation requires roughly 1M of space on your hard drive.

Summary

This chapter has described conventions and differences. The conventions used in Windows programs include Hungarian notation and MFC and AFX prefixes. The chapter also covered data types—data types used in Windows as well as data types that have changed in the move from a 16-bit environment to a 32-bit environment.

Because data types are only one of the Windows elements that have changed, this chapter also took a brief look at some other Windows types being replaced with MFC class equivalents. Further, because the changes in Windows programming resulting from the Microsoft Foundation Classes go far beyond types and data elements, this chapter also discussed the structural changes produced by message mapping. We've also touched briefly on thunking, on OLE 2, on MAPI, and on networking protocols.

The changes you are faced with are not just changes caused by moving from a 16-bit to a 32-bit environment. Because you are working with both Windows NT and Windows 95, you're also concerned with differences between these two operating systems—even though these changes are more a matter of appearance than function.

This chapter introduced the differences and changes rather than covered them in depth; all these topics will reappear in later chapters, where their effects are both more immediately relevant and more visible. For the moment, the point is simply that you be aware of these topics so that they will not come as a complete surprise when they reappear later.

Chapter 4, "Using Message Boxes," returns to application design—using the Microsoft Foundation Classes. You will see many of these topics reappear in practical settings.

PART II

The User Interface

Part II • The User Interface

Folk wisdom holds that, if you build a better mousetrap, the world will beat a path to your door. More recently, this adage has been replaced with one concerning baseball diamonds built in corn fields but the point is the same: if you create something people want, whether mouse trap or ball field, you'll gain their attention.

However, creating something people want is only half the battle. Too often, the more important half is creating something people *perceive* as something they want. Toward this end—perception—Madison Avenue annually spends enough to finance a minor international war, send men to Mars, and find the cure for the common cold.

As a software developer—unless you're already so rich that there's no point in your reading this book anyway—you're not likely to have the budget for the Madison Avenue approach. To ensure that people perceive your product favorably, you need a different course of action.

Like advertising, fancy packaging is expensive. Unless, of course, your packaging is electronic...in which case, your user interface is your best package and your best advertising.

There's nothing new in any of this. Windows itself is a winner not because it is technically superior to OS/2, for example, but because it is *perceived* as superior. And it is perceived as superior in part because people see the user interface as superior. The evaluation is subjective, not objective.

Of course, getting too far into this subject is on a par with discussing religion or politics; the results can only be disagreement and aggravation and will settle nothing. The important point is that how people perceive your program—subjectively—is at least as important as how good it is technically. Probably more so.

In view of the importance of perception, the overall topic in this part of the book is about how to design your user interface.

Obviously, your user interface depends on the Windows interface and Windows features. But these are only tools; it is how you use them to package your application that is important.

However, I cannot design your interface. What I can and will do is show you the tools, show you how to use them, and suggest the best ways various tools can be employed. The rest is up to you.

CHAPTER 4

Using Message Boxes

Because you really don't have to do anything to create them, the simplest graphic elements in your application are message dialog boxes. Message boxes are stock dialog boxes supplied by Windows and Visual C++ and are not—unlike most other dialog boxes—application resource elements. Of course, because application resource dialog boxes haven't been introduced yet, this last assertion deserves a word of explanation.

Most dialog boxes, as you see in Chapter 7, "Designing Custom Dialog Boxes," must be designed as application resources before they can be displayed and used by the application. Message boxes, on the other hand, can be used on-the-fly. As their name implies, message boxes provide a means to display a brief message, such as a warning, a caution, a query, an error report, or some other bit of simple information.

In addition to displaying information, message boxes can offer a series of buttons to present the user with choices; depending on the user's selection, the message box can return simple responses to the application. And finally, message boxes can include a selection of simple, predefined icons.

> Tip: Most often, message boxes are used to present information to the user. As a developer, you may find these boxes useful to present information to yourself for debugging or for tracking execution during development.

This chapter looks at several programming elements. To begin, you examine several styles of message boxes. In the process of doing so, you also learn to use the ClassWizard to create class methods and link menu items to them.

Further, to show the responses from the message boxes, you will create a class member variable to receive the responses. After each message box closes, you will display a text message in the View window that reports which button was selected.

Last, you will modify the standard Exit menu item so that, instead of the default handling that provides an immediate exit, you display your own message box requesting confirmation before exiting.

MessageBox Displays

In conventional Windows applications, the `MessageBox` API requires four parameters, beginning with a window handle. In an MFC application (assuming that you are using a class derived from the `CWnd` class), the window handle parameter is not required because the application window handle is already a member variable within the class instance. In addition, because you are working with MFC applications, you'll use the `CWnd::MessageBox` format here and in the Dialog_1 example program in this chapter.

The `CWnd::MessageBox` method is defined as follows:

```
int MessageBox( LPCTSTR lpszText,
                LPCTSTR lpszCaption = NULL,
                UINT nType = MB_OK );
```

The MFC `MessageBox` function can be called with one, two, or three parameters.

At a minimum, the `MessageBox` function is called with a text string, which may be either a NULL-terminated string constant (`LPCTSTR`) or a `CString` instance. The calling string is the message displayed in the dialog box. The dialog box is automatically sized to accommodate the text being displayed.

For long strings, you have two choices:

- ◆ You can supply the long string and allow Windows to size the box and break the string on a best-fit basis according to its own internal rules.
- ◆ You can insert newline symbols (\n) in the text string to force line breaks.

Chapter 4 • Using Message Boxes

> Note: Elaborate formatting is not supported in `MessageBox` dialog boxes. When special formatting is required, you should consider either `AfxMessageBoxes` (described later in this chapter), or custom dialog boxes (described in Chapter 7, "Designing Custom Dialog Boxes").

The `LPCTSTR lpszCaption` parameter, the caption string, is defined as NULL by default. If no `lpszCaption` parameter is supplied, this default parameter is used. However, if a caption parameter is supplied, it can be either a NULL-terminated string constant or a `CString` instance.

> Note: Caption strings too long to fit the message box header are arbitrarily truncated and end with an ellipsis (...) when displayed.

The `nType` parameter, the dialog type, defines the appearance (graphics and buttons) and behavior of the message box and is also defined with a default value. If no dialog type is supplied, the default is an OK button. Dialog style flags and options are discussed later in this chapter.

The `MB` parameter may be a combination of a graphic icon specifier, a button group specifier, a default button identifier, and a dialog modality specifier. Each of these is defined by constants. The dialog type parameter is defined by ORing two or more of these constants together. The following sections discuss each group of style constants.

> Note: When multiple parameters are defined and one or more parameters are optional (that is, they are supplied with default definitions), two rules apply:
>
> ◆ The optional parameters always appear following all required parameters.
>
> ◆ When two or more parameters are optional but are supplied in the function call, they must be supplied in strict order. (Using the `MessageBox` function as an example, although the `lpszCaption` parameter can be specified without specifying the `nType` parameter, the `nType` parameter cannot be supplied unless the `lpszCaption` parameter has already been supplied.)

All message boxes exit when any of their control buttons are clicked; they return a value on exit, based on the buttons supplied and the selection made. The button selections and values returned by each are discussed later in this chapter. However, if the system cannot display a message box (because of memory limitations or other errors), the return value is zero. This is the only error result returned directly by a message box.

MessageBox Icons

A message box can display an optional graphic icon in the upper-left corner of the dialog. Four icons are supplied as system resources (refer to Figures 4.1 through 4.4; the icons are shown in both Windows 95 and Windows NT formats). The icon constants are listed and described in Table 4.1.

You can specify only one message box icon for each message box.

Table 4.1. `MessageBox` icons.

Icon Constant	Description	Figure
MB_ICONASTERISK	See MB_ICONINFORMATION	4.1
MB_ICONEXCLAMATION	Exclamation-point icon	4.1
MB_ICONHAND	See MB_ICONSTOP	4.2
MB_ICONINFORMATION	Lowercase *i* icon	4.3
MB_ICONQUESTION	Question-mark icon	4.4
MB_ICONSTOP	Stop-sign icon (WinNT) or *X*-in-circle icon (Win95)	4.2

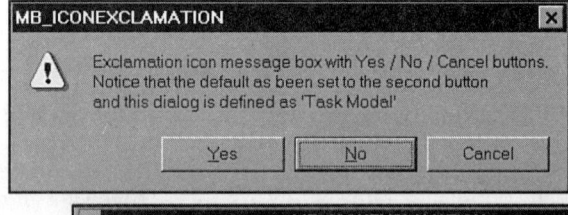

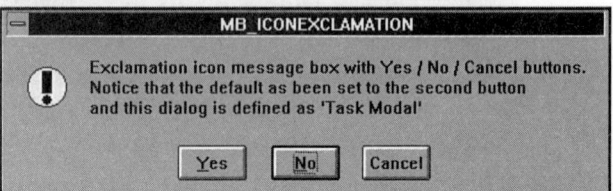

Figure 4.1. *Examples of the exclamation-point icons and the Yes, No, and Cancel buttons in Windows 95 (top) and Windows NT (bottom) formats.*

Figure 4.2. *Examples of the stop icons and the Abort, Retry, and Ignore buttons in Windows 95 (top) and Windows NT (bottom) formats.*

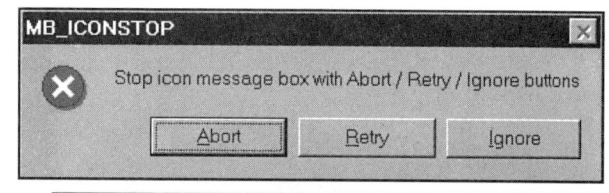

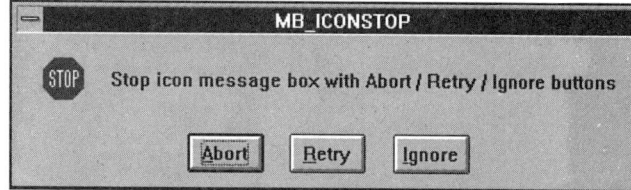

Figure 4.3. *Examples of the information icons and the OK button in Windows 95 (top) and Windows NT (bottom) formats.*

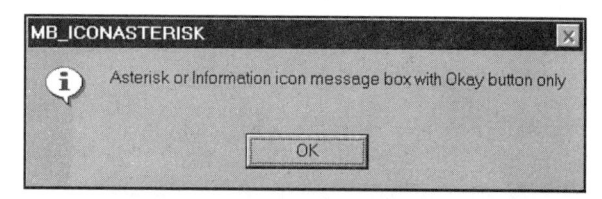

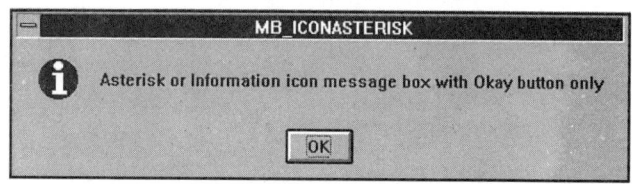

Figure 4.4. *Examples of the question-mark icon and the OK and Cancel buttons in Windows 95 (top) and Windows NT (bottom) formats.*

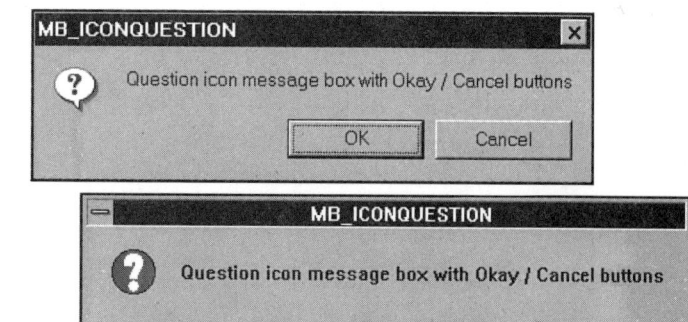

MessageBox Buttons

MessageBox buttons are supplied as one of six predefined groups. The button constants that define those groups are listed in Table 4.2. Refer to Figures 4.1 through 4.4 for some examples of the button groups.

Table 4.2. `MessageBox` button groups.

Button Constant	Buttons Created	Figure
MB_ABORTRETRYIGNORE	Displays three buttons: Abort, Retry, and Ignore	4.2
MB_OK	Displays a single OK button	4.3
MB_OKCANCEL	Displays two buttons: OK and Cancel	4.4
MB_RETRYCANCEL	Displays two buttons: Retry and Cancel	none
MB_YESNO	Displays two buttons: Yes and No	none
MB_YESNOCANCEL	Displays three buttons: Yes, No, and Cancel	4.1

If no dialog type parameter is specified or if no button group is specified, the `MB_OK` button is displayed by default. Button group constants are ORed with other style specifications to produce the desired message box appearance and behavior.

The button group selected determines which message values can be returned by the `MessageBox` function. Return values are shown in Table 4.4.

Unless otherwise specified, the first button in each group is the default button; pressing the Enter key is the same as clicking the default button. You can use the default button constants listed in Table 4.3 to change the default button.

Table 4.3. `MessageBox` default button constants.

Button Defaults	Function
MB_DEFBUTTON1 (default)	Specifies the first button as the default button. This is the default unless either `MB_DEFBUTTON2` or `MB_DEFBUTTON3` has been specified earlier.
MB_DEFBUTTON2	Specifies the second button as the default.
MB_DEFBUTTON3	Specifies the third button as the default.

Default button constants are ORed together with the button group identifier and any other style identifiers to produce the desired message box appearance and behavior.

MessageBox Responses

Message boxes are used for a variety of purposes. They can call the user's attention to information, such as reporting the completion of a task; they can also be used for more important purposes, such as reporting a serious error condition.

If the message box is used for the former purpose (reporting an event of some sort), displaying a simple OK button is generally sufficient.

In other circumstances, such as when the message box reports a serious error for which instructions are needed from the user, a single response button is inappropriate. In these cases, you can supply two or three buttons for responses, such as Abort/Retry/Ignore, OK/Cancel, Retry/Cancel, Yes/No, or Yes/No/Cancel.

The possible message values that can be returned by a message box are listed in Table 4.4.

Table 4.4. `MessageBox` return values.

Return Value	Button	Value
NULL	Display of message box failed	0
IDOK	OK button selected	1
IDCANCEL	Cancel button selected	2
IDABORT	Abort button selected	3
IDRETRY	Retry button selected	4
IDIGNORE	Ignore button selected	5
IDYES	Yes button selected	6
IDNO	No button selected	7

If a message box has a Cancel button, the `IDCANCEL` value is returned if either the Esc key is pressed or the Cancel button is selected. If there is no Cancel button, pressing Esc has no effect.

Obviously, if multiple buttons are supplied, the procedure that issues the message box should watch for the return value and respond accordingly.

MessageBox Modality

Three modes are defined for message boxes, as shown in Table 4.5. These modes are mutually exclusive; you can apply only one modality selection to each message box.

Table 4.5. `MessageBox` modality.

Modal Constant	Function
`MB_APPLMODAL` (default)	Application Modal forces the user to respond to the message box before continuing work in the current application window; it does not prevent the user from moving to another application window to work.
`MB_SYSTEMMODAL`	System Modal suspends all applications until the user responds to the message box. This mode is used for message boxes that notify the user of a serious condition requiring immediate attention. System Modal message boxes should be used sparingly.
`MB_TASKMODAL`	Task Modal is similar to Application Modal but is reserved for a calling application or library that does not have a window handle. It disables all top-level windows belonging to the current task. (Not useful within an MFC application.)

> Note: When the `MB_ICONSTOP` and `MB_SYSTEMMODAL` flags are combined, the message box is displayed regardless of the available memory. The message text length, however, is limited to three lines and automatic line breaks are not supplied. Embedded line breaks (\n), however, can be used to break text lines.

In addition to the mode, button, and icon flags defined in Tables 4.1 through 4.5, two miscellaneous flags are defined (see Table 4.6). You can combine these two flags with each other and with any of the preceding flags. These two flags were originally defined for Windows NT and have no function in Windows 3.1 applications. Their functionality under Windows 95, however, appears somewhat uncertain.

Table 4.6. Miscellaneous `MessageBox` flags.

Miscellaneous Flag	Function
`MB_DEFAULT_DESKTOP_ONLY`	If the desktop currently receiving input is not a default desktop (that is, one on which an application runs after the user logs on), the `MessageBox` function fails and no dialog is displayed.
`MB_SETFOREGROUND`	Calls the `SetForegroundWindow` API to make the message box the new foreground window, even if the parent application issuing the message box does not have the foreground focus.

AfxMessageBox Displays

In addition to the MessageBox API and the CWnd::MessageBox method, a third form of message box is available: the AfxMessageBox API. The AfxMessageBox API is defined in two forms, both of which are similar to the MessageBox API/method but with distinct differences.

In one version, the AfxMessageBox accepts a text parameter, a style parameter, and a Help-context ID. In the second version, instead of a text parameter, the first argument is an integer that references an entry in the application's string table.

You can use the functions AfxFormatString1 and AfxFormatString2 to format the message box text display. In general, however, a custom dialog box is recommended for any text display that requires heavy formatting.

Further information on the AfxMessageBox, AfxFormatString1, and AfxFormatString2 functions is available through Visual C++'s online help and Books Online.

Dialog_1: A Message Box Demo

Stock message boxes can be called from any routine or subroutine within a Windows application. For demo purposes, however, you will create an application whose only purpose is to display a selection of message boxes that use different icon styles and button options in response to a simple menu.

The first step is to create an application skeleton, following the procedures demonstrated in Chapter 2, "Creating an MFC Application." For this example, called Dialog_1, you use AppWizard to create a framework that has a single document interface and a standard menu but no toolbar or status bar support.

Once the skeleton application is complete, use the AppStudio (described in Chapter 5, "Introducing AppStudio and Application Resources") to modify the default menu by removing all items except the Exit item and the separator bar preceding that item. Then change the main File menu item to Message Boxes and add four new entries to produce the menu shown in Figure 4.5.

To modify the menu, double-click the Dialog-1.RC file from the Project Workspace dialog box in the Developer Studio (Visual C++ version 4.0) or from the project list in Visual Workbench (Visual C++ version 2.*x*).

From the resource list, select Menu and IDR_MAINFRAME to load the default menu for editing. From the **F**ile menu, simply highlight the current entries and press the Delete button. Then use the Insert button to add the new entries listed in Table 4.7.

Figure 4.5. The Dialog_1 menu.

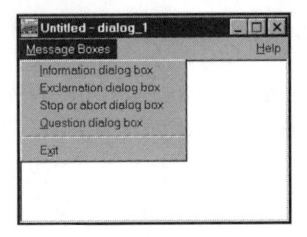

Adding menu entries is not, in itself, sufficient because you need identifier constants before you can use the ClassWizard to tie the menu to a series of methods (procedures). The menu item identifiers used in this example application are shown in Table 4.7.

Table 4.7. Menu items and identifiers.

Menu Entry	Identifier Constant	Source
Information message box	ID_DLG_INFO	Programmer supplied
Exclamation message box	ID_DLG_EXCL	Programmer supplied
Stop or abort message box	ID_DLG_STOP	Programmer supplied
Question message box	ID_DLG_QUESTION	Programmer supplied
E**x**it	ID_APP_EXIT	Defined by AppWizard

Display the Menu Item Properties dialog box by double-clicking any menu item. To create the menu, type the Menu Entry (listed in Table 4.7) in the Caption field; type the corresponding Identifier Constant in the ID field. Values for these constants are generated automatically and appear in the Resource.H source file.

> Note: The Resource.H header file does not appear in the project file list and is not intended for direct editing. This header file does, however, contain definitions for all application-specific resource identifiers. These entries are managed by AppWizard and by the resource editors. Change them only with great care.

Linking Menu Items to Class Methods

Once the menu is created, the next step is to call the MFC ClassWizard from the **P**roject menu. The ClassWizard is shown in Figure 4.6.

In the Message Maps tab of the ClassWizard, select the Class **N**ame pull-down list box. This list box offers a choice of five classes: CAboutDlg, CDialog_1App, CDialog_1Doc, CDialog_1View, and CMainFrame. Because all these classes are implemented in Dialog_1, the question is, where do you want to implement the responses to the menu items?

Figure 4.6. *Using the ClassWizard.*

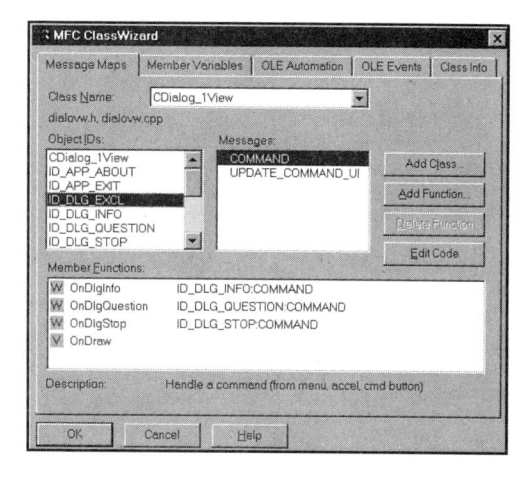

	Classes
Class	*Purpose*
CAboutDlg	Used to handle the default, AppWizard-created About dialog box. The message box menu items are not visible from this class.
CDialog_1App	Used to handle global operations for the application. The message box menu items could be handled here; many menu selections would be, particularly those that have global relevance or that affect or call for operations in more than one class.
CDialog_1Doc	Provided to handle document-specific operations. The message box menu items could be handled here but document-related operations (such as opening or closing files) are more appropriate in this class.
CDialog_1View	Used to handle application client window activities such as drawing the application display. For demonstration purposes, the message box menu items are handled here so that we can conveniently report which buttons are selected from each dialog box.
CMainFrame	Used primarily to handle operations affecting the application frame window (such as resizing, moving, or positioning the application). Again, the message box menu items could be handled through the mainframe class but they are not particularly relevant to the application framework.

Some elimination is possible at this point. For example, if you select the CAboutDlg class from the list, you'll find that CAboutDlg and IDOK are the only object IDs available. Obviously, then, the CAboutDlg class is not appropriate for responding to the menu commands.

> Note: You use the Message Maps tab in the MFC ClassWizard dialog box to browse a list of object IDs—and the messages or control notifications associated with each—and to create the required handler routines as appropriate.

The remaining four classes, however, are all capable of responding to the menu messages we're concerned with—that is, the four object IDs with the form ID_DLG_xxxx. Depending on the purpose of the menu item, you may want to respond to some messages with the application class (CDialog_1App), others with the document class (CDialog_1Doc), and still others with the CMainFrame class.

Here, however, the view class (CDialog_1View) is most appropriate—not because of the dialog messages, but simply because the view class reports which button is selected. Keeping the methods that call the message boxes in the same class in which you report results simplifies your options. The reasons for this are given in a moment.

But the immediate task is to use the ClassWizard to generate methods (think of these as procedures, if you prefer) from which the message boxes will be called. Figure 4.6 shows three of the methods already created; the fourth is ready to be created by clicking the **A**dd Function button.

The method names (OnDlgInfo, OnDlgQuestion, and OnDlgStop) are generated automatically by the ClassWizard and are derived from the ID constants. Although these method names and message identifiers can be edited and modified (feel free to do so if you feel the need), the attempt involves multiple source files and is certainly a whole lot more trouble than any functional results, real or imagined, warrant (that is, it isn't recommended).

As you can see in Figure 4.6, ID_DLG_EXCL is selected in the Object **I**Ds list and COMMAND is selected in the Messa**g**es list. When **A**dd Function is selected, a new member function is generated—along with message mapping—that will be called to respond when the Exclamation dialog box menu item is selected.

The link between the menu item and skeletal function in the CDialog_1View class source files (DialoVW.CPP and DialoVW.H) is supplied by ClassWizard. The functional response within the skeletal function must be supplied by the programmer.

Table 4.8 offers an overview of the elements in the Message Maps tab of the ClassWizard dialog box.

Table 4.8. Elements in the Message Maps tab of the ClassWizard.

Element	Function or Purpose
Class **N**ame	Lists the names of all classes in the application.
Object **I**Ds	Lists IDs for objects that can generate messages, such as menu items, dialog box controls, and so on. The first entry is always the name of the current class and can be used to generate responses for other messages such as system events that are not directly visible as separate objects.

Element	Function or Purpose
Messa**g**es	Lists messages that the selected item in the Object **I**Ds list can handle. If a class associated with a window in the Object **I**Ds list is selected (such as the current class itself), the Messa**g**es list shows which Windows messages the class instance can receive.
Member **F**unctions	Lists the member functions belonging to the selected class. These functions may be message-handler functions (identified with a *W*) or MFC virtual functions (identified with a *V*).
Add C**l**ass	Calls the Add Class dialog box, from which you can create a derived class.
Add Function	Adds a member function (method) to the Member **F**unctions list box and creates a skeleton function in the class source file.
Delete Function	Deletes the member function declaration from the header file and the function reference from the message map for the selected function. Any implementation code in the source file must be removed manually.
Edit Code	Opens an editor window positioned at the selected member function, ready for editing. You can use this feature to implement the response a member function takes when the corresponding object receives a message.

Implementing a Member Function

After you generate a member function for `OnDlgExcl` (ID_DLG_EXCL:COMMAND), ClassWizard generates the skeletal function shown in Listing 4.1.

> Note: Portions of code generated by AppWizard are shown with a gray background; portions of code added by the programmer are shown with a white background.

Listing 4.1. The skeletal function `OnDlgExcl`, generated by ClassWizard.

```
///////////////////////////////////////////////////////////////////
// CDialog_1View message handlers

void CDialog_1View::OnDlgExcl()
{
    // TODO: Add your command handler code here
}
```

As it stands, this member function does nothing except provide a function to be called. You have to provide the implementation, as shown in Listing 4.2.

Listing 4.2. The finished function `OnDlgExcl`.

```
///////////////////////////////////////////////////////////////
// CDialog_1View message handlers

void CDialog_1View::OnDlgExcl()
{
    // TODO: Add your command handler code here
    m_nResponse =
        MessageBox( "Exclamation icon message box "
                    "with Yes / No / Cancel buttons.\n"
                    "Notice that the default as been "
                    "set to the second button\n"
                    "and this dialog is defined as 'Task Modal'",
                    "MB_ICONEXCLAMATION",
                    MB_ICONEXCLAMATION | MB_YESNOCANCEL |
                    MB_DEFBUTTON2 | MB_TASKMODAL );
    Invalidate();
}
```

The code added to the `OnDlgExcl` function accomplishes the following:

1. Calls a `MessageBox` function for display.
2. Assigns the value returned by the `MessageBox` function to the `m_nResponse` member variable.
3. Invalidates the view window when finished.

In the first step, calling the `CWnd::MessageBox` method, hard line breaks (`\n`) were inserted in the text to format the display. Several style flags were also applied. The first flag, `MB_ICONEXCLAMATION`, provides the exclamation icon. The `MB_YESNOCANCEL` flag provides the three buttons, and the `MB_DEFBUTTON2` flag sets the second button (the No button) as the default.

The last flag, `MB_TASKMODAL`, is actually redundant and has no effect here because the `CDialog_1View` class is derived from the `CWnd` class and `CWnd` has a window handle. If this flag had been omitted, the `MB_APPMODAL` flag would have been used by default and the results would have been exactly the same. The only reason `MB_TASKMODAL` is included is to show how the flag is used (even though modality flags are not commonly employed).

The second step accomplished by the added code (assigning the value returned by the `MessageBox` function to the `m_nResponse` member variable) requires some explanation if only because the `m_nResponse` member is not a default element in this class. Instead, `m_nResponse` must be declared in the DialoVW.H header file, as shown in the following code fragment:

```
class CDialog_1View : public CView
{
protected: // create from serialization only
    CDialog_1View();
    DECLARE_DYNCREATE(CDialog_1View)
    int    m_nResponse;
```

Because the member name m_nResponse uses Hungarian notation, you already know that it is an integer variable. The fact that this is a protected member variable (rather than private or public) is not so obvious: To get this snippet of information, you must look at the declaration (it is not encoded in the member name).

> ### Public, Private, and Protected Class Member Variables
>
> Class member variables and class member functions can be declared as private, protected, or public. These conditions are briefly defined as follows:
>
> **Private** means that the member or function can only be accessed indirectly through another member function or through a friend of the class. It cannot be accessed externally or directly from a derived class. Private is the default for all members (both functions and variables) of a class.
>
> **Protected** means that the member or function can be called both by member functions and friends of the class. It can also be called from derived classes but are not accessible publicly.
>
> **Public** identifies member functions and member variables that can be accessed from outside the class and by friends of the class or derived classes. All class members (particularly method functions) intended to be called by applications to access the class must be declared public.

Just like any variable, m_nResponse must be initialized before it can be used. The logical place for initialization is in the constructor method:

```
CDialog_1View::CDialog_1View()
{
    // TODO: add construction code here
    m_nResponse = 0;
}
```

A class's *constructor method*, which always bears the same name as the class itself, is called automatically when the class instance is created. It offers the opportunity to initialize the instance and any member variables within the class.

In similar fashion, the *destructor method*, which also bears the name of the class but is preceded by a tilde (~), is called automatically when a class instance goes out of scope but may also be called deliberately to destroy an instance. The destructor also offers an opportunity for any clean-up required before the class instance terminates.

The last step in responding to the ID_DLG_EXCL message is a call to the Invalidate method. Invalidate is defined in the CWnd ancestor class; by default, it invalidates the entire window region, erasing the window background before repainting. The purpose of the Invalidate instruction is to ensure that the view window is repainted after the message box closes. When the view window is repainted, the button selection used to close the message box is displayed as the rest of the code executes.

The remaining three handler methods are shown in Listing 4.3.

Listing 4.3. The `OnDlgInfo`, `OnDlgQuestion`, and `OnDlgStop` methods used in the Dialog_1 sample application.

```
void CDialog_1View::OnDlgInfo()
{
    // TODO: Add your command handler code here
    m_nResponse =
        MessageBox( "Asterisk or Information icon message box "
                    "with Okay button only",
                    "MB_ICONASTERISK", MB_ICONASTERISK | MB_OK );
    Invalidate();
}

void CDialog_1View::OnDlgQuestion()
{
    // TODO: Add your command handler code here
    m_nResponse =
        MessageBox( "Question icon message box "
                    "with Okay / Cancel buttons",
                    "MB_ICONQUESTION", MB_ICONQUESTION | MB_OKCANCEL );
    Invalidate();
}

void CDialog_1View::OnDlgStop()
{
    // TODO: Add your command handler code here
    m_nResponse =
        MessageBox( "Stop icon message box "
                    "with Abort / Retry / Ignore buttons",
                    "MB_ICONSTOP", MB_ICONSTOP | MB_ABORTRETRYIGNORE );
    Invalidate();
}
```

In each case, the same pattern as shown for the `OnDlgExcl` function is followed: the message box is created, the return result is assigned to the `m_nResponse` variable, and the view window is invalidated for repainting.

Reporting Button Selections

Although they are not really necessary, the provisions to report button selection (or, more accurately, to report the results returned by the message boxes) are quite simple. The `OnDraw` method is provided in the `CDialog_1View` class by default—primarily because AppWizard assumes that there will be something to be displayed. The `OnDraw` method provides a convenient place for your own report display. The necessary code is shown in Listing 4.4.

Listing 4.4. The completed `OnDraw` method, used to report which button was selected to close a message box.

```
void CDialog_1View::OnDraw(CDC* pDC)
{
    CDialog_1Doc* pDoc = GetDocument();
    ASSERT_VALID(pDoc);

    // TODO: add draw code for native data here
    CString csText;

    csText = "The last response was ";
    switch( m_nResponse )
    {
        case IDABORT:   csText += "Abort";   break;
        case IDCANCEL:  csText += "Cancel";  break;
        case IDIGNORE:  csText += "Ignore";  break;
        case IDNO:      csText += "No";      break;
        case IDOK:      csText += "Okay";    break;
        case IDRETRY:   csText += "Retry";   break;
        case IDYES:     csText += "Yes";     break;
    }
    if( m_nResponse )
    {
        pDC->TextOut( 10, 10, csText );
        m_nResponse = 0;
    }
}
```

For those new to MFC, the `CString` class is MFC's replacement for the familiar strings defined as arrays of char. Unlike arrays of char, however, `CString` objects follow a different set of rules (a more flexible set, as it were); they are described in greater detail in the following section.

Before looking at `CString`s at length, however, you should notice a few elements in the implementation of the `OnDraw` method.

First, the `CString csText` declaration is local to this function and has no scope outside the `OnDraw` method. This means that the `csText` instance is initialized (including memory allocation for dynamic storage) when `OnDraw` is called and is deallocated (by its own destructor method) when `OnDraw` concludes. The `m_nResponse` variable, on the other hand, is a member of the `CDialog_1View` class and is not destroyed until the application concludes.

Second, where conventional Windows draw functions had to retrieve a device context before doing anything else, the `OnDraw` method receives a pointer to a device context when it is called. Using MFC, however, instead of a pointer to a handle for a device context, the pointer is a pointer to a device context class that incorporates its own member functions.

Thus, instead of calling API functions for output, output calls are made to the equivalent member functions. Although these member functions duplicate the familiar API functions, the calling parameters (and the types of parameters permitted) differ.

For example, for text output in a conventional Windows application, you would have written a call like this one:

```
TextOut( hDC, 10, 10, szText, strlen( szText ) );
```

But because you have a pointer to a device context class instance, your output function call is much simpler. Because TextOut is an overloaded function, your output function call can take either of the following two forms:

```
pDC->TextOut( 10, 10, szText, strlen( szText ) );
pDC->TextOut( 10, 10, csText );
```

In these latter two examples, you do not have to provide the device context handle because it belongs to the class instance already.

The first of these two forms uses a LPCSTR (char array) and, therefore, requires a length argument—just as the original API example does. The second of these two forms uses a CString argument and no longer requires the length argument (probably because the length is already a member element in the CString class).

Note: *Overloaded functions* are functions that have two or more calling formats; the calling formats are distinguished by the number and type of calling parameters. In most cases, the overloaded functions perform essentially the same function; in some cases, however, overloaded functions may perform drastically different tasks.

Overloaded Functions and Overloaded Operators

Although the idea of *overloaded functions* (functions that accept different parameters and perform different tasks) may sound odd, it is actually nothing new. What may be more familiar, however (and serves well for examples), are the *overloaded operators*, which have been an unremarked feature of programming languages almost from their inception.

Consider the addition operator represented by the plus (+) sign. The addition (or concatenation) operator has always been an overloaded operator. The activities involved in the calculation 1 + 2 are not the same as those involved in the calculation 1.00 + 2.00. We *think* of these as the same (they're both addition operations), but the first example involves integer values and the second involves floating point values.

Even if we perform this task using paper and pencil, the task itself is so familiar that we do not consciously recognize the fact that there are two different operations involved.

We can create a third version by stating the equation this way: 1.00 + 2 (adding a floating point value and an integer). This third form (and the fourth form if we reverse the order) is not automatically covered by an overloaded operator and may require that we use typecasting to instruct the system to treat the integer as a floating point value.

> The point, however, is that this practice of overloading operators has been extended to overloading functions by the simple process of allowing us to create two or more forms of a function with the same name—as long as the functions can be distinguished by the types of parameters used to call them.
>
> In the end, this is not a case of having one function that examines the calling parameters and makes a decision about what should be done with them. Rather, it's a case of which version of a function is called as determined by the number and types of the parameters passed as arguments.
>
> Although it may not be obvious, this means that a function cannot be called with just any parameter list. If an overloaded function has not been defined with a particular list of arguments—and provided with the necessary operations code to use those arguments—the function cannot be called with that set of arguments.
>
> Another form (typified by the `printf` function) does accept and parse a variable parameter list. These forms, however, begin with one or more predefined parameters and have provisions to check the stack to see how many additional parameters have been passed, to retrieve these variable parameters, and to parse them according to their own rules. In the case of the `printf` function, this takes the form of a format string as a fixed parameter and uses codes in the format string to help determine what additional arguments should be expected, what the types of each should be, and how they should be treated.
>
> This form has the advantage of being more flexible than an overloaded function but is also more complicated to program correctly.

For simplicity, the `CString` format is used wherever possible in this book. The `CString` format is also recommended for general use.

The *CString* Class

The `CString` class fills a long-standing gap in C/C++ functionality. Conventional strings (that is, char arrays) have always been an inconvenience at best—and a major annoyance at worst. Using MFC, the `CString` object class offers much of the functionality conventional C/C++ string handling has so long lacked.

Like conventional strings, a `CString` object consists of a sequence of characters. But unlike conventional strings, a `CString` object has a variable length and can expand and shrink as required. Further, the `CString` class provides functions and operators similar to those found in BASIC, permitting strings to be concatenated, substrings to be extracted, and string comparisons to be made. The end result is that `CString` objects are both more convenient and easier to use than conventional character arrays.

The `CString` class is based on the `TCHAR` data type. This means that—if `_UNICODE` is defined in your application—`TCHAR` and `CString` are defined as type `wchar`, a 16-bit character type. If `_UNICODE` is not defined, `CString` objects are created from 8-bit characters.

Other important characteristics of CStrings are listed here:

- CString objects can grow by concatenation.
- CString objects follow "value semantics" and can therefore be treated as actual strings rather than as pointers to strings.
- CString objects can be substituted for const char * and LPCTSTR arguments in functions.
- CString object characters are directly accessible as a read-only array using a conversion operator, making the CString object behave like a C-style string.

> Note: When possible, you can save memory by allocating CString objects on the frame rather than on the heap. Doing so also simplifies parameter passing.

Table 4.9 lists CString operators and methods and provides a brief explanation of each.

Table 4.9. CString operators and method functions.

CString Member	Purpose
CString	Constructor: initializes the CString instance.
GetLength	Returns the number of characters in a CString object.
IsEmpty	Returns TRUE if CString object is empty.
Empty	Forces CString object to have 0 length.
GetAt	Returns the character at a given position.
(operator) [ ]	Returns the character at a given position. The [] brackets perform as an operator version of the GetAt() method: the value within the brackets identifies an offset within the string. In effect, this is the same as indexing an array of char.
SetAt	Sets a character at a given position.
(operator) LPCTSTR ()	Directly accesses characters stored in a CString object as a C-style string.

Assignment/Concatenation Operators

CString Member	Purpose
(operator) =	Assigns a new value to a CString object.
(operator) +	Concatenates two strings and returns a new string.
(operator) +=	Concatenates a new string to the end of an existing string.

Comparison Operators

CString Member	Purpose
(operators) ==, <, >, and so on	Comparison operators (case sensitive).
Compare	Compares two strings (case sensitive).
CompareNoCase	Compares two strings (case insensitive).
Collate	Obsolete; see Compare.

Extraction Methods

CString Member	Purpose
Mid	Extracts the middle part of a string. Requires arguments to specify the beginning and ending character positions.
Left	Extracts the left *n* characters of a string.
Right	Extracts the right *n* characters of a string.
SpanIncluding	Extracts a substring that contains only the characters in a specified set.
SpanExcluding	Extracts a substring that contains only the characters *not* in a specified set.

Conversion Methods

CString Member	Purpose
MakeUpper	Converts all the characters in string to uppercase characters.
MakeLower	Converts all the characters in string to lowercase characters.
MakeReverse	Reverses the order of characters in string.
Format	Formats a string following the same insertion rules as the sprintf function.
TrimLeft	Trims leading whitespace characters from string.
TrimRight	Trims trailing whitespace characters from string.

Search Methods

CString Member	Purpose
Find	Finds a character or substring inside a larger string.
ReverseFind	Finds a character inside a larger string; starts from the end.
FindOneOf	Finds the first matching character from a set.

Archive/Dump Methods

CString Member	Purpose
(operator) <<	Inserts a CString object into an archive or dump context.
(operator) >>	Extracts a CString object from an archive.

continues

Table 4.9. continued

Buffer Access CString Member	Purpose
GetBuffer	Returns a pointer to the characters in the CString; must be followed by a call to ReleaseBuffer.
GetBufferSetLength	Returns a pointer to the characters in the CString, truncating the buffer to the specified length.
ReleaseBuffer	Releases control of the buffer returned by GetBuffer.
FreeExtra	Removes any overhead of this string object by freeing any extra memory previously allocated to the string.

Examples of some of these methods can be found in various example programs throughout this book. Complete details about each of these methods are available through online help in the Visual Workbench and in Books Online on your distribution CD.

Creating a Custom Exit

So far, this chapter has demonstrated a number of message boxes that operate on a standalone basis—that is, they haven't been tied into any functional code waiting for a response. However, there is one area in every application menu for which a message box can be quite appropriate: the Exit option.

The AppWizard and MFC provide a default Exit option in every application menu (or, if there is no menu, they provide an Exit button and an Exit option in the system menu). In many cases, however, you will want to either provide your own exit option or use a message box to query the user before exiting (as in this example).

In a conventional Windows application, the exit code for a message box that queries the user before exiting might have looked like this:

```
case ID_EXIT:
    if( MessageBox( hWnd,
                    "Are you sure you want to exit?",
                    "Leaving so soon?",
                    MB_ICONQUESTION | MB_YESNO ) == IDYES )
        PostQuitMessage( 0 );
    break;
```

The PostQuitMessage instruction is used to send a terminate instruction to the application. In an MFC application, the instruction can also be used in exactly this fashion. However—you knew there was a catch coming, didn't you?—in an MFC application, issuing a PostQuitMessage instruction may cause the application to terminate without an orderly shutdown.

In some cases, a disorderly shutdown may make no particular difference. Depending on your application, however, a disorderly shutdown can also leave files open, leave buffers unflushed, or otherwise leave the system in an awkward or unstable state.

To perform a more orderly shutdown while still having the option of querying the request, return to the ClassWizard. This time, however, select the CMainFrame class and add a function to respond to the ID_APP_EXIT object (see Figure 4.7).

This is accomplished with the same steps used earlier to link the four menu items to the skeleton functions that call the individual message boxes and report the responses to each. From the ClassWizard, select the CMainFrame class and then the ID_APP_EXIT message. Then select COMMAND from the Messages list and click the **A**dd Function button to create a skeleton function.

Finally, click the **E**dit Code button; you are positioned in the appropriate source file at the created function, ready to implement the necessary provisions.

Figure 4.7. Creating a custom exit procedure.

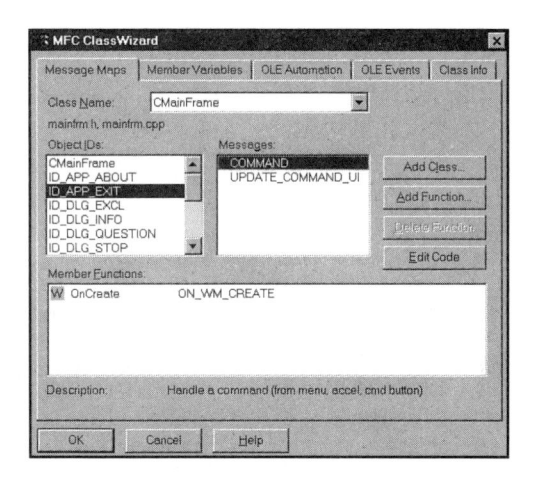

In the resulting OnAppExit function in MainFram.CPP, you can now install the implementation shown in Listing 4.5 to call a message box to query the user.

Listing 4.5. The completed OnAppExit method, used to call a message box to query the user before terminating the application.

```
void CMainFrame::OnAppExit()
{
   // TODO: Add your command handler code here
   if( MessageBox( "Are you sure you want to exit?",
                   "Leaving so soon?",
                   MB_ICONQUESTION | MB_YESNO ) == IDYES )
      OnClose();
}
```

Notice that, rather than issuing a `PostQuitMessage` instruction (which, even here, can still result in a disorderly shutdown), the `OnClose` function is called if the user response is affirmative.

The `OnClose` function is a member function in `CWnd`; it, in turn, calls the `DestroyWindow` member function to send the appropriate messages to the window to deactivate it, and remove the input focus. In addition, `DestroyWindow` destroys the window's menu, flushes the application queue, destroys outstanding timers, removes Clipboard ownership, and breaks the Clipboard viewer chain if `CWnd` is at the top of the viewer chain.

If the window is the parent of any windows, the `DestroyWindow` member function destroys child windows first and then the window itself. The `DestroyWindow` member function also destroys modeless dialog boxes created by `CDialog::Create`.

The end result is that the application shuts down in an orderly manner without you having to trouble with all the details.

Of course, if you have any special shutdown requirements, you could execute these in response to the MessageBox dialog…or, better by far, you could use object classes to ensure that the class destructor methods incorporate the appropriate shutdown provisions.

> Tip: Check the `OnCreate` method in `CMainFrame`; you will find a line of code that positions and sizes this application when it is initially executed.
>
> Although some initialization can be handled in the class constructor method (such as initializing member variables), other tasks cannot be carried out at this time because they require information that does not exist yet. Examples include resizing and positioning the application window because, when the constructor method is called, the application window does not yet exist.
>
> Instead, the `OnCreate` method (which is not called immediately but is called after the window has been created) provides a second initialization opportunity for tasks of this type.

Source Code

Source code listings for `DialoVW.H`, `DialoVW.CPP`, and `MainFram.CPP` appear in Listings 4.6, 4.7, and 4.8, respectively. The remaining source files used to create the Dialog_1 example remain as they were created by AppWizard and are available on the CD-ROM that accompanies this book.

Listing 4.6. Source code for DialoVW.H.

```
// dialovw.h : interface of the CDialog_1View class
//
/////////////////////////////////////////////////////////////////////

class CDialog_1View : public CView
```

```
{
protected: // create from serialization only
      CDialog_1View();
      DECLARE_DYNCREATE(CDialog_1View)
intm_nResponse;
// Attributes
public:
      CDialog_1Doc* GetDocument();

// Operations
public:

// Overrides
      // ClassWizard generated virtual function overrides
      //{{AFX_VIRTUAL(CDialog_1View)
      public:
      virtual void OnDraw(CDC* pDC);  // overridden to draw this view
      protected:
      //}}AFX_VIRTUAL

// Implementation
public:
      virtual ~CDialog_1View();
#ifdef _DEBUG
      virtual void AssertValid() const;
      virtual void Dump(CDumpContext& dc) const;
#endif

protected:

// Generated message map functions
protected:
      //{{AFX_MSG(CDialog_1View)
      afx_msg void OnDlgExcl();
      afx_msg void OnDlgInfo();
      afx_msg void OnDlgQuestion();
      afx_msg void OnDlgStop();
      //}}AFX_MSG
      DECLARE_MESSAGE_MAP()
};

#ifndef _DEBUG  // debug version in dialovw.cpp
inline CDialog_1Doc* CDialog_1View::GetDocument()
   { return (CDialog_1Doc*)m_pDocument; }
#endif

/////////////////////////////////////////////////////////////////////////////
```

Listing 4.7. Source code for DialoVW.CPP.

```
// dialovw.cpp : implementation of the CDialog_1View class
//

#include "stdafx.h"
#include "dialog_1.h"

#include "dialodoc.h"
```

continues

Listing 4.7. continued

```
#include "dialovw.h"

#ifdef _DEBUG
#undef THIS_FILE
static char BASED_CODE THIS_FILE[] = __FILE__;
#endif

/////////////////////////////////////////////////////////////////////////////
// CDialog_1View

IMPLEMENT_DYNCREATE(CDialog_1View, CView)

BEGIN_MESSAGE_MAP(CDialog_1View, CView)
    //{{AFX_MSG_MAP(CDialog_1View)
    ON_COMMAND(ID_DLG_EXCL, OnDlgExcl)
    ON_COMMAND(ID_DLG_INFO, OnDlgInfo)
    ON_COMMAND(ID_DLG_QUESTION, OnDlgQuestion)
    ON_COMMAND(ID_DLG_STOP, OnDlgStop)
    //}}AFX_MSG_MAP
END_MESSAGE_MAP()

/////////////////////////////////////////////////////////////////////////////
// CDialog_1View construction/destruction

CDialog_1View::CDialog_1View()
{
    // TODO: add construction code here
    m_nResponse = 0;
}

CDialog_1View::~CDialog_1View()
{
}

/////////////////////////////////////////////////////////////////////////////
// CDialog_1View drawing

void CDialog_1View::OnDraw(CDC* pDC)
{
    CDialog_1Doc* pDoc = GetDocument();
    ASSERT_VALID(pDoc);

    // TODO: add draw code for native data here
    CString csText;

    csText = "The last response was ";
    switch( m_nResponse )
    {
        case IDABORT:   csText += "Abort";   break;
        case IDCANCEL:  csText += "Cancel";  break;
        case IDIGNORE:  csText += "Ignore";  break;
        case IDNO:      csText += "No";      break;
        case IDOK:      csText += "Okay";    break;
        case IDRETRY:   csText += "Retry";   break;
        case IDYES:     csText += "Yes";     break;
    }
```

```
      if( m_nResponse )
      {
         pDC->TextOut( 10, 10, csText );
         m_nResponse = 0;
      }
}

/////////////////////////////////////////////////////////////////////////////
// CDialog_1View diagnostics

#ifdef _DEBUG
void CDialog_1View::AssertValid() const
{
   CView::AssertValid();
}

void CDialog_1View::Dump(CDumpContext& dc) const
{
   CView::Dump(dc);
}

CDialog_1Doc* CDialog_1View::GetDocument() // non-debug version is inline
{
   ASSERT(m_pDocument->IsKindOf(RUNTIME_CLASS(CDialog_1Doc)));
   return (CDialog_1Doc*)m_pDocument;
}
#endif //_DEBUG

/////////////////////////////////////////////////////////////////////////////
// CDialog_1View message handlers

void CDialog_1View::OnDlgExcl()
{
   // TODO: Add your command handler code here
   m_nResponse =
      MessageBox( "Exclamation icon message box "
                  "with Yes / No / Cancel buttons.\n"
                  "Notice that the default as been "
                  "set to the second button\n"
                  "and this dialog is defined as 'Task Modal'",
                  "MB_ICONEXCLAMATION",
                  MB_ICONEXCLAMATION | MB_YESNOCANCEL |
                  MB_DEFBUTTON2 | MB_TASKMODAL );
   Invalidate();
}

void CDialog_1View::OnDlgInfo()
{
   // TODO: Add your command handler code here
   m_nResponse =
      MessageBox( "Asterisk or Information icon message box "
                  "with Okay button only",
                  "MB_ICONASTERISK", MB_ICONASTERISK | MB_OK );
   Invalidate();
}

void CDialog_1View::OnDlgQuestion()
{
```

continues

Listing 4.7. continued

```
        // TODO: Add your command handler code here
        m_nResponse =
            MessageBox( "Question icon message box "
                        "with Okay / Cancel buttons",
                        "MB_ICONQUESTION", MB_ICONQUESTION | MB_OKCANCEL );
        Invalidate();
    }

    void CDialog_1View::OnDlgStop()
    {
        // TODO: Add your command handler code here
        m_nResponse =
            MessageBox( "Stop icon message box "
                        "with Abort / Retry / Ignore buttons",
                        "MB_ICONSTOP", MB_ICONSTOP | MB_ABORTRETRYIGNORE );
        Invalidate();
    }
```

Listing 4.8. Source code for MainFram.CPP.

```
// mainfrm.cpp : implementation of the CMainFrame class
//

#include "stdafx.h"
#include "dialog_1.h"

#include "mainfrm.h"

#ifdef _DEBUG
#undef THIS_FILE
static char BASED_CODE THIS_FILE[] = __FILE__;
#endif

/////////////////////////////////////////////////////////////////////////////
// CMainFrame

IMPLEMENT_DYNCREATE(CMainFrame, CFrameWnd)

BEGIN_MESSAGE_MAP(CMainFrame, CFrameWnd)
    //{{AFX_MSG_MAP(CMainFrame)
    ON_WM_CREATE()
    ON_COMMAND(ID_APP_EXIT, OnAppExit)
    //}}AFX_MSG_MAP
END_MESSAGE_MAP()

/////////////////////////////////////////////////////////////////////////////
// CMainFrame construction/destruction

CMainFrame::CMainFrame()
{
    // TODO: add member initialization code here
}

CMainFrame::~CMainFrame()
{
```

```
}
/////////////////////////////////////////////////////////////////////////////
// CMainFrame diagnostics

#ifdef _DEBUG
void CMainFrame::AssertValid() const
{
   CFrameWnd::AssertValid();
}

void CMainFrame::Dump(CDumpContext& dc) const
{
   CFrameWnd::Dump(dc);
}

#endif //_DEBUG

/////////////////////////////////////////////////////////////////////////////
// CMainFrame message handlers

int CMainFrame::OnCreate(LPCREATESTRUCT lpCreateStruct)
{
   if (CFrameWnd::OnCreate(lpCreateStruct) == -1)
      return -1;

   // TODO: Add your specialized creation code here
   MoveWindow( 0, 0, 320, 240, FALSE );
   return 0;
}

void CMainFrame::OnAppExit()
{
   // TODO: Add your command handler code here
   if( MessageBox( "Are you sure you want to exit?",
                   "Leaving so soon?",
                   MB_ICONQUESTION | MB_YESNO ) == IDYES )
      OnClose();
}
```

Summary

In this chapter, you were introduced to message boxes and how they are used. You also learned how to use the ClassWizard to link menu items to class member functions, and were introduced to CStrings. Finally, you learned how to create a custom exit procedure.

Chapter 5, "Introducing AppStudio and Application Resources," takes a look at the Visual C++ AppStudio; you will learn how you can create your own custom application resource elements.

CHAPTER 5

Introducing AppStudio and Application Resources

◆

In DOS applications—back in the old and unlamented 16-bit world—any elements used by an application were expected to be loaded into active memory when the application started. Granted, there were some exceptions (such as overlays), but these exceptions were both rare and limited in application. And unfortunately, it didn't matter whether all these elements—code and data—were being used at any one time; it all had to be loaded from the start. The result was that, generally, any application requiring more than 600K for application code and data was out of luck.

A number of schemes have been introduced at various times and in various operating systems to circumvent these memory limitations. DLLs, for example, can be thought of as shared overlays that are loaded only when needed; but they can be loaded (used) by many different applications and the DLLs aren't part of the application code at all.

Another important development—and one more immediately relevant to our purposes—is the separation of certain application data elements, or application resources. When you separate application resources, even if they are part of the application's executable file, the resources are not loaded into memory on execution. Instead, application resources under Windows (or under OS/2) are loaded on an as-needed basis and are discarded when no longer needed.

Because application resources are functionally separate from the executable portion of an application, resources can be edited directly from an executable (with the appropriate utility) without recompiling the executable. Such changes, however, cannot alter the functionality of the resource, only the appearance or the arrangement of elements within the resource.

To many, the biggest advantage of resources (and certainly one of the major propaganda points) is that this independence makes it possible to adapt applications to other languages without having to revise—and potentially introduce errors into—the source code. Because all dialog boxes and display elements are contained in the resources and because all display strings can be drawn from string tables, the application resources can be edited and translated into different languages without any revisions to the original application code. Indeed, these changes can be made without touching or recompiling the application at all.

Application Resource Types

An *application resource* is binary data created by a resource compiler or developer and added to an application's executable file. Standard resources describe accelerator tables, bitmaps, cursors, dialog boxes, fonts, icons, menus, message-table entries, string-table entries, or version information. Custom or application-defined resources also consist of binary data but have a format and function defined by the application itself. The standard resource types are briefly introduced in this section and detailed in the following chapters.

Figure 5.1 shows the resource file for an application created by AppWizard.

Figure 5.1. *A collection of application resources.*

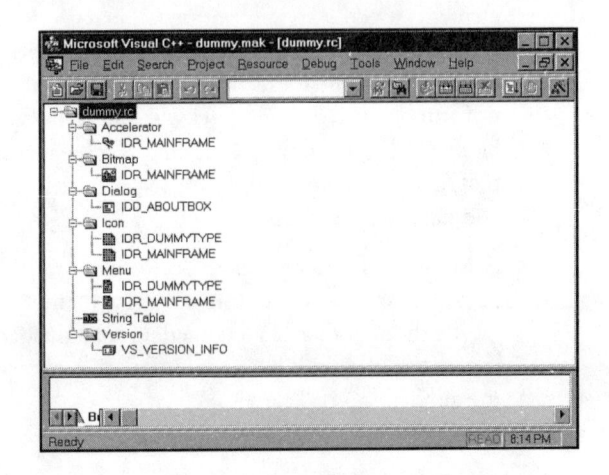

In Figure 5.1, the application resources are arranged by type in a tree list. Groups representing resource types can be expanded to show individual resources; double-clicking individual resource items brings up the resource editor for the selected item.

The **R**esource menu in version 2.*x* and either the **I**nsert, **R**esource option or the resource buttons on the toolbar in version 4.0 can be used to add new resource items to an application. Simply select the resource type from the menu or toolbar and a new, blank resource is created by opening the editor for that resource type. However, at the same time AppWizard creates your skeletal application files, it also creates skeletal application resource files (as shown in Figure 5.1) as part of the project. These include accelerators, menus, a toolbar bitmap, default icons, a string table, an About dialog box, and version information. All these elements can be edited, revised, deleted, or modified as desired.

Accelerator Keys

An *accelerator key* is a key or key combination that can be used to initiate an action within an application. In most cases, accelerators are used as keyboard shortcuts for program commands that are also available on a menu or toolbar. Accelerator keys can also be used to initiate commands not associated with conventional interface objects. Examples of system-defined accelerator keys are using the Ctrl+Delete, Shift+Delete, or Shift+Insert keys to copy, cut, or paste information to or from the Clipboard.

Accelerator tables are Windows resources that contain lists of accelerator keys and their associated command identifiers. Applications can contain more than one accelerator table and can load different accelerator tables—with different key combinations and actions—at different times or in response to user preferences.

> Tip: You can use the ClassWizard to hook accelerator key commands directly to class functions.

Dialog Boxes

Dialog boxes are commonly seen as message or input windows. But they can also be child windows used to organize information for display. Although you can construct dialog boxes as scripts (text files), the dialog box editor provides an interactive environment in which the dialog elements (buttons, list boxes, edit fields, scrollbars, and so on) can be selected, sized, and positioned exactly as they are to appear on screen.

Further, the dialog box editor provides the means to align dialog elements and set tab orders and groups; it even permits dialog boxes to be tested during construction.

Dialog boxes are discussed further in Chapter 7, "Designing Custom Dialog Boxes," and Chapter 8, "Customizing Dialog Boxes with Additional Controls."

Font Resources

Fonts—files containing character images—are also resource elements. With the development and current popularity of TrueType fonts, however, the use of resource fonts has become increasingly uncommon; font resources are no longer supported by most resource editors.

Image Resources

Image resources include three principal resource types: bitmaps (BMP), cursors (CUR), and icons (ICO). In actual fact, all three are bit images but each is stored in a different format; different rules and organization are also applied to the creation of each. The fourth image type, toolbars, are actually bitmap images (BMP) that receive special handling within the application.

The simplest form of image resource is the *bitmap image*. These pixel images can be any size and can contain 2, 16, or 256 colors. Individual bitmap images can be as large as a full screen (or larger), medium-sized (as are the card images used in the Solitaire or Hearts games), or as small as the few dozen pixels required for a checkmark image. Bitmap images are limited, however, in that they can consist of only foreground pixels and do not contain any transparent areas.

Icon image resources are commonly used to represent applications in program groups or on the desktop. They are special-purpose bitmaps; unlike conventional bitmaps, icon images are fixed in size and can contain transparent areas or have pixels that interact with and invert background image pixels.

Cursor images are the third type of bitmap resource and consist of fixed-size (32×32-bit) monochrome images. Like icons, however, cursor images can contain transparent areas or, for maximum contrast, pixels that invert background pixels. Cursor images also contain a reference point or *hotspot*: a pixel location within the image that defines the cursor position.

Toolbar images are a specialized form of bitmap consisting of one or more equally sized images arranged in a strip. By default, each button is 15 pixels high and 16 pixels wide (the only button size originally supported). With Visual C++ 4.0, however, you can change both the height of the bitmap strip and the width of the buttons. All buttons in a specific toolbar, however, continue to be the same width.

The spacing and grouping of buttons in a toolbar is not defined in the toolbar bitmap but is determined in the application code as you discover in Chapter 6, "Using Menus, Toolbars, and Status Bars."

Bitmaps, cursors, icons, and toolbars are discussed further in Chapter 6.

Menu Resources

Menu resources provide selections of application options in the form of pull-down lists. Menu entries can call additional menu lists, call dialog boxes, or initiate immediate execution of a selected action. Like dialog boxes, menus can be constructed using ASCII scripts but are more conveniently constructed using the menu editor to design, arrange, and test menus. Menus are discussed further in Chapter 6, "Using Menus, Toolbars, and Status Bars."

String Tables

String resources are text strings that may be used by an application in any situation in which any other text might be displayed. The advantages of string resources over embedded strings are the conservation of memory and the convenience in editing.

Version Information

The *version resource* consists of VS_VERSION_INFO keys that identify file, product, and operating system versions. These keys also contain product names, copyright and trademark information, and internal and source filenames. This data is available—and editable—using the version information editor in AppStudio.

Application Files and File Types

Figure 5.2 shows an application file tree created by AppWizard. The 16 source files shown are the standard files used to create an application using AppWizard's default settings. An actual application may have more files than this, or may omit some of these files and include their functionality in other sources or omit them entirely. Alternatively, a project can include other file types.

Figure 5.2. *A project file tree.*

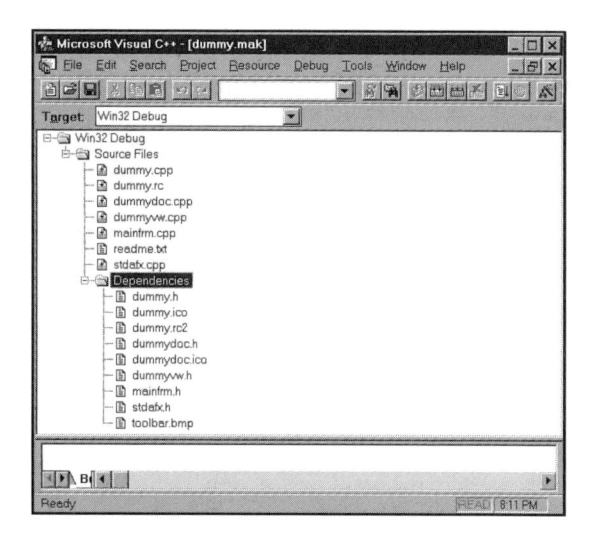

The files shown in Figure 5.2 are not, however, the only files you may find in your directories. The files shown in this tree are only the source files used to build the application; the tree does not include other files generated by Visual C++ that contain browse information, file organization and positioning, object class organization, and so on.

Table 5.1 shows some of the files generated during compile and link for a dummy application created by AppWizard. Even though the dummy application has no real functionality, these work files—which are superfluous once an application is finished—take more than 4.5M of disk space.

Table 5.1. Work files generated by Visual C/C++.

Extension	Typical Size	Function
APS	31K	Used by Visual C++ to organize application files and windows.
BSC	700K	Browse file containing class mapping information.
CLW	2K	Contains information used by the ClassWizard to edit existing classes or add new classes; also stores information needed to create and edit message maps and dialog data maps and to create prototype member functions.
ILK	170K	Microsoft Link database.
OBJ	10K to 40K	Object file used by linker to produce executable application.
PCH	2,300K	Precompiled header file; saves recompiling source files that have not been modified.
PDB	500K	Microsoft C/C++ program database.
SBR	0K to 600K	Debug information.
VCP	11K	Record file used by Visual C++ during project compile/link.

Of course, if you have unlimited disk space, 4.5M of work files for a dummy application produces no particular strain on your system. For most of us, however, deleting these files after use frees up an important block of disk space. After all, if you need these files later, they are very easy to regenerate.

Unfortunately, Visual C++ does not include a utility that cleans up after a project by deleting the remnant files.

Resource File Types

In addition to the work files generated by the Visual C/C++ compiler, AppStudio also uses—and may generate—a variety of files containing individual resources, resource groups, or resource scripts. These file types are listed in Table 5.2.

Table 5.2. Resource file types.

Extension	Type	Description
BMP	Bitmap image	An individual bitmap image file.
CUR	Cursor image	An individual cursor image file.
DAT	Resource	Raw data resource used for custom resource types; may be copied, edited, renamed, or deleted but is not supported by the Visual Workbench. Instead, some custom utility or application may be needed to work with DAT resources.
DLG	Dialog resource	Script file describing a resource dialog box.
DLL	Executable	Dynamic link library module that may contain executable code or compiled application resources.
DRV	Device driver	Compiled device driver; like an EXE file, a device driver can contain resource elements, dialog boxes, and so on.
EXE	Executable	Executable program code that combines application resources and compiled program code.
FNT	Font typeface	File containing a single typeface font.
FON	Font library	File containing one or more fonts belonging to a single typeface.
H	Header file	Header file containing symbolic names for identifier constants used for resources and messages.
ICO	Icon image	An individual icon image file.
RC	Resource script	An ASCII (text) script containing one or more application resources that can be edited by AppStudio.
RC2	Resource script	An ASCII (text) script containing one or more application resources that cannot be edited by AppStudio.
RES	Resource	Compiled (binary) resource file.

Compiling and Linking Resources

Although you can use AppStudio to create and edit application resources, you normally create these resources in the form of scripts (for dialog boxes, menus, and accelerator and string tables) or in the form of individual binary files (for bitmaps, icons, and cursors). Before you can link these resources to an executable, however, you must compile them into a single binary file identified with the RES resource extension.

Once a binary RES file has been created, these resources can be linked with the compiled executable at any time. Further, resources can be edited; as long as they remain functionally the same and the application's OBJ files are still available, the resources can be recompiled and linked without recompiling the rest of the executable.

Dynamic Link Libraries

Dynamic link libraries (DLLs, pronounced *dills*) are executable library modules that may contain application executable code and/or application resources. A dynamic link library is similar to a runtime library except that the DLL is not linked to the application during the compile/link process. Instead, DLLs are dynamically linked during execution, when and as library routines or resources are required.

Dynamic link libraries have several advantages over runtime libraries:

- DLLs can be shared between applications. This means that several applications can simultaneously use code or resources from a single DLL—and that a single application can draw on code or resources from more than one DLL.
- DLL resources and functions are shared without duplicating them in multiple applications. This also means that your application can use third-party DLLs in addition to those you develop yourself.
- Just as executable resources can be edited without requiring a complete rebuild, DLL resources can also be edited—with the appropriate utilities—without having to recompile the library.

> Note: Earlier resource compilers provided capabilities for opening and editing fully compiled resources, including RES resource files, EXE executables, and DLL dynamic link libraries. These features, however, have not appeared in any of the Microsoft Visual C++ packages—possibly to prevent annoyed users from modifying (or worse, "borrowing") resources from Microsoft applications. You may, however, still be able to find other resource editors that retain this useful feature.

Header Files

Header files serve several purposes. They are often used to contain constants used in an application or to contain macro definitions. For Windows applications, however, header files serve another very important function: they provide the link between application source code and application resources.

All application resources are identified by numbers; although numbers are convenient for computers, they're not particularly convenient for programmers. Therefore, instead of remembering numbers, we use mnemonic identifiers, which are defined in the header files, in place of raw numbers.

Of course, once the resources and the application are compiled, both mnemonic identifiers and their numerical equivalents are replaced by new numbers—addresses within the resource segment. (By that time, however, they're only for the computer's convenience and we're no longer concerned with them.)

AppStudio

Visual C++'s AppStudio is not a separate application but is a general term for a collection of utilities contained in the Visual C++ Application Workbench. These utilities are not accessed separately and, with some exceptions, application resources are not created as separate files. Instead, in most cases, application resources are created as a part of an *application project*.

Figure 5.1, earlier in this chapter, showed an application resource tree that listed resources by type and by resource identifier. Table 5.3 lists those resources. You can edit any of these predefined application resources simply by clicking the resource item to bring up the appropriate resource editor for that type.

Table 5.3. Resources defined for Dummy project.

Resource Type	Identifier	Comments
Accelerator	IDR_MAINFRAME	The accelerator table defines hotkeys for menu and toolbar.
Bitmap	IDR_MAINFRAME	Bitmap used for application toolbar.
Dialog	IDR_ABOUTBOX	A simple dialog box that names the application and the version number and provides a copyright statement. This may be modified and expanded as needed.
Icon	IDR_MAINFRAME	Application icon; uses the default AFX icon image.
	IDR_DUMMYTYPE	Document icon; uses the default document icon image.
Menu	IDR_MAINFRAME	Standard application menu (brief form).
	IDR_DUMMYTYPE	Standard application menu (long form).
String Table		Standard string resources. Because there is only one string table, instead of the table having an identifier, individual identifiers are assigned to each entry in the string table.
Version	VS_VERSION_INFO	Version and copyright information.

As you may have noticed, four of these resource elements share the identifier IDR_MAINFRAME. These resources identify the application icon, accelerator table, menu, and toolbar bitmaps used by default. The two IDR_DUMMYTYPE resources offer an icon for documents and an expanded application menu that is loaded after a file (document) is opened. The IDR_ABOUTBOX identifier is standard for the About dialog box; VS_VERSION_INFO is predefined for the version information resource.

Although these predefined resources are useful—and can and should be modified—the odds are that you'll want to add your own resource elements.

Managing Resources

The **R**esource menu in Visual C++ (see Figure 5.3) offers a number of options for managing application resources. You can use the menu to create new resource items, edit resources as binary data, import and export resources, browse resource symbols, and manage symbolic header and include files for your project. These options are discussed further in the following sections.

Figure 5.3. The Visual C++ Resource menu.

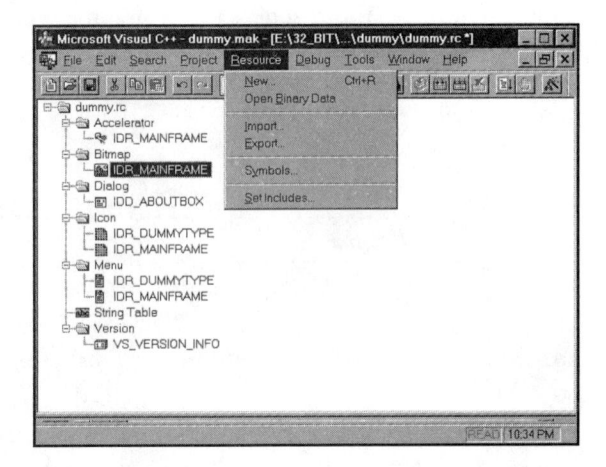

Creating a New Resource

From the **R**esource menu, you use the **N**ew option to call the New Resource dialog box (see Figure 5.4).

Figure 5.4. The New Resource dialog box.

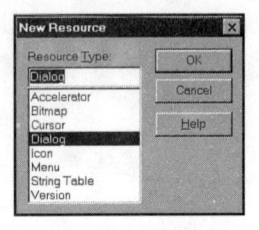

The New Resource dialog box contains a list box with a selection of eight resource types. Select a resource type by highlighting the selection and clicking OK or by double-clicking the resource type in the list. A new resource item is created in the current project and C++ takes you to the editor for the selected resource type.

Editing a Resource as Binary Data

The Open **B**inary Data option on the **R**esource menu is enabled only if an existing resource is already selected from the resource tree (in the RC file). Select a resource item and then choose Open **B**inary Data to call a binary (hexadecimal) editor for the compiled resource (see Figure 5.5).

Figure 5.5. The binary editor.

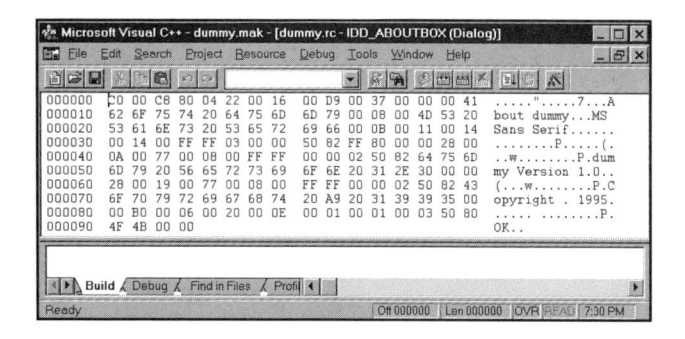

Importing and Exporting Resource Items

The **I**mport option on the **R**esource menu opens the Import Resource dialog box (see Figure 5.6). Use this dialog box to import a bitmap, cursor, or icon image into the current resource file.

Figure 5.6. The Import Resource dialog box.

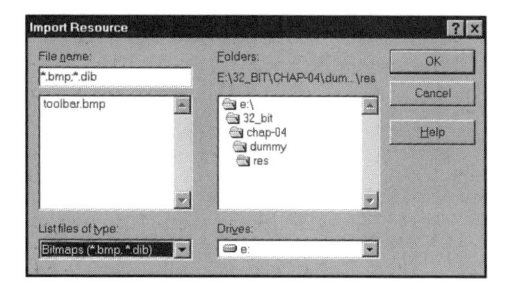

If a bitmap, cursor, or icon is already selected in the resource tree, the **E**xport option on the **R**esource menu is also enabled. Use the **E**xport option to save the selected resource as a separate file.

> Note: Some resource utilities also support the import and export of menus, dialog boxes, and other nonimage resources.

Using the Symbol Browser Dialog Box

The **Sy**mbols option on the **R**esource menu opens the Symbol Browser dialog box (see Figure 5.7). Use this dialog box to browse through and edit symbols used in the resources for the active file. The **N**ew button is used to create a new symbolic name; the **C**hange button is used to edit an existing identifier. The **V**iew Use button shows the resource item identified by the selected symbolic name.

Figure 5.7. The Symbol Browser dialog box.

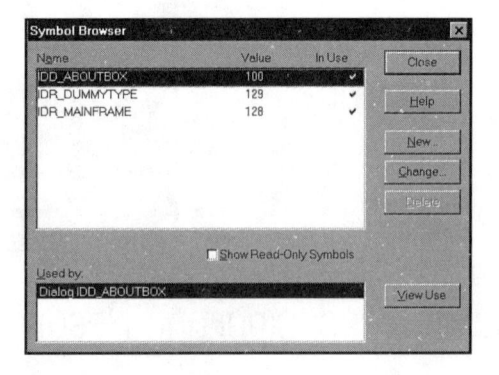

Using the Set Includes Dialog Box

The **S**et Includes option on the **R**esource menu calls a dialog box of the same name (see Figure 5.8). Use this dialog box to manage the symbols header file or to include files containing other symbols or resources for your project. The Set Includes dialog box displays the name of the symbolic header file for the project resource file, a list of read-only symbol directives, and a list of compiler directives.

Figure 5.8. The Set Includes dialog box.

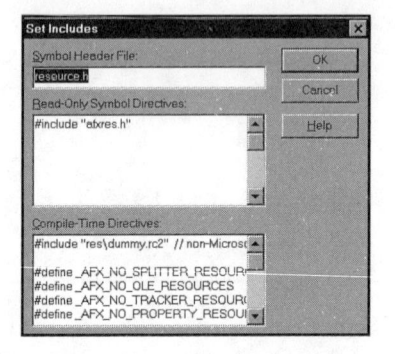

You can also use the Set Includes dialog box to change the name of the symbols header file or to include files containing symbols or resources for your project.

Summary

The AppStudio provides facilities to manage application resources ranging from acceleration keys and dialog boxes to image resources (bitmaps, icons, and cursors) to menus, string tables, and version information. Resource elements are displayed using a tree arrangement and are edited by clicking individual resource items to call the appropriate resource editors.

This chapter also looked at the files generated by the AppWizard, not only for application resources but also as work files during application compiling and linking.

The following chapters take a closer look at the individual resource elements and how the various resource editor utilities are used.

CHAPTER 6

Using Menus, Toolbars, and Status Bars

Perhaps the first element to look at in any application is the menu. If you are unfamiliar with an application, generally begin by checking the menu. Expect the choices listed to give a hint about what the program can do, and what options are available. When uncertain about how to do something, check the menu again. Look for a relevant selection or something that might lead to relevant options.

Menus are not new to Windows. They have been an application feature since programs first passed beyond the stage of command-line execution. This happened long before Windows appeared, and even before MS-DOS became a product.

Further, although there have been attempts to move beyond menus, Microsoft's Bob (the much publicized and entirely too-cute cartoon interface) is only the latest in a long line of totally graphic replacements for the functionally illiterate. Menus remain the principal entry point for those who have mastered the fundamentals of the written or printed word, who expect a lot from an application's menus, and who, perhaps, expect everything.

Admittedly, when everything else fails, you may finally turn to the online help. Even so, the main menu remains the starting point. In effect, the menu is the index to an application, and the framework which tells the user where they are, what they can expect, and what to look for.

A Starting Point

This chapter concentrates on menus. At the same time, it also looks at toolbars and status bars. The real emphasis, however, is on the application menus themselves.

Menus come in many forms. The most familiar are *static menus*—menus designed using the Developer Studio menu resource editor. Static, however, is something of a misnomer because there are a number of ways that menus can be modified (see "Switching Menus," later in this chapter).

> Note: You may also want to refer to Chapter 18, "Using Simple OLE Operations," for more about object linking and embedding. Depending on how an OLE server is called, different menus appear by default.

In addition to menus, there are the *application toolbars*. These are graphic supplements to the standard menus. Although these toolbars are not widely accepted as replacements for menus, they do offer convenient access to high-use options. In this form, graphic menus are widely accepted and very popular. Similar to menus, toolbars must be more than static. The toolbar used in one circumstance may be totally useless in other situations; toolbars must be able to change.

Both menus and toolbars are often cryptic—toolbar icons are not marvels of clarity and menu entries are often unclear. Both the *status bar* and the tool help *popup menus* offer the opportunity to amplify otherwise brief, therefore cryptic, menu items as well as offer text amplification for toolbar icons.

Menus and Menu Structures

The simplest form of menu consists of one or more primary menu entries, which are always visible on the menu bar. Each primary menu entry may activate an application function or produce a popup menu with additional options. For example, the standard menu supplied by AppWizard (see Figure 6.1) has four primary entries, each of which calls a popup menu that contains from one to nine entries.

Figure 6.1. The default IDR_MAINFRAME menu.

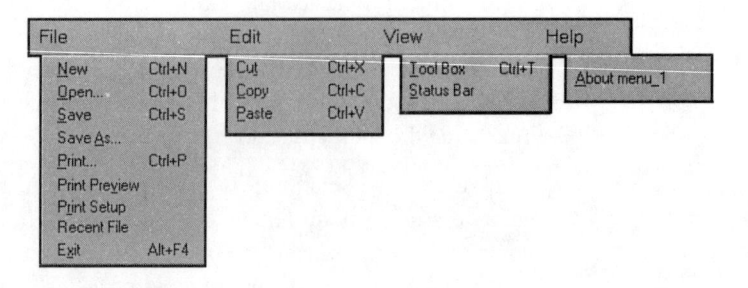

Creating a Menu

If you use Developer Studio for the Menu_1 demo application, the first step in creating a menu is to select the Menu button from the toolbar. (Alternatively, select **I**nsert, **R**esources from the menu bar and then select **M**enu from the Resources dialog box.) In response, the Project Workspace dialog box appears to display the Resource tab (see Figure 6.2).

Figure 6.2. The Project Workspace Resource tab.

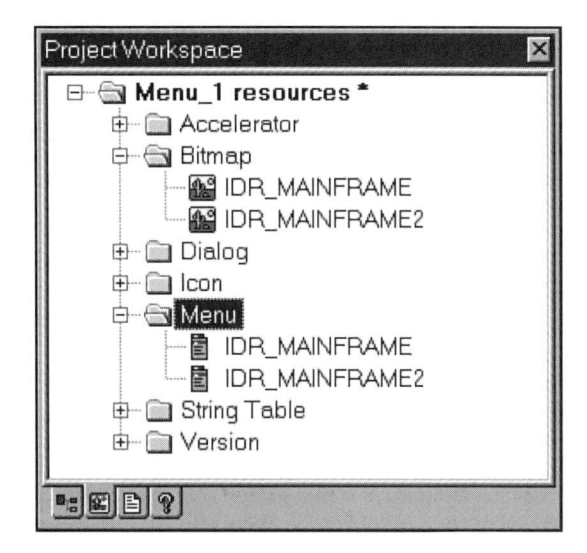

The resource tree shows two menus and two bitmaps, identified as IDR_MAINFRAME and IDR_MAINFRAME2. Originally, both the IDR_MAINFRAME menu and bitmap were stock resources generated by AppWizard. Here, however, although the original IDR_MAINFRAME bitmap has been retained, both menus are new, with the second menu corresponding to the second toolbar bitmap.

> Note: The identifier names given to the bitmaps and menus can be changed according to your preferences and requirements.

The new IDR_MAINFRAME menu is shown in Figure 6.3. Most of the entries in this demo menu are intended only for demonstration purposes and are named simply to reflect their position in the menu. The exception is the Toolbar item, which does have an actual function: switching between the two toolbars used for this demo.

Figure 6.3. A new IDR_MAINFRAME menu.

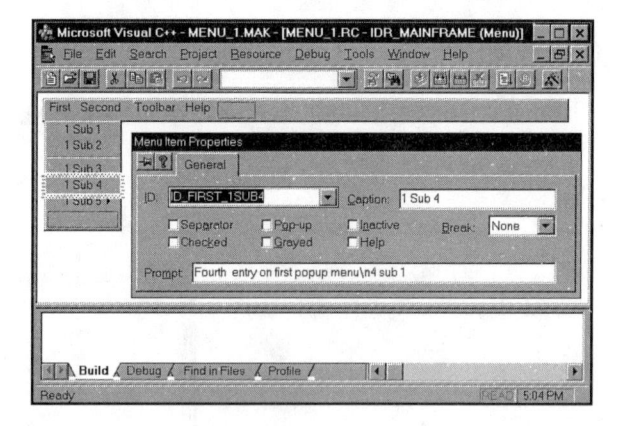

In the Properties dialog box, the Caption edit field shows the menu item text. To make one of the characters in the menu item caption the mnemonic hotkey, precede the character with an ampersand (&).

The ID list box shows the menu item resource identifier. The resource ID may be a symbol supplied by Visual C++ or by the programmer. This is defined in the H file created as part of your project.

At the bottom of the dialog box, the Prompt field displays two text elements, delimited by the \n newline character. The first part of this string entry appears on the status bar when the menu item is selected. The second, briefer part of the string appears as a small tool help popup when the mouse cursor pauses on the menu item entry. The Prompt string is placed in the string table using the menu item identifier. This is available only in resource files with MFC support.

Structured Menus

The main bar at the top of the menu and the popup menus can use several different formats, detailed in Table 6.1. By default, the main menu bar appears as a single row of entries. The Help item, normally the last item on the primary menu, can be set off by placing it at the far right end of the menu.

If the primary menu is too long to appear on a single line, the menu bar is broken into two or more lines. This happens, for example, if the application window is too small. Alternatively, column and bar breaks can also be used to separate primary menu items into several rows.

By default, pull-down menus appear as a straight column of options, as shown for the First menu option in Figure 6.4. However, pull-down menus often use column and bar breaks, as shown for the Second menu option, to organize popup (pull-down) menus into multiple columns. Further, popup menus may themselves have popup menu entries as shown in Figure 6.4, where item *1 Sub 5* calls another popup menu.

Figure 6.4. A custom IDR_MAINFRAME menu.

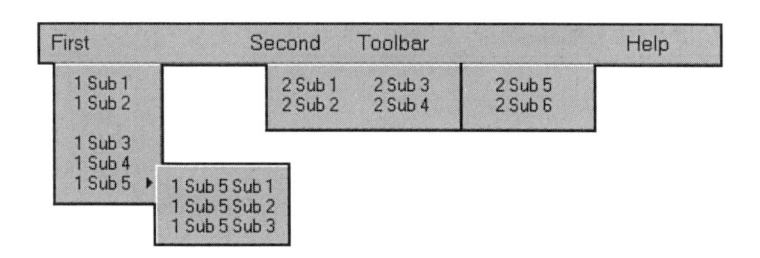

Individual menu item properties are assigned using the checkboxes described in Table 6.1, and the Break options described in Table 6.2.

Table 6.1. Menu item properties checkboxes.

Checkbox	Purpose
Separator	If set, identifies the menu item as a separator, which is a horizontal line used to group menu items. Separator items do not have IDs, captions, or prompts.
Checked	If set, a checkmark is displayed to the right of the menu entry.
Pop-up	If set, identifies the menu item as the label for a popup menu. Popup items do not have IDs or prompts, but do have caption entries. Selecting Pop-up creates a single item popup menu as a child of the current item. The default is to set this flag to TRUE for all top-level menu items or FALSE otherwise.
Grayed	If set, the menu item is "grayed" and is not selectable. The default is FALSE.
Inactive	If set, the menu item appears normal but is not selectable. The default is FALSE.
Help	Applies only to primary menu items. If set, the menu item is positioned to the right end of the menu. This is normally used only for Help menu items. The item must be the last item on the menu bar. The default is FALSE.

> Note: From a design standpoint, setting a menu item as Inactive is not recommended. A visible menu option that cannot be selected is generally seen by the users as an error (or simply annoying). Instead, use the grayed option to disable menu items when appropriate.

Break settings, shown in Table 6.2, are applied to individual menu items.

Table 6.2. Break settings.

Break	Property
None	Default
Column	For static, primary menu bar items, the item is placed on a new line.
	For popup menus, the item is placed in a new column with no dividing line between the columns. Separator items do not have IDs, captions, or prompts.
Bar	For static, primary menu bar items, the item is placed on a new line.
	For popup menus, the item is placed in a new column with a vertical dividing line between the columns. Separator items do not have IDs, captions, or prompts.

> Note: Setting a break property affects the appearance of the menu only at runtime. These settings have no effect in the menu editor.

> Note: Primary menu items that call popup menus don't display status bar prompts or tool hints because they don't have associated IDs. Primary menu items that issue commands or instructions to the application do have associated IDs and will display status bar prompts and tool hints. Also, popup menu items that have column or bar break properties assigned do not display status bar prompts or tool hints.

Menu Conventions and Formatting

A few conventions apply to application menus. These conventions give the user clues about what specific menu entries do; the conventions also show the user alternative entries or options. These options include action items such as hotkeys and accelerator keys as well as conventions identifying items calling popups and dialog boxes.

Hotkeys for menu items are created by preceding the corresponding character with an ampersand (&); in the working menu, that character appears underscored. For example, the *F* in **F**ile or the *E* in **E**dit are hotkeys; the entries in the menu script appear as `&File` and `&Edit`.

When *accelerator keys* are defined for a function, the usual custom is to show the associated accelerator key in the menu. For example, Ctrl+N identifies the Control-plus-N key as an accelerator key combination. Other combinations are Alt+H, Shift+Ctrl+B, or Shift+Ctrl+Alt+K. In the menu editor, accelerator key entries are preceded by the `\t` tab character, which causes the accelerator key entry to appear flush right.

Popup menu items that call dialog boxes are commonly indicated by ellipses (…) following the menu entry. Examples are the **O**pen…, Save **A**s…, and **P**rint… items from the **F**ile popup menu shown in Figure 6.1. These must be entered as part of the text entry in the menu script; for example through the menu editor.

Popup menu items that call further popups are identified by arrow pointers following the menu item. These arrows are supplied by the resource compiler and don't require provisions by the programmer.

Last, *separators* and *menu breaks* are used to provide additional functional groupings for menu entries. Separators are fairly common. For example, in the stock menu demonstrated in the Menu_2 application, the first four items in the menu are followed by a separator bar, which appears as a horizontal line. These items deal with file operations. The next three items, which deal with print operations, are also followed by a separator bar. The final **E**xit item, common with most applications, is preceded by a menu separator.

Menu Limits

The only practical limits on the number of primary entries are how many items can fit across the screen. If they exceed the fit (that is, the width of the window), the menu displays on multiple lines. Too many items on the menu makes the menu difficult to read and use. Likewise, there are no real limits on how many items a popup menu can contain. However, remember that too long a list makes it difficult to find the item you want.

The solution is to minimize primary menu entries; use the primary menu entries as categories for popups that offer further choices. Within a popup menu, anything over a dozen entries becomes confusing but popup entries themselves can call other popup menus. In effect, you can create a hierarchy of menus. Remember that a complicated hierarchy may also make things hard to find and use.

Toolbars

Application *toolbars*, the graphic button bars below the menu bar, offer an alternative to the standard menu. Unlike menus, toolbars can be switched at any time. This gives the user a choice of tool shortcuts appropriate to changing situations or tasks. See "Switching Menus," later in this chapter.

AppWizard supplies a default toolbar bitmap that corresponds to the default menu with each application shell. When using toolbars, the odds are that you also want to create your own custom toolbars. This means creating a custom bitmap.

Creating Toolbar Bitmaps

The resource toolkit offers excellent support in its bitmap editor with default provisions to support toolbar images; toolbar bitmaps are not particularly difficult to create.

From Developer Studio, double-click the New Toolbar button on the toolbar to bring up the toolbar editor shown in Figure 6.5.

> Note: Under Visual C++ version 2.*x*, select **N**ew, **B**itmap from the menu to call the bitmap editor to create a toolbar image.
>
> In version 2.*x*, the initial, default bitmap for a new resource is a 47×47-pixel field, overlaid by a grid with 15×14-pixel spacing. This is precisely the spacing required for a toolbar bitmap. To create a new toolbar bitmap, simply drag the supplied drawing field to match the grid: one unit (14 pixels high) and as wide (in 15-pixel multiples) as you need buttons.

Initially, the toolbar editor shows a bitmap sized for a single button image (15 pixels wide by 14 pixels high). The button may be resized horizontally or vertically if you want, but the displayed size is the default button size.

> Note: All buttons in a toolbar are resized equally. Although some Microsoft applications (such as Microsoft Word 7.0) use toolbars in which some buttons differ in width, the default toolbar handler does not make provisions for variations in button width or height within a toolbar image. You can experiment by using more than one image (using different widths) on a single toolbar display.

As an image is drawn for the button (or pasted from another source), the toolbar editor adds an additional blank button to the end of the bitmap. Any blank that is not filled with something is ignored when the toolbar bitmap resource is saved. Figure 6.5 shows the IDR_TOOLBAR1 bitmap; five buttons have been drawn and a sixth blank button provides space for an additional image.

Figure 6.5. Creating a toolbar bitmap.

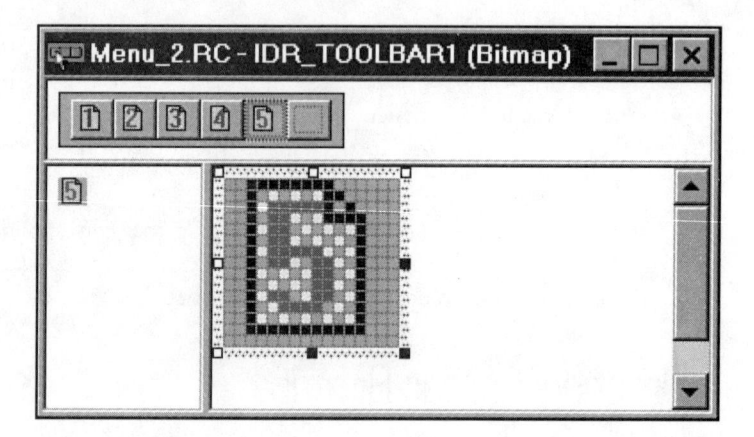

> Tip: Keep button images simple and avoid the use of complicated color schemes. When the toolbar image is displayed, the default system palette is used. Colors too elaborate may not be visible.

The toolbar image is drawn as a single strip of button images without spacing between the buttons. Spacing between buttons or groups of buttons is supplied in the toolbar declaration (see the example declaration in the following section, "Linking Messages and IDs to Toolbars") by including ID_SEPARATOR constants in the declaration.

That is all there is to preparing the bitmap. Just draw the button images and save the image as part of the resource file. The rest of the story is in the linking.

> Note: Although Visual C++ 4.0 makes a distinction between bitmap images and toolbar images, Visual C++ 2.x does not. In both cases, however, the toolbar images are simply bitmaps and are distinguished in use only in how the resource script references the bitmap. Therefore, in the demo applications in this book, existing toolbar bitmaps appear simply as bitmaps in the resource lists even though new toolbar images created using Developer Studio may be identified explicitly as toolbar resources, as shown in Figure 6.6.

Figure 6.6. *A toolbar entry in the resource tree.*

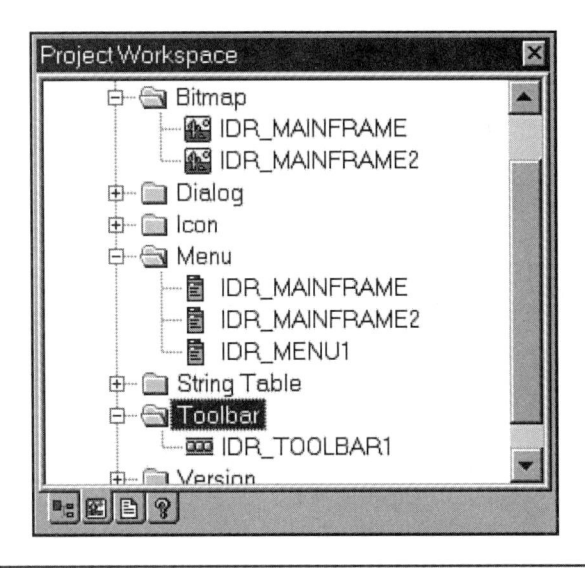

Linking Messages and IDs to Toolbars

Before you enable docking and set toolbar styles, the first step is to define links between the toolbar buttons and application functions (or, at least, the application messages).

In Visual C++ 2.x, AppWizard has already supplied the necessary links for the default toolbar in MainFram.CPP in the form of a series of ID assignments. These assignments are shown here:

```
// toolbar buttons - IDs are command buttons
static UINT BASED_CODE buttons[] =
{
    // same order as in the bitmap 'toolbar.bmp'
    ID_FILE_NEW,
    ID_FILE_OPEN,
    ID_FILE_SAVE,
        ID_SEPARATOR,
    ID_EDIT_CUT,
    ID_EDIT_COPY,
    ID_EDIT_PASTE,
        ID_SEPARATOR,
    ID_FILE_PRINT,
    ID_APP_ABOUT,
};
```

In C++ version 4.0, using Developer Studio and a toolbar resource instead of a bitmap used as a toolbar, the preceding assignments have been moved to the resource script (RC), where they appear as follows:

```
/////////////////////////////////////////////////////////////////////////
//
// Toolbar
//

IDR_MAINFRAME TOOLBAR DISCARDABLE  16, 15
BEGIN
    BUTTON      ID_FILE_NEW
    BUTTON      ID_FILE_OPEN
    BUTTON      ID_FILE_SAVE
        SEPARATOR
    BUTTON      ID_EDIT_CUT
    BUTTON      ID_EDIT_COPY
    BUTTON      ID_EDIT_PASTE
        SEPARATOR
    BUTTON      ID_FILE_PRINT
    BUTTON      ID_APP_ABOUT
END
```

In this second sample, notice that the resource is identified first by the constant IDR_MAINFRAME and then as a toolbar resource. The DISCARDABLE keyword says that this resource can be discarded from memory when not in use (the default for all resources); the 16, 15 values specify the width and height of the individual buttons contained in the image.

> Tip: The change from bitmaps used as toolbar images to toolbar-specific images does not mean that your existing toolbars must be redone or that your existing code must be rewritten for Visual C++ version 4.0. The older usage and format are still supported in C++ 4.0 and your applications will compile and execute just as they did under version 2.x.

When using Developer Studio to create a toolbar resource, because the identifying links between the buttons have been moved from a macro in the application's MainFrame source file to the resource script, a means is still required to define these links. You can, of course, edit the RC script but this really isn't necessary.

Instead, from the toolbar editor, double-click a button from the toolbar sample (not from the edit window). The Toolbar Button Properties dialog box appears (see Figure 6.7).

Figure 6.7. *Using the Toolbar Button Properties dialog box.*

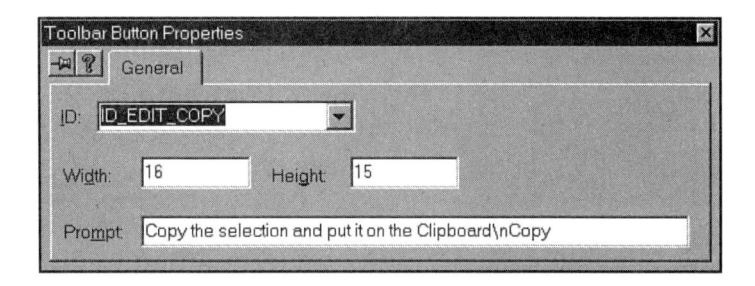

The ID field shows the identifying constant linked to the button. Although you can enter a new identifier here, this field is normally used to select from existing IDs.

Remember that the Width and Height fields apply to all buttons in the toolbar. Changing either value affects the entire toolbar.

> Tip: One advantage of the toolbar resource over the bitmap used as a toolbar is that the buttons can be resized without having to redraw or adjust the spacing of the button images.

Last, the Prompt field contains the string for the Status Line prompt. Follow that string with the new line \n character and then the text of the tool tip. The Prompt entry is, of course, an entry in the string table with the same identifier as the button.

> Note: Although Visual C++ version 4.0 has changed how toolbars are handled, the toolbar editor does not appear to include any provisions for inserting separators in the toolbars. (See the preceding listing for the IDR_MAINFRAME toolbar for examples of the separators in the RC script listing.) In this respect, if you require separators in your custom toolbar, the only recourse appears to be to edit the RC script directly.

In both version 2.*x* and 4.0 applications, even though the toolbar assignments have moved, the status bar links still appear in the MainFrame source file as follows:

```
static UINT BASED_CODE indicators[] =
{
    ID_SEPARATOR,           // status line indicator
    ID_INDICATOR_CAPS,
    ID_INDICATOR_NUM,
    ID_INDICATOR_SCRL,
};
```

These three default ID assignments cover the three indicator buttons on the status bar. These assignments are CAPS, NUM LOCK, and SCRL LOCK.

Using Visual C++ 2.x, for the second toolbar bitmap, a new series of IDs are required. These also appear in the MainFrame source file as follows:

```
static UINT BASED_CODE buttons2[] =
{
    // same order as in the bitmap 'toolbar2.bmp'
    ID_DOC_ONE,
    ID_DOC_TWO,
    ID_DOC_THREE,
    ID_DOC_FOUR,
    ID_DOC_FIVE
};
```

Even though the toolbar is visible, without these links the buttons are also grayed out and disabled until provisions are made to link the toolbar buttons to application functions or application messages.

Using C++ version 4.0 and the Developers Studio, just as with the previous IDR_MAINFRAME example, the corresponding toolbar identifier assignments are made using the Toolbar Button Properties dialog box. They appear in the RC script as shown here:

```
IDR_MAINFRAME2 TOOLBAR DISCARDABLE  16, 15
BEGIN
    BUTTON      ID_DOC_ONE
    BUTTON      ID_DOC_TWO
    BUTTON      ID_DOC_THREE
    BUTTON      ID_DOC_FOUR
    BUTTON      ID_DOC_FIVE
END
```

The application shell source code also includes provisions for installing the toolbar with the following two versions of the code. The first code sample is the Visual C++ 2.x version of the code:

```
int CMainFrame::OnCreate(LPCREATESTRUCT lpCreateStruct)
{
    if (CFrameWnd::OnCreate(lpCreateStruct) == -1)
        return -1;
```

For Visual C++ 2.x, the toolbar is created from a bitmap resource thus:

```
    if (!m_wndToolBar.Create(this) ||
        !m_wndToolBar.LoadBitmap(IDR_MAINFRAME) ||
        !m_wndToolBar.SetButtons(buttons,
            sizeof(buttons)/sizeof(UINT)))
    {
```

For Visual C++ 4.0, the corresponding provisions create the toolbar from a toolbar resource, as shown here:

```
if (!m_wndToolBar.Create(this) ||
    !m_wndToolBar.LoadToolBar(IDR_MAINFRAME))
{
```

Because the button size is defined in the toolbar resource but not in the bitmap image, the SetButtons() function in the first example is not required in the second example. Other than this fragment, the two versions of the application are essentially identical; both continue with the same provisions:

```
    TRACE0("Failed to create toolbar\n");
    return -1;      // fail to create
}
if (!m_wndStatusBar.Create(this) ||
    !m_wndStatusBar.SetIndicators(indicators,
      sizeof(indicators)/sizeof(UINT)))
{
    TRACE0("Failed to create status bar\n");
    return -1;      // fail to create
}
    // TODO: Delete these three lines if you don't want the toolbar to
    // be dockable
m_wndToolBar.EnableDocking(CBRS_ALIGN_ANY);
EnableDocking(CBRS_ALIGN_ANY);
DockControlBar(&m_wndToolBar);
```

After creating the toolbar and the status bar, the EnableDocking function is called twice. Once for the toolbar itself, m_wndToolBar, and once for the application frame window. If this seems a bit odd, realize that the toolbar itself has its own window and has to be enabled for docking here as well as in the frame window. The EnableDocking function is called with a parameter that specifies which side or sides of the parent window can be used to dock the control bar (see Table 6.3).

Table 6.3. Docking options.

Parameter	Function
CBRS_ALIGN_TOP	Toolbar can be docked at the top of the client area.
CBRS_ALIGN_BOTTOM	Toolbar can be docked at the bottom of the client area.
CBRS_ALIGN_LEFT	Toolbar can be docked on the left side of the client area.
CBRS_ALIGN_RIGHT	Toolbar can be docked on the right side of the client area.
CBRS_ALIGN_ANY	Toolbar can be docked on any side of the client area.

One additional parameter is allowed for the frame window, but not for the toolbar window.

CBRS_FLOAT_MULTI   Permits multiple floating control bars in a miniframe window.

By default, control bars for frame windows are docked in the following order: top, bottom, left, and right.

> Note: The side specified for the toolbar window must match one of the sides specified for the destination frame window. Otherwise, the control bar cannot be docked in the frame window.

Tool Tips

The tool tips displayed for toolbar items must also be enabled, as shown in the following code:

```
    // TODO: Remove this if you don't want tool tips
m_wndToolBar.SetBarStyle(m_wndToolBar.GetBarStyle() |
    CBRS_TOOLTIPS | CBRS_FLYBY);
m_nToolbar = 1;
    return 0;
}
```

The SetBarStyle function accepts multiple ANDed flag parameters. In the preceding example, the GetBarStyle function is called to return the settings made in the EnableDocking function call, ANDing the returned value with two new flag values. These additional flag values are listed in Table 6.4.

Table 6.4. SetBarStyle parameters.

Parameter	Function
CBRS_BORDER_TOP	Adds a border to the top edge of the control bar.
CBRS_BORDER_BOTTOM	Adds a border to the bottom edge of the control bar.
CBRS_BORDER_LEFT	Adds a border to the left edge of the control bar.
CBRS_BORDER_RIGHT	Adds a border to the right edge of the control bar.
CBRS_TOOLTIPS	Displays tool tips for the control bar.
CBRS_FLYBY	Message text in the status bar is updated at the same time as tool tips.

Also, because you will be switching toolbars, the nToolbar variable is initialized here during CMainFrame::OnCreate. This particular provision is for convenience in the demo application only, and may or may not be relevant in other circumstances.

Switching Toolbars

One of the advantages of toolbars is that they can be switched during execution. In the Menu_1 demo, the Toolbar menu option switches between the two toolbars by loading the appropriate bitmap, calling SetButtons to assign the appropriate set of IDs and, lastly, setting nToolbar to identify the current bitmap. (The Visual C++ 2.*x* and 4.0 versions of the function differ in how the toolbars are loaded but are otherwise identical.)

```
/////////////////////////////////////////////////////////////////////////
// CMainFrame message handlers
void CMainFrame::OnSwitchtool()
{
    // TODO: Add your command handler code here
    switch( m_nToolbar )
    {
       case 1:
```

Visual C++ version 2.x:

```
          if( ! m_wndToolBar.LoadBitmap( IDR_MAINFRAME2 ) ||
              ! m_wndToolBar.SetButtons( buttons2, sizeof(buttons2) /
                                           sizeof(UINT) ) )
```

Visual C++ version 4.0:

```
          if( ! m_wndToolBar.LoadToolBar(IDR_MAINFRAME2) )
```

Both versions continue:

```
          {
              TRACE0("Failed to create toolbar\n");
              return;     // fail to create
          }
          m_nToolbar = 2;
          break;

       case 2:
       default:
```

Visual C++ version 2.x:

```
          if( ! m_wndToolBar.LoadBitmap( IDR_MAINFRAME ) ||
              ! m_wndToolBar.SetButtons( buttons, sizeof(buttons) /
                                           sizeof(UINT) ) )
```

Visual C++ version 4.0:

```
          if( ! m_wndToolBar.LoadToolBar(IDR_MAINFRAME) )
```

Both versions continue:

```
          {
              TRACE0("Failed to create toolbar\n");
              return;     // fail to create
          }
          m_nToolbar = 1;
          break;
    }
    m_wndToolBar.Invalidate();
}
```

After switching toolbars, the Invalidate method is called to ensure that the toolbar is redrawn using the new bitmap image.

> Note: The m_wndToolBar.Create() function is not called a second time. Once the toolbar has been created, a new bitmap button image can be loaded at any time.

Switching Menus

If switching toolbars is so easy, you might wonder why nothing has been discussed concerning switching menus. You should be able to switch and modify menus, but Windows 95 has distinct problems in this area. The problems in Win95 may partially be a case of remaining bugs in the Beta version used to write this book, or it may be a bug in the Visual C++ 2.1 libraries.

First, however, we'll use Windows NT to see how changing a menu is supposed to work. Figure 6.8 shows the Menu_2 application that begins with the standard default menu supplied by AppWizard, which then inserts two new menu entries: Menu and Toolbar.

Figure 6.8. *The default menu (Menu_2 under WinNT).*

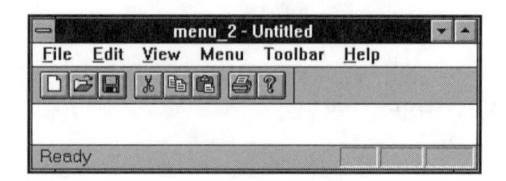

Rather than accomplishing this alteration to the default menu by editing the menu using the resource editor, a brief addition is made in the `CMainFrame::OnCreate` function:

```
int CMainFrame::OnCreate(LPCREATESTRUCT lpCreateStruct)
{
   if (CFrameWnd::OnCreate(lpCreateStruct) == -1)
      return -1;
   ...
   if (!m_wndToolBar.Create(this) ||
      !m_wndToolBar.LoadBitmap(IDR_MAINFRAME) ||
      !m_wndToolBar.SetButtons(buttons,
        sizeof(buttons)/sizeof(UINT)))
   {
      TRACE0("Failed to create toolbar\n");
      return -1;      // fail to create
   }

   if (!m_wndStatusBar.Create(this) ||
      !m_wndStatusBar.SetIndicators(indicators,
        sizeof(indicators)/sizeof(UINT)))
   {
      TRACE0("Failed to create status bar\n");
      return -1;      // fail to create
   }

   // TODO: Delete these three lines if you don't want the toolbar to
   //  be dockable
   m_wndToolBar.EnableDocking(CBRS_ALIGN_ANY);
   EnableDocking(CBRS_ALIGN_ANY);
   DockControlBar(&m_wndToolBar);

   // TODO: Remove this if you don't want tool tips
   m_wndToolBar.SetBarStyle(m_wndToolBar.GetBarStyle() |
      CBRS_TOOLTIPS | CBRS_FLYBY);
```

```
    m_nMenu = 1;
    m_nToolbar = 1;
    CMenu * pMenu = GetMenu();
    pMenu->InsertMenu( 3, MF_BYPOSITION | MF_STRING, IDM_SWITCHMENU, "Menu" );
    pMenu->InsertMenu( 4, MF_BYPOSITION | MF_STRING, IDM_SWITCHTOOL, "Toolbar" );
    return 0;
}
```

The two new entries are inserted by identifying their positions in the menu (that is, the positions at which they will be inserted) along with the ID values and the text for the new menu entry.

The `CMenu::InsertMenu` function has two forms:

```
BOOL InsertMenu( UINT nPosition, UINT nFlags, UINT nIDNewItem = 0,
                 LPCTSTR lpszNewItem = NULL );
BOOL InsertMenu( UINT nPosition, UINT nFlags, UINT nIDNewItem,
                 const CBitmap* pBmp );
```

The `InsertMenu` parameters act in several fashions, depending primarily on the flags passed in the `nFlags` parameter.

Parameter	*Comments*
nPosition	The existing menu item position that the new menu item will precede. The nPosition parameter is further interpreted by the nFlags parameter.
nFlags	The nFlags parameter is used to interpret nPosition as described in the following paragraphs.
MF_BYCOMMAND	nPosition specifies the command ID of the existing menu item. This is default if neither MF_BYCOMMAND nor MF_BYPOSITION is set.
MF_BYPOSITION	nPosition specifies the position of the existing menu item. The first item is at position 0. If nPosition is ×1, the new menu item is appended to the end of the menu.
MF_POPUP	Combined with either the MF_BYCOMMAND or MF_BYPOSITION flags, the inserted menu is a popup menu rather than a single item.
MF_STRING	lpszNewItem contains a long pointer to a NULL-terminated string. (Default interpretation)
MF_OWNERDRAW	lpszNewItem contains an application-supplied 32-bit value the application can use to maintain additional data associated with the menu item. This 32-bit value is available to the application in the itemData member of the structure supplied by the WM_MEASUREITEM and WM_DRAWITEM messages. These messages are sent when the menu item is initially displayed or is changed.

continues

Parameter	Comments
	MF_SEPARATOR Combined with either the MF_BYCOMMAND or MF_BYPOSITION flags, inserts a menu separator.
nIDNewItem	This may be either the command ID of the new menu item or, if nFlags is set to MF_POPUP, the menu handle (HMENU) of the popup menu. The nIDNewItem parameter is ignored (not needed) if nFlags has MF_SEPARATOR set.
lpszNewItem	Specifies the content of the new menu item.
pBmp	Pointer to a CBitmap object to be used as the menu item.

In either form or configuration, the InsertMenu function returns 0 on failure and returns a non-zero value on success.

Although the provisions in the CMainFrame::OnCreate function add a menu item to allow you to switch menus, you also need handling to respond to this menu entry. This is provided in the OnSwitchMenu function, shown here:

```
void CMainFrame::OnSwitchmenu()
{
   // TODO: Add your command handler code here
   CMenu cMenu;
   switch( m_nMenu )
   {
      case 1:
         cMenu.LoadMenu( IDR_MAINFRAME2 );
         m_nMenu = 2;
         break;

      case 2:
      default:
         cMenu.LoadMenu( IDR_MAINFRAME );
         cMenu.InsertMenu( 3, MF_BYPOSITION | MF_STRING,
                     IDM_SWITCHMENU, "Menu" );
         cMenu.InsertMenu( 4, MF_BYPOSITION | MF_STRING,
                     IDM_SWITCHTOOL, "Toolbar" );
         m_nMenu = 1;
         break;
   }
   SetMenu( &cMenu );
   cMenu.Detach();
   DrawMenuBar();
}
```

There are two important items to notice here:

- The member variable m_nMenu is used to track which menu is active. Remember, both the original IDR_MAINFRAME menu and the second IDR_MAINFRAME2 menu contain the Menu option; both return the same message, which calls OnSwitchMenu. Therefore, the m_nMenu variable is your only guide to which menu is sending the message and which menu is now being requested.

- The provisions to restore the original menu begin by loading the IDR_MAINFRAME menu and then continue, as in the `OnCreate` function, by inserting the two additional menu entries.

On the other hand, when loading the IDR_MAINFRAME2 menu, these latter provisions are not required because these two entries are part of the resource menu definition.

> Note: Immediately after the `SetMenu()` function is called to establish the new menu as the window's menu, the `Detach` method is called to release the menu handle from the `CMenu` object. This is done to prevent the new menu from being destroyed when the `CMenu` instance goes out of scope—which will happen when the current function terminates.
>
> Interestingly, this last provision appears to be unnecessary under WinNT but is absolutely essential under Win95.

In operation, selecting the Menu option does exactly what you want; the changed application appears as shown in Figure 6.9 with the new menu bar.

Figure 6.9. Changing menus (Menu_2 under WinNT).

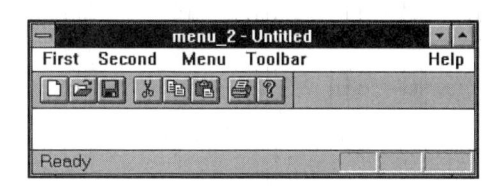

Clicking on the Menu option from here restores the original menu with the inserted Menu and Toolbar options, just as designed.

Summary

This chapter covers a good bit of ground; it describes both application toolbars and menus, how they're drawn or defined, how you insert items in existing menus, how menus are implemented in the application, and how to swap menus and toolbars on-the-fly.

You also learned how to create complex menus with submenu popups, how to use column breaks and column bar breaks, and other ways of arranging menu entries to group options.

Even with all this, we've barely scratched the surface. Menus offer a world of possibilities; this chapter has only been an introduction. Accept this strong recommendation: menus are worth a bit of work and deserve some study. The possibilities are more than minor, but they aren't always simple.

CHAPTER 7

Designing Custom Dialog Boxes

Although it is possible to write a Windows application without using dialog boxes, it's rather hard to imagine doing so...or even to imagine a reason why you'd want to try. Dialog boxes are simply too useful to ignore. Granted, you can do a lot with menus, but you can do a lot more with dialog boxes—particularly if you use the new common controls provided with Visual C++ under Windows 95.

This chapter looks at how dialog boxes are designed and, at the same time, how information is passed to and retrieved from dialog boxes.

Dialog Box Design

Proper dialog box design is an area in which there are lots of theories but no real rules. The design of a dialog box depends entirely on the task or tasks you want the dialog box to accomplish. The only two real criteria in designing a dialog box are these: does the dialog box accomplish the intended task and is the dialog box design such that the user can readily understand its purpose and find it convenient to use.

Of course, as a programmer, the first criteria (the dialog box's purpose) has paramount importance. However, if you intended to be a *successful* programmer, it is the second criteria (how the user regards the dialog box) that is more important.

Toward both purposes, here are a few suggestions:

- **Keep your dialog boxes simple:** Don't try to put everything in a single dialog box. If you have more than ten controls in a dialog box (count checkboxes and radio buttons as groups, not individually), consider creating more than one dialog box. Better yet, consider using the tabbed dialog boxes, introduced in Chapter 8, "Customizing Dialog Boxes with Additional Controls."
- **Split complex dialog boxes:** When necessary, break up a too-large or too-complex dialog box into several simpler dialog boxes. Keep the primary, high-use options in one dialog box and add a button (or buttons) to call other, supplementary dialog boxes to handle secondary options.
- **Group controls:** Use group boxes to organize controls logically and keep related controls together.
- **Label groups of controls:** Granted, each of the buttons in an array of radio buttons has a label. But using a group box—with a label for the group—makes using the controls much easier for the user.
- **Test your design:** Naturally, as a programmer, you test your dialog box from a functional standpoint. But, more important, have someone else—someone who is not writing the dialog box code—test your dialog box design from a user's perspective.
- **Be flexible:** After asking someone to test your design, listen carefully to criticism. Don't argue. Don't explain. If your tester says something is hard to use or doesn't work, just change it.

Although these guidelines won't solve all your problems (we're not promising miracles), following these suggestions should simplify your design process.

Creating a Dialog Box

A few years ago, creating a dialog box was a matter of first writing a script, calling a resource compiler to create a binary resource, and then testing the result to see how it looked and whether you'd managed to keep controls from overlapping and had them sized correctly. Under these circumstances, many programmers turned to designing dialog boxes on paper—graph paper—before writing their scripts.

Naturally, such an awkward approach to design prompted programmers to find better methods; companies such as Blue Sky entered the market with visual design tools that, for obvious reasons, quickly became the *de facto* standards.

Of course, if you really want to do so, you can still do your design by writing a script and drawing your design on paper...but then you're probably not interested in other approaches anyway.

For the rest of us, the first step in creating a dialog box is to select **R**esource, **N**ew and then select Dialog from the New Resource Dialog list. In response, AppStudio creates a new, blank dialog box with two buttons (OK and Cancel) and a dialog identifier with the format `IDD_DIALOGx`.

Chapter 7 • Designing Custom Dialog Boxes

Along with the blank dialog box, a toolbar like the one in Figure 7.1 appears, offering a choice of dialog box controls.

Figure 7.1. The Developer Studio dialog box controls.

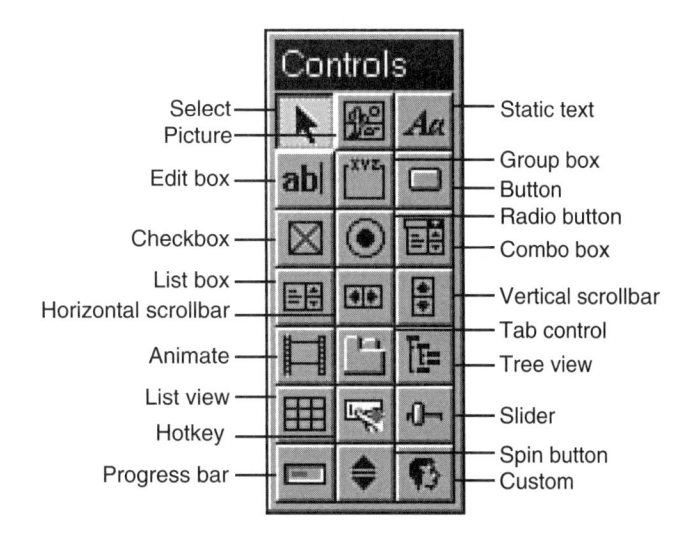

```
Controls
Select ———— ▶    ———— Static text
Picture ———       
                  ———— Group box
Edit box ———      ———— Button
                  ———— Radio button
Checkbox ———      ———— Combo box
List box ———      
Horizontal scrollbar ——  ———— Vertical scrollbar
                  ———— Tab control
Animate ———       ———— Tree view
List view ———     
Hotkey ———        ———— Slider
                  ———— Spin button
Progress bar ———  ———— Custom
```

> **Note:** Eight new controls (animate, tab control, tree view, list view, hotkey, slider, progress bar, and spin button) are currently supported only by Windows 95 (they are not supported by Windows NT 3.5). These controls are, however, expected to be supported by later versions of Windows NT and Win32.

Within this *tabula rasa* (blank slate), you are free to add anything you want and can change anything—including the buttons provided and the identifying labels—you don't like.

Individual controls are created by selecting the control type from the toolbar and then clicking inside the dialog box (click and drag if you want to resize the control).

After you create a control, you can modify it in several ways. Click on any control—or on the dialog box itself—to display a selection border with four corner and four side tabs. Click any of these tabs and drag to resize the control. Click within the control and drag to move the control.

> **Tip:** For fine positioning, click a control to display the selection border and then use the arrow keys to reposition the control.

Select multiple controls by holding the Shift key as you click each control; you can then align, position, or resize the group of controls using the dialog box toolbar at the bottom of the AppWizard screen (see Figure 7.2 in the following sidebar).

The Dialog Toolbar Offers Six Groups of Buttons

Beginning at the left of the toolbar shown in Figure 7.2, the Switch button allows you to test your dialog box functionally during design. Click the Switch button to display a run version of the dialog box, which permits you to check radio button groups, test entries in edit boxes, check tab orders and groups, and so on. To end your test, click the OK or Cancel button in the dialog box you are testing (or click any other button returning `IDOK` or `IDCANCEL`); alternatively, use the close button (the × button) on the caption bar.

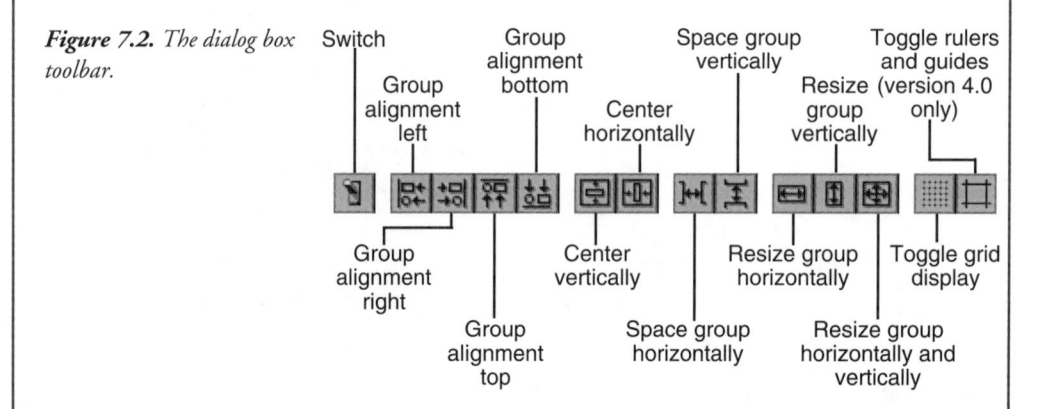

Figure 7.2. The dialog box toolbar.

- Switch
- Group alignment left
- Group alignment right
- Group alignment bottom
- Group alignment top
- Center horizontally
- Center vertically
- Space group vertically
- Space group horizontally
- Resize group vertically
- Resize group horizontally
- Resize group horizontally and vertically
- Toggle rulers and guides (version 4.0 only)
- Toggle grid display

Note: If you remove the OK and Cancel buttons from your dialog box, do not disable the close button (the × button) on the caption bar or you may find yourself with no way to close the dialog box during testing.

The next four buttons on the dialog box toolbar are used to align groups of controls. Select multiple controls by holding the Shift key as you click the desired controls. The last control selected—shown by the highlighted selection frame—is the reference control; the other controls selected are aligned with the reference.

The next two buttons center a control vertically or horizontally within the dialog box. If multiple controls are selected, they are centered as a group with their relative positions unchanged.

The next two buttons are used to equally space a group of controls either horizontally or vertically. Spacing uses the first and last control in the selected group as references and adjusts the positions of the remaining members.

The three-button group toward the right of the dialog box toolbar is used to resize two or more controls. As with other multiple-control operations, the last control selected is used as the reference and the remaining controls in the group are resized (horizontally, vertically, or both) to match the reference.

> The next control on the dialog box toolbar toggles the dialog grid display. When enabled, the dialog grid appears as a field of dots using a default spacing of 5 DLU (dialog logical units). By default, when the grid appears, the Snap to Grid option is also enabled, causing position and size adjustments to align with grid units. To adjust grid spacing, select **G**rid (in version 4.0, select **G**uide Settings) from the **L**ayout menu.
>
> Version 4.0 has one additional button that toggles rulers and a guide outline. When enabled, a vertical and horizontal rule are shown at the top and left of the dialog box and an outline frame appears inside the dialog box. The inside offset for the outline frame is preset.
>
> Note: In version 4.0, selecting the grid option turns off the guide outline and vice versa. To turn off both grid and guide, select **G**uide Settings from the **L**ayout menu and click the **N**one button in the dialog box.

The Standard Controls Dialog Box

Figure 7.3 shows the Standard Controls dialog box with an edit box at the top, two checkboxes, four radio buttons, a combo box, and three buttons (OK, Cancel, and Special).

Figure 7.3. *The Standard Controls dialog box.*

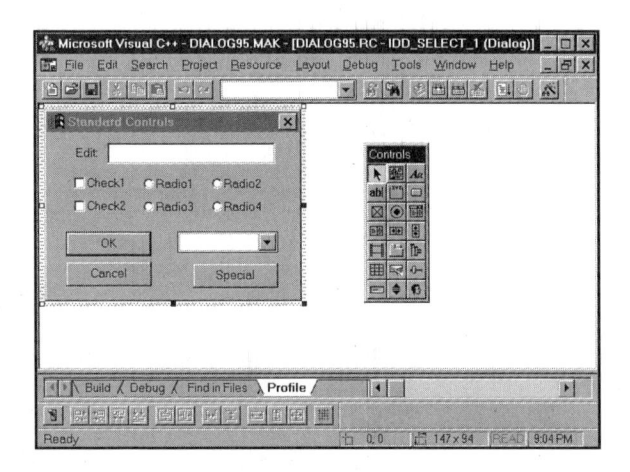

In this example, the combo box had five entries defined when the dialog box was designed (these entries do not appear in Figure 7.3 but are contained in the resource definition). More often, however, you may want to use the `CComboBox::AddString` or `CComboBox::InsertString` method to build your combo box at run time rather than during design.

Assigning Member Variables

Setup for this example dialog box is minimal; the ClassWizard is called to assign member variables for each of the checkbox, edit box, and combo box controls (see Figure 7.4). Notice, however, that the four radio buttons are not represented by control IDs and do not have member variables.

Figure 7.4. Assigning member variables for dialog box controls.

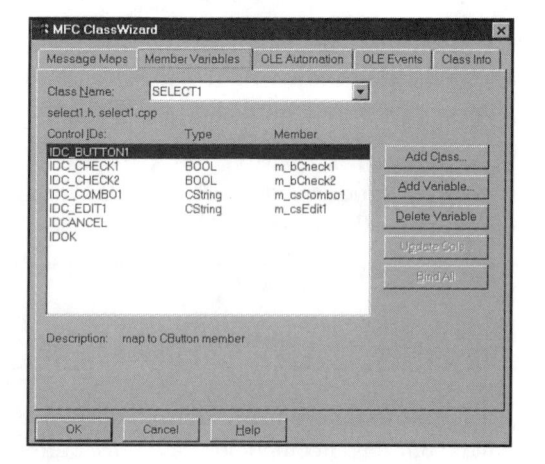

When assigning member variables to dialog box controls, you generally have a choice of the type of variable. For example, when you assign a variable to a checkbox, the default options (see Figure 7.5) are Category: Value and Variable Type: BOOL. These options are perfectly satisfactory for a Boolean transfer (which is all you really want here). However, you can select Category: Control and Variable Type: CButton to map the control to a `CButton` member.

Figure 7.5. Adding a member variable.

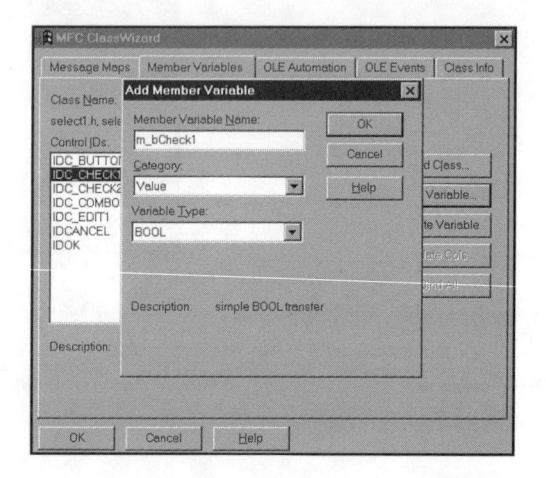

Likewise for this example, both the edit box and the combo box are mapped to a CString member (because all you really want to retrieve from either of these controls is a string). Alternatively, you could have mapped the combo box to a CComboBox member variable and, from there, transferred an entire combo box structure from the calling application to the dialog handler—complete with initialization strings.

Using the ClassWizard to assign member variables, the variable definitions were added to the Select1.H header, as shown in the following code fragment (code lines without background shading show what was added):

```
CString    m_csEdit1;
CString    m_csCombo1;
BOOL       m_bCheck1;
BOOL       m_bCheck2;
UINT       m_nRadio;
```

Although the ClassWizard supplies four of the variable definitions, the fifth (which is used to track the radio button selection) must be added manually.

Initializing Member Variables

Initialization is also supplied by ClassWizard for the four controls that have had member variables assigned. The initialization appears in the SELECT1 constructor (in Select1.CPP) as shown in the following code fragment:

```
SELECT1::SELECT1(CWnd* pParent /*=NULL*/)
    : CDialog(SELECT1::IDD, pParent)
{
    //{{AFX_DATA_INIT(SELECT1)
    m_csEdit1 = _T("");
    m_csCombo1 = _T("");
    m_bCheck1 = FALSE;
    m_bCheck2 = FALSE;
    //}}AFX_DATA_INIT
}
```

This default initialization ensures that both the edit box and the combo box fields are cleared and that both checkboxes are cleared. However, no default initialization has been supplied for the radio buttons; you can include this here by calling member functions as shown here:

```
CButton *pRB = (CButton *) GetDlgItem(IDC_RADIOx);
pRB->SetCheck( 1 );
```

Alternatively, you can use the following, even simpler, method of initializing the radio buttons:

```
GetDlgItem(IDC_RADIOx).SetCheck(1);
```

The three buttons (OK, Cancel, and Special) are also represented by control IDs but, for our purposes, don't require member variables. However, two of the buttons (OK and Special) do have message maps and associated methods defined in Select1.CPP; the third button (Cancel) receives default handling and does not require a message map.

Retrieving Values from Dialog Box Controls

Assigning member variables to the controls is only one part of the operation. In Select1.CPP, in the OnOK method, you must make provisions to query the radio buttons and decide whether any have been selected. Remember that you have not set any of the radio buttons by default, but you have initialized nRadio as 0.

Although ClassWizard provides the OnOK skeleton function, you still have to supply the validation code to read the radio button controls from the dialog box, as shown here:

```
void SELECT1::OnOK()
{
   // TODO: Add extra validation here
   CButton * pRB;
   UINT      i;

   for( i = IDC_RADIO1; i <= IDC_RADIO4; i++ )
   {
      pRB = (CButton *) GetDlgItem(i);
      if( pRB->GetCheck() )
         m_nRadio = i - IDC_RADIO1 + 1;
   }
   CDialog::OnOK();
}
```

To determine whether any of the radio buttons have been selected, use a loop to poll the buttons. Design the loop to return a value of 1..4 instead of returning the button identifier. If no selection has been made, the loop should return the default value 0.

> Tip: If necessary, edit the RESOURCE.H header to give grouped controls sequential IDs. Sequential IDs can be useful when you work with groups of checkboxes and, particularly, radio buttons. Sequential IDs allow your application to step through groups using a for loop rather than referencing each checkbox or radio button individually.

Notice that the variable m_nRadio was initialized here, in the OnOK method, before calling the loop to decide whether another value should be assigned. As experienced programmers, you may wonder why we've waited until now to do this. Why didn't we initialize the variable back in the Select1.H header when it was defined?

The answer, of course, is that initialization of member variables is not allowed during declaration because the class instance does not exist at that point (only the structure definition exists) and no memory has yet been allocated to hold a variable instance value. Initialization can, however, be done within the class constructor method or any time thereafter.

Closing the Dialog Box

The final step, because you also expect a response from the Special button in this dialog box, is to provide some control notification here as well. Remember that the IDOK and IDCANCEL codes from the OK and Cancel buttons provide automatic termination of the dialog box. However, the third button does not have such provisions; you must add them, as shown here:

```
void SELECT1::OnButton1()
{
   // TODO: Add your control notification handler code here
   EndDialog( IDC_BUTTON1 );
}
```

Even though you intend for the Special button to call another dialog box, you want the current dialog box to close first rather than remaining open while the second dialog is called. Therefore, the simple solution is to call the EndDialog function with an argument that is returned to the calling application.

What argument you return isn't particularly important as long as you can recognize the return value to act on. Remember that if the OK or Cancel button is selected to close the dialog box, these buttons return values of, respectively, IDOK (1) and IDCANCEL (2).

Alternatively, if you want a custom closure, you can assign some other method of initiating the EndDialog call—and return anything or nothing. One alternative—using a timer and a progress bar control—is demonstrated later in this chapter during the discussion of the Select2 dialog handler.

Figure 7.6 shows the Standard Controls dialog box in operation (the Win95 version is on the left and the WinNT version is on the right).

Figure 7.6. *Two versions of the Standard Controls dialog box.*

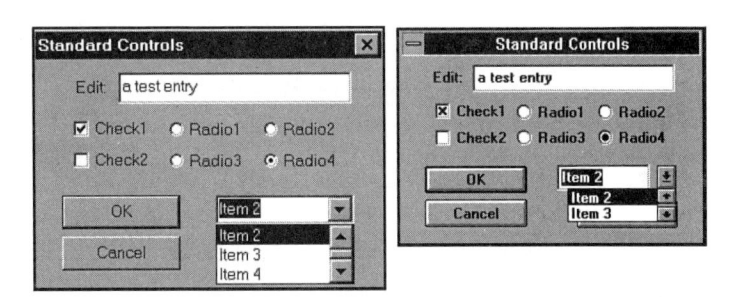

When you compare these two versions of the dialog box, you can see that Win95 and WinNT present the dialog box quite differently, even though both are produced by the same executable program and, in both cases, the screen display used is 800 × 600. You frequently may notice this discrepancy: fonts that are nominally the same size appear larger in Win95 than in Win31 or WinNT; dialog box layouts are sized differently; buttons and controls are larger in Win95 and spacing differs.

Although you can't do much about these differences, it may help to be aware of the differences—just in case you have an application where it matters.

Initializing Dialog Box Elements

In Chapter 4, "Using Message Boxes," when message dialog boxes were demonstrated, there was no need for initialization. In this Standard Controls dialog box example, there isn't much opportunity for initialization, either. However, you will initialize the radio buttons in the Standard Controls dialog box example.

In the DialoVW.CPP source example, the dialog box is called from CDialog_1View, which begins by declaring an instance of the SELECT1 class. However, before calling the dialog box itself as dlg.DoModal(), you have the opportunity to pass one value to the dialog box before it is displayed.

```
void CDialog_1View::OnDialogsStandard()
{
   // TODO: Add your command handler code here
   SELECT1    dlg;
   UINT       nResult;

   dlg.m_nRadio = 0;
   switch( nResult = dlg.DoModal() )
{
```

The call dlg.m_nRadio = 0; assigns a value to the SELECT1 member variable. In this case, it is for initialization only; in other circumstances, you can pass a number of values by assigning them to member variables. Then, within the class, in response to OnDlgCreate—after the dlg.DoModal() call—you can use these member variables to initialize dialog box elements.

In the Standard Controls dialog box example, there hasn't been much to initialize. The CComboBox element was initialized with a selection of strings when the dialog box was designed. More commonly, you will probably want to pass a set of arguments to initialize the list, which you can do by using a CString variable with delimiters separating the elements. Then, within the SELECT1 class handling (in Select_1.CPP), provisions in OnDlgCreate can break down the CString into individual entries and add these to the combo box using the CComboBox::AddString and CComboBox::InsertString methods.

> Note: A similar technique is shown in the Select_2.CPP source file in the WinNT Standard Controls dialog box (in the DialogNT example) when the ListBox member is initialized.

Retrieving Dialog Box Results

In Chapter 4, "Using Message Boxes," when message dialog boxes were introduced, the only value retrieved from the dialog box was the exit code indicating which button had been selected. For the Standard Controls dialog box, however, you must retrieve several values. There are two string entries (one from the edit box and one from the combo box), the settings of the checkboxes, and a radio button result—all of which must be reported to the procedure that called the dialog box.

Chapter 7 • Designing Custom Dialog Boxes

In the OnOK method, the dialog box control values were copied to member variables. Now you must transfer these values, which are members of the dialog class SELECT1, to local variables that can be used by the calling procedure for other operations.

Returning to the OnDialogsStandard method in DialoVW.CPP, add the following, unshaded code so that, if the SELECT1 dialog box returns IDOK, the dialog class members are copied to local members for further use.

```
void CDialog_1View::OnDialogsStandard()
{
   ...
   switch( nResult = dlg.DoModal() )
   {
      case IDOK:
         csEdit1  = dlg.m_csEdit1;
         csCombo1 = dlg.m_csCombo1;
         bCheck1  = dlg.m_bCheck1;
         bCheck2  = dlg.m_bCheck2;
         nRadio   = dlg.m_nRadio;
         nReport = 1;
         break;
```

Because you used CString variables, transferring string information is every bit as simple as copying a Boolean or an integer.

Once this becomes local information (local to the CDialog_1View class), you're finished with dialog box class instance and can move along. But remember that the dialog box class instance has a strictly limited scope within CDialog_1View. If you don't retrieve the information to a local variable *now*, the information will be lost entirely once the dialog instance passes out of scope.

Other Response Provisions

In response to an IDOK result message, you have retrieved the strings, checkbox settings, and radio button results. When the view window is redrawn, you can display these results.

More immediate, however, is the question of what to do if an IDC_BUTTON1 or IDCANCEL result is returned.

In the case of an IDC_BUTTON1 result, the simple response is to call the OnDialogsSpecials() method, which, in turn, will call the second example dialog box:

```
case IDC_BUTTON1:
   OnDialogsSpecials();
   break;
```

If any other result is reported, the appropriate response is to clear the local variables:

```
        default:
           csEdit1.Empty();
           csCombo1.Empty();
           bCheck1 = FALSE;
           bCheck2 = FALSE;
```

```
            nRadio  = 0;
            nReport = 0;
        }
        Invalidate();
    }
```

The final step in the response is to call the `Invalidate()` method to ensure that the view window is redrawn after the dialog box terminates so that you can display the selections made in the dialog box.

The Special Controls Dialog Box—WinNT Version

The Standard Controls dialog box designed and explained in the first part of this chapter made use of a fairly simple set of widely used dialog box controls. The second dialog box, the Special Controls dialog box, uses a set of somewhat more complex controls, including a few of the new common controls supplied by Visual C++ and supported by Win95.

Because these controls are not supported by current versions of Windows NT (that is, by WinNT versions 3.1 and 3.5), we'll begin by creating two versions of the demo program, naming them (very imaginatively) DialogNT and Dialog95.

The DialogNT version of the Special Controls dialog box offers horizontal and vertical control bars, a single list box, and, of course, the usual Cancel and OK buttons (see Figure 7.7).

Figure 7.7. The DialogNT Special Controls dialog box.

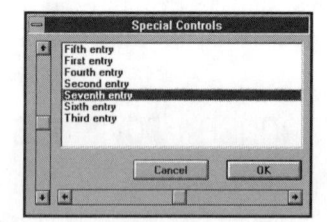

Of these controls, the list box is not particularly different from the combo box in the Standard Controls dialog box. In this instance, however, the list box entries are created in the `OnDlgCreate` method, which is called when the dialog box is initialized.

```
BOOL SELECT2::OnInitDialog()
{
    CDialog::OnInitDialog();

    // TODO: Add extra initialization here
    m_HScroll.SetScrollRange(0,100);
    m_HScroll.SetScrollPos(50);
    m_VScroll.SetScrollRange(0,100);
    m_VScroll.SetScrollPos(50);
    m_List1.AddString( "First entry" );
    m_List1.AddString( "Second entry" );
    m_List1.AddString( "Third entry" );
    m_List1.AddString( "Fourth entry" );
```

```
    m_List1.AddString( "Fifth entry" );
    m_List1.AddString( "Sixth entry" );
    m_List1.AddString( "Seventh entry" );
    return TRUE;  // return TRUE unless you set the focus to a control
                  // EXCEPTION: OCX Property Pages should return FALSE
}
```

In addition to loading strings in the list box, the OnInitDialog method is used to initialize the two scrollbars by establishing their ranges and their initial settings.

Although these scrollbars don't actually accomplish anything in the dialog box, scrollbar handling code is required and the resulting settings are passed back to the calling procedure. Scrollbar controls—unlike most controls—absolutely *must* be initialized because, if they are not, the default range is 0..0—not a very useful size.

Scrollbar Event Messages

In addition to initializing a scrollbar, the dialog class must include message handling provisions for the scrollbar. Without this code, the scrollbar does not respond at all.

For the horizontal scrollbar—or more accurately, for *all* horizontal scrollbars, regardless of their ranges, step sizes, or other characteristics—the OnHScroll method contains the necessary code to allow the scrollbar thumbpad to be dragged and for the thumbpad to move in response to hits on the scrollbar body and the end pads. Vertical scrollbars—all vertical scrollbars—receive their corresponding handling through the OnVScroll method. With the exception of the vertical and horizontal directional differences, the two methods are otherwise identical.

Using OnHScroll as the example for both, the method is called with three parameters:

- ◆ The first parameter is the nSBCode parameter, which supplements the horizontal scroll message by telling where on the scrollbar the message was generated. Depending on the nSBCode message, the scrollbar may have been hit on either end (SB_LINEUP and SB_LINEDOWN scroll events), on the body to one side or the other of the thumbpad (SB_PAGEUP and SB_PAGEDOWN scroll events), or by dragging the thumbpad (an SB_THUMBPOSITION event).

- ◆ The second parameter is the nPos parameter. If the scrollbar event is SB_THUMBPOSITION, nPos specifies the new thumbpad position. For any other event, the nPos parameter should be 0 but, in any case, should be ignored.

- ◆ The third parameter, pScrollBar, is a pointer to the scrollbar instance that generated the scroll message.

Using this third parameter, the first step is to retrieve the scrollbar position and then retrieve the range for this specific scrollbar.

In the Select2.CPP source file, the OnHScroll method responds to all scrollbar messages—from all horizontal scrollbars. For vertical scrollbars, an OnVScroll method is used. In situations where more than one horizontal or vertical scrollbar may be generating the message events, the `nSBCode` parameter identifies the individual scrollbar.

```
void SELECT2::OnHScroll(UINT nSBCode, UINT nPos, CScrollBar* pScrollBar)
{
    // TODO: Add your message handler code here and/or call default
    int    iMin, iMax, nScrollPos;

    nScrollPos = pScrollBar->GetScrollPos();
    pScrollBar->GetScrollRange( &iMin, &iMax );
```

With the range and position for this specific scrollbar in hand, it's time to respond to the event message.

For the `SB_PAGEUP` and `SB_PAGEDOWN` events, the response decided on in the following code is to move the scrollbar one-quarter of the total range. This movement can take many different forms. If this were scrollbar handling for the Visual C++ editor, for example, the movement would be the page (display) width horizontally (vertically, it would be the page height). But the distance the scrollbar moves can be anything—it's your choice.

```
switch( nSBCode )
{
    case SB_PAGEUP:
        nScrollPos = max( iMin, nScrollPos - ( ( iMax - iMin ) / 4 ) );
        break;

    case SB_PAGEDOWN:
        nScrollPos = min( iMax, nScrollPos + ( ( iMax - iMin ) / 4 ) );
        break;
```

For the `SB_LINEUP` or `SB_LINEDOWN` events (the endpads on the scrollbar), the response decided on in the following code is one-tenth of the total range. Again, the distance the scrollbar moves can be anything depending on the application and its requirements.

```
    case SB_LINEUP:
        nScrollPos = max( nScrollPos - 10, iMin );
        break;

    case SB_LINEDOWN:
        nScrollPos = min( nScrollPos + 10, iMax );
        break;
```

In the final event, `SB_THUMBPOSITION`, the `nPos` parameter contains a new position. All that's required here is to copy the new position to the `nScrollPos` variable:

```
    case SB_THUMBPOSITION:
        nScrollPos = nPos;
        break;
```

Now that you have the new position information, the last step is to call the `SetScrollPos` method to reset the scrollbar:

```
}
pScrollBar->SetScrollPos( nScrollPos );
```

Notice, however, that the ClassWizard has provided a default handler, `CDialog::OnHScroll`:

```
//    CDialog::OnHScroll(nSBCode, nPos, pScrollBar);
}
```

Unfortunately, this default handler doesn't really do anything—and certainly doesn't make the scrollbar work. Bad planning in MFC? Probably…but that's how it is.

On the other hand, in the Special Controls dialog box, you see a special scrollbar that does have its own handling—even though it continues to funnel messages through the `OnHScroll` (or `OnVScroll`) methods.

Closing the Special Controls Dialog Box

The cleanup necessary to retrieve the two scrollbar positions should be familiar by this time. Getting the current selection from the list box, however, is a slightly different process because it requires two steps: calling the `GetCurSel` method to retrieve the selection index and then calling the `GetText` method, with the index value, to retrieve the actual string. The following code shows how this is accomplished:

```
void SELECT2::OnOK()
{
   // TODO: Add extra validation here
   int nIndex;

   m_nHScroll = m_HScroll.GetScrollPos();
   m_nVScroll = m_VScroll.GetScrollPos();
   nIndex = m_List1.GetCurSel();
   if( nIndex >= 0 )
      m_List1.GetText( nIndex, m_csList );
   else
      m_csList.Empty();
   CDialog::OnOK();
}
```

Of course, if there is no current selection, the index returned is –1 (remember that list box entries begin at 0, not at 1); a call to `GetText` with this argument would result in an assertion error. Instead, the preceding code ensures that that `m_csList` is empty.

Just as with the Standard Controls dialog box, code in the DialoVW.CPP file reports the result of the dialog box but the provisions should be perfectly clear.

The following section looks at the Win95 version of the Special Controls dialog box—with the new common dialog box controls that, hopefully, are a bit more interesting.

The Special Controls Dialog Box—Win95 Version

Visual C++ version 2.5 and Windows 95 offer a new group of controls not available under Windows NT. These controls appear on the Visual Workbench (refer back to Figure 7.1) as eight of the bottom nine controls on the toolbar (the final control type is Custom). The Win95 Special

Controls dialog box shown in Figure 7.8 demonstrates five of these eight controls: the tree view, the hotkey edit box, the spin button, the slider, and the progress bar. The remaining three (the animation tool, tab control, and list view tool) are discussed later in this chapter.

Figure 7.8. *The Win95 version of the Special Controls dialog box uses five new controls not available in WinNT.*

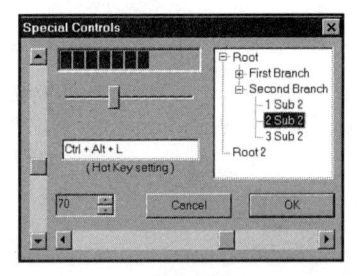

The Win95 Special Controls dialog box also incorporates the vertical and horizontal scrollbars demonstrated in the WinNT version—not because they behave differently in Win95 but because the slider control (as you may ascertain by tracking event messages) also uses the `OnHScroll` method if it is present. Alternatively, if no special `OnHScroll` method is provided, the trackbar (a.k.a. *slider*) control class has its own default handling.

The first requirement in using any of the new dialog box controls is to add the following `include` statement to your STDAFX.H file:

```
#include <afxcmn.h>
```

This `include` statement enables the new controls by defining the MFC COMCTL32 Control Classes including the `CAnimateCtrl`, `CHotKeyCtrl`, `CListCtrl`, `CProgressCtrl`, `CSliderCtrl`, `CSpinButtonCtrl`, `CTabCtrl`, and `CTreeCtrl` classes.

The Hotkey Control

A *hotkey control* is a special form of edit window designed to allow a user to create or define a hotkey combination. The hotkey edit window accepts any valid hotkey combination from the keyboard (including Ctrl, Alt, and Shift keys in combination with a valid character key) and displays the result.

> **Warning:** The `CHotKeyCtrl.GetHotKey` method is not well documented and the member `CHotKeyCtrl.SetHotKey` method causes an application error in Visual C++ 2.1. Although this is an interesting function, it does not appear, at the time of this writing, to be fully functional. See notes on partial workarounds in the following sections.

The `CHotKeyCtrl.GetHotKey` method is documented as returning the character code (the virtual key code) in one WORD parameter and the flags in a second. However, the method is also documented as follows:

The virtual-key code is in the low-order byte, and the modifier flags are in the high-order byte.

This statement seems to refer to a single WORD argument...except that the `GetHotKey` method has two implementations: one requiring two WORD arguments passed by address and returning VOID and the other requiring no arguments but returning a DWORD result.

The bottom line is that this class appears to be garbage, both in documentation and implementation.

If you want to get the result back from the `GetHotKey` member function, the following code will work:

```
m_dwKey = m_HotKey.GetHotKey();
```

Here, the `GetHotKey` method is called without parameters and returns a DWORD value. In the returned DWORD, the character code is found in the low byte of the low word; the flags are found in the high byte of the low word. The high word is NULL.

The modifier flags are defined as follows:

Constant	Meaning
HOTKEYF_ALT	Alt key
HOTKEYF_CONTROL	Ctrl key
HOTKEYF_EXT	Extended key
HOTKEYF_SHIFT	Shift key

As for implementing the use of the hotkey...well, this and further details will just have to wait until the `CHotKeyCtrl` class is more fully functional.

The Progress Control

A *progress control* or *progress bar* is a control used to indicate the progress of a lengthy operation. The progress control consists of a rectangle that is gradually filled (from left to right) as an operation progresses. The fill color used is the system's selected highlight color.

In the Win95 version of the Special Controls dialog box, when the dialog box is initialized, the progress bar is given a range of 1..100, a step size of 1, and an initial position of 0. When the timer is started, the progress bar is incremented in one-second steps.

The code required to set up the progress bar in the `OnInitDialog` method is as follows:

```
BOOL SELECT2::OnInitDialog()
{
   CDialog::OnInitDialog();

   // TODO: Add extra initialization here
   ...
   // setup for progress bar
   m_ProgressBar.SetRange( 1, 100 );
   m_ProgressBar.SetStep( 1 );
```

```
    m_ProgressBar.SetPos( 0 );
    SetTimer( 1, 1000, NULL );
    ...
    return TRUE;   // return TRUE unless you set the focus to a control
                   // EXCEPTION: OCX Property Pages should return FALSE
}
```

Each time a timer message is received, the progress bar `StepIt()` method is called to increment progress, as specified in the following code fragment:

```
void SELECT2::OnTimer(UINT nIDEvent)
{
    // TODO: Add your message handler code here and/or call default
    if( m_ProgressBar.StepIt() == 100 ) OnOK();
//    CDialog::OnTimer(nIDEvent);
}
```

Because the `StepIt()` method returns the previous value even as it increments, the progress bar is used in this example to close the dialog box after 100 seconds have elapsed by calling the `OnOK()` method. Of course, this is equivalent to clicking the OK button but, if you want a different exit result, you can call the `EndDialog(arg)` function instead.

A bit of explanation is in order to better understand how the progress bar operates:

◆ By default, if no other settings are established, the progress bar is incremented in ten steps.

◆ The progress bar is filled in only ten increments. That is, a filled progress bar shows ten segments, regardless of the length or range of the bar (refer back to Figure 7.8).

◆ As soon as the progress bar position is incremented (past 0 in this example), the first segment is filled in. When 11 is reached, the second segment appears. And so forth.

Quite frankly, if you really want a smooth progress bar, even a simple owner-draw control would probably look much better than this one.

Happily, the rest of the special controls demonstrated in the Win95 Special Controls dialog box are not as flawed as the first two.

Progress Bar Methods

Refer to online documentation for details on parameters and return values.

Method	Description
OffsetPos(nPos)	Advances the current position of the progress bar control by the specified increment and redraws the bar.
SetPos(nPos)	Sets the current position for the progress bar control and redraws the bar.
SetRange(nLower, nUpper)	Sets the minimum and maximum ranges for the progress bar control and redraws the bar.

Method	Description
SetStep(nStep)	Specifies the step increment for the progress bar control.
StepIt()	Advances the current position for the progress bar control by the specified step increment and redraws the bar.

The Slider Control

A *slider control* (also known as a *trackbar*) is a window containing a slider and optional tick marks. When the user moves the slider using either the mouse or the direction keys, the control sends notification messages to indicate the change. In action, these notification messages are the same as scrollbar messages except, of course, that there are no end pads and the only messages received are SB_THUMBPAD, SB_PAGEUP, and SB_PAGEDOWN.

> Note: Unlike the scrollbar controls and despite similarities, the slider control does not require any additional provisions to handle positioning or to update the slider position.

Unlike the progress bar, the slider control is rather well designed and allows you to set positions on the slider and specify tick marks, frequency, and other characteristics. With these capabilities, slider controls allow the user to select a discrete value or a set of consecutive values in a range. Examples are setting the keyboard repeat rate or the mouse acceleration rate.

At any rate, this control is worth experimenting with.

Initializing a slider control is simplicity itself. Do it in the OnInitDialog method as shown here:

```
m_Slider.SetRange(0,100,FALSE);
```

Of course, for more elaborate slider controls, you may also want to set tick marks and positions or use the SetPos method to position the slider or accomplish a variety of other customizations appropriate to your application. Toward this purpose, take a look at the various methods (the slider control offers a great variety) documented in the online help.

Retrieving the slider control position is quite simple and parallels the methodology for a scrollbar control. In the OnOK method, the slider position is retrieved as shown here:

```
m_nSlider = m_Slider.GetPos();
```

That is about all that can be said of the slider control. It works quite nicely and quite simply. If you need to elaborate, a number of customizations are provided. Have fun.

Slider Control Methods

Refer to online documentation for details on parameters and return values.

Method	Description
ClearSel	Clears the current selection in the slider control.
ClearTics	Clears the current tick marks from the slider control.
GetChannelRect	Gets the size of slider control's channel (or bounding rectangle).
GetLineSize	Gets the line size of the slider control.
GetNumTics	Gets the number of tick marks in the slider control.
GetPageSize	Gets the page size of the slider control.
GetPos	Gets the current position of the slider.
GetRange	Gets the minimum and maximum positions for the slider.
GetRangeMax	Gets the maximum position for the slider.
GetRangeMin	Gets the minimum position for the slider.
GetSelection	Gets the range of the current selection.
GetThumbRect	Gets the size of the slider control's thumbpad.
GetTic	Gets the position of a specified tick mark.
GetTicArray	Gets the array of tick-mark positions for a slider control.
GetTicPos	Gets the position of a specified tick mark, in client coordinates.
SetLineSize	Sets the line size of the slider control.
SetPageSize	Sets the page size of the slider control.
SetPos	Sets the current position of the slider.
SetRange	Sets the minimum and maximum positions for the slider.
SetRangeMax	Sets the maximum position for the slider.
SetRangeMin	Sets the minimum position for the slider.
SetSelection	Sets the range of the current selection.
SetTic	Sets the position of a specified tick mark.
SetTicFreq	Sets the frequency of tick marks per slider control increment.
VerifyPos	Verifies that the position of a slider control is zero.

The Spin Button Control

A *spin button control* (also known as an *up-down control*) is a pair of arrow buttons that the user can click to increment or decrement a value, such as a scroll position or a number displayed in a companion control, or *buddy window*. The value associated with a spin button control is called its *current position*.

The spin button control is one control element that has been much anticipated. It is particularly useful, for example, in setting dates (using separate spin buttons for day, month, and year) or in incrementing any type of sequential counter for which a limited range of values is expected.

Before the introduction of the spin button, a truncated scrollbar could have been used in a similar capacity but the spin button has several advantages:

- A spin button and its optional buddy window not only behave, quite automatically, as a single unit, they also store a result and limit the result to a preset range.
- Association between a spin control and its buddy window are established, in the absence of other provisions, by the tab order of the controls. For example, in the Win95 Special Controls dialog, the IDC_EDIT2 control (a conventional edit box) is associated with the adjacent spin control button automatically by tab order with the edit box's tab order (tab order 6) immediately preceding the spin control's (tab order 7).
- No internal coding provisions are required to synchronize values between the spin control and the edit box buddy window. Synchronization is handled internally through the association; as the spin control is incremented, the edit window is updated to reflect these changes. Of course, if the edit window is changed, the spin control value also changes to match (assuming, of course, that the edit window has not been flagged with a read-only status in the resource script).
- A spin button control can also be assigned a relative position to its buddy window (for example, to the left or right of the buddy window). When this is done, the position established during the dialog design is overridden during execution.

Note: Because the spin button control can move during execution to assume a position relative to its buddy, and because the control tab order establishes the buddy relationship in the absence of other provisions, an error in tab order may mean that your dialog box will behave quite oddly during execution.

In the Win95 Special Controls dialog box, the spin button control is initialized quite simply in the OnInitDialog method, as shown here:

```
m_SpinButton.SetRange( 1, 100 );
```

However, because the associated edit box has not been initialized, the edit box does not display any value until the spin button is activated. Of course, even though the spin button assumes a minimum initial value when the range is set, specifically initializing either the edit box or the spin control initializes both.

You can retrieve a value from the spin control and its buddy window after closing the dialog box in a few ways. First, in the OnOK method, you can use the GetPos() method to query the spin button control directly, as in the following code sample:

```
void SELECT2::OnOK()
{
    ...
    m_nSpinButton = m_SpinButton.GetPos();
    CDialog::OnOK();
}
```

Alternatively, because the spin button has an associated edit box, you can use a second retrieval method, as a `CString` value in DialoVW.CPP, after the dialog box closes, as shown in the following code sample:

```
if( dlg.DoModal() == IDOK )
{
    ...
    csEdit2 = dlg.m_csEdit2;
    ...
}
```

Remember, however, that this second retrieval approach returns a string rather than an integer value.

Spin Button Methods

Refer to online documentation for details on parameters and return values.

Method	Description
GetAccel	Retrieves acceleration information for a spin button control.
GetBase	Retrieves the current base for a spin button control.
GetBuddy	Retrieves a pointer to the current buddy window.
GetPos	Retrieves the current position of a spin button control.
GetRange	Retrieves the upper and lower limits (range) for a spin button control.
SetAccel	Sets the acceleration for a spin button control.
SetBase	Sets the base for a spin button control to base 10 (default) or base 16 (hexadecimal).
SetBuddy	Sets the buddy window for a spin button control. The default is the preceding control in the z-order (tab order).
SetPos	Sets the current position for the control.
SetRange	Sets the upper and lower limits (range) for a spin button control.

The Tree View Control

A *tree view control* is a window displaying a hierarchical list of items, such as the headings in a document, the entries in an index, or the files and directories on a disk (the resource tree in the Visual C++ editor offers a good example of the `CTreeCtrl` control box).

Within the tree, each item, or node, consists of a label and, optionally, a bitmapped image. Further, each item may have a list of associated subitems; individual items can be clicked to expand or collapse the associated subitem list.

The tree control also offers an option to supply default node images (in the form of boxes with a + for nodes that can be expanded or a – for nodes that can be collapsed). These options are found in the resource general settings for the tree control object along with an edit labels flag and a disable drag/drop flag.

Operationally, the CTreeCtrl class offers a wealth of member functions that allow you to control the appearance of the tree, to include bitmap images, trace items and parent nodes, add and retrieve entries, and carry out virtually any other task you may find appropriate.

However, to use a CTreeCtrl control, you need two structures to enter and retrieve node information: TV_ITEM and TV_INSERTSTRUCT.

TV_ITEM

The TV_ITEM structure defines the contents and properties of a tree node and is defined as follows:

```
typedef struct _TV_ITEM
{
   UINT       mask;
   HTREEITEM  hItem;           // item this structure refers to
   UINT       state;
   UINT       stateMask;
   LPSTR      pszText;
   int        cchTextMax;
   int        iImage;
   int        iSelectedImage;
   int        cChildren;
   LPARAM     lParam;           // 32-bit value to associate with item
} TV_ITEM;
```

For purposes of the example dialog box, our interest is primarily in the *mask* and *pszText* fields of the TV_ITEM structure (we simply ignore the other fields). If you wanted to incorporate bitmap images, however, you also need the *iImage* and *iSelectedImage* fields that index the normal and selected images to be used for this item.

The TV_ITEM structure fields are detailed in the following chart:

Field	Comments
mask	An array of flags that indicate which of the other structure members contain valid data or are to be filled in. The array can be a combination of the following values:
	TVIF_CHILDREN cChildren member is valid
	TVIF_HANDLE hItem member is valid
	TVIF_IMAGE iImage member is valid

Field	Comments	
	TVIF_PARAM	lParam member is valid
	TVIF_SELECTEDIMAGE	iSelectedImage member is valid
	TVIF_STATE	state and stateMask members are valid
	TVIF_TEXT	pszText and cchTextMax members are valid
state and stateMask	Current state and valid states of the item can be any valid combination of state values.	
pszText	If the structure specifies item attributes, this is the address of a NULL-terminated string containing item text.	
	If this is an LPSTR_TEXTCALLBACK value, the parent window is responsible for storing the name. The tree control sends the parent window a TVN_GETDISPINFO notification message when it needs the item text for displaying, sorting, or editing; the tree control also sends a TVN_SETDISPINFO notification when the item text changes.	
	If the structure is receiving item attributes, this member is the address of the buffer receiving the item text.	
cchTextMax	The size of the buffer pointed to by the pszText member if the structure is receiving item attributes (ignored if the structure specifies item attributes).	
iImage and iSelectedImage	Indexes of the icon image and selected icon image within the image list.	
	If either member is the I_IMAGECALLBACK value, the parent window is responsible for storing the corresponding images. The tree view control sends the parent a TVN_GETDISPINFO notification message when it needs to display the images and a TVN_SETDISPINFO notification message when the images change.	
cChildren	Number of child items associated with the item.	
	If this is an I_CHILDRENCALLBACK value, the parent window is responsible for drawing the child items. The tree view control sends the parent a TVN_GETDISPINFO notification message when it needs to display the child items and a TVN_SETDISPINFO notification message when the attributes of a child item change.	

TV_INSERTSTRUCT

The `TV_INSERTSTRUCT` structure defines the position, within the tree, where the `TV_ITEM` node will appear. It is defined as follows:

```
typedef struct _TV_INSERTSTRUCT
{
   HTREEITEM hParent;
   HTREEITEM hInsertAfter;
   TV_ITEM   item;
} TV_INSERTSTRUCT;
```

The fields in the `TV_INSERTSTRUCT` structure are detailed in the following chart:

Field	Comments
hParent	The handle of the parent item. If `TVI_ROOT` or `NULL`, the item is inserted at the root of the tree view control.
hInsertAfter	Can be the handle of the item after which the new item is to be inserted or can be one of the following values: `TVI_FIRST` Inserts the item at beginning of the list `TVI_LAST` Inserts the item at end of the list `TVI_SORT` Inserts the item into the list in alphabetical order
item	The `TV_ITEM` structure defining the item to be added to the tree view control.

Adding Nodes to a Tree View Control

In the Win95 Special Controls dialog box, three levels of nodes are added to the tree structure—beginning, of course, with a root note. To create these nodes, `TV_ITEM` and `TV_INSERTSTRUCT` instances are required along with two `HTREEITEM` variables. (The `HTREEITEM` variables are simply handles for previously inserted nodes.)

Although all of the nodes used in the following example are text labels (`TVIF_TEXT`), items can be mixed. The first node is inserted as a root entry (`TVI_ROOT`) and is placed at the first of the list (`TVI_FIRST`).

```
BOOL SELECT2::OnInitDialog()
{
   CDialog::OnInitDialog();
   ...
   //   setup for tree

   TV_ITEM           tvi;
   TV_INSERTSTRUCT   tvIS;
   HTREEITEM         hItem1, hItem2;
```

After calling the `InsertItem` method, as shown in the following sample, the returned value is stored in `hItem2`.

```
tvi.mask = TVIF_TEXT;
tvi.pszText = "Root";
tvIS.item = tvi;
tvIS.hParent = TVI_ROOT;
tvIS.hInsertAfter = TVI_FIRST;
hItem2 = m_TreeView.InsertItem( &tvIS );
```

> Note: Although a pointer to TV_INSERTSTRUCT is defined as LPTV_INSERTSTRUCT, attempts to use pointers rather than structures cause access violations at run time.

The next two entries are child branches inserted as children of the first entry:

```
tvi.mask = TVIF_TEXT;
tvi.pszText = "First Branch";
tvIS.item = tvi;
tvIS.hParent = hItem2;
tvIS.hInsertAfter = TVI_LAST;
hItem1 = m_TreeView.InsertItem( &tvIS );

tvi.mask = TVIF_TEXT;
tvi.pszText = "Second Branch";
tvIS.item = tvi;
tvIS.hParent = hItem2;
tvIS.hInsertAfter = TVI_LAST;
hItem2 = m_TreeView.InsertItem( &tvIS );
```

Notice that separate HTREEITEM handles have been retained for each of these branches so that subsequent entries can be added to both.

In the following code fragment, additional child entries are added, first to the "first branch" node and then to the "second branch" node:

```
tvi.mask = TVIF_TEXT;
tvi.pszText = "1 Sub 1";
tvIS.item = tvi;
tvIS.hParent = hItem1;
tvIS.hInsertAfter = TVI_LAST;
m_TreeView.InsertItem( &tvIS );

tvi.mask = TVIF_TEXT;
tvi.pszText = "2 Sub 1";
tvIS.item = tvi;
tvIS.hParent = hItem1;
tvIS.hInsertAfter = TVI_LAST;
m_TreeView.InsertItem( &tvIS );

tvi.mask = TVIF_TEXT;
tvi.pszText = "1 Sub 2";
tvIS.item = tvi;
tvIS.hParent = hItem2;
tvIS.hInsertAfter = hItem2;
hItem1 = m_TreeView.InsertItem( &tvIS );
```

Chapter 7 • Designing Custom Dialog Boxes

```
    tvi.mask = TVIF_TEXT;
    tvi.pszText = "3 Sub 2";
    tvIS.item = tvi;
    tvIS.hParent = hItem2;
    t+vIS.hInsertAfter = TVI_LAST;
    m_TreeView.InsertItem( &tvIS );

    tvi.mask = TVIF_TEXT;
    tvi.pszText = "2 Sub 2";
    tvIS.item = tvi;
    tvIS.hParent = hItem2;
    tvIS.hInsertAfter = hItem1;
    m_TreeView.InsertItem( &tvIS );
```

And finally, another root entry is placed at the end of the tree list:

```
    tvi.mask = TVIF_TEXT;
    tvi.pszText = "Root 2";
    tvIS.item = tvi;
    tvIS.hParent = TVI_ROOT;
    tvIS.hInsertAfter = TVI_LAST;
    m_TreeView.InsertItem( &tvIS );
```

As you can see, this is a very cumbersome method of building a tree. In actual practice, you will want a more elegant—and flexible—process for this purpose. In practice, you would probably pass a pointer to a data array with the data elements in order. Each data element would contain a field to define which data elements were children of which preceding elements and an HTREEITEM field to store a return handle as each item is added. Then, as the tree is populated, you would decrypt these data records to retrieve the appropriate parent handles for each item.

Of course, if a more elegant approach occurs to you, feel free to experiment.

Retrieving a Node from a Tree View Control

Retrieving a node from a tree view control is relatively simple. Several methods are provided to select nodes, select parent nodes, or select child nodes. For demonstration purposes, however, operations are limited to retrieving a selected (highlighted) item from the tree (assuming, of course, that a selection has been made).

The CTreeCtrl::GetSelectedItem method returns an HTREEITEM handle from the tree if a selection has been made. If nothing has been selected from the tree, the returned value is NULL. This process is handled in the OnOK method as follows:

```
void SELECT2::OnOK()
{
    ...
    tvItem.hItem = m_TreeView.GetSelectedItem();
    if( tvItem.hItem )
    {
```

Assume that an item was selected and the query returned a valid HTREEITEM handle to the tvItem instance. The next step is to set the mask to indicate that you are passing a valid handle and want to retrieve the item label:

```
        tvItem.mask  = TVIF_HANDLE | TVIF_TEXT;
```

You must also provide a buffer which, in this case, is the buffer belonging to a `CString` variable. The following example specifies a size of 100 bytes both when `GetBuffer()` is called and in the `cchTextmax` field:

```
tvItem.pszText = m_csTree.GetBuffer(100);
tvItem.cchTextMax = 100;
m_TreeView.GetItem( &tvItem );
```

With the buffer and buffer size ready, you can call `GetItem()` and then—and this is important—call `ReleaseBuffer` for your `CString` instance:

```
m_csTree.ReleaseBuffer();
```

At this point, you have the item label in the `CString` buffer. No further transfer is required and, in brief, the job is done.

However, if the original test—`if( tvItem.hItem )`—failed, you must still handle the `else` branch to set the `CString m_csTree` to empty. Here's how that is done:

```
   }
   else
      m_csTree.Empty();
   ...
   CDialog::OnOK();
}
```

Overall, the `CTreeCtrl` is a fairly clean and elegant addition to our dialog resources. Perhaps the handling is a bit awkward and, certainly, there are advantages in working out a cleaner method of passing information into the control. How you will choose to use this—and how you will choose to pass information in—depends on what features of the tree view you want to use and what kind of information you plan to display.

But, in any case, have fun. This one is worth a little effort.

Tree View Methods

Refer to online documentation for details on parameters and return values.

Method	*Description*
`CreateDragImage`	Creates a dragging bitmap for a specified tree view item.
`DeleteAllItems`	Deletes all items in the tree view control.
`DeleteItem`	Deletes an item in the tree view control.
`EditLabel`	Edits a specified tree view item in place.
`EnsureVisible`	Ensures that the tree view item is visible in the tree view control.
`Expand`	Expands or collapses child items of a specified tree view item.
`GetChildItem`	Gets the child of a specified tree view item.

Method	Description
GetCount	Gets a number of tree items associated with the tree view control.
GetDropHilightItem	Gets the target of a drag-and-drop operation.
GetEditControl	Gets the handle of the edit control used to edit a specified tree view item.
GetFirstVisibleItem	Gets the first visible item of a specified tree view item.
GetImageList	Gets the handle of an image list associated with the tree view control.
GetIndent	Gets the offset (in pixels) of a tree view item from the parent.
GetItem	Gets attributes of a specified tree view item.
GetItemRect	Gets the bounding rectangle of the tree view item.
GetNextItem	Gets the next tree view item matching the specified relationship.
GetNextSiblingItem	Gets the next sibling of a specified tree view item.
GetNextVisibleItem	Gets the next visible item of a specified tree view item.
GetParentItem	Gets the parent of a specified tree view item.
GetPrevSiblingItem	Gets the previous sibling of a specified tree view item.
GetPrevVisibleItem	Gets the previous visible item of a specified tree view item.
GetRootItem	Gets the root of a specified tree view item.
GetSelectedItem	Gets the currently selected tree view item.
GetVisibleCount	Gets the number of visible tree items associated with the tree view control.
HitTest	Returns the current position of the cursor related to the CTreeCtrl object.
InsertItem	Inserts a new item in the tree view control.
Select	Selects, scrolls into view, or redraws the specified tree view item.
SelectDropTarget	Redraws the tree item as the target of a drag-and-drop operation.
SelectItem	Selects a specified tree view item.
SetImageList	Sets the handle of the image list associated with a tree view control.
SetIndent	Sets the offset (in pixels) of a tree view item from the parent.
SetItem	Sets the attributes of a specified tree view item.
SortChildren	Sorts the children of a given parent item.
SortChildrenCB	Sorts the children of a given parent item using an application-defined sort function.

Summary

Although dialog boxes and graphics controls play an important part in most applications, the Microsoft Foundation Classes and the ClassWizard offer new convenience in creating dialog box control handling. For most common dialog box controls, the foundation classes provide default handling that leaves the application with little to do except watch return codes and retrieve resulting dialog box selections and values.

Some dialog box controls (such as scrollbars), however, require handling code within the dialog class; others (such as the new slider control), although functionally the same as a scrollbar, perform complex tasks entirely on their own.

Visual C++ has also introduced several new control classes supported by Windows 95. Although these classes are expected to be supported by future versions of Windows NT, they are not supported by current Windows NT versions (3.1 or 3.5) nor are they supported by any 16-bit versions of Windows.

Further, as mentioned in this chapter, some of the new controls do not work at all and others work only partially; unfortunately, all are badly documented to boot. Still, a few of these controls are worth your attention: the tree view, spin button, and slider controls. On the other hand, although the progress bar is functional, it isn't particularly well done—and the hotkey class is both badly documented and, in one respect at least, seriously flawed.

This caveat aside, please experiment with all these controls. Hopefully, the flaws will not remain forever.

CHAPTER 8

Customizing Dialog Boxes with Additional Controls

Chapter 7, "Designing Custom Dialog Boxes," looked at several elements of dialog box design, including the use of a number of the new common dialog box controls. This chapter looks at two additional common controls, one of which (the tab control class) will likely prove very useful to you; the second (the animation control class) is of less-certain value. Both these controls, however, are compatible only with Windows 95 and with Windows NT versions 3.51 or later (they are not functional under Windows 3.x or Windows NT 3.5).

> Note: To use common dialog box controls, add `#include <afxcmn.h>` to the list of includes in the STDAFX.H file for your project.

The Tab Control

The tab control—the `CTabCtrl` class—creates a graphic analog of tabbed file folders or tabbed pages in which each page, or tab window, acts as a separate item and displays separate information or offers a separate set of controls. Granted, the description of a tab control is not distinctively different from a series of windows or a series of dialog boxes—and this is as it should be. A tab control is, in function, a series of dialog boxes or windows.

What is different (as you will see in the Dialog2 program used in this chapter) is that the tabs offer a means of switching between views of these different dialog boxes or windows. The user selects each by its tab rather than closing one to open another. The difference is one of appearance and convenience, even if the operations themselves remain familiar.

> Note: Incidentally, Word 6.0 offers an excellent example of a dialog box that uses tabs: select **T**ools, **O**ptions. Visual C++ version 2.1 offers a set of four tabs in the output window: Build, Debug, Find in Files, and Profile.

Creating a Tab Control

Figure 8.1 shows a dialog box with a single tab control (one tab control supports multiple tabs) filling the dialog box window. The TabControl Properties dialog box in the lower right of Figure 8.1 is itself another tab control with two tabs; the Styles tab is shown with the default tab style settings.

Figure 8.1. Creating a tab control.

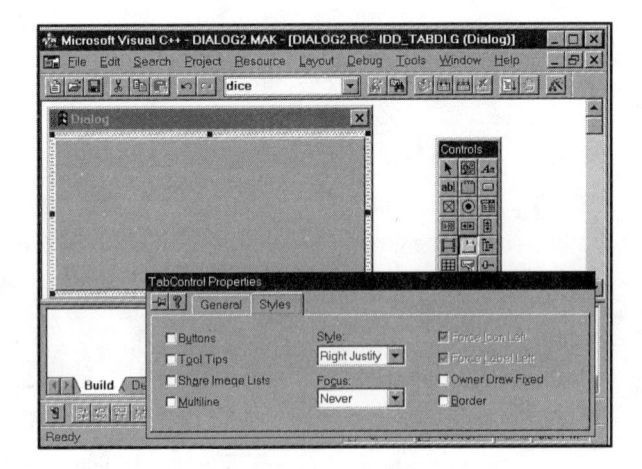

The tab control image in the resource editor doesn't look like much. When you create it, it's just a blank box: there are no tabs. No dialog box appears to ask you to enter tab labels nor are you given the opportunity to connect the tab to anything. As a matter of fact, using the tab control is a lot like old-style programming: you have to do the work instead of depending on Visual C++ to set everything up for you.

But in just a moment, I'll show you how to do the work…and why.

First, however—because you will be creating three tabs for this demonstration program—you must design three more dialog boxes. Note that these will be child windows, not popups. The first of these dialog boxes, POP2, is shown in Figure 8.2.

Chapter 8 • Customizing Dialog Boxes with Additional Controls

Figure 8.2. A child dialog box to be used with a tab control.

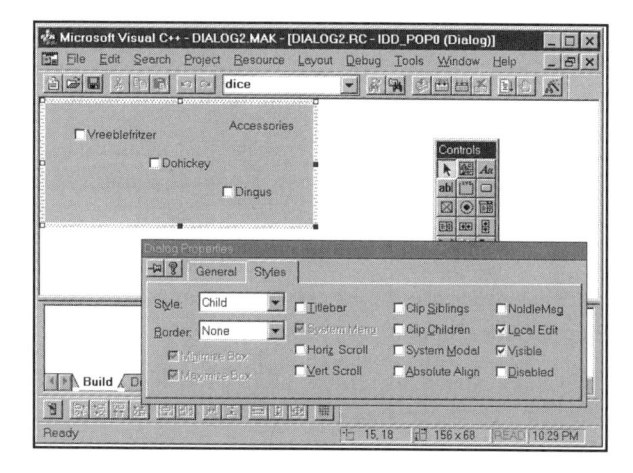

On the Styles tab of the Dialog Properties dialog box (shown in the lower right of Figure 8.2), the dialog box is defined as a child with no border and no title bar. On the General tab of the Dialog Properties dialog box (not shown in Figure 8.2), an offset is set with an x-position of 15 and a y-position of 18. This offset is relative to the parent window (which, in operation, is the tab control). The vertical offset allows room for the tabs themselves (you don't want the dialog box to cover the tabs); the horizontal offset centers the child relative to the parent window.

The rest of the POP2 dialog box—three checkboxes and a label—are purely for demonstration. The remaining two popup dialog boxes used with the tab control (POP1 and POP2) are created with the same size, the same style, and the same offsets but use different controls.

You must first do some preparation work. In the TabDlg.H header, add `include` statements for the three child dialog boxes:

```
/////////////////////////////////////////////////////////////////////////////
// TabDlg dialog


#include "pop0.h"
#include "pop1.h"
#include "pop2.h"

class TabDlg : public CDialog
{
// Construction
public:
    TabDlg(CWnd* pParent = NULL);   // standard constructor

// Dialog Data
    //{{AFX_DATA(TabDlg)
    enum { IDD = IDD_TABDLG };
    //}}AFX_DATA

    CTabCtrl   m_Tab;
    UINT       m_nStyle;
    BOOL       m_bAccessory[3];
```

```
CString   m_csModel;
POP0      cDlg0;
POP1      cDlg1;
POP2      cDlg2;
```

Also in the preceding code, member variables are declared for the CTabCtrl control, the three child dialog boxes, and an assortment of data member variables.

The three child dialog boxes have their own class definitions, header files, and source files but these are for internal handling (that is, for handling operations and selections internal to the dialog box itself). And because these operations are not particularly different from examples in other chapters in this book, they are not discussed here.

How these dialogs are called and displayed, however, *is* relevant. These tasks are handled within the TabDlg source file.

But before handling the dialog boxes, the tab itself must be set up. This task begins with the m_Tab member, defined in TabDlg.H (which is connected to the IDC_TAB control in the dialog box by way of the data exchange statement in TabDlg.CPP):

```
void TabDlg::DoDataExchange(CDataExchange* pDX)
{
    CDialog::DoDataExchange(pDX);
    //{{AFX_DATA_MAP(TabDlg)
    DDX_Control(pDX, IDC_TAB, m_Tab);
    //}}AFX_DATA_MAP
}
```

With this connection established, the next task is to set up the three tabs. This is accomplished in the OnInitDialog procedure in TabDlg.CPP as shown following example:

```
/////////////////////////////////////////////////////////////////////////////
// TabDlg message handlers

BOOL TabDlg::OnInitDialog()
{
    CDialog::OnInitDialog();

    // TODO: Add extra initialization here
    TC_ITEM tci;

    tci.mask = TCIF_TEXT;
    tci.iImage = -1;
    tci.pszText = "Accessories";
    m_Tab.InsertItem( 0, &tci );
    tci.pszText = "Style";
    m_Tab.InsertItem( 1, &tci );
    tci.pszText = "Model";
    m_Tab.InsertItem( 2, &tci );
    return TRUE;  // return TRUE unless you set the focus to a control
                  // EXCEPTION: OCX Property Pages should return FALSE
}
```

In the preceding sample of code, several tasks are accomplished. The TC_ITEM structure, introduced in Chapter 7, "Designing Custom Dialog Boxes," is used here to contain text labels that, with the InsertItem method, create three tabs in the tab control.

The `InsertItem` method is called with two arguments: a zero-based index (tab position) and the `TC_ITEM` structure containing the label text. In response, each tab is sized appropriately to the supplied label.

> Note: Although a zero-based index used for the tab position is documented with the implicit suggestion that this index governs the tab ordering, the truth is that the index does *not* directly govern the tab order...at least, not by the usual rules. Most importantly, the argument values do not assign the index values returned by the `GetCurSel` function described later in this chapter.
>
> If you want to experiment, try changing the 0..1..2 arguments to something like 9..5..2 and observe the results.
>
> On the other hand, if you change all three arguments to 0, the results are slightly more interesting.
>
> Of course, there is a certain logic to how these arguments work, but it isn't obvious. However, have fun as you figure it out (or you can check the solution at the end of this chapter).
>
> Remember that, for all practical purposes, if you simply number your entries sequentially, you should not have any problems or surprises.

The `OnInitDialog` provisions are enough to create three tabs with the labels defined in the code. On execution, the `TabCtrl` instance displays these tabs and allows tab selection. However, the labels aside, the tab pages will be blank. Really not much use as is.

Because you need to know when the tabs change (even though the tab display itself is already taken care of), ClassWizard was invoked to establish four very important member functions, as shown in the following sample code:

```
BEGIN_MESSAGE_MAP(TabDlg, CDialog)
    //{{AFX_MSG_MAP(TabDlg)
    ON_NOTIFY(TCN_SELCHANGING, IDC_TAB, OnSelchangingTab)
    ON_NOTIFY(TCN_SELCHANGE, IDC_TAB, OnSelchangeTab)
    ON_WM_SHOWWINDOW()
    ON_WM_DESTROY()
    //}}AFX_MSG_MAP
END_MESSAGE_MAP()
```

The `TCN_SELCHANGING` and `TCN_SELCHANGE` messages are sent, respectively, before a tab is deselected and after a new tab is selected. Or, if you prefer, the `TCN_SELCHANGING` message indicates that tab selection is about to change and `TCN_SELCHANGE` indicates that tab selection has changed. Using these two messages, you can handle any cleanup necessary before a tab loses the focus and then do any setup as another tab receives the focus.

Using Child Dialog Boxes

So far in this example, you have created a tab control and added three tabs. The next step is to add some functionality by connecting the three child dialog boxes to the three tabs.

You can accomplish this in several ways. You can initialize each dialog box when the appropriate tab is selected and close the dialog box when the tab changes; but the simpler approach is to initialize all three tab (child) dialog boxes when the parent dialog box is called.

However, if you create these dialog boxes too soon (say, in response to the WM_INITDIALOG message), the three dialog boxes would be created without the appropriate parent—and would be positioned relative to the parent *application*, not the dialog box.

Therefore, by waiting for the OnShowWindow event, and checking bShow to ensure that the dialog box is being created rather than being destroyed, you can create the three dialog box instances with the proper parent and the proper positions:

```
void TabDlg::OnShowWindow(BOOL bShow, UINT nStatus)
{
    CDialog::OnShowWindow(bShow, nStatus);

    // TODO: Add your message handler code here
    CButton * pRB;

    if( bShow )
    {
        //=== setup for third tab dialog
        cDlg2.Create( IDD_POP2, m_Tab.GetActiveWindow() );
        cDlg2.m_csSelect = "Mark I";
        cDlg2.ShowWindow( SW_HIDE );
        //=== setup for second tab dialog
        cDlg1.Create( IDD_POP1, m_Tab.GetActiveWindow() );
        pRB = (CButton *) cDlg1.GetDlgItem(IDC_RADIO1);
        pRB->SetCheck(1);
        cDlg1.ShowWindow( SW_HIDE );
        //=== setup for first tab dialog
        cDlg0.Create( IDD_POP0, m_Tab.GetActiveWindow() );
        pRB = (CButton *) cDlg0.GetDlgItem(IDC_CHECK1);
        pRB->SetCheck(1);
        pRB = (CButton *) cDlg0.GetDlgItem(IDC_CHECK2);
        pRB->SetCheck(1);
        pRB = (CButton *) cDlg0.GetDlgItem(IDC_CHECK3);
        pRB->SetCheck(1);
        cDlg0.ShowWindow( SW_SHOW );
    }
}
```

By creating the child dialog boxes in reverse order and calling ShowWindow(SW_HIDE) for the first two, you are left with the first child dialog box (which matches and belongs with the first tab) showing, active and on top.

With the three child dialog boxes in place and one of them visible, the next step is to make the visible dialog box vanish when the current tab is deselected:

```
void TabDlg::OnSelchangingTab(NMHDR* pNMHDR, LRESULT* pResult)
{
   // TODO: Add your control notification handler code here
   switch( m_Tab.GetCurSel() )
   {
      case 0:   cDlg0.ShowWindow( SW_HIDE );   break;
      case 1:   cDlg1.ShowWindow( SW_HIDE );   break;
      case 2:   cDlg2.ShowWindow( SW_HIDE );   break;
   }
   *pResult = 0;
}
```

Because the `TCN_SELCHANGING` message (which calls the `OnSelchangingTab` function) is received *before* the tab changes, the `GetCurSel` method retrieves the old tab index. Calling `ShowWindow( SW_HIDE )` conceals the dialog box before the tab is inactivated.

Following the `TCN_SELCHANGING` message, the `TCN_SELCHANGE` message reports a new tab selection; another call to `GetCurSel` will return the new tab index:

```
void TabDlg::OnSelchangeTab(NMHDR* pNMHDR, LRESULT* pResult)
{
   // TODO: Add your control notification handler code here
   switch( m_Tab.GetCurSel() )
   {
      case 0:   cDlg0.ShowWindow( SW_SHOW );   break;
      case 1:   cDlg1.ShowWindow( SW_SHOW );   break;
      case 2:   cDlg2.ShowWindow( SW_SHOW );   break;
   }
   *pResult = 0;
}
```

Just as `SW_HIDE` concealed and inactivated each dialog box, `SW_SHOW` reveals and activates the desired dialog box. The results are shown in Figure 8.3.

Figure 8.3. A tab control dialog box in two views.

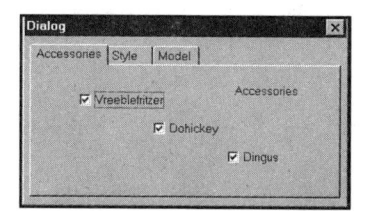

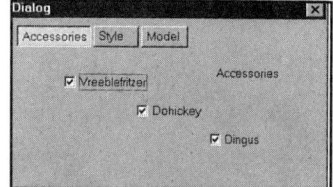

> Tip: The tab style for the dialog box shown on the right side of Figure 8.3 (the one using buttons instead of card tabs) is achieved by selecting the B**u**ttons option on the Styles tab of the TabControl Properties dialog box (refer back to Figure 8.1). Functionally, both tab styles operate identically.

At this point, you have created three tabs and have the capabilities of displaying and hiding the separate dialog boxes based on the tab selection. There is now only one additional requirement: retrieving information from the dialog boxes before they're destroyed.

Information retrieval is accomplished in two steps: retrieving the settings from the individual child dialog boxes to the TabDlg dialog box and then retrieving this same information from TabDlg to the main application. Although this seems rather indirect, because the child dialog boxes belong to the TabDlg dialog box, it is the only reliable sequence of retrieval.

If you're worried about wasting memory, remember that the memory used by the member variables—as well as the class instances—is released automatically when the TabDlg instance closes.

In addition, because the sample dialog box does not have an OK button, the only way to close the TabDlg dialog box is to click the close button in the upper-right corner. The obvious close response to watch for is the WM_DESTROY (OnDestroy) message.

> Note: The absence of an OK or Cancel button is not a requirement; either or both can be incorporated in the TabDlg dialog box or the child dialog boxes. If you choose to place these buttons in the child dialog boxes, be sure to place them in *all* the child dialog boxes. If you choose to put the buttons in the TabDlg dialog (or some other parent), make sure that the child dialog boxes don't cover and conceal the buttons.

The OnDestroy method is used to retrieve information from the tab boxes before the dialog box is destroyed. Remember: Even though two of the three tabs are invisible, they still exist and still contain information. But when the parent dialog box is destroyed, the three child dialog boxes are also destroyed.

```
void TabDlg::OnDestroy()
{
   CDialog::OnDestroy();

   // TODO: Add your message handler code here
   CButton * pRB;
   UINT      i;

   //=== get third tab results
   m_csModel = cDlg2.m_csSelect;

   //=== get second tab results
   for( i=IDC_RADIO1; i<=IDC_RADIO3; i++ )
   {
      pRB = (CButton *) cDlg1.GetDlgItem(i);
      if( pRB->GetCheck() )
      {
         m_nStyle = i - IDC_RADIO1 + 1;
         break;
      }
   }
   if( m_nStyle < 1 || m_nStyle > 3 ) m_nStyle = 1;   // set default

   //=== get first tab results
   for( i=IDC_CHECK1; i<=IDC_CHECK3; i++ )
   {
```

```
            pRB = (CButton *) cDlg0.GetDlgItem(i);
            m_bAccessory[i-IDC_CHECK1] = pRB->GetCheck();
    }
}
```

The retrieval process used in the preceding program excerpt should be familiar from previous examples (except for a few changes in the names, the retrieval processes shown here are identical to earlier examples such as the Standard Controls dialog box described in Chapter 7, "Designing Custom Dialog Boxes").

Aside from reporting the returned results (which is trivial in execution), you have now completed the tab control demonstration.

The tab controls are useful, even if they are a little cumbersome. They provide an excellent way to organize a large number of controls or options in a single dialog box by grouping an otherwise unwieldy collection into smaller functional selections—without using multiple-screen dialog boxes.

> Tip: A collection of separate dialog boxes requires a commitment—by the user—to the selections made in each (before one dialog box is closed and another is opened). On the other hand, a tabbed dialog box allows the user to move back and forth between child dialog boxes, which are presented as tabs, so that he or she can make a large number of choices before accepting or rejecting them all as a group.

Using Additional *CTabCtrl* Methods

The `CTabCtrl` class offers a wide variety of functions beyond those demonstrated in the Dialog2 example program described in the first part of this chapter. Although you may not need this degree of versatility (most tab dialog boxes will not), it's nice to have the functions available. The additional `CTabCtrl` methods are listed in Table 8.1 with brief descriptions of each. Further details are available through Visual C++'s online help.

Table 8.1. `CTabCtrl` member function categories.

Function	Description
`AdjustRect`	Calculates the display area required for a tab control to fit a window rectangle or the window rectangle required to fit a tab's display area.
`Create`	Creates a tab control, attaching it to an instance of a `CTabCtrl` object.
`DeleteAllItems`	Removes all tabs from a tab control.

continues

Table 8.1. continued

Function	Description
`DeleteItem`	Removes a tab from a tab control.
`DrawItem` (overridable)	Draws a specified item of a tab control.
`HitTest`	Determines which tab, if any, matches a specific screen position.
`InsertItem`	Inserts a new tab in a tab control.
`RemoveImage`	Removes an image from a tab control's image list.

Attribute Functions

Function	Description
`GetBkColor`	Gets the background color of a tab control.
`GetCurFocus`	Gets the tab with the current focus of a tab control.
`GetCurSel`	Determines the currently selected tab in a tab control.
`GetImageList`	Gets the image list associated with a tab control.
`GetItem`	Gets information about a tab in a tab control.
`GetItemCount`	Gets the number of tabs in the tab control.
`GetItemRect`	Gets the bounding rectangle for a tab in a tab control.
`GetRowCount`	Gets the current number of rows of tabs in a tab control.
`GetTextBkColor`	Gets the background color for text used in a tab control.
`GetTextColor`	Gets the text, or foreground, color of a tab control.
`GetTooltips`	Gets the handle of the tool tip control associated with a tab control.
`SetBkColor`	Sets the background color of a tab control.
`SetCurSel`	Selects a tab in a tab control.
`SetImageList`	Assigns an image list to a tab control.
`SetItem`	Sets some or all of a tab's attributes.
`SetItemExtra`	Sets the number of bytes per tab reserved for application-defined data in a tab control.
`SetItemSize`	Sets the width and height of an item.
`SetPadding`	Sets padding space around each tab's icon and label in a tab control.
`SetTextBkColor`	Sets the background color for text used in a tab control.
`SetTextColor`	Sets the text, or foreground, color of a tab control.
`SetTooltips`	Assigns a tool tip control to a tab control.

The Animation Control

As computers with sound cards have moved from rarities to virtually commonplace—a change motivated in part by increasingly sophisticated computer games and in part by the popularity of CD players—AVI (Audio Video Interleaved, the standard Windows audio-video format) files have also become popular. In recognition of this popularity, contemporary versions of Windows provide AVI playback utilities such as the Media Player application that supports both audio (with a sound card) and video playback capabilities.

Applications may, of course, play AVI files by launching Media Player. To date, however, applications that wanted to incorporate AVI files within their own programs faced the difficulty of providing their own AVI handlers.

The new common controls supplied by Visual C++ 2.1 include an animation control—the CAnimateCtrl class—in the form of a rectangular window designed to play the video portion of an AVI audio-video file. However, the audio portion of an AVI file (even when a sound card and drivers are installed) is not supported, limiting the usefulness of the CAnimateCtrl class.

> Warning: At this writing, the CAnimateCtrl class appears to have serious functional defects. It does not function per design. The description and application presented in this chapter are designed according to the *documented* functional specifications of the CAnimateCtrl class. Presumably, the current defects will be corrected in future releases.

Like other members of the common control classes, the CAnimateCtrl class is not supported by Windows 3.1 or Windows NT version 3.5; it is expected to be supported by future versions of WinNT.

Requirements for Animation Control AVIs

Animation controls are limited to displaying only simple AVI clips that meet the following requirements:

- The AVI file must have no more than one video stream and must be at least one frame in length.
- The AVI file must not have more than two streams total, including one audio stream. (The second audio stream is ignored by the animation control.)
- AVI file formats must be either uncompressed or RLE8 (Run-Length Encoded, 8-bit color) compression. All other compression schemes are not supported at this time.
- Palette changes in the AVI video stream are not supported.

- AVI clips can accompany applications as separate AVI files or, with some diligence, incorporated in an application's resources as an AVI resource. The current versions of the resource workbench do not, however, offer direct support for incorporating AVI resources.

Because an AVI clip is executed by a separate thread from the application itself, one common use for an animation control is to show system activity during prolonged operations. One example of an AVI file used in this fashion is found in the Win95 Explorer's Find dialog box, where a moving magnifying glass is displayed while Explorer searches for a file.

Typically, an animation control is used according to the following sequence:

1. An instance of a `CAnimateCtrl` object is constructed within an application.
2. The `Create` member function is called to initialize the animation control and to attach it to a `CAnimateCtrl` object in a dialog box.
3. The `Open` member function is called to open an AVI clip from an external file or as an application resource.
4. The `Play` member function is called to initiate playback of the AVI clip. The application thread continues separate execution while the AVI clip is playing. Alternatively, the `Seek` member function can be called to statically display a single frame from the AVI clip.
5. The `Close` member function is called when the AVI clip concludes to terminate and remove the clip from memory.

The `Stop` member function can be called at any time to stop playback. The last executed frame remains displayed when the clip concludes or when `Stop` is called.

Creating a *CAnimateCtrl* Dialog Box

Figure 8.4 shows a dialog box that uses `CAnimateCtrl` and three buttons: Play, Stop, and Close.

Figure 8.4. *A CAnimateCtrl dialog box.*

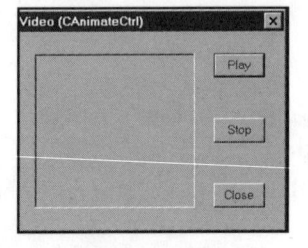

The video dialog box is implemented in the VideoDlg source file as the `CVideoDlg` class. The `OnCreate` message handler is used to connect the `cVid` instance to the `IDC_VIDEO1` control in the dialog resource:

Chapter 8 • Customizing Dialog Boxes with Additional Controls

```
/////////////////////////////////////////////////////////////////////
// CVideoDlg message handlers

int CVideoDlg::OnCreate(LPCREATESTRUCT lpCreateStruct)
{
   if (CDialog::OnCreate(lpCreateStruct) == -1)
      return -1;

   // TODO: Add your specialized creation code here
   CRect  cRect;
   CWnd   * pWnd;

   pWnd = FromHandle( m_hWnd );
   cRect.SetRect( 10, 12, 93, 88 );
   cVid.Create( WS_CHILD | WS_VISIBLE | ACS_CENTER,
                cRect, pWnd, IDC_VIDEO1 );
   return 0;
}
```

The `CAnimateCtrl::Create` member function is called with four parameters, as shown in this example. The following chart explains the parameters.

```
BOOL Create( DWORD dwStyle, const RECT& rect, CWnd* pParentWnd, UINT nID );
```

Parameter	Explanation
dwStyle	Animation control's style; may be any combination of window and animation control styles listed in Table 8.2.
rect	Animation control's position and size; may be either CRect *object* or RECT *structure*.
pParentWnd	Animation control's parent window, usually a CDialog; must not be NULL.
nID	Animation control's ID.

The animation control's size and the control's ID can be copied from the RC script; the style can be any combination of the flag values listed in Table 8.2. The pointer to the parent window, however, must be derived from the dialog box's `m_hWnd` member using the `FromHandle` function.

Table 8.2. Animation Control Styles

Animation Styles	Comments
WS_CHILD	Always used.
WS_VISIBLE	Commonly used.
WS_DISABLED	Rarely used; it disables the animation control.

continues

Table 8.2. continued

Animation Styles	Comments
One or More of the Following Animation Control Styles May Also Be Applied:	
ACS_CENTER	Centers the AVI clip in the animation control's window, leaving the control's size and position unchanged when the AVI clip opens.
	If ACS_CENTER is not specified, the control is resized to match the image size of the AVI clip.
ACS_TRANSPARENT	The AVI clip is drawn using a transparent background instead of the background color specified in the AVI clip.
ACS_AUTOPLAY	The AVI clip begins playing immediately on opening and repeats automatically on completion.

For this example, the WS_CHILD, WS_VISIBLE, and ACS_CENTER style flags were selected.

On return, the Create member function returns zero on failure or nonzero on success.

The following code shows how the Play button in the Video (CAnimateCtrl) dialog box is used to open a preset AVI file and initiate playback:

```
void CVideoDlg::OnPlay()
{
   // TODO: Add your control notification handler code here
   UINT nResult;

   nResult = cVid.Open( "CLOCK.AVI" );
   if( ! nResult )
   {
      MessageBox( "AVI file not found" );
      EndDialog(0);
   }
   else
   if( ! cVid.Play( 0, (UINT) -1, 1 ) )
   {
      MessageBox( "Can't play AVI file" );
      EndDialog(0);
   }
}
```

Opening the AVI file, however, is the point at which the current version of the CAnimateCtrl control fails: it returns a zero result to report failure.

Assuming success, however, the next step (because the ACS_AUTOPLAY style has not been selected) is to call the Play method to initiate playback. The second button, Stop, is mapped to the OnStop method, which calls the Stop member function to terminate playback. The following code shows how this is accomplished:

```
void CVideoDlg::OnStop()
{
   // TODO: Add your control notification handler code here
   if( ! cVid.Stop() )
   {
      MessageBox( "Can't close AVI file" );
      EndDialog(0);
   }
}
```

The third and final button, Close, actually returns an IDOK message to close the dialog box—not the AVI file. The AVI file closes automatically when the CVid class instance terminates on the closure of the dialog box.

Notifying Parent Windows

The CAnimateCtrl class is capable of sending notification messages (ACN_START and ACN_STOP) to the parent window (that is, the dialog window class). The parent application, however, is not required to respond to either message.

To handle either of these notification messages, use the ClassWizard to add to the parent window class an ON_CONTROL message map entry and message handler functions for one or both notifications. These messages *must* be handled by the parent; they cannot be handled by the control class.

Notification messages take the following form:

```
ON_CONTROL( wNotifyCode, idChild, memberFxn )
```

In this syntax, *wNotifyCode* is the notification code sent by the control (ACN_START or ACN_STOP). The *idChild* parameter provides the child window ID for the control sending the message; the *memberFxn* parameter provides the name of the parent function handling notification.

If needed, additional information about notification messages is available in Visual C++'s online help.

Constructing AVI Files

Utilities for the preparation of AVI files are not supplied by Visual C++ or by Windows 95. Third-party vendors supply some very good utility programs you can use to create AVI files; however, these utilities are subject to a few limitations:

- **Size.** Video standards require either 15 or 30 frames per second (900 or 1,800 images per minute).
- **Color.** A *small* image (captured from a camera or video tape) uses a 120×160-pixel format with 8-bit (one byte) color per pixel. This comes to 19,200 bytes per frame, raising the ante to 17,280,000 bytes per minute of video. That's 16.5M per minute! (The more usual 16-bit, 30 frames per second raises the ante to 66M/minute or 1.1M/second.)

Most video systems support several compression standards that reduce the size of such unwieldy image files. However, the `CAnimateCtrl` class accepts only uncompressed or RLE8 files (and RLE8 compression is not particularly efficient).

> Note: The maximum uncompressed image that can fit on a 1.44M floppy disk is 1.6 minutes at 32×32 pixels, 15 frames per second, and 8-bit color. That's 1K per frame or 900K per minute. Good compression can reduce storage requirements by as much as two thirds without unacceptable losses.

When dealing with AVI files, right from the start you're faced with extremely unwieldy file size. To distribute your applications, you'll need recordable CDs as your media.

You'll also need a video capture card (costs range from $300 to $900) and a video source (any video camera should be acceptable). You'll also need the software to control the video capture card and to edit the captured image files. Most better video capture cards are bundled with the appropriate software (usually from one of the better third-party designers). On the other hand, high-end video editing software can cost several times the price of a good capture card but, in general, is necessary only when elaborate special effects are required.

Not to overlook the obvious, you can create an AVI file on a frame-by-frame basis using a paint program to draw the individual images (at 15 images per second for your finished product). If you have the time and patience to go this route, I recommend a good AVI editor, such as Asymetrix, to combine and order your images.

Finally, if you are interested in creating your own AVI editor or a utility to produce AVI files, please note that, from a programming standpoint, this topic is not within the scope of this book.

A Useful AVI Control Class

As stated earlier in this chapter, even if it is working, the `CAnimateCtrl` control class is not a particularly versatile or useful video display class. It is limited to only video, has no sound track capability, accepts only the most rudimentary AVI formats, and does not promise much in the way of future versatility.

Here are two opportunities for third-party developers: to develop (and market, of course) a comprehensive AVI class—`CAVICtrl`—and to create an editor designed to work with BMP files to create simple AVI files.

The `CAVICtrl` class should include the capabilities to do the following:

- Recognize and play all compression formats
- Support palette changes and palette encoding
- Play back the audio track (assuming the presence of a supported sound card)
- Support both external AVI files and internal AVI resources

Alternatively, an invisible Media Player analog that can accept position and size instructions from a calling application could be used by other applications to play back AVI files within their own client windows.

The AVI editor should provide a few minimal capabilities, including the ability to do the following:

- Edit images frame by frame
- Import BMP files
- Reorder frame images both individually and by groups
- Include AVI files as a custom control element in a resource file and link these to dialog boxes

With a little thought, you can probably come up with a few other criteria and features that would make these truly useful. The preceding suggestions are intended only as minimums. In any case, there are definitely opportunities here.

Summary

This chapter has looked at two of the new common controls supplied by Visual C++ 2.1: the tab control and the animation control.

The tab control can be useful and versatile, even if it is a bit unwieldy in a few characteristics. The primary objection to the tab control is the awkwardness of how child dialog boxes are positioned relative to a tab. This minor annoyance aside, once the tab control is designed, it works quite well and offers a much needed and appreciated addition to your dialog box tools.

The animation control and the `CAnimateCtrl` class is the opposite of the tab control. Although outwardly simple to use, the animation control suffers from the even simpler fact that it does not work. Even if the control/class *did* function as documented, it is overly restricted in the types of AVI files accepted, in its inability to incorporate AVI files as resources, and in lacking any audio playback capabilities.

This chapter concludes the examination (for the present) of the new common control features for dialog boxes. In the next chapter, you see how you can create your own custom controls using the OCX object extensions.

Solution to the Tab-Ordering Conundrum

The index position governs where an entry is inserted in the sequence of tabs. If three entries are indexed 0..1..2 or 1..2..3 or 5..6..7, they are entered as the 0th, 1st, and 2nd tabs.

On the other hand, if the sequence 3..2..1 is used, the first item again becomes the 0th entry because there are no previous entries. The entry indexed as 2, being greater than 0, becomes

continues

the 1st entry. The result is this sequence (according to the original indexes): (0th)3..(1st)2. When the final entry, indexed as 1, is added, it is inserted in the second (1st) position, bumping the previous 1st (indexed 2) entry to the 2nd position to produce this sequence: (0th)3..(1st)1..(2nd)2.

There you have it. There *is* a method to the madness…or, if you prefer, a madness to the method.

CHAPTER 9

Using Customized OCX Controls

Chapters 7 and 8 looked at a number of common dialog box controls and how they add new possibilities for applications. Although the common controls are useful, they're hardly the answer to all your programming prayers.

But, what about designing your own custom controls? And I don't mean using VBX[1].

Originally, dynamic link libraries (DLLs) were the end-all and be-all of programming extensibility because they allowed function libraries to be shared between applications. Of course, DLLs continue to be valuable programming tools. After all, you use DLLs every time you write a Windows application—for that matter, every time you write almost any application except, perhaps, the simplest DOS applications (and no one really writes those very much any more).

Unfortunately, DLLs don't offer much help in designing Windows dialog boxes. At least, the usual DLLs don't.

---

[1] VBX (Visual Basic eXtension) was developed as a means of extending the Visual Basic programming environment to allow programmers to design new, custom controls to augment the standard Windows dialog box control set. Unfortunately, VBX controls are inherently 16-bit controls and do not transport readily to other environments.

Introducing OLE Custom Controls (OCX)

Visual Basic and VBX extensions suffer from portability limitations; conventional DLLs simply aren't versatile enough to conveniently create dialog box controls. But OLE 2[2] custom controls (commonly referred to as OCX controls, the acronym derived from OLE Control eXtensions) offer an avenue to creativity without imposing heavy overhead memory penalties or execution restrictions.

OCX controls consist of two components: the OCX control itself—as a compiled library function (actually a DLL with an OCX extension)—and the application's OLE 2 container that provides the interface for the embedded OCX control's functionality.

> Note: Visual C++ 1.51 can be used to develop 16-bit OCX controls; 32-bit OCX controls require Visual C++ 2.0 or later.

OCX controls are defined by three interface types: properties, events, and methods.

OCX Properties

Properties are named values within an OCX control. Examples of properties are color, size, or range values; state identifiers; and behavioral flags. For example, an OCX control can have the properties of a red background, a size of 32 × 32 pixels, a state of disabled, and flags identifying whether the control can be tab selected. OCX control properties are commonly classified as shown in the following chart:

Property	Type/Examples
Stock	Standard properties needed by most controls such as captions. Implementation for stock properties is provided by Microsoft's CDK in the OCX control runtime DLL. May be overridden for custom implementation.
Ambient	Read-only properties providing information about the container (for example, the foreground color of the OCX control).
Extended	Properties managed by the container such as width, height, or position.
Custom	Properties implemented by the OCX control itself and governing the internal performance of the OCX control.

---

[2] OLE (Object Linking and Embedding) was designed from the beginning as an open standard. It lacks the portability and extendibility limitations of the VBX controls and is inherently supported by both the 16-bit and 32-bit C/C++ compilers.

OCX Methods

Methods may be stock or custom; they are functions within an OCX control that can be called externally by the container. For example, an application can call an OCX control method to initialize the control's appearance or state.

OCX Events

Events may be stock or custom; they are occurrences triggered by the OCX control in response to some action such as a mouse click or a keyboard event. The OCX control translates these occurrences into event notifications that are sent to the container as instructions to execute some action such as a change of state or appearance. Further, events can be accompanied by parameters such as the mouse coordinates or Shift-key states.

The *COleControl* Class

Each OCX control object also inherits a powerful set of features from its MFC base class, COleControl. The features include customizable painting and serialization. The COleControl base class also provides the functionality of an MFC window object as well as the ability to fire events.

Constructing an OLE 2 Custom Control (OCX) Using Visual C++ Version 2.*x*

Although much of this section is relevant to both Visual C++ versions 2.*x* and 4.0, if you are using version 4.0, the OLE Custom Development Kit is already installed as an integral part of Developer Studio. At the same time, the instructions for invoking the MFC ControlWizard are irrelevant for version 4.0. Instead, you may want to skip to "Constructing an OLE 2 Custom Control (OCX) Using Visual C++ Version 4.0," later in this chapter.

Installing the OLE Custom Development Kit

If you are using Visual C++ 2.1, and the ControlWizard option does not appear on your **T**ools menu, you must install the OLE Custom Development Kit (CDK). (For Visual C++ 4.0, the OLE CDK is installed automatically.)

Use the Setup utility in the MSVCCDK directory on your Visual C++ 2.1 CD to add the OLE CDK to your Visual C++ installation; alternatively, run the original Setup utility for Visual C++ and select the OLE Custom Development Kit (CDK) button.

The CDK utilities and files are installed in \MSVC20\CDK32 as follows:

Directory	Contents
\BIN	Executables for ControlWizard, Test Container, and Register Control tools.
\HELP	Online documentation and help files for the CDK.
\INCLUDE	Include files required to develop OLE controls.
\LIB	Libraries required to develop OLE controls.
\SAMPLES	OLE control samples in subdirectories containing samples to demonstrate various features of OLE controls.
\SRC	Source code for OLE control classes in the class library.

The first step in constructing an OCX control is to call the ControlWizard from the **T**ools menu to create a set of OCX starter files (refer to Figure 9.1). The starter set includes source, header, and resource files; a module-definition file; a project file; an object description language file, and so on. Subsequently, the ClassWizard can be used to define the OCX control's events, properties, and methods.

Figure 9.1. The MFC ControlWizard dialog box.

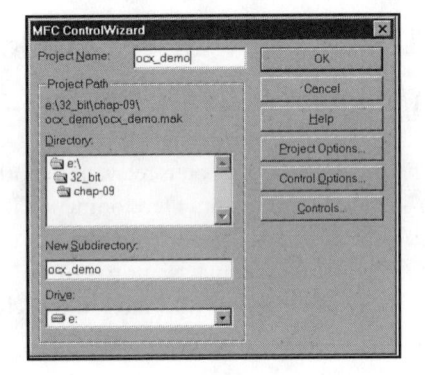

Selecting Options

Click the **P**roject Options button in the ControlWizard dialog box to display the Project Options dialog box (see Figure 9.2). Use the Project Options dialog box to select options for context-sensitive help, for generating an external makefile, for including source comments, and for including license validation capabilities. The following chart better explains what the checkbox options do:

Chapter 9 • Using Customized OCX Controls

Figure 9.2. The Project Options dialog box.

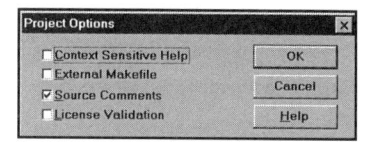

Option	Purpose
Context-Sensitive Help	Generates a set of help files to provide context-sensitive help. Help support is created with the Help compiler provided with Visual C++.
External Makefile	Creates an external NMAKE makefile instead of the default project file.
Source Comments (default)	Includes comments in the source and header files.
License Validation	Provides several function calls and a separate LIC file to support licensing for the control(s).

Click the Control **O**ptions button in the ControlWizard dialog box to display the Control Options dialog box (see Figure 9.3). Use the Control Options dialog box to select options for each control. Use the **C**ontrol pull-down list box at the top of the dialog box to select the control whose options are to be modified. The following chart describes the options available in the Control Options dialog box:

Figure 9.3. The Control Options dialog box.

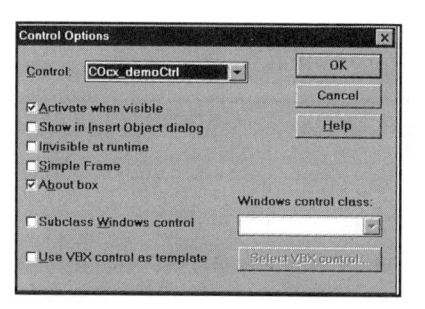

Option	Function
Activate when Visible	The OCX control is activated automatically when it is visible. ***Note:*** The container class may not support this option.
Show in **I**nsert Object Dialog	Causes the OCX control to appear in the Insert Object dialog boxes of all OLE container applications.

continues

Option	Function
	Note: Because not all OLE containers are "control aware" and may not provide a means of activating controls using the mouse, this option also adds an "edit" verb to the control's set of verbs (that is, the action objects).
I**n**visible at Runtime	Allows the control to be invisible at runtime but visible during development. *Note:* Some containers may ignore this option.
Simple Frame	Allows the control to behave as a simple frame.
A**b**out Box	Creates a standard About dialog box for the control. The control's About dialog box can be called by a container to display information about the control (such as copyright and source information).
Subclass **W**indows Control	Allows common Windows controls (such as buttons, scrollbars, and edit controls) to be subclassed. If this option is enabled, you select Windows control classes from the popup list box at the right. (Subclassing an existing control is a quick method of developing a custom OCX control by inheriting the methods and capabilities of the subclassed control.)
Use VBX Control as Template	Allows an existing VBX control to be used as a project framework. If this option is enabled, the Select VBX Control button allows you to select a VBX control.

Modifying the Controls

Click the **C**ontrols button in the ControlWizard dialog box to display the Controls dialog box (see Figure 9.4). The Controls dialog box lists the OCX controls in the current project. When you select a control from the **C**ontrols list box, the other fields list the classes and files for the control selected. You can modify the classes created by the ControlWizard and add additional control classes to a project. The names of the classes and files are based on the project name specified in the Project **N**ame box in the ControlWizard dialog box.

The C**l**ass drop-down list box is used to select either the control class or the property page class for modification. With this option, you can modify the class name, header, and implementation filenames.

Figure 9.4. *The Controls dialog box.*

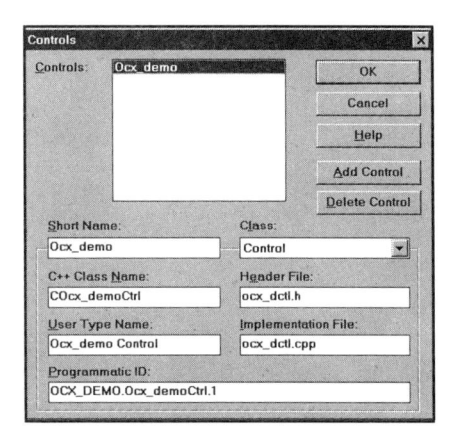

> Note: Changing the control class's short name or selecting another class from the Class list box automatically updates the several edit boxes for the selected class.

Use the **A**dd Control button to add a new control class and property page to the project. The header and implementation files must be named for each new control class.

Use the **D**elete Control button to delete the selected control from the project. Both the control and property page classes are deleted.

Select OK when you're finished editing the selections. In response, the New Control Information dialog box appears.

Accepting Control Information

The New Control Information dialog box, shown in Figure 9.5, shows the options and specifications selected for the new skeleton control project.

Figure 9.5. *The New Control Information dialog box.*

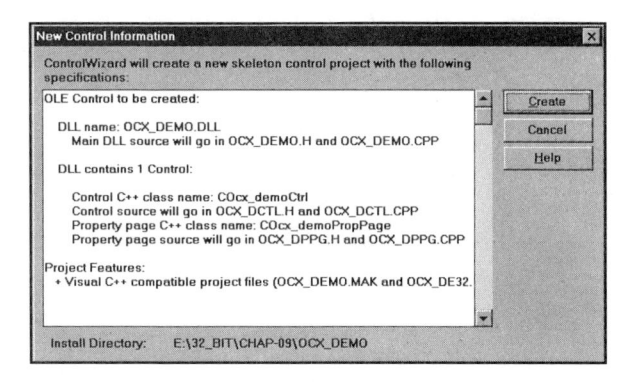

The New Control Information dialog box includes information about the DLL to be created, including the DLL name, the names of the control's classes, the files making up the project, and the features of the control. If all the information in the dialog box is correct, click the **C**reate button; the ControlWizard creates the control as specified. If the information is not correct, click Cancel; return to the ControlWizard dialog box and make any necessary changes to the definition of the control. When the ControlWizard finishes, the newly created OCX project is automatically opened in the development environment.

Constructing an OLE 2 Custom Control (OCX) Using Visual C++ Version 4.0

Visual C++ version 4.0 definitely simplifies the development of OCX controls, beginning by including the OLE ControlWizard as an integral part of the Developer Studio. Using C++ version 4.0 to create an OCX control, begin by selecting **F**ile, **N**ew; from the New dialog box, select Project Workspace. In response, the New Project Workspace dialog box shown in Figure 9.6 appears.

Figure 9.6. The New Project Workspace dialog box.

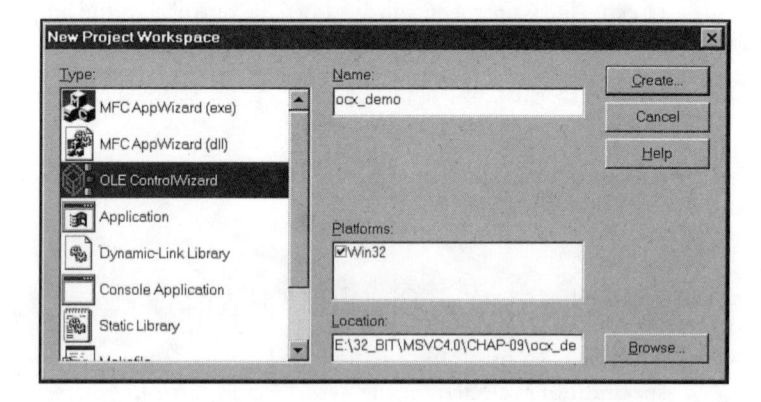

Next, select OLE ControlWizard from the **T**ype menu and enter a name for the OCX control project in the **N**ame edit box. As with any project, you can enter a location or use the **B**rowse button to select a directory location.

> Tip: Use the **B**rowse button to select a root directory for your project before entering a name for the OCX project. Once the root directory is selected, the project name is used to generate a subdirectory of the same name for the project files.

Click the **C**reate button to proceed. The OLE ControlWizard appears (see Figure 9.7) with a series of options.

Chapter 9 • Using Customized OCX Controls

Figure 9.7. The OLE ControlWizard, Step 1 of 2.

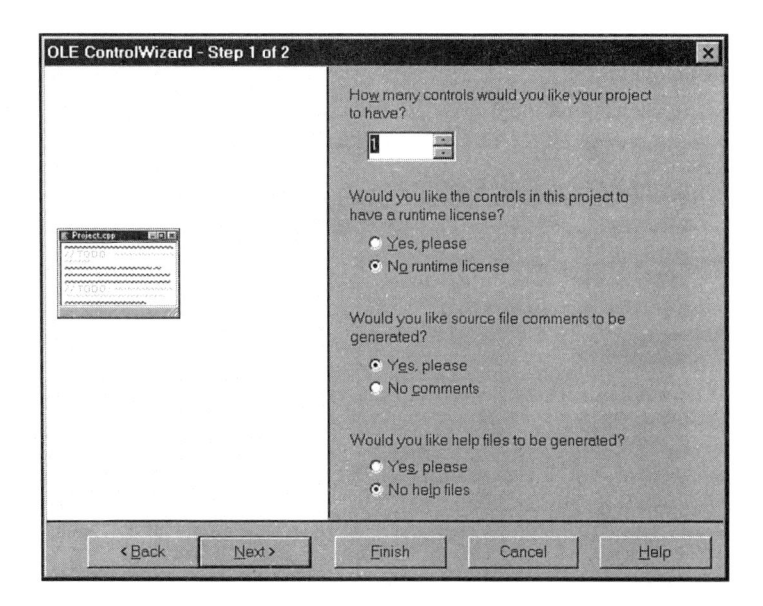

Although an OCX project can include any number of controls desired, the default—and minimum—is one. Use the spin button or enter a new value if desired. If multiple controls are selected, ControlWizard generates names using the project name and an incremental number for each (for example, Ole_demo1, Ole_demo2, and so on).

> Note: In the Step 2 dialog box that follows, you have the opportunity to select new names, control options, and individual class and file names for each control.

In the Step 1 dialog box, select options for including a runtime license, generating source comments, and generating help files according to your requirements. Click **N**ext to continue with the Step 2 dialog box (see Figure 9.8).

The OLE ControlWizard presents a pull-down list of the controls to be generated. Select features by clicking the checkboxes for each control and select an existing Windows class to be *subclassed* (that is, to be used as a basis for the OCX control). Click the **E**dit Names button to display the Edit Names dialog box, shown in Figure 9.9.

The Edit Names dialog box shows the control selected from the list box in Step 2. Use this dialog box to enter a new name for the control or to rename the control and property page classes individually; you can also rename everything.

Beginning with the **S**hort Name field (the name of the control itself), any changes you make are reflected automatically in the Control and Property Page class name, header file, type name, implementation file, and type IDs.

Figure 9.8. *The OLE ControlWizard, Step 2 of 2.*

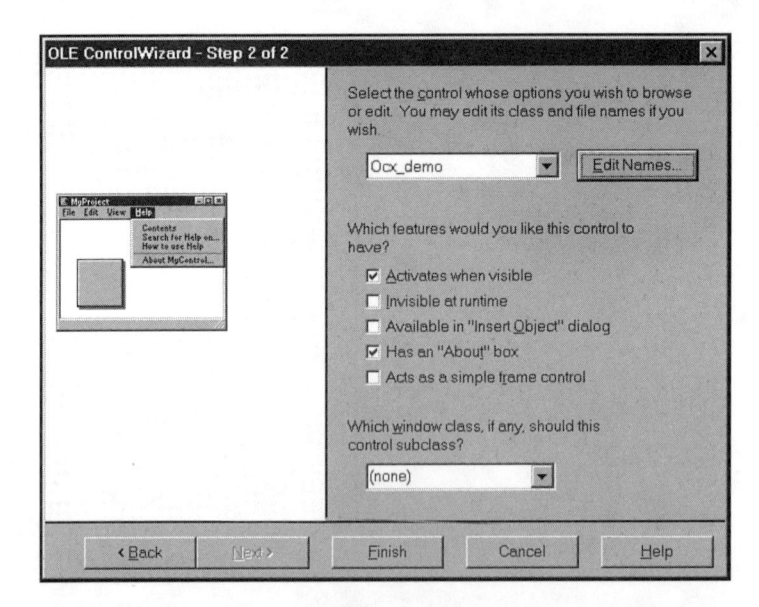

Figure 9.9. *The Edit Names dialog box.*

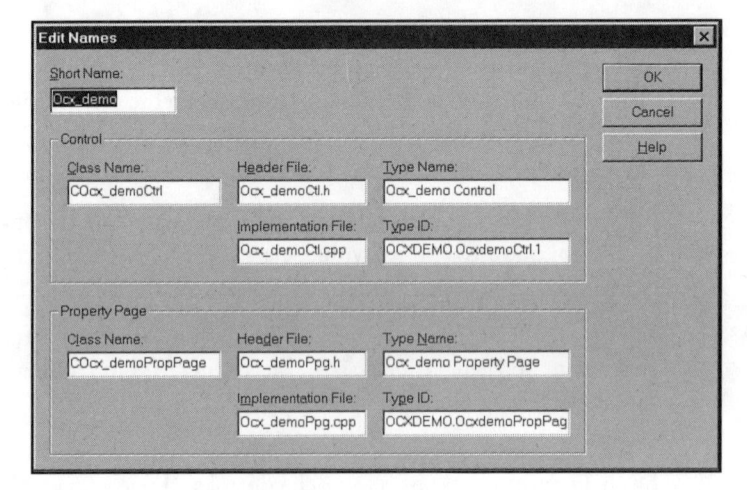

Alternatively, you can edit each of these entries individually.

When you have finished naming this control, click OK to return to the Step 2 dialog box and repeat these actions for however many controls you've selected.

Finally, from the Step 2 dialog box, click the **F**inish button to conclude.

The New Product Information dialog box, shown in Figure 9.10, lists the project files, the selected controls, and a description of the classes, class files, and options for each control.

If these are satisfactory, select OK. ControlWizard generates the skeleton project and project files.

Figure 9.10. *The New Product Information dialog box.*

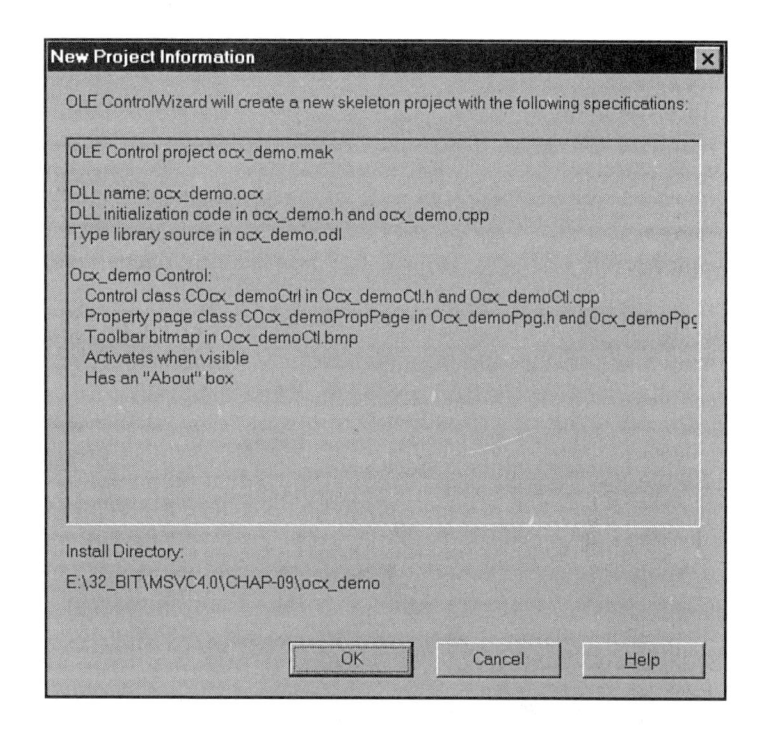

Of course, this is only the first part of creating an OCX control. To create *functional* OCX controls, each of the controls in the project must be programmed individually—a topic we'll return to in just a moment.

ControlWizard Files

Like AppWizard, ControlWizard generates a number of project source files. The following chart lists the files:

File	Function
OCX_DEMO.MAK	Project makefile for building a 16-bit OLE custom control, compatible with the Visual C++ 1.5 Workbench or with the NMAKE utility.
OCX_DE32.MAK	Project makefile for building a 32-bit OLE custom control, compatible with the Visual C++ 2.0 Workbench or with the NMAKE utility.
OCX_DEMO.MDP	Project makefile for building a 32-bit OLE custom control, compatible with the Visual C++ 4.0 Developer Studio.

continues

File	Function
MAKEFILE	Makefile allowing NMAKE to run from the command prompt. Use the following parameters with NMAKE: `DEBUG = 0` Release version `DEBUG = 1` Debug version (default) `WIN32 = 0` 16-bit version (default) `WIN32 = 1` 32-bit version `UNICODE = 0` ANSI/DBCS version (default when `WIN32 = 0`) `UNICODE = 1` Unicode version (default when `WIN32 = 1`)
OCX_DEMO.H	Main include file for the OLE custom control DLL. It includes other project-specific includes such as RESOURCE.H.
OCX_DEMO.CPP	This is the main source file containing OLE DLL initialization, termination, and other bookkeeping.
OCX_DEMO.RC	Project resource file, including palette or toolbar bitmap, property page dialog box, and a default About dialog box.
OCX_DEMO.RC2	This file contains resources not edited by the resource editor. Initially, this file contains a `VERSIONINFO` resource you can customize for your OLE custom control DLL, and a `TYPELIB` resource for your DLL's type library. Place other manually maintained resources in this file.
OCX_DEMO.DEF	This file contains information about the OLE custom control DLL that must be provided to run with Microsoft Windows. It defines parameters such as the name and description of the DLL and the size of the initial local heap. The numbers in this file are typical for OLE custom control DLLs.
OCX_DE32.DEF	Project module definition file, including the name and description of the control plus the size of the runtime heap.
OCX_DEMO.CLW	Defines a project's object classes and provides data used to generate event, dispatch, and message maps.
OCX_DEMO.ODL	Object Description Language source code used by the Make Type Library Tool to generate a type library for the OCX control. The Type library exposes the control's interface to OLE automation clients.
OCX_DEMO.ICO	The icon to appear in the About box (which is itself included in the main resource file OCX_DEMO.RC).

File	Function
OCX_DCTL.CPP	Implementation of the COcx_demoCtrl C++ class derived from COleControl. Includes skeleton implementations for member functions to initialize, draw, and serialize (load and save) a control as well as message, event, and dispatch maps.
OCX_DCTL.H	Declaration of the COcx_demoCtrl C++ class.
OCX_DPPG.CPP	Implementation for the COcx_demoPropPage C++ class, derived from CPropertyPageDialog. Includes a skeletal member function, DoDataExchange, to implement data exchange and validation.
OCX_DPPG.H	Declaration for the COcx_demoPropPage C++ class.
OCX_DCTL.BMP	Image representing the OCX control in a toolbar or palette.

Other Standard Files

File	Function
STDAFX.H and STDAFX.CPP	These files are used to build a precompiled header (PCH) file named STDAFX.PCH and a precompiled types (PCT) file named STDAFX.OBJ.
RESOURCE.H	This is the standard header file, which defines new resource IDs.

> Note: *Unicode* refers to the 16-bit character format used to support international alphabets. In Unicode, all characters are 16 bits rather than 8 bits; therefore, they require corresponding provisions in string handling functions and so on to accommodate this difference. All MFC/Windows string functions are written to accept both 8-bit and 16-bit Unicode strings.

Optional ControlWizard Files

If Help or License options are selected, the following files are generated in the project's \HLP subdirectory.

Help Option	Description
MAKEHELP.BAT	Used to create the help file PRJNAME.HLP for your OLE control.
OCX_DEMO.HPJ	The Help Project file used by the Help compiler to create your OLE control's Help file.
CTRLCORE.RTF	Standard Help topics for the common properties, events, and methods supported. Edit this file to add new control-specific topics or to remove existing topics.

continues

License Option	Description
*.BMP	Bitmaps are used by standard Help topics for MFC Library commands.
OCX_DEMO.LIC	User license file; must be present in the same directory as the control's DLL to allow an instance of the control to be created in a design-time environment. Typically, this file is distributed with a control set to developers but is not distributed to end users.

OCX Runtime Files

In addition to the OCX files generated to contain your custom OCX controls, applications created using Visual C++ 2.*x* also require the OC25.DLL runtime file for 16-bit systems and the OC30.DLL runtime file for 32-bit systems. If you are using Visual C++ 4.0, these libraries are not required nor supplied; see the following sidebar, "Converting Version 2.1 OLE CDK Projects to Version 4.0."

As a developer, you will find four versions (two for Windows 3.1 and 3.11) of the DLL in your \WINDOWS\SYSTEM or \WINNT\SYSTEM32 directory:

Library	Description
OC25.DLL	16-bit OLE release version (Windows 3.1 and 3.11 only)
OC25D.DLL	16-bit OLE debug version (Windows 3.1 and 3.11 only)
OC30.DLL	32-bit OLE release version with ANSI/DBCS support
OC30D.DLL	32-bit OLE debug version with ANSI/DBCS support
OC30U.DLL	32-bit OLE release version with Unicode support
OC30UD.DLL	32-bit OLE debug version with Unicode support

Only the first (or third, if you have Unicode support) of these files is required for distribution with your application.

Converting Version 2.1 OLE CDK Projects to Version 4.0

OCX controls developed under Visual C++ 2.1 require no adaptation to be used with Visual C++ 4.0. The project MAK files, however, do require one modification before they can move from version 2.1 to version 4.0.

If you attempt to compile an OCX MAK project file created under Visual C++ 2.1 using the Visual C++ 4.0 Developer Studio, you will probably get a linker error reporting that the ocs30d.lib file cannot be opened. This is perfectly reasonable because this library file does not exist in Visual C++ 4.0.

In the version 2.1 MAK file, find the following instructions:

Chapter 9 • Using Customized OCX Controls

```
LINK32=link.exe
# ADD BASE LINK32 ocs30d.lib /nologo /subsystem:windows /dll /machine:IX86
↪/out:"obj32/ocx_demo.ocx"
# SUBTRACT BASE LINK32 /pdb:none /nodefaultlib
# ADD LINK32 ocs30d.lib /nologo /subsystem:windows /dll /machine:IX86 /out:"obj32/
ocx_demo.ocx"
# SUBTRACT LINK32 /pdb:none /nodefaultlib
LINK32_FLAGS= ocs30d.lib /nologo /subsystem:windows /dll /incremental:no\
```

Using an ASCII editor (such as Notepad or Write), remove the three references to the ocx30d.lib library but *do not remove* the rest of the instruction lines. The results should look like this:

```
LINK32=link.exe
# ADD BASE LINK32 /nologo /subsystem:windows /dll /machine:IX86 /out:"obj32/
↪ocx_demo.ocx"
# SUBTRACT BASE LINK32 /pdb:none /nodefaultlib
# ADD LINK32 /nologo /subsystem:windows /dll /machine:IX86 /out:"obj32/
↪ocx_demo.ocx"
# SUBTRACT LINK32 /pdb:none /nodefaultlib
LINK32_FLAGS= /nologo /subsystem:windows /dll /incremental:no\
```

With these changes, the debug version of the OCX control should be ready to compile and link. However, before saving the MAK file, repeat this same operation for three occurrences of the string `ocs30.lib` to correct the link instructions for the release version.

With these changes made, save the MAK file. Then open the Developer Studio. From the menu, select **F**ile, Open **W**orkspace. In the Open Project Workspace dialog box, select Makefiles (*.mak) from the Files of Type list box.

Last, locate the revised MAK file and open the project.

Tip: After importing the MAK file, save the project as an MDP project file.

Initializing the OCX Control

Like any object, an OCX control requires initialization. As is usual with objects, the OCX control properties are set in the constructor method:

```
COcx_demoCtrl::COcx_demoCtrl()
{
   InitializeIIDs(&IID_DOcx_demo, &IID_DOcx_demoEvents);

   // TODO: Initialize your control's instance data here.
   m_nNumber = 0;
   m_nScale  = 2;      // default is twice bitmap size
   SetInitialSize( m_nScale * BMP_SIZEX, m_nScale * BMP_SIZEY );
}
```

Although the `m_nNumber` member variable sets the initial value for the control, `m_nScale` establishes the scale size for the control button and is discussed further under "OCX Control Properties," later in this chapter. For the moment, it is sufficient to say that the `SetInitialSize` function sets the initial horizontal and vertical size for the OCX control. (Without this last provision, the default size is a rectangle and the bitmap is stretched to fit.)

Drawing the OCX Control

In many respects, painting an OCX control is the same as painting any MFC application window. However, unlike normal application windows, OCX controls have two states: active or inactive.

An active OCX control is represented by a child window in an OLE container. Like any window, the OCX control is responsible for painting itself on receipt of a WM_PAINT message. By default, the control's base class, COleControl, handles this message in its OnPaint function by calling the OnDraw function in the control's implementation class.

For an inactive control, however, the control's window may not be visible or may be nonexistent; in either case, the control's window does not receive a WM_PAINT message. Instead, the control's container calls the control's OnDraw function directly, bypassing the base class's OnPaint function entirely.

In both situations, the OCX control's implementation class (the COcx_demoCtrl class in the Ocx_Demo application) is called to execute the OnDraw function to paint the control. Although both calls produce essentially the same result, the process of painting the control follows two different routes, depending on whether the control is active or inactive. Of course, the key is that you cannot depend on trapping the WM_PAINT message directly; nor can you depend on the base class's OnPaint function.

The OCX *OnDraw* Function

The OnDraw member function is called with three parameters: a pointer to the device context and two CRect objects, one for the area occupied by the control and a second with an invalidated rectangle area (the area of the control that actually requires a repaint).

For an active OCX control, the area occupied by the control has upper-left coordinates of 0,0; the supplied device context is the child window containing the control. If the control is inactive, the upper-left coordinates are the control's position within the control container—not the control window itself—and the device context is that of the container rather than the control.

The ControlWizard supplies the following default OnDraw function:

```
/////////////////////////////////////////////////////////////////////////
// COcx_demoCtrl::OnDraw - Drawing function

void COcx_demoCtrl::OnDraw(
          CDC* pdc, const CRect& rcBounds, const CRect& rcInvalid)
{
    // TODO: Replace the following code with your own drawing code.
    pdc->FillRect(rcBounds,
                  CBrush::FromHandle((HBRUSH)GetStockObject(WHITE_BRUSH)));
```

```
    pdc->Ellipse(rcBounds);
}
```

The default `OnDraw` function draws an ellipse (or circle, depending on the bounding rectangle) that fills the control window. This ellipse is fine for a simple demo but is not what we have in mind for this control.

For this particular demonstration, I have a more interesting function in mind:

- The `Ocx_Demo` control will be designed as a button that displays a number from 0 through 9.
- When a button is clicked—as long as the mouse button is not released—the button will change state for a 3D effect.
- When the button is clicked with the left mouse button, the button will increment itself, rolling over from 9 to 0; when the button is clicked with the right mouse button, the button will decrement, rolling over from 0 to 9.

To provide these effects, begin with two sets of bitmaps: one set showing the numbers 0 through 9 on buttons in the up (normal) position and one set showing the numbers 0 through 9 on buttons in the pressed (selected) position. In this example, each image is 20 pixels by 20 pixels (this is not a limitation; the bitmap images can be any size you want).

The normal set of buttons is shown in Figure 9.11.

Figure 9.11. *Ten OCX buttons in the normal position.*

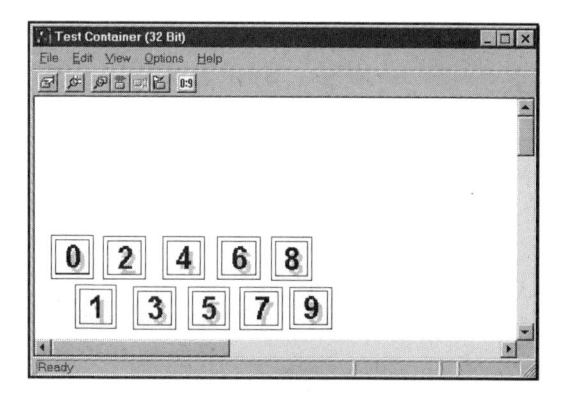

The 20 button images are identified as `IDB_BTN_UP0` through `IDB_BTN_UP9` for the normal button state and `IDB_BTN_DN0` through `IDB_BTN_DN9` for the selected state. Each set of identifiers is numbered sequentially.

> Tip: When creating a set of controls in which sequential numbering is important, always check the RESOURCE.H header to ensure that the identifiers are assigned sequential and continuous values. If they are not, edit the values shown; also be sure to update the `_APS_NEXT_RESOURCE_VALUE` defined at the end of the header.

After creating the bitmap images for the control, the next step is to implement an appropriate `OnDraw` function to replace the ellipse-drawing function supplied by the ControlWizard. The following code shows the first part of the altered `OnDraw` function.

```
/////////////////////////////////////////////////////////////////////////////
// COcx_demoCtrl::OnDraw - Drawing function

void COcx_demoCtrl::OnDraw(
            CDC* pdc, const CRect& rcBounds, const CRect& rcInvalid)
{
    CBitmap       bitmap;
    BITMAP        bmp;
    CRect         rcSrcBounds;
    UINT          btnBitmap;
    CPictureHolder picHolder;

    // Load button bitmap
    if( m_btnState )           // button is up
       btnBitmap = IDB_BTN_UP0 + m_nNumber;
    else                       // button is down
       btnBitmap = IDB_BTN_DN0 + m_nNumber;
    bitmap.LoadBitmap( btnBitmap );
```

This first item in the new `OnDraw` response checks the button state (up or down as identified by the `m_btnState` member) and selects the appropriate bitmap identifier using the `m_nNumber` member before calling the `LoadBitmap` function to load the bitmap from the control resources.

After loading the bitmap, the bitmap size is retrieved to set the source rectangle bounds (more about this in a moment):

```
    bitmap.GetObject(sizeof(BITMAP), &bmp);
    rcSrcBounds.right = bmp.bmWidth;
    rcSrcBounds.bottom = bmp.bmHeight;
```

Finally, the `CreateFromBitmap` and `Render` methods are called to paint the bitmap in the supplied display context:

```
    // Create picture and render
    picHolder.CreateFromBitmap( btnBitmap );
    picHolder.Render( pdc, rcBounds, rcSrcBounds );
}
```

As a draw function, this example is pretty simple. It is also effective—which is the whole point.

However, two object member functions have been introduced here; they deserve a bit of explanation. The first is the `CPictureHolder::CreateFromBitmap` method, which can be called in three forms:

```
BOOL CreateFromBitmap( UINT idResource );
BOOL CreateFromBitmap( CBitmap* pBitmap, CPalette* pPal = NULL,
                       BOOL bTransferOwnership = TRUE );
BOOL CreateFromBitmap( HBITMAP hbm, HPALETTE hpal = NULL );
```

In the first and simplest version, `CreateFromBitmap` is called with the resource ID for a bitmap resource.

The second version of `CreateFromBitmap` requires the following three parameters:

Parameter	Description
pBitmap	Pointer to a `CBitmap` object.
pPal	Pointer to a `CPalette` object.
bTransferOwnership	If TRUE, the picture object is expected to take ownership of the bitmap and palette objects.
	If `bTransferOwnership` is TRUE, ownership of the bitmap and palette are passed to the picture object and cannot be used subsequently by the calling function. If FALSE, the calling function remains responsible for both and must ensure that the bitmap and palette remain valid throughout the life of the picture object.

In the third version, `CreateFromBitmap` is called with the following two parameters:

Parameter	Description
hbm	Handle to the bitmap from which the `CPictureHolder` object is created.
hpal	Handle to the palette used for rendering the bitmap.

If you're planning to use palette animation for an OCX bitmap control, either the second or third form is probably appropriate. In most other cases, the first and simplest form is more than adequate.

All three forms return zero on failure; they return nonzero on success.

The second function introduced here is the `CPictureHolder::Render` method, which renders the picture in the rectangle referenced by the `rcRender` rectangle. The `Render` method is called as follows:

```
void Render( CDC* pDC, const CRect& rcRender, const CRect& rcWBounds );
```

The `Render` method is called with the following three parameters:

Parameter	Description
pDC	Pointer to the display context in which the picture is to be rendered.
rcRender	Rectangle in which the picture is to be rendered.
rcWBounds	Represents the bounding rectangle of the object rendering the picture. For a control, this rectangle is the `rcBounds` parameter passed to an override of `COleControl::OnDraw`.

If you want to play with Render's resize capability, the member variable m_nScale has been provided. To use this scale factor, begin by revising the OnDraw method as shown here:

```
...
CRect     rcRender;
...
rcSrcBounds.right  = bmp.bmWidth  * m_nScale;
rcSrcBounds.bottom = bmp.bmHeight * m_nScale;
rcRender.left = rcBounds.left;
rcRender.top  = rcBounds.top;
rcRender.right  = rcBounds.left + ( bmp.bmWidth  * m_nScale );
rcRender.bottom = rcBounds.top  + ( bmp.bmHeight * m_nScale );
// Create picture and render
picHolder.CreateFromBitmap( btnBitmap );
picHolder.Render( pdc, rcRender, rcSrcBounds );
```

To complete this method, add an OnSize method that resizes the button to match. This provision is left as an exercise for the reader to figure out; this chapter proceeds to discuss other, more important methods.

> Note: When you use the OnDraw method, do not make any assumptions about the state of the device context supplied. In particular, do not assume that the device context has been initialized to the default state. Therefore, if your drawing operation needs colors, fonts, or other resources, all these resources should be explicitly selected. Also, do not assume that the rectangle's upper-left point is set at 0,0; however, at the same time, be careful not to draw beyond the limits of the supplied rectangle.

Mouse Messages in the OCX Control

In addition to drawing the control button, you also need provisions to recognize mouse events, to set the button state (up or down), and to increment the button count. To handle these functions, the ClassWizard is used to create OnLButtonDown, OnLButtonUp, OnRButtonDown, and OnRButtonUp methods.

When the left (primary) mouse button is pressed, the OnLButtonDown method function is called with three tasks:

```
void COcx_demoCtrl::OnLButtonDown(UINT nFlags, CPoint point)
{
    // TODO: Add your message handler code here and/or call default
    m_btnState = FALSE;
    SetCapture();
    Invalidate();
}
```

The first task is to flip the m_btnState method variable to FALSE, indicating that the button has been clicked on.

The second task is to call the SetCapture() method to ensure that the current button instance continues to receive the mouse messages (at least, until the mouse button is released). Without this provision, the mouse could be moved off the OCX button before the mouse button was released; if that happened, the control would never receive the button release message. For this control design, the button release message is essential.

Other provisions in the OCX scheme handle events of this nature (such as triggers and the FireMouseClick, FireMouseDown, and FireMouseUp methods in the COleControl class), but sometimes the simplest provisions are the best.

The last task for the OnLButtonDown method function is to call the Invalidate() method to ensure that the control is redrawn to reflect the change in state. This call comes back to the OnDraw method and completes the first half of the button's cycle.

In the OnLButtonUp method, the mouse button release event finishes one cycle of the button's operation by restoring the button state to TRUE (released), releasing the mouse capture, incrementing the button's counter (m_nNumber), and having the button redrawn:

```
void COcx_demoCtrl::OnLButtonUp(UINT nFlags, CPoint point)
{
   // TODO: Add your message handler code here and/or call default
   m_btnState = TRUE;
   ReleaseCapture();
   if( ++m_nNumber > 9 ) m_nNumber = 0;
   Invalidate();
}
```

Remember that when the mouse button was pressed, all subsequent mouse events were captured by the OCX control's instance…until now, when the mouse button is released. Any mouse events (which are pretty much limited to movements anyway) that may have been directed to another control have been intercepted by the mouse capture. Once the button is released, however, another control or window is free to receive mouse messages.

For the right mouse button, the OnRButtonDown and OnRButtonUp methods are essentially the same as the methods that handle the left mouse button except that the m_nNumber variable is decremented rather than incremented:

```
void COcx_demoCtrl::OnRButtonDown(UINT nFlags, CPoint point)
{
   // TODO: Add your message handler code here and/or call default
   m_btnState = FALSE;
   SetCapture();
   Invalidate();
// COleControl::OnRButtonDown(nFlags, point);
}

void COcx_demoCtrl::OnRButtonUp(UINT nFlags, CPoint point)
{
   // TODO: Add your message handler code here and/or call default
   m_btnState = TRUE;
   ReleaseCapture();
   if( —m_nNumber < 0 ) m_nNumber = 9;
   Invalidate();
```

```
//   COleControl::OnRButtonUp(nFlags, point);
}
```

The only remaining provision with any real validity for the demo OCX class is the initialization of the class instance. This is carried out in the object constructor as follows:

```
COcx_demoCtrl::COcx_demoCtrl()
{
    InitializeIIDs(&IID_DOcx_demo, &IID_DOcx_demoEvents);

    // TODO: Initialize your control's instance data here.
    m_nNumber = 0;
    m_nScale  = 2;
    SetControlSize( m_nScale * BMP_SIZEX, m_nScale * BMP_SIZEY );
}
```

There's not really much here—just an initial value for the `m_nScale` and `m_nNumber` members. Hardly worth worrying about, right?

OCX Control Properties

Although you probably know that object instances possess member variables (such as the `m_nNumber` and `m_nScale` variables in the current example), OCX control class instances possess another type of member variables called *properties*. Table 9.1 lists eight stock properties that belong to all OCX controls.

Table 9.1. Stock properties of OCX controls.

Property	*Purpose*
BackColor	Background color value for the control
BorderStyle	Border style for the control
Caption	Text caption for the control
Enabled	Status (enabled or disabled)
Font	Character font used by the control
ForeColor	Foreground color value for the control
hWnd	Control's window handle
Text	Text to display within the control

When the ControlWizard was used to create the `OCX_Demo` control class, the project files created included the Ocx_DPpg.CPP and Ocx_DPpg.H files that define the property page for the object class. Also, in the Ocx_Demo.RC script, a default dialog box, `IDD_PROPAGE_OCX_DEMO`, is supplied in which controls can be installed to set properties.

Once defined (or if defined, because it is optional), the property page is called from the resource editor when an OCX control is installed in a dialog box. Alternatively, the property page dialog box can also be called from the Test Container menu. (The Test Container is a utility used to test OCX controls during development and is discussed later in this chapter.)

Adding a Property to an OCX Control

The first step in adding a property to an OCX control is to call the ClassWizard, select the OLE Animation tab, and then select the control class (`COcx_demoCtrl` in this case) from the Class **N**ame list (see Figure 9.12).

Figure 9.12. The ClassWizard's OLE Animation tab.

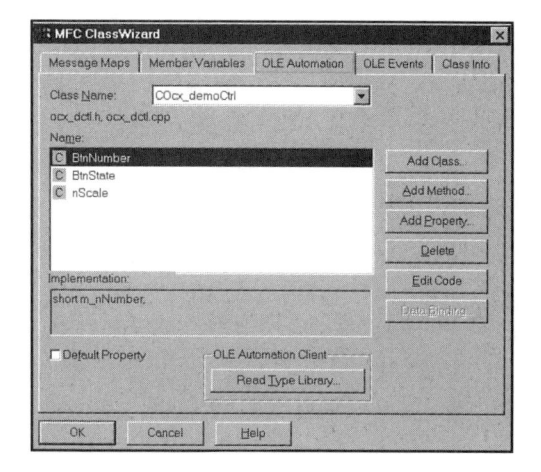

The OLE Automation tab is used to create and expand the OLE animation capabilities of an application, including the following:

- Adding classes to support OLE animation.
- Adding methods and properties to existing classes that already support OLE automation.
- Creating C++ classes for other OLE automation objects such as Microsoft Word.

The Na**m**e box lists the names of defined properties and methods. Entries are identified as stock properties (S), custom properties (C), or methods (M); default properties are indicated by making the item bold.

The Implementation field shows how the property or method selected in the Na**m**e field is implemented in your C++ class. The type and identifier name are listed.

The OLE Automation tab provides a variety of options for adding classes, methods, and data bindings. The available buttons and checkboxes are listed in Table 9.2.

Table 9.2. OLE animation options.

Option	Purpose
Add Class	Calls the Add Class dialog box; use this box to add a new message-handling class to an application.
Add Method	Calls the Add Method dialog box; use this box to add new OLE automation methods used by other classes to make requests of this class. The ClassWizard automatically updates the dispatch map when methods are added or deleted. (Available only when a class supporting OLE automation is selected.)
Add Property	Calls the Add Property dialog box (shown in Figure 9.8); use this box to add a new OLE automation property.
Delete	Deletes the currently selected item from the Name list.
Edit Code	Opens the editor window for the selected property or method.
Data Binding	Defines data binding for a property.
Default Property	Makes the selected property the default property for this OLE object.
Read Type Library	Opens the Type Library Tool dialog box; use this box to add C++ classes representing other OLE automation objects such as Microsoft Excel.

Adding A New Property

In most cases like the OCX_Demo example, the principal purpose of OLE animation is to add a new property to an OCX control, using the Add Property dialog box shown in Figure 9.13.

Figure 9.13. *The Add Property dialog box.*

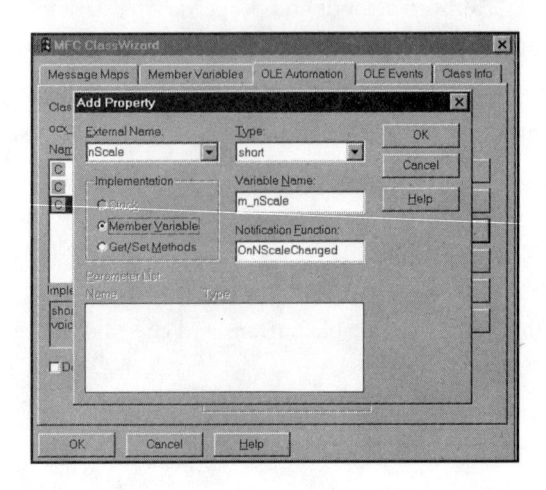

Chapter 9 • Using Customized OCX Controls

Use the Add Property dialog box to add new OLE automation properties to your class. *Properties* are attributes of your class that can be changed by OLE automation clients. The ClassWizard automatically updates the dispatch map of your class when you add or delete properties. The following chart lists the options available in the Add Property dialog box.

> Note: *Dispatch map* refers to the macro mechanisms supplied by MFC to call methods and access properties across applications. The dispatch map designates internal and external names for object functions and properties as well as the data types of the properties and of the function arguments.

Option/Field	Description
External Name	The external name for the property is used by automation clients to make changes to the property. Rather than defining a new property, you can select from the predefined properties in the list box.
Implementation	Choose from the following:
	Stoc**k** — Indicates use of the default implementation of this property.
	Member **V**ariable — Implementation allows direct access to the member variable; commonly used for properties that do not affect the user interface when changed.
	Get/Set **M**ethods — Implementation allows controlled access to the property; used when value changes must be entered or when a property value is calculated; commonly used for properties that affect the user interface when changed.
Type	Specifies the property type (required).
Variable **N**ame	Class member variable name or function name associated with the property. Available only when Member **V**ariable is selected as the Implementation.
Notification **F**unction	The function called whenever the property value is changed. Available only when Member **V**ariable is selected as the Implementation (see Figure 9.13).
Get Function	The member function that returns the current value of a property. Available only when Get/Set **M**ethods is selected as the Implementation (see Figure 9.14).

continues

Option/Field	Description
Set Function	The member function that sets the value of a property. Available only when Get/Set **M**ethods is selected as the Implementation (see Figure 9.14).
Parameter List	Optional parameters used with Get/Set **M**ethod functions (see Figure 9.14).

Name	The internal name of the parameter to be added. To add a name, double-click the first empty row under the Name label and enter the variable name.
Type	The parameter type; double-click the first empty row under the Type label to display the drop-down list and then select a type for the parameter variable.

Figure 9.14. *The Add Property dialog box, showing Get/Set Method Implementation variations.*

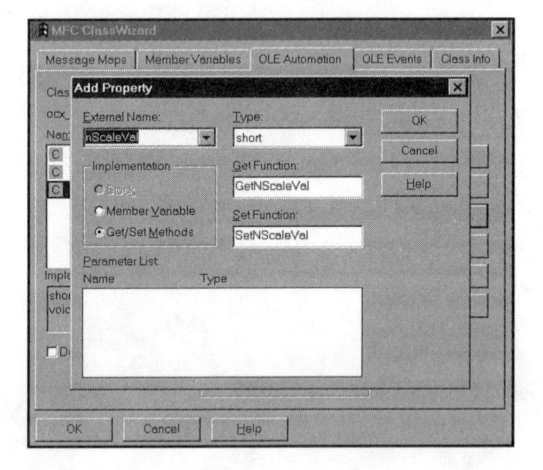

Note: To create a read-only property, leave the **S**et Function field blank. To create a write-only property, leave the **G**et Function field blank.

Properties in the OCX_Demo Example

In the OCX_Demo example, three member variables are provided with the external names BtnNumber, BtnState, and nScale. Internally, these are m_nNumber, m_btnState, and m_nScale.

You may expect these variables to be initialized in the constructor method; after all, this is common practice. However, following is the constructor for the COcx_demoCtrl class; notice that the only initialization is the control's size (and even this is not engraved in stone).

Chapter 9 • Using Customized OCX Controls

```
COcx_demoCtrl::COcx_demoCtrl()
{
    InitializeIIDs(&IID_DOcx_demo, &IID_DOcx_demoEvents);

    // TODO: Initialize your control's instance data here.
    SetControlSize( 2 * BMP_SIZEX, 2 * BMP_SIZEY );
}
```

If you compare this segment with the OnNScaleChanged method that follows, you'll notice that the later code uses the m_nScale member variable; the preceding fragment uses a hard-coded 2 for the multiplier. Why the difference?

Even though the m_nScale variable is initialized, the initialization does not take place until later and no set value is available at this point.

Instead of m_nScale being initialized in the constructor method, because the m_nScale member is a persistent custom property (as are m_btnState and m_nNumber), the DoPropExchange method contains the PX_ functions that both initialize and validate all three of these member variables. The DoPropExchange method is shown here:

```
void COcx_demoCtrl::DoPropExchange(CPropExchange* pPX)
{
    ExchangeVersion(pPX, MAKELONG(_wVerMinor, _wVerMajor));
    COleControl::DoPropExchange(pPX);

    // TODO: Call PX_ functions for each persistent custom property.
    PX_Bool( pPX, _T("BtnState"), m_btnState, TRUE );
    PX_Short( pPX, _T("BtnNumber"), m_nNumber, 0 );
    PX_Short( pPX, _T("nScale" ), m_nScale, 2 );
}
```

Both PX_Bool and PX_Short are overloaded functions with the following two forms:

```
BOOL PX_Bool( CPropExchange* pPX, LPCTSTR pszPropName, BOOL& bValue );
BOOL PX_Bool( CPropExchange* pPX, LPCTSTR pszPropName, BOOL& bValue,
              BOOL bDefault );

BOOL PX_Short( CPropExchange* pPX, LPCTSTR pszPropName, short& sValue );
BOOL PX_Short( CPropExchange* pPX, LPCTSTR pszPropName, short& sValue,
               short sDefault);
```

In the current examples (as is true in most cases), the second form is used to ensure that default values are in place. On the other hand, if you assign default values in the constructor method, the short form can be used here.

PX_Bool and Other Functions

The PX_Bool function is called from a control's DoPropExchange function to serialize or initialize a class property. The property's value is read from or written to the referenced variable, as appropriate. The following chart lists and defines the parameters used by the PX_Bool function.

Parameter	Description
pPX	Pointer to the `CPropertyExchange` object (generally supplied as a parameter to the `DoPropExchange` function).
pszPropName	Name of the property being exchanged; uses the external name defined when the property was defined, not the internal variable name.
bValue	Variable in which the property is stored (normally a member variable).
bDefault	Default value.

Other `PX_` property functions are also provided, including `PX_Currency`, `PX_Double`, `PX_Float`, `PX_Font`, `PX_IUnknown`, `PX_Long`, `PX_Picture`, `PX_Short`, `PX_String`, `PX_ULong`, and `PX_UShort`. The parameter list for each varies according to the type of property handled and the requirements. Consult the online documentation for details.

Responding to a Property Change

The process of responding to a value change is simple. When you created the `nScale` property (`m_nScale`), the ClassWizard also created the shell for the `OnNScaleChanged` member function:

```
void COcx_demoCtrl::OnNScaleChanged()
{
    // TODO: Add notification handler code
    SetControlSize( m_nScale * BMP_SIZEX, m_nScale * BMP_SIZEY );
    SetModifiedFlag();
}
```

One addition to this function—calling the `SetControlSize` function—is sufficient for a response; the additional function makes the control resizable in response to any changes in the scale parameter.

Using the Get and Set Property Methods

Provisions have also been made to return the `m_nScale` value through the `GetNScaleVal` method:

```
short COcx_demoCtrl::GetNScaleVal()
{
    // TODO: Add your property handler here
    return m_nScale;
//  return 0;
}
```

The `SetNScaleVal` method sets a new `m_nScale` value:

```
void COcx_demoCtrl::SetNScaleVal(short nNewValue)
{
    // TODO: Add your property handler here
    if( ( nNewValue > 0 ) && ( nNewValue < 9 ) ) // limit values to 1..8
        m_nScale = nNewValue;
```

```
    SetModifiedFlag();
}
```

Both methods are simple and should be familiar without further explanation. Now let's move on to the Property Page dialog box.

Defining the Property Page Dialog Box

When the OCX_Demo control was first created, the ControlWizard provided a default property page in the OCX_DPPG.CPP and OCX_DPPG.H files. In the OCX_DEMO.RC script, the dialog box is identified as IDD_PROPAGE_OCX_DEMO.

Initially, the Property Page dialog box is simply a blank, borderless, child dialog box. Sound familiar? Sound like something you were introduced to Chapter 8? Like one of the popup dialog boxes used with a tab control? It should, because that's exactly how it will be used. But the present task is to put something into it.

Because the OCX_Demo control has only one property worth setting—the scale factor for sizing the button—the Property Page dialog box will be very simple, containing one label and one edit field (see Figure 9.15).

Figure 9.15. A simple Property Page dialog box.

Notice that this dialog box does not have an OK or Cancel button, has no caption or system menu, and has nothing else except the label and edit field, IDC_EDIT1, for the property value.

Of course, if there are other properties to be set, you can also place them in this dialog box. If necessary, you can create multiple property pages. In any case, you do not need OK and Cancel buttons because these are supplied by the parent dialog box. All this child dialog box should contain are the actual properties to be edited.

One other task is required for setting the property page: setting a member variable for the IDC_EDIT1 field.

To set this member variable, call the ClassWizard and select the Member Variables tab (see Figure 9.16). Then select COcx_demoPropPage from the Class **N**ame list.

Highlight the IDC_EDIT1 entry, click the Add **V**ariable button, and identify the member variable as an integer named m_nScale. Because you want to limit the size of the control buttons, also specify a minimum value of 1 and a maximum value of 8. Remember, these are multipliers applied to the original size of the button image.

Figure 9.16. The Member Variables tab of the ClassWizard dialog box.

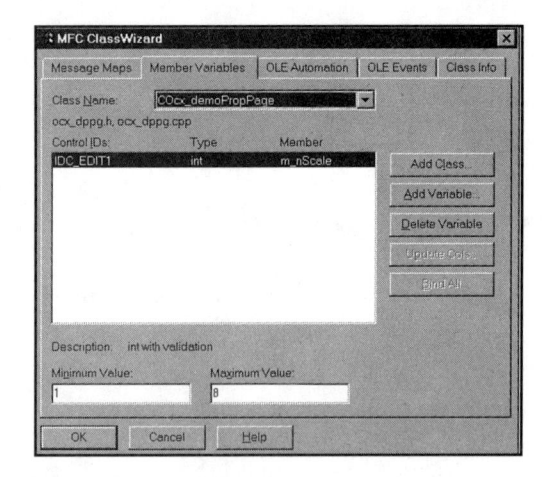

When this is done, the OCX_DPPG.CPP file is updated to initialize the m_nScale member. However, the initial value supplied by the ClassWizard (in the COcx_demoPropPage constructor) does not match the limits just set because the ClassWizard initializes all numerical member variables to 0. Because limits of 1..8 have been set, this code segment must also be revised, as follows:

```
COcx_demoPropPage::COcx_demoPropPage() :
    COlePropertyPage(IDD, IDS_OCX_DEMO_PPG_CAPTION)
{
    //{{AFX_DATA_INIT(COcx_demoPropPage)
    m_nScale = 2;          // ClassWizard sets this to 0 by default
    //}}AFX_DATA_INIT
}
```

More important is the DoDataExchange method, in which the ClassWizard has provided the data exchange handling to copy the m_nScale variable between the property page and the OCX control. The DoDataExchange method also contains the limit test: the DDV_MinMaxInt provision, shown in the following code fragment:

```
void COcx_demoPropPage::DoDataExchange(CDataExchange* pDX)
{
    //{{AFX_DATA_MAP(COcx_demoPropPage)
    DDP_Text(pDX, IDC_EDIT1, m_nScale, _T("nScale") );
    DDX_Text(pDX, IDC_EDIT1, m_nScale);
    DDV_MinMaxInt(pDX, m_nScale, 1, 8);
    //}}AFX_DATA_MAP
    DDP_PostProcessing(pDX);
}
```

This is all the handling required—but it is also absolutely essential. Otherwise, the application cannot receive any changes.

At this point, the OCX control is ready for testing.

Testing the OCX Control

Normally, an executable application is tested simply by running it. However, dynamic link libraries require that you write a shell to call the DLL functions. Even though OCX controls are technically dynamic link library functions, there is a much easier method to test them than constructing an application for the purpose: the Test Container utility.

> Note for 16-Bit Programmers: To allow another application to use an OCX control, a Type library is required. A Type library is generated by the MkTypLib.EXE utility using the project's ODL file (the ODL file is generated automatically when the ControlWizard is used).

> Note for 32-Bit Programmers: The 32-bit CDK creates both the Type library and the ODL files through the project's makefile. The MkTypLib utility is not required.

Before we can use the Test Container, you must begin by registering the OCX control.

Registering an OCX Control

OCX controls are registered through the RegSrv utility called from the C++ **T**ools menu as Register Control. Because the service registered is the current project's OCX services, no parameters or arguments are required. Figure 9.17 shows the results reported by RegSvr.

Figure 9.17. The RegSvr.EXE utility, reporting success.

The RegSvr utility loads the control's DLL into memory and calls the OCX library's `DllRegisterServer` function, which provides information about the control, its Type library, and its property page to the Windows' registration database.

An OCX control class can also be unregistered by calling the Unregister Control command from the **T**ools menu. In turn, the library's `DllUnregisterServer` function is summoned and the entry is removed from the Windows' registration database.

Using the Test Container Utility

The Test Container utility provides an OLE Container service. You can use this service to conveniently test OCX controls for both function and performance.

To test an OCX control, select Test Container from the Visual C++ **T**ools menu. The Test Container utility appears.

Select Insert OLE Control from the Test Container's **E**dit menu. The Insert OLE Control dialog box appears (see Figure 9.18). This dialog box contains a list of all registered OCX controls. Select the desired control from the list and click OK.

Figure 9.18. The Insert OLE Control dialog box.

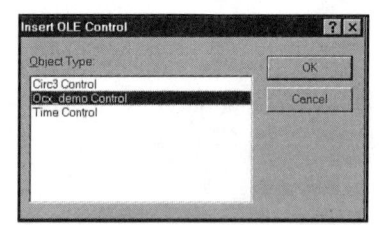

The icon for the selected control is added to the Test Container's toolbar (Figure 9.11, earlier in this chapter, shows the Test Container with the ten OCX_Demo controls).

> Note: If your control is not listed, make sure that the control class has been registered with the Register Control command from the **T**ools menu.

Testing an OCX Control

Selecting an OCX control from the Insert OLE Control dialog box places the control's icon on the toolbar, but it also creates an instance of the control in the Test Container window. Operations of the OCX control can be tested directly from there: Use the mouse to click or manipulate the control, just as if the control existed within an application (except, of course, that only internal operations of the control can be tested).

In Figure 9.11 (earlier in this chapter) and in Figure 9.19, most of the OCX button states have been changed from the default 0 to another value by clicking the various buttons—a strictly internal operation.

Testing Control Properties

OCX control properties and events can also be tested by selecting the Properties option from the Test Container's **V**iew menu. In response, the Properties dialog box appears (refer to the upper-right dialog box in Figure 9.19).

Figure 9.19. *The Properties and OCX_Demo Control Properties dialog boxes.*

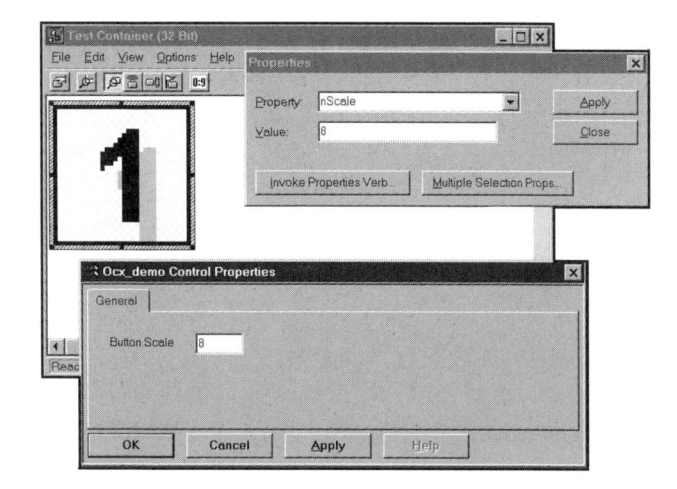

From the **P**roperty list box in the Properties dialog box, select a property to examine. The current value for the selected property appears in the **V**alue field and can be edited there. For example, the button state (BtnState) or the button number (BtnNumber) for the selected button can be changed.

The button scale property (nScale) is handled through the OCX_Demo Control Properties dialog box (see the dialog box at the bottom of Figure 9.19). Although this value can also be changed in the Test Container Properties dialog box, the OCX_Demo Control Properties dialog box is more important (or, at least, more relevant).

In the OCX_Demo Control Properties dialog box in Figure 9.19, the rather simple child dialog box identified as IDD_PROPAGE_OCX_DEMO (designed earlier in this chapter) appears as a full-fledged tab control together with OK, Cancel, and Apply buttons. (The Help button is disabled because no help was provided for this topic.)

If you change the value shown in the Button Scale edit field and then click the Apply button, the control instance in the Test Container is redrawn (assuming that the application is written correctly) to reflect the change. In this example, the button has been resized to 8 times the original bitmap size.

Testing Events

Assuming that the control class uses events, you can test events in a manner similar to the way you test properties. To test an event, select Event Log from the **V**iew menu and then perform any action that causes an event to be fired. The corresponding event appears in the Event Log window.

> Note: Events have not been demonstrated in the OCX control class demonstration in part because the author regards them as trivial and, more importantly, because there was no particular need for events in the control design.

Source Code

The complete source code for the Ocx_DCtl.CPP demonstration program is shown in Listing 9.1; the entire project files for the OCX_Demo controls are on the disc that accompanies this book.

Listing 9.1. Source code for the `Ocx_DCtl.CPP` demonstration program.

```cpp
// ocx_dctl.cpp : Implementation of the COcx_demoCtrl OLE control class.

#include "stdafx.h"
#include "ocx_demo.h"
#include "ocx_dctl.h"
#include "ocx_dppg.h"

#ifdef _DEBUG
#undef THIS_FILE
static char BASED_CODE THIS_FILE[] = __FILE__;
#endif

IMPLEMENT_DYNCREATE(COcx_demoCtrl, COleControl)

/////////////////////////////////////////////////////////////////////////////
// Message map

BEGIN_MESSAGE_MAP(COcx_demoCtrl, COleControl)
    //{{AFX_MSG_MAP(COcx_demoCtrl)
    ON_WM_LBUTTONDOWN()
    ON_WM_LBUTTONUP()
    ON_WM_RBUTTONDOWN()
    ON_WM_RBUTTONUP()
    //}}AFX_MSG_MAP
    ON_OLEVERB(AFX_IDS_VERB_PROPERTIES, OnProperties)
END_MESSAGE_MAP()

/////////////////////////////////////////////////////////////////////////////
// Dispatch map

BEGIN_DISPATCH_MAP(COcx_demoCtrl, COleControl)
    //{{AFX_DISPATCH_MAP(COcx_demoCtrl)
    DISP_PROPERTY(COcx_demoCtrl, "BtnNumber", m_nNumber, VT_I2)
    DISP_PROPERTY_NOTIFY(COcx_demoCtrl, "BtnState", m_btnState,
                        OnBtnStateChanged, VT_BOOL)
    DISP_PROPERTY_NOTIFY(COcx_demoCtrl, "nScale", m_nScale,
                        OnNScaleChanged, VT_I2)
    //}}AFX_DISPATCH_MAP
    DISP_FUNCTION_ID(COcx_demoCtrl, "AboutBox", DISPID_ABOUTBOX,
                    AboutBox, VT_EMPTY, VTS_NONE)
END_DISPATCH_MAP()

/////////////////////////////////////////////////////////////////////////////
// Event map

BEGIN_EVENT_MAP(COcx_demoCtrl, COleControl)
    //{{AFX_EVENT_MAP(COcx_demoCtrl)
    // NOTE - ClassWizard will add and remove event map entries
    //    DO NOT EDIT what you see in these blocks of generated code !
```

```
    //}}AFX_EVENT_MAP
END_EVENT_MAP()

//////////////////////////////////////////////////////////////////////
// Property pages

// TODO: Add more property pages as needed.  Remember to increase the count!
BEGIN_PROPPAGEIDS(COcx_demoCtrl, 1)
    PROPPAGEID(COcx_demoPropPage::guid)
END_PROPPAGEIDS(COcx_demoCtrl)

//////////////////////////////////////////////////////////////////////
// Initialize class factory and guid

IMPLEMENT_OLECREATE_EX(COcx_demoCtrl, "OCX_DEMO.Ocx_demoCtrl.1",
    0x25c92ee0, 0x9e7f, 0x11ce, 0xbb, 0x7, 0x8e, 0x97, 0xe5, 0xbd, 0xd7, 0xdc)

//////////////////////////////////////////////////////////////////////
// Type library ID and version

IMPLEMENT_OLETYPELIB(COcx_demoCtrl, _tlid, _wVerMajor, _wVerMinor)

//////////////////////////////////////////////////////////////////////
// Interface IDs

const IID BASED_CODE IID_DOcx_demo =
        { 0x25c92ee1, 0x9e7f, 0x11ce,
            { 0xbb, 0x7, 0x8e, 0x97, 0xe5, 0xbd, 0xd7, 0xdc } };
const IID BASED_CODE IID_DOcx_demoEvents =
        { 0x25c92ee2, 0x9e7f, 0x11ce,
            { 0xbb, 0x7, 0x8e, 0x97, 0xe5, 0xbd, 0xd7, 0xdc } };

//////////////////////////////////////////////////////////////////////
// Control type information

static const DWORD BASED_CODE _dwOcx_demoOleMisc =
    OLEMISC_ACTIVATEWHENVISIBLE |
    OLEMISC_SETCLIENTSITEFIRST |
    OLEMISC_INSIDEOUT |
    OLEMISC_CANTLINKINSIDE |
    OLEMISC_RECOMPOSEONRESIZE;

IMPLEMENT_OLECTLTYPE(COcx_demoCtrl, IDS_OCX_DEMO, _dwOcx_demoOleMisc)

//////////////////////////////////////////////////////////////////////
// COcx_demoCtrl::COcx_demoCtrlFactory::UpdateRegistry -
// Adds or removes system registry entries for COcx_demoCtrl

BOOL COcx_demoCtrl::COcx_demoCtrlFactory::UpdateRegistry(BOOL bRegister)
{
    if (bRegister)
        return AfxOleRegisterControlClass(
            AfxGetInstanceHandle(),
            m_clsid,
            m_lpszProgID,
            IDS_OCX_DEMO,
            IDB_OCX_DEMO,
            FALSE,                      // Not insertable
            _dwOcx_demoOleMisc,
```

continues

Listing 9.1. continued

```
            _tlid,
            _wVerMajor,
            _wVerMinor);
    else
        return AfxOleUnregisterClass(m_clsid, m_lpszProgID);
}

/////////////////////////////////////////////////////////////////////////////
// COcx_demoCtrl::COcx_demoCtrl - Constructor

COcx_demoCtrl::COcx_demoCtrl()
{
    InitializeIIDs(&IID_DOcx_demo, &IID_DOcx_demoEvents);

    // TODO: Initialize your control's instance data here.
    m_nNumber = 0;
    m_nScale  = 2;      // default is twice bitmap size
    SetControlSize( m_nScale * BMP_SIZEX, m_nScale * BMP_SIZEY );
}

/////////////////////////////////////////////////////////////////////////////
// COcx_demoCtrl::~COcx_demoCtrl - Destructor

COcx_demoCtrl::~COcx_demoCtrl()
{
    // TODO: Cleanup your control's instance data here.
}

/////////////////////////////////////////////////////////////////////////////
// COcx_demoCtrl::OnDraw - Drawing function

void COcx_demoCtrl::OnDraw(
            CDC* pdc, const CRect& rcBounds, const CRect& rcInvalid)
{
    // TODO: Replace the following code with your own drawing code.
//  pdc->FillRect(rcBounds,
//          CBrush::FromHandle((HBRUSH)GetStockObject(WHITE_BRUSH)));
//  pdc->Ellipse(rcBounds);

    CBitmap    bitmap;
    BITMAP     bmp;
    CRect      rcSrcBounds;
    UINT       btnBitmap;
    CPictureHolder picHolder;

    // Load button bitmap
    if( m_btnState )        // button is up
        btnBitmap = IDB_BTN_UP0 + m_nNumber;
    else                    // button is down
        btnBitmap = IDB_BTN_DN0 + m_nNumber;
    bitmap.LoadBitmap( btnBitmap );
    bitmap.GetObject(sizeof(BITMAP), &bmp);
    rcSrcBounds.right  = bmp.bmWidth;
    rcSrcBounds.bottom = bmp.bmHeight;

    // Create picture and render
    picHolder.CreateFromBitmap( btnBitmap );
    picHolder.Render( pdc, rcBounds, rcSrcBounds );
```

```cpp
}

//////////////////////////////////////////////////////////////////////
// COcx_demoCtrl::DoPropExchange - Persistence support

void COcx_demoCtrl::DoPropExchange(CPropExchange* pPX)
{
    ExchangeVersion(pPX, MAKELONG(_wVerMinor, _wVerMajor));
    COleControl::DoPropExchange(pPX);

    // TODO: Call PX_ functions for each persistent custom property.
    PX_Bool( pPX, _T("BtnState"), m_btnState, TRUE );
    PX_Short( pPX, _T("BtnNumber"), m_nNumber, 0 );
    PX_Short( pPX, _T("nScale" ), m_nScale, 2 );
}

//////////////////////////////////////////////////////////////////////
// COcx_demoCtrl::OnResetState - Reset control to default state

void COcx_demoCtrl::OnResetState()
{
    COleControl::OnResetState();  // Resets defaults found in DoPropExchange
    // TODO: Reset any other control state here.
}

//////////////////////////////////////////////////////////////////////
// COcx_demoCtrl::AboutBox - Display an "About" box to the user

void COcx_demoCtrl::AboutBox()
{
    CDialog dlgAbout(IDD_ABOUTBOX_OCX_DEMO);
    dlgAbout.DoModal();
}

//////////////////////////////////////////////////////////////////////
// COcx_demoCtrl message handlers

void COcx_demoCtrl::OnBtnStateChanged()
{
    // TODO: Add notification handler code
    SetModifiedFlag();
}

void COcx_demoCtrl::OnLButtonDown(UINT nFlags, CPoint point)
{
    // TODO: Add your message handler code here and/or call default
    m_btnState = FALSE;
    SetCapture();
    Invalidate();
//  COleControl::OnLButtonDown(nFlags, point);
}

void COcx_demoCtrl::OnLButtonUp(UINT nFlags, CPoint point)
{
    // TODO: Add your message handler code here and/or call default
    m_btnState = TRUE;
    ReleaseCapture();
    if( ++m_nNumber > 9 ) m_nNumber = 0;
    Invalidate();
```

continues

Listing 9.1. continued

```
//  COleControl::OnLButtonUp(nFlags, point);
}

void COcx_demoCtrl::OnRButtonDown(UINT nFlags, CPoint point)
{
    // TODO: Add your message handler code here and/or call default
    m_btnState = FALSE;
    SetCapture();
    Invalidate();
//  COleControl::OnRButtonDown(nFlags, point);
}

void COcx_demoCtrl::OnRButtonUp(UINT nFlags, CPoint point)
{
    // TODO: Add your message handler code here and/or call default
    m_btnState = TRUE;
    ReleaseCapture();
    if( —m_nNumber < 0 ) m_nNumber = 9;
    Invalidate();
//  COleControl::OnRButtonUp(nFlags, point);
}

void COcx_demoCtrl::OnNScaleChanged()
{
    // TODO: Add notification handler code
    SetControlSize( m_nScale * BMP_SIZEX, m_nScale * BMP_SIZEY );
    SetModifiedFlag();
}

short COcx_demoCtrl::GetNScaleVal()
{
    // TODO: Add your property handler here
    return m_nScale;
}

void COcx_demoCtrl::SetNScaleVal(short nNewValue)
{
    // TODO: Add your property handler here
    if( ( nNewValue > 0 ) && ( nNewValue < 9 ) ) // limit values to 1..8
        m_nScale = nNewValue;
    SetModifiedFlag();
}
```

Summary

This chapter detailed the basics of constructing OCX (OLE 2) custom controls. However, to cover all the details and all the possibilities inherent in custom controls, this book would have to be devoted to the topic to the exclusion of all else.

For example, stock control properties are mentioned only in passing. Events (which can be used for keyboard or mouse interactions) have not been covered at all (because they are not particularly important). A number of other minor features have not even been mentioned.

Fortunately, additional information and examples are available through the OcxPg.HLP and OcxTut.HLP files. These files are located in your \MSVC20\HELP directory and in additional help files and examples on the Visual C++ 2.1 distribution CD. The files easily contain enough material to fill a moderately sized book; hopefully, they will contain far more than you ever need to know about OCX controls.

If you are using Visual C++ 4.0, you'll want to check the distribution CD; the MSDEV/Samples/MFC/Controls directory holds a variety of OCX control examples. Copy these to your hard drive to compile and run them (use File Manager to clear the Read Only flags from the files after you copy them). These files offer a number of interesting examples and can serve as starting points for your own designs.

CHAPTER 10

Using Common Dialog Boxes, Fonts, and Colors

Previous chapters have examined various aspects of dialog boxes ranging from common controls to custom OCX controls. To bring the topic of dialogs to a close, this chapter takes a look at *common dialog boxes*, dialog boxes provided by the CommDlg.DLL or ComDlg32.DLL library (in the Windows\System directory). These DLL-supplied common dialog boxes include printer, font, and color selection dialog boxes as well as search and replace dialog boxes.

A second type of common dialog box is supplied by the Microsoft Foundation Class/AppWizard system in the form of the File Open, Save, and Save As dialog boxes. Although these latter common dialog boxes are members of the CommDlg library and are listed in the CommDlg.H header, they do not have exposed class equivalents but are "built in" to the AFX services provided by MFC.

Unlike previous dialog box examples, common dialog boxes are not defined in RC resource scripts and do not require command provisions within your application.

There's nothing new about these dialog boxes; common dialog boxes have been around since Windows 3.1 and do not require object classes to invoke them. However, because you are using Visual C++ and because Visual C++ has provided object classes for invoking common dialog boxes, the object versions of the common dialog boxes (or, more accurately, the object classes invoking the common dialog boxes) are used here.

Understanding Common Dialog Boxes and Data Types

Table 10.1 lists the common dialog boxes defined in the CommDlg/ComDlg32 library by entry functions. The MFC class equivalents and the data structures used with each are also listed.

Table 10.1. Common dialog boxes, classes, and data structures.

Entry Function	Class Equivalent	Data Structure
ChooseColor	CColorDialog	CHOOSECOLOR
ChooseFont	CFontDialog	CHOOSEFONT
FindText	CFindReplaceDialog	FINDREPLACE
ReplaceText	CFindReplaceDialog	FINDREPLACE
GetOpenFileName	CFileDialog	OPENFILENAME
GetSaveFileName	CFileDialog	OPENFILENAME
PageSetupDlg	CPageSetupDialog	PAGESETUPDLG
PrintDlg	CPrintDialog	PRINTDLG

With MFC, most of these common dialog boxes are effectively stock functions. The File Print, and Find and Replace dialog boxes are invoked by default menu options supplied by AppWizard when an application is generated. Because the Color and Font dialog boxes require explicit invocation, this chapter begins with these two common dialog boxes, shown in the FontDlg application.

Selecting Fonts and Colors

The FontDlg application calls the `CFontDialog` class to display the Font dialog box; this dialog box is used to select character font, point size, attributes, and text color. The application calls the `CColorDialog` class to select a background color specification. To store the information returned by these dialog boxes and to initialize the dialog boxes when called, four member variables are declared in the `CFontdlgView` class:

```
// fontdvw.h : interface of the CFontdlgView class
    ...
public:
    CFontdlgDoc* GetDocument();
```

```
    int     nPoints;                    // font size in points * 10
    DWORD   rgbColor, rgbBackColor;     // foreground / background colors
    LOGFONT logFont;                    // logical font structure
```

The `logFont` member is a structure, defined in CommDlg.H, used to specify the type of font requested. The `rgbColor` member contains the foreground color specification; the `nPoints` member receives the actual point size (in tenths of a point) of the font selected through the dialog box.

The `rgbBackColor` member is used with the `CColorDialog` class to contain a color selection returned by the Color dialog box and, of course, to initialize the Color dialog box when called.

Figure 10.1 shows the FontDlg application with a menu offering two options: Font and Color.

Figure 10.1. *The FontDlg application.*

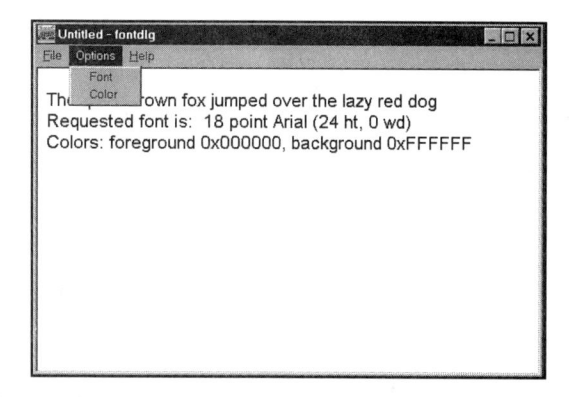

The FontDlg application is relatively simple. The Options, Font menu item calls the Font selection dialog box. The Font dialog box allows the user to choose typeface, point size, and font color, as well as bold, italic, underscore, and strikethrough characteristics. The foreground (text) color value is selected from a pull-down list with a limited (16-entry) palette.

The Options, Color menu item calls the Color selection dialog box. The Color dialog box allows the user to choose an RGB color value. The returned value is used both to fill the client window and as background for the text display. However, you may find that the fill color and the text background color do not match precisely because the `TextOut` function is less versatile and maps the color selection to the nearest system palette entry rather than using the actual RGB color specification.

The results are used to display a sample line of text together with the typeface name, point size, character height and width, and the RGB color values for the foreground and background colors.

Before the Font selection dialog box can be called, however, an initial font specification is expected. You do this with the `LOGFONT` structure.

The *LOGFONT* Structure

The LOGFONT structure is used to set parameters requesting a matching font from those available on a system. A font request is not explicit because there is no guarantee that any specific font is present on any specific system. Instead, the LOGFONT structure is used to define a font request that the GDI uses to select the closest matching font from those available on the system.

The LOGFONT structure is defined as follows and is detailed in Table 10.2:

```
typedef struct tagLOGFONT
{       LONG  lfHeight;
        LONG  lfWidth;
        LONG  lfEscapement;
        LONG  lfOrientation;
        LONG  lfWeight;
        BYTE  lfItalic;
        BYTE  lfUnderline;
        BYTE  lfStrikeOut;
        BYTE  lfCharSet;
        BYTE  lfOutPrecision;
        BYTE  lfClipPrecision;
        BYTE  lfQuality;
        BYTE  lfPitchAndFamily;
        CHAR  lfFaceName[LF_FACESIZE];
} LOGFONT;
```

Table 10.2. The LOGFONT Structure.

LOGFONT *Field*	*Purpose*
lfHeight	The height of fonts, in logical units, taking one of three forms:
	lfHeight > 0 The value in device units is matched against the cell height of the available fonts.
	lfHeight = 0 A reasonable default size is used.
	lfHeight < 0 The value in absolute device units is matched against the character height of the available fonts.
	The font mapper looks for the largest font that does not exceed the requested size. If this condition cannot be satisfied, the font mapper looks for the smallest font available.
lfWidth	The average width, in logical units, of characters in the font.
	For lfWidth == 0 (the usual default), the font mapper looks for a match between the device aspect ratio and the digitization aspect ratio of the available fonts, selecting the closest match according to the absolute value of the difference.

LOGFONT Field	Purpose
lfEscapement	The angle, in tenths of degrees, relative to the bottom of the page for each line of text. The default value of 0 produces normal text; a value of 180 produces an inverted line (upside down, right to left).
lfOrientation	The angle, in tenths of degrees, relative to the bottom of the page for each character's base line. This value can be used to adjust the angle of an italic font.
lfWeight	Specifies a font weight in the range 0 through 1000. For lfWeight == 0, a default weight is used. *Note:* A weight of 400 is normal; 700 is bold. Most fonts do not currently support other weights.
lfItalic	If TRUE, specifies an italic font.
lfUnderline	If TRUE, specifies an underlined font.
lfStrikeOut	If TRUE, specifies a strikeout font.
lfCharSet	Selects a character set. May be one of the following predefined values: ANSI_CHARSET — (default) OEM_CHARSET — The OEM character set is system dependent. OEM (Original Equipment Manufacturer) character sets are generally supplied by the video-card manufacturer. SYMBOL_CHARSET — Includes dingbat and other symbol sets. UNICODE_CHARSET — 16-bit Unicode characters provide international alphabets. Other character sets may exist on some systems. However, if an application uses a font from an unknown character set, strings rendered in the unknown font should not be translated or interpreted.
lfOutPrecision	Output precision defines how closely the output must match the requested font's height, width, character orientation, escapement, and pitch. The following constants specify output precision options: OUT_CHARACTER_PRECIS OUT_DEFAULT_PRECIS (default) OUT_STRING_PRECIS OUT_STROKE_PRECIS

continues

Table 10.2. continued

LOGFONT Field	Purpose
lfClipPrecision	Clipping precision defines how characters that fall partially outside the clipping region are clipped:

	CLIP_CHARACTER_PRECIS	Clips entire characters.
	CLIP_DEFAULT_PRECIS	Clips character strokes at the clipping region boundary.
	CLIP_STROKE_PRECIS	Clips entire strokes that cross the clipping region boundary.

lfQuality	Output quality defines how carefully the graphics device interface (GDI) must attempt to match the logical-font attributes to those of an actual physical font. The lfQuality field can have one of the following values:

	DEFAULT_QUALITY	Appearance is unimportant.
	DRAFT_QUALITY	Appearance is less important than it is with PROOF_QUALITY.
		For GDI fonts, DRAFT_QUALITY enables scaling, making more font sizes available and reducing quality. Bold, italic, underline, and strikeouts are synthesized as necessary.
	PROOF_QUALITY	Character quality is more important than the exact matching of the logical-font attributes.
		For GDI fonts, PROOF_QUALITY disables scaling and selects the font closest in size. Font quality is high without any distortion. Bold, italic, underline, and strikeouts are synthesized as necessary.

lfPitchAndFamily	Font families are used when an exact typeface is not available; you can specify the look of a font rather than a specific font. The lfPitchAndFamily value is set by ORing a pitch constant with a family constant.
	Defined pitch constants are listed here:
	DEFAULT_PITCH
	FIXED_PITCH
	VARIABLE_PITCH

LOGFONT Field	Purpose	
	Defined font family constants are listed here:	
	FF_DECORATIVE	Novelty fonts such as Old English.
	FF_DONTCARE	Don't care or don't know.
	FF_MODERN	Fixed-pitch fonts (constant character width), with or without serifs such as Pica, Elite, or CourierNew.
	FF_ROMAN	Proportionally spaced fonts (variable character widths) with serifs such as Times New Roman.
	FF_SCRIPT	Fonts resembling handwriting such as Script or Cursive.
	FF_SWISS	Proportionally spaced fonts (variable character widths) without serifs such as Arial.
lfFaceName	Points to a NULL-terminated string of 32 characters or less that specifies the font name. If lfFaceName is NULL, a default typeface is used.	

> Note: As an alternative to the Font dialog box, you can call the ::EnumFonts function to retrieve a list of the typeface names of all currently available fonts and allow your application to select a font from the list.

Initializing the *LOGFONT* Structure

In the FontDlg application, the logFont variable is initialized in the view class constructor as follows:

```
CFontdlgView::CFontdlgView()
{
   // TODO: add construction code here
   //=== initialize font specification
   logFont.lfHeight        = 24;
   logFont.lfWidth         = 0;
   logFont.lfEscapement    = 0;
   logFont.lfOrientation   = 0;
   logFont.lfWeight        = 400;
   logFont.lfItalic        = FALSE;
   logFont.lfUnderline     = FALSE;
   logFont.lfStrikeOut     = FALSE;
   logFont.lfCharSet       = ANSI_CHARSET;
   logFont.lfOutPrecision  = OUT_DEFAULT_PRECIS;
   logFont.lfClipPrecision = CLIP_DEFAULT_PRECIS;
```

```
logFont.lfQuality       = DEFAULT_QUALITY;
logFont.lfPitchAndFamily = DEFAULT_PITCH | FF_SWISS;
strcpy( logFont.lfFaceName, "Arial" );
//=== default point size to match font spec
nPoints = 180;
//=== default foreground / background colors
rgbColor = 0;
rgbBackColor = 0x00FFFFFF;
}
```

In this example, the salient points in the request are a character height of 24 and the Arial typeface.

> **Note:** A character height of 24 does not mean a 24-point typeface. Requesting a character height of 24 (which includes the interlinear spacing as well as the actual character size) results in the selection of an 18-point font.
>
> To approximate the character height for a desired point size, add roughly 1/3 for the character descenders and interlinear spacing. For example, for a 30-point font, set a height of 40 (remember that this is an approximation and varies with different fonts). Use the point size only when you need to fit a font to a particular vertical spacing.
>
> Otherwise, because the Font dialog box allows you to choose the font by point size rather than height, this discrepancy in sizes shouldn't present a problem.

In addition, because the Arial typeface may or may not be available on a given system, the specification also calls for the ANSI character set and, for the lfPitchAndFamily field, the DEFAULT_PITCH and FF_SWISS values.

Also, the default foreground color is specified as black (0x000000) and the background color as white (0xFFFFFF).

> **Note:** To select other colors, refer to Chapter 13, "Working with Colors, Palettes, and Drawing Modes," for details on how to specify RGB color values.

Choosing a Font

The FontDlg demo application uses an instance of the CFontDialog class to call the Font dialog box. However, before invoking the CFontDialog class instance, we'll use a couple provisions to initialize the Font dialog box. The relevant code appears following:

```
void CFontdlgView::OnFont()
{
   // TODO: Add your command handler code here
   CFontDialog   cfDlg;

   cfDlg.m_cf.lpLogFont = &logFont;
   cfDlg.m_cf.rgbColors = rgbColor;
   cfDlg.m_cf.Flags |= CF_INITTOLOGFONTSTRUCT | CF_EFFECTS;
```

```
   if( cfDlg.DoModal() == IDOK )
   {
      nPoints  = cfDlg.m_cf.iPointSize;
      rgbColor = cfDlg.m_cf.rgbColors;
      Invalidate();
   }
}
```

Before calling the `DoModal` member for the `CFontDialog` instance, the FontDlg `logFont` member (which was initialized in the `CFontDVw` constructor) is assigned to `CFontDialog`'s `m_cf.lpLogFont`. The FontDlg `rgbColor` member (which contains the foreground color) is assigned to the `m_cf.rgbColors` member.

Last but essential, the `CF_INITTOLOGFONTSTRUCT` and `CF_EFFECTS` flags are set by ORing them with the existing `m_cf.Flags` member.

However, because the `m_cf` member of `CFontDialog` is an instance of the `CHOOSEFONT` structure defined in CommDlg.H, why not simply replace the entire `CHOOSEFONT` structure with one of your own?

The answer is that the existing `CHOOSEFONT` structure, `m_cf`, has already been initialized when the `CFontDialog` instance was declared. The `CHOOSEFONT` structure contains fields for which we do not have the appropriate information—unless we extracted these from the `m_cf` member (which would simply be a case of taking a tour of Robin Hood's barn). Instead, it's easier to replace values you want to specify or, in the case of the flags, ORing your flags with the existing flags.

In other circumstances, you may want to replace the flags entirely to remove default flags. In this example, however, that is unnecessary.

If the Font dialog box returns `IDOK`, the color and point size are retrieved from the `m_cf` member. Because the local `logFont` member was assigned by address to the `m_cf` member, `logFont` already contains the returned `CHOOSEFONT` structure and does not require an assignment for retrieval.

Figure 10.2 shows the Font dialog box in operation. The **F**ont, Font St**y**le, and **S**ize list boxes allow you to select a typeface, style, and point size. In the Effects group, the Stri**k**eout and **U**nderline checkboxes are disabled by default and the **C**olor pull-down list box offers a selection of standard colors. The Sample display window shows the chosen font in the size, style, and color selected.

Figure 10.2. The Font dialog box.

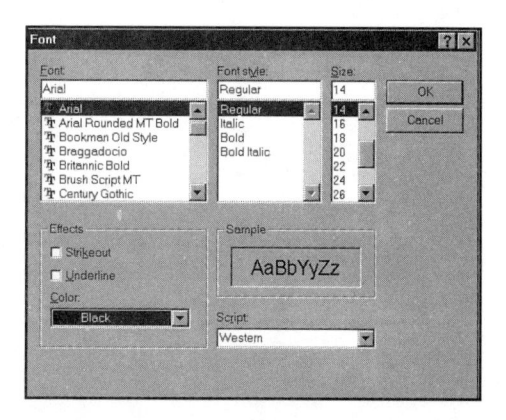

> Note: The WinNT version of the Font dialog box is functionally the same as the Win95 version shown in Figure 10.2 but does differ in appearance.

The Script pull-down list at the bottom of the Font dialog box lists only Western (that is, European) scripts. If you have other fonts such as Japanese Kanji, additional options appear here.

In use, the Font dialog box is simplicity itself. But despite its simplicity, you should be familiar with the CHOOSEFONT structure, which is defined as follows:

```
typedef struct
{   DWORD          lStructSize;
    HWND           hwndOwner;
    HDC            hDC;
    LPLOGFONT      lpLogFont;
    INT            iPointSize;
    DWORD          Flags;
    DWORD          rgbColors;
    DWORD          lCustData;
    LPCFHOOKPROC   lpfnHook;
    LPCTSTR        lpTemplateName;
    HANDLE         hInstance;
    LPTSTR         lpszStyle;
    WORD           nFontType;
    WORD           __MISSING_ALIGNMENT__;
    INT            nSizeMin;
    INT            nSizeMax;    } CHOOSEFONT;
```

The CHOOSEFONT structure contains information the operating system uses to initialize the system-defined Font dialog box. After the Font dialog box closes, the structure returns information about the selections made in the dialog box. The CHOOSEFONT fields and flag values are detailed in Tables 10.3 and 10.4.

Table 10.3. The CHOOSEFONT (m_cf) structure.

Field	Function
lStructSize	The size, in bytes, of the structure.
hwndOwner	The window owning the dialog box; NULL if the dialog box has no owner.
hDC	The printer device or information context whose fonts are listed in the dialog box. Used only if the Flags field specifies CF_PRINTERFONTS; otherwise hDC is ignored.
lpLogFont	Pointer to a LOGFONT structure. If the lpLogFont structure is initialized before calling the ChooseFont function and the CF_INITTOLOGFONTSTRUCT flag is set, the Font dialog box is initialized with the closest possible match.
	After the dialog box closes, the LOGFONT structure is returned with the user's final selection.

Field	Function
iPointSize	Returns the size of the selected font in tenths of a point.
Flags	Initialization flags; *see* Table 10.4.
rgbColors	If the CF_EFFECTS flag is set, rgbColors contains an RGB value specifying the initial text color and returns with the RGB value of the user's color selection.
lCustData	If the CF_ENABLEHOOK flag is set, lCustData provides application-defined data to be passed to the hook function identified by lpfnHook as the lParam argument accompanying the WM_INITDIALOG message.
lpfnHook	If the CF_ENABLEHOOK flag is set, lpfnHook provides a pointer to a hook function that processes dialog box messages.
lpTemplateName	If the CF_ENABLETEMPLATE flag is set, lpTemplateName points to a NULL-terminated string naming the dialog box template to be substituted for the standard dialog box template.
hInstance	If the CF_ENABLETEMPLATE flag is set, hInstance identifies a data block containing the dialog box template specified by lpTemplateName.
lpszStyle	If the CF_USESTYLE flag is set, lpszStyle points to a buffer containing style data used to initialize the style control. Returns the string in the dialog's style control in this buffer.
nFontType	Selected font type; may contain one of the following values: SIMULATED_FONTTYPE — Font simulated by the graphics device interface (GDI). PRINTER_FONTTYPE — Printer font. SCREEN_FONTTYPE — Screen font.
nSizeMin	If the CS_LIMITSIZE flag is set, nSizeMin specifies the minimum point size that can be selected.
nSizeMax	If the CS_LIMITSIZE flag is set, nSizeMax specifies the maximum point size that can be selected.

The Flags member is used during initialization to determine which fields and features are enabled or disabled in the Font dialog box. The available flags are listed in Table 10.4.

Table 10.4. The CHOOSEFONT flags.

Flag	Meaning
CF_APPLY	Enables the Apply button in the Font dialog box.
CF_ANSIONLY	Allows only the fonts using the Windows character set. (Disallows fonts containing only symbols.)

continues

Table 10.4. continued

Flag	Meaning
CF_BOTH	Lists the available printer and screen fonts; the hDC member identifies the device context (or information context) associated with the printer.
CF_TTONLY	Lists only TrueType fonts.
CF_EFFECTS	Enables strikeout, underline, and color effects allowing the lfStrikOut, lfUnderline, and rgbColors members to be set before the Font dialog box is called.
CF_ENABLEHOOK	Enables the hook function specified in lpfnHook.
CF_ENABLETEMPLATE	Indicates that hInstance identifies a data block containing a dialog box template identified by lpTemplateName.
CF_ENABLETEMPLATEHANDLE	Indicates that hInstance identifies a data block containing a preloaded dialog box template (lpTemplateName is ignored).
CF_FIXEDPITCHONLY	Only fixed-pitch fonts can be selected.
CF_FORCEFONTEXIST	Reports an error condition if a nonexistent font or style is selected.
CF_INITTOLOGFONTSTRUCT	Uses the LOGFONT structure indicated by lpLogFont to initialize the dialog box controls.
CF_LIMITSIZE	Limits font size selection to the range specified by nSizeMin and nSizeMax.
CF_NOOEMFONTS	OEM font selections are not allowed (*see* CF_NOVECTORFONTS).
CF_NOFACESEL	Disables an initial face name selection (usually because no single face name applies).
CF_NOSTYLESEL	Disables an initial style selection (usually because no single style applies).
CF_NOSIZESEL	Disables an initial size selection (usually because no single size applies).
CF_NOSIMULATIONS	Disables graphics device interface (GDI) font simulation selection.
CF_NOVECTORFONTS	Vector font selections are not allowed (*see* CF_NOOEMFONTS).
CF_PRINTERFONTS	Lists only the fonts supported by the printer associated with the device context (or information context) identified by the hDC member.
CF_SCALABLEONLY	Allows selection only of scalable fonts (includes vector fonts, scalable printer fonts, TrueType fonts, and fonts scaled by other technologies).
CF_SCREENFONTS	Lists only the screen fonts supported by the system.
CF_SHOWHELP	If set, the dialog box shows a Help button. *Note:* The hwndOwner member must not be NULL.
CF_USESTYLE	The lpszStyle member points to a buffer containing style data used to initialize the Font Style selection. Style data for the selection is returned in this buffer.

Flag	Meaning
CF_WYSIWYG	Allows selection only of fonts available on both the printer and the display. Should be set in combination with the CF_BOTH and CF_SCALABLEONLY flags.

> ### Customizing Common Dialog Boxes
>
> Common dialog boxes can be customized by combining existing common dialog handling provisions with your own custom dialog box template. Using the Font dialog box as an example, you can set CF_ENABLETEMPLATE or CF_ENABLETEMPLATEHANDLE together with the lpTemplateName and hInstance fields. In this fashion, you can redesign the appearance of the dialog box without re-creating the functional code provisions. You must, however, ensure that you include all the appropriate fields of the original dialog box along with the same ID names.
>
> Although this procedure is not for the faint hearted, all common dialog boxes can be "rewritten" in this fashion.

Selecting Colors

Invoking the Color dialog box brings up an array of 48 palette entries plus 16 (blank) custom color entries. A color selection can be made from the defined palette entries (refer to the left side of Figure 10.3) by clicking any entry. In the Win95 version of the dialog box shown in the figure, the selected entry is indicated by a 3D border; in the WinNT version of the dialog box, the selected color is indicated by a border surrounding the selection.

Figure 10.3. *The expanded Color dialog box.*

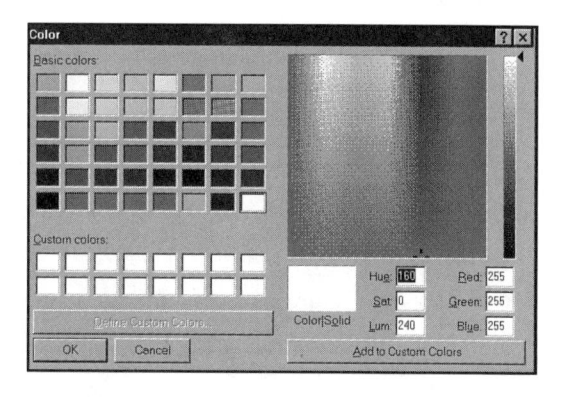

> Note: The WinNT version of the Color dialog box is functionally the same as the Win95 version shown in Figure 10.3 but does differ in appearance.

The **D**efine Custom Colors button under the palette array expands the Color dialog box to show the customization controls shown on the right side of Figure 10.3.

Notice the Color|S**o**lid box, which shows each palette or custom color in two forms: the actual (fill) color on the left and the equivalent color used for solids (such as text background) on the right. Although the two values are often the same, they may not always match.

Before invoking the Color dialog box, the `rgbResult` field in the `m_cc` member variable is loaded with the current background color; the existing `Flags` field is ORed with the `CC_RGBINIT` flag to ensure that the Color dialog box is correctly initialized. The `m_cc` member (a `CHOOSECOLOR` structure) is detailed later in this section. The following code fragment from FontdVw.CPP shows the initialization of the Color dialog box:

```
void CFontdlgView::OnColor()
{
    // TODO: Add your command handler code here
    CColorDialog ccDlg;

    ccDlg.m_cc.rgbResult = rgbBackColor;
    ccDlg.m_cc.Flags |= CC_RGBINIT;
    if( ccDlg.DoModal() == IDOK )
    {
        rgbBackColor = ccDlg.GetColor();
        Invalidate();
    }
}
```

Assuming that the Color dialog box returns an `IDOK` value, the `GetColor()` member function is called to retrieve the RGB value selected in the dialog box.

The Color dialog box is easily invoked and easily used. The preceding code fragment demonstrated only one of the possibilities—the `CHOOSECOLOR` structure and its member are worth a moment's review.

The `CHOOSECOLOR` structure is defined in CommDlg.H as follows:

```
typedef struct
{   DWORD           lStructSize;
    HWND            hwndOwner;
    HWND            hInstance;
    DWORD           rgbResult;
    LPDWORD         lpCustColors;
    DWORD           Flags;
    DWORD           lCustData;
    LPCCHOOKPROC    lpfnHook;
    LPCTSTR         lpTemplateName;   } CHOOSECOLOR;
```

The `CHOOSECOLOR` structure contains information used to initialize the Color dialog box. After the Color dialog box closes, the structure returns information about selections made in the dialog box. The `CHOOSECOLOR` fields are detailed in Table 10.5.

Chapter 10 • Using Common Dialog Boxes, Fonts, and Colors

Table 10.5. The CHOOSECOLOR (m_cc) structure.

Field	Purpose
lStructSize	The size, in bytes, of the structure.
hwndOwner	The window owning the dialog box; NULL if the dialog box has no owner.
hInstance	If the CF_ENABLETEMPLATE flag is set, hInstance identifies a data block containing the dialog box template specified by lpstrTemplateName.
rgbResult	The RGB color value used to initialize the Color dialog box selection and to return the selection when the Color dialog box closes. If the CC_RGBINIT flag is set and the rgbResult value does not match the available colors, the nearest matching solid color is selected. If rgbResult is NULL, the initial color selection is black.
lpCustColors	A pointer to an array of 16 DWORD values containing RGB values for the custom color boxes in the Color dialog box. Values in the array are updated as changes to custom colors are made in the dialog box.
Flags	Initialization flags; may be a combination of the following:
	CC_ENABLEHOOK — Enables the hook function specified by lpfnHook.
	CC_ENABLETEMPLATE — Indicates that hInstance identifies a data block containing a dialog box template identified by lpTemplateName.
	CC_ENABLETEMPLATEHANDLE — Indicates that hInstance identifies a data block containing a preloaded dialog box template (lpTemplateName is ignored).
	CC_FULLOPEN — Causes the entire dialog box, including the portion used to create custom colors, to appear when the dialog box is opened.
	CC_PREVENTFULLOPEN — Disables the Define Custom Colors button, blocking the creation of custom colors.
	CC_RGBINIT — Identifies the rgbResult member as the initial color selection.
	CC_SHOWHELP — If set, the dialog box shows a Help button. *Note:* The hwndOwner member must not be NULL.
lCustData	If the CC_ENABLEHOOK flag is set, lCustData provides application-defined data to be passed to the hook function identified by lpfnHook as the lParam argument accompanying the WM_INITDIALOG message.

continues

Table 10.5. continued

Field	Purpose
lpfnHook	If the CC_ENABLEHOOK flag is set, lpfnHook provides a pointer to a hook function that processes dialog box messages.
lpTemplateName	If the CC_ENABLETEMPLATE flag is set, lpTemplateName points to a NULL-terminated string naming the dialog box template to be substituted for the standard dialog box template.

Although information can be entered and retrieved directly from the CColorDialog m_cc (CHOOSECOLOR) member, three useful member functions are also provided:

Function	Description
GetColor	Returns the RGB value for the selected color.
GetSavedCustomColors	Retrieves the array of custom colors defined in the Color dialog box.
SetCurrentColor	Sets the current color selection to the color specified.

Using the File Open, Save, and Save As Dialog Boxes

The CFileDialog class provides a standard dialog box for opening or saving files or for any other operation requiring a path, filename, or extension (see Figure 10.4). A CFileDialog dialog box is customized by setting or modifying values in the m_ofn structure (refer to "The OPENFILENAME Structure," later in this chapter) before calling the DoModal function to display the dialog box.

Figure 10.4. The File Open common dialog box (Win95 version).

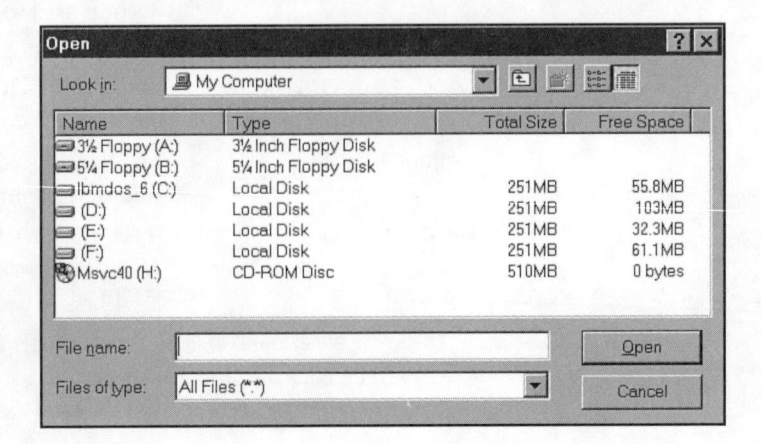

On exit, the `CFileDialog` dialog box returns either `IDOK` or `IDCANCEL`, depending on the button selected by the user. If the user selects the Cancel button, no further action is appropriate. If the user selects the OK button, the following member functions can be used to return information from the dialog box:

Member Function	Purpose
GetPathName[1]	Returns the fully qualified path for a selected file, including the drive, path, filename, and extension.
GetFileName	Returns only the filename for a selected file; does not include the path or file extension.
GetFileExt	Returns only the file extension for a selected file; does not include path or filename information.
GetFileTitle	Returns the complete title—both filename and extension—for a selected file.
GetReadOnlyPref	Returns TRUE if the ReadOnly checkbox (in the File Open and File Save As dialog boxes) is checked.

Three overridable member functions are also defined as follows. These member functions are normally handled by the `CFileDialog` class but may be overridden to provide custom application handing. Refer to Visual C++'s Books Online for details.

Member Function	Purpose
OnShareViolation	Notification that a share violation has occurred.
OnFileNameOK	Request from the dialog box to validate the filename entry.
OnLBSelChangedNotify	Notification that the list box selection has changed.

The *OPENFILENAME* Structure

The `OPENFILENAME` structure provides the `m_ofn` data member for the `CFileOpen` object class. `OPENFILENAME` is defined in CommDlg.H as follows:

```
typedef struct _OFN   // ofn
{   DWORD         lStructSize;         HWND      hwndOwner;
    HINSTANCE     hInstance;           LPCTSTR   lpstrFilter;
    LPTSTR        lpstrCustomFilter;   DWORD     nMaxCustFilter;
    DWORD         nFilterIndex;        LPTSTR    lpstrFile;
    DWORD         nMaxFile;            LPTSTR    lpstrFileTitle;
    DWORD         nMaxFileTitle;       LPCTSTR   lpstrInitialDir;
    LPCTSTR       lpstrTitle;          DWORD     Flags;
    WORD          nFileOffset;         WORD      nFileExtension;
    LPCTSTR       lpstrDefExt;         DWORD     lCustData;
```

---

[1] If the `OFN_ALLOWMULTISELECT` flag is set, this function applies only to the first file item.

```
    LPOFNHOOKPROC lpfnHook;            LPCTSTR lpTemplateName;
} OPENFILENAME;
```

The information contained in the OPENFILENAME structure is used to initialize the system-defined Open or Save As dialog boxes and to return information about the user's selections after the dialog boxes close.

The OPENFILENAME structure members are detailed in Table 10.6.

Table 10.6. OPENFILENAME structure members.

Member	Purpose
lStructSize	The size, in bytes, of the OPENFILENAME structure.
hwndOwner	The handle of the window owning the dialog box; NULL if there is no owner.
hInstance	If the OFN_ENABLETEMPLATE flag is set, hInstance identifies the data block containing the dialog block template identified by lpTemplateName.
lpstrFilter	A pointer to the buffer holding NULL-terminated filter strings; refer to "Filter Strings," later in this chapter.
lpstrCustomFilter	A pointer to the buffer holding user-defined filter strings; refer to "Filter Strings," later in this chapter.
nMaxCustFilter	The size, in characters, of the lpstrCustomFilter buffer. Must be a minimum of 40 characters. This field is ignored if lpstrCustomFilter is NULL or points to a NULL string.
nFilterIndex	An index into the lpstrFilter buffer; refer to "Filter Strings," later in this chapter.
lpstrFile	A pointer to a buffer containing a filename used to initialize the File Name edit control. For MFC applications, buffer space is allocated by the CFileOpen object class.
nMaxFile	The size, in characters, of the lpstrFile buffer (supplied by CFileOpen).
lpstrFileTitle	A pointer to a buffer receiving the title of the selected file.
nMaxFileTitle	The size, in characters, of the lpstrFileTitle buffer (supplied by CFileOpen).
lpstrInitialDir	A pointer to a string specifying the initial file directory; if NULL, the current directory is used.
lpstrTitle	A pointer to a string for the dialog box title bar; if NULL, the default title Open or Save As is used.

Member	Purpose
nFileOffset	The zero-based offset in the `lpstrFile` buffer to the initial character in the filename. For example, for a path/filename of `c:\dirpath1\dirpath2\filename.ext`, the offset value is 21.
nFileExtension	The zero-based offset in the `lpstrFile` buffer to the initial character in the filename extension. For example, for a path/filename of `c:\dirpath1\dirpath2\filename.ext`, the offset value is 30. If `lpstrDefExt` is NULL and no extension has been supplied, the offset indicates the terminating NULL character. If a wildcard (*.*) is entered for the filename and extension, the offset returns zero.
lpstrDefExt	A pointer to a string containing a default extension; if no extension is supplied, the default extension is appended to the filename. The string pointed to by `lpstrDefExt` may be any length but must not contain a period. Only the first three characters are appended. If `lpstrDefExt` is NULL and no user-supplied extension is provided, no extension is appended.
lCustData	Application-defined data passed to the hook function identified by `lpfnHook` is passed in the `lParam` argument of the `WM_INITDIALOG` message.
lpfnHook	If the `OFN_ENABLEHOOK` flag is set, `lpfnHook` contains a pointer to the hook function that processes dialog box messages.
lpTemplateName	If the `OFN_ENABLETEMPLATE` flag is set, `lpTemplateName` contains a pointer to a NULL-terminated string that names the dialog template to replace the standard dialog box.
Flags	Dialog creation flags; may be a combination of the flags listed in Table 10.7.

Table 10.7. OPENFILENAME structure flags.

Member	Purpose
OFN_ALLOWMULTISELECT	If set, multiple file selections are allowed. (If a custom dialog box template is used, the File Name list box must be created with `LBS_EXTENDEDSEL`.)
OFN_CREATEPROMPT	If set, the dialog box prompts the user before creating a file that does not exist. (Automatically uses the `OFN_PATHMUSTEXIST` and `OFN_FILEMUSTEXIST` flags.)

continues

Table 10.7. continued

Member	Purpose
OFN_ENABLEHOOK	If set, enables the hook function specified in the lpfnHook member.
OFN_ENABLETEMPLATE	If set, the dialog box is created using the template identified by the hInstance and lpTemplateName members.
OFN_ENABLETEMPLATE	If set, the hInstance member identifies HANDLE (a data block containing a preloaded dialog box template); the lpTemplateName member is ignored.
OFN_EXTENSIONDIFFERENT	If set, reports that the user has entered a filename extension that does not match the extension specified by lpstrDefExt. If lpstrDefExt is NULL, this flag is not used.
OFN_FILEMUSTEXIST	If set, the user is limited to existing filenames only (no new files can be created). If an invalid filename is entered, a warning message is displayed. If set, the OFN_PATHMUSTEXIST flag is also set automatically.
OFN_HIDEREADONLY	If set, the Read Only checkbox is hidden.
OFN_NOCHANGEDIR	If set, the current directory is restored to the active directory when the dialog box was called.
OFN_NONETWORKBUTTON	If set, the Network button is disabled and hidden.
OFN_NOREADONLYRETURN	If set, reports that the returned file does not have the Read Only flag set and is not in a write-protected directory.
OFN_NOTESTFILECREATE	If set, specifies that the file cannot be created before the dialog box closes. This flag is used when a file is saved on a create-nonmodify network sharepoint. When set by the application, the library does not check for write protection, full disk, open drive door, or network protection. Applications using this flag must perform file operations carefully because the file cannot be reopened once it is closed.
OFN_NOVALIDATE	If set, indicates that invalid characters are allowed in the returned filename.
OFN_OVERWRITEPROMPT	If set, the Save As dialog box requests confirmation before overwriting an existing file.
OFN_PATHMUSTEXIST	If set, allows the user to enter only valid paths and filenames. If an invalid path or filename is entered in the File Name entry field, a warning message box is displayed.
OFN_READONLY	If set on creation, checks the Read Only checkbox. Returns the state of the Read Only checkbox when the dialog box closes.
OFN_SHAREAWARE	If set, network sharing violations on file opens are ignored and the dialog box returns the given filename.

Member	Purpose
	If not set, the registered message for SHAREVISTRING is sent to the hook function with a pointer to a NULL-terminated string for the path and filename in the lParam parameter.
	The hook function responds with one of the following flags:
OFN_SHAREFALLTHROUGH	If set, the filename is returned by the dialog box.
OFN_SHARENOWARN	If set, no further action is taken.
OFN_SHAREWARN	If set, the standard warning message for this error is returned (as if there were no hook function).
OFN_SHOWHELP	If set, the dialog box displays the Help button; the hwndOwner member must not be NULL.

Filter Strings

The lpstrFilter member points to a buffer containing pairs of NULL-terminated filter strings with the last string in the buffer terminated by two NULL characters.

The first string in each pair describes a filter (such as *Text Files* or *Bitmap Images*); the second string specifies the filter pattern (such as *.TXT* or *.BMP*). If multiple filters are desired (such as *All Images*), individual filters can be separated in a single string by semicolons: *.BMP;*.PCX;*.GIF*.

The first string in each pair is the file type description and is listed in the List Files of Type popup list box. When a selection is made from this list, the corresponding filter pattern is applied to select the files displayed in the File Name list box.

The File dialog box assumes that the filter strings are in the order desired; no sorting is applied. If lpstrFilter is NULL, no filters are displayed and the user must supply his or her own filter specification.

The nFilterIndex member provides an index value to select the initial filter description and filter pattern from those defined in lpstrFilter with the first entry indexed at 1 (not 0). On return, nFilterIndex contains an index to the user-selected filter string pair.

If nFilterIndex is zero, the custom filter defined in lpstrCustomFilter is used.

The lpstrCustomFilter member contains a custom filter defined by the user; lpstrCustomFilter returns this value to initialize the file filter the next time the file dialog box is called. If lpstrCustomFilter is NULL, the dialog box lists user-defined filter strings but does not save them.

Multiple File Selection

To allow the selection of multiple files from the File dialog lists, set the OFN_ALLOW_MULTISELECT flag before calling DoModal and replace the m_ofn.lpstrFile member with a pointer to an application-defined and allocated buffer large enough to contain the selections.

Using the Print Dialog Box

When the OnPrint method is invoked, MFC supplies two parameters: a pointer to a device context (the printer or printer context) and a pointer to a CPrintInfo object that contains information about the print job. The CPrintInfo object is created when the Print or Print Preview command is invoked; it is destroyed when the task is completed. The CPrintInfo object is used during the printing process to exchange information between the application framework and the view class.

The CPrintInfo object contains data about the print job, including the range of pages to be printed and the current status of the print job. The CPrintInfo object also contains information from the CPrintDialog dialog box, which is invoked when the Print or Print Preview menu command is selected; this information includes the beginning and ending page numbers to be printed (see Figure 10.5).

Figure 10.5. The Print common dialog box.

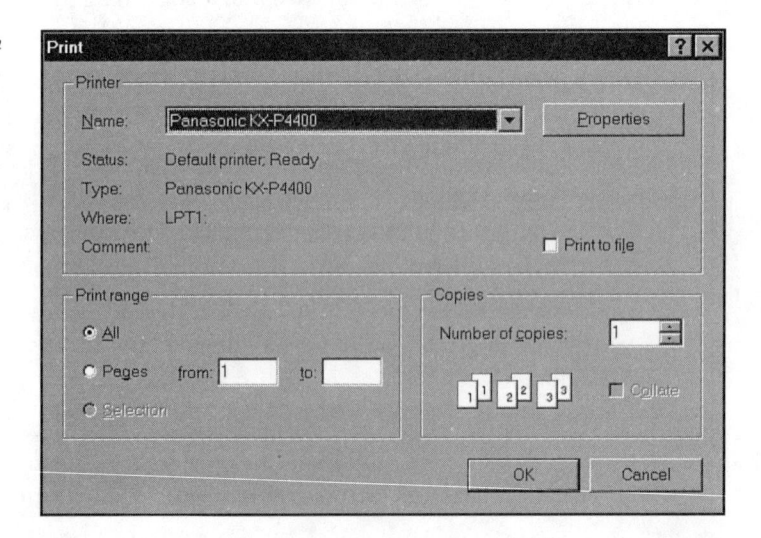

In operation, the framework assigns a page to the m_nCurPage member of CPrintInfo to tell the view class which document page must be drawn. In turn, the view class retrieves the m_nCurPage value to perform the actual printing by drawing the specified page.

When the document length is undetermined, the view class can test for the end of the document as each page is processed; when the end is reached, the view class can set m_bContinuePrinting member to FALSE to instruct the frame class to terminate the print loop.

Table 10.8 shows the member variables and methods for the CPrintInfo class. Additional details are available in Visual C++'s online help.

Table 10.8. The CPrintInfo class.

Member	Comments
m_pPD	A pointer to the CPrintDialog object used for the Print dialog box.
m_bPreview	If TRUE, the document is being previewed.
m_bContinuePrinting	If TRUE, the framework should continue the print loop until the job is completed.
m_nCurPage	The number of the page currently being printed.
m_nNumPreviewPages	The number of pages in the preview window (1 or 2).
m_lpUserData	A pointer to a user-created structure used to store printing data outside of the view class.
m_rectDraw	The rectangle defining the current usable page area in logical coordinates; used to track the remaining usable area after printing headers, footers, and so on.
m_strPageDesc	The format string used to display page numbers during print preview. Consists of two substrings, each terminated by a \n character, for single and double page display. Has the following default format string: Page %u\nPages %u-%u\n.
SetMinPage	Sets the page number for the first page of the document.
SetMaxPage	Sets the page number of the last page of the document; if the document length is not known until printing is finished, set the m_bContinuePrinting member to control the print loop.
GetMinPage	Retrieves the number of the first page of the document.
GetMaxPage	Retrieves the number of the last page of the document.
GetFromPage	Retrieves the page number specified in the Print dialog box for the first page to be printed. If nothing is specified, the default is the first page of the document.
GetToPage	Retrieves the page number specified in the Print dialog for the last page to be printed. If nothing is specified, the default is the last page of the document.

Using the Find and Find/Replace Dialog Boxes

The `CFindReplaceDialog` class provides a standard dialog box for both search and search-and-replace operations (see Figure 10.6). Because the Find and Find/Replace dialog boxes are modeless (unlike other common dialog boxes), other operations can be handled without first closing the Find or Find/Replace dialog boxes.

Figure 10.6. The Find/Replace common dialog box (Win95 version).

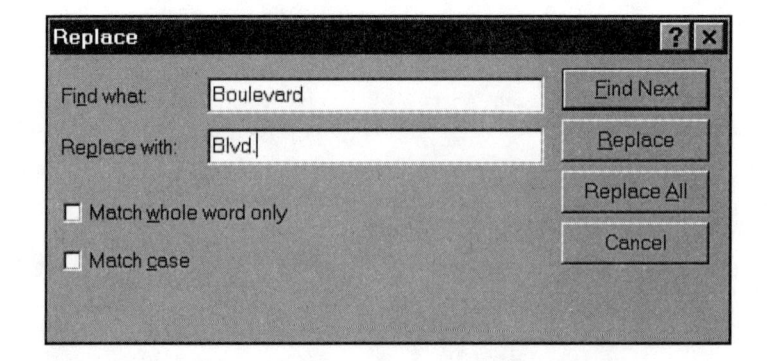

The Find and Find/Replace dialog boxes do not execute find or find/replace operations; they provide a standard interface for users to specify search and replace strings, search directions, and other options. The actual search or replace operations are carried out by the application itself in response to the dialog box selections.

The `CFindReplaceDialog` class instance is invoked in the usual fashion: by calling the constructor. It requires no arguments. It is then initialized through the `m_fr` member, which is an instance of the `FINDREPLACE` structure detailed later in this section.

The `Create` member function is then called to create and display the dialog box and to select either the Find or the Replace dialog box format.

The `CFindReplaceDialog::Create` function is called as follows:

```
BOOL Create( BOOL     bFindDialogOnly,
             LPCTSTR  lpszFindWhat,       LPCTSTR lpszReplaceWith = NULL,
             DWORD    dwFlags = FR_DOWN, CWnd * pParentWnd = NULL );
```

The following chart details the parameters in the `CFindReplaceDialog::Create` function.

Parameter	Purpose
`bFindDialogOnly`	If TRUE, displays the Find dialog box; if FALSE, displays the Find/Replace dialog box.
`lpszFindWhat`	Pointer to the initial search string. May be a `CString` parameter.

Parameter	Purpose
lpszReplaceWith	Pointer to the initial replacement string. May be a `CString` parameter.
dwFlags	Flags used to customize the dialog box settings; refer to Table 10.10, which lists the `FINDREPLACE` structure flags.
pParentWnd	A pointer to the dialog box's parent or owner window that receives the special messages indicating whether find or replace actions are requested. If NULL, the application's main window is assumed.

To have the parent window (normally the frame window) notified of find/replace requests, the Windows `RegisterMessage` function is called. In addition, the `ON_REGISTERED_MESSAGE` message map macro is included in the window class that will handle the registered message.

For subsequent operations, call the following member functions from the frame window's callback function.

> Note: In addition to the following member functions, the `CFindReplaceDialog m_fr` member (an instance of the `FINDREPLACE` structure, detailed later in this section) can also be used to initialize the Find or Find/Replace dialog box.

Operation	Purpose
FindNext	Call this function to determine whether or not the user wants to find the next occurrence of the find string.
GetNotifier	Retrieves the `FINDREPLACE` structure in the registered message handler.
GetFindString	Retrieves the current find string.
GetReplaceString	Retrieves the current replace string.
IsTerminating	If TRUE, the user has requested termination.
MatchCase	If TRUE, the search operation must match the case of the find string.
MatchWholeWord	If TRUE, the search operation must match entire words only.
ReplaceAll	If TRUE, all occurrences of the search string should be replaced.
ReplaceCurrent	If TRUE, the current occurrence of the search string should be replaced.
SearchDown	If TRUE, the search is executed from the current position to the end of the file. If FALSE, the search is executed from the current position to the beginning of the file.

The FINDREPLACE structure (the `m_fr` member) holds information used to initialize the system-defined Find and Replace dialog boxes and to return information about selections made by the user in these dialog boxes. The FINDREPLACE structure is defined as follows:

```
typedef struct      // fr
{   DWORD          lStructSize;
    HWND           hwndOwner;
    HINSTANCE      hInstance;
    DWORD          Flags;
    LPTSTR         lpstrFindWhat;
    LPTSTR         lpstrReplaceWith;
    WORD           wFindWhatLen;
    WORD           wReplaceWithLen;
    LPARAM         lCustData;
    LPFRHOOKPROC   lpfnHook;
    LPCTSTR        lpstrTemplateName;
} FINDREPLACE;
```

Table 10.9 lists the members in the FINDREPLACE structure.

Table 10.9. FINDREPLACE structure members.

Member	Comments
lStructSize	The size, in bytes, of the FINDREPLACE structure.
hwndOwner	The handle of the window owning the dialog box; may be any valid window handle but may not be NULL.
hInstance	If the FR_ENABLETEMPLATE flag is set, hInstance identifies the data block containing the dialog template specified by the lpstrTemplateName member.
lpstrFindWhat	A pointer to the string or character array to search for. The application must allocate a buffer for the string with a minimum size of 80 characters.
	If a string is specified in lpstrFindWhat when the dialog box is initialized, the string appears in the Find What edit box.
lpstrReplaceWith	For the ReplaceText function, a pointer to the string or character array used for replacement. This field is ignored by the FindText function.
wFindWhatLen	The length, in bytes, of the buffer pointed to by lpstrFindWhat.
wReplaceWithLen	The length, in bytes, of the buffer pointed to by lpstrReplaceWith.
lCustData	Specifies application-defined data that the system passes to the hook function identified by the lpfnHook member. The system passes the data in the lParam parameter of the WM_INITDIALOG message.

Member	Comments
lpfnHook	Points to a hook function that processes messages intended for the dialog box. An application must specify the FR_ENABLEHOOK flag in the Flags member to enable the function; otherwise, the system ignores this member. The hook function should return FALSE to pass a message on to the standard dialog box procedure or TRUE to discard the message.
lpstrTemplateName	Points to a NULL-terminated string that names the dialog box template resource to be substituted for the standard dialog box template. An application can use the MAKEINTRESOURCE macro for numbered dialog box resources. This member is used only if the Flags member specifies the FR_ENABLETEMPLATE flag; otherwise, this member is ignored.
Flags	Dialog setting and initialization flags; may be a combination of the flags listed in Table 10.10.

Table 10.10. FINDREPLACE structure flags.

Flag	Comments
FR_DIALOGTERM	If set, indicates that the dialog box is closing and that the window handle returned by the FindText or ReplaceText function is not valid.
FR_DOWN	If set, a document is searched from the current position to the end of the document. If cleared, the search is from the current position to the first of the document. Corresponds to the dialog box's Up/Down controls.
FR_FINDNEXT	If set, the application should search for the next occurrence of the lpstrFindWhat string.
FR_MATCHCASE	Indicates case-sensitive searches.
FR_REPLACE	If set, the application should search for and replace only the next occurrence of the lpstrFindWhat string with the lpstrReplaceWith string.
FR_REPLACEALL	If set, the application should search for and replace all occurrences of the lpstrFindWhat string with the lpstrReplaceWith string.
FR_WHOLEWORD	Sets the Whole Word checkbox. If TRUE, only whole words matching the search string are considered.

The flags listed in Table 10.11 are used only during initialization of the dialog box and do not have any subsequent meaning.

Table 10.11. `FINDREPLACE` structure initialization flags.

Flag	Comments
FR_ENABLETEMPLATE	If set, the dialog box template identified by the `hInstance` and `lpTemplateName` members is used to create the dialog box.
FR_ENABLETEMPLATEHANDLE	If set, the `hInstance` member identifies a data block containing a preloaded dialog box template; the `lpTemplateName` member is ignored.
FR_ENABLEHOOK	If set, the hook function specified in `lpfnHook` is enabled.
FR_HIDEMATCHCASE	If set, hides the Match Case checkbox.
FR_HIDEUPDOWN	If set, hides the Direction checkbox and the Up and Down radio buttons.
FR_HIDEWHOLEWORD	If set, hides the Whole Word checkbox.
FR_NOMATCHCASE	Disables the Match Case checkbox.
FR_NOUPDOWN	Disables the direction radio buttons.
FR_NOWHOLEWORD	Disables the Whole Word checkbox.
FR_SHOWHELP	Enables (displays) the Help button; if set, the `hwndOwner` member must not be NULL.

> Note: The `CFindReplaceDialog` class relies on the COMMDLG.DLL library shipped with Windows 3.1 and Windows NT or the COMDLG32.DLL library shipped with Windows 95.

The Find or Find/Replace dialog box can be customized by deriving a class from the `CFindReplaceDialog` and providing a custom dialog template and a message map to process notification messages from the dialog box controls. All unprocessed messages should be sent to the base class for processing.

Summary

This chapter discussed the Windows common dialog boxes and covered a range of territory. It described not only the common dialog boxes themselves and the data structures used for each but also their MFC class equivalents and how they can be initialized on entry. Notes on how these elements can be customized were given.

The common dialog boxes include the Font and Colors dialog boxes, the File dialog boxes used for Open, Save, and Save As operations, the Print dialog box, and the Find and Find/Replace dialog boxes.

Several of these (especially the Print, File, Find and Find/Replace dialog boxes) should be familiar because they are common to many applications, including all word processors and the Visual C++ editor.

The Colors and Font dialog boxes are also widely shared but are less common. Fonts are often handled by custom provisions such as pull-down lists on word processor toolbars; colors are not a common selection outside of graphics paint programs (even then, color selection is usually limited to restricted palettes or to custom selections)—which is a pity, considering the color resolutions offered by most of today's systems. (Speaking of colors, as a programmer, you should be planning for tomorrow's display capabilities, not working around yesterday's restrictions.)

In any case, the real importance of the common dialog boxes is that they save you from having to recreate the same utilities over and over. Equally important, common dialog boxes offer users the convenience of familiarity. Use them; they're worth it.

PART III

Graphics Operations

Part III • Graphics Operations

On a number of the earliest personal computers and pre-MS-DOS operating systems, there was no difference between text and graphics modes. All memory was directly addressable and text and pixel graphics could mix without distinction. Later (partially because IBM-design standards save money by limiting expensive video RAM), graphics were relegated to low-resolution 320 × 200 pixels with a choice of four colors from predefined palettes.

Although such limited graphics resolutions didn't last long, the distinction between text and graphics mode remained entirely too long. It wasn't until the introduction of Windows 3.0 that this artificial distinction began to disappear.

Today, in both Windows NT and Windows 95, the old text mode (except as emulated support in the DOS shell) has been firmly retired and all displays are graphic, whether they are used for drawing images or diagrams. Even with most word processors, the graphic displays are used principally for drawing text.

Of course, this is oversimplification. By operating entirely in graphics mode, we have a far greater choice of fonts than the old, hard-wired (PROM-based) text modes and images. Drawings can now be incorporated in documents without distinguishing between text and graphics.

But where there are possibilities, there are also penalties. Unlike the earliest systems in which we wrote our own graphics primitives (remember when drawing a straight line between two screen-coordinate points required writing a special subroutine?), modern systems supply a host of drawing routines. They even delegate some operations to video card-based graphics coprocessors.

To use these graphic services, we have to understand the rules—all the rules. It isn't enough to understand how to draw a line between two points. We must also understand the coordinate systems (the mapping modes) that translate our drawing space to the screen display. In addition, we must understand how colors are defined and how drawing operations interact with existing screen images. And because we have a host of drawing primitives, including functions to create shapes and to fill regions, we must understand these as well.

And then there are image files (BMP bitmaps or some other format), which are written to store images and read display images. None of this is entirely automatic—and all of it is integral to contemporary graphics applications.

In brief, the topic of graphics isn't brief at all. In this part of the book, we cover the territory—if not in total detail, at least in enough detail to provide a sound and comprehensive grounding in all of the basics and in some of the advanced topics.

CHAPTER 11

Understanding Device Capabilities and Mapping Modes

One of the advantages of Windows is that, as a programmer, you do not have to know the capabilities of the system on which your application executes. You do not have to ask users what the graphics resolutions of their systems happen to be, nor do you query for details about the printer type or mouse. Windows (together with the various device drivers) handles these details and provides you with a single *virtual* environment in which programs execute, insulated from the mundane details of the requirements of the system hardware.

On the other hand, there may be many reasons (simple curiosity aside) when you *do* want to know these things. For example, you may want to know how large a screen the user has so that you can scale a presentation appropriately. You may want to know what color capabilities are supported by the video graphics card. Or whether the printer is black and white or supports color. Or even whether the video (or printer) offers special graphics support to speed drawing operations.

After all, given the average user's expectations, we programmers want our applications to perform as quickly and smoothly as possible, right?

Okay, okay...99 percent of the time, it really doesn't matter. We really don't care and have no intention of optimizing our applications for those few users who have relatively limited systems. Besides, if it's important, they can always upgrade, right? But what about that other 1 percent of the time when we really do need to optimize? Or, in other cases, simplify?

At these times, you have to know how to query the system and find out just exactly what the system's limitations and strengths are. This is the whole purpose behind the GetDeviceCaps function.

The *GetDeviceCaps* Function

The GetDeviceCaps function is explained by the DCApp application discussed in this chapter and included on the CD-ROM that accompanies this book. The function offers convenient access to device-specific information relevant to a requested output device. More accurately, the GetDeviceCaps function can access information relevant to a specific device *driver*—the physical devices themselves are mute concerning their capabilities and limitations.

Before querying the GetDeviceCaps API (or the CDC class method of the same name), you must have either a device context (HDC) for the queried device driver or a CDC class instance. However, because you are interested only in information about a device, rather than calling CreateDC for an output device context, it's cleaner to call the CreateIC function, either directly as the Windows API or as the CDC class method, to return a handle to an information context.

The DCApp Demo

The DCApp demo menu contains two pull-down menus. The first, Device, allows selection of either the display device or the printer; the second menu, Capabilities, offers reporting of device capabilities by categories. The various capability categories are discussed later in this chapter together with the flags used to query each.

The *CreateIC* Function

The CreateIC function creates an information context for a requested device. Whether calling the Windows API or the CDC function, the parameters required by the CreateIC function are the same:

```
HDC CreateIC
  { LPCTSTR lpszDriver,           // driver name
    LPCTSTR lpszDevice,           // device name
    LPCTSTR lpszOutput,           // port or file name
    CONST DEVMODE* lpdvmInit };   // optional initialization data
```

Chapter 11 • Understanding Device Capabilities and Mapping Modes

Parameter	Comments
lpszDriver	Pointer to a null-terminated string (or CString) specifying the name of the device driver such as *Epson* or *DISPLAY* (for system video).
lpszDevice	Pointer to a null-terminated string (or CString) specifying the name of the output device. For a printer, this is the name shown by the Print Manager (such as *HP LaserJet IID*). If the requested device is the system video, this parameter can be ignored.
lpszOutput	Pointer to a null-terminated string (or CString) specifying the file or device name for the physical output medium (file or output port). This parameter is ignored and is provided only for Windows 3.1 compatibility.
lpdvmInit	Optional pointer to a DEVMODE structure holding initialization data for the device driver. Use the DocumentProperties function to fill this structure for a specific device or pass this argument as NULL to use the default initialization (if any) set by the user though the Control Panel.

GetDeviceIC returns a handle for an information context; if the function fails, it returns NULL.

In the DCApp demo, printer-specific data is retrieved from the Printer common dialog box (which was introduced in Chapter 10, "Using Common Dialog Boxes, Fonts, and Colors") to display the capabilities of the printer, plotter, fax, and so on.

To query the video driver settings, you can use an even simpler form of the CreateIC query:

```
hIC = ::CreateIC( "DISPLAY", "", "", NULL );
```

The identifier DISPLAY is all that is required to identify the current video driver and video mode.

Once you retrieve an information device context, the next step is to call the GetDeviceCaps function. The Windows API function is called as follows:

```
nReport = GetDeviceCaps( hIC, nIndex );
```

The GetDeviceCaps function is called with two parameters: the device (or information) context handle and an index identifying the particular device capability being queried.

Alternatively, if you use a CDC instance, the GetDeviceCaps function requires only one parameter: the index argument identifying the queried device capability:

```
nReport = hIC.GetDeviceCaps( nIndex );
```

In this second example, the information context instance already "knows" what the device context is and does not require the additional parameter. Internally, of course, the class version still calls the API function using the first syntax shown above.

Driver Versions and Hardware Types

Two flags are defined that query a device driver to return the driver version number and identify the type of technology used by the device.

Index Flag	Identifies
DRIVERVERSION	The device driver version—the major version number is in the low-order byte; the minor version number is in the high-order byte.
TECHNOLOGY	Device technology—any of the following values:
DT_PLOTTER	Vector plotter
DT_RASDISPLAY	Raster display
DT_RASPRINTER	Raster printer
DT_RASCAMERA	Raster camera
DT_CHARSTREAM	Character stream
DT_METAFILE	Metafile
DT_DISPFILE	Display file

If the TECHNOLOGY query identifies the device context as a metafile, use GetObjectType to determine whether it is an enhanced metafile DC. If it *is* an enhanced metafile, the device technology is the device passed to the CreateEnhMetaFile function.

The driver version number (shown later in this chapter in Figure 11.2) is most likely to be of interest to the hardware manufacturer. This information may be important in other circumstances, particularly if you've written a specialty application that depends on features or capabilities supported by certain models or by specific device drivers.

The device technology can be important in many situations. For example, if you are writing to a plotter rather than a printer, you definitely want to use vector drawing operations and not pixel drawing—and even vector operations are slow. (Of course, plotters are a vanishing breed but are still used for special purposes.)

Video and Printer Resolutions

The flags listed in Table 11.1 are used to query the video and print resolution capabilities of a device.

Table 11.1. Flags used to query video and print resolution.

Index Flag	Identifies
HORZSIZE	Screen (or page) width in millimeters.
VERTSIZE	Screen (or page) height in millimeters.
HORZRES	Width in pixels (screen) or in dots (printer).
VERTRES	Height in pixels (screen) or in dots (printer).
LOGPIXELSX	Pixels (screen) or dots (printer) per logical inch (width).
LOGPIXELSY	Pixels (screen) or dots (printer) per logical inch (height).
ASPECTX	Pixel (or dot) aspect (relative width) on x-axis.
ASPECTY	Pixel (or dot) aspect (relative height) on y-axis.
ASPECTXY	Diagonal pixel (or dot) size.
BITSPIXEL	Color bits per pixel.
PLANES	Number of color planes.
NUMBRUSHES	Number of device-specific brushes.
NUMPENS	Number of device-specific pens.
NUMFONTS	Number of device-specific fonts.
NUMCOLORS	Number of entries in the device's color table.
PDEVICESIZE *	Reserved.
CLIPCAPS *	Boolean flag for device clipping capabilities: a value of 1 means the device can clip to a rectangle.
SIZEPALETTE	Entries in the system palette; valid only if the device driver sets the RC_PALETTE bit in the RASTERCAPS index.
NUMRESERVED	Reserved entries in the system palette; valid only if the device driver sets the RC_PALETTE bit in the RASTERCAPS index.
COLORRES	Actual color resolution of device (bits per pixel); valid only if the device driver sets the RC_PALETTE bit in the RASTERCAPS index.
PHYSICALWIDTH *	(Printer) Physical width in device units; see HORZSIZE.
PHYSICALHEIGHT *	(Printer) Physical height in device units; see VERTSIZE.
PHYSICALOFFSETX *	(Printer) Physical printable area horizontal margin.
PHYSICALOFFSETY *	(Printer) Physical printable area vertical margin.
SCALINGFACTORX *	(Printer) Horizontal scaling factor.
SCALINGFACTORY *	(Printer) Vertical scaling factor.
VREFRESH	(Display only) Device vertical refresh rate in cycles per second (Hz).

continues

Table 11.1. continued

Index Flag	Identifies
DESKTOPHORZRES	(Display only) Width, in pixels, of the virtual desktop; may exceed HORZRES for virtual desktops or multiple displays.
DESKTOPVERTRES	(Display only) Height, in pixels, of the virtual desktop; may exceed VERTRES for virtual desktops or multiple displays.
BLTALIGNMENT	Preferred horizontal drawing alignment in pixels; for optimum drawing performance, all windows should be horizontally aligned on some multiple of this value. Zero indicates an accelerated device (any alignment can be used).

* Not demonstrated in DCApp application.

Flags and Windows

Although flags are used as Boolean indicators (TRUE if set or FALSE if cleared), multiple flags are commonly combined in a single WORD or DWORD value by assigning individual flags to bit positions within the value.

For example, the following chart shows eight flags both in decimal and binary format.

Constant	Value	Binary	Constant	Value	Binary
FLAGONE	1	0000 0001	FLAGFIVE	16	0001 0000
FLAGTWO	2	0000 0010	FLAGSIX	32	0010 0000
FLAGTHREE	4	0000 0100	FLAGSEVEN	64	0100 0000
FLAGFOUR	8	0000 1000	FLAGEIGHT	128	1000 0000

Because these flags are set by bit values, any of these eight flags can be combined—ORed—to create a WORD variable defining a set of flags.

Thus, a WORD value of 37 (0010 0101 in binary) has FLAGONE, FLAGTHREE, and FLAGSIX set and the remaining five flags cleared.

To test an individual flag, AND the WORD value with the flag constant. If the result of this operation is TRUE, the flag is set. If the result is FALSE, the flag is clear.

Most flag constants defined in Windows use this format with related flags grouped together so that a combination of flags can be passed as a single WORD or DWORD parameter.

> In the case of the flags used to query video and printer device resolution (listed in Table 11.1), a total of 31 flags have been defined. This means that a 32-bit value—a DWORD—is required to contain these flags and that the individual flag values are defined as DWORD constants.

Several of these query flags produce overlapping reports. For example, both PHYSICALWIDTH and HORZSIZE return the physical size of a device. Of course, the reported size may or may not be accurate, depending on the nature of the device. For example, if the device is a printer, the driver probably knows the paper size and the printer limitations. On the other hand, if you query the video, the driver knows all about the video card but nothing about the actual monitor used—which could be a 14-inch screen or a 10-foot projector. A bit of caution (and skepticism) is suggested.

To clear up a point of possible confusion: Understand that PLANES is usually 1 but the BITSPIXEL result reports the actual color resolution supported. On some older systems, however, multiple color planes were used; in such cases, the BITSPIXEL result is generally 1. Early color plotters that used pen carousels offer one example of this form.

Figure 11.1 shows the pixel and color capabilities reported for the author's display device. The capabilities reported for your system may differ.

Figure 11.1. *Pixel and color capabilities.*

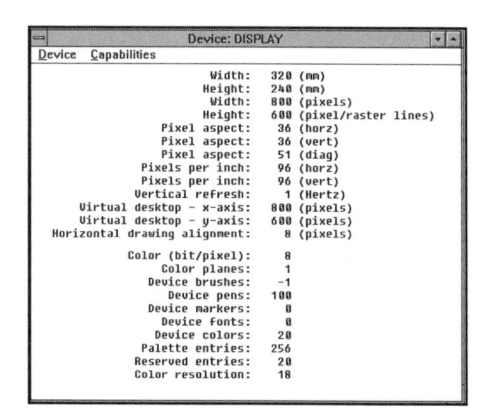

```
                    Device: DISPLAY
 Device  Capabilities
                       Width:   320 (mm)
                      Height:   240 (mm)
                       Width:   800 (pixels)
                      Height:   600 (pixel/raster lines)
                Pixel aspect:    36 (horz)
                Pixel aspect:    36 (vert)
                Pixel aspect:    51 (diag)
              Pixels per inch:   96 (horz)
              Pixels per inch:   96 (vert)
             Vertical refresh:    1 (Hertz)
       Virtual desktop - x-axis: 800 (pixels)
       Virtual desktop - y-axis: 600 (pixels)
   Horizontal drawing alignment:   8 (pixels)
            Color (bit/pixel):    8
                Color planes:     1
              Device brushes:    -1
                 Device pens:   100
              Device markers:     0
                Device Fonts:     0
               Device colors:    20
             Palette entries:   256
            Reserved entries:    20
            Color resolution:    18
```

> **Caution: A Discrepancy in Full Measure**
>
> Although the display characteristics reported by the GetDeviceCaps function are relatively accurate under Windows 3.1 and Windows NT 3.x, the same cannot be said under Windows 95. The following table compares the results reported for physical display characteristics for the same system, video card, and monitor under both WinNT and Win95.

	Display Characteristics According To:	
	WinNT	*Win95*
Screen width	320 mm (12.6 in)	169 mm (6.7 in)
Screen height	240 mm (9.4 in)	127 mm (5.0 in)
Width (pixels)	800	800
Height (pixels)	600	600
Pixels / inch (horizontal)	96	120
Pixels / inch (vertical)	96	120

The results reported under Windows NT are essentially correct for the 15-inch monitor used. Under Windows 95, however, the dimensions reported suggest that the monitor is expected to measure roughly 8.3 inches diagonally.

Interestingly, experiments with the DCApp utility under Windows 95 on a laptop machine with a 640×480 graphics display returned essentially the same results as shown here except that the pixel resolution was reported (correctly) as 96 pixels per inch. The screen height and width, however, were returned with measurements essentially the same as those shown here but were, coincidentally, correct for the portable's LCD display.

The reason for this discrepancy appears to be connected to the Win95 desktop settings at resolutions higher than 640×480 when the Large Fonts option has been selected from the desktop's Display Properties/Settings dialog box. If the standard Small Font option is selected, the display size is reported correctly.

More is said about this discrepancy in Chapter 12, "Working with Mapping Modes."

Caution: At the present time, do not rely too heavily on Windows 95 reporting the physical display characteristics with any reasonable accuracy.

Happily, most of the remaining device characteristics (thus far) appear to be reported with a fair degree of accuracy.

RASTERCAPS

Raster capabilities are pretty basic to video systems and also appear in most printers. For plotters and other vector devices, however, raster capabilities are not generally supported.

The RASTERCAPS query in the DCApp demo reports the device's raster capabilities using the flags listed in Table 11.2.

Table 11.2. Flags used with the RASTERCAPS query.

Index Flag	Meaning
RC_BANDING	Requires banding support.
RC_BITBLT	Supports bitmap transfers.
RC_BITMAP64	Supports bitmaps larger than 64K.
RC_DI_BITMAP	Supports the SetDIBits and GetDIBits functions.
RC_DIBTODEV	Supports the SetDIBitsToDevice function.
RC_FLOODFILL	Supports flood fills.
RC_GDI20_OUTPUT	Supports Windows 2.0 features.
RC_PALETTE	Supports palette-based device.
RC_SCALING	Supports scaling.
RC_STRETCHBLT	Supports the StretchBlt function.
RC_STRETCHDIB	Supports the StretchDIBits function.

Figure 11.2 shows the raster and clipping capabilities reported for the author's display device. The capabilities reported for your system may differ.

Figure 11.2. *Device, technology, and raster capabilities.*

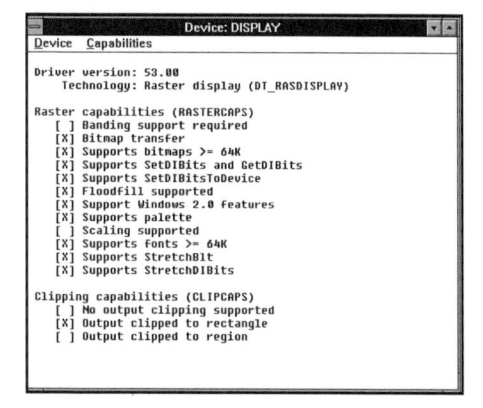

TEXTCAPS

Obviously, you expect all devices to support text capabilities (some of us remember when text was the *only* thing supported). However, in a graphics system, text support means much more than a simple character-based display. You expect to be able to display different fonts in different sizes, to scale them, twist them, and position them with great precision.

The TEXTCAPS query reports the text-support capabilities of a device using the index flags listed in Table 11.3.

Table 11.3. Flags used with the `TEXTCAPS` query.

Index Flag	Feature
`TC_OP_CHARACTER`	Supports character output precision.
`TC_OP_STROKE`	Supports stroke output precision.
`TC_CP_STROKE`	Supports stroke clip precision.
`TC_CR_90`	Supports 90-degree character rotation.
`TC_CR_ANY`	Supports any character rotation.
`TC_SF_X_YINDEP`	Supports independent x and y scaling.
`TC_SA_DOUBLE`	Supports doubled character scaling.
`TC_SA_INTEGER`	Supports only integer multiples for character scaling.
`TC_SA_CONTIN`	Supports any multiples for exact character scaling.
`TC_EA_DOUBLE`	Supports double-weight characters.
`TC_IA_ABLE`	Supports italicized characters.
`TC_UA_ABLE`	Supports underlining.
`TC_SO_ABLE`	Supports strikeouts.
`TC_RA_ABLE`	Supports raster fonts.
`TC_VA_ABLE`	Supports vector fonts.
`TC_RESERVED`	Reserved; must be zero.
`TC_SCROLLBLT`	Cannot scroll using bit-block transfer ***Note:*** Meaning may be the opposite of what is expected.

Figure 11.3 shows the text capabilities reported for the author's display device. The capabilities reported for your system may differ.

Figure 11.3. *Text capabilities.*

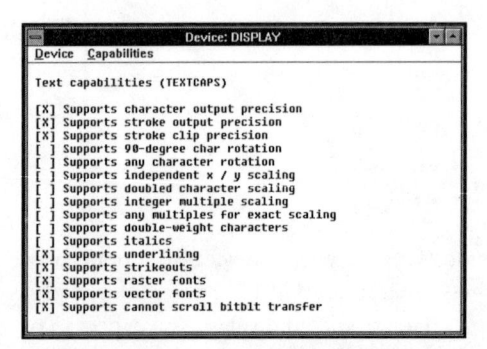

The presence or absence of these support capabilities does not necessarily mean that these features are not supported—only that the device does not provide on-board support for these features. In such cases, the unsupported feature must be handled by the system CPU, a request that is often computation intensive and may drastically slow the system.

LINECAPS

Line-drawing operations are not generally considered computation intensive. (After all, how much processing does it take to draw a line from point A to point B?) If you're familiar with graphic primitives (try writing a few if you're skeptical), you already know that there's more to a line—for a computer—than simple addition. Add styling, wide lines, and markers and you've got a real challenge for your CPU. There are advantages to off-loading the work to a graphics processor.

The LINECAPS query reports the line-drawing capabilities of a device using the flags listed in Table 11.4.

Table 11.4. Flags used with the LINECAPS query.

Index Flag	Features
LC_NONE	Lines not supported.
LC_POLYLINE	Supports polylines.
LC_MARKER	Supports markers.
LC_POLYMARKER	Supports multiple markers.
LC_WIDE	Supports wide lines.
LC_STYLED	Supports styled lines.
LC_WIDESTYLED	Supports both wide and styled lines.
LC_INTERIORS	Supports drawing interiors.

CURVECAPS

Curve capabilities are another excellent example of operations that, if accomplished by the CPU, can be time and computation intensive. Whenever possible, curve operations should be handed by device-supported dedicated graphics processors.

The CURVECAPS query reports the curve-drawing capabilities of a device using the flags listed in Table 11.5.

Table 11.5. Flags used with the CURVECAPS query.

Index Flag	Feature
CC_NONE	Curves not supported.
CC_CIRCLES	Supports circles.
CC_PIE	Supports pie wedges.
CC_CHORD	Supports chord arcs.

continues

Table 11.5. continued

Index Flag	Feature
CC_ELLIPSES	Supports ellipses.
CC_WIDE	Supports wide borders.
CC_STYLED	Supports styled borders.
CC_WIDESTYLED	Supports both wide and styled borders.
CC_INTERIORS	Supports drawing interiors.
CC_ROUNDRECT	Supports rounded rectangles.

Figure 11.4 shows the curve drawing capabilities reported for the author's display device. The capabilities reported for your system may differ.

Figure 11.4. Curve-drawing capabilities.

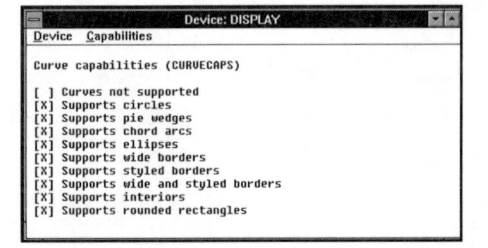

POLYGONALCAPS

Polygons probably fall somewhere between lines and curves in terms of their processing demands. In any case, a good graphics processor can provide a lot of off-loaded support.

The POLYGONALCAPS query reports the polygon-drawing support capabilities of a device using the flags listed in Table 11.6.

Table 11.6. Flags used with the POLYGONALCAPS query.

Index Flag	Feature
PC_NONE	Polygons not supported.
PC_POLYGON	Supports alternate-fill polygons.
PC_RECTANGLE	Supports rectangles.
PC_WINDPOLYGON	Supports winding-fill polygons.
PC_SCANLINE	Supports single scanline.
PC_WIDE	Supports wide borders.

Index Flag	Feature
PC_STYLED	Supports styled borders.
PC_WIDESTYLED	Supports wide and styled borders.
PC_INTERIORS	Supports interiors.

Figure 11.5 shows the polygon drawing capabilities reported for the author's display device. The capabilities reported for your system may differ.

Figure 11.5. *Polygon-drawing capabilities.*

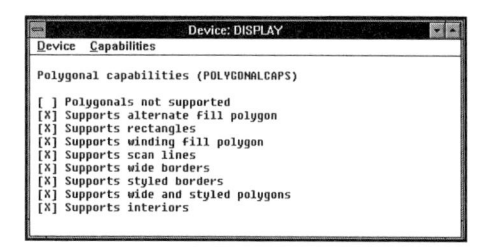

```
                    Device: DISPLAY
 Device  Capabilities

 Polygonal capabilities (POLYGONALCAPS)

 [ ] Polygonals not supported
 [X] Supports alternate fill polygon
 [X] Supports rectangles
 [X] Supports winding fill polygon
 [X] Supports scan lines
 [X] Supports wide borders
 [X] Supports styled borders
 [X] Supports wide and styled polygons
 [X] Supports interiors
```

Summary

Details about device capabilities may be the feature you will use least in your application development. Truth be told, most programmers *never* feel the need to query device capabilities. If you ever do need details about devices, the areas you'll probably want to query are color resolutions and screen sizes. But whatever snippet of information you find yourself needing, knowing that you *can* get this information is invaluable.

Now let's move on to a more interesting subject: Chapter 12, "Working with Mapping Modes," looks at mapping modes and how you can use them to tailor an environment for your application—and do so independently of the actual system hardware and its limitations.

CHAPTER 12

Working with Mapping Modes

In Chapter 11, "Understanding Device Capabilities and Mapping Modes," the point was made that you do not have to be aware of a system's device capabilities before you can use the system. Windows provides a virtual environment in which applications can execute without your worrying about hardware limitations. This statement was, however, a simplification.

The truth is much more complex because the virtual environment provided by Windows is not simply a single uniform environment. It is a very flexible environment you can adjust to fit the needs of an application—rather than fitting an application to the environment.

The virtual environment is, of course, the graphics environment—the display space in which applications communicate with the user (ignore the audio aspects, which are quite a different matter). In line with the adage that a picture is worth a thousand words, we consider graphics our primary avenue of expression—at least, in the computer.

Mapping modes allow you to create a virtual environment that, at any given instant, is scaled to the requirements of your application. What this means, in practical terms, is not the easiest thing to explain but may be easily understood by example.

If you want to draw a graph using time (say, months) on the x-axis and dollars on the y-axis, the usual approach is to calculate horizontal and vertical scales in terms of screen pixels and then draw bars or lines accordingly.

But why not simply create an environment scaled horizontally in months (or in as many horizontal units as you need) and scaled vertically in dollar units? With this approach, you may want a horizontal scale of 12 (for months) and 10,000 vertically (for dollars). You can then draw vertical bars at x=1, x=2, ..., x=12 in however many dollars are appropriate:

```
for( x=1; x<=12; x++ )
{
   MoveTo( x, 1 );
   LineTo( x, nDollars[x] );
}
```

If you did this in pixels, you'd have a graph that is less than a single character in width and which extends from the top of the screen down many dozens of times beyond the bottom of the screen.

If you do this same drawing in a virtual space, where 1 unit horizontal is mapped to perhaps 50 pixels, and where 102,000 vertical units are mapped to 300 pixels, suddenly you have a graph that appears at least reasonable and fits the confines of the screen.

Of course, the graph still starts at the top and extends down; you probably prefer drawing bars from the bottom up. You can fix this by changing the coordinate system and putting the 0,0 origin at the lower left with positive values extending up and right.

This is not, however, a task you have to incorporate in your application. You do not have to "translate" your virtual map to the screen. Instead, change the screen coordinates to anything you want—both in terms of horizontal and vertical scales and in terms of where you want to locate the origin and which directions are positive and negative on each axis.

On the other hand, always having to define a special mapping mode can be a headache. Therefore, Windows offers a selection of standard mapping modes designed to satisfy most common environmental requirements.

Standard Mapping Modes

Windows supplies eight mapping modes, beginning with the default MM_TEXT mode, in which the map and the screen pixels are equivalent.

There are also five stock special-purpose modes: MM_HIENGLISH, MM_HIMETRIC, MM_LOENGLISH, MM_LOMETRIC, and MM_TWIPS. These special-purpose modes are useful for applications that require physically meaningful units (such as inches or millimeters).

The list of modes concludes with the MM_ISOTROPIC and MM_ANISOTROPIC modes, which can be scaled to fit any unit system required. MM_ISOTROPIC ensures a 1:1 aspect ratio (useful in preserving the exact shape of an image); MM_ANISOTROPIC permits independent x and y coordinate scales.

Each mapping mode creates a virtual environment in which drawing operations occur in logical units with the logical units defined by the active mode. In turn, Windows maps drawing operations from the logical units of the mapping mode to the physical (pixel) units of the actual display.

> Note: Different mapping modes can be used for different drawing operations in a single window. You can draw a graph using a custom MM_ANISOTROPIC mode and then add labels after switching to MM_TEXT or MM_TWIPS mode.

The *SetMapMode* Function

The SetMapMode function selects the active mapping mode. The mapping mode defines the unit of measure used to convert logical units to device units as well as the orientation of the device's x and y-axes. The GDI (graphics device interface) uses the mapping mode to convert logical coordinates into the appropriate device coordinates.

The SetMapMode function can be called as a member of the CDC device context, in this fashion:

```
void CWinmodesView::OnDraw( CDC* pDC )
{
   ...
pDC->SetMapMode( nMapMode );
   ...
}
```

The function can also be called directly as a Windows API function:

```
void Draw( HDC hDC )
{
   ...
SetMapMode( hDC, nMapMode );
   ...
}
```

In either form, the return value is the previously active mapping mode. Both the return value and the nMapMode parameter can be any of the following values:

MM_TEXT
MM_HIENGLISH or MM_LOENGLISH
MM_HIMETRIC or MM_LOMETRIC
MM_TWIPS
MM_ISOTROPIC or MM_ANISOTROPIC

MM_TEXT Mode

The MM_TEXT mode is the system's default mapping mode and allows applications to work in device pixels. In MM_TEXT mode, each logical unit is equal to one device pixel with the origin point at the upper-left corner of the mapping space. Positive x-axis values increase to the right; positive y-axis values increase down (see Figure 12.1).

Figure 12.1. *Screen measurements in MM_TEXT mode.*

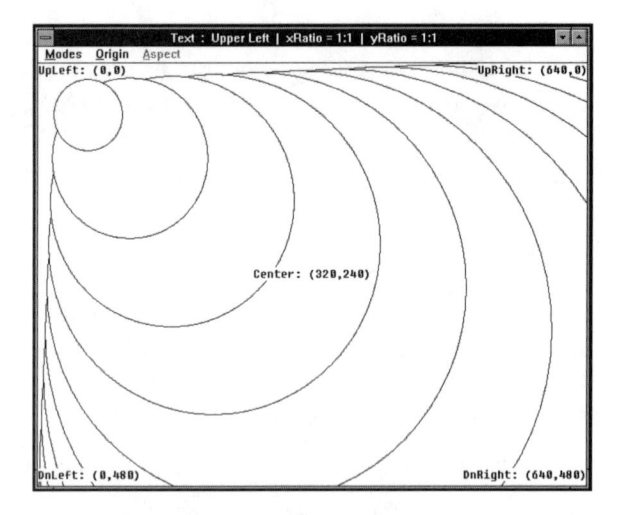

Note: The physical size of a pixel varies from device to device.

MM_HIENGLISH and MM_LOENGLISH Modes

The MM_HIENGLISH and MM_LOENGLISH modes map logical drawing units to 0.001 (HI) and 0.01 (LO) inches, respectively. In both modes, the default origin point is the lower-left corner of the window. Positive x-axis values increase to the right; positive y-axis values increase up (see Figures 12.2 and 12.3).

These two mapping modes are useful for drawings in inches—which should appear on-screen in essentially the same size as their unit measurements.

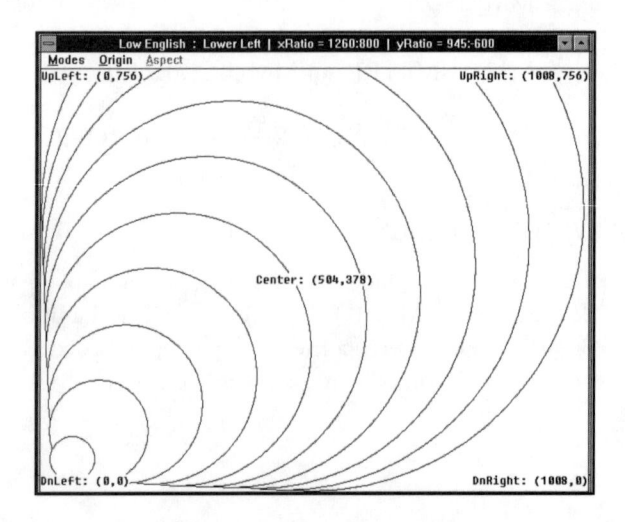

Figure 12.2. *Screen measurements in MM_LOENGLISH mode.*

Figure 12.3. *Screen measurements in MM_HIENGLISH mode.*

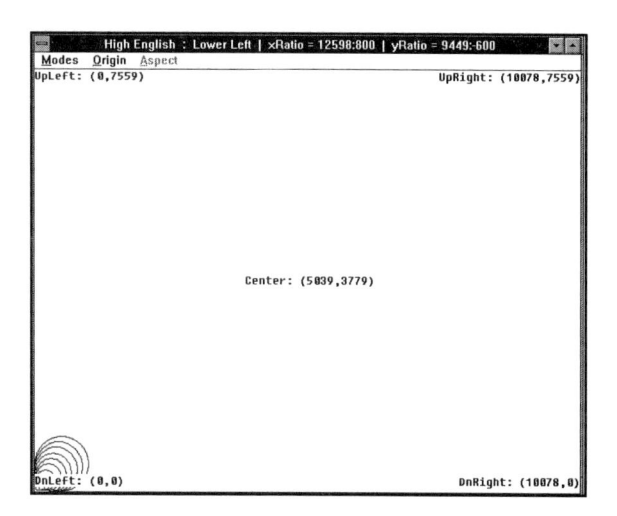

Compare the two windows in Figures 12.2 and 12.3; notice that the circles that fill the window in MM_LOENGLISH mode become an almost obscure detail in the lower-left corner in MM_HIENGLISH. In every case, the circles are drawn by the same set of instructions and are the same size—in logical units. But as the mapping scale increases from LOENGLISH to HIENGLISH, changing by a factor of ten, these same circles are mapped to a much smaller area in the display with the largest circle in the higher resolution the same as the smallest circle in the lower resolution.

> Caution: Because monitor sizes vary and because screen dimensions are subject to adjustments, these measurements remain approximate at best. Refer to the sidebar with the title, "A Discrepancy in Full Measure," in Chapter 11, "Understanding Device Capabilities and Mapping Modes."

MM_HIMETRIC and MM_LOMETRIC Modes

The MM_HIMETRIC and MM_LOMETRIC modes map logical drawing units to 0.01 (HI) and 0.1 (LO) millimeters, respectively. In both modes, the default origin point is at the lower-left corner of the window. Positive x-axis values increase to the right and positive y-axis values increase up (see Figures 12.4 and 12.5).

These two mapping modes are useful for drawings in millimeters—which should appear on-screen in essentially the same size as their unit measurements.

Figure 12.4. Screen measurements in MM_LOMETRIC mode.

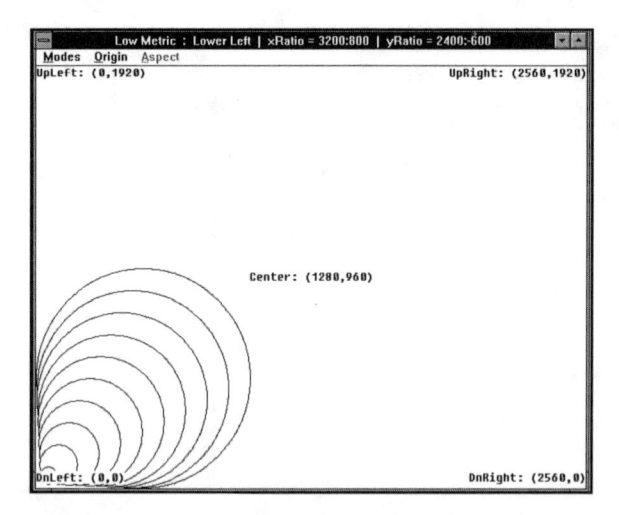

Figure 12.5. Screen measurements in MM_HIMETRIC mode.

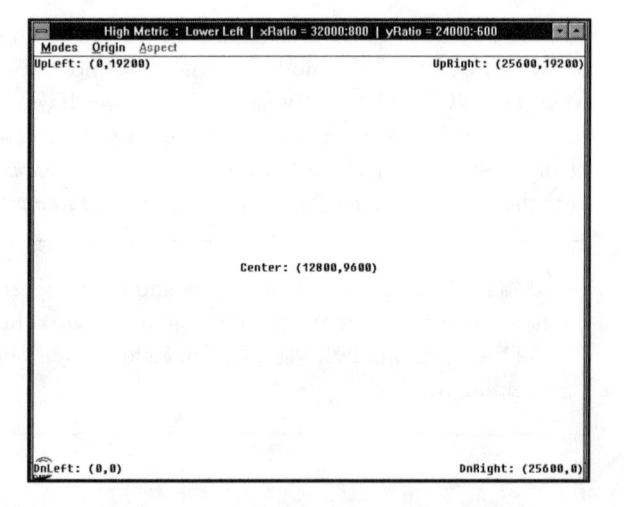

As you noticed when you compared the figures for the MM_LOENGLISH and MM_HIENGLISH modes, notice that Figures 11.4 and 11.5 show the MM_LOMETRIC and MM_HIMETRIC modes. The series of circles were drawn using the same set of instructions and are the same size—in logical units. Again, as the mapping scale increases from LOMETRIC to HIMETRIC, these same circles are mapped to a much smaller area in the display; the largest circle in the higher resolution is the same as the smallest circle in the lower resolution.

> Caution: Because monitor sizes vary and because screen dimensions are subject to adjustments, these measurements remain approximate at best. Refer to the sidebar with the title, "A Discrepancy in Full Measure," in Chapter 11, "Understanding Device Capabilities and Mapping Modes."

MM_TWIPS Mode

The MM_TWIPS mode maps logical units to 1/20 of a point (a *twip*), or 1/1440th of an inch. The default origin point is at the lower-left corner of the window; positive x-axis values increase to the right and positive y-axis values increase up (see Figure 12.6).

MM_TWIPS mode is designed for typesetting. Points and twips are established printer's measures (72 points equals 1 inch in height). A printed 36-point font is a half-inch in height, measured from the base of one line to the base of the next. By using the MM_TWIPS mapping mode, you can describe individual characters in great detail—200 vertical units for a 10-point typeface—allowing complex typefaces to be reproduced cleanly on the screen or printer.

Figure 12.6. *Screen measurements in MM_TWIPS mode.*

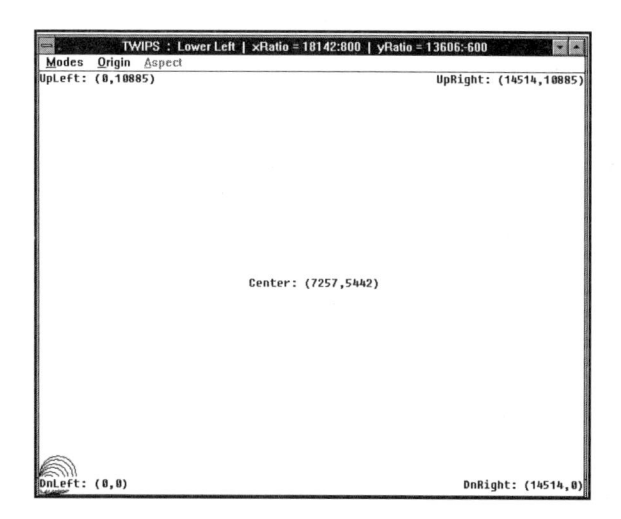

Caution: Because monitor sizes vary and because screen dimensions are subject to adjustments, these measurements remain approximate at best. Refer to the sidebar with the title, "A Discrepancy in Full Measure," in Chapter 11, "Understanding Device Capabilities and Mapping Modes."

MM_ISOTROPIC and MM_ANISOTROPIC Modes

The MM_ISOTROPIC and MM_ANISOTROPIC mapping modes allow you to set up any custom mapping scales your application may require. (The MM_ISOTROPIC and MM_ANISOTROPIC modes are demonstrated and contrasted in the Life application, which is included on the CD-ROM that accompanies this book but which is not discussed in any detail. Please feel free, however, to experiment with the Life demo.)

The MM_ISOTROPIC mode allows you to use the `SetWindowExt` and `SetViewportExt` functions to establish a space measured in logical units and a mapping ratio to physical (screen) units. X-axis and y-axis units use the same scale and mapping ratio (see Figure 12.7).

> Note: *Isotropic* is from the Greek; it means simply "the same in all directions."

Figure 12.7. Screen measurements in MM_ISOTROPIC mode.

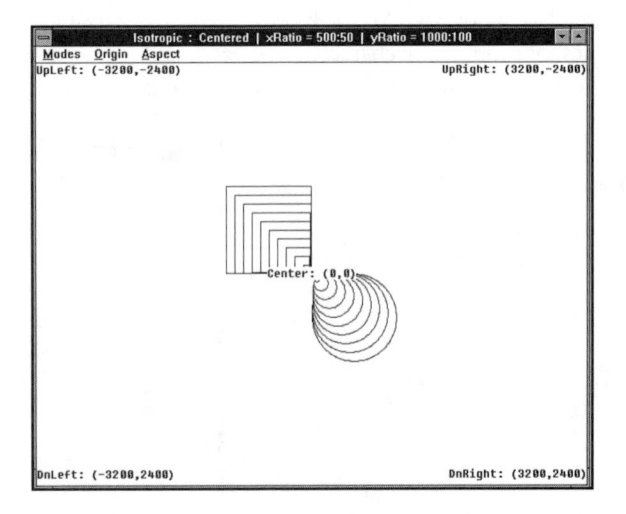

In MM_ISOTROPIC mode, you can experiment by changing the x and y extents for both the window and viewport using the Aspect dialog box. Changes affect the extents and the metrics reported; however, notice that the squares remain square and the circles remain circular.

> Note: The Aspect dialog box is called from the Aspect menu item. This menu item, however, is disabled (grayed out) until either the MM_ISOTROPIC or MM_ANISOTROPIC mode is selected.

The MM_ANISOTROPIC mode allows separate x-axis and y-axis logical units and mapping ratios to the physical screen (see Figure 12.8).

> Note: *Anisotropic* is also from the Greek; it means simply "not the same in all directions."

Figure 12.8. *Screen measurements in MM_ANISOTROPIC mode.*

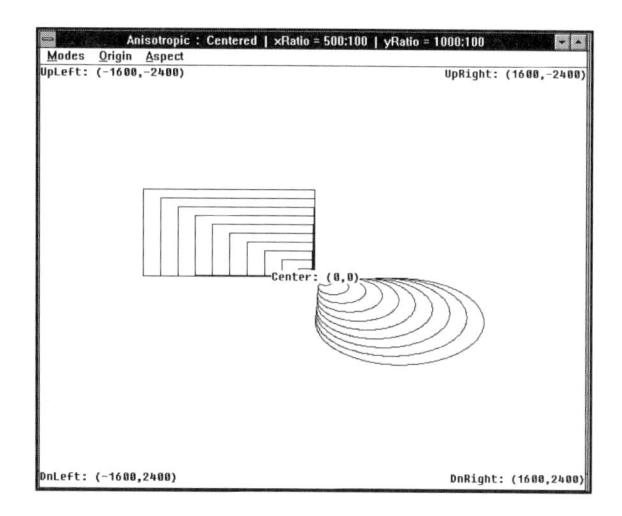

In this example, the squares from Figure 12.7 become rectangles and the circles become elliptical. Of course, if you set the two sets of extents equally, you restore the anisotropic mode to match the isotropic mode (which is precisely what the MM_ISOTROPIC mode does in the first place).

In both cases, the origin point can be located anywhere in the window—or even outside the window entirely. See the following section, "Origins, Windows, and Viewports."

> Note: Selecting the MM_ISOTROPIC or MM_ANISOTROPIC mode does not change the current window or viewport settings. To change the units, orientation, and scaling, call the SetWindowExt and SetViewportExt member functions.

Origins, Windows, and Viewports

Customarily, the application window is referred to as the space, both in memory and on the screen, in which drawing operations are executed. In actual fact, however, drawing operations occur in a *virtual space*—the device context—which, physically and effectively, is separate from the video memory and the screen display.

More important, because there is both a virtual drawing space (called a *window*) as well as a display space (a *viewport*), you can treat each of these separately. This is precisely what the mapping modes described in the preceding sections accomplish.

In MM_TEXT mode, the window and the viewport are essentially one and the same. One logical unit in the virtual window space is mapped to one pixel in the viewport display. In the metric, English, and twips modes, the horizontal and vertical units are determined by the (approximate) physical size of the display according to the ratios shown in Table 12.1. Remember that the value 120 in the recorded ratios comes from the pixels-per-inch reported by the `GetDeviceCaps` function described in Chapter 11. This value differs based on the display device (that is, according to the device driver's expectations).

Table 12.1. Comparing mapping modes.

Mode	O/S	Horizontal	Vertical	X-Axis Ratio	Y-Axis Ratio	Notes
MM_TEXT	WinNT	800	562	1:1	1:1	
	Win95	800	519	1:1	1:1	(1)
MM_LOMETRIC	WinNT	3,200	2,248	3200:800	2400:–600	
	Win95 (3)	1,693	1,099	254:120	–254:120	(2)
MM_HIMETRIC	WinNT	32,000	22,480	32000:800	24000:–600	
	Win95 (3)	16,933	10,986	2540:120	–2540:120	(2)
MM_LOENGLISH	WinNT	1,260	885	1260:800	945:–600	
	Win95 (3)	667	431	100:96	–100:96	(2)
MM_HIENGLISH	WinNT	12,598	8,851	12598:800	9449:–600	
	Win95 (3)	6667	4313	1000:96	–1000:96	(2)
MM_TWIPS	WinNT	18,142	12,744	18142:800	13606:–600	
	Win95 (3)	9600	6228	1440:120	–1440:120	(2)
MM_ISOTROPIC		variable	variable	= y-axis ratio	variable	
MM_ANISOTROPIC		variable	variable	variable	variable	

1. Both WinNT and Win95 report the MM_TEXT mode window size and ratios correctly. The single discrepancy between the two systems is the window's vertical measurement reported as 562 instead of 519; this discrepancy is accounted for by the icon bar at the bottom of the Win95 screen and by differences in the size of the application title bar and frame under Win95.

2. In all cases, Win95 incorrectly reports the physical window size much smaller than does WinNT. Win95 also grossly varies reports on both the x-axis and y-axis ratios. If you are relying on the MM_HI- or MM_LOENGLISH and MM_HI- or MM_LOMETRIC modes or on the MM_TWIPS mode for typefaces, the resulting displays are nowhere close (with the possible exception of some laptops) to the expected scale.

3. These measurements were recorded with Large Fonts selected from the desktop's Display dialog box. Changing the font selection to Small Fonts changes the reported sizes. Neither setting, however, yields ranges or ratios that match the values reported by WinNT nor the values that would be expected on the basis of the installed video card's characteristics.

> ### A Discrepancy in Full Measure, Part 2
>
> The discrepancies between the window sizes and aspect ratios reported by Windows 95 and Windows NT are much more than a mere mathematical inconvenience. Figure 12.9 shows three typeface samples as reproduced by Win95 (left) and the same three typefaces as reproduced by WinNT (right). 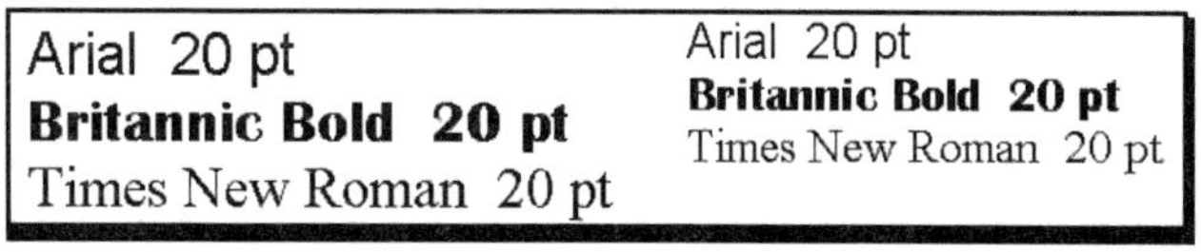
>
> *Figure 12.9.* Comparing Win95 (left side) and WinNT (right side) in MM_TWIPS mode.
>
> | Arial 20 pt | Arial 20 pt |
> | **Britannic Bold 20 pt** | **Britannic Bold 20 pt** |
> | Times New Roman 20 pt | Times New Roman 20 pt |
>
> Perhaps the only defense that can be offered for these errors is that they are consistent among themselves. That is, a ruler drawn using MM_LOENGLISH mode correctly measures a 36-point font drawn using MM_TWIPS. However, neither the on-screen ruler nor the font correspond at all with a physical ruler or a font rule.
>
> Fortunately, corresponding discrepancies do not appear in the printer metrics (also reported by the `GetDeviceCaps` function). Even if the screen display is somewhat enlarged under Win95, actual printer output corresponds to the requested font sizes, spacing, and so on.

The *SetWindowExt* and *SetViewportExt* Functions

The `SetWindowExt` and `SetViewportExt` functions are used to establish ratios between the virtual window device context and the screen viewport. These two functions ***do not*** affect the window size; they ***do*** affect the virtual window size.

This next example uses an application with a client window size of 612 pixels horizontal and 314 pixels vertical. Using the `SetWindowExt` and `SetViewportExt` functions, Table 12.2 shows the measurements reported as the window:viewport ratios are changed.

Table 12.2. Window:viewport ratios and virtual window sizes.

Window	Viewport	Ratio	X-Axis	Y-Axis
100	10	10:1	6120	3140
100	100	1:1	612	314
100	1000	1:10	61	31

For practical purposes, the `SetWindowExt` and `SetViewportExt` functions are rather awkwardly designed (a pair of functions with the names `SetXAxisRatio` and `SetYAxisRatio` would not only be simpler to use, they would also be more logically named). But the former are the supplied API functions (the latter can be easily designed but are left as an exercise for those who feel the need).

Both the `SetWindowExt` and `SetViewportExt` functions can be called either with two parameters (an x-axis and a y-axis value) or with a single `CSize` object instance supplying effectively the same arguments. In either format, these functions return `CSize` objects containing the previous window or viewport extents (in logical units). Alternatively, if an error occurs, the returned coordinates are both zero.

The `SetWindowExt` and `SetViewportExt` functions are relevant only when the MM_ISOTROPIC or MM_ANISOTROPIC mode is used. You are cautioned, however, to call the `SetWindowExt` function before calling the `SetViewportExt` function.

> Note: The x-axis and y-axis ratios are simply ratios, nothing more. A ratio of 1000:100 produces exactly the same results as a ratio of 10:1. Thus, the magnitudes of the values used to express the ratios are irrelevant. Only the proportions matter.

Related Mode, Viewport, and Window Functions

Although the `SetWindowExt` and `SetViewportExt` functions are the two you're most likely to use to change the display mapping, a variety of other functions deal with modes and window and viewport extents. Although most of these functions are not demonstrated in either the WinModes or Life applications (included on the CD-ROM that accompanies this book), they are briefly discussed in the following sections.

The *GetMapMode* Function

The `GetMapMode` function can be called directly, as an API function, with a single parameter identifying the device context being queried. It can also be called as the CDC member function without parameters. In either form, the `GetMapMode` function returns the current, active mapping mode for the device context. The `GetMapMode` function is called in one of the following ways:

```
nMode = GetMapMode( hdc );
nMode = pDC->GetMapMode();
```

In the event of failure, the `GetMapMode` function returns 0.

Additional Window and Viewport Extent Functions

The `SetWindowExt` and `SetViewportExt` functions have already been introduced. These functions have retrieval counterparts (called `GetWindowExtEx` and `GetViewportExtEx`) that can be invoked either as CDC member functions or as direct API calls.

If the CDC member function is used, `GetWindowExt` or `GetViewportExt` returns a `CSize` member containing the x and y extents of the window or viewport as follows:

```
cSizeWindow = pDC->GetWindowExt();
cSizeViewport = pDC->GetViewportExt();
```

The direct API functions can also be invoked in the following manner:

```
GetWindowExtEx( hDC, lpSize );
GetViewportExtEx( hDC, lpSize );
```

In both cases, the x and y extents of the window or viewport are reported in the `LPSIZE` structure; the functions each return Boolean arguments reporting success or failure.

In addition to setting the window or viewport extents, two functions are supplied to scale the extents: `ScaleWindowExt` and `ScaleViewportExt`. The `ScaleWindowExt` and `ScaleViewportExt` members are each called with four integer parameters, as follows:

```
cSizeWindow = ScaleWindowExt( xNum, xDenom, yNum, yDenom );
cSizeViewport = ScaleViewportExt( xNum, xDenom, yNum, yDenom );
```

The `xNum` and `yNum` parameters are used to multiply the current x and y extents; the `xDenom` and `yDenom` parameters are used to divide the x and y extents after they are multiplied.

> Note: Because the results of the operations are always integers, multiplication is performed *before* division so that round-off errors are minimized.

Assume that the existing viewport extent is 10, 10 for the x and y axes. Calling `ScaleViewportExt ( 5, 4, 3, 2 )` multiplies the x-axis extent by 5 and then divides by 4, making the new x-axis extent 12 (the 0.5 fraction is dropped). Likewise, the y-axis extent is multiplied by 3 and divided by 2 to become 15.

In each case, the returned `CSize` object reports the previous window or viewport extents in logical units.

If you prefer to call the Windows API functions directly, the corresponding functions are `ScaleWindowExtEx` and `ScaleViewportExtEx`. Call these functions in the following manner:

```
ScaleWindowExtEx( hDC, xNum, xDenom, yNum, yDenom, lpSize );
ScaleViewportExtEx( hDC, xNum, xDenom, yNum, yDenom, lpSize );
```

In each case, a Boolean return value indicates success or failure; the `LPSIZE` structure reports the previous window or viewport extents.

Window and Viewport Origins

Although the various mapping modes each have their default origins, you can use the `SetWindowOrg` function with any mapping mode to change the 0,0 origin point within the application window. The WinModes demo application menu offers a choice of three origins: upper-left, centered, and lower-right. You can use the `SetWindowOrg` function to place the origin point anywhere inside or outside the application window.

The `SetWindowOrg` member function can be called either with two integer parameters for the x and y origins or with a single `CPoint` object or a `POINT` structure argument:

```
pDC->SetWindowOrg( xOrg, yOrg );
pDC->SetWindowOrg( cPoint );
```

In any of these forms, the returned value is a `CPoint` object containing the previous origins.

If you prefer to call the API function directly, the `SetWindowOrgEx` function requires four parameters:

```
SetWindowOrgEx( hDC, xOrg, yOrg, lpPoint );
```

In this form, `SetWindowOrgEx` returns a Boolean result reporting success or failure; the previous origin point is reported in the `LPPOINT` structure.

A similar member function, `SetViewportOrg`, is provided for the viewport extent.

The `GetWindowOrg` and `GetViewportOrg` member functions can be used to query the current window and viewport origins. The `OffsetWindowOrg` and `OffsetViewportOrg` member functions can be called to modify the origin points relative to the current positions.

The WinModes Demo

The WinModes application is written to demonstrate both the standard mapping modes and the custom mapping modes (refer back to Figures 12.1 through 12.8). The mechanisms used in this demo are relatively simple but are discussed briefly to explain how the mapping modes function.

Although a good portion of the WinModes demo is devoted to the responses to the several menu options and to the Aspect dialog box, the portion most relevant to the topics discussed in this chapter is found in the `CWinmodesView::OnDraw` function, which is responsible for drawing the client window display.

This limitation of relevance should be no particular surprise to most. Still, the point bears reiteration: All display activities take place in the `OnDraw` method (or, of course, in functions called from the `OnDraw` method). When dealing with mapping modes, remember that the appropriate mapping mode—as well as any associated operations such as window and viewport extents—must be handled every time the screen is redrawn.

Certain preparations must be made for each screen redraw. Any special conditions, such as window or viewport extents, must be nonvolatile and available for reuse. For example, an application cannot simply select MM_TWIPS mode and then expect this mode to be valid each time the application window is redrawn. The mode must be reset each time the window is redrawn.

Another point (that may not be so obvious) is that you can select more than one mapping mode during a single screen-drawing operation. Because you can combine mapping modes—or, more accurately, *switch* mapping modes—you can use different mapping modes for different parts of a drawing operation even though the end result is a single screen image. This is exactly what you see in the WinModes application.

Because of the nature of the display, the application begins with a potpourri of local variables. Further, because the device context represented by pDC is initially and by default set to MM_TEXT mode, we also query the system font for text metrics and retain the average character width and height for later use.

```
void CWinmodesView::OnDraw(CDC* pDC)
{
    TEXTMETRIC   tm;
    CRect        cRect;
    CSize        cSizeWindow, cSizeView;
    CString      csBuff, csTitle;
    int          cxChr, cyChr, OrgDC, i, j;
    int          xLeft, xRight, yTop, yBottom, xCenter, yCenter;

    CWinmodesDoc* pDoc = GetDocument();
    ASSERT_VALID(pDoc);

    pDC->SelectObject( GetStockObject( SYSTEM_FIXED_FONT ) );
    pDC->GetTextMetrics( &tm );
    cxChr = tm.tmAveCharWidth;
    cyChr = tm.tmHeight + tm.tmExternalLeading;
    OrgDC = pDC->SaveDC();
```

Before proceeding, call the SaveDC() method to retrieve the current (active) device context so that it can later be restored (after we finish changing the device context for our own purposes). Although this conservative approach is not mandatory, it is a good idea and is recommended as a general practice.

Next, check the m_nCurMode member variable to see which mode has been selected from the **M**odes menu and then set the device context to this mode:

```
switch( m_nCurMode )
{
    case IDM_TEXT:
        pDC->SetMapMode( MM_TEXT );
        break;

    case IDM_LOMETRIC:
        pDC->SetMapMode( MM_LOMETRIC );
        break;
```

```
        case IDM_HIMETRIC:
            pDC->SetMapMode( MM_HIMETRIC );
            break;

        case IDM_LOENGLISH:
            pDC->SetMapMode( MM_LOENGLISH );
            break;

        case IDM_HIENGLISH:
            pDC->SetMapMode( MM_HIENGLISH );
            break;

        case IDM_TWIPS:
            pDC->SetMapMode( MM_TWIPS );
            break;

        case IDM_ISOTROPIC:
            pDC->SetMapMode( MM_ISOTROPIC );
            pDC->SetWindowExt( theApp.m_cSizeWindow );
            pDC->SetViewportExt( theApp.m_cSizeView );
            break;

        case IDM_ANISOTROPIC:
            pDC->SetMapMode( MM_ANISOTROPIC );
            pDC->SetWindowExt( theApp.m_cSizeWindow );
            pDC->SetViewportExt( theApp.m_cSizeView );
            break;
}
```

In the case of the MM_ISOTROPIC or MM_ANISOTROPIC mode, we also call the SetWindowExt and SetViewportExt functions. Notice that SetWindowExt is called first and SetViewportExt is called second: an ordering that is cautioned in Microsoft's documentation but that is not explained.

Because provisions have been made to override the standard origins for each mode, we use GetClientRect to request the size of the client window and then call the SetWindowOrg function using the retrieved size:

```
AfxGetMainWnd()->GetClientRect( cRect );
pDC->DPtoLP( cRect );
switch( m_nCurOrg )
{
    case IDM_UPLEFT:
        pDC->SetWindowOrg( 0, 0 );
        break;

    case IDM_DNLEFT:
        pDC->SetWindowOrg( 0, -cRect.BottomRight().y );
        break;

    case IDM_CENTER:
        pDC->SetWindowOrg( - ( cRect.Width() / 2 ),
                           - ( cRect.Height() / 2 ) );
        break;
}
```

Strictly for demonstration purposes (to show how drawing operations are affected by differences in the active mapping mode), the next operation is to draw a series of ten circles and ten squares:

```
for( i=10; i>0; i-- )
{
   j = 20 - ( 2 * i );
   pDC->Ellipse( j, j, 100*i, 100*i );
   pDC->Rectangle( -j, -j, -(100*i), -(100*i) );
}
```

After drawing the pattern, the cRect variable, which contains the limits of the application client window (in the selected mapping mode but expressed in device points), is converted to logical points:

```
pDC->DPtoLP( cRect );
xLeft    = cRect.TopLeft().x;
xRight   = cRect.BottomRight().x;
yTop     = cRect.TopLeft().y;
yBottom  = cRect.BottomRight().y;
xCenter  = ( xRight + xLeft ) / 2;
yCenter  = ( yBottom + yTop ) / 2;
cSizeWindow = pDC->GetWindowExt();
cSizeView = pDC->GetViewportExt();
```

After conversion, the left, right, top, and bottom limits of the window are in logical points and are extracted; the center coordinates (also in logical points) are calculated. Finally, the window extent and viewport extent are retrieved. All the retrieved or calculated values are eventually used to report the characteristics. But before doing so, because we are finished with the current drawing mode, the original mode is restored by calling the RestoreDC function:

```
pDC->RestoreDC( OrgDC );
```

Once again, we query the size of the client rectangle. When this was done a moment ago, a different drawing mode was in effect. The size retrieved was in units appropriate to the active mode. This time, with the original text mode restored, the retrieved size is in pixels:

```
AfxGetMainWnd()->GetClientRect( cRect );
pDC->DPtoLP( cRect );

csBuff.Format( "UpLeft: (%d,%d)", xLeft, yTop );
pDC->TextOut( cRect.TopLeft().x,
              cRect.TopLeft().y,
              csBuff );

csBuff.Format( "DnLeft: (%d,%d)", xLeft, yBottom );
pDC->TextOut( cRect.TopLeft().x,
              cRect.BottomRight().y - (cyChr+5),
              csBuff );

csBuff.Format( "Center: (%d,%d)", xCenter, yCenter );
pDC->TextOut( ( cRect.Width() - ( csBuff.GetLength() * cxChr ) ) / 2,
              ( cRect.Height() - cyChr ) / 2,
                csBuff );

csBuff.Format( "UpRight: (%d,%d)", xRight, yTop );
pDC->TextOut( cRect.BottomRight().x - ( csBuff.GetLength() * cxChr ),
              cRect.TopLeft().y,
              csBuff );
```

```
csBuff.Format( "DnRight: (%d,%d)", xRight, yBottom );
pDC->TextOut( cRect.BottomRight().x - ( csBuff.GetLength() * cxChr ),
              cRect.BottomRight().y - ( cyChr + 5 ),
              csBuff );
```

Attempting to report the device context mapping-mode parameters while still in the various mapping modes is not impossible but is certainly difficult. Look back at Figures 12.1 through 12.8 and refresh your memory of how the circles and rectangles appeared as different sizes (not to mention different positions) in each mode; now imagine the scaling and positioning necessary to place text on the screen at the four corners of the window and in the center and to ensure that the text is appropriately sized in each instance.

Instead, for text reports, it's much simpler to revert to MM_TEXT mode (which was done when the original device context was restored) and then write the text captions using the TextOut function. Of course, it's also much simpler to calculate the positions for each text string without having to mess with complicated conversions.

In addition, because not quite everything we want to report fits conveniently on the screen (at least, not without becoming cluttered), we report the aspect ratio, mode, and origins on the title bar:

```
csBuff.Format( "xRatio = %d:%d ¦ yRatio = %d:%d",
               cSizeWindow.cx, cSizeView.cx,
               cSizeWindow.cy, cSizeView.cy );
csTitle = csCurMode[ m_nCurMode - IDM_TEXT ] + " : " +
          csCurOrg[ m_nCurOrg - IDM_UPLEFT ] + " ¦ " + csBuff;
AfxGetMainWnd()->SetWindowText( csTitle );
}
```

Because the last drawing operation is conducted in a separate window and is quite independent of the operations in the client window, it is quite unaffected by the mapping mode used—or by any other aspect of the client window's device context.

The remainder of the WinModes demo is devoted to setting conditions and selections for the drawing operation and needs no particular explanation here.

The Life Demo

A second demo program, called Life, is provided to graphically demonstrate the differences between the isotropic and anisotropic mapping modes. It also shows a somewhat more practical use of the custom mapping modes.

The Life program is not particularly complex but it does use a mapping mode to fit a 50×50 grid on the display. By using custom mapping, the Life application can combine the convenience of a grid (to track events in a simulated world and display the results) at a size convenient for viewing without having to perform complicated calculations to draw a recognizable map display.

Equally important, the mapping is independent of both the size of the application window and of the video mode used by the display. Both of these factors can otherwise make drawing calculations complicated (or, at the very least, inconvenient).

By using mapping, the simulation can execute recognizably regardless of the size of the client window, regardless of how the window is resized, and regardless of the graphics capabilities of the executing system.

For demonstration purposes, the Life grid can be displayed in either MM_ISOTROPIC or MM_ANISOTROPIC mode.

The Game of Life

The game of Life used for this demo is a simple game (or simulation). In the years BC (before computers), the game was played with paper and pencil (a tedious exercise at best). The rules are not complicated.

The game is played on a field, or grid, of whatever size you choose. Initially, any point in the grid can be turned on (made *alive*) or off (made *dead*); you can begin with whatever arrangements you like.

After the initial setup, the game proceeds by generations: the status of each cell in each following generation is determined by the state of the surrounding cells in the previous generation.

In each generation, the status of every point in the grid is recalculated according to the number of cells in the previous generation that border the current cell:

```
if( GetLastGeneration( i, j ) ) Neighbors = -1;
                          else Neighbors =  0;
for( k=-1; k<=1; k++ )
{
   x = i + k;
   if( x <     0 ) x += GRID;
   if( x >= GRID ) x -= GRID;
   for( l = -1; l <= 1; l++ )
   {
      y = j + l;
      if( y <     0 ) y += GRID;
      if( y >= GRID ) y -= GRID;
      if( GetLastGeneration( x, y ) ) Neighbors++;
   }
}
```

Here the count `Neighbors` is initialized as −1 if the cell is alive; if the cell is dead, it is initialized as 0. This is a simple trick to allow the two loops, which count from −1 to 1 around the cell, to count all nine cells without having to make elaborate provisions to skip the center cell during the loop. The reason, of course, is that you want the count to reflect the neighboring cells but not to include the center cell.

As you can see from the preceding code, provisions have been included to cause the grid to wrap both left-to-right and top-to-bottom, making the grid a "closed universe." In this fashion, the lifeforms can grow across the edges of the world—a better simulation than imposing border conditions.

After checking the number of neighboring cells that are alive, four rules are applied:

1. If a cell has two live neighbors in the last generation, its current state in this generation remains unchanged. If the cell is currently alive, it remains alive. If the cell is dead, it remains dead.
2. If a cell has three live neighbors in the last generation, the cell is alive in this generation, regardless of its previous state. If a dead cell has three live neighbors, it becomes alive. If a live cell has three live neighbors, it remains alive.
3. If a cell has less than two live neighbors, it dies of loneliness.
4. If a cell has more than three live neighbors, it dies of overcrowding.

In computer terms, these rules are implemented with a simple `switch` statement:

```
switch( Neighbors )
{
   case 2:
       SetThisGeneration( i, j, GetLastGeneration( i, j ));
       break;      // two neighbors, remains as it was

   case 3:
       SetThisGeneration( i, j, TRUE );
       break;      // three neighbors, it's alive

   default:
       SetThisGeneration( i, j, FALSE );
}                  // all other conditions, the cell dies
```

To make it easier to see how Life grows, as each generation is drawn, the cells that were live in the previous generation are drawn in yellow before the current generation's live cells are drawn in green.

Menu options allow you to start and stop (pause) the Life program, to randomly seed the grid, to launch a life form called a *flyer* (watch this one "fly" across the grid as it recreates itself in successive generations going through a cycle of four steps) or to operate in a second mode called Forest.

Forest Life

The Forest version of the game of Life is an alternative simulation. It uses the same 50×50 grid but follows a different set of rules.

Briefly stated, each cell can be alive or dead; but once alive, the cell ages through ten generations.

Live cells can randomly seed adjoining cells if they are not already alive.

Cells die after ten generations; after another generation, that cell becomes bare ground and can be reseeded by neighbors.

As a forest simulation, Forest is a simplistic program (it mirrors an actual forest in only vague terms). If you want a more complicated simulation, experiment by adding other growth factors (such as rainfall) and other death factors (such as forest fires and winds).

As you can observe, the Forest version of the game of Life uses gradations of green to show the age of each grid point. On a more sophisticated simulation, fires can be shown in red; burned-off areas can be shown in black and gray; and bare ground can be shown in brown.

It's worth playing with. It's a fascinating simulation—try it. And in the process, notice how much simpler mapping modes make drawing your display.

Summary

Together with window and viewport extents, mapping modes can make complicated graphics operations much simpler to handle. Although mapping modes are not a cure-all, they *are* convenient and useful.

At least for the present, you must also remain aware of the problems with Win95's metric reporting and the fact that, except for the default MM_TEXT mode, the reported and calculated screen sizes are not accurate.

Even with this caveat, the mapping modes can still be used relatively successfully. Just don't depend on them for accuracy in dimensions until the reporting problem is resolved.

CHAPTER 13

Working with Colors, Palettes, and Drawing Modes

Not too long ago, computers were commonly supported by black-and-white monitors. If you did have color, it was amber or green or you were hooked up to a TV with a 320×200 pixel display.

Color was simply too expensive—not so much in terms of color monitors as in terms of memory—to support a more elaborate display. Monochrome required only one bit per pixel; color took eight times as much RAM, and RAM was expensive.

It wasn't simply a matter of expensive RAM. Color monitors were rare, and TVs couldn't support the resolutions needed. In addition, there were no standards for color videos. When IBM entered the market, thinking they could set standards and dominate the industry, their brilliant concept of color (CGA) was to select a palette of four hues from a total of 16.

The later EGA and VGA standards were the products of dropping memory prices and an understandable dissatisfaction with the CGA color scheme. Today's SVGA standards have become so common that even low-end notebooks support at least 256 colors.

It would be very difficult to imagine Windows without color. Black and white is barely acceptable for DOS text, and not at all acceptable for anything else.

It is understandable that the results of this frantic competition for color resolution are reflected in rather gaudy applications. However, unless your name happens to be Claude Monet or Georges Seurat, an excess of color rarely does anything to improve your program, and color is certainly no cure for a badly designed application.

The word processor I used to write this book displays black text on a white background. The scrollbars and status bar use grays and blacks; the toolbar does show a few traces of yellow and blue, but these are unobtrusive and are more highlights than anything else.

This is not a book on the aesthetics of color in application design. The general rule is to minimize colors where they are used simply for emphasis. The other side of the coin is that colors are absolutely wonderful when they are needed.

After all, a Gantt chart in black and white isn't nearly as easy to read as one that uses color to distinguish features. A CAD program without color may be usable, but not nearly as readable as one using color to supply shading and depth. As for 3D modeling without color…well, you can write your own depreciating description.

The topic of this chapter is not color design but *creating colors*, which begins with the Windows palettes.

> Note: The author's illustrations show the richness of colors available through the Windows display system. However, those colors cannot be satisfactorily reproduced within the confines of this printed text. Therefore, the presentation in the book is in gray scale. The full-color figures have been placed on the CD accompanying this book in the Figures directory and have names as shown in their captions. They can be viewed using the Paint program supplied with any Windows product.

Windows Palettes

Device palettes were mentioned briefly in Chapter 11, "Understanding Device Capabilities and Mapping Modes," where the GetDeviceCaps function reported the color bits per pixel and the number of color planes. The color device capabilities reported depend entirely on the installed video drivers because most video cards can support a selection of video resolutions. The standard video resolutions are discussed here.

The old **CGA** systems, which used four color planes, provided palettes with 16 entries. Each palette entry contained a 4-bit color identifier, providing a choice of 16 colors—8 bright and 8 dark. The use of color planes was ingenious. Three of the color planes were devoted to the red, green, and blue color guns; the fourth provided an intensity control—high for bright colors and low for dark colors. The results were limited and palette entries were identified as RGBI (red, green, blue, intensity) format.

EGA/VGA continued to use color planes but used 6 bits instead of 4 by providing 2 bits per plane and a possible total of 64 colors instead of 16. Windows continued to treat SVGA as a 16-color palette system even though the 16 VGA colors were much better than the old EGA palette. The color codes used by EGA/VGA were commonly referred to as an rgbRGB format (denoting the high and low red, green, and blue intensity bits).

The **SVGA** standard (the current standard) uses 8 bits per pixel to reference a palette with a total of 256 entries. Each palette entry contains a 24-bit value, which raises the total number of hues from which you can select to 16,777,216.

More recently, two new standards have appeared: High Color and True Color.

The **High Color** standard abandons palettes entirely and uses 16 bits of RAM for each pixel in the screen display, providing a total of 64K colors. Because a 640×480 screen has 300,000 pixels, this is still a limitation. It does not supply an indefinite range of hues for each pixel, but it comes close enough to satisfy most requirements.

How High Color is implemented can vary depending on the video card. If you figure 5 bits each for the red, green, and blue values for each pixel, plus a 16th intensity bit, this is a pretty good approximation. The results, even for very exacting requirements and superior color vision, are superb.

The **True Color** standard goes one step further and uses a full 24 bits of color information for each screen pixel, providing a total of 16 million possible hues. Because 24-bit color provides hue resolution higher than even superior color vision can recognize, there is little point in even considering higher color resolutions. What you need is at least 2M of video RAM for a 1024×768 display at 24 bits per pixel.

> Note: A few years ago, before either High Color or True Color became common, special video boards and very expensive monitors supported both of these standards as displays for digital video output. At the time, I was involved in designing a system to image gem stones and had the opportunity to show simultaneous displays at both 16 and 24 bits per pixel. No one, including jewelers and gemologists, could distinguish between the two.
>
> In sum, the 16-bit-per-pixel color was every bit as good as the 24-bit-per-pixel—and this was according to a very critical audience.

However, both the High Color and True Color video modes have their drawbacks (at least compared to the 256-color SVGA mode). Because SVGA video operations involve manipulating 8 bits per pixel versus 16 and 24, SVGA operations are faster.

Depending on the situation, this may or may not be relevant. If the most important aspect of your application is how good your video display is, you should use either the 16-bit or 24-bit mode. On the other hand, if speed is important, 8-bit SVGA has the advantage.

In either case, a good graphics accelerator chip on your video card makes a lot more difference in speed than your choice of color resolution does.

Three standard color resolutions are detailed in Table 13.1, as reported by the DC utility.

Table 13.1. Graphics color capabilities.

Graphics Type	Color Planes	Bits/ Pixel	Palette Size	System Palette	Possible Colors
SVGA	1	8	256	20	256 of 16,777,216 possible
High Color	1	16	0	0	65,536
True Color	1	24	0	0	16,777,216

Color Definitions

The video color palettes defined by DOS systems used a rather simple system of setting high and low intensity bits for the red, blue, and green color guns. The problem with such a system is that only a limited number of colors were possible, and the precise hues of each color were determined by hardware rather than by software.

Some time ago, both the Windows and OS/2 operating systems abandoned this restrictive method of color definition in favor of a more flexible system. As a result, the RGBTriplet or RGBQuad color values have become standard. In each form, 3-byte values are used to define a pixel color with the red, green, and blue intensities, each defined by a byte value with a range of 0 to 255.

The Windows-standard RGB values, called RGBQuad structures, reserve the high byte of the high word for a flag value to indicate the type of COLORREF value. (COLORREF types are discussed later in this chapter.)

Table 13.2 compares a conventional 16-item EGA/VGA color palette using the rgbRGB color system with the equivalent Windows RGB palette entries.

Chapter 13 • Working with Colors, Palettes, and Drawing Modes   301

Table 13.2. System color definitions.

Color	EGA/VGA	Colors	Windows RGB Color Values
Binary		r g b R G B	0x.. BBGGRR
Black	000000	- - - - - -	0x00 00 00 00
Dark Blue	000001	- - - - - B	0x00 77 00 00
Dark Green	000010	- - - - G -	0x00 00 77 00
Dark Cyan	000011	- - - - G B	0x00 77 77 00
Dark Red	000100	- - - R - -	0x00 77 00 00
Dark Magenta	000101	- - - R - B	0x00 77 00 77
Brown	010100	- g - R - -	0x00 00 77 CC
Light Gray	000111	- - - R G B	0x00 80 80 80
Dark Gray	111000	r g b - - -	0x00 3F 3F 3F
Light Blue	111001	r g b - - B	0x00 FF 00 00
Light Green	111010	r g b - G -	0x00 00 FF 00
Light Cyan	111011	r g b - G B	0x00 FF FF 00
Light Red	111100	r g b R - -	0x00 00 00 FF
Light Magenta	111101	r g b R - B	0x00 FF 00 FF
Yellow	111110	r g b R G -	0x00 00 FF FF
White	111111	r g b R G B	0x00 FF FF FF

In the Windows RGB system, each palette entry or pixel color in 16-bit or 24-bit color mode is defined by a long integer (4-byte) value using the format 0x00BBGGRR. In this form, the red value is found in the low byte of the low word, the green value in the high byte of the low word, the blue value in the low byte of the high word, and the most significant byte is zero.

> Note: The most significant byte in a Windows RGB value is reserved for a flag indicating the type of color reference. For absolute RGB values, this byte remains zero but may also have values of 1 and 2 for palette-index COLORREF values and palette-relative COLORREF values. These three palette types are discussed further in following section.

For video systems supporting only 256 colors, these 4-byte values are written to palettes. Actually, only the three least-significant bytes are written to the palettes because the flag value is unnecessary once the palette is created. In turn, each pixel address in the video memory receives an index value referring to the appropriate palette entry.

For video systems supporting High Color or True Color, the color palettes are omitted in favor of writing the individual color values for each pixel on the screen directly to the video memory.

One of the major strengths of Windows is that it relieves you and your applications of the tedium of having to know and adapt to each system's hardware limitations and capabilities. One of the tasks you generally do not want to contend with is defining the colors for every element on the screen.

For this purpose, even though palettes are not necessarily required by the video system, Windows continues to supply a standard palette consisting of 20 static colors. On an EGA/VGA system, only the first 16 of these colors are available.

Standard Color Palettes

If you refer back to the DC application in Chapter 11, "Understanding Device Capabilities and Mapping Modes," you may recall that for a 256-color video system, the `GetDeviceCaps` function reported only 236 available palette entries. This was not a mistake but recognition of the fact that 20 of the 256 palette entries were already reserved by Windows for the 20 stock palette entries. These first 20 entries are predefined by Windows and cannot normally be overwritten by your applications.

The Color1 demo application shown in Figure 13.1 offers a convenient look at these reserved palette entries by creating a client window with five horizontal divisions and four vertical, filling each with one of the stock palette colors.

Figure 13.1. *The stock Windows palette.*

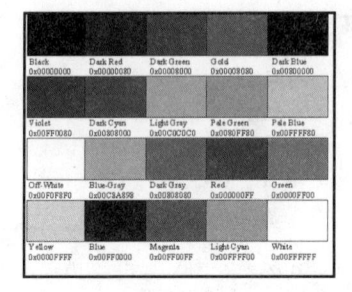

These reserved entries can be changed if you change the system colors, but they are used by all applications and cannot be revised by an individual application. Although applications may attempt to assign 256 palette entries, when the application's palette is mapped to the display, the 20 reserved entries remain as they are, and the final 20 entries in the application's virtual palette are ignored. Because palettes are usually arranged in order of importance, this loss of 20 entries is usually not particularly noticeable because the missing colors are mapped to their closest approximations in the effective palette.

When more than two applications use custom palettes, very real palette contentions can be observed quite easily. Suppose that you have a 256-color wallpaper on your desktop and you load Visual C++. When the elaborate C++ bitmap is displayed, the colors in the wallpaper image are abruptly reduced to a few simple shades. All the fine gradations of color are mapped to their nearest equivalents in the active display palette, which is temporarily dominated by the 200+ shades of blue in the C++ bitmap.

The rule is simple: The active window's palette always takes precedence, and any other windows' images are mapped to the nearest equivalent colors in the active palette.

Because the color mapping algorithm is quite efficient as long as the active palette is relatively varied, the inactive window images should retain most of their colors, or at least approximations of their colors. Again, in a tribute to the algorithm's efficiency, palette switching as different windows take precedence is quite rapid and very smooth.

If you are operating in High Color or True Color mode, all the preceding limitations can simply be ignored. Without palettes, there are no palette conflicts, no palette switching, and no color mapping to fit one image to another image's hues.

Color Composition

Color is an elusive characteristic. People talk about colors with the assumption that everyone—unless they are blind or color-deficient—understands what is meant by blue, red, green, or yellow. We act as if we are referring to something concrete, substantial, and immutable. This was how people though about color for a very long time: colors were realities; colors did not change; colors had mystic properties; colors could cure illness; colors were responsible for everything under the sun. White was special: immaculate; sacred; indivisible; irreducible.

Then Isaac Newton used a prism to split white light into a spectrum of colors.

Perhaps this revelation wasn't as earth-shaking as Galileo's assertions, but it did have an impact, and in its own way, it did change the world. If nothing else, it certainly changed how we look at the world.

For centuries, painters from the Niaux caves to the Left Bank in Paris have relied on the characteristic colors of materials to create their paintings. Burnt umber is not a color but a material. Cinnabar (an oxide of mercury) is a red-orange pigment. Lead oxides are white. Rouge, saffron, indigo…all colors on the painter's palette were materials.

> Note: My apologies to those whose cultural backgrounds include a better knowledge of color than the pre-Newtonian Europeans. Still, it's the European tradition and the European scientific method that are relevant here, because this is the line of learning and education that resulted in Technicolor film and color television and color video monitors for your PCs.

The painter's basic colors can be combined. If you mix red and blue, you make purple. Red and green come out closer to black—some colors simply don't mix well. If you mix a blue pigment and a yellow pigment, the result is usually a green. If you mix black, yellow, and red, you create brown. If you mix several colors, you get black, or maybe a muddy gray.

However, when Newton mixed red and green light from his arrangement of prisms, he didn't get a dark, blackish color. Instead, he got yellow! Bright yellow! Combining blue and green produced cyan. Mixing red and blue didn't make purple; instead, the result was magenta.

It took a while, but soon enough, experimenters and thinkers came up with new theories on the nature and composition of colors. The difference between these new theories and the old Aristotelian theories is that the new, revolutionary rules of color *worked*.

You are concerned with only two color schemes: the RGB color scheme used in your TV, your video monitor, and at the movie theater; and the CMYK color scheme used in print for everything from the *Playboy* centerfold to the Sunday comics.

The RGB color scheme is important because that is the system you use in your computer applications. Less common in your everyday applications is the basic scheme used by every color printer, color plotter, raster camera, and other multihued hard copy device in this industry.

The RGB color wheel is shown in the left half of Figure 13.2. Inside the face of the video tube, you have a fine array of dots of red, green, and blue phosphors. Depending on which of these dots are excited by the beam from the tube's electron guns—and how strongly—you produce all the colors of the rainbow, or at least enough of them to fool your eyes into seeing a rainbow. If you excite all three dots strongly and equally, you see white. If none of the pixels are emitting light, you have black.

Figure 13.2. The RGB and CMYK color wheels.

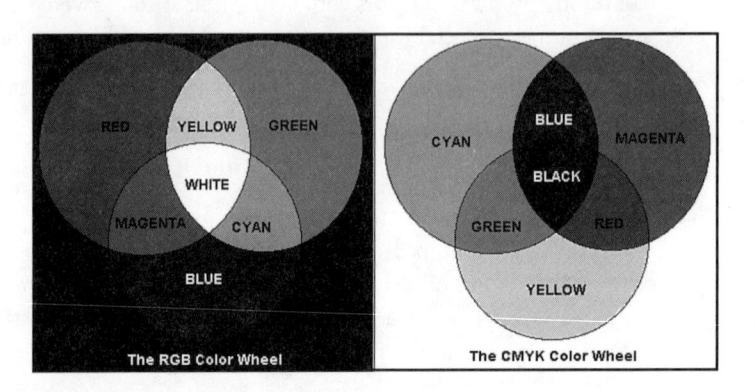

With portable computers, the same effect is produced by opening tiny liquid crystal windows to allow light to shine through colored lenses, either from behind or reflected. You can also turn on tiny colored LEDs to emit colors in varying combinations and strengths.

In either case, the results are the same. You combine red, green, and blue light in varying combinations and strengths to produce the entire spectrum of colors.

For printed color, the process is the reverse of the video tube. On paper, canvas, or print film, you depend on a source of white light, such as the sun or indoor lighting, and use pigments to absorb the colors you don't want. This process is referred to as the CMYK (cyan, magenta, yellow, and black) color system.

A cyan pigment absorbs reds but reflects greens and blues—the same two colors you combined on screen to create cyan. If you combine cyan pigments with magenta, which absorbs greens but reflects reds and blues, both the red and green are absorbed, leaving only the blue reflected, as the CMYK color wheel shows in Figure 13.2.

In color printing, you don't combine these pigments directly; you use tiny dots of each color, a process called *half-toning*, and vary the intensity of each by varying the size of the dots. As long as the dots are small and close together, the result is exactly as desired. You don't see the dots, only the colors produced by the combinations.

> Tip: Use a good magnifying glass and take a close look at the Sunday comics, or use a stronger glass and examine any good color artwork in a magazine.

In theory, you can combine yellow, cyan, and magenta pigments to produce black, except that you aren't actually combining pigments, and you aren't using enough density to produce a real black. The best you can do might be a dark gray. Therefore, the CMYK process includes a separate black element that is used with cyan, magenta, and yellow to produce darker colors as well as grays and blacks.

Your applications are not required to support both the RGB and CMYK color schemes unless you are writing color printer drivers. The majority of programmers can rely on the printer drivers supplied with Windows to handle the translation from the RGB colors to the hard copy device's CMYK color scheme.

The Color1 Program

The Color1 program shown in Figure 13.1 is created simply to demonstrate the Windows stock color palette; it contains no menus or dialog boxes and no elaborate resources. Still, the Color1 application does have a few points worth attention.

In the Color1Vw.CPP source file, where the actual drawing operations take place, the `OnDraw` method uses the `CreateSolidBrush()` method to create brushes using the 20 stock palette colors:

```
////////////////////////////////////////////////////////////////////
// CColor1View drawing

void CColor1View::OnDraw(CDC* pDC)
{
    CColor1Doc* pDoc = GetDocument();
    ASSERT_VALID(pDoc);
```

```
         // TODO: add draw code for native data here
         int     i, j;
         CRect   cRect;

         AfxGetMainWnd()->SetWindowText( "Standard Palette Colors" );
         for( j=0; j<ySteps; j++ )
            for( i=0; i<xSteps; i++ )
            {
               CBrush cBrush;

               cBrush.CreateSolidBrush( 0x01000000 +
                                        ( i + ( j * xSteps ) ) );
               cRect.SetRect( i * m_xSize, j * m_ySize,
                              ( i + 1 ) * m_xSize - 1,
                              ( j + 1 ) * m_ySize - 1 );
               pDC->FillRect( cRect, &cBrush );
            }
```

The argument (`0x01000000` + (i + (j * xSteps))) is a convenient shorthand method of generating a series of values from 0x01000000 through 0x01000014. As RGB colors, these values would be shades of black to slightly off-black. However, because the high byte in each value is 01, these are identified as palette-index color values—a slightly different matter. As each brush is created, the color used is the RGB color value from the system palette.

There are other ways to access the system palette. For one, you can use an `HPALETTE` structure and call the `GetSystemPaletteEntries` function, as follows:

```
HPALETTE    hPal

GetSystemPaletteEntries( hDC, 0, 20, hPal );
```

In this example, `GetSystemPaletteEntries` is asked to start with the 0th palette entry and to retrieve 20 entries. Thus, on return, the `hPal` structure contains the RGB values for palette entries 0 to 19. Because you are calling a Windows API function, not a class method, you first have to retrieve a device context handle to pass to the `GetSystemPaletteEntries` function. Once you have done this, you can request as many entries as you want—up to 256.

Alternatively, you can use the `CPalette` class method `GetPaletteEntries()` to retrieve entries from a custom palette. If you retrieve a handle to the system palette to create a `CPalette` class, this method can also be used to retrieve system palette entries.

Still, the system palette isn't something you are likely to need frequently. The odds are much more likely that you will want to access a custom palette. The next section looks first at how COLORREF values are defined and then continues with custom palettes and palette definitions.

Three Formats for COLORREF Values

All COLORREF values are 4-byte (DWORD) variables; the value in the high byte determines how the COLORREF entry is interpreted. A 0 in the high byte identifies an absolute RGB value; a 1 in the high byte indicates a palette-index value; a 2 in the high byte indicates a palette-relative value.

Absolute RGB COLORREF Values

Absolute RGB COLORREF values use the format 0x00*bbggrr*, where *bb*, *gg*, and *rr* are byte values setting the blue, green, and red intensities.

> Note: Referring to these as RGB values and then setting the actual bytes in the reverse order (*bbggrr*) is perfectly understandable in computer terms. This dates back to the good old days when values were always loaded onto the stack in reverse order because, when needed, they would be retrieved in Last In, First Out order. Thus *RGB* is pseudo-English and *bbggrr* is computerese.

When setting color parameters, as in calling the CreatePen or CreateSolidBrush function, perhaps the most common format is to pass an absolute RGB color value to set the pen or brush color. The absolute RGB COLORREF value is identified by the 0 value in the high byte; the remaining three bytes provide the red, green, and blue intensities for the color.

Individual red, green, and blue values can be combined using the RGB macro, as follows:

```
RGB( bRed, bGreen, bBlue )
```

The returned value takes the form (COLORREF) 0x00bbggrr and is accepted as an absolute color specification.

Palette-Index COLORREF Values

The second COLORREF format is a palette-index format identified by a 1 in the high byte. It takes the format 0x0100*nnnn*, where the low word (*nnnn*) is the index value to a logical palette. In the Color1 demo, the palette index value is generated directly.

You can also use the PALETTEINDEX macro, as follows:

```
PALETTEINDEX( i )
```

The returned COLORREF value has the form 0x01bbggrr and is accepted as a reference to an entry in a logical palette.

Palette-Relative COLORREF Values

The third COLORREF format is the palette-relative format, which is identified by a 2 in the high byte. You can also use the PALETTERGB macro, as follows:

```
PALETTERGB( bRed, bGreen, bBlue )
```

Again, the returned value is a COLORREF value with the form 0x02bbggrr.

For devices that support logical palettes, such as 256-color video devices, the palette-relative RGB value is matched to the nearest color in the device context's logical palette as if this were a palette-index specification.

If the output device does not support palettes, such as a True Color display, the palette-relative RGB value is treated as an absolute RGB color specification.

Dithered Colors

Although 256-color palettes have become the minimum standard for today's systems, earlier, less-versatile color ranges necessitated a practice known as *dithering* to attempt to display colors that were not directly supported. Today, even though dithering is not as necessary as in the past, tradition continues to dictate its presence.

In practice, dithering is a high-tech counterpart to the color half-tones mentioned earlier except that, instead of using the CYMK pigments, dithered colors are composed of two, three, or four colors in an 8×8 array. For example, a good dithered pink may be composed of a mixture of red, yellow, and white selected from the 20 system palette entries.

If you call the Win95 Paint program and double-click any of the palette entries, the Edit Colors dialog box appears. Select the Define Custom Colors button to expand the dialog box (see Figure 13.3). Choose colors from the palette selection on the left until the Color|Solid box on the right shows two different entries: one for Color and another for Solid.

Figure 13.3. *A dithered color entry in the Edit Colors dialog box.*

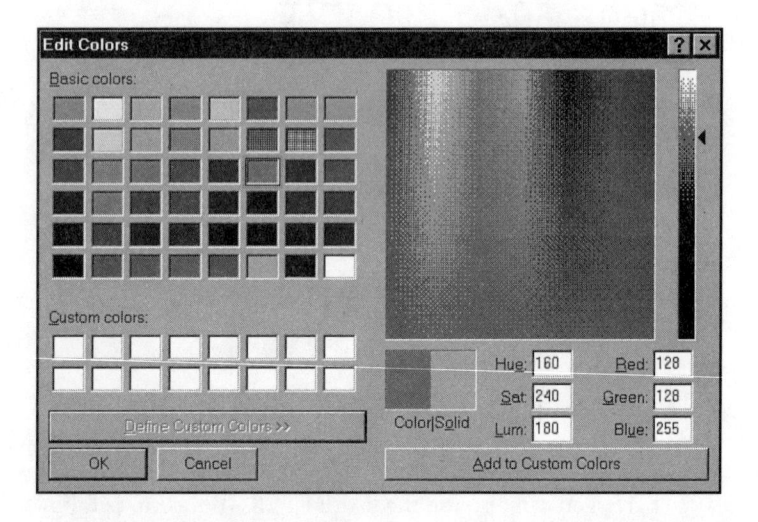

In the figure, the selected color entry is a soft blue produced by dithering a combination of light blue and white. Because dithered colors cannot be used for some purposes such as lines, the Solid entry shown is a gray of roughly equivalent intensity (see "Colors to Grays," later in this chapter). If you select this palette entry for a line, the gray equivalent shown is used; the dithered blue is used for area fills.

Although dithered patterns are provided by and supported by Windows and don't really demand your attention, there are a few points worth noting:

- Dithered colors are always an 8×8 pattern, using a minimum of 64 pixels for the simulated color.
- Dithered colors are never used for lines. Lines are always drawn using the nearest equivalent solid color supported by the palette.
- Dithered colors are composed of two, three, or four individual shades, never more.
- Dithered colors can be used to fill irregular outlines. However, individual pixels can combine visually with borders and outlines. The results may appear to the eye as irregularities or flaws in the outline.

Custom Colors

The Color2 demo program, shown in Figure 13.4, offers an opportunity to see directly how RGB color specifications are translated to screen colors. If you have a 16-color system or reset your video driver to 16-color resolution, you can also experiment with dithering, although this is not the intended purpose.

In addition to experimenting with color values, the Color2 demo program offers an opportunity to demonstrate how keyboard events are trapped using the Tab key and the four arrow keys to step between color rectangles.

However, rather than relying on the following description, it may be worthwhile to copy the demo application to your hard drive and recompile it so that you can use the debugger to follow events as they are described here.

Figure 13.4. *The Custom Colors dialog box in the Color2 demo program.*

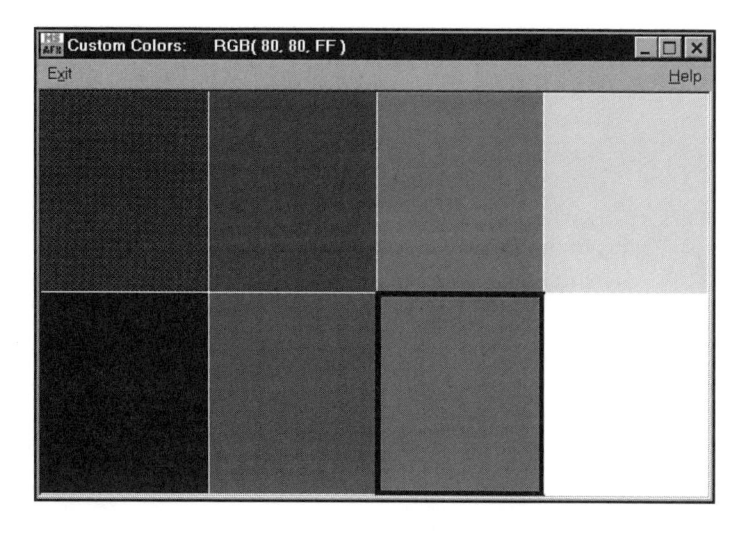

More important, the Color2 application demonstrates how the Color dialog box can be used to set color specifications; it also shows how MFC methods can be used to trap keyboard events.

The Color2 program arranges eight color blocks using an array of RGB member variables, with the selected block identified by a black border. The selected block can be changed by clicking the block with the mouse or by using the Tab or arrow keys to move the selection.

Double-clicking a block calls the Color dialog box with the current block's color. Selecting a new color value from the dialog box resets the RGB color in the member variable array.

Displaying the custom colors is quite simple and is handled in the CColor1View::OnDraw method.

In the OnDraw method, you begin by declaring a few variables, including an array of eight brushes for these eight colors, as follows:

```
/////////////////////////////////////////////////////////////////////
// CColor1View drawing

void CColor1View::OnDraw(CDC* pDC)
{
    CColor1Doc* pDoc = GetDocument();
    ASSERT_VALID(pDoc);
```
```
    int      i, j, k;
    CRect    cRect;
    CString  cString;
    CPen    * pOldPen, cNewPen( PS_SOLID, 5, (COLORREF) 0 );
    CBrush   cBrush[8];
```

The eight m_RGB values initialized in the CColor1View constructor are now used to create an array of brushes that are used to draw the eight color blocks:

```
    for( i=0; i<8; i++ )
        cBrush[i].CreateSolidBrush( m_RGB[i] );
    for( j=0; j<2; j++ )
       for( i=0; i<4; i++ )
       {
          k = i + ( j * xSteps );
          cRect.SetRect( i * m_xSize, j * m_ySize,
                         ( i + 1 ) * m_xSize - 1,
                         ( j + 1 ) * m_ySize - 1 );
          if( m_nSelection != k )
             pDC->FillRect( cRect, &cBrush[ k ] );
```

Seven of the blocks are drawn without borders, using the same FillRect method you used in the Color1 demo. For the eighth block (whichever block is identified by the m_nSelection member variable), you have a few other tasks to carry out.

As shown in the following code, the GetRValue, GetGValue, and GetBValue functions are used to retrieve the current red, green, and blue values from the RGB value and to report these as part of the application title bar. Next, to identify the selected block, you want to create a black pen to draw a rectangle around the block.

```
      else
      {
         cString.Format( "Custom Colors:     RGB( %02X, %02X, %02X )",
                         GetRValue( m_RGB[k] ),
                         GetGValue( m_RGB[k] ),
                         GetBValue( m_RGB[k] ) );
         AfxGetMainWnd()->SetWindowText( cString );
         pDC->SelectObject( &cBrush[ k ] );
         pOldPen = pDC->SelectObject( &cNewPen );
         pDC->Rectangle( cRect );
         pDC->SelectObject( pOldPen );
      }
   }
}
```

There's nothing really complicated involved in these processes. Because brushes and pens are all objects, they are automatically deallocated when they go out of scope after leaving this function. There is no need for cleanup or freeing memory—one of the conveniences of object classes.

One bit of routine, but probably unnecessary, cleanup is handled here: saving the pOldPen when selecting a new one for the outline rectangle, and then restoring the old pen when you are finished. This is unnecessary because the original, default, pen is never used anyway (at least not within the scope of this OnDraw procedure). It is also unnecessary because the pen selection in this method does not affect any drawing operations in any other windows. However, this wasn't always true, and old habits can be hard to break.

Trapping Keyboard Events

Although the Microsoft Foundation Classes and AppWizard supply full-featured edit windows and dialog boxes that handle keyboard events without application provisions, there are still occasions when your application needs or wants to trap keyboard events directly. The Color2 demo offers a good opportunity to demonstrate such handling.

Your first instinct, regarding the choices offered by the ClassWizard, might be to select the WM_CHAR message to create an OnChar method, as shown here:

```
void CColor1View::OnChar(UINT nChar, UINT nRepCnt, UINT nFlags)
{
   // custom handling for key event goes here before
   // CView::OnChar method provides default handling for key event
   CView::OnChar(nChar, nRepCnt, nFlags);
}
```

The OnChar method receives three parameters, as shown in Table 13.3.

Table 13.3. The parameters for the `OnChar` method.

Parameter	Purpose
nChar	Virtual-key (character) code for the key event.
nRepCnt	The repeat count; number of times the keystroke has repeated since the last `OnChar` message. Normally 1, but can be higher if a key is held down.
nFlags	Scan code, key-transition code, previous key state, and context codes, as shown in Table 13.4.

Table 13.4. Codes for the `nFlags` parameter.

Flag Bits	Description
0 to 7	Keyboard scan code (OEM-dependent value).
8	Extended key flag (function keys or numeric keypad). This flag is set (1) for extended key events.
9 to 10	Not used.
11 to 12	Used internally by Windows.
13	Alt key context code. Set (1) if Alt key was down when key event occurred.
14	Prior key state. Set (1) if key was down before key event occurred.
15	Transition state. Set (1) if the key is being released. Clear (0) if the key is being pressed.

For many circumstances, the `OnChar` method is fine and provides a wealth of information about what's going on, but in the Color2 demo, it is a total disaster.

You want to trap the Tab key and the four arrow keys as events. Using the `OnChar` method, the only keyboard event that comes through in a trappable fashion is the Tab key. The arrow keys simply are not visible using the `OnChar` method because they are not recognized as characters.

To trap the events you really want, select the `WM_KEYDOWN` message and generate an `OnKeyDown` method, as shown here:

```
void CColor1View::OnKeyDown(UINT nChar, UINT nRepCnt, UINT nFlags)
{
    switch( nChar )
    {
        case VK_TAB:
        case VK_RIGHT:   m_nSelection++;          Invalidate();   break;
        case VK_LEFT:    m_nSelection—;           Invalidate();   break;
        case VK_UP:      m_nSelection -= xSteps;  Invalidate();   break;
        case VK_DOWN:    m_nSelection += xSteps;  Invalidate();   break;
    }
```

Chapter 13 • Working with Colors, Palettes, and Drawing Modes

```
    if( m_nSelection >= ( xSteps * ySteps ) )
                    m_nSelection -= ( xSteps * ySteps );
    if( m_nSelection < 0 ) m_nSelection += ( xSteps * ySteps );
    CView::OnKeyDown(nChar, nRepCnt, nFlags);
}
```

Like the OnChar method, the OnKeyDown method receives three calling parameters: nChar with the character code; nRepCnt with the key repeat count; and nFlags.

There are only a few real differences. First, in the nFlags parameter, the context code (bit 13) is always 0, meaning that the Alt key is ignored at this point. The key-transition code (bit 15) must also be 0, because this is a key-down event.

> Note: On a key-down event, it is possible for the nRptCnt parameter to be greater than 1. This would require multiple key presses (not a key held down) while another process was dominating the CPU and preventing the application from retrieving keyboard messages. Even though this is not likely, you should keep the possibility in mind when designing your application, just in case you have to respond to multiple key-down events.

Second, and most important, the nChar parameter is not filtered for valid character codes but is received for every keyboard event, regardless of whether the key generates a valid character.

Within the OnKeyDown method, a simple switch...case statement handles your responses by incrementing or decrementing the m_nSelection variable, invalidating the window, and checking that m_nSelection remains valid.

In this example, the response is quite simple; there is no particular need to check flags or repeat counts, and you are interested in only five keyboard events. Under other circumstances, however, you may want to be able to respond to a much wider variety of conditions, or to more complicated conditions.

Other Keyboard Events

In addition to the OnKeyDown and OnChar methods, ClassWizard is also prepared to respond to WM_KEYUP messages. These have an OnKeyUp method that functions essentially the same as the OnKeyDown method except, of course, for the event occurring when a key is released, rather than when a key is pressed.

There are four other keyboard messages, although you won't find these listed in ClassWizard's Message Map Messages list. Instead, if you need these, you must write your own workarounds. These are the WM_DEADCHAR, WM_SYSCHAR, WM_SYSKEYDOWN, and WM_SYSKEYUP messages.

The WM_DEADCHAR and WM_SYSCHAR messages are generally used by non-US keyboards. They supply accents or diacritical marks, provide other special functions or, for Unicode applications, generate special selections. Because these keys do not generate characters directly, they are called *dead keys*.

The WM_SYSKEYDOWN and WM_SYSKEYUP messages are generally intended for the system rather than the application. They include such events as the Alt+Tab and Alt+Esc combinations used to switch the active window or the system menu accelerators. Although these keys can be used directly by the application under special circumstances, they are normally left to the Windows system for handling.

Trapping Mouse Events

Mouse events are always useful and often essential. Many aspects of your applications rely on default handling to recognize and respond to mouse messages for everything from resizing application windows to menu selections and titlebar buttons. However, there will always be a need for your applications to recognize and respond directly to where the mouse is and what is happening.

For this purpose, several mouse messages are supplied, as shown in Table 13.5.

> Note: Because Windows allows the right and left mouse buttons to be swapped, the LBUTTON messages always come from the primary mouse button and RBUTTON messages always come from the secondary mouse button, regardless of whether these are actually the right or left buttons.
>
> Also, because Windows mouse drivers do not currently support three-button mice, until new drivers are provided or OEM mouse manufacturers create new 32-bit drivers, the MBUTTON messages are simply not supported.

Table 13.5. Mouse messages.

Message	*Method*	*Purpose*
WM_MOUSEMOVE	OnMouseMove	Reports any movement of the mouse.
WM_LBUTTONDBLCLK	OnLButtonDblClk	Reports a double-click of the primary mouse button.
WM_LBUTTONDOWN	OnLButtonDown	Reports a single-click of the primary mouse button.
WM_LBUTTONUP	OnLButtonUp	Reports the primary mouse button release.
WM_MBUTTONDBLCLK	OnMButtonDblClk	Reports a double-click of the third mouse button.
WM_MBUTTONDOWN	OnMButtonDown	Reports a single-click of the third mouse button.
WM_MBUTTONUP	OnMButtonUp	Reports the third mouse button release.
WM_RBUTTONDBLCLK	OnRButtonDblClk	Reports a double-click of the secondary mouse button.
WM_RBUTTONDOWN	OnRButtonDown	Reports a single-click of the secondary mouse button.
WM_RBUTTONUP	OnRButtonUp	Reports the secondary mouse button release.

In each case, the mouse message is accompanied by two arguments. The first is a `CPoint` instance that contains the x and y coordinates of the mouse at the time the event occurred. Because these coordinates are always expressed in logical units relative to the client window origin (the upper-left corner), there is no need for elaborate conversions or offsets.

The second argument is an `nFlags` parameter that indicates the state of various virtual keys at the instant the mouse key was pressed or the mouse was moved. These options are shown in Table 13.6.

Table 13.6. The `nFlags` parameters.

Parameter	Purpose
MK_CONTROL	Right or left Ctrl key was down.
MK_LBUTTON	Left mouse button was down.
MK_MBUTTON	Middle mouse button was down.
MK_RBUTTON	Right mouse button was down.
MK_SHIFT	Right or left Shift key was down.

Including the mouse button states in the flags might seem a bit redundant. However, the `WM_MOUSEMOVE` message is generated by movement, not by a button operation, and the mouse is used for various types of drag-and-drop operations. Therefore, there are ample reasons for wanting to know at any instant whether a button has been released.

Also, for other operations, such as File Manager copy and move operations, the state of the Ctrl and Shift keys becomes relevant. Although you can query these separately, they are also included in all mouse messages.

> Note: Querying button states, whether keyboard or mouse, at the time the message is processed does not guarantee that the reported states will be the same as they were at the time the mouse event was generated.

Although these mouse messages are commonly messages directed to your application, or directed to specific application windows, there are also occasions in which you may want to trap mouse events outside your application. This can be accomplished by using the `SetCapture` API to ensure that all mouse messages are passed to your application for attention. One example of this usage is when you want to capture a screen image by using the right mouse button to trigger capture, or by clicking and holding the right mouse button while selecting an area of the screen.

If you are not going to respond to them yourself, these messages should still be returned for processing by the intended window. Refer also to the `GetCapture` and `ReleaseCapture` APIs.

Mouse Messages in the Color2 Demo

For the Color2 demo, you are interested in only two of the mouse messages: the WM_LBUTTONDOWN and WM_LBUTTONDBLCLK messages. These are mapped to the OnLButtonDown and OnLButtonDblClk methods, respectively.

The OnLButtonDown method is used to identify which area in the client window—which color block—the user has clicked. The OnLButtonDown method is shown here:

```
void CColor1View::OnLButtonDown(UINT nFlags, CPoint point)
{
    m_nSelection = ( point.x / m_xSize ) +
                 ( ( point.y / m_ySize ) * xSteps );
    Invalidate();
    CView::OnLButtonDown(nFlags, point);
}
```

OnLButtonDown is called with two parameters: the nFlags variable and the point argument. For the purposes of this example, you are interested only in the mouse position being reported in the CPoint instance. A simple calculation transforms the point.x and point.y values to an appropriate value for the m_nSelection member.

In the OnLButtonDblClk method, shown next, the block selection has already been carried out by the first click of the left mouse button and does not need to be repeated here. Instead, the only tasks required here are to retrieve the current color value and place it in ccDlg.m_cc.rgbResult and to set the ccDlg.m_cc.Flags value to CC_RGBINIT, ensuring that the Color dialog box is initialized with the current color.

```
void CColor1View::OnLButtonDblClk(UINT nFlags, CPoint point)
{
    CColorDialog ccDlg;

    ccDlg.m_cc.rgbResult = m_RGB[m_nSelection];
    ccDlg.m_cc.Flags |= CC_RGBINIT;
    if( ccDlg.DoModal() == IDOK )
    {
        m_RGB[m_nSelection] = ccDlg.GetColor();
        Invalidate();
    }
    CView::OnLButtonDblClk(nFlags, point);
}
```

If the Color dialog box returns IDOK, the current m_RGB selection receives the returned color value, and the window is invalidated so that it will be redrawn with the new color.

Colors to Grays

Earlier, when discussing colors and color composition, I mentioned that color printing was handled by the printer drivers and wasn't really a concern of your applications. For black-and-white printers, essentially the same is true; the printer drivers handle converting colors to gray scales for reproduction.

How well the printer drivers handle the conversion is an open question. Many of them do very well, but not all. It is hardly proper to raise a question like this without offering at least a minimal solution, so I offer a few notes on converting colors to grays.

The principal issue in printing color on a black-and-white printer is to have the gray-scaled image resemble the color image as closely as possible. Therefore, the first requirement is a method of converting colors to gray tones.

The human eye does not recognize colors equally, in terms of absolute intensity. Taking the three primary colors you use on the monitor—red, green, and blue—the human eye perceives green almost twice as well as red, and the eye's response to blue is only a third of the red response.

A gray-scale formula approximating this response is written as follows:

```
Red * 0.30 + Green * 0.59 + Blue * 0.11
```

To convert the Windows RGB values, which use colors in the range 0 to 255, the equivalent formula for an RGB color specification is shown here:

$$W = \frac{(R * 0.30)}{255} + \frac{(G * 0.59)}{255} + \frac{(B * 0.11)}{255}$$

In this formula, W is the percentage of white in the corresponding gray.

The black percentage for the printer is `B = 100 - W`.

Returning to the palette shown in Figure 13.1 (the Windows default palette), you can apply this formula to the RGB values for these shades to calculate a percent white and to write an equivalent RGBgray specification. Also, for convenience, you can reorder the list according to gray intensities, as shown in Table 13.7.

Table 13.7. Colors to grays.

Color	R	G	B	White %	RGB Gray
Black	00	00	00	0.0%	0x000000
Dark Blue	00	00	80	5.5%	0x0E0E0E
Blue	00	00	FF	11.0%	0x1C1C1C
Dark Red	80	00	00	15.0%	0x262626
Violet	80	00	FF	26.0%	0x424242
Dark Green	00	80	00	29.6%	0x4C4C4C
Red	FF	00	00	30.0%	0x4D4D4D
Dark Cyan	80	80	80	35.1%	0x5A5A5A
Magenta	FF	00	FF	41.0%	0x696969
Gold	80	80	00	44.6%	0x727272

continues

Table 13.7. continued

Color	R	G	B	White %	RGB Gray
Dark Gray	80	80	80	50.2%	0x808080
Green	00	FF	00	59.0%	0x969696
Blue-Gray	98	A8	C8	65.4%	0xA7A7A7
Light Cyan	00	FF	FF	70.0%	0xB3B3B3
Light Gray	C0	C0	C0	75.3%	0xC0C0C0
Pale Green	80	FF	80	79.6%	0xCBCBCB
Pale Blue	80	FF	FF	85.0%	0xD9D9D9
Yellow	FF	FF	00	89.0%	0xE3E3E3
Off-White	F0	F8	F0	96.0%	0xF5F5F5
White	FF	FF	FF	100.0%	0xFFFFFF

Notice that dark green and red are almost indistinguishable as grays—a problem that many color-blind individuals are well aware of.

> Tip: Instead of the formula shown, try calculating the average of the red, green, and blue color values. Compare the results produced this way against the color response results.

This is hardly the answer to all your questions about gray-scale conversions, but it's a start.

Raster Drawing Operations (ROP2)

I have talked about how colors are defined and about how colors are displayed, but thus far not much has been said about how drawing operations are carried out. Before going into detail on drawing operations in Chapter 14, "Using Drawing Tools," I want to discuss one other aspect of screen operations that affects colors: the drawing modes.

Drawing modes, known as *ROP2 modes* or *binary drawing modes*, determine how drawing operations interact with the underlying screen. Normally, drawing operations are carried out using the default R2_COPYPEN mode, in which the drawing operation simply overwrites the existing screen image.

However, suppose that you want to write text across a complex background image so that you can ensure that the text was distinctly visible at all points. Further, assume that the background is a chessboard of black and white squares.

If you use a black pen, this shows up nicely against the white squares but disappears against the black squares. If you use a white pen, the reverse is true. Another option is to use the R2_NOT drawing mode, which simply inverts the existing screen wherever you are writing and ignores your drawing color entirely.

The result is precisely what you need: black letters against a white background; white letters against a black background; and half-and-half letters where the background color changes. Try doing that with conventional techniques.

In theory, dozens of ROP2 drawing modes are possible; in practice, Windows defines 16 such operations in WinGDI.H. These operations are listed in Table 13.8 and are shown in the Color3 demo shown in Figure 13.5.

Table 13.8. ROP2 binary drawing operations.

ROP2 Constant	Logical Operation*	Result
R2_NOP	S	Screen image is not affected (no operation)
R2_NOT	~ S	Existing screen image is inverted
R2_COPYPEN	P	Pen overwrites screen image (default operation)
R2_NOTCOPYPEN	~ P	Inverted pen overwrites screen image
R2_MASKPEN	P & S	Pen ANDed with screen image
R2_MASKNOTPEN	~ P & S	Inverted pen ANDed with screen image
R2_MASKPENNOT	P & ~ S	Pen ANDed with inverted screen image
R2_NOTMASKPEN	~ (P & S)	Pen ANDed with screen image, then result inverted
R2_MERGEPEN	P | S	Pen ORed with screen image
R2_MERGENOTPEN	~ P | S	Inverted pen ORed with screen image
R2_MERGEPENNOT	P | ~ S	Pen ORed with inverted screen image
R2_NOTMERGEPEN	~ (P | S)	Pen ORed with screen image, then result inverted
R2_XORPEN	P ^ S	Pen XORed with screen image
R2_NOTXORPEN	~ (P ^ S)	Pen XORed with screen image, then result inverted
R2_BLACK	0	Black line (drawing color ignored)
R2_WHITE (R2_LAST)	1	White line (drawing color ignored)

*S = screen, P = pen

> Note: These ROP2 codes are not listed in the order of their identifying constants; they are grouped functionally.

The Color3 demo, shown in Figure 13.5, uses the default palette to draw 20 vertical color bars to serve as background. The color menu offers a selection of eight colors used against the color-bar background to draw lines using the 16 ROP2 drawing modes. The modes used for these horizontal lines are in the order listed in Table 13.8.

Figure 13.5. The Color3 demo with ROP2 drawing modes.

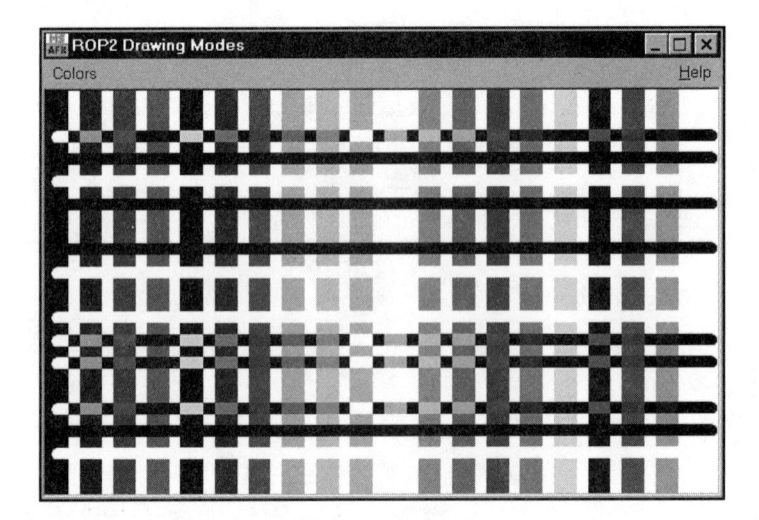

> Tip: Because the first line is drawn using the R2_NOP mode (which does nothing), it has no effect on the background and therefore is invisible.

The Color3 Demo Program

Back in Chapter 12, "Working with Mapping Modes," when mapping modes were introduced, a number of uses for the anisotropic mapping mode were suggested. The Color3 demo, described here, describes another use.

In the Color3 demo, you draw 20 vertical color bars and then draw 16 horizontal bars. One way to do this is to get the size of the client window and calculate the positions and widths for each.

You can also take the easy route.

The easy route, after selecting MM_ANISOTROPIC for the mapping mode, is to set the viewport extent to match the client window size and then set the window extent to an arbitrary, but convenient, horizontal and vertical size, as shown here:

```
//////////////////////////////////////////////////////////////////
// CColor3View drawing

void CColor3View::OnDraw(CDC* pDC)
{
    CColor3Doc* pDoc = GetDocument();
    ASSERT_VALID(pDoc);
```

```
CBrush   cBrush[20];
CRect    cRect;
CPen     cPen;
int      i;

pDC->SetMapMode( MM_ANISOTROPIC );
AfxGetMainWnd()->GetClientRect( &cRect );
pDC->SetViewportExt( cRect.right, cRect.bottom );
pDC->SetWindowExt( nHorz, nVert );
```

In this case, *convenient* is a horizontal size of 60 units and a vertical size of 18, which is how nHorz and nVert are defined in ColorVw.H.

With the virtual window extent set to your preferred dimensions, the next step is to initialize a set of brushes using the default palette entries and draw the vertical color bars as rectangles positioned at increments of three logical units with a width of two units, as shown here:

```
AfxGetMainWnd()->SetWindowText( "ROP2 Drawing Modes" );
   for( i=0; i<20; i++ )
      cBrush[i].CreateSolidBrush( 0x01000000 + i );
   for( i=0; i<20; i++ )
   {
      cRect.SetRect( i*3, 0, i*3+2, nVert );
      pDC->FillRect( &cRect, &cBrush[i] );
   }
```

A rectangle only two pixels wide wouldn't exactly fit the requirements. But a rectangle of two *logical* units with these viewport and window extents produces a very satisfactory series of color bars separated by white space half the width of the bars.

For the horizontal lines, the next step is to create a pen using the color selected from the menu and then to draw 16 horizontal lines, switching ROP2 modes for each line, as shown here:

```
cPen.CreatePen( PS_SOLID, 1, m_RGB[m_nSelection] );
   for( i=0; i<16; i++ )
   {
      pDC->SetROP2( m_DrawMode[i] );
      pDC->SelectObject( &cPen );
      pDC->MoveTo( 1, i+1 );
      pDC->LineTo( nHorz-1, i+1 );
   }
}
```

Again, the lines have a width of one logical unit and consequently produce a series of horizontal lines that demonstrate the several ROP2 interactions.

> Note: In theory, the horizontal lines drawn using these settings should not leave gaps between. The fact that they do so when executed under Win95 is not readily discernible. It can be assumed to be simply another symptom of the previously mentioned idiosyncrasies in the Win95 mapping modes. For comparison, execute this same demo under WinNT, where the lines are sized correctly and the horizontal gaps vanish.

Summary

This chapter discussed color, including system color capabilities and standard palettes, and how colors are defined. Because not all systems support all possible colors, dithered colors were also introduced.

For users who have at least 256-color palette capabilities, the Color2 demo shows how the RGB color specifications affect the on-screen display. It also demonstrates trapping both keyboard and mouse events, as well as using the Color dialog box to set color values.

Because color printers, unlike monitors, are neither standard nor common, I have touched briefly on how colors can be converted to true grays.

Last, having demonstrated colors, the ROP2 drawing modes were introduced and used to show how colors interact in different drawing modes.

Chapter 14, "Using Drawing Tools," continues the coverage of drawing operations with the introduction of drawing tools.

CHAPTER 14

Using Drawing Tools

Today's programming languages commonly provide a good variety of drawing functions, or graphic primitives, to handle everything from drawing a straight line to composing complex shapes. But this has not always been the case; having had considerable first-hand experience in creating graphic primitives, I can say that the introduction of drawing functions in Turbo Pascal years ago was more than a minor relief. Today, any programming language lacking such graphics support would be laughed out of the market—even spreadsheets and databases support some form of drawing operations.

Even though the available drawing tools for Visual C++ are less elaborate than those in, for example, CorelDRAW!, they are nonetheless a fairly sophisticated selection. Unfortunately, in some cases, they are also more sophisticated in their operation than in their interface design.

Shape and Line Tools

Windows APIs (and the MFC CDC class methods) provide a variety of shape primitives ranging from simple lines to circular and elliptical curves, rectangles, and complex polygons. You are provided with a variety of logical pens and brushes for drawing and filling shapes.

Although there are more options and forms among these than it is practical to demonstrate, the Draw1 and Draw2 programs offer illustrations of most of the principal drawing tools. Let's begin with the tools themselves.

Logical Pens

A *logical pen* is defined by three elements: line pattern (style), width, and color. Pens can also be defined by end styles and join (corner) styles, although these are normally left at the default values.

Three standard pens selected using the `CPen::GetStockObject` function are defined in Table 14.1.

Table 14.1. Stock pens.

Style ID	Pen Style
BLACK_PEN	Black pen
NULL_PEN	NULL pen
WHITE_PEN	White pen

If your application begins drawing without first selecting a pen, the stock BLACK_PEN is used by default.

Because you have been using the MFC classes, the simplest pen to examine is the CPen class.

The CPen class is defined with three overloaded constructors, as follows:

```
CPen( );

CPen( int nPenStyle, int nWidth, COLORREF crColor )
    throw( CResourceException );

CPen( int nPenStyle, int nWidth, const LOGBRUSH* pLogBrush,
      int nStyleCount = 0, const DWORD* lpStyle = NULL )
    throw( CResourceException );
```

When the first (empty) constructor is called, the CPen object must be initialized using the CreatePen, CreatePenIndirect, or CreateStockObject member function. If you use the second or third constructor, no further initialization is required. The parameters for these constructors are explained in Table 14.2.

> Note: Constructors with arguments can throw an exception if errors are encountered. The empty constructor is always successful unless memory limitations are encountered.

Table 14.2. Parameters for the second and third constructors.

Parameter	Function
nPenStyle	Specifies the pen style. This parameter in the first version of the constructor can be one (or more) of the values shown in Tables 14.3 and 14.4.

Parameter	Function
nWidth	Specifies the width of the pen. If set to 0, the width defaults to 1 pixel. If nPenStyle is PS_GEOMETRIC, the width is in logical units. If nPenStyle is PS_COSMETIC, the width must be set to 1.
crColor	RGB color specification for the pen.
pLogBrush	LOGBRUSH structure. If nPenStyle is PS_COSMETIC, the lbColor member (of the LOGBRUSH structure) specifies the color of the pen, and the lbStyle member must be BS_SOLID. If nPenStyle is PS_GEOMETRIC, all members are required to specify the brush attributes for the pen.
nStyleCount	Size in DWORD units of the lpStyle array, or 0 if nPenStyle is not PS_USERSTYLE.
lpStyle	Array of DWORD values. The first value specifies the length of the first dash in a user-defined style. The second value specifies the length of the first space. Must be NULL if nPenStyle is not PS_USERSTYLE.

For most purposes, one of the standard pen styles shown in Table 14.3 is sufficient.

Table 14.3. Standard pen styles.

Style ID	Line Style	Example	Line Width
PS_SOLID	Solid	────────────	Variable
PS_DASH	Dashed (pen width must be 1)	− − − − − − − − − − −	1
PS_DOT	Dotted (pen width must be 1)	. . . .	1
PS_DASHDOT	Alternates dashes and dots (pen width must be 1)	−.−.−.−.−.−.	1
PS_DASHDOTDOT	Alternates dashes and double dots	−..−..−..−.−.	1
PS_NULL	No line (blank)		0

continues

Table 14.3. continued

Style ID	Line Style	Example	Line Width
PS_INSIDEFRAME	Pen is restricted to draw only inside the frame created by a closed shape function (such as an `Ellipse`, `Rectangle`, `RoundRect`, `Pie`, or `Chord`). Used with open shape functions (such as `LineTo` or `Arc`), the drawing area is not limited. If the pen width is 1, PS_INSIDEFRAME is treated as PS_SOLID.		Variable

The third CPen constructor offers a chance to customize the CPen style by including combined style sets by ORing the type, style, end cap, and join attributes. The extended style specifiers are shown in Table 14.4.

Table 14.4. Additional pen styles.

Pen Styles	
PS_GEOMETRIC	Geometric pen
PS_COSMETIC	Cosmetic pen
PS_ALTERNATE	Pen alternates pixels (must be cosmetic pen)
PS_USERSTYLE	Pen uses styling array; see `lpStyle` parameter
End Cap Styles	
PS_ENDCAP_ROUND	Rounded ends
PS_ENDCAP_SQUARE	Square ends
PS_ENDCAP_FLAT	Flat ends
Joint Styles	
PS_JOIN_BEVEL	Beveled joins
PS_JOIN_MITER	Joins are mitered if within limits set by the ::SetMiterLimit function; otherwise, the join is beveled
PS_JOIN_ROUND	Rounded joins

Creating a Logical Pen

Conventionally, a logical pen is created using the ::CreatePen function with specifications for the style, width, and color, as follows:

```
hPen = ::CreatePen( nLineStyle, nPenWidth, rgbColor );
hOldPen = ::SelectObject( hdc, hPen );
```

After creating the pen, calling SelectPen associates the pen with the device context and, optionally, returns a handle to the previous pen.

You can also create an array of pens, selecting each as needed using SelectObject(), but this wastes memory without offering much in the way of advantages.

After you finish with each pen, you must dispose of it:

```
::SelectObject( hdc, hOldPen );
::DeleteObject( hPen );
```

After restoring the original pen, the DeleteObject function gets rid of the pen.

> Caution: Do not delete a pen or brush while it is associated with an active device context, unless the device context is about to be closed.

Using a CPen object offers a simple approach:

```
cPen.CreatePen( nLineStyle, 1, rgbColor );
pDC->SelectObject( &cPen );
```

Although the declaration and selection are essentially the same, with the CPen object there is no need to delete the object when you are finished with it. The object destructor handles this automatically when the object goes out of scope.

Logical Brushes

Logical pens are provided to draw lines; *logical brushes* are used to paint areas. Like logical pens, logical brushes are defined by a color specification and a pattern. A width does not apply to a brush because brushes are used for area fill operations.

The seven standard brushes selected using the GetStockObject function are defined in Table 14.5.

Table 14.5. Stock brushes.

Style ID	Brush Style
BLACK_BRUSH	Black brush
DKGRAY_BRUSH	Dark gray brush
GRAY_BRUSH	Gray brush

continues

Table 14.5. continued

Style ID	Brush Style
HOLLOW_BRUSH	Hollow brush (equivalent to NULL_BRUSH)
LTGRAY_BRUSH	Light gray brush
NULL_BRUSH	Null brush (equivalent to HOLLOW_BRUSH)
WHITE_BRUSH	White brush

> Caution: The DKGRAY_BRUSH, GRAY_BRUSH, and LTGRAY_BRUSH stock objects should be used only in windows with the CS_HREDRAW and CS_VREDRAW styles. Using any of these three brushes in a window without the redraw styles can result in a misalignment of brush patterns after a window is moved or sized.

Stock brushes aside, logical brushes are defined by style, color, and pattern values in the LOGBRUSH structure passed to the CBrush::CreateBrushIndirect method.

The LOGBRUSH structure is defined as follows:

```
typedef struct tagLOGBRUSH
{
    UINT     lbStyle;
    COLORREF lbColor;
    LONG     lbHatch;
} LOGBRUSH;
```

The lbStyle value can be any of the BS_ identifiers listed in Table 14.6.

Table 14.6. Brush styles.

Style ID	Fill Style
BS_SOLID	Solid fill
BS_NULL	No fill; lbColor is ignored
BS_HOLLOW	Same as BS_NULL
BS_HATCHED	Uses hatch patterns (see Table 14.8). The lbColor value sets the foreground color for the hatch pattern. (Background color is set by the SetBkMode and SetBkColor functions.)
BS_PATTERN	Pattern brush defined by a memory bitmap. lbColor is ignored. lbHatch contains a handle to the bitmap pattern.
BS_INDEXED	Undocumented
BS_DIBPATTERN	A pattern brush defined by a device-independent bitmap (DIB) specification. If lbStyle is BS_DIBPATTERN, the lbHatch member contains a handle to a packed DIB.

Style ID	Fill Style
BS_DIBPATTERNPT	A pattern brush defined by a device-independent bitmap (DIB) specification. If lbStyle is BS_DIBPATTERNPT, the lbHatch member contains a pointer to a packed DIB.
BS_PATTERN8X8	Undocumented
BS_DIBPATTERN8X8	Undocumented

> Note: Unfortunately, three brush styles listed are not documented or explained. Feel free to experiment.

If lbStyle is identified as BS_DIBPATTERN or BS_DIBPATTERNPT, the low-order word of lbColor specifies whether the bmiColors members of the BITMAPINFO structure contain explicit red, green, and blue (RGB) values or indexes into the currently realized logical palette. The lbColor member must be one of the values listed in Table 14.7.

Table 14.7. Color table identifiers for logical brushes.

Color ID	Definition
DIB_PAL_COLORS	Color table consists of an array of 16-bit indexes to the active palette.
DIB_RGB_COLORS	Color table contains literal RGB values.

Hatch Patterns

Several hatch-fill patterns are provided and identified by constants defined in WinGDI.H. These hatch-fill patterns are listed in Table 14.8.

Table 14.8. Hatch-fill patterns.

Hatch Fill Style	Value	Pattern
HS_HORIZONTAL	0	Horizontal lines
HS_VERTICAL	1	Vertical lines
HS_FDIAGONAL	2	Forward diagonal, coarse spacing, approximately 45°
HS_BDIAGONAL	3	Backward diagonal, coarse spacing, approximately 45°
HS_CROSS	4	Horizontal cross-hatch
HS_DIAGCROSS	5	Diagonal cross-hatch

> Note: Originally, an additional 13 hatch-fill patterns were defined for WinNT and identified by the following constants: `HS_FDIAGONAL1`, `HS_BDIAGONAL1`, `HS_SOLID`, `HS_DENSE1`...`HS_DENSE8`, `HS_NOSHADE`, and `HS_HALFTONE`. These are no longer defined and are not supported by Win95.

Creating a Logical Brush

A logical hatch-fill brush is created in the same fashion as the logical pens described previously and subject to the same restrictions. In the Draw1 demo program, the logical brushes are created as follows:

```
if( nFillStyle == -1 )
{
   logBrush.lbStyle = BS_HOLLOW;
   logBrush.lbHatch = NULL;
}
else
{
   logBrush.lbStyle = BS_HATCHED;
   logBrush.lbHatch = nFillStyle;
}
logBrush.lbColor = rgbColor;
cBrush.CreateBrushIndirect( &logBrush );
pDC->SelectObject( &cBrush );
```

A fill style of −1 has been defined outside WinGDI.H to provide for a hollow-fill selection. This provision aside, the logical brush is created using a `CBrush` object in essentially the same fashion as was done with the logical pens.

Other Logical Brush Methods

The `CBrush::CreateDIBPatternBrush` method initializes a brush with the pattern specified by a device-independent bitmap (DIB).

A packed DIB consists of a `BITMAPINFO` data structure immediately followed by the array of bytes defining bitmap pixels. For fill patterns, bitmaps should be 8 pixels by 8 pixels. If a larger bitmap is used, only the first 8 rows from the first 8 columns are used—that is, the 8×8 array from the upper-left corner of the bitmap.

The `CBrush::CreatePatternBrush` method is similar to the `CBrush::CreateDIBPatternBrush` method except that the bitmap is typically initialized by using the `CBitmap::CreateBitmap`, `CBitmap::CreateBitmapIndirect`, `CBitmap::LoadBitmap`, or `CBitmap::CreateCompatibleBitmap` functions. The brush created can subsequently be selected for any device context supporting raster operations.

> Note: Bitmap pattern brushes can be deleted without affecting the associated bitmaps. Thus, the bitmap can be used to create any number of pattern brushes without having to be reloaded.

The `CBrush::CreateSolidBrush` method is called with an RGB color value to initialize a solid color brush.

The `CBrush::CreateHatchBrush` method is called with an index to a hatch pattern (refer back to Table 14.8) and an RGB color value to initialize a hatch brush.

Standard Drawing Shapes

Styled lines and patterned brushes are of little use by themselves. To use lines and brushes, drawing tools are necessary as well. Visual C++ provides a selection of shape tools as listed in Table 14.9.

Table 14.9. Shape-drawing tools.

Function	Shape
Arc	Any open curve; can be elliptical or circular
ArcTo	Any open curve; can be elliptical or circular
Chord	An arc with the end points connected by a chord
Ellipse	A closed curve; can be elliptical or circular
LineTo	A simple line connecting two points
Pie	Any open curve with the end points connected to the center point; can be elliptical or circular
Polygon	Any multisided figure
PolyPolygon	Multiple multisided figures
Rectangle	A rectangle or square with square corners
RoundRect	A rectangle or square with rounded corners

> Note: In Windows 95, the `RoundRect` function requires that the sum of the coordinates of the bounding rectangle cannot exceed 32,767.

The *LineTo* Function

The `CDC::LineTo` method uses the selected logical pen to draw a line beginning at the current position to a specified point. The specified end point can be supplied in either of two forms: as separate x and y coordinates or as a `POINT` or `CPoint` coordinate pair.

The origin point for the line is determined by the current position. The *current position* is a location maintained within the device context like an invisible cursor. The current position is always set at the end point of the last drawing operation.

The `GetCurrentPosition` method can be used to retrieve the current position; the `MoveTo` method can be used to set the current position without a drawing operation.

In the Draw1 demo program, select the line tool from the menu or the toolbar. Click the left (or primary) mouse button to set the start point for the line and call the `MoveTo` function to set the current position to the mouse coordinates. Release the button to set the end point.

As long as the mouse button is down, each time the mouse moves, a dotted line is drawn from the start point to the current mouse position.

To be more accurate, a dotted line is drawn from the start point to the previous end point, then the end point is updated and the line is drawn once more. Refer to the `DrawDotLine` procedure shown in Listing 14.1.

Listing 14.1. The `DrawDotLine` function.

```
void CDraw1View::DrawDotLine( CDC *pDC )
{
    CPen        cPen;

    pDC->MoveTo( rFrame.left, rFrame.top );
    pDC->SetROP2( R2_XORPEN );
    cPen.CreatePen( PS_DOT, 1, RGB(0,0,0) );
    pDC->SelectObject( &cPen );
    pDC->LineTo( rFrame.right, rFrame.bottom );
}
```

First, notice that the `MoveTo` function is called to reset the current position each time. Remember that after the line is drawn, the new current position becomes the end point of the drawing operation. If the device context has closed and then reopened, the current position is reset, nominally to the device context origin point. The moral is to not rely on the current position.

Second, because you are using the `R2_XORPEN` drawing mode, each time the line is drawn, it is XORed with the existing image. Drawing the same line a second time has the effect of erasing the line, which is exactly what is desired.

Finally, the `PS_DOT` pen style gives you a dotted line.

The end result is that you produce a dotted line that is an inversion of the background image. It is anchored at the start point and follows the mouse as it moves.

When the mouse button is released, the `DrawDotLine` function is called a final time to erase the dotted line before the solid line is drawn using a solid pen in the selected color.

The *Rectangle* Function

The `CDC::Rectangle` function is called either with four individual coordinates or with a `RECT` structure or `CRect` member defining the rectangle position. Like the `LineTo` drawing function, the `Rectangle` function uses the selected logical pen. In addition, the `Rectangle` function uses the selected brush to fill the interior of the rectangle.

A square is simply a special case of a rectangle in which the horizontal and vertical dimensions are equal. This can be created quite easily, as follows:

```
Rectangle( xUL, yUL,    // creates a square
           xUL + min( xLR-xUL, yLR-yUL ),
           yUL + min( xLR-xUL, yLR-yUL ) );
```

You can perform similar adjustments in several other fashions. For another approach, refer to the `AdjustRect()` function in the Draw1VW.CPP source file (see the Draw1 demo application included on the CD-ROM that accompanies this book).

> Note: In addition to drawing rectangles, the `Rectangle` function also serves as the basis for the `Ellipse`, `Arc`, `Chord`, and other curve functions, all of which are defined by a bounding rectangle.

Just as the `DrawDotLine` function was used to trace a line as the mouse moved, the `DrawOutline` function does the same for shapes (see Listing 14.2).

Listing 14.2. The `DrawOutline` function.

```
void CDraw1View::DrawOutline( CDC *pDC )
{
    CPen     cPen;
    CBrush   cBrush;
    LOGBRUSH logBrush;

    pDC->SetROP2( R2_XORPEN );
    logBrush.lbStyle = BS_HOLLOW;
    logBrush.lbColor = NULL;
    logBrush.lbHatch = NULL;
    cBrush.CreateBrushIndirect( &logBrush );
    pDC->SelectObject( &cBrush );
    cPen.CreatePen( PS_DOT, 1, RGB(0,0,0) );
    pDC->SelectObject( &cPen );
    pDC->Rectangle( &rFrame );
}
```

For simplicity, the DrawOutline function is used for all shapes. The actual shape—rectangle, arc, chord, circle, ellipse, or pie section—is drawn by the DrawShape function only after the mouse button is released.

The *RoundRect* Function

The RoundRect function is called in a similar fashion to the Rectangle function. The differences are that two additional individual coordinates are supplied, for a total of six individual coordinates, or a POINT or CPoint argument is supplied in addition to the RECT or CRect structure defining the rectangle.

These two additional coordinates, whether individual values or a POINT or CPoint argument, provide the x and y values for the ellipses forming the corners for the rounded rectangles. The corner x value specifies the width of the corner ellipse (in logical units); the corner y value specifies the height.

Nominally, the x and y corner sizes should be equal to produce smoothly circular corners, but this is not a requirement. Instead, the corner ellipses can be elongated in either the horizontal or vertical direction, as shown in Figure 14.1.

Figure 14.1. *How rounded corners are drawn with* RoundRect.

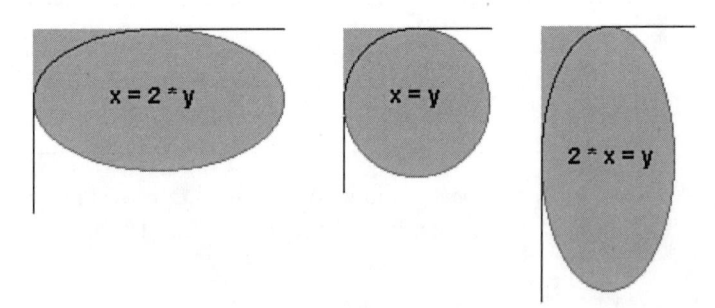

The RoundRect function is not demonstrated in the Draw1 program.

The *Ellipse* Function

Customarily, ellipses are defined in terms of x and y radii and center coordinates. In the Windows GDI, however, an ellipse is defined by a theoretical bounding rectangle. Thus, the Ellipse function is called in exactly the same fashion as the Rectangle function, with either four discrete parameters or a RECT or CRect argument defining the bounding rectangle.

As with a square, a circle is simply a special case of an ellipse in which the horizontal and vertical sizes are equal.

Figure 14.2 shows three ellipses with bounding rectangles. In actual operation, the bounding rectangles would not be drawn.

Figure 14.2. *Three ellipses.*

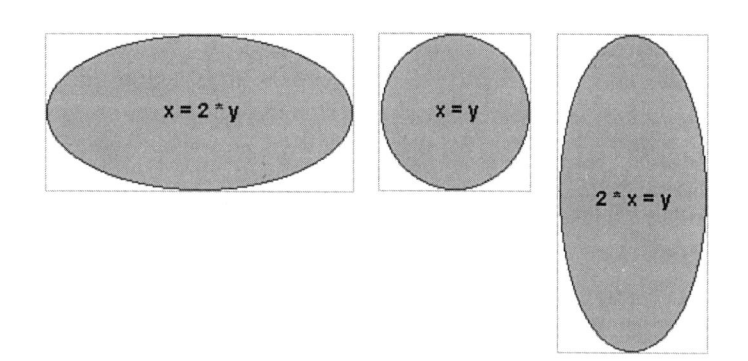

Arcs, Chords, and Pie Sections

Figure 14.3 shows the arc, chord, and pie forms.

Figure 14.3. *Arc, chord, and pie shapes.*

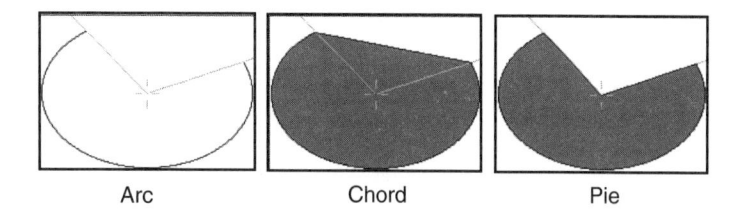

An *arc* is simply a section of an ellipse; because it is an open line, it is drawn without a fill brush.

A *chord* is an arc closed by a straight line drawn between the end points of the arc. Because a chord is a closed figure, it is drawn using the selected fill brush and appears as a solid (unless a NULL brush is used).

> Note: The actual end points of the ellipse section are used, rather than the xStart, yStart and xEnd, yEnd points used to define the radii intersecting the ellipse.

A *pie section* is also defined by an arc but adds two radii drawn from the center to the end points of the arc to complete and close the figure. As with the chord, the pie figure is drawn using the selected fill brush and appears as a solid.

Defining an Arc, Chord, or Pie Section

An arc is created in the same fashion as an ellipse but requires two further coordinate pairs to determine the end points of the arc.

Logically, you might have expected the end points to be determined by beginning and ending angles, either in degrees or radians. Indeed, the original Borland Graphics Interface (BGI) used just such a definition, as do many other graphics drawing systems, including CAD systems and other engineering applications.

In general, the simple approach to defining an ellipse is to define a center point and define the x and y axes—not merely because this is the engineering approach, but also because the graphic primitive requires this information to calculate the points comprising the line of the ellipse. To create an arc, start and end angles (in radians or degrees) would conclude the process.

The Arc function, as well as the Chord and Pie functions, accept two pairs of coordinates: xStart, yStart and xEnd, yEnd. These are assumed to lie somewhere on a radius drawn from the hypothetical center of the ellipse. Where the ellipse intersects these hypothetical radii, the arc is determined to begin and end. These points are not required to lie on the circumference of the ellipse, nor even within the bounding rectangle.

> Note: Although this approach resembles a hack by a programmer who failed high school mathematics, it is vaguely possible that there is some elegance in the internal implementation of the function that makes this approach reasonable, no matter how awkward it is for the application programmers using these functions.

Figure 14.4 shows how an arc is defined. The bounding rectangle sets the size of the ellipse. The ellipse is drawn counterclockwise; it begins at the intersection with the first radius, drawn from the center to the xStart, yStart coordinates, and ends at the intersection with the second radius, determined by the xEnd, yEnd coordinates.

Figure 14.4. Defining arc angles.

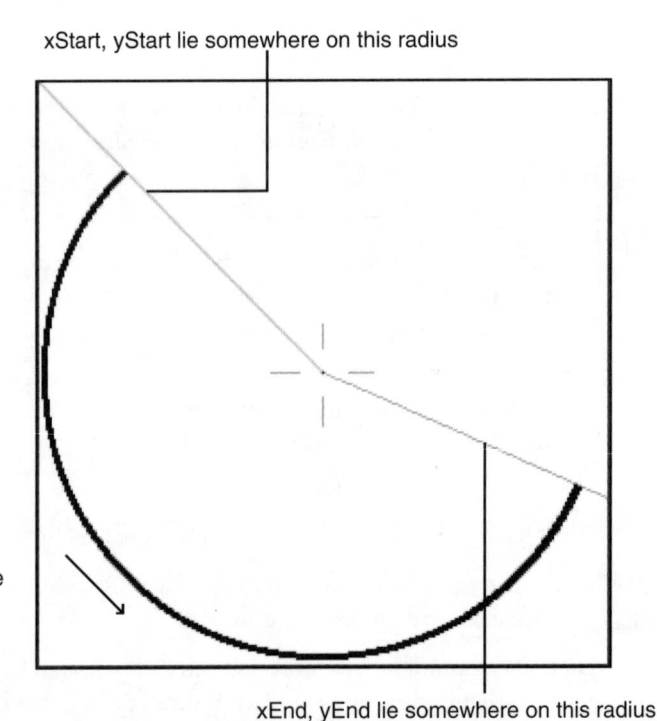

In the Draw1 demo program, arbitrary start and end point pairs, derived from the corner coordinates of the device context, are used for the Arc, Chord, and Pie functions. Only the bounding rectangle is determined by the mouse button-down and button-up positions.

The CDC::Arc function is called in either of two forms, as follows:

```
BOOL Arc( int xUL, int yUL, int xLR, int yLR,
          int xStart, int yStart, int xEnd, int yEnd );
BOOL Arc( LPCRECT lpRect, POINT ptStart, POINT ptEnd );
```

The CDC::Chord function is also called in either of two forms, as follows:

```
BOOL Chord( int xUL, int yUL, int xLR, int yLR,
            int xStart, int yStart, int xEnd, int yEnd );
BOOL Chord( LPCRECT lpRect, POINT ptStart, POINT ptEnd );
```

The CDC::Pie function is also called in either of two forms:

```
BOOL Pie( int xUL, int yUL, int xLR, int yLR,
          int xStart, int yStart, int xEnd, int yEnd );
BOOL Pie( LPCRECT lpRect, POINT ptStart, POINT ptEnd );
```

As you can see, all three forms are created using the same arguments and are simply variations on a theme.

The Draw1 Demo Program

The Draw1 demo program, shown in Figure 14.5, offers a choice of colors, line styles, fill styles, and shape tools to draw simple figures. A selection of shapes and fill styles are shown in the figure.

Figure 14.5. The Draw1 demo.

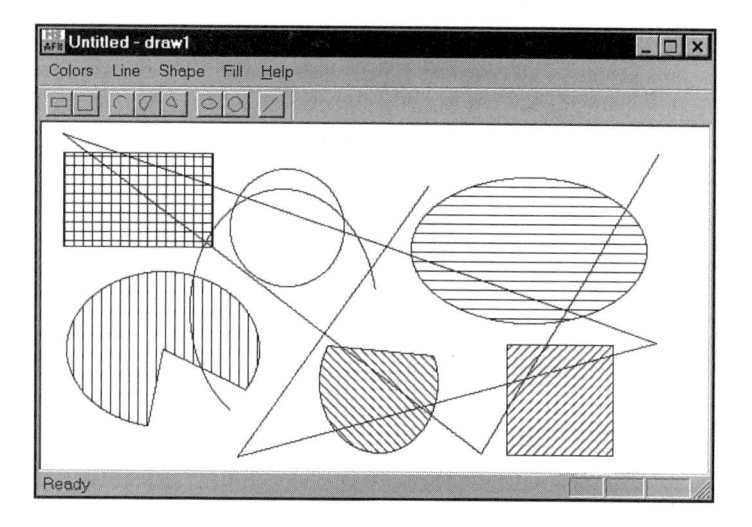

Creating Pie Graphs

Although not shown in the Draw1 or Draw2 program, one popular use for the Pie function is to create pie graphs, commonly used to illustrate financial expenditures or income by category. For this purpose, the Pie function itself is very poorly designed, but it can be supplemented rather easily by creating a function to convert angles into coordinate positions suitable for the pie section end points. (A similar procedure is used in the Draw2 demo program to calculate points for the five-pointed and seven-pointed stars.)

Assume that you have to create eight pie sections to show a breakdown by category for the year's expenses.

The first step is as follows:

```
int TotVal[8];

TotVal[0] = 0;    // a starting point
for( i=0; i<8; i++ )
   TotVal[i+1] = TotVal[i] + Account[i];
```

This loads the TotVal[] array with the incremented values necessary to calculate an angle for each expense category. The last element in the array contains the total for all categories.

For simplicity of discussion, you can set a mapping mode for the device context, with the origin centered where you want the center of the pie graph to appear. Select a radius for the graph before stepping through the pie sections, as follows:

```
for( i=0; i<8; i++ )
{
   LOGBRUSH logBrush;
   CBrush  *pBrush;
   CPen    *pPen( nLineStyle[i], 1, rgbColor[i] );

   pDC->SelectObject( pPen );
   logBrush.lbStyle = BS_HATCHED;
   logBrush.lbHatch = nFillStyle[i];
   logBrush.lbColor = rgbColor[i];
   pBrush->CreateBrushIndirect( &logBrush );
   pDC->SelectObject( pBrush );
   pDC->Pie( -Radius, Radius, Radius, -Radius,
             (int)( Radius * cos( PI2 * TotVal[i]   / TotVal[8] ) ),
             (int)( Radius * sin( PI2 * TotVal[i]   / TotVal[8] ) ),
             (int)( Radius * cos( PI2 * TotVal[i+1] / TotVal[8] ) ),
             (int)( Radius * sin( PI2 * TotVal[i+1] / TotVal[8] ) ) );
}
```

There you have it—a very simple process to draw a series of pie sections.

Because the CPen and CBrush object instances are declared within the for loop, there is no need for an explicit destructor call for either. Instead, the drawing objects simply go out of scope on each loop and are cleaned up by the default destructor method and then are reinitialized on the next loop.

The *Polygon* and *PolyPolygon* Functions

The `Polygon` and `PolyPolygon` functions, like the previous shape-drawing functions, also create closed, bordered figures that are filled using the selected brush. For polygons, however, there are a few differences.

First, even though a polygon is a closed figure, the enclosed area is not necessarily contiguous. That is, a single continuous border can enclose multiple areas. Thus, two different fill modes are supported for polygon figures.

Second, the figures created by the polygon functions are not simple, predefined shapes; as shown in the Draw2 demo, the polygon functions can create quite complex shapes. In either of the polygon methods, shapes are defined by an array of vertices and created by connecting these vertices with straight lines.

The `Polygon` function is called with two parameters:

```
Polygon( lpPoints, nCount );
```

The `lpPoints` argument is a pointer to an array of `POINT` or `CPoint`, each of which identifies one vertex in the figure. The second argument, `nCount`, simply identifies the number of points to be used from the array. To create the figure, the `Polygon` function simply begins at the first coordinate pair and draws a line from there to the next coordinate pair in the array, continuing until the last point, indicated by `nCount`, is reached.

If the first and last points correspond, the figure is complete as-is. If not, the figure is completed automatically by adding a final segment to connect the last vertex with the first.

> Note: The array of points for a polygon must contain at least two elements. Three elements are necessary for an actual shape rather than a line.

The `PolyPolygon` function is called with three parameters:

```
PolyPolygon( lpPoints, lpPolyCounts, nCount );
```

The `lpPoints` argument is a pointer to an array of `POINT` or `CPoint`, with each element identifying one vertex in a polygon. The second argument, `lpPolyCounts`, is a pointer to an array of integers, with each element specifying the number of vertices in one of the polygons. Finally, the `nCount` argument identifies the number of entries in the `lpPolyCounts` array.

Assume that you want to draw a triangle, a trapezoid, and a pentagram. The first is defined by three `CPoint` elements, the second by four, and the third by five. Thus, `lpPoints` points to an array of 12 `POINT` or `CPoint` instances; the `lpPolyCounts` array consists of the values 3, 4, and 5; and `nCount` is 3.

```
POINT Points[] =
    {   0,   0,  20, 100, 100,  20,      // triangle
      125,  10, 125, 150, 255, 150, 255,  10,   // trapezoid
```

```
        350,  75, 230, 125, 185, 185, 115, 225,  75, 260 };  // pentagram
int PolyCounts[] = { 3, 4, 5 };
PolyPolygon( &Points, &PolyCounts, 3 );
```

> Note: One assumption was included in the previous example. This description assumes that each of the polygons is described by the minimum number of points and that closure is automatic. That is, rather than using four points to describe a triangle, with the first and last points the same, the `Polygon` function is allowed to connect the first and third points for closure. The minimum points were used to define the trapezoid and pentagram as well.
>
> Earlier versions of the `PolyPolygon` function required each polygon to be explicitly closed. That is, the last vertex in each array had to match the first vertex, and the function did not support automatic closure. This shortcoming is no longer found in the `PolyPolygon` function.
>
> You must be quite certain that the values in `lpPolyCounts` and the array of points in `lpPoints` agree. Even a minor error can produce far-reaching results (as shown later in Figure 14.8).

Polygon Fill Modes

The Draw2 demo program uses the `Polygon` function to create the two polygons shown in Figure 14.6: a pentagonal star and a septagonal star.

Figure 14.6. Two polygons using Alternate fill.

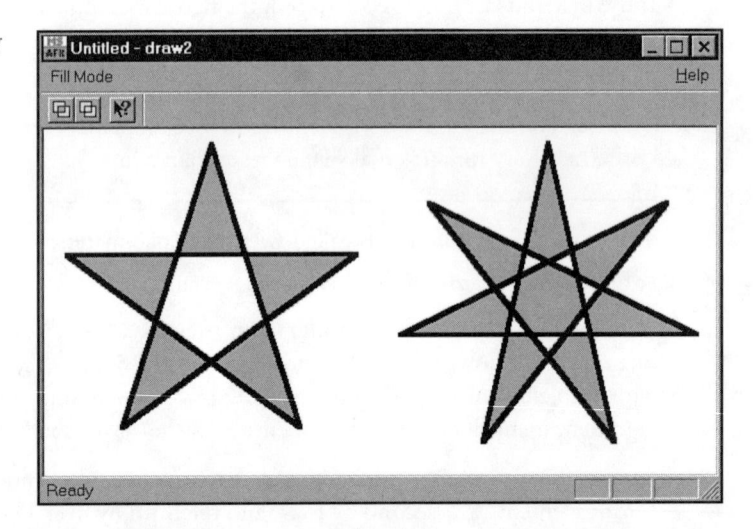

In Figure 14.6, the default Alternate fill mode was used. As you can see, the interior pentagon on the left and seven interior triangles on the right are left unfilled.

The Alternate fill mode considers areas within a figure to be interior if and only if they are reached by crossing an odd number of boundaries. It treats all other areas as exterior, regardless of whether they are surrounded by a boundary. The Alternate fill mode has the advantage of fast execution, requiring only a linear scan of the figure, starting fill when an odd-numbered boundary is crossed and stopping when an even-numbered boundary is reached.

The fill mode used is set by calling the CDC::SetPolyFillMode method as follows:

SetPolyFillMode(nPolyFillMode);

The two fill modes supported are Alternate and Winding. When called, the SetPolyFillMode function returns the previous fill mode or returns 0 (FALSE) on failure.

Figure 14.7 shows the same two polygons after selecting the Winding fill mode.

Figure 14.7. Two polygons using Winding fill.

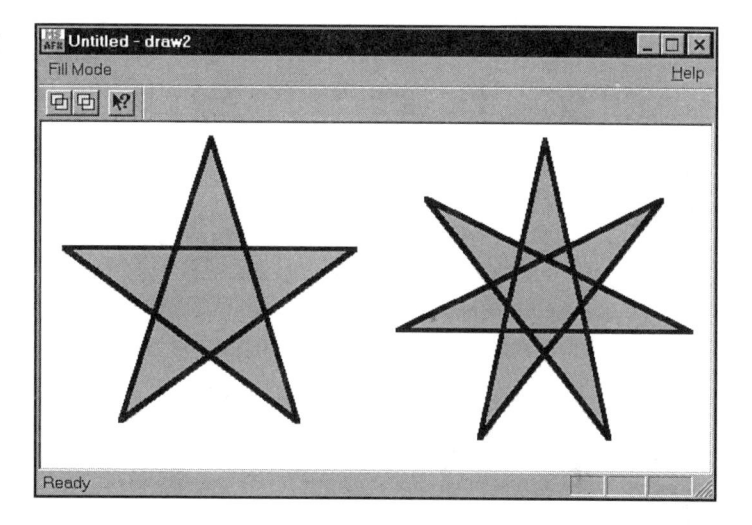

Although the Winding fill mode is slower to process, it has the advantage of reliably filling all—or almost all—interior regions, regardless of the boundary crossings. In Winding mode, the GDI uses the direction the figure is drawn to determine which areas are interior and should be filled.

Each line segment in a polygon is drawn either clockwise or counterclockwise. To determine whether a region is interior to the polygon, an imaginary line is drawn from each enclosed area to the outside of the figure. If the imaginary line passes through a clockwise line segment, the boundary count is incremented. If the line passes through a counterclockwise line segment, the boundary count is decremented. When the imaginary line reaches the exterior of the figure, if the boundary count is not zero, the area is filled.

PolyPolygon with Errors

A brief mention was made previously of the fact that even a minor error in indexing in the PolyPolygon arrays can have serious consequences. The Draw3 demo program is a duplicate of the Draw2 program except for the inclusion of one indexing error. The result is shown in Figure 14.8.

Figure 14.8. PolyPolygon *with errors.*

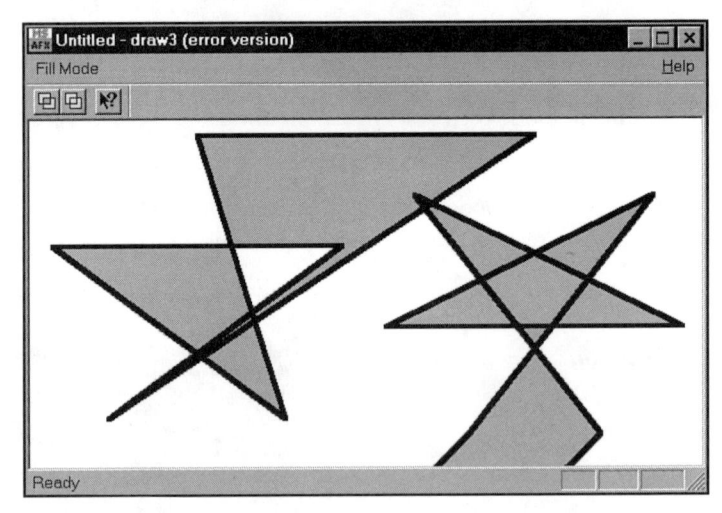

The Draw3 demo uses the Winding fill mode but, as you can see, there is a region in the left figure that, although technically enclosed, is topologically exterior (at least according to the rules in the Winding mode).

Other Drawing Functions

In addition to the drawing functions described in this chapter, the CDC class also provides the PolyPolyline, PolyDraw, PolyBezier, and BeginPath methods.

The *PolyPolyline* Function

The PolyPolyline function is used to draw multiple (connected) line segments. The line segments are drawn using the current pen but, unlike the Polygon or PolyPolygon functions, the resulting figure is neither closed nor filled. The PolyPolyline function is called as follows:

```
PolyPolyline( lpPoints, lpPolyPoints, nCount );
```

The PolyPolyline function is very much like the PolyPolygon function. The lpPoints argument points to an array of POINT or CPoint containing consecutive vertices. The lpPolyPoints array identifies the number of points from the lpPoints array for each polyline figure. The nCount parameter identifies the number of values in lpPolyPoints, or the total number of polyline figures.

> Note: The current position is not used in the PolyPolyline operation and is not updated.

The *PolyBezier* Function

The `PolyBezier` function is used to draw cubic Bézier splines by defining the end points and control points in the `lpPoints` parameter. A single spline requires four `POINT` or `CPoint` values, with the first and fourth points defining the beginning and end points for the spline. The second and third points provide the control points for the curve (see the following sidebar).

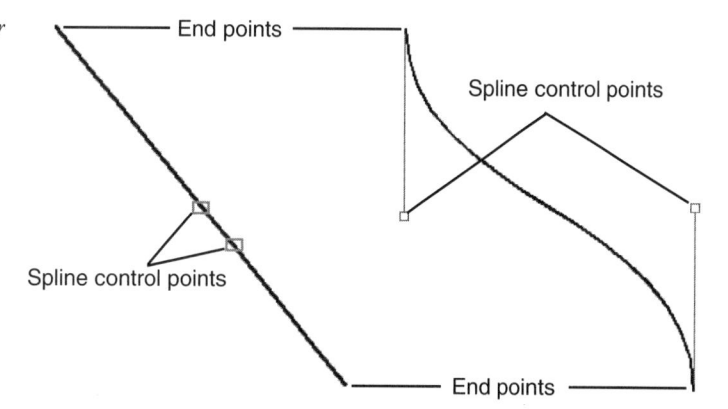

> ### Bézier Spline Curves
>
> A *Bézier spline* segment is a curve defined by four points: two end points and two control points. Figure 14.9 shows two splines.
>
> The first spline on the left positions the two control points (indicated by small squares) on the line connecting the end points. In this configuration, the result is simply a straight line with zero curvature.
>
> The spline on the right positions the two control points outside the line; their positions, relative to the end points, cause the line to be distorted in a smooth curve. The radius and degree of curvature are controlled by the linear separation between the control point and end point and by the angle between the line drawn from the end point to its control point and a line drawn between the two end points.
>
> **Figure 14.9.** *Two Bézier spline curves.*
>
> As each control point moves closer to its respective endpoint, the size of the arc decreases. Increasing the separation increases the size of the arc (or, more accurately, the *curve*, because these are not simple arc segments). In effect, the angle of the control point "drags" the curve with it.
>
> Likewise, the closer a control point lies to a line between the end points, the shallower the curve. Conversely, as the angle between the control point and a line connecting the end point increases, the resulting curve deepens.

> Incidentally, CorelDRAW! offers a good example of Bézier curves and provides the capabilities to manipulate the control points interactively. CorelDRAW! is an excellent platform for experimenting.

When multiple splines are drawn, each subsequent spline requires three POINT or CPoint values, with the last point in the previous spline serving as the first point in the subsequent spline.

Splines are drawn using the current pen, but the figure is not filled even if it is closed.

The PolyBezier function is called as follows:

```
PolyBezier( lpPoints, nCount );
```

The lpPoints argument points to an array of POINT or CPoint data elements containing the end points and control points for the splines. The nCount parameter specifies the number of points in the lpPoints array. Because each spline requires three point values plus a starting point value for the first spline, this value must be a multiple of three, plus one (for example, 4, 7, 10, 13, 16, 19).

> Note: The current position is not used in the PolyBezier function and is not updated.

The *PolyDraw* Function

The PolyDraw function combines line segments and Bézier splines in a single drawing operation. You can use the MoveTo, LineTo, and PolyBezierTo functions in consecutive calls to create similar figures; alternatively, you can use the PolyDraw function to combine these operations into a single operation.

Both lines and splines are drawn using the current pen. Figures are not filled even if they are closed.

If an active path has been started, the PolyDraw function adds to the path. (Refer to Paths and the BeginPath function in Visual C++'s Books Online for more information on this topic.)

The PolyDraw function is called as follows:

```
PolyDraw( lpPoints, lpTypes, nCount );
```

The lpPoints argument is a pointer to an array of POINT or CPoint data elements that provide the end points for each line segment and the end points and control points for the Bézier splines.

The lpTypes argument is a pointer to an array of values specifying how the lpPoints values should be used. The lpTypes values can be any of those shown in Table 14.10.

Table 14.10. The `lpTypes` values.

`lpTypes` Values	Purpose
PT_MOVETO	The point begins a disjoint figure and becomes the new current position.
PT_LINETO	A line is drawn from the current position to this point, which becomes the new current position.
PT_BEZIERTO	The point can be either a control point or an end point for a Bézier spline. `PT_BEZIERTO` points always occur in sets of three. Because the current position provides the starting point for the spline, the first two points in the triplet are control points; the third is the end point and sets the new current position. If three consecutive `PT_BEZIERTO` points are found, an error occurs.
PT_CLOSEFIGURE	This flag can be ORed with the `PT_LINETO` or `PT_BEZIERTO` flags to indicate that the corresponding point is the final point in a figure and that the figure should be closed. A line is drawn from this point to the most recent `PT_MOVETO` or `MoveTo` point.

The `nCount` parameter specifies the number of `POINT` or `CPoint` entries in the `lpPoints` array.

Note: The `PolyDraw` function uses and updates the current position.

Summary

This chapter covered the highlights of the various shape and line tools: from simple lines and logical pen styles to fill styles for solid shapes and the polygon tools. It also touched briefly on the polyline and Bézier curve tools.

Although the coverage of these topics was not comprehensive, it should be sufficient to offer you a grounding in the basics and enable you to pursue your own experimentation.

Chapter 15, "Using Bitmaps and Screen Images," looks at another aspect of graphics operations: how to capture a screen image and write a bitmap file.

CHAPTER 15

Using Bitmaps and Screen Images

Over the years, many different image standards and formats have come and gone. Under DOS, the standard image format was the PCX image, originally developed by ZSoft but supported by a wide variety of applications. Others included the GIF (Graphics Image Format) standard championed by CompuServe, the TGA format developed by TARGA, the BMP OS/2 image format, and the PIC format used by Apple.

Because of the popularity of the Windows operating system, the Windows BMP image format has become its own standard. Over the years, the Windows standard has also evolved, and today it is represented by two file extensions: BMP and DIB.

The BMP extension is derived from BitMaP; DIB is an acronym for Device-Independent Bitmap. Both refer to variations of a single format and, for all practical purposes, they are interchangeable.

> Note: Although the DIB extension was intended to replace the BMP extension and to identify device-independent images as opposed to device-dependent images, today the two extensions are used interchangeably. The popular BMP extension identifies what are actually DIB format images, and the DIB extension is almost unknown.

The basic characteristics of a Device-Independent Bitmap, regardless of the extension, are described next.

BMP versus DIB

The original BMP bitmaps, introduced under Windows 1.0, were highly device specific. The images were structured for display only on a device with specific characteristics and capabilities (for example, a video driver, video card, or monitor). The problem was that these images were not transportable to or compatible with other devices.

In contrast, DIB bitmaps are an extension of the OS/2 version 1.0 Presentation Manager bitmap format (jointly developed by Microsoft, IBM, and ZSoft). However, with the split between Microsoft and IBM, the current OS/2 and Windows versions of the DIB image format are not quite the same.

Where both of these are similar, however, is in the design of the image record. Although the original bitmap images depended on the system video capabilities, device-independent bitmaps added information beyond the image itself, including image sizes, palettes, palette sizes, number of colors used, and resolution data. With this information, applications are able to adapt the images to display them to the best advantage, independent of the platform's capabilities. In brief, DIB images can be fitted to the system, as opposed to having to be written to fit the system.

The original device-dependent bitmap format is now an obsolete and defunct format of little more than historical interest. In the future, whenever I refer to a BMP image, I will be talking about the DIB format.

DIB Image Files

All DIB image files consist of four sections: a DIB header record, a bitmap info header, a bitmap color table, and the image data itself.

Beginning with the DIB header, this is the BITMAPFILEHEADER defined in WinGDI.H:

```
typedef struct tagBITMAPFILEHEADER {
        WORD    bfType;
        DWORD   bfSize;
        WORD    bfReserved1;
        WORD    bfReserved2;
        DWORD   bfOffBits;
} BITMAPFILEHEADER, FAR *LPBITMAPFILEHEADER, *PBITMAPFILEHEADER;
```

Table 15.1 shows the breakdown of the information included here.

Table 15.1. BITMAPFILEHEADER example.

Field	Size	Example	Value	Description
bfType	WORD	42 4D	BM	Image identifier
bfSize	DWORD	1E 51 01 00	1511Eh	Total file size
bfReserved1	WORD	00 00	0h	Reserved, always 0
bfReserved2	WORD	00 00	0h	Reserved, always 0
bfOffBits	DWORD	36 04 00 00	436h	Offset from first of file to beginning of bitmap image

The `bfType` field is always set to the value BM to identify the image file as a bitmap.

The `bfSize` field provides the total size of the image file and offers a check for file validity. Notice that the 4-byte value is arranged with the least significant byte first and the most significant byte last. Thus, the bytes 1E 51 01 00 decode as 1511Eh.

The `bfOffBits` field is the offset in the file where the actual image data begins. Again, the bytes are arranged with the least significant byte first, making the sequence 36 04 00 00 decode as 436h, or 1078 (decimal). This gives you the size of the BITMAPFILEHEADER plus the BITMAPINFOHEADER and the color palette, all of which precede the image data.

The *BITMAPINFOHEADER*

The BITMAPINFOHEADER table contains information identifying the size and dimensions of the bitmap image, whether image compression has been used, the ideal resolution of the image, how many colors are used in the image, and how many of these colors are important. The BITMAPINFOHEADER structure is detailed in Table 15.2.

Table 15.2. The BITMAPINFOHEADER structure.

Field	Size	Data	Value	Description
biSize	DWORD	28 00 00 00	28h	Size of BITMAPINFOHEADER
biWidth	LONG	40 01 00 00	140h	Bitmap width in pixels
biHeight	LONG	D2 00 00 00	D2h	Bitmap height in pixels
biPlanes	WORD	01 00	1h	Color planes (always 1)
biBitCount	WORD	08 00	8h	Color bits per pixel (1, 4, 8, 24)
biCompression	DWORD	00 00 00 00	0h	Compression scheme (0 = none)
biSizeImage	DWORD	E8 4C 01 00	14CE8h	Bitmap image size (used as check if image is compressed)

continues

Table 15.2. continued

Field	Size	Data	Value	Description
biXPelsPerMeter	LONG	00 00 00 00	0h	Horizontal resolution (pixels/meter)
biYPelsPerMeter	LONG	00 00 00 00	0h	Vertical resolution (pixels/meter)
biClrUsed	DWORD	00 00 00 00	0h	Number of colors used in image
biClrImportant	DWORD	00 00 00 00	0h	Number of important colors

The biSize field defines the size of the BITMAPINFOHEADER structure itself and is always 28h bytes.

The biWidth and biHeight fields give the horizontal and vertical sizes of the image in pixels. In this example, the values 140h and D2h identify an image that is 320×210 pixels.

The biPlanes and biBitCount fields identify the number of color planes and the color bits per pixel. In this example, the image uses one color plane and 8 bits per pixel for a 256-color image. (Color planes and bits per pixel were discussed in Chapter 13, "Working with Colors, Palettes, and Drawing Modes.") A value of 1 bit per pixel identifies a monochrome image, 4 is a 16-color image, and 24 is a True Color image.

The biCompression field can be used to identify an image compression format such as RLE (Run-Length Encoding). When compression is used, the biSizeImage field provides the uncompressed image size for use as a check during decoding. Standard compression formats are discussed later.

The biXPelsPerMeter and biYPelsPerMeter fields are not commonly used and are generally 0. These fields can be used to identify the size of the screen where the image was created and, therefore, the absolute size of the image.

The biClrUsed and biClrImportant fields provide two pieces of image information that are not generally supplied and that, when supplied, are usually ignored. Optionally, however, the biClrUsed field identifies the number of colors in the image; the biClrImportant field specifies how many of these colors are important. These two values can be useful when mapping high-resolution color images to displays with more limited capabilities. Both values default to 0.

BITMAPINFO versus *BITMAPCOREINFO*

The Windows BMP/DIB format uses the BITMAPINFO structure, consisting of the BITMAPINFOHEADER and an RGBQUAD palette. OS/2 bitmaps use the BITMAPCOREINFO structure, which consists of a BITMAPCOREHEADER and an RGBTRIPLE palette. The two structures are defined in the WinGDI.H header as follows:

```
typedef struct tagBITMAPINFO {
    BITMAPINFOHEADER    bmiHeader;
    RGBQUAD             bmiColors[1];
} BITMAPINFO, FAR *LPBITMAPINFO, *PBITMAPINFO;
```

```
typedef struct tagBITMAPCOREINFO {
    BITMAPCOREHEADER    bmciHeader;
    RGBTRIPLE           bmciColors[1];
} BITMAPCOREINFO, FAR *LPBITMAPCOREINFO, *PBITMAPCOREINFO;
```

Although this chapter does not spend much time on OS/2 format bitmaps, the BmpImage program can distinguish between the two formats and, therefore, can read both Windows and OS/2 format images.

The DIB Bitmap Color Table

The bitmap color table follows BITMAPINFOHEADER and can contain 2, 16, or 256 entries. For 24-bit true-color images, it may be missing entirely. Because the size of this table is variable, the bfOffBits field in the BITMAPFILEHEADER structure provides the offset to the beginning of the image data.

Each entry in the DIB palette consists of a 32-bit RGBQUAD structure. This consists of three 8-bit values for the red, green, and blue components, with the fourth 8-bit value a 0.

For OS/2 format images, palette entries consist of RGBTRIPLEs, which also consist of three 8-bit values for the red, green, and blue components but lack the fourth 8-bit value.

DIB Image Data

The final portion of the DIB image is the pixel data itself. The organization of the image data depends on three factors:

- The number of bits per pixel reported in the biBitCount field in the BITMAPINFOHEADER.
- Each row in the bitmap image, regardless of the actual width of the image, is always a DWORD size, with the bits in each row padded with NULLs as necessary. Thus, each row is read as an integral number of DWORD values, but the biWidth field is necessary to determine how many pixels to display.

    To set the size for a scan row, the WIDTHBYTES macro offers a solution:

    ```
    #define WIDTHBYTES(bits) ( ( ( bits ) + 31 ) / 32 * 4 )
    ```
- Bitmap images are stored in inverted order. In other words, the first row in the image data is the bottom row in the image proper, and so forth.

OS/2 versus Windows Images

To distinguish between OS/2 and Windows images, the biSize field in the BITMAPFILEHEADER is checked against the size of the BITMAPINFOHEADER (Windows) and BITMAPCOREHEADER (OS/2) structures.

The `IS_WIN30_BMP` macro is used for checking:

```
#define IS_WIN30_BMP(pBMI) ((*(LPDWORD)(pBMI)) == sizeof(BITMAPINFOHEADER))
```

The Capture and Display of Screen Images

Because all displays under Windows are graphic, a graphic screen capture utility is a natural tool for many purposes. A screen capture utility can be used to save graphics information for documentation, to transfer image information between applications, or simply to save images for future use. Further, under Windows, the capture process is relatively simple.

First, there is a built-in capture process. Simply press the Print Screen button on your keyboard, and the entire desktop image is copied to the Clipboard. From here, the ClipBook utility can be used to view the image and, optionally, save the image to a file. Unfortunately, the ClipBook utility saves information only in a Clipboard format, using the CLP extension, and does not support writing BMP image files. (Although the Clipboard handles several types of information, each with its own format, only the graphics image format is relevant here.)

Second, you could use the MSPaint utility under Win95 to view the captured image and, from MSPaint, save the image in a BMP format. Any other paint utility that supports the paste function from the Clipboard could be used in a similar fashion.

Both of these are rather clumsy processes, which makes it worthwhile to have a single utility to perform a capture, display the results, and write the image to a bitmap as a single integrated process.

There are utilities on the market for this purpose, or you can use (and modify as desired) the Capture utility included on the CD-ROM that accompanies this book.

> Note: This is an unsolicited plug for Snapshot3 from Beacon Hill Software. Snapshot3 is a 32-bit screen capture utility that is well designed and well implemented and also offers features not incorporated in the Capture program described here. Beacon Hill can be contacted at Box 8494, Boston, MA 02114 or through CompuServe at 74130,2452. Beacon Hill Software is not associated with the author, and this recommendation is made solely at the author's discretion in recognition of a timely and well-designed utility.

The Capture Utility

The Capture utility is written with several options. Capture begins with options to capture either to the Clipboard, like the Print Screen feature, or directly to a BMP (or DIB) file. It also offers a choice of capturing the entire desktop or capturing only the active window.

Capture incorporates a seven-second time delay, allowing time to pull down menus or call dialog boxes to be included in the capture. Capture also offers a choice of display modes—either displaying the Clipboard contents at the original size (the default) or sizing the image to fit the display window.

If the Clipboard contains an image clip when Capture is called, the Clipboard contents are displayed automatically.

There are no provisions for saving an image displayed from the Clipboard—only an image captured directly.

Figure 15.1 shows the Capture program after capturing the Win95 desktop. Because the Capture client window is considerably smaller than the desktop, the captured image is shrunk to fit, and some distortion is unavoidable.

Figure 15.1. The Capture application.

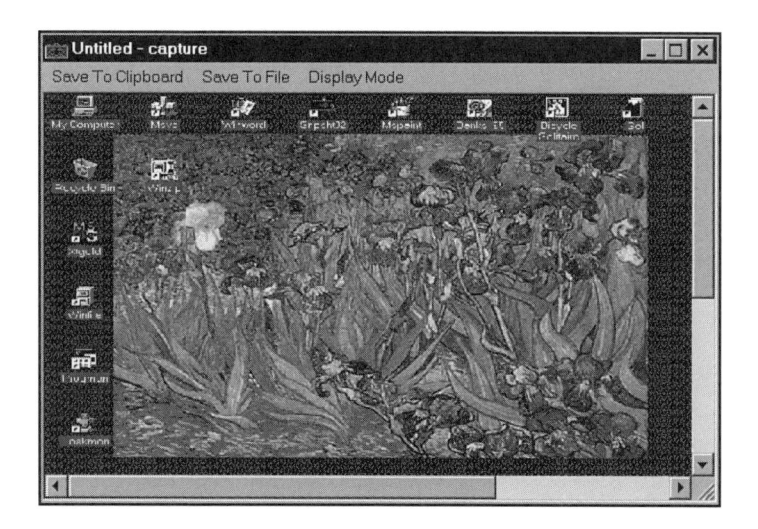

Setup and Cleanup Provisions

Before capturing an image to the Clipboard or to a file, one important setup item is required: creating a new CDC. Initializing the m_Action and m_fExpand members is simply routine:

```
CCaptureView::CCaptureView()
{
   // TODO: create a memory device context
   m_pDCMem = new CDC;
   m_Action = NONE;
   m_fExpand = FALSE;
}
```

For cleanup, you need to delete your bitmap object and delete the device context created during initialization:

```
CCaptureView::~CCaptureView()
{
   delete m_pDCMem->SelectObject( CBitmap::FromHandle( m_hBM ) );
   delete m_pDCMem;
}
```

Further Initialization

Although the constructor method is a useful place for some initialization—particularly for member variables that should be set before anything else is done—other initialization actions need to wait a little longer. One of these, for a `CScrollView` window, is setting the window scroll sizes:

```
int CCaptureView::OnCreate(LPCREATESTRUCT lpCreateStruct)
{
   if (CScrollView::OnCreate(lpCreateStruct) == -1)
      return -1;
   SetScrollSizes( MM_TEXT,          // set scrollview to desktop size
               CSize( ::GetSystemMetrics( SM_CXSCREEN ),
                     ::GetSystemMetrics( SM_CYSCREEN ) ),
               CSize( 20, 20 ), CSize( 4, 4 ) );
```

How the window scroll sizes are set is pretty immaterial at this point. You don't know yet what image size will be displayed, if any, but you need to provide some default scroll sizes before the application window is updated and drawn. If you prefer, the defaults could be supplied as follows:

```
SetScrollSizes( MM_TEXT, CSize( 1, 1 ) );
```

In any case, you reset the scroll sizes as appropriate later; all that matters here is that you supply some initial values.

> Tip: Try commenting out the `SetScrollSizes` instruction, then recompile and execute the Capture demo.

Next, although the `m_pDCMem` device context was created in the constructor method, it still needs to be turned into a compatible device context using `CreateCompatibleDC`:

```
   // TODO: make memory device context compatible with display
   CClientDC   dc(this);
   m_pDCMem->CreateCompatibleDC( &dc );
   m_Action = DESKTOPTOCLIPBD;
   OnImageDisplay();
   return 0;
}
```

Last, you call the `OnImageDisplay` member function to update the screen display. In this fashion, if there is a bitmap image in the Clipboard when Capture is called, that image is retrieved and shown. The `OnImageDisplay` method is also called at other times for the same purpose. If you are not interested in seeing an existing Clipboard image, simply disable the instruction here, and the Clipboard is not checked until after a screen or window image has been captured.

The *OnImageDisplay* Procedure

The `OnImageDisplay` procedure is used to retrieve an image from the Clipboard and write the results to a memory context. This begins by opening the Clipboard and requesting a bitmap image from the Clipboard:

```
void CCaptureView::OnImageDisplay()
{
   // TODO: retrieve from clipboard, write to memory context
   HBITMAP   hBitmap;
   CBitmap  *pBM;

   if( OpenClipboard() )
   {
      if( hBitmap = (HBITMAP) ::GetClipboardData( CF_BITMAP ) )
```

The `GetClipboardData` API is called with the `CF_BITMAP` specification identifying the type of Clipboard data. If the Clipboard does not contain a bitmap image, `hBitmap` is NULL and the process skips directly to the `CloseClipboard()` API.

However, if the Clipboard does contain a bitmap, a handle is returned to the bitmap, `hBitmap`, which is then used by the `FromHandle` function to initialize the `CBitmap` object. Then, from `pBM`, the size is retrieved for possible use by `StretchBitBlt` and also for use after selecting the bitmap into the device context to set the scroll range for the `CScrollView` window:

```
      {
         pBM = CBitmap::FromHandle( hBitmap );
         pBM->GetObject( sizeof(m_BM), &m_BM );  // need for StretchBitBlt
         m_pDCMem->SelectObject( pBM );
         SetScrollSizes( MM_TEXT,          // set scrollview to fit bitmap
                         CSize( m_BM.bmWidth, m_BM.bmHeight ),
                         CSize( 20, 20 ), CSize( 4, 4 ) );
      }
      CloseClipboard();
   }
   Invalidate();
}
```

Recall that a dummy range was set in the `OnCreate` method; this scroll range is now being updated to fit the bitmap being displayed. This is the `SetScrollSizes` call, which ensures that the `CScrollView` window is able to correctly scroll and display the bitmap image.

The initial `SetScrollSizes` call was also important simply because there is no provision in the `CScrollView` class for a default scroll range. Unless this is explicitly set, the `CScrollView` window simply does not display.

After opening the Clipboard, an explicit call to `CloseClipboard` is expected. Because the Clipboard is a shared resource, trying to retain ownership of the Clipboard is not good form.

Capturing Screen Information

To explain how to capture screen information, the simplest place to start is in the `CCaptureView::CaptureScreen` procedure. After declaring variables for a memory device context and a bitmap handle, this procedure begins by setting the cursor to the wait cursor (the hour glass):

```
void CCaptureView::CaptureScreen()
{
   HDC        hdcMem;
```

```
        HBITMAP    hBitmap;
        int        LnPad = 0;
        CRect      cRect;

        SetCursor( LoadCursor( NULL, IDC_WAIT ) );
        switch( m_Action )
        {
```

The `m_Action` member reflects the type of capture selected from the Capture menu. Because two options are offered—capturing the desktop and capturing the active window—two different sets of provisions are used to determine the rectangular coordinates for the area to capture.

In the first instance, where you want to capture the active window, you begin by getting a handle to the active window. You use this handle to get the window's device context, using `GetWindowDC`, and to retrieve the window's coordinates. Notice that both the window handle and the device context are retrieved as member variables, because these may be wanted later in the process in a different procedure:

```
           case ACTIVETOCLIPBD:
           case ACTIVETOFILE:
              m_hSrcWnd = ::GetForegroundWindow();
              m_hdcSrc  = ::GetWindowDC( m_hSrcWnd );
              ::GetWindowRect( m_hSrcWnd, &cRect );
              m_xSize = cRect.Width();
              m_ySize = cRect.Height();
              break;
```

From the retrieved rectangular coordinates, the width and height are also retrieved and stored as member variables.

For the instance where you want to capture the entire desktop, you set the source window handle to `HWND_DESKTOP` before calling `GetDC` to retrieve the device context:

```
           case DESKTOPTOCLIPBD:
           case DESKTOPTOFILE:
              m_hSrcWnd = HWND_DESKTOP;
              m_hdcSrc  = ::GetDC( m_hSrcWnd );
              m_xSize = GetDeviceCaps( m_hdcSrc, HORZRES );
              m_ySize = GetDeviceCaps( m_hdcSrc, VERTRES );
              break;
        }
```

This time, instead of asking for the window rectangle, you simply ask `GetDeviceCaps` for the horizontal and vertical resolution.

Now that you know the size and have a handle to the source device context, you can create a compatible device context in memory and create a compatible bitmap of the appropriate size. Then call `StretchBlt` to copy the image from the screen or window to your memory device context:

```
        hdcMem = CreateCompatibleDC( m_hdcSrc );
        hBitmap = CreateCompatibleBitmap( m_hdcSrc, m_xSize, m_ySize );
        if( hBitmap )
        {
           SelectObject( hdcMem, hBitmap );
```

```
    StretchBlt( hdcMem,   0, 0, m_xSize, m_ySize,
                m_hdcSrc, 0, 0, m_xSize, m_ySize, SRCCOPY );
    OpenClipboard();
    EmptyClipboard();
    SetClipboardData( CF_BITMAP, hBitmap );
    CloseClipboard();
    Invalidate();
}
```

After you capture the screen image, you open the Clipboard, discard any existing contents, and write the new bitmap to the Clipboard. Then you invalidate your application window so that it is redrawn in a moment.

You do have a bit of cleanup:

```
    DeleteDC( hdcMem );
    ::ReleaseDC( HWND_DESKTOP, m_hdcSrc );
    SetCursor( LoadCursor( NULL, IDC_ARROW ) );
    AfxGetMainWnd()->OpenIcon();
    OnImageDisplay();
    return;
}
```

Displaying the Clipboard

The Capture utility automatically displays the contents of the memory device context, m_pDCMem, using either StretchBlt or BitBlt depending on whether the image is being sized to fit or displayed as the original size.

For a size-to-fit operation, the COLORONCOLOR stretch mode is used with the entire bitmap image fitted to the display window, as shown here:

```
void CCaptureView::OnDraw(CDC* pDC)
{
    CCaptureDoc* pDoc = GetDocument();
    ASSERT_VALID(pDoc);

    if( m_Action )
    {
        if( m_fExpand )
        {
            pDC->SetStretchBltMode( COLORONCOLOR );
            pDC->StretchBlt( 0, 0, m_cxWnd, m_cyWnd,
                             m_pDCMem, 0, 0, m_BM.bmWidth, m_BM.bmHeight,
                             SRCCOPY );
        }
        else
        {
            CPoint cPoint = GetDeviceScrollPosition();
            pDC->BitBlt( cPoint.x, cPoint.y,
                         m_cxWnd + cPoint.x, m_cyWnd + cPoint.y,
                         m_pDCMem, cPoint.x, cPoint.y, SRCCOPY );
        }
    }
}
```

For an image displayed at the original size, because the image may be larger than the display window, provisions are added for scrolling the image by calculating an offset from the current scroll positions.

Writing a Bitmap File

The `WriteToFile` procedure is used to write a bitmap image to a disk file and begins with a block of variable declarations. Many of these should be familiar from other operations, or in the case of the bitmap file header and info structures, from previous discussion in this chapter.

```
void CCaptureView::WriteToFile()
{
   // TODO: Add your command handler code here
   HDC       hdcMem;      // handle to memory device context
   HANDLE    hFil;        // handle to file
   HBITMAP   hBitmap;     // handle to bitmap
   LPVOID    pBits;       // pointer to image bits
   char      *pszNull[8]; // pointer to null array
   RGBQUAD   RGBQuad;
   CRect     cRect;
   DWORD     ImgSize, plSize, dwWritten;
   int       i, CRes, LnWidth, LnPad = 0;
   BITMAPFILEHEADER    bmFH;
   BITMAPINFO          bmInfo;
   LPLOGPALETTE        pPal;
```

Before doing anything else, use `memset` to set the `pszNull` array to NULLs. This is used later to image scan pad lines as they are written to the image file:

```
memset( pszNull, '\0', 8 );
```

Now, because you already have a filename and path specification in the member variable `m_csFileName`, you can start by opening a file for write. (The filename was supplied by a call to the File Open dialog box in this case, but it could also have been supplied automatically as an incremented filename.)

```
      SetCursor( LoadCursor( NULL, IDC_WAIT ) );
//=== open file for write ================================
   hFil = CreateFile( m_csFileName, GENERIC_WRITE, 0,  NULL,
           CREATE_ALWAYS, FILE_ATTRIBUTE_NORMAL, NULL );
   if( hFil == NULL )
   {
      MessageBox( "Can't open file" );
      return;
   }
   switch( m_Action )
   {
```

If the create process fails, you simply report failure and back out. If it succeeds, you can proceed by checking whether you are supposed to be writing the active window or the desktop:

```
      case ACTIVETOFILE:
         m_hSrcWnd = ::GetForegroundWindow();
         m_hdcSrc  = ::GetWindowDC( m_hSrcWnd );
         ::GetWindowRect( m_hSrcWnd, &cRect );
```

```
    m_xSize = cRect.Width();
    m_ySize = cRect.Height();
    break;
```

Under Win95, a maximized window reports a horizontal size larger than the physical screen by an amount that is twice the frame width. In effect, Win95 is reporting the window size as the full frame, despite the fact that the frame itself is off-screen at both the right and left.

The solution is to check the reported width against the horizontal size reported by `GetDeviceCaps` and use the smaller of the two:

```
    case DESKTOPTOFILE:
        m_hSrcWnd = HWND_DESKTOP;
        m_hdcSrc  = ::GetDC( m_hSrcWnd );
        m_xSize = GetDeviceCaps( m_hdcSrc, HORZRES );
        m_ySize = GetDeviceCaps( m_hdcSrc, VERTRES );
        break;
}
```

The only real difference between these two cases is where you are retrieving the size information, and this provision parallels the process used during the screen capture discussed earlier.

The next step is to query the memory context that holds the bitmap image for the number of palette entries. You use this to calculate the size of the palette. You also need the bits per pixel, which is written directly to the `bmInfo.bmiHeader.biBitCount` field:

```
CRes = GetDeviceCaps( m_hdcSrc, SIZEPALETTE );
plSize = CRes * sizeof( RGBQUAD );           // palette size
bmInfo.bmiHeader.biBitCount = GetDeviceCaps( m_hdcSrc, BITSPIXEL );
if( bmInfo.bmiHeader.biBitCount == 8 )
   LnWidth = m_xSize;
else
   LnWidth = m_xSize / 2;
if( LnWidth % sizeof(DWORD) )
   LnPad = sizeof(DWORD) - ( LnWidth % sizeof(DWORD) );
ImgSize = (DWORD)( (DWORD)( LnWidth + LnPad ) * m_ySize );
```

Depending on the bits per pixel value, you can calculate the line width (`LnWidth`) and the image size (`ImgSize`) values. As for the bits per pixel, a hidden assumption is that the reported bits per pixel value is either 4 or 8 for a 16-color or 256-color palette and does not accommodate 24-bit-per-pixel images or monochrome images. To use Capture for either would require additional provisions.

Now that you have the basic information on the image, it's time to start writing the bitmap header:

```
bmFH.bfType      = 0x4D42;              // Type is "BF"
bmFH.bfReserved1 = 0L;
bmFH.bfReserved2 = 0L;
bmFH.bfOffBits   = plSize +             // bitmap offset
                   sizeof( BITMAPINFO ) +
                   sizeof( BITMAPFILEHEADER );
bmFH.bfSize      = ImgSize +            // file size
                   bmFH.bfOffBits;
WriteFile( hFil, &bmFH, sizeof( bmFH ),
           &dwWritten, NULL );          // write file header
```

After writing the bitmap header to the output file, the next step is to prepare the BITMAPINFOHEADER and write this to the output file as well:

```
bmInfo.bmiHeader.biSize =
    (DWORD) sizeof( BITMAPINFOHEADER );
bmInfo.bmiHeader.biWidth         = m_xSize;
bmInfo.bmiHeader.biHeight        = m_ySize;
bmInfo.bmiHeader.biPlanes        = 1;
bmInfo.bmiHeader.biCompression   = BI_RGB;
bmInfo.bmiHeader.biSizeImage     = 0L;
bmInfo.bmiHeader.biXPelsPerMeter = 0L;
bmInfo.bmiHeader.biYPelsPerMeter = 0L;
bmInfo.bmiHeader.biClrUsed       = 0L;
bmInfo.bmiHeader.biClrImportant  = 0L;
WriteFile( hFil, &bmInfo.bmiHeader,
           sizeof( bmInfo.bmiHeader ),
           &dwWritten, NULL );       // write info header
```

This is all quite straightforward. You are not using file compression, so all that's needed is the size information. The color resolution (bits per pixel) has already been set.

This brings you to the palette information. Here you need to translate the PALETTEENTRY data from the bitmap to RGBQUAD values for the file. The PALETTEENTRY and RGBQUAD definitions appear next:

```
Palette Entry              RGBQUAD for Bitmap file

typedef struct             typedef struct tagRGBQUAD
{                          {
   BYTE   peRed;              BYTE   rgbBlue;
   BYTE   peGreen;            BYTE   rgbGreen;
   BYTE   peBlue;             BYTE   rgbRed;
   BYTE   peFlags;            BYTE   rgbReserved;
} PALETTEENTRY;            } RGBQUAD;
```

Notice that the PALETTEENTRY structure is in R..G..B..flags order; the RGBQUAD structure runs B..G..R..reserved. The two are not identical, so the red, green, and blue color values must be assigned individually to the correct fields in each.

To create a palette, begin by declaring a new LOGPALETTE structure and filling in the number of entries and the version information:

```
lp = new LOGPALETTE;
lp->palNumEntries = CRes;
lp->palVersion    = 0x0300;
```

The GetSystemPaletteEntries function retrieves CRes entries from the memory context to the LOGPALETTE structure:

```
GetSystemPaletteEntries( m_hdcSrc, 0, CRes,
                         lp->palPalEntry );
RGBQuad.rgbReserved = 0;
for( i=0; i<=CRes; i++ )
```

```
    {
        RGBQuad.rgbRed   = lp->palPalEntry[i].peRed;
        RGBQuad.rgbGreen = lp->palPalEntry[i].peGreen;
        RGBQuad.rgbBlue  = lp->palPalEntry[i].peBlue;
        WriteFile( hFil, &RGBQuad, sizeof( RGBQuad ),
                   &dwWritten, NULL );
    }
    delete []lp;
```

Having retrieved the palette information, a simple loop is all that's needed to write the values to the file. Notice that the RGBQuad.rgbReserved field has been set to 0 for all entries. Also, once the palette information is written, the lp LOGPALETTE array is deleted.

It's time to write the image data to the file.

The first step is to create another memory device context, then create a compatible bitmap. In both cases, you use the m_hdcSrc device context and then select the bitmap into the memory context:

```
hdcMem = CreateCompatibleDC( m_hdcSrc );
hBitmap = CreateCompatibleBitmap( m_hdcSrc, m_xSize, 1 );
SelectObject( hdcMem, hBitmap );
```

Note that the bitmap, hBitmap, is the width of the image but is only one pixel tall. In other words, this bitmap can hold only one scan line from the source image.

The new operator is used to allocate an array of bytes as a buffer before starting a loop at the bottom of the bitmap to copy one scan line of the image from m_hdcSrc to hdcMem. After each line is copied to hdcMem, the next step is to copy the bits to the pBits buffer, and from there write the bits to the image file, then write any necessary padding to the image file:

```
pBits = new BYTE[ LnWidth * m_ySize ];
for( i = m_ySize - 1; i >= 0; i-- )
{
    BitBlt( hdcMem,  0, 0, m_xSize, 1,
            m_hdcSrc, 0, i, SRCCOPY );
    GetBitmapBits( hBitmap, m_xSize, pBits );
    WriteFile( hFil, pBits, LnWidth, &dwWritten, NULL );
    WriteFile( hFil, pszNull, LnPad, &dwWritten, NULL );
}
```

Finally, when the loop is completed, the pBits array is deleted, the memory contexts are released, and the file is closed:

```
    delete []pBits;
    DeleteDC( hdcMem );                        // delete and release
    ::ReleaseDC( HWND_DESKTOP, m_hdcSrc );     // the device contexts
    CloseHandle( hFil );                       // and close the file
    SetCursor( LoadCursor( NULL, IDC_ARROW ) );
    return;
}
```

If this looks like a rather complex method of writing a bitmap to a file, that's because it is. In a moment, I discuss an alternative approach that makes better use of the MFC and is notable for its relative simplicity.

As mentioned previously, the Capture utility was originally written for WinNT; at that time, Visual C++ and the MFC classes had not been created. However awkward, the present `WriteToFile` procedure does have a purpose in that it shows in detail how a bitmap file is written.

Unlike the bitmap file write procedure, demonstrated next, this process is easily modified if you want to include some form of image compression, for example.

Bitmap Compression Formats

Bitmap image compression is used to reduce both memory and disk-storage requirements. At the present time, two image compression formats are supported: one for 4-bit-per-pixel images (16-color) and one for 8-bits-per-pixel (256-color).

BI_RLE4 for 16-Color Images

The BI_RLE4 image compression format incorporates two modes: Absolute and Encoded. Both modes can be used anywhere within an individual bitmap.

Remember that pixel values are 4-bit indexes to a 16-color palette.

An image using BI_RLE4 encoding is identified by the `biCompression` flag:

```
bmInfo.bmiHeader.biCompression    = BI_RLE4;
```

The Encoded mode uses WORD values, with the first byte in each word specifying a number of consecutive values (01h..FFh) to be drawn using the two-color indexes in the second byte. Because the second byte contains two color indexes—one in the high nibble and one in the low nibble—the sequence of pixels is drawn alternating the two indexes. Thus, the first pixel would use the first color index, the second nibble the second index, the third nibble the first index, and so on. The sequence terminates when the specified number of pixels in the first byte have been painted. For a sequence in which all pixels are the same color, both the high and low nibbles would contain the same index, but the drawing process would be the same.

The exception occurs when the first byte is a 0, initiating an escape sequence. Escape sequences, shown in Table 15.1, denote an end of scan line, an end of bitmap image, an offset to the next pixel position, or a sequence of uncompressed pixels.

> Note: If the first palette entry (the 0 index entry) is the same as the window background (white), blank areas can be drawn using the delta offsets instead of drawing the pixels individually.

Table 15.1. Compression escape sequences.

First Byte	Second Byte	Definition
00	00	End of scan line.
00	01	End of bitmap image.
00	02	Delta: The next two bytes following the escape sequence contain the horizontal and vertical offsets for the next pixel position relative to the current pixel position.
00	03..FF	Second byte contains the absolute number of pixels following that are not compressed. The following uncompressed sequence is padded to a DWORD size (excluding the escape sequence) with NULL bytes.

The end of scan line and end of image escapes are self-explanatory. The delta escape is always followed by two bytes, with the first byte containing a horizontal offset (00h..FFh) and the second byte containing a vertical offset (00h..FFh). These offsets are relative to the current (last drawn) pixel and always extend down and right but never cross the bottom or right margins of the image. That is, offsets in an image do not wrap.

Following is an example of an RLE4-compressed bitmap image, together with the decompressed results:

Raw Data: 06 04 05 06 00 06 45 56 67 00 04 77 00 02 05 01 04 78 00 00 09 1E

Compressed Bytes	Mode	Decompressed Results/ Pixel Indexes
06 04	Absolute	4 0 4 0 4 0
05 06	Absolute	0 6 0 6 0
00 06 45 56 67 00	Encoded	4 5 5 6 6 7 (write six uncompressed pixels)
04 77	Absolute	7 7 7 7 7 7 7
00 02 05 01	Encoded	Move right 5 pixels, move down 1 pixel
18 78	Absolute	7 8 7 8 7 8 7 8 7 8 7 8 7 8 7 8 7 8 7 8 7 8 7 8
00 00	Encoded	End of scan line
09 1E	Absolute	1 E 1 E 1 E 1 E 1
00 01	Encoded	End of RLE bitmap

As you can see, RLE4 compression is most efficient where a sequence of single-color or two-color alternating pixels needs to be drawn. RLE4 compression is inefficient where an odd number of pixels needs to be drawn or where a short sequence of pixels cannot be compressed. Still, compression can save considerable space in most images.

BI_RLE8 for 256-Color Images

Like RLE4 compression, the BI_RLE8 image compression format incorporates two modes: Absolute and Encoded. Both modes can be used anywhere within an individual bitmap.

Remember that pixel values are 8-bit indexes to a 256-color palette.

An image using BI_RLE8 encoding is identified by the `biCompression` flag:

    bmInfo.bmiHeader.biCompression   = BI_RLE8;

Again, the Encoded mode uses WORD values, with the first byte in each word specifying a number of consecutive values (01h..FFh) to be drawn using the color index in the second byte. The sequence terminates when the specified number of pixels in the first byte have been painted.

The exception occurs when the first byte is a 0, initiating an escape sequence. Escape sequences, shown in Table 15.3, denote an end of scan line, an end of bitmap image, an offset to the next pixel position, or a sequence of uncompressed pixels.

Following is an example of an RLE8-compressed bitmap image, together with the decompressed results:

Raw data: 03 04 05 06 00 03 45 56 67 00 0F 78 00 02 05 01 74 78 00 00 09 1E 00 01

Compressed Bytes	Mode	Decompressed Results/ Pixel Indexes
03 04	Absolute	04 04 04
05 06	Absolute	06 06 06 06 06
00 03 45 56 67 00	Encoded	45 56 67 (write three uncompressed pixels)
0F 78	Absolute	78 78 78 78 78 78 78 78 78 78 78 78 78 78 78
00 02 05 01	Encoded	Move right 5 pixels, move down 1 pixel
74 78	Absolute	78 78 ... 78 78 (repeats 74h times)
00 00	Encoded	End of scan line
09 1E	Absolute	1E 1E 1E 1E 1E 1E 1E 1E 1E
00 01	Encoded	End of RLE bitmap

Again, RLE8 compression is most efficient when a sequence of single-color pixels needs to be drawn. Like RLE4, RLE8 compression is inefficient when a short sequence of pixels cannot be compressed. Still, compression can save considerable space in most images.

Reading and Displaying Images

Given the graphics orientation of the Windows OS—whether Win3.1, WinNT, or Win95—and the standardization of the BMP/DIB image format, it seems strange that neither Windows nor Visual C++ has yet provided a simple API or object class specifically for the purpose of loading, displaying, and saving bitmap images. Further, as shown in the preceding Capture demo, handling a bitmap image can be a laborious process.

Granted, the process demonstrated was somewhat more complex than absolutely necessary, and partial support for bitmaps has been provided by MFC, but the point remains that no single integrated operation is provided.

Therefore, what is needed is a package providing complete read and write facilities for bitmap images, which is exactly what the BmpImage demo program provides. For convenience, these bitmap APIs are packaged separately—in the source files ImageAPI.CPP and ImageAPI.H—making these utility functions available for easy reuse.

> Note: Alternatively, you can compile these utility functions as a DLL for shared use by multiple applications.

The ImageAPI service consists of three primary APIs: `ReadDIBFile` and `SaveDIBFile` to read and write bitmap files to and from the disk, and `PaintDIB` to paint a bitmap to a device context. Three utility APIs are also included: `CreateDIBPalette`, which loads a `CPalette` member with color information from a bitmap; `GetColorCount`, which checks the color resolution of a bitmap; and `CopyBlock`, which provides Clipboard support by copying a global memory block.

The *ReadDIBFile* API

The `ReadDIBFile` API function accepts a `CFile` parameter, which is presumably an opened bitmap file, and reads the contents before returning a handle to a DIB bitmap image:

```
HDIB WINAPI ReadDIBFile( CFile &cFile )
{
   BITMAPFILEHEADER bmfHeader;
   DWORD dwBitsSize;
   HDIB  hDIB;
   LPSTR pDIB;

   dwBitsSize = cFile.GetLength();
   if( cFile.Read( (LPSTR)&bmfHeader, sizeof(bmfHeader) ) !=
      sizeof(bmfHeader) ) return NULL;
   if( bmfHeader.bfType != DIB_HEADER_MARKER )
      return NULL;
```

Initially, `ReadDIBFile` checks the total file size before reading the bitmap file header (`bmfHeader`) and checking the `bfType` field, which must be `BM`.

After confirming that the file is a bitmap image, memory is allocated for the entire file, and the rest of the file is read into the allocated memory:

```
hDIB = (HDIB) GlobalAlloc(GMEM_MOVEABLE | GMEM_ZEROINIT, dwBitsSize);
if( hDIB == 0 ) return NULL;
pDIB = (LPSTR) GlobalLock((HGLOBAL) hDIB);
if( cFile.ReadHuge( pDIB, dwBitsSize - sizeof(BITMAPFILEHEADER) ) !=
    dwBitsSize - sizeof(BITMAPFILEHEADER) )
{
   GlobalUnlock((HGLOBAL) hDIB);
   GlobalFree((HGLOBAL) hDIB);
   return NULL;
}
GlobalUnlock((HGLOBAL) hDIB);
return hDIB;
}
```

If the second read fails—no bitmap is retrieved—the allocated memory is unlocked and freed, and `ReadDIBFile` returns a NULL result.

On success, the allocated memory is unlocked and the handle returned to the calling function.

This is a very simple process that is passed an open `CFile` and retrieves the contents as a bitmap that is written to globally allocated memory before returning a handle for the calling function's use.

The *SaveDIBFile* API

Earlier, in the Capture program, a detailed and complex process was used to write a bitmap file to disk. Now, `SaveDIBFile` demonstrates a simpler process.

The `SaveDIBFile` API is called with two arguments: a handle to a bitmap image and an opened `CFile` where the image should be written.

```
BOOL WINAPI SaveDIBFile( HDIB hDIB, CFile& cFile )
{
   BITMAPFILEHEADER    bmFH;           // Header for Bitmap cFile
   LPBITMAPINFOHEADER  pDIB;           // Pointer to DIB info structure
   DWORD               dwFileSize;

   if( hDIB == NULL ) return FALSE;
   // get pointer to DIB memory and BITMAPINFO struct
   pDIB = (LPBITMAPINFOHEADER) GlobalLock((HGLOBAL) hDIB);
   if( pDIB == NULL ) return FALSE;
```

The `hDIB` handle is checked for validity before locking the memory object and returning a pointer to the `BITMAPINFOHEADER`. If either `hDIB` or `pDIB` is NULL, `SaveDIBFile` returns failure.

Next, using the `BITMAPINFOHEADER`, the bitmap is checked for validity to ensure that this is indeed a version 3.0 (device-independent) bitmap:

```
   if( ! IS_WIN30_DIB(pDIB) )
   {
      GlobalUnlock((HGLOBAL) hDIB);
      return FALSE;    // not a DIB, can't save it
   }
```

If this is a DIB image, the `bfType` field is set to BM and the file size is initialized:

```
bmFH.bfType = DIB_HEADER_MARKER;   // first 2 bytes must be "BM"
dwFileSize = *(LPDWORD)pDIB + PALETTESIZE(pDIB);
```

Next, a check is required to determine whether this is a compressed bitmap because this affects how the total file size is calculated:

```
if( ! ISCOMPRESSED(pDIB) ) // not compressed, size = W * H * bits/pixel
    pDIB->biSizeImage = pDIB->biHeight *
        SCANWIDTH( pDIB->biWidth * (DWORD)pDIB->biBitCount );
```

If this is a compressed file, the `biSizeImage` field already contains the total image size. If not, the image size is calculated from the height, width, and bits per pixel; the result is entered in the `biSizeImage` field.

In either case, the next step is to add the image size to the file size before completing the file header:

```
dwFileSize += pDIB->biSizeImage;   // add biSizeImage field to total
bmFH.bfSize = dwFileSize + sizeof(BITMAPFILEHEADER);
bmFH.bfReserved1 = 0;
bmFH.bfReserved2 = 0;
// calc image offset in cFile
bmFH.bfOffBits = (DWORD)sizeof(BITMAPFILEHEADER) + pDIB->biSize
                 + PALETTESIZE(pDIB);
```

Having completed the file header, all that remains is to write the file header to the output file and then write the bitmap itself (which already includes the DIB header, palette, and image bits):

```
TRY
{
   cFile.Write( (LPSTR) &bmFH, sizeof(BITMAPFILEHEADER) ); // write header
   cFile.WriteHuge( pDIB, dwFileSize );   // write DIB header and image bits
}
CATCH (CFileException, e)
{
   GlobalUnlock((HGLOBAL) hDIB);
   THROW_LAST();
}
END_CATCH
GlobalUnlock((HGLOBAL) hDIB);
return TRUE;
}
```

The actual file output operation is done using the TRY..CATCH..END_CATCH exception handling and concludes by unlocking the hDIB handle.

Notice that you did not have to construct a DIB header or a palette and you did not have to write the image scan line by scan line from the bottom up. Instead, you simply wrote the entire bitmap, from memory, to the file, without process.

The *PaintDIB* API

Painting a device-independent bitmap can be quite convenient, as handled by the PaintDIB API.

The `PaintDIB` API is called with five parameters, beginning with a device context handle (`hDC`) and an output rectangle—the client rectangle in the device context. Next is a handle to the bitmap, a second `CRect` containing the bitmap dimensions, and a `CPalette` containing the bitmap colors. The `CPalette` argument is created using the `CreateDIBPalette` API, which is also part of the ImageAPI utilities:

```
BOOL WINAPI PaintDIB( HDC    hDC,   CRect *pDCRect,
                      HDIB hDIB, CRect *pDIBRect,
                      CPalette* pPal )
{
   LPSTR    pBMI;                    // pointer to BITMAPINFOHEADER
   LPSTR    pDIBits;                 // pointer to DIB bits
   BOOL     bSuccess = FALSE;
   HPALETTE hPal = NULL;             // DIB palette
   HPALETTE hOldPal = NULL;          // original palette

   if( hDIB == NULL ) return FALSE; // invalid handle
```

As usual, the `hDIB` handle is checked for validity before proceeding. If it is a valid handle, memory is locked and a pointer to the bitmap image bits is retrieved:

```
pBMI = (LPSTR) GlobalLock( (HGLOBAL) hDIB );
pDIBits = pBMI + *(LPDWORD)pBMI + PALETTESIZE(pBMI);
```

Next, a check is made to determine whether the palette is valid (non-NULL). If so, the palette is selected into the display device context:

```
if( pPal != NULL )    // get DIB palette, select into DC
{
   hPal = (HPALETTE) pPal->m_hObject;
   hOldPal = SelectPalette( hDC, hPal, TRUE );
}
```

A NULL palette is not cause for aborting the drawing operation because not all bitmaps have palettes. For example, if the bitmap is a 24-bit-per-pixel image, the color information is in the bits themselves and there is no palette.

Because two options for drawing are provided, the `COLORONCOLOR` `StretchBlt` mode is selected before deciding whether to call the `StretchDIBits` API to size the image to the window or simply to call the `SetDIBitsToDevice` API to paint the image without alteration:

```
SetStretchBltMode( hDC, COLORONCOLOR );
if( pDCRect->EqualRect( pDIBRect ) )
```

The decision on fitting the image to the window is made using the `CRect::EqualRect` method to compare the bitmap rectangle to the client window rectangle. If the two match, the `SetDIBitsToDevice` API is used to draw the image. If the two are different sizes, the `StretchDIBits` API sizes the image to fit.

> Note: Because the BmpImage program uses `CScrollView` windows with the scroll size set to the bitmap image size to be displayed, the `EqualRect` function always returns TRUE, and only the `SetDIBitsToDevice` drawing method is used. In this demo, images are never resized to fit the display window.

Because the `SetDIBitsToDevice` API is not a member function of the CDC class, the API has to be called directly using a device context handle and a host of individual parameters to specify the destination rectangle (there is no overloaded version accepting a `CRect` parameter). Parameters are also supplied for the source x and y origins, the image start scan line, the number of scan lines, a pointer to the image bits, the bitmap info structure, and a palette type constant:

```
         bSuccess =
            ::SetDIBitsToDevice( hDC,          // device context
                    pDCRect->left,             // destination x-origin
                    pDCRect->top,              // destination y-origin
                    pDCRect->Width(),          // destination width
                    pDCRect->Height(),         // destination height
                    pDIBRect->left,            // source x-origin
             (int) DIBHEIGHT(pBMI) -
                   pDIBRect->top -
                   pDIBRect->Height(),         // source y-origin
                    0,                         // nStartScan
           (WORD)  DIBHEIGHT(pBMI),            // nNumScans
                   pDIBits,                    // lpBits
(LPBITMAPINFO)pBMI,                            // lpBitsInfo
                   DIB_RGB_COLORS );           // palette type
```

Although the details are pretty awkward, the fact that you are using a scroll view window simplifies matters and relieves you of the details of calculating offsets and other tedium. Instead, even though provisions have been made here for a vertical offset calculation, you can simply assume that the bitmap and window fit and let it go at that.

If this were a normal window and you were relying on the `StretchDIBits` API for sizing, the process would not be greatly different. Both image and window rectangles are supplied as individual origin and size parameters extracted from the two `CRect` arguments passed to the `PaintDIB` function in the first place:

```
     else
        bSuccess =
           ::StretchDIBits( hDC,               // device context
                    pDCRect->left,             // destination x-origin
                    pDCRect->top,              // destination y-origin
                    pDCRect->Width(),          // destination width
                    pDCRect->Height(),         // destination height
                    pDIBRect->left,            // source x-origin
                    pDIBRect->top,             // source y-origin
                    pDIBRect->Width(),         // source width
                    pDIBRect->Height(),        // source height
                    pDIBits,                   // lpBits
(LPBITMAPINFO)pBMI,                            // lpBitsInfo
                    DIB_RGB_COLORS,            // palette type
                    SRCCOPY );                 // ROP2 copy mode
```

The remaining arguments are a pointer to the image data and the bitmap info structure, plus a palette type constant and an ROP2 copy mode.

Whichever drawing mode was used, the bitmap handle is unlocked, the original palette restored, and the results reported back:

```
   GlobalUnlock((HGLOBAL) hDIB);        // always unlock memory
   if( hOldPal != NULL )                // reset original palette
      SelectPalette( hDC, hOldPal, TRUE );
   return( bSuccess );
}
```

Perhaps the reliance on the StretchDIBits and SetDIBitsToDevice APIs is less elegant than using a CDC member function, but there are no CDC member functions supplying the equivalent capabilities. Also, because these are in place inside the PaintDIB API, there really isn't any further need to be concerned with them.

Other Utility Functions in ImageAPI

The ImageAPI files also include a couple of utility functions.

The CreateDIBPalette API function has been mentioned previously and is called with a handle to a bitmap and a pointer to a CPalette instance that is returned with the color values from the bitmap. Internally, this function should be familiar from previous operations and doesn't require explanation here.

The GetColorCount API function also parallels operations that have been discussed earlier. It doesn't warrant further explanation here aside from saying that it is called with a pointer to the bitmap and returns a color count that can be the biClrUsed value or can be 2, 16, or 256 palette entries.

The final utility function, CopyBlock, warrants at least a brief explanation. The CopyBlock API function is used to retrieve information from or load information to the Clipboard. The CopyBlock function is called with a handle to a memory object and returns a handle to a duplicate object. This is accomplished by first checking the size of the object passed and allocating memory for a second block of the same size:

```
HANDLE WINAPI CopyBlock( HANDLE h )
{
   BYTE    *lpCopy;
   BYTE    *lp;
   HANDLE  hCopy;
   DWORD   dwLen;

   if( h == NULL ) return NULL;
   dwLen = GlobalSize((HGLOBAL) h);
   if( ( hCopy = (HANDLE) GlobalAlloc(GHND, dwLen) ) != NULL )
   {
```

If memory cannot be allocated, the CopyBlock function simply returns NULL. If memory has been allocated, pointers are set by locking both the original and the duplicate memory addresses and using a loop to copy the contents of the original to the duplicate:

```
      lpCopy = (BYTE *) GlobalLock( (HGLOBAL) hCopy );
      lp     = (BYTE *) GlobalLock( (HGLOBAL) h );
```

```
        while( dwLen-- ) *lpCopy++ = *lp++;
        GlobalUnlock( (HGLOBAL) hCopy );
        GlobalUnlock( (HGLOBAL) h );
    }
    return hCopy;
}
```

Once the copy is finished, both memory blocks are unlocked and the handle to the duplicate is returned.

The BmpImage Demo

The BmpImage demo application has several features. First, using a multidocument interface, BmpImage can display multiple bitmaps, each in a separate CScrollView window. Second, BmpImage can save bitmaps to the Clipboard or load images from the Clipboard. Third, BmpImage accepts drag-and-drop files. Finally, bitmap images can be printed.

Even though there are no image editing capabilities, because a bitmap can be retrieved from the Clipboard, there are provisions to save an image to a file.

The BmpImage application is shown in Figure 15.2 with four bitmap files open. Because this figure is reproduced in black-and-white instead of color, some aspects of this multiple view of separate bitmaps may not be as easily distinguished here as they are on-screen. However, the four bitmaps displayed consist of one 16-color bitmap (Winnt.BMP, upper-left) and three 256-color bitmaps.

Figure 15.2. BmpImage and views.

Because this display was run on a 256-color video driver, only the active bitmap window (the WinLogo bitmap at the upper-right) and the 16-color bitmap appear in the correct colors. The remaining two 256-color bitmaps are both quite distorted.

The reason for this is simple. Because the system can support only one 256-color palette, the palette in the active window takes precedence, and the two remaining 256-color bitmaps are mapped to the nearest colors in the active palette. This mapping, however, does not produce a very appealing result, nor are the contents of the inactive windows very recognizable.

The single 16-color bitmap is unaffected, because it is using the default system palette in the first place.

On a system using a 24-bit true-color video, this problem would not occur because each of these images would be displayed using their exact color values, regardless of their internal palettes. As the focus changes from one window to another, the palette belonging to the active window becomes the dominant palette, and the image in that window is displayed correctly, to the detriment of the inactive windows.

Clipboard Operations in BmpImage

One aspect of the BmpImage program that has not been discussed previously in any application is the process of retrieving an image from the Clipboard or copying an image to the Clipboard. In the Capture demo, the Clipboard contents were displayed, but this was a passive operation and any changes in the Clipboard contents were simply reflected in the display as an update.

In the BmpImage program, a different approach is used. A copy is made of the Clipboard DIB, if there is one, and the image copy is displayed, quite independent of any changes that may occur on the Clipboard.

This operation is accomplished in the `OnEditPaste` procedure and begins by opening the Clipboard and calling `GetClipboardData` to return a handle to any DIB image on the Clipboard:

```
void CBmpimageView::OnEditPaste()
{
   HDIB hNewDIB = NULL;

   if( OpenClipboard() )
   {
      BeginWaitCursor();
      hNewDIB = (HDIB) CopyBlock( GetClipboardData(CF_DIB) );
      CloseClipboard();
```

If the Clipboard does not have a bitmap image, the returned value is NULL, and the `CopyBlock` operation returns a NULL handle to `hNewDIB`. In either case, the Clipboard is closed before proceeding.

If `hNewDIB` is not NULL and you did retrieve a bitmap image, the `CBmpimageDoc::GetDocument` function is called for a pointer to a new document window that is loaded with the retrieved bitmap and initialized:

```
        if (hNewDIB != NULL)
        {
           CBmpimageDoc* pDoc = GetDocument();
           pDoc->ReplaceHDIB(hNewDIB); //
           pDoc->InitDIBData();         // set up new size & palette
           pDoc->SetModifiedFlag(TRUE);
```

In addition, before the new window is displayed, the `SetScrollSizes` method is called to set the window scroll size to the document size, which is also the bitmap size:

```
        SetScrollSizes( MM_TEXT, pDoc->GetDocSize(),
                                 CSize( 20, 20 ), CSize( 4, 4 ) );
        OnDoRealize( (WPARAM) m_hWnd, 0 );  // realize the new palette
```

Because this new window is the top-most window in the active display, the `OnDoRealize` method is called to make the new bitmap's palette the active and dominant palette in the display. This was discussed earlier when explaining why, with multiple windows open, not all the images were distinguishable.

Last, the `UpdateAllViews` method is called to repaint all the multiple windows:

```
        pDoc->UpdateAllViews(NULL);
     }
        EndWaitCursor();
  }
}
```

This concludes the Clipboard retrieval. The retrieved image is now displayed in a document window and can be saved to a disk file if desired.

The second Clipboard operation—copying to the Clipboard—is even simpler and is handled in the `OnEditCopy` function. The image copied is the image in the active document window.

The Clipboard copy process begins by opening the Clipboard and emptying it before calling the `SetClipboardData` function with the `CF_DIB` type constant and the `CopyBlock` function to return a handle to a copy of the current bitmap:

```
void CBmpimageView::OnEditCopy()
{
   CBmpimageDoc* pDoc = GetDocument();

   if( OpenClipboard() ) // clean clipboard and copy bitmap
   {
      BeginWaitCursor();
      EmptyClipboard();
      SetClipboardData( CF_DIB, CopyBlock((HANDLE) pDoc->GetHDIB()) );
      CloseClipboard();
      EndWaitCursor();
   }
}
```

The Clipboard is closed and the operation is completed. It couldn't be simpler.

Summary

This chapter talked about bitmap formats, the development of the contemporary device-independent bitmap, and the file and data structures used for bitmaps. In addition, you learned how to capture an image from the screen and save the image to a disk file. The chapter also touched briefly on the OS/2 bitmap format and looked at the RLE4 and RLE8 image compression schemes.

I also discussed the need for generic bitmap file and display APIs and, in the ImageAPI.CPP and ImageAPI.H files, constructed a set of utilities to read and write bitmap files and to paint a bitmap to a device context.

In conclusion, you learned how to copy bitmap images to and from the Clipboard.

Chapter 16, "Interfacing Data with Object Classes," leaves the graphics aspect of programming and looks at how application data elements are mapped to object class members and how data can be retrieved from external files and from the registry for use in dialog boxes and applications.

PART IV

Other Elements in Visual C++

Previous parts of the book have talked about conversion and changing from 16 to 32 bits, about creating the user interface, and about graphics. Although all these topics are important, there are still a number of other important topics we have not yet covered.

The next several chapters fill a few of these gaps. We begin by looking at how data and applications—or, more accurately, data and objects—are connected, both using conventional file access and using Open DataBase Connectivity (ODBC).

Because applications today must work together and must be able to interact, we move on to discuss OLE (object linking and embedding) and how OLE allows application interactions. Remember that another aspect of OLE—OCX controls—were introduced back in Chapter 9.

And because we've been relying on the Microsoft Foundation Classes to provide most of our functional services in all the applications discussed or used as examples in this book, we return to the MFC classes for an overview of the existing classes supported in both Visual C++ 2.*x* and in 4.0. Then we continue with deriving descendent classes and creating our own dynamic link libraries.

Last (because by their nature, classes are neither self-contained nor simple to examine), we look at the Developer Studio's debugging capabilities and how Developer Studio and other applications can be used to trace class ancestry and look beyond the obvious.

CHAPTER 16

Interfacing Data with Object Classes

Perhaps the biggest problem that has faced programmers since computers were invented is the simple question of getting data into the computer. The famous, and now obsolete, punchcard originated as a device for controlling lace-making looms. Later, when the punchcard format was adapted to store information for the census bureau, the data storage and computation operations were integrated, and the computer revolution began. It wasn't fancy, but it was the beginning.

Computer punchcards became a standard of everyday life. Punchcards arrived with your monthly utility bills. Book and record clubs sent out punchcards; voting booths turned to punchcards; and "do not fold, spindle, or mutilate" was heard even in households where computers were thought of as having lots of flashing lights and spinning tapes.

For most people, magnetic floppy disks and hard drives were the real harbingers of the computer revolution. PCs have never had much use for punchcards.

Regardless of how you store data, transferring data from storage to your applications has always been a problem.

File Access Methods

With contemporary systems, file access is essentially independent of the media—backup tapes excepted. Reading a file is the same whether the file is read from a floppy disk, a hard drive, a magnetic optical, or a CD. Regardless of the media, all you do is tell your application the drive, path, and file name.

The details of how to handle different types of hardware, what format the media uses, which port and interrupt calls to use, and which drivers to load are left to the operating system. This is true not only under Win95 or WinNT but also under DOS. All your application has to do is call the C/C++ open function with permission and operation flags, and the file is ready for access.

Once the file is opened, the question becomes what to read. Is this a flat ASCII text file? Does the file consist of records defined by a structure? Is the structure defined in the data?

You are probably familiar with all of these formats. Certainly if you have been programming for any length of time you have used all these formats and more.

MFC File Capabilities

Whereas C/C++ replaced the old DOS interrupts with superior file handling functions, the Microsoft Foundation Classes offer new access methods in the CFile and CStdioFile classes to make file I/O easier and more convenient.

The CFile class has been introduced in previous examples. In Chapter 15, "Using Bitmaps and Screen Images," for example, the CFile class was used to read and write bitmap files. The Open dialog box was introduced in Chapter 10, "Using Common Dialog Boxes, Fonts, and Colors," as one of the common dialog box utilities. Although these demonstrate programming techniques and capabilities, there hasn't been much reason so far for using file access.

For most real applications, however, file access is important and integral, and the CFile class is where application file access begins. The CFile class is descended from the CObject class and offers a wide variety of function methods for handling file operations. Table 16.1 shows an overview of the CFile class members.

Table 16.1. CFile members.

Data Members	
m_hFile	Normally contains the operating system file handle.
Construction	
CFile	Constructor method; creates a CFile object from a path or file handle.
Open	Opens a file with error-testing options.
Close	Closes a file and deletes the CFile object.

Abort	Closes a file. All warnings and errors are ignored.
Duplicate	Constructs a duplicate `CFile` object.
Input/Output	
Read	Reads data from a file at the current position. `Read` is not buffered but is limited to blocks smaller than 64K.
ReadHuge	Reads blocks of data larger than 64K. `ReadHuge` is not buffered.
Write	Writes data to a file at the current position. `Write` is not buffered but is limited to blocks smaller than 64K.
WriteHuge	Writes blocks of data larger than 64K. `WriteHuge` is not buffered.
Flush	Flushes any data remaining in the file buffer, writing the data to the file. Note that `Flush` does not guarantee flushing of `CArchive` buffers. For `CArchive` buffers, call `CArchive::Flush` before calling `CFile::Flush`.
File Position	
Seek	Positions the file pointer to a specified location (offset) in the file.
SeekToBegin	Positions the file pointer at the beginning of the file.
SeekToEnd	Positions the file pointer at the end of the file.
GetPosition	Returns the file pointer position (offset) in the file.
GetLength	Returns the current file length.
SetLength	Changes the file length. Be careful, because changes will extend or truncate the open file.
File Locking	
LockRange	Locks a range of bytes in a file.
UnlockRange	Unlocks a range of bytes in a file.
File Status	
GetStatus	Returns the status of an open file.
GetFileName	Returns the filename of a selected file.
GetFileTitle	Returns the title of a selected file.
GetFilePath	Returns the full file path for a selected file.
SetFilePath	Sets the full file path for a selected file.
Static Functions	
Rename	Renames the specified file; equivalent to the REN function.
Remove	Deletes the specified file. Path can be relative or absolute but cannot contain a network name. This is equivalent to the DEL command except that the `Remove` member function throws an exception if the specified file is open or if the file cannot be removed. Note that the `Remove` method does not delete a directory.

continues

Table 16.1. continued

GetStatus	Returns a CFileStatus structure containing file dates, attributes, and absolute path name.
SetStatus	Uses a CFileStatus structure to set file dates, attributes, and so forth. Note that fields in the CFileStatus structure that are NULL are not updated.

Opening a File Using *CFile*

Opening a CFile instance can be handled directly or indirectly.

Indirectly, a CFile instance is declared by using the CFile constructor, which requires no parameters, and then calling the CFile::Open method with a file specification and flags, as follows:

```
BOOL Open( LPCTSTR lpszFileName, UINT nOpenFlags,
           CFileException* pError = NULL );
```

The lpszFileName parameter is the path to the desired file and can be relative or absolute but cannot contain a network name. Unaccountably, the Open method is not overloaded to accept a CString argument.

The nOpenFlags parameter is a UINT value defining the file's sharing and access modes and specifies the action to take on opening the file. Access and share flags are listed in Table 16.2. Option flags can be combined using the bitwise OR (|) operator. One access permission and one share option are required. The modeCreate and modeNoInherit modes are optional.

The Open method returns nonzero if successful. If there is an error, it returns zero, with pError pointing to an existing file-exception object reporting the completion state of the Open operation.

A second CFile constructor method is called with the lpszFileName and nOpenFlags parameters, as follows:

```
CFile( LPCTSTR lpszFileName, UINT nOpenFlags )
    throw( CFileException );
```

The opening parameters are the same as those passed to the Open method; in this form, a CFileException is thrown if the constructor fails.

The third CFile constructor is called with a handle to a file that has already been opened:

```
CFile( int hFile );
```

In this form, because the file is already opened, no error checking is supplied within the constructors.

A fourth way of opening a file is demonstrated in the ARRL_HAM application, where the `CWinApp::OnFileOpen` parent method is called in lieu of supplying application-specific custom handling. This provision is found in the message map in the ARRL_HAM.CPP source file, shown here:

```
BEGIN_MESSAGE_MAP(CAarl_hamApp, CWinApp)
    //{{AFX_MSG_MAP(CAarl_hamApp)
    ON_COMMAND(ID_APP_ABOUT, OnAppAbout)
    //}}AFX_MSG_MAP
    // Standard file based document commands
    ON_COMMAND(ID_FILE_NEW, CWinApp::OnFileNew)
    ON_COMMAND(ID_FILE_OPEN, CWinApp::OnFileOpen)
END_MESSAGE_MAP()
```

The file open provision has been supplied by AppWizard as a default. It removes all need for supplying additional handling unless there's a reason or circumstance demanding a different type of handling or a different set of permission and access flags.

Also supplied by default, the `InitInstance` method includes a simple provision allowing the application to be called with the name of the data source file as a command-line parameter:

```
BOOL CAarl_hamApp::InitInstance()
{
    ...
    // simple command line parsing
    if (m_lpCmdLine[0] == '\0')
        OnFileNew();                         // create a new (empty) document
    else
        OpenDocumentFile(m_lpCmdLine);       // open an existing document
    return TRUE;
}
```

In this default configuration, if a command-line parameter is supplied, the specified data source is opened as the application is initialized. If no source is specified, an empty data file is created.

Access and Share Flags

Under DOS, files were opened for read or write or with a flag to truncate (reset) a file. Because Windows is a multitasking environment, several additional modes and permission are required. You now have five mode flags, five share permissions, and two type flags.

The five mode (or access) flags replace the original DOS file open flags and determine how the file is opened. The `modeNoInherit` flag has no parallel under DOS. The five share flags, which were not required under a single-tasking system, determine if and how other processes are allowed access to an opened file. The two type flags are text and binary. Although these do have historical parallels, they are used by MFC as special-purpose flags used by descendant classes. Table 16.2 lists the access and share flags.

Table 16.2. File access and share flags.

Access (Mode) Flags

`CFile::modeCreate`	Creates a new file or truncates an existing file to length 0 (optional).
`CFile::modeRead`	Opens file for read only.
`CFile::modeReadWrite`	Opens file for read and write.
`CFile::modeWrite`	Opens file for write only.
`CFile::modeNoInherit`	File cannot be inherited by child processes (optional).
`CFile::modeNoTruncate`	Combined with `modeCreate` to prevent an existing file from being truncated. This ensures that either an existing file is opened or a new file is created.

Share Flags

`CFile::shareDenyNone`	Opens file without denying read or write access to other processes. Operation fails if this file is currently opened by any other process in `shareCompat` mode.
`CFile::shareDenyRead`	Opens file and denies other processes read access to the file. Operation fails if this file is currently opened by another process in `shareCompat` mode or with read access.
`CFile::shareDenyWrite`	Opens file and denies other processes write access to the file. Operation fails if this file is currently opened by another process in `shareCompat` mode or with write access.
`CFile::shareExclusive`	Opens file in exclusive mode, denying both read and write access to other processes. Operation fails if this file is currently opened in any other mode for read or write access. This applies even if the file has been previously opened by the current process.
`CFile::shareCompat`	The `shareCompat` mode enables access to a file to be shared between different applications. Operation fails if this file is already open in any other sharing modes.

Type Flags

`CFile::typeText`	Text mode provides special processing for carriage-return/line-feed pairs. Used in derived classes only.
`CFile::typeBinary`	Explicitly sets binary mode. Used in derived classes only.

Serialization

In object-oriented programming, *objects* refers not only to processes and procedures but also to data objects—any type of structured record. Phrased simply, *serialization* is the process of file I/O applied to objects. If you prefer, it is the process of reading or writing object data from or to a storage file. The serialization process is supplied by the MFC through the `CObject` class and is inherited by object classes derived from the `CObject` class.

The idea behind serialization is that an object should be capable of writing its state (its member variables) to a file. The converse of serialization—deserialization—is simply the process of retrieving data members from a file. Generically, both of these processes are referred to simply as serialization.

Serialization is handled by MFC's `CArchive` class, which provides the file I/O operations and operators. `CArchive` objects are associated with `CFile` objects and, like `iostreams`, use the overloaded insertion (<<) and extraction (>>) operators.

> Note: Although serialization is similar to the general-purpose `iostreams`, the two should not be confused. The `iostreams` are designed for formatted text; `CArchive` objects are used for binary format serialized objects.

Saying that `CArchive` objects are used for binary format files is something of an oversimplification and may be misleading. For example, an editor application might use serialization to read and write simple text files with a `CArchive` object without reflecting on the nature of the data. For example, the application document class might handle serialization as follows:

```
////////////////////////////////////////////////////////////////
// CEditorDoc serialization

void CEditorDoc::Serialize( CArchive& ar )
{
    ((CEditView*)m_viewList.GetHead())->SerializeRaw(ar);
}
```

Here, the standard `Serialize` method expects to find object description data. Because this example is handling text data that has no structure, the `SerializeRaw` method is called to pipe the data to and from the file without object description data.

Customizing Serialization

Serialization is often used to write structured data, but for this purpose you need to supply a custom serialization method designed specifically for the data being handled.

In a conventional application such as DOS, an application using structured records begins by opening a file in binary mode and then reading as many bytes as required for the target data structure buffer, repeating this operation for as many records as needed.

Under MFC, using serialization, a custom serialize method is created that knows how to read or write the object data. An example of custom serialization is found in the AARL_HAM demo application where the `CAarl_hamDoc::Serialize` and `CRepeater::Serialize` methods handle `m_repeaterList` data records.

Customization begins in the AARL_DOC.H header, where an overridden Serialize method is declared:

```
public:
    virtual ~CAarl_hamDoc();
    CObList* GetList() {   return &m_repeaterList;    }
    virtual void Serialize(CArchive& ar);    // overridden for document i/o
```

Next, the overridden Serialize method is implemented in the AARL_DOC.CPP source, as follows:

```
void CAarl_hamDoc::Serialize(CArchive& ar)
{
    m_repeaterList.Serialize(ar);
}
```

Obviously, the CAarl_hamDoc::Serialize method can't handle serialization for data members belonging to another class. Therefore, as you can see, the overridden method does nothing on its own except to refer to the object method belonging to the data class.

Implementing a Custom Serialization Method

Implementing a custom serialization method begins by calling the IMPLEMENT_SERIAL macro. This call appears in the Repeater.CPP source file:

```
IMPLEMENT_SERIAL( CRepeater, CObject, 0 )
```

The first argument is the object class being serialized. The second argument is the base class that provides the functionality for the serialization process. The third argument, nominally 0, is a version number. Using a version number is normally done to enable later versions of the process to recognize and handle data files created by earlier versions of the application, or if earlier versions are not supported, to ensure that only current data files are accepted.

The IMPLEMENT_SERIAL macro generates the C++ code needed to give the CObject-derived class runtime access to the class name and position with the hierarchy.

> Note: If a versionable object is implemented, the CArchive::GetObjectSchema method is called before reading any records to retrieve the object version information. Given a version number, an application can then call different serialization methods appropriate to the version.

Following class implementation, the custom serialization method is implemented in the Repeater.CPP source as follows:

```
void CRepeater::Serialize(CArchive& ar)
{
    if( ar.IsStoring() )
        ar << m_csCallSign << m_csLocation << m_csNotes <<
            m_csSponsor << m_csOutput << m_csInput;
```

```
    else
        ar >> m_csCallSign >> m_csLocation >> m_csNotes >>
            m_csSponsor >> m_csOutput >> m_csInput;
}
```

You can see the overloaded insertion (<<) and extraction (>>) operators in use. More importantly, notice that both input and output are handled by a single function. The choice of operation is controlled by the `CArchive::IsStoring()` function, which returns TRUE if `CArchive` is being used for output and FALSE if `CArchive` is used to retrieve from a file.

Conversely, the `CArchive::IsLoading()` function returns FALSE for output and TRUE for input.

The Insertion and Extraction Operators

The insertion (<<) and extraction (>>) operators have overloaded definitions for the BYTE, WORD, LONG, DWORD, float, and double data types. Operators are not defined for int and short int data types, however, because these have system-dependent sizes. (The size of an int or short int depends on the operating system and is not constant.)

Table 16.3 shows the standard data types supported by the insertion and extraction operators and their sizes (for a 32-bit system). The √ identifies those data types supported; the × identifies those data types not supported.

Table 16.3. Data types supported by insertion and extraction operators.

Type	Supported	Size	Aliases
int	×	*	signed, signed int
unsigned int	×	*	unsigned
BYTE	√	1	none
char	×	1	signed char
unsigned char	×	1	none
short	×	2	short int, signed short int
unsigned short	×	2	unsigned short int
WORD	√	2	none
long	×	4	long int, signed long int
unsigned long	×	4	unsigned long int
LONG	√	4	none
enum	×	2	none
float	√	4	none
double	√	8	none
DWORD	√	8	none
long double	×	10	none

If custom data types require special support, overloaded definitions for the insertion and extraction operators can be defined. In most cases, however, it is easier to cast an undefined type to a supported type.

The *CArchive* Class

The CArchive class is used with CFile objects to implement persistent storage for objects through the serialize and deserialize processes. The CArchive class members are described in Table 16.4.

Table 16.4. CArchive class members.

Data Members	
m_pDocument	Pointer to the CDocument object being serialized.
Construction	
CArchive	Constructor method creates a CArchive object, specifying whether it will be used for loading or for storing objects.
Close	Flushes any unwritten data before disconnecting from the associated CFile object.
Input/Output	
Flush	Flushes unwritten data from the archive buffer; called automatically before exit unless the bNoFlushOnDelete flag was set when the constructor was called.
>> (extraction)	Loads objects and primitive types from the archive. Overloaded insertion operators are defined for all standard data types and additional custom operators can be defined as required.
<< (insertion)	Stores objects and primitive types to the archive. Overloaded extraction operators are defined for all standard data types and additional custom operators can be defined as required.
Read	Reads a specified number of raw bytes from the source file to the buffer.
Write	Writes a specified number of raw bytes from the buffer to the archive (file).
ReadString	Reads a single line of text from a source file, stopping when a CR/LF pair is read, when the end of file is reached, or when the buffer size is exceeded.
WriteString	Writes a single line of text to a file, stopping when a terminating NULL is reached. A CR/LF pair is not automatically supplied.

I/O Status

GetFile	Returns a pointer to the CFile object for this archive.
GetObjectSchema	Called from the Serialize function to determine the version of the object that is being deserialized when IsLoading returns TRUE. This should be the first call to the Serialize function and should be called only once. A return value of –1 indicates that the version number is unknown. CObject-derived classes can use the VERSIONABLE_SCHEMA ORed with the version number in the IMPLEMENT_SERIAL macro to create an object version.
SetObjectSchema	Used to set a particular version to be read in a Serialize function of a derived class.
IsLoading	Returns TRUE if an archive is being loaded, FALSE if it is being stored.
IsStoring	Returns TRUE if an archive is being stored, FALSE if it is being loaded.
IsBufferEmpty	Used during a Windows Sockets receive process to determine whether the buffer has been emptied. Returns TRUE if the buffer is empty, FALSE if the buffer still contains data.

Object I/O

ReadObject	Reads object data from the archive, constructing an object of the appropriate type. This function is usually called by the extraction (>>) operator overloaded for a CObject pointer. In turn, the Serialize function for the archived class is called.
WriteObject	Writes object data to an archive. This function is usually called by the insertion (<<) operator overloaded for a CObject pointer. In turn, the Serialize function for the archived class is called.

New Methods in MFC 4.0

MapObject	Places objects in the map that are not serialized and stored in the output file but that are available for other subobjects to reference.
SetStoredParams	Used when storing CObject-derived objects in an archive. Sets the hash table and block size in the map used to identify unique objects during serialization
SetLoadParams	Used to set the size for the load array.
ReadClass	Used to retrieve version and class information previously stored using the WriteClass member.
WriteClass	Used to store version and class information for a base class during serialization of the derived class.
SerializeClass	Reads or writes class references to the CArchive object.

> Note: Before archiving an object, you should finish creating, deleting, or updating the object. If modifications and archiving are mixed, the archive may be corrupted.

Random File Access

Just as DOS file operations offered random file access through file offset positioning, the `CFile` class provides these same features through a series of methods: `Seek`, `SeekToBegin`, and `SeekToEnd`.

The `CFile::Seek` method is called with two parameters:

`Seek( lOff, nFrom );`

The `lOff` argument is an offset in bytes to move the file pointer; the `nFrom` argument specifies where to offset from. `nFrom` must be one of these three values:

`CFile::begin`   File pointer is offset `lOff` bytes forward from the beginning of the file.

`CFile::current` File pointer is offset `lOff` bytes forward from the current position in the file.

`CFile::end`   File pointer is offset `lOff` bytes backward from the end of the file.

Because `lOff` is a signed long value, negative offsets are permitted, but when `CFile::end` is specified, the `lOff` value is assumed to be a positive value offset backwards from the end of the file.

> Note: If the requested position is legal, `CFile::Seek` returns the new current file position. If the requested position is invalid, the return value is undefined and a `CFileException` object is thrown.

To query the current file position, the `CFile::GetPosition()` method returns the file pointer position in the file. In addition, the `SeekToBegin` and `SeekToEnd` methods position the current file pointer to the beginning or end of the file, respectively.

There is one problem with the file positioning functions when you are using a `CFile` object with the `CArchive` class for I/O. The problem, shown in Listing 16.1, is that the data records are variable rather than fixed length. That is, each field in the record is preceded by a byte value giving the length of that individual field; each record, beginning with the second, is preceded by the flag bytes 01 80.

Listing 16.1. An excerpt from the Repeater.RPT data file.

```
000000  06 00 FF FF 00 00 09 00   43 52 65 70 65 61 74 65   ........CRepeate
000010  72 05 4B 44 36 4C 43 0A   53 6F 6E 6F 6D 61 20 28   r.KD6LC.Sonoma (
000020  35 29 04 6F 70 65 6E 00   06 31 34 37 2E 31 32 06   5).open..147.12.
000030  31 34 34 2E 35 37 01 80   06 57 42 36 53 58 43 0A   144.57...WB6SXC.
000040  53 6F 6E 6F 6D 61 20 28   36 29 06 42 20 32 31 30   Sonoma (6).B 210
```

```
000050  30 0C 53 6F 6E 6F 6D 61    20 4D 74 20 52 53 06 31    0.Sonoma Mt RS 1
000060  34 36 2E 39 31 06 31 34    34 2E 35 37 01 80 06 57    46.91.144.57...W
000070  42 36 52 48 50 0A 53 6F    6E 6F 6D 61 20 28 31 29    B6RHP.Sonoma (1)
000080  04 6F 70 65 6E 06 57 42    36 52 48 50 06 31 34 35    .open.WB6RHP.145
```

In Listing 16.1, the contents of the Repeater.RPT file are shown in both hexadecimal (left) and ASCII (right) formats. In the hexadecimal display, the record headers, record flags, and field lengths are shown in bold; the actual field data is shown with a half-tone background.

Notice also that the record begins with the record header, where the first two bytes in the record header are an offset to a second two-byte offset. This second offset points to the position of the first record. Following this second offset, a single field record names the class associated with the data file—the class that contains the structure and the insertion and extraction methods for this data.

However, the `CFile::Seek` methods are not particularly useful with this data structure, simply because the data must be read serially to find the beginning of each record and each field.

In other situations, where a more consistently structured record is used, the `CFile::Seek` methods would be much more useful. Alternatively, they could be used with a raw data file, using `SerializeRaw`, or in any other situation where the appropriate offsets could be calculated.

The *CStdioFile* Class

The `CStdioFile` class is derived from the `CFile` class and represents a C runtime stream file that normally would have been opened using the `_fopen` function. Stream files are buffered and can be opened in either text (default) or binary mode.

In text mode, special processing is provided for CR/LF (carriage-return/line-feed) pairs. When a newline character (0x0A) is written to a `CStdioFile` object (in text mode), a CR/LF two-byte pair (0x0A,0x0D) is written to the file. On read, when the CR/LF pair is encountered, it is translated into a single 0x0A byte.

> Note: The `CFile` methods `Duplicate`, `LockRange`, and `UnlockRange` are not implemented in `CStdioFile`. These are relevant only for structured file I/O in a shared access environment. Calling these functions results in a `CNotSupportedException`.

CStdioFile Text Input

The `CStdioFile` class provides the `ReadString` method for text input from a file. `ReadString` is called with two arguments: a pointer to a user-supplied buffer to receive a NULL-terminated string, and an unsigned int specifying the maximum number of characters to read.

For example, using a `CString` object as the buffer, the `ReadString` function is called as follows:

```
CString csBuffer;
if( ! ReadString( csBuffer.GetBuffer( nMax ), nMax ) return FALSE;
```

In response, `ReadString` reads up to `nMax` characters from the file, stopping either when `nMax` characters have been read or when a CR/LF pair is encountered. The CR/LF pair is translated into a single CR character. In either case, a single NULL character is appended to the end of the returned string.

> Note: The `nMax` argument must be one less than the size of the buffer to allow space for the terminating NULL character.

The `ReadString` method returns a pointer to the buffer containing the text data, or NULL if the end of file was reached.

CStdioFile Text Output

The `CStdioFile` class provides the `WriteString` method for text output to a file. The `WriteString` function is called with a single argument—the buffer containing the data to be output. Any newline characters in the buffer contents are translated to CR/LF pairs on output. Using a `CString` object as a data source, the `WriteString` method can be called as follows:

```
CString csBuffer;
WriteString( csBuffer );
```

`WriteString` does not return a value but throws an exception in response to an error condition.

The advantage of using the `ReadString` and `WriteString` methods lies in their string orientation. For example, if the `CFile::Write` method was used instead of `CStdioFile::Write`, an explicit number of bytes would be written from the buffer to the file rather than writing a string from the buffer and terminating. These bytes could include any NULL terminator and any garbage characters following.

The AARL_HAM Demo

The AARL_HAM application demonstrates the use of the `CFile` and `CArchive` classes by reading and writing records of two-meter repeater stations. When the AARL_HAM application is called, the Open dialog box shown in Figure 16.1 appears, listing source files to be opened.

The file type specification is found in the RC source file; the initial directory information is automatically stored in the AARL_HAM.INI file (located in the Windows directory).

The AARL_HAM.INI file contains very little:

```
[Recent File List]
File1=E:\32_BIT\CHAP-16\REPEATER\Repeater.rpt
```

Figure 16.1. *The Open dialog box (Win95 version).*

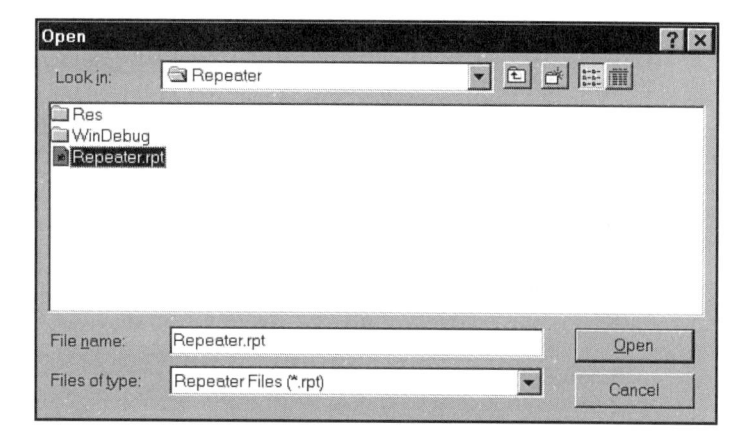

The handling for this INI file, including its creation, has been provided by the application document class and is maintained without need of any special provisions.

Once the data file has been opened (a sample data file is provided along with the application source code), the application shows the records individually using a dialog box (see Figure 16.2).

Figure 16.2. *The ARRL_HAM application, showing the 2-Meter Repeater Listing.*

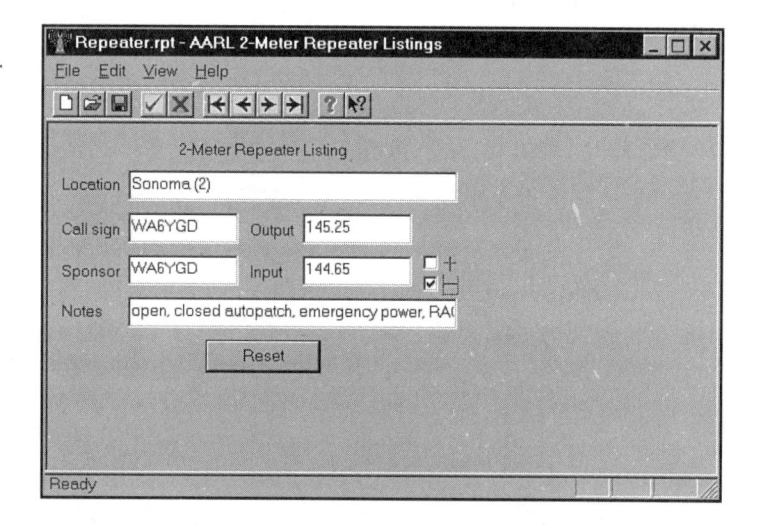

There are several elements of interest in this application. For one, the toolbar shown uses a yellow background for several of the buttons. However, instead of shadowed button images provided by the common gray-on-white buttons, these appear as a solid dark gray when disabled. This is a minor point, but it is worth observing.

Second, any of the fields can be edited, but a few rules apply to the Output and Input fields and to the two buttons (+ and –) next to the Input edit box.

> **Note:** For those of you who aren't amateur radio operators, *two-meter repeaters* are rebroadcast stations operated by groups or individuals. These are called on an input frequency and retransmit their received signal on their output frequency, allowing a transmission to be received over a wider area than the originating (often handheld) radios could reach. Repeater stations are listed by their output frequency, and a station's input frequency is commonly 600 KHz above or below (+ or –) the output. Some repeaters, however, may use other frequency pairs or may operate on a single frequency (simplex operation).

The Output frequency can be changed, but if either the + or – button is selected, the Input frequency reflects the changes in the Output edit box, remaining 600 KHz above or below the Output.

Alternatively, if the Input field is changed, unless the resulting entry has a 600 KHz value, both the + and – buttons are disabled (grayed out). Changes in the Input field do not affect the Output value.

Conversely, clicking either the + or – button changes the value in the Input field to reflect a 600 KHz offset.

These changes are reflected in the data record on exit, assuming that changes are saved.

Reading and Writing *CArchive* Records

The hat trick, so to speak, in the AARL_HAM application is found in two places.

In the Repeater.CPP file, a custom `Serialize` method handles reading and writing output records:

```
void CRepeater::Serialize(CArchive& ar)
{
   if( ar.IsStoring() )
      ar << m_csCallSign << m_csLocation << m_csNotes <<
            m_csSponsor << m_csOutput << m_csInput;
   else
      ar >> m_csCallSign >> m_csLocation >> m_csNotes >>
            m_csSponsor >> m_csOutput >> m_csInput;
}
```

The `ar.IsStoring()` method tells the `Serialize` method whether this operation is for input or output; other than this, the actual serialization is about as simple as you could ask. The only restraints here are that the fields for both input and output are listed in the same order.

Although the Repeater.CPP source is minimal, the Repeater.H source file is also worth your attention. It is the header file in which several custom operators are defined, as well as the usual member variables and two overloaded constructor methods:

```
class CRepeater : public CObject
{
   DECLARE_SERIAL(CRepeater)
```

```
public:
   CString m_csLocation;
   CString m_csCallSign;
   CString m_csNotes;
   CString m_csSponsor;
   CString m_csOutput;
   CString m_csInput;
```

The member variables in this application are all CString members, making operations convenient.

The first overloaded constructor method—called without parameters—simply makes all the CString members empty. It is very simple and straightforward:

```
CRepeater()
{
   m_csLocation.Empty();
   m_csCallSign.Empty();
   m_csNotes.Empty();
   m_csSponsor.Empty();
   m_csOutput.Empty();
   m_csInput.Empty();
}
```

The second overloaded constructor is called with string arguments corresponding to each member variable and simply assigns the values accordingly:

```
CRepeater( const char* szLocation, const char* szCallSign,
           const char* szNotes,    const char* szSponsor,
           const char* szOutput,   const char* szInput )
{
   m_csLocation = szLocation;
   m_csCallSign = szCallSign;
   m_csNotes    = szNotes;
   m_csSponsor  = szSponsor;
   m_csOutput   = szOutput;
   m_csInput    = szInput;
}
```

Overloaded Operators

Perhaps of more interest than the constructors are the overloaded =, ==, and != operators provided for the CRepeater class. The first is the set equal (=) operator:

```
const CRepeater& operator = (const CRepeater& s)
{
   m_csLocation = s.m_csLocation;
   m_csCallSign = s.m_csCallSign;
   m_csNotes    = s.m_csNotes;
   m_csSponsor  = s.m_csSponsor;
   m_csOutput   = s.m_csOutput;
   m_csInput    = s.m_csInput;
   return *this;
}
```

Notice that the overloaded set equal operation accounts for each member variable individually but also assumes that the operation is carried out with a member of the same class as the right-hand object.

Another overloaded set equal operator could be defined with a different class or element as the right-hand object and would not necessarily have to match all member variables. All members should, however, be accounted for in one fashion or another.

Next, the equality operator (==) is defined as a series of tests ANDed together to return the appropriate result:

```
BOOL operator == (const CRepeater& s) const
{
   if( ( m_csLocation == s.m_csLocation ) &&
       ( m_csCallSign == s.m_csCallSign ) &&
       ( m_csNotes == s.m_csNotes ) &&
       ( m_csSponsor == s.m_csSponsor ) &&
       ( m_csOutput == s.m_csOutput ) &&
       ( m_csInput == s.m_csInput ) )
      return TRUE;
   else
      return FALSE;
}
```

Again, additional overloaded operators can be defined with other right-hand members or elements. This test can be defined to check nonidentical objects by testing only fields common between the two.

Finally, a not-equal operator (!=) is defined that simply returns the inverse result of the equality operator:

```
BOOL operator != (const CRepeater& s) const
{
   return !( *this == s );
}
```

If multiple equality operators are defined, each version should be paralleled by an inequality operator—each with the appropriate replacement for the CRepeater class—even though the body of each operation is identical because all refer to the overloaded equality operators.

The *GetEntry* Function

The GetEntry function copies information from the CRepeater class member, which performs the actual I/O, to CAarl_hamView member variables. Notice that even though the member variables in each class are named the same and are the same types, they are not the same elements. The GetEntry function makes the information read by the CRepeater class available for display by the CAarl_hamView class:

```
void CAarl_hamView::GetEntry(POSITION position)
{
   double  fIn, fOut, fDiff;
   int     iDiff;
   if( position )
   {
      CRepeater* pRepeater = (CRepeater*) m_pList->GetAt(position);
      m_csLocation = pRepeater->m_csLocation;
```

Chapter 16 • Interfacing Data with Object Classes

```
m_csCallSign = pRepeater->m_csCallSign;
m_csNotes    = pRepeater->m_csNotes;
m_csSponsor  = pRepeater->m_csSponsor;
m_csOutput   = pRepeater->m_csOutput;
m_csInput    = pRepeater->m_csInput;
```

Once this data has been transferred to the `CAarl_hamView` class instance, a call to `UpdateData()` invokes the `DoDataExchange` method to update the dialog box.

> Note: The `DoDataExchange` method should never be called directly but invoked only by calling the `CWnd::UpdateData` method. (See "The `UpdateData` Function," later in this chapter.)

Before calling `UpdateData`, one other detail needs to be handled. The two checkboxes labeled + and – must be set to reflect the Input and Output frequencies for this record. Remember, these do not have any values or settings stored as part of the data record; these are calculated for each data record.

```
//=== check 600KHz difference between Input / Output ===
fIn  = atof( m_csInput );
fOut = atof( m_csOutput );
fDiff = (fIn-fOut)*1000;          // may show fractional error
iDiff = (int)( ( fIn*1000 ) - (fOut*1000) );
if( abs(iDiff) == 600 )  // standard offset
{
   if( fIn > fOut )
   {
      CheckDlgButton(IDC_PLUS,  1);
      CheckDlgButton(IDC_MINUS, 0);
   }
   else
   {
      CheckDlgButton(IDC_PLUS,  0);
      CheckDlgButton(IDC_MINUS, 1);
   }
}
else   // non-standard offset, set gray buttons
{
   CheckDlgButton(IDC_PLUS,  2);
   CheckDlgButton(IDC_MINUS, 2);
}
```

This is nothing terribly complicated, but it is still necessary.

> Note: Although radio buttons might seem more appropriate here, a three-state display was needed, and the radio buttons supplied by Win95 did not perform according to expectations (or documented design). Therefore, checkboxes have been used.

Finally, if the position parameter supplied when the GetEntry function was called is NULL, the OnReset method is called to handle an empty record:

```
    }
    else
        OnReset();
    UpdateData(FALSE);
}
```

After all these provisions have been taken care of, the UpdateData function is invoked.

The *UpdateData* Function

The CWnd::UpdateData function is used to invoke the DoDataExchange function to transfer information to or retrieve information from a dialog box. UpdateData is called with a single Boolean parameter indicating whether a dialog box is being initialized (FALSE) or data is being retrieved from the dialog box (TRUE).

If the operation is successful, a Boolean TRUE is returned. If data is being retrieved from a dialog box, a TRUE result also indicates that the data has been validated correctly.

Summary

This chapter examined file I/O using the CFile class and the access and share operators. It also looked at serialization using the CArchive class and the insertion and extraction operators. You also looked at how overloaded operators are defined and how serialization is customized.

You also learned about other file operations, including random access methods and the CStdioFile class, concluding with the AARL_HAM demo program, which uses many of the methods and techniques discussed.

Chapter 17, "Understanding the ODBC Connection," takes a different look at retrieving records, but instead of using CFile and CArchive, you use ODBC (Open DataBase Connectivity) to access an Access database.

CHAPTER 17

Understanding the ODBC Connection

Microsoft's Open DataBase Connectivity (ODBC) provides an alternative to serialized data access and makes it possible for applications to use database sources created by other applications such as Paradox, SQL Servers, and Microsoft Access.

To use ODBC before you design your application, however, you must install ODBC and the data source—or, instead of a data source, the network connections to your data servers.

The data sources you plan to use must be registered with the ODBC. This is accomplished by selecting the ODBC utility from the Control Panel. In response, the Data Sources dialog box shown in Figure 17.1 appears.

In this figure, one database source, created using Microsoft Access, is already registered with the ODBC.

If this is your first time setting up ODBC, you may want to begin by calling the Drivers dialog box, shown in Figure 17.2, to select an installed ODBC driver or to call the Add Drivers dialog box to install ODBC drivers.

For the AARL2 and AARL3 demo programs (included on the CD-ROM that accompanies this book), Microsoft Access has been used to define the initial database and is the preferred driver. For other applications, of course, you may select whichever driver is appropriate to the task. The application design and creation is essentially the same in all cases because the selected ODBC driver handles all the database transactions for the application.

Figure 17.1. Selecting an ODBC data source.

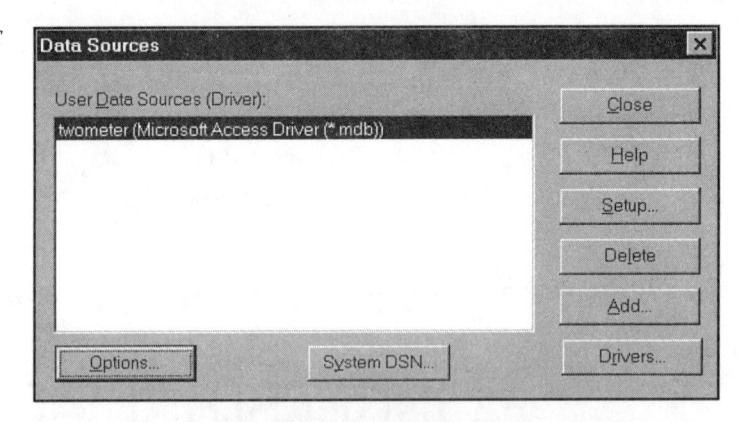

Figure 17.2. Selecting an ODBC driver.

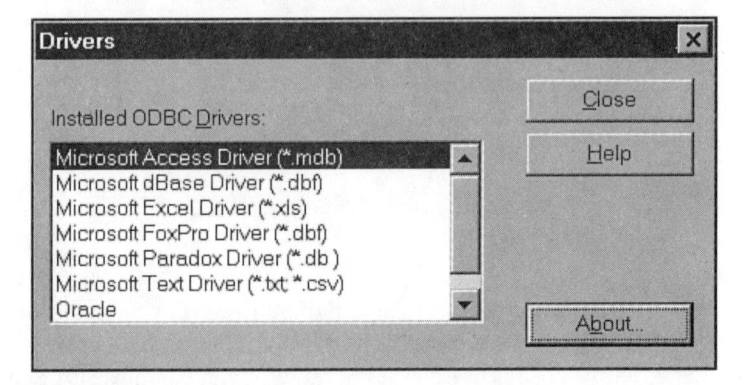

If the desired data source is not yet registered—for example, to run the AARL2 or AARL3 demo programs—use the Setup option from the Data Sources dialog box to bring up the ODBC Data Source Setup dialog box shown in Figure 17.3.

Figure 17.3. ODBC Data Source setup.

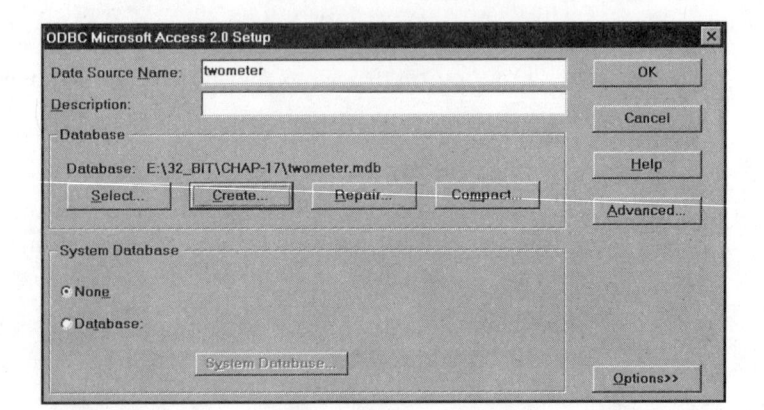

From the Data Source Setup dialog box, use the **S**elect button to bring up the Select Database dialog box shown in Figure 17.4. The Select Database dialog box may look familiar: it is another variation of the File Open dialog box. In this case, however, the default file extension for Access database files, MBD, is specified.

> Note: At the time of this writing, Microsoft has provided limited distribution of a new version of the Microsoft Access database application, identified as version 7.0. (There aren't any versions 3.0 through 6.0; the version numbers jump directly from 2.0 to 7.0.) Although Access 7.0 does have interesting features and can import databases from earlier versions of Visual C++ applications, you cannot use Visual C++ version 2.x or 4.0 to access Access version 7.0 database files. Although this should change in the near future, please be aware of this shortcoming.

Figure 17.4. The Select Database dialog box.

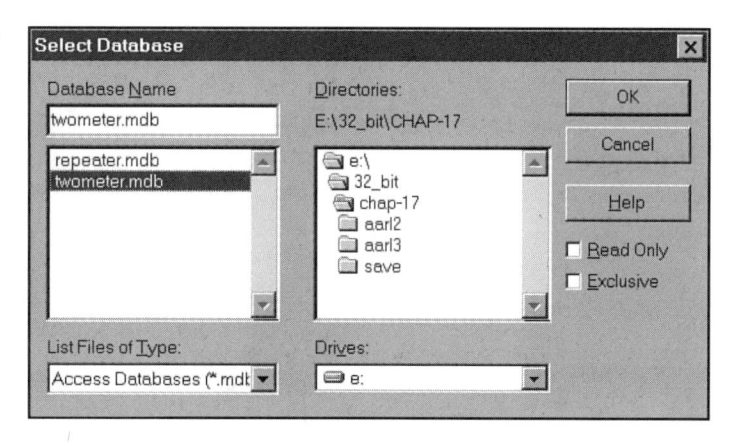

From the Select Database dialog box, select the twometer.mdb database file. In the Data Source Setup dialog box, add any description you want to include.

This concludes the ODBC setup process. For your own applications, however, you can register a variety of different databases, using as many protocols as you have drivers installed.

Creating an ODBC Application

You create an ODBC application in the same way you begin any other application: using AppWizard and selecting a single document interface. In the end, the new program will be a dialog-based application. Nonetheless, the initial setting is a single document.

When AppWizard asks whether to include database support, select the Database View with File Support option because you want to be able to write to and read from the database.

Alternatively, if you want to access information from the database but do not intend to write changes back, the option Database View without File Support is appropriate. Figure 17.5 shows AppWizard's Step 2 dialog box, from which database support is selected.

Figure 17.5. Creating an application using ODBC.

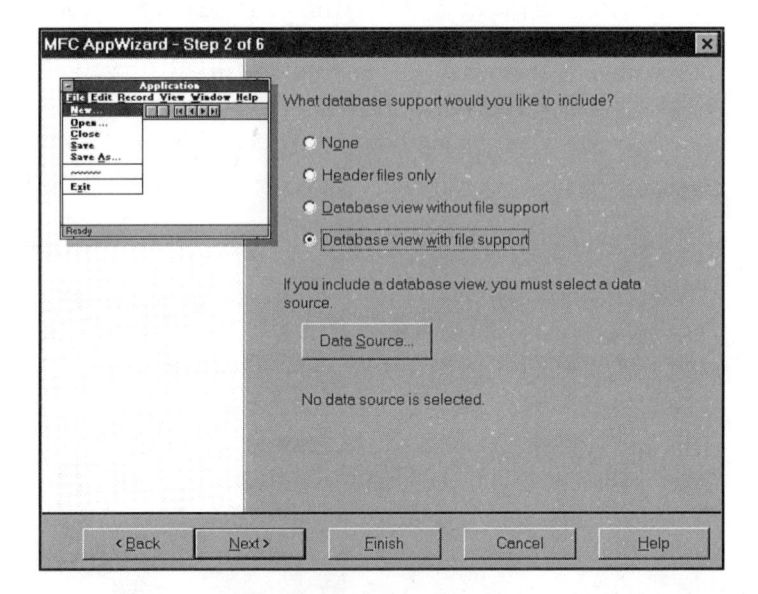

After selecting database support, but before proceeding further with AppWizard, use the Data Source button to call the Database Options dialog box (see Figure 17.6).

Figure 17.6. Selecting a data source.

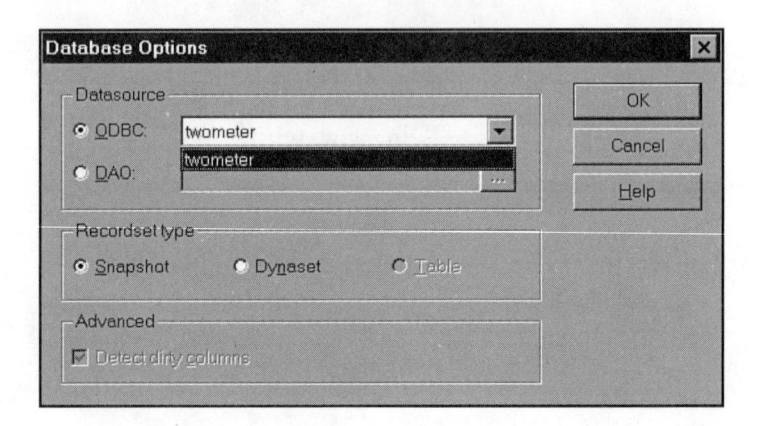

The Database Options dialog box shows the database sources registered with ODBC. Select the twometer database and click OK to proceed.

The Select Database Tables dialog box lists the tables in the twometer database (see Figure 17.7). In this example, there is only one table, Repeaters, which is the obvious selection as well as the correct choice.

Figure 17.7. The Select Database Tables dialog box.

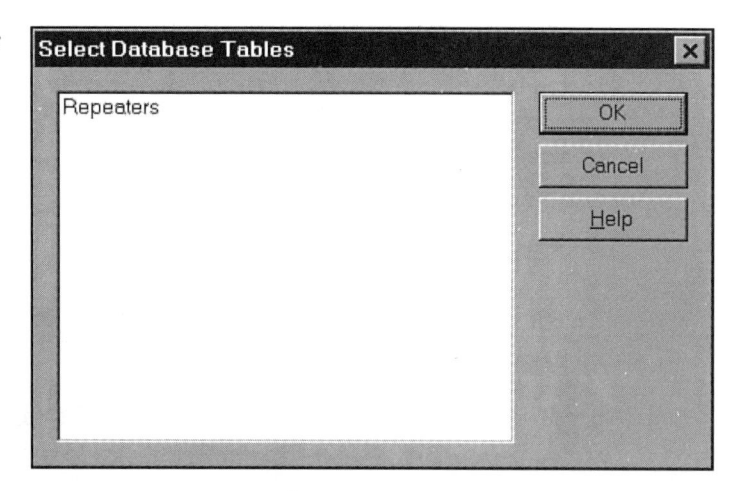

After selecting a database and database table, you can proceed with AppWizard in the usual fashion. When you are done with the AppWizard, the New Project Information dialog box, shown in Figure 17.8, lists the files and classes to be created for the application.

Notice that you are provided with a `RecordView` and a `Recordset` class; the `Recordset` class is connected to the table Repeaters in the data source twometer.

What isn't shown here, however, is that a blank dialog box, identified as IDD_AARL2_FORM, has been created in the application resource file. For this sample application, lift the dialog fields from the AARL_HAM demo and paste them into the IDD_AARL2_FORM dialog box, as shown in Figure 17.9.

Delete the Reset button because this feature isn't necessary. Then assign member variables in the `CArrl2Set` class (see Figure 17.10).

Notice that the Member Variables tab lists the column names from the database. For simplicity, the member names are the same except for the `m_` prefix.

In the `CArrl2View` class, another set of member variables requires assignment. In this case, however, even though the dialog tab shows the familiar control IDs, the assignments are not quite as simple as before (see Figure 17.11).

Figure 17.8. *The New Project Information dialog box.*

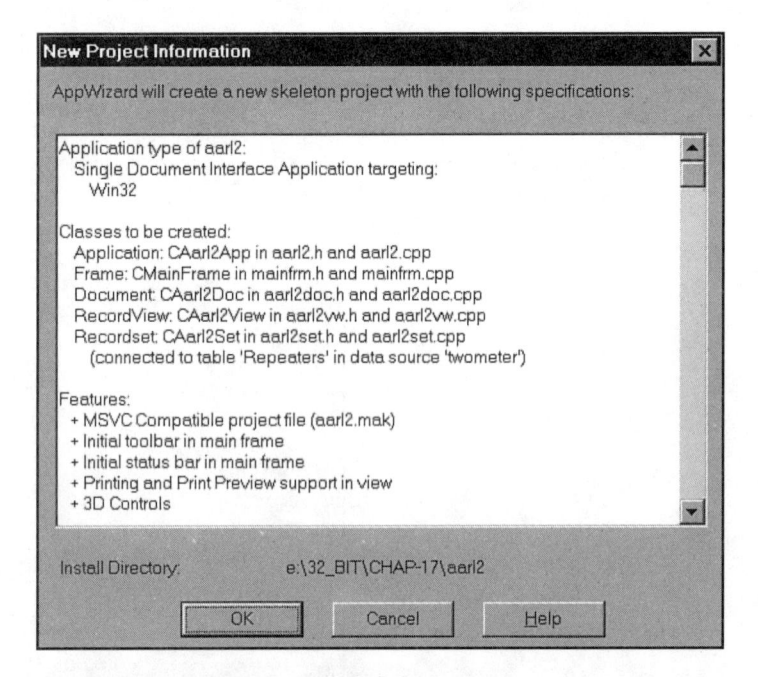

Figure 17.9. *The FORM dialog box.*

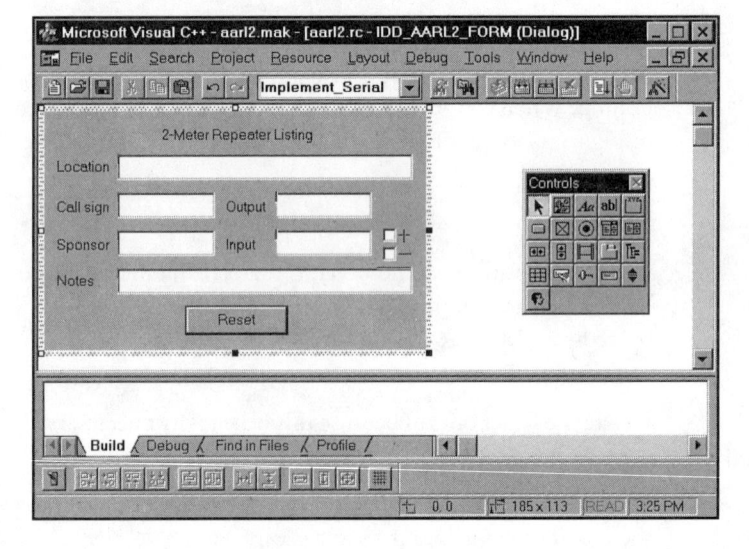

Chapter 17 • Understanding the ODBC Connection

Figure 17.10. Assigning member variables in `CArr12Set`.

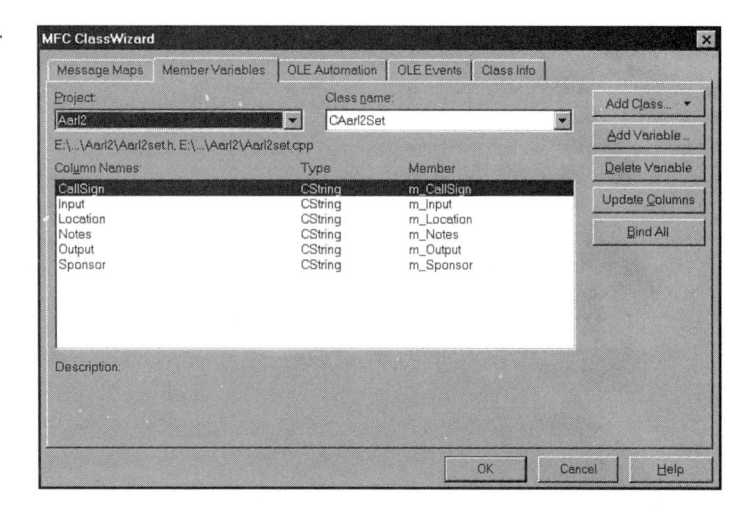

Figure 17.11. Assigning member variables in `CArr12View`.

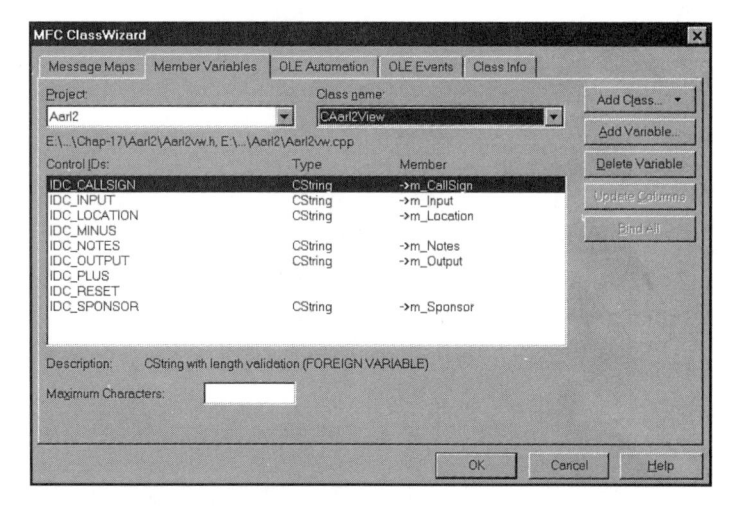

Notice that although the member names for `CArr12View` parallel the member names assigned for the `CArr12Set` class, all are identified as `->m_Nnnnnn`. What you can't see is the left side of the pointer.

When you add a member variable, however, the Add Member Variable dialog box (shown in Figure 17.12) shows the rest of the story: the full member name is entered as `m_pSet->m_Sponsor`.

Figure 17.12. Adding a member variable in `CArrl2View`.

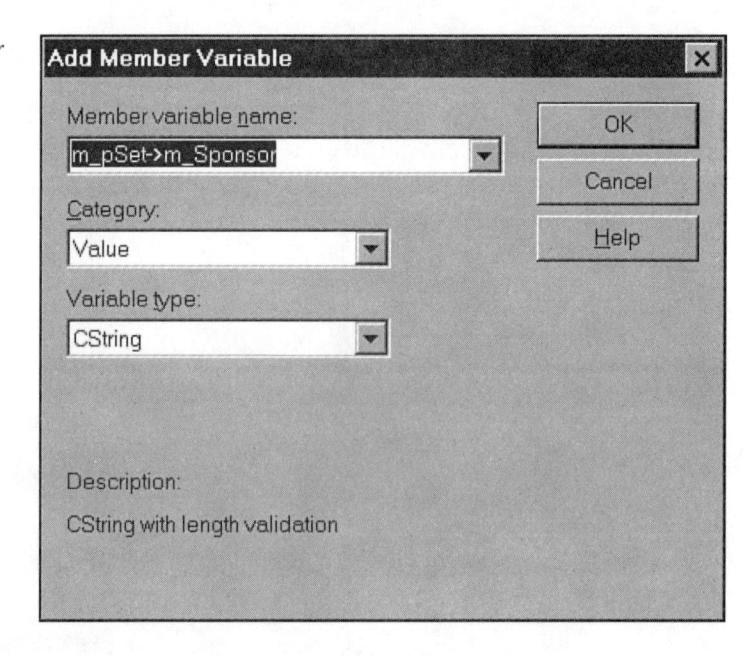

You may wonder how the `m_pSet` variable appeared. The `m_pSet` variable was defined by AppWizard in `CArrl2View` as `CAarl2Set* m_pSet`, a pointer to the `CAarl2Set` class in which the members were assigned to database table columns.

When these assignments are finished, so is the application; the ARRL2 application is ready to compile and run. The results are shown in Figure 17.13. Notice that the default toolbar supplied by AppWizard has the appropriate arrow buttons to step through the displayed database.

Figure 17.13. The ARRL2 application.

The Default Database

Before leaving the AARL2 application, you should be aware that the application has two hard-coded specifications for the database connection and the database table. These are found in the Aarl2Set.CPP source file:

```
CString CAarl2Set::GetDefaultConnect()
{
    return _T("ODBC;DSN=twometer;");
}

CString CAarl2Set::GetDefaultSQL()
{
    return _T("Repeaters");
}
```

A Quick Review

The first part of this chapter provided a tour of setting up ODBC drivers, registering a database, and creating an application to use the database. Because the tour was quick, you haven't seen that no programming was done except for the minor details of creating the dialog view and assigning member variable names.

Not one line of source code was written for the ARRL2 application. The entire source code was created by the AppWizard and by ClassWizard—and it runs.

What's wrong with this picture? Actually, if all you want is a quick viewer for a database table, nothing is wrong. You may want more than that, however. For example, you *did* specify an application with both a view and file support, but what you have in ARRL2 is only a view. Also, the + and – buttons, to the right of the Input edit box, don't work at all. You certainly can't edit any of these entries. And, if you could edit them, you couldn't save the results. Still, this is, so far, probably the easiest program you've ever written, right?

The AARL3 Demo

The AARL3 program begins as a duplicate of the AARL2 demo, exactly as it was left after assigning the m_pSet->m_Xxxx member variables in the CAarl2View class. Remember that you left the AARL2 demo in a completed, ready-to-execute form. Its only shortcoming was that AARL2 was a viewer; beyond viewing records from the database, it did not have any real functionality.

The AARL3 application adds this missing functionality by including complete support for the two + and – buttons as well as complete editing support for all fields of the database. The first step is to modify the Aarl3VW source files.

Beginning with Aarl3VW.H header, add an enum member variable m_Offset as a flag to identify the status of the plus and minus buttons. Later, in the Aarl3VW.CPP file, provisions are added to test the m_Offset flag; if m_Offset is None, both buttons are grayed; otherwise, both buttons are enabled. If m_Offset is Minus, the minus button is selected; if m_Offset is Plus, the plus button is selected.

Before getting into details, some setup is required, as shown in the following listing—beginning with the enum statement:

```
class CAarl3View : public CRecordView
{
protected: // create from serialization only
    CAarl3View();
    DECLARE_DYNCREATE(CAarl3View)

public:
    //{{AFX_DATA(CAarl3View)
    enum { IDD = IDD_AARL3_FORM };
    CAarl3Set* m_pSet;
    //}}AFX_DATA

// Attributes
public:
    enum { None, Minus, Plus } m_Offset;
    CAarl3Doc* GetDocument();
// Operations
public:
    void    UpdateButtons();
    void    CheckFrequencies();
```

Last, define two utility methods: UpdateButtons() and CheckFrequencies(). The functional portion of these two utilities is supplied in a moment.

With these provisions made, it's time to call the ClassWizard and provide message map functions for the dialog controls:

```
// Generated message map functions
protected:
    //{{AFX_MSG(CAarl3View)
    afx_msg void OnPlus();
    afx_msg void OnMinus();
    afx_msg void OnChangeCallsign();
    afx_msg void OnChangeInput();
    afx_msg void OnChangeLocation();
    afx_msg void OnChangeNotes();
    afx_msg void OnChangeOutput();
    afx_msg void OnChangeSponsor();
    //}}AFX_MSG
    DECLARE_MESSAGE_MAP()
};
```

The plus and minus button messages are triggered by a single click. The remaining edit field message map functions are all handled in response to the EN_CHANGE event messages, which indicate that a change has been made in one of the edit fields.

Because you have defined a total of 10 new member functions, it's time to go to the Aarl3VW.CPP source file and fill in some functionality.

For simplicity of explanation, let's begin with the OnChangeCallsign, OnChangeLocation, OnChangeNotes, and OnChangeSponsor methods. Although the edit box functions provide complete editing capabilities, the trick is to make sure that the edit changes are retrieved from the dialog box and are written to the database. The solution is simple, but this is an area that is only vaguely documented.

The functional solution is shown in the following code fragment for the OnChangeCallsign function; the remaining three edit functions are identical in their provisions:

```
void CAarl3View::OnChangeCallsign()
{
    m_pSet->Edit();        // set record for edit
    UpdateData(TRUE);      // get change from dialog
    m_pSet->Update();      // update record
    UpdateData(FALSE);     // update dialog
}
```

The first step is to call the CRecordset::Edit method for the m_pSet record, the active record displayed in the dialog box. The Edit function is called to enable changes to the current record. After the Edit function is called, you can change field data members by resetting their values (that is, by editing them).

The Edit function saves the value of the recordset's data members. If Edit is called, changes are made, and Edit is called again, the changes are lost and the recordset's data members are restored to their original values. Changes are also lost—the original values are restored—if the application is scrolled to a new record before the edit operation is completed by calling the CRecordset::Update function.

> **Note:** A CDBException is thrown if Edit is called for a recordset that cannot be updated or if there is no current record.

After calling the CRecordset::Edit method, the CRecordView::UpdateData function is invoked with a TRUE argument to retrieve changes from the dialog box fields. Remember that this operation invokes the DoFieldExchange function and retrieves the values from all the dialog box fields, not just the field currently being changed.

After retrieving the changes, the CRecordset::Update method is called to terminate the edit process and to write the updated changes to the database.

You conclude by calling the CRecordView::UpdateData function a second time with a FALSE argument to update the dialog box with the changed data.

The key is that you must call the Edit method to begin making changes to the record and then call the Update method to conclude and write the changes to the database. Without these two provisions, even though the dialog box is updated, these changes are not retained.

In the OnChangeInput method, the same four statements appear, but this time conclude with a call to the CheckFrequencies method, which (after the input frequency is changed), checks the frequency offset and updates the + and – buttons.

```
void CAarl3View::OnChangeInput()
{
    m_pSet->Edit();         // set record for edit
    UpdateData(TRUE);       // get change from dialog
    m_pSet->Update();       // update record
    UpdateData(FALSE);      // update dialog
    CheckFrequencies();
}
```

You can observe the same Edit(), UpdateData(TRUE), Update(), UpdateData(FALSE) sequence in the remaining OnChangeXxxxx methods. In the later methods, however, the sequence is interrupted with other provisions.

The OnChangeOutput method is a good example of this expansion but also offers an illustration of another interesting element required when working with a database.

Indirect Editing—An Idiosyncrasy

The OnChangeOutput method begins innocently enough by calling the Edit function to enable an update to the database and then calls the UpdateData function to retrieve changes from the edit boxes:

```
void CAarl3View::OnChangeOutput()
{
    int      i, iLen;
    CString  csNew;
    double   fOut;

    //=== first update the Output frequency
    m_pSet->Edit();         // set record for edit
    UpdateData(TRUE);       // get changes from dialog
```

The problem is that you also want changes in the output frequency to be reflected in the input frequency edit field, as demonstrated in the AARL_HAM application in Chapter 16, "Interfacing Data with Object Classes."

In AARL_VW.CPP, this was handled as follows:

```
m_csInput.Format( "%3.3f", fOut + 0.600 );
```

You might expect that the parallel in AARL3VW.CPP would take this form:

```
m_pSet->m_Input.Format( "%3.3f", ( fOut + 0.600 ) );
```

This is the fly in the ointment. Although this statement compiles and executes, there is a hidden operation involved (which normally doesn't matter). With ODBC operations, this hidden operation becomes a serious problem when the Update function is called. The result is an address violation in the ODBC handler.

When you call the CString::Format method, the hidden operation allocates a new buffer for the CString data and deallocates the original buffer. After this happens, the ODBC handler is subjected to terminal confusion when it finds that the original and new addresses of the CString buffer are no longer the same.

The solution, to provide indirect editing, is a bit of a work-around, thus:

```
fOut = atof( m_pSet->m_Output );
switch( m_Offset )
{
    case None:   csNew = m_pSet->m_Input;                        break;
    case Minus:  csNew.Format( "%3.3f", (fOut-0.600) );          break;
    case Plus:   csNew.Format( "%3.3f", (fOut+0.600) );          break;
}
iLen = csNew.GetLength();
for( i=0; i<iLen; i++ )
    m_pSet->m_Input.SetAt( i, csNew.GetAt(i) );
```

If the + or – buttons are selected, a separate CString object instance is used to format the new frequency string. After this is done, a simple loop is used to copy the characters from the new buffer to the old, replacing the original.

After the buffer is updated with the new information, but still at the old address, the Update and UpdateData functions are called to conclude the process:

```
m_pSet->Update();
UpdateData(FALSE);
}
```

A similar technique is used in the OnPlus and OnMinus functions, where the input field is also updated.

The process described here is a work-around, but there are also some problems inherent in this approach. The most obvious problem is when the original buffer is smaller than the updated information to be added to it. Of course, if the original buffer is larger than the replacement data, the buffer can always be padded with NULLs. If the original buffer is too small, consider using the CString.GetBufferSetLength method to resize the buffer.

How these operations interact with the CRecordset.Edit and Update functions is an open question. I suggest some experimentation before relying on these operations.

Alternatively, you can insert a new record, with whatever information was required, and delete the original. This may be the simplest solution of all.

> Note: Refer to the CRecordset class in your online documentation for further capabilities of this object type. Although the preceding AARL3 application demonstrates the basics required for an ODBC-interactive application, the CRecordset class offers a variety of methods that allow you to customize and extend operations.

Summary

For most circumstances, ODBC offers an excellent avenue for applications to access databases, particularly databases that have been created by other applications or that are shared with other applications. Furthermore, because ODBC provides drivers for different database systems, your custom operations are nearly independent of the type of database that supplies information.

As you have seen, creating an ODBC-dependent application is extremely easy and can be accomplished with a minimum of bother. Because custom serialization methods are not required, the ODBC version of the repeater database application is simpler to create than the earlier version demonstrated in Chapter 16, "Interfacing Data with Object Classes."

Just as the Win95 interface has started the move from application-centric to document-centric operations, the ODBC services move database files away from application dependence. Continuing in this venue, Chapter 18, "Using Simple OLE Operations," examines how object linking and embedding further enables applications to use services and data from other applications.

CHAPTER 18

Using Simple OLE Operations

Object Linking and Embedding (OLE) is the newest item in a long history of attempts to make separate applications work together by sharing data and services. OLE is not, however, a simple topic and is not covered here in depth. Instead, this chapter offers an introduction to OLE and gives examples of simple OLE container and server applications.

For further information on OLE and for advanced and custom OLE container or server applications, a variety of books are available—devoted entirely to the subject of OLE programming. These books go far beyond the coverage possible in this chapter. If you are really interested in customizing OLE operations, start with *Teach Yourself OLE Programming in 21 Days*, by Lawrence Harris (published by Sams Publishing).

Integrating Applications

Even before Windows, a variety of Terminate and Stay Resident (TSR) utilities were available to copy and paste text between separate applications. Later, Windows (as a multitasking environment) offered the Clipboard to perform similar services.

Clipboard Services

The Clipboard should not be confused with the Clipbrd.EXE or ClipBook.EXE viewer utilities. The Clipboard is a service that allows one application to write an object (which may be text, raw data, a graphic, or some other record format) to memory before transferring ownership of the object (that is, the memory block) to the Clipboard. Subsequently, another application (or the same application) can retrieve a copy of the stored memory block for its own use.

However, like the earlier TSRs, the Clipboard is static. There was a real demand for *dynamic* information exchange. This demand led to the development of the Dynamic Data Exchange (DDE) protocols.

Dynamic Data Exchange

The Dynamic Data Exchange protocols allowed compatible applications to transfer not only data but instructions and requests for data. Using the DDE, applications could define their own formats for data exchange when the standard formats were not acceptable; they could also pass messages requesting specific data or notifying a client application that data previously supplied had changed or updated.

Despite its potentials, DDE messaging has been a major headache for developers. Applications had to be able to recognize (that is, agree on) message protocol and transfer formats. And there were no easy standards that allowed independent applications to communicate.

More recently, the original DDE APIs have been improved and integrated into the DDE Management Library (DDEML.DLL), relieving programmers of many of the original headaches.

Metafiles

Because Windows is a graphics environment, there was also a need for a method of scripting graphics operations for later playback by other applications (*shared graphics*, if you will). This need was filled by the graphics *metafile*. Metafiles are nominally memory objects and can be stored as disk files. More commonly, however, they are replayed by the originating application or, through the Clipboard, are shared with other applications.

Today, metafiles are still in use. But with the development of OLE, they have become less important.

Object Linking and Embedding

The newest medium for dynamic information exchange is the OLE2 protocols that operate through a system of OLE containers and servers. OLE allows one application to call another, independent application to provide services. The requested services may consist simply of providing data or may include processing and displaying the results of data operations. With OLE, a spreadsheet can call a graphics package to paint an image and can call a word processor to format text to accompany pie charts; a word processor can call a spreadsheet to include a graph or financial report.

> Note: The first part of this chapter oversimplified the discussion of the progress from the original TSR and Clipboard transfers to the contemporary OLE operations by inferring that each step in the process supplanted and replaced its predecessors. The truth is that OLE continues to use both DDE and Clipboard services but also extends these in forms that the earlier services did not provide or support.

Figure 18.1 shows a Microsoft Word document with an embedded Quattro Pro spreadsheet opened for editing. Notice that the menus and toolbars belong to Quattro Pro, not to Microsoft Word.

Figure 18.1. An embedded spreadsheet opened for editing.

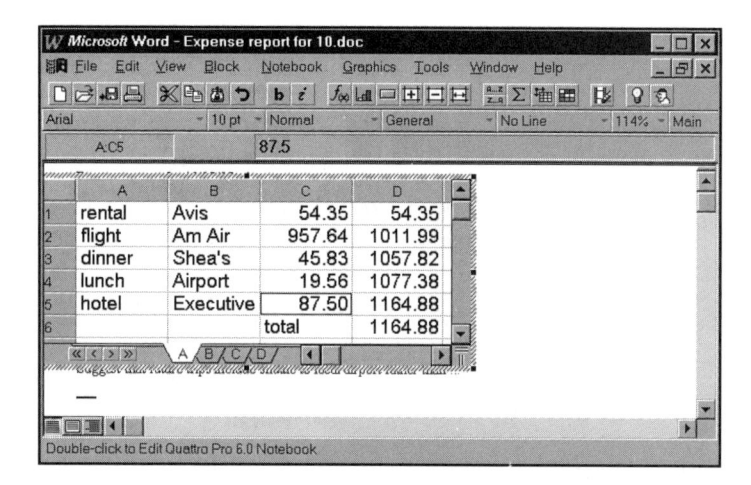

Figure 18.2 shows the same document with the same embedded spreadsheet except that the object is not opened for editing. The cursor is in the paragraph following the spreadsheet and the menu and toolbars shown now belong to Microsoft Word.

Figure 18.2. An embedded spreadsheet after editing.

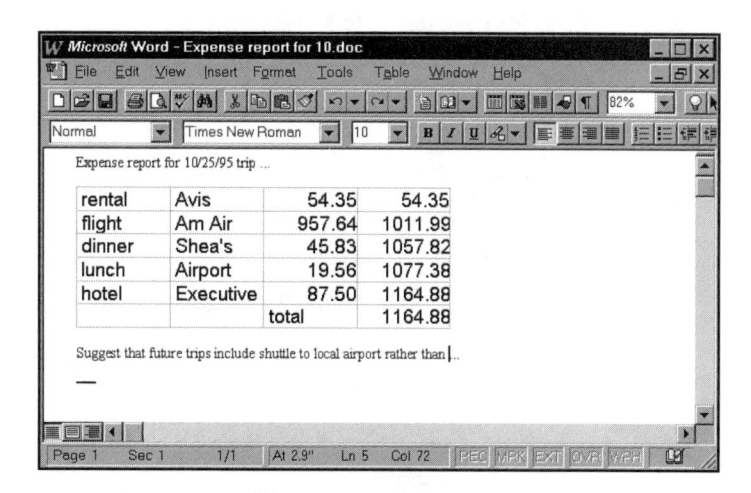

Even when it is not open for editing, the embedded object is still subject to some of Word's operations and is immune to others. For example, the object can be selected as a paragraph and centered or given additional leading points because the positioning and size of the object are under Word's control.

On the other hand, you cannot change fonts or change to bold or italic because the internal appearance of the spreadsheet is under Quattro Pro's control. Of course, you can reopen the object and use Quattro Pro to change the fonts, edit the numbers, or change any other internal formatting.

Compound Documents

In today's applications, the term *document* has come to mean much more than simply a paper containing words and images. In computer terminology, the term *document* includes everything from a worksheet produced by a spreadsheet or database, a CAD image file, a voice or video clip, and even the conventional word processor file.

Following this expanded definition, a *compound document* is simply a document that incorporates data objects from two or more sources. The compound document is created by embedding data objects produced by other applications or by linking data objects from other applications. For example, a compound document produced by a word processor may include a project drawing from a CAD program, a block of cells from a spreadsheet calculating costs, and a timeline from a task planner showing a production schedule. In this fashion, changes in scheduling can be reflected in the cost calculations—and so can changes in the project design.

By using OLE, users do not have to be concerned with compatible data formats or with locating or initiating separate applications to support the various embedded objects. Instead, when the document is created, the embedded or linked objects are simply selected from a list—through the registry—of OLE server applications. (See "OLE Server Registration and Selection," later in this chapter.)

Of course, once an application is embedded or linked in a compound document, the supporting applications are called automatically (when requested) to handle changes or updates to the document.

Linked versus Embedded Objects

Even when limited to the programming realm, the term *object* has many meanings that are not always consistent. In OLE, an object is any data that can be included by embedding or linking in a compound document and subsequently manipulated by the user.

When an object is *linked* to a document, the document provides only minimal storage for the object's data (the link to the server application). The displayed object is updated automatically whenever the data in the linked server changes.

This means that the linked data is stored outside the compound document in its own document, which belongs to the server application. The compound document (the OLE container) contains only a link to the server and server data. If the linked object is spreadsheet calculations based on information from a database, and the database information changes, the displayed calculations provided by the spreadsheet also change immediately.

Conversely, for an *embedded* object, both the data and operation instructions associated with the object are stored as a part of the compound document. The object is updated by calling the server application when and only when the object in the document is selected. To use the previous example, even though changes occur in the database, the spreadsheet display in the document does not change or be recalculated until the embedded object is selected.

In summary, it is more advantageous to link dynamic objects so that they are updated and corrected automatically. Static objects such as bitmaps that do not require frequent changes can be embedded. In this fashion, linked objects are updated as changes occur and embedded objects save overhead but can still be edited when required.

Packages

A *package* is an OLE object that encapsulates another object, a file, or even a command-line instruction represented as a graphic icon (or bitmap). An example of an OLE package is a sound clip that is embedded (not linked) in a compound document and represented as an icon of a microphone (under Windows 95, the icon is a speaker). When you double-click the embedded object to select it, the embedded object is activated—together with its associated application, of course.

In the example of a sound clip, double-clicking the microphone (or speaker) icon activates the WAV sound file for playback through the Windows and SoundBlaster application utilities.

Packages themselves can be documents containing other packages, giving OLE a functionality similar to hyperlinks to allow documents to be connected (included within other documents) for interactive selection.

Figure 18.3 shows the same Word document shown in Figures 18.1 and 18.2—except that now the Quattro Pro spreadsheet, which is embedded in the Word document, has its own embedded object: the speaker icon to the left of the *total* entry. The embedded spreadsheet has become a package encapsulating a sound (AVI) file.

Figure 18.3. An OLE package.

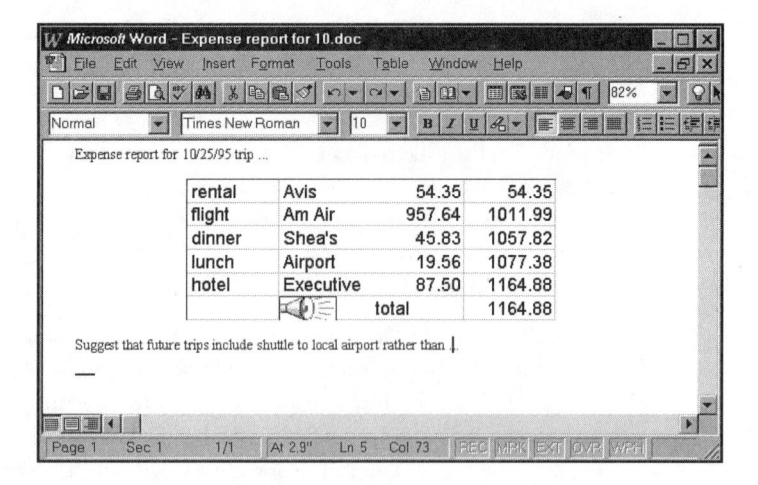

OLE Verbs

Although some OLE objects support only one action, others support more than one. In both cases, the server application responds to an OLE *verb* that tells the object what is to be done.

For example, when it is an OLE object, the Microsoft Paint (Paintbrush Picture) utility responds automatically to the verb Edit, which is generated when you select the Paint utility. The Edit verb allows you to edit the embedded image.

> Note: MSPaint also offers a second verb, Open, which calls Paint as a stand-alone application so that you can edit the embedded bitmap image. The Open verb is common to all OLE applications supporting embedded objects (which, effectively, includes all OLE applications).

A second example uses the Sound Recorder as an OLE object in a Microsoft Word document. When you select the sound recorder icon and then open Word's **E**dit menu, you see an entry for the Wave Sound **O**bject at the end of the menu (see Figure 18.4). Select the Wave Sound **O**bject entry to bring up a submenu that lists two action verbs: **P**lay and **E**dit.

> Note: The third submenu item in Figure 18.4, Con**v**ert, is not an action verb but is used to convert an OLE item to another form or file format. In this case, the embedded Sound Recorder is a package item and there is no conversion appropriate (possible conversions are listed in the Convert dialog box if any exist). For a better example of conversion, you can convert an embedded image to an internal graphic image to minimize file size.

Figure 18.4. The **E**dit, Wave Sound **O**bject menu.

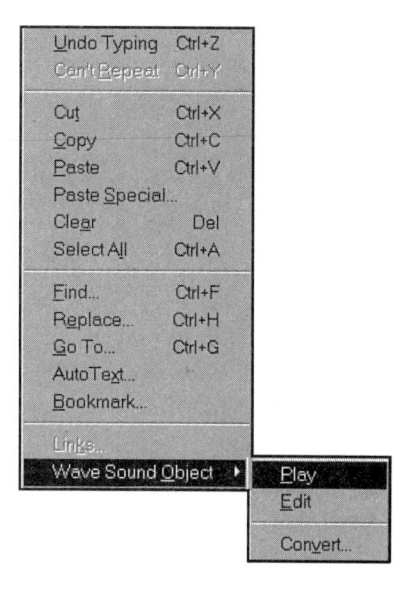

The verb **P**lay—which is also the default verb activated when you double-click the sound recorder icon—causes the embedded WAV file to be played. The verb **E**dit calls up the Sound Recorder to allow the sound file to be reviewed, edited, or re-recorded.

Normally, the primary and secondary verbs are defined by the application. For packaged objects, however, the primary verb is set by the application and the secondary verb is always Edit Package (which calls the Packager.EXE utility). From the packager, any additional secondary object verbs are available.

Verbs, Objects, and the Packager

The primary verb for an OLE object is the action taken by the embedded object when it is double-clicked in a document. In most cases, the action verb is Edit; in some cases, however (such as in the Sound Recorder), the primary action is to play the sound file and the Edit verb is available as a secondary verb.

An OLE object can have only one primary verb. It may, however, have multiple secondary verbs activated through a submenu (this submenu is usually reached through the **E**dit, **O**bject menu entries from the OLE client).

The object packager (Packager.EXE) is a dual-purpose utility. It provides package support for OLE applications as well as a standalone tool you can use to create packages from non-OLE applications and insert them into a document. OLE packages can be inserted only into applications that support OLE drag-and-drop functions.

OLE Containers versus OLE Servers

OLE applications come in two basic types: *containers* (or clients) and *servers*. Servers come in two types: *full servers* and *mini-servers*. Although containers and servers are not mutually exclusive (a container application can also be a server and vice versa), many applications incorporate only one aspect without attempting to incorporate both.

Some applications such as Microsoft Word or Quattro Pro are both containers and servers. They accept OLE objects from other servers and can act as OLE servers to other client applications.

On the other hand, both Windows Write and Cardfile are only OLE client (container) applications. Windows Write accepts three OLE types: graphics (images), sound files, and text. Cardfile accepts the same three OLE types as well as spreadsheet objects.

Windows MSPaint, on the other hand, is an OLE server. It supplies images to container applications. Because MSPaint is a standalone application as well as an OLE server, MSPaint is a *full server*. In contrast, a *mini-server* application cannot operate as a standalone application and cannot open or save files; but mini-servers do provide services to OLE client applications.

Servers of either type (full server or mini-server) can offer more than one type of service. For example, Quattro Pro provides the choice of Quattro Pro Graph or Quattro Pro Notebook (which was the choice in Figures 18.1 through 18.3). In like fashion, Microsoft Word offers a choice of Microsoft Word Document or Microsoft Word Picture objects.

Creating an OLE Container

Creating an OLE container with the help of AppWizard is easier than you expect. The Ole_Cntr demo application, which can be found on the CD-ROM that accompanies this book, provides an example of a simple OLE container constructed using AppWizard.

Using MFC's AppWizard, build the skeleton for your application—with one addition: In AppWizard's Step 3, you find options to include OLE compound document support; the default option, N**o**ne, is checked by default. For a simple OLE container, select the **C**ontainer option from the list and then continue (see Figure 18.5).

When you finish, MFC creates a multidocument interface with the usual object classes and with one new object class: the container item, `COle_cntrCntrItem` (see Figure 18.6).

Surprise! You now have an OLE container application ready to compile and execute. More important, the OLE container application is fully functional and adequate for most purposes.

At this point, of course, the application doesn't do anything except accept OLE support because no other functionality has yet been written. Given the scope of OLE operations, this in itself is a big start—a ***really*** big start!

Chapter 18 • Using Simple OLE Operations

Figure 18.5. Creating an OLE container application: AppWizard—Step 3.

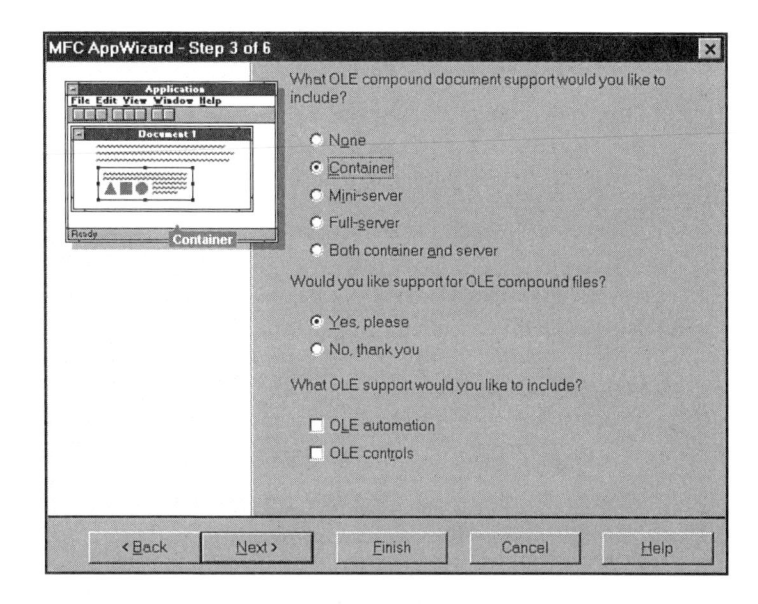

Figure 18.6. The OLE container application.

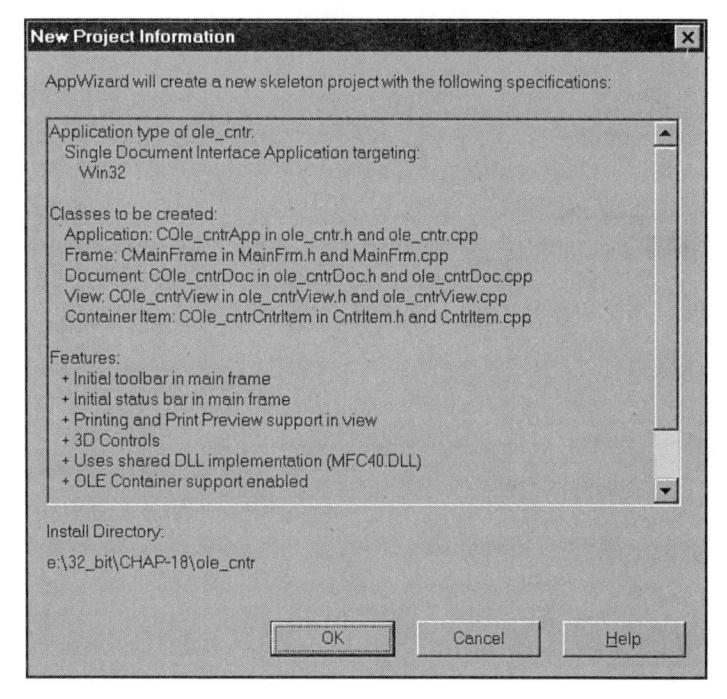

The heart of OLE operations is found in the deceptively simple `COle_cntrCntrItem` class, which is derived from the MFC `COleClientItem` class and partially from the `COle_cntrView` class (derived from `CView`).

The *COle_cntrView* Class

When you instruct AppWizard to provide OLE container support, the wizard provides the COle_cntrView class with seven OLE client support functions. Although these functions are fully implemented as provided, they are presented and discussed briefly here.

The default OnDraw function provides two areas of functionality. First, as in other programs, OnDraw is where the application's drawing operations are implemented. In the current example, no application-specific drawing operations have been defined or implemented, but OnDraw remains the appropriate method for implementing the drawing functionality.

Second, OnDraw is where all OLE objects in the document must be drawn—even though the drawing operations are actually carried out by the server applications.

In the following default implementation, each object is drawn at an arbitrary position and size. This function should be redesigned to provide individual positioning and sizing for each item. Still, for demonstration purposes, the following implementation is satisfactory as provided, even if it is also limited.

```
void COle_cntrView::OnDraw(CDC* pDC)
{
    COle_cntrDoc* pDoc = GetDocument();
    ASSERT_VALID(pDoc);
    // TODO: add draw code for native data here

    // TODO: also draw all OLE items in the document
    // TODO: remove this code when final draw code is complete.
    if (m_pSelection == NULL)
    {
        POSITION pos = pDoc->GetStartPosition();
        m_pSelection = (COle_cntrCntrItem*)pDoc->GetNextClientItem(pos);
    }
    if (m_pSelection != NULL)
        m_pSelection->Draw(pDC, CRect(10, 10, 210, 210));
}
```

The OnInitialUpdate function needs little if any explanation. It simply initializes the m_pSelection member (a pointer to a COle_cntrCntrItem object) to NULL:

```
void COle_cntrView::OnInitialUpdate()
{
    CView::OnInitialUpdate();

    // TODO: remove this code when final selection model code is written
    m_pSelection = NULL;    // initialize selection
}
```

As provided, the IsSelected method implementation is adequate to handle COle_cntrCntrItem objects (objects created by MFC-based servers). You should revise the implementation provided if you need other selection mechanisms for variant server classes.

```
BOOL COle_cntrView::IsSelected(const CObject* pDocItem) const
{
   // TODO: implement this function that tests for a selected OLE client item
   return pDocItem == m_pSelection;
}
```

The OnInsertObject method has two purposes: invoking the standard Insert Object dialog box to select an OLE object (see "Server Registration and Selection," later in this chapter) and then, assuming that an OLE object has been selected, connecting the item to the application document.

```
void COle_cntrView::OnInsertObject()
{
   COleInsertDialog dlg;
   if (dlg.DoModal() != IDOK)
      return;
   BeginWaitCursor();
   COle_cntrCntrItem* pItem = NULL;
   TRY
   {
      COle_cntrDoc* pDoc = GetDocument();
      ASSERT_VALID(pDoc);
      pItem = new COle_cntrCntrItem(pDoc);
      ASSERT_VALID(pItem);
      if (!dlg.CreateItem(pItem))
         AfxThrowMemoryException();  // any exception will do
      ASSERT_VALID(pItem);
```

The first task handled in the OnInsertObject method is to initialize (create) the selected OLE item from the data supplied by the dialog box.

After initialization (assuming that the item was created from the OLE class list rather than from a file), the next task is to invoke the OLE server for the item:

```
      if (dlg.GetSelectionType() == COleInsertDialog::createNewItem)
         pItem->DoVerb(OLEIVERB_SHOW, this);
      ASSERT_VALID(pItem);
      // TODO: reimplement selection as appropriate for your application
      m_pSelection = pItem;   // set selection to last inserted item
      pDoc->UpdateAllViews(NULL);
```

In the preceding code, the selection is arbitrarily set to the last item inserted. Your implementation could revise this section of code if you want a different selection mechanism.

Last, the CATCH handling provides standard error trapping for error exceptions:

```
   }
   CATCH(CException, e)
   {
      if (pItem != NULL)
      {
         ASSERT_VALID(pItem);
         pItem->Delete();
      }
      AfxMessageBox(IDP_FAILED_TO_CREATE);
   }
   END_CATCH
   EndWaitCursor();
}
```

The `OnCancelEditCntr` method provides a standard keyboard interface that allows the user to cancel an in-place editing session. For this purpose, the OLE container application—not the server—handles the deactivation.

```
void COle_cntrView::OnCancelEditCntr()
{
   // Close any in-place active item on this view.
   COleClientItem* pActiveItem = GetDocument()->GetInPlaceActiveItem(this);
   if (pActiveItem != NULL)
   {
      pActiveItem->Close();
   }
   ASSERT(GetDocument()->GetInPlaceActiveItem(this) == NULL);
}
```

Finally, the `OnSetFocus` and `OnSize` methods make special provisions for OLE containers and allow an object to be edited in place:

```
void COle_cntrView::OnSetFocus(CWnd* pOldWnd)
{
   COleClientItem* pActiveItem = GetDocument()->GetInPlaceActiveItem(this);
   if (pActiveItem != NULL &&
      pActiveItem->GetItemState() == COleClientItem::activeUIState)
   {
      // need to set focus to this item if it is in the same view
      CWnd* pWnd = pActiveItem->GetInPlaceWindow();
      if (pWnd != NULL)
      {
         pWnd->SetFocus();   // don't call the base class
         return;
      }
   }
   CView::OnSetFocus(pOldWnd);
}

void COle_cntrView::OnSize(UINT nType, int cx, int cy)
{
   CView::OnSize(nType, cx, cy);
   COleClientItem* pActiveItem = GetDocument()->GetInPlaceActiveItem(this);
   if (pActiveItem != NULL)
      pActiveItem->SetItemRects();
}
```

The *COle_cntrCntrItem (COleClientItem)* Class

The `COle_cntrCntrItem` class is derived from the `COleClientItem` class and provides the application's client side with a connection to an embedded or linked OLE item. However, although the functionality provided by the AppWizard in the `COle_cntrCntrItem` class is minimal, the real functionality is found in the parent `COleClientItem` class, which provides methods for handling OLE objects.

Rather than detailing the more than 70 OLE-handling methods here, this section provides a general overview of the methods. If you need more detail, refer to the online documentation.

The `COleClientItem` creation methods include functions to create both embedded and linked items from the Clipboard, from data objects, or from files; it can also create new OLE items by launching a selected OLE server.

In part, status methods provide functions to retrieve various OLE item aspects, including the item's class ID, the view aspect, and the OLE type and descriptive string. The `ActivateAs` and `ConvertTo` methods allow items to be activated as or converted to another OLE type.

A series of Clipboard operations are provided to retrieve OLE items from the Clipboard, to place items on the Clipboard, and to support drag-and-drop operations.

Additional methods allow OLE items to be drawn, closed, released, or executed. OLE object activation is provided by a series of functions that handle the different aspects of activation. One item of particular interest in this group is the `SetItemRects` method, which allows you to resize an OLE item. If you're going to provide your own implementation of resizing, look at the `SetExtent` method for embedded OLE items.

I have hit only a few of the highlights; there are still more than 20 overridable functions for various other aspects of OLE container operations. Which brings us to the real point of all this: aren't you glad that you, as a developer, don't have to write all these yourself?

Although you may find it worthwhile to modify or extend some of these methods, the basic functionality has been provided for you. For most purposes, that functionality should be adequate.

OLE Server Registration and Selection

Before an OLE container application can request an object from a server, the client application has to know which servers are available and what object types are supported. However, it is hardly practical for the client application to search the hard drive and query every file (or even every EXE and DLL) on the system to discover which offer server functions and what object types each provide. On the other hand, without this information, OLE simply isn't practical.

To circumvent this quandary, Windows supplies a system registration database that contains, among other elements, a thorough list of server applications and key information on each. To access this information directly, use the RegEdit utility, located in your \WINDOWS\SYSTEM directory.

The RegEdit Utility

Neither WinNT nor Win95 install the RegEdit utility in a program group or program menu for ready access. This is not an oversight; the RegEdit utility is not intended for casual use nor is it intended for the average user. The RegEdit utility provides access to a variety of data settings which, if changed unwisely or unknowingly, can too easily disrupt system operations irrevocably.

For most purposes, there is no need to access the registry directly. Instead, many mechanisms for indirect access are available, such as the `COleInsertDialog` discussed in the following section, which provide safe—if restricted—access to registry information.

Still, you may have occasion to directly access the registry, if only for information. Figure 18.7 shows the Registry Editor (the RegEdit utility) after the Edit, Find function was called to locate the Ole_Srvr application registry.

Figure 18.7. *The Registry Editor.*

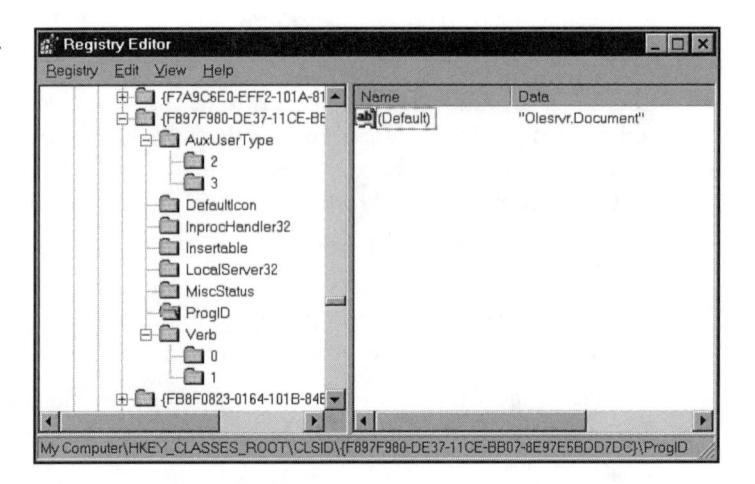

Because there are hundreds of entries in the registry and because the desired application was found under the HKEY_CLASSES_ROOT\CLSID\ branch where it is identified by a unique (generated) class ID (CLSID) entry (F897F980-DE37-11CE-BBC7-8E975BDD7DC), simply looking for this entry by scrolling through the list would have been rather futile.

> Note: This particular application also appears in the registry under the branch HKEY_CLASSES_ROOT\Olesrvr.Document as Ole_sr Document with the same CLSID. This duplication is not unusual because many items need to be locatable several ways.

Instead, when you need to locate an item in the registry, the easiest—and only practical—method is to use the Find function to locate a string identifier or some other known value.

Once you locate the desired item, you can see quite a bit of information. Although Figure 18.7 shows the ProgID (Olesrvr Document), other branches under this entry show where the OLE registry application is located, where the application icon is found, what action verbs the server responds to, whether insertable objects are supported, and so on.

> Note: The registry contains much more than server registration. You can use it to find information on most applications installed on the system, user configuration information, system configuration information, and other data.

> Caution: Before you use RegEdit to change anything, make sure that you know what you're changing—and how to recover from mistakes. It's also a good idea to first make a copy of the registry files to reuse in case you make a severe mistake.

In many ways, the RegEdit utility is a very awkward utility. Awkward or not, it does provide access to key information about your system and applications. Alternatively, you can experiment with the OLE2View utility, described later in this chapter.

Selecting a Server: *COleInsertDialog*

Normally, when you want to locate a server application to insert an object into a document, you call an instance of the COleInsertDialog to display the Insert Object dialog box shown in Figure 18.8 (refer to the code showcasing the OnInsertObject function in "The COle_cntrView Class," earlier in this chapter).

Figure 18.8. The Insert Object dialog box.

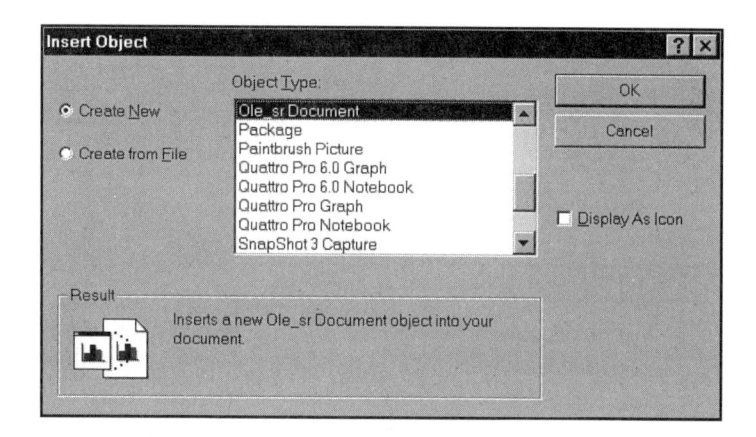

By default, the Insert Object dialog box names all registered object types in a list box; the Result box shows a brief explanation of the selected item.

The **D**isplay As Icon checkbox at the right offers the option of inserting an OLE item as an icon instead of as an active item. The advantage is that an iconized item does not have to be drawn and remains inactive until it is double-clicked.

The Create from **F**ile radio button is used to select a file of any type to insert as an OLE object (see Figure 18.9). The **B**rowse button calls the standard file-selection dialog box. In Figure 18.9, the ReadMe.Txt file from the Ole_Cntr project has been selected. Click the OK button to insert the file in the application. Note that when you insert a file as an OLE object, the object is always an icon, regardless of whether or not you select the **D**isplay As Icon checkbox.

Figure 18.9. Inserting a file object.

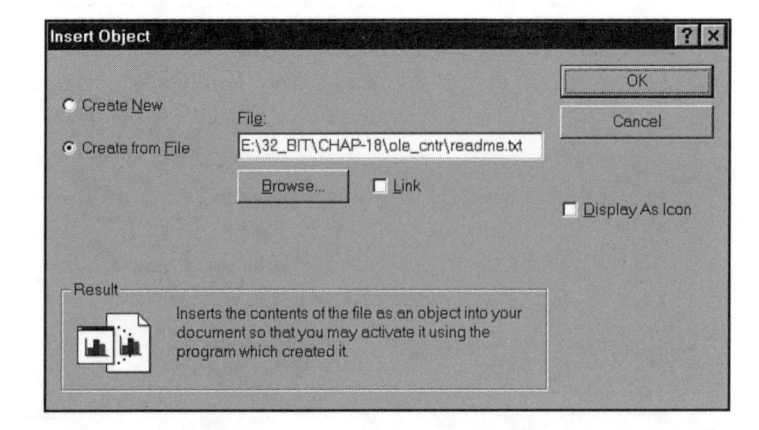

When a file is inserted as an OLE object, you also have the option of selecting the **L**ink checkbox. When you link the OLE file object, any changes to the file through external sources are immediately reflected in the linked object.

> Note: AppWizard does not provide full in-place editing for files. To fully support embedded or linked files, you can either modify your container application or use the **E**dit, **P**ackager option to call the appropriate supporting utility.

Registering an OLE Server

The preceding sections talked about the system registry and how to select a registered server; the following section describes how to create an OLE server. But before moving on to creating a server, this section takes a quick look at how server applications register themselves—and, of course, how they don't.

Full server applications register themselves virtually automatically. A full server application is executed as a standalone process by invoking the `COleServerRegister` member. If your server application was created using MFC and the AppWizard, this function is already installed in the `InitInstance` procedure as a call to the `COleTemplateServer::RegisterAll()` function (which is described later in this chapter).

For mini-server applications that do not run standalone, a different approach is required. When you use AppWizard to create your server application (whether it is a mini-server or a full server), AppWizard also creates a REG script, like the following one:

```
REGEDIT
; This .REG file may be used by your SETUP program.
;    If a SETUP program is not available, the entries below will be
;    registered in your InitInstance automatically with a call to
;    CWinApp::RegisterShellFileTypes and COleObjectFactory::UpdateRegistryAll.
HKEY_CLASSES_ROOT\Olesrvr.Document = Ole_sr Document
HKEY_CLASSES_ROOT\Olesrvr.Document\protocol\StdFileEditing\server = OLE_SRVR.EXE
HKEY_CLASSES_ROOT\Olesrvr.Document\protocol\StdFileEditing\verb\0 = &Edit
HKEY_CLASSES_ROOT\Olesrvr.Document\Insertable =
HKEY_CLASSES_ROOT\Olesrvr.Document\CLSID = {F897F980-DE37-11CE-BB07-8E97E5BDD7DC}
HKEY_CLASSES_ROOT\CLSID\{F897F980-DE37-11CE-BB07-8E97E5BDD7DC} = Ole_sr Document
HKEY_CLASSES_ROOT\CLSID\{F897F980-DE37-11CE-BB07-8E97E5BDD7DC}\DefaultIcon =
➥OLE_SRVR.EXE,1
HKEY_CLASSES_ROOT\CLSID\{F897F980-DE37-11CE-BB07-8E97E5BDD7DC}\LocalServer32 =
➥OLE_SRVR.EXE
HKEY_CLASSES_ROOT\CLSID\{F897F980-DE37-11CE-BB07-8E97E5BDD7DC}\ProgId =
➥Olesrvr.Document
HKEY_CLASSES_ROOT\CLSID\{F897F980-DE37-11CE-BB07-8E97E5BDD7DC}\MiscStatus = 32
HKEY_CLASSES_ROOT\CLSID\{F897F980-DE37-11CE-BB07-8E97E5BDD7DC}\AuxUserType\3 =
➥ole_srvr
HKEY_CLASSES_ROOT\CLSID\{F897F980-DE37-11CE-BB07-8E97E5BDD7DC}\AuxUserType\2 = Ole_sr
HKEY_CLASSES_ROOT\CLSID\{F897F980-DE37-11CE-BB07-8E97E5BDD7DC}\Insertable =
HKEY_CLASSES_ROOT\CLSID\{F897F980-DE37-11CE-BB07-8E97E5BDD7DC}\verb\1 = &Open,0,2
HKEY_CLASSES_ROOT\CLSID\{F897F980-DE37-11CE-BB07-8E97E5BDD7DC}\verb\0 = &Edit,0,2
HKEY_CLASSES_ROOT\CLSID\{F897F980-DE37-11CE-BB07-8E97E5BDD7DC}\InprocHandler32 =
➥ole32.dll
```

Normally, you want the REG script to be executed by your application's installation program. However, during development, you can also use the RegEdit utility to execute this script directly.

From the menu of the RegEdit utility, select **R**egistry, **I**mport Registry File to call the file selection dialog box. From the Import Registry File dialog box, select the application's REG script and click the Open button. After a few seconds, RegEdit advises you that the registry information has been entered in the system. That's all that's required.

Creating an OLE Server

When you use the Microsoft Foundation Classes and the AppWizard, you have only two choices for creating an OLE server application: a mini-server or a full server application. There are, however, more than these two possible server types, as described in the following section.

OLE Server Types

OLE server applications have defined four base classes: the COleServerDoc and COleServerItem classes used by all server applications, the COleServer class used by mini-server applications, and the COleTemplateServer class used by full server applications. Server architecture variations include those listed in Table 18.1.

Table 18.1. Single Document Interface (SDI) server, multiple instances.

Class Type	Classes	Mini-Server Objects	Full Server Objects
Server	1	1	1
Document	1	1	1
Item	1	1	many

SDI servers are probably the most common type of OLE servers—they are also the simplest to implement. An SDI server uses a single server object and a single document object. For each client requesting service, a new server instance is launched.

Because mini-servers do not support links, they provide only one item object; full servers supply multiple item objects when two or more clients are linked to the same disk-based document (see Table 18.2).

Table 18.2. Multiple Document Interface (MDI) server, single server type, single instance.

Class Type	Classes	Mini-Server Objects	Full Server Objects
Server	1	1	1
Document	1	many	many
Item	1	many	many

These single-instance MDI servers are used when DGROUP memory constraints preclude multi-instance servers or when a full server has to be MDI in standalone mode. For mini-servers, there is only one item per document.

Table 18.3. Multiple Document Interface (MDI) server, multiple instances.

Class Type	Classes	Full Server Objects
Server	many	many
Document	many	1
Item	many	many

The multi-instance MDI servers listed in Table 18.3 include applications such as Microsoft Excel, which provides both charts (graphic objects) and spreadsheets. Each server class has one document class and each server object has one document object. Because full servers support links, a single document can have multiple item objects and a document class can have multiple item classes.

Using AppWizard to Create an OLE Server

Earlier in this chapter, AppWizard was used to create an OLE container application and to show how MFC automatically provides virtually all the necessary functionality. For the OLE server application, the story is not quite as simple.

Because the design of an OLE server is much more application specific than the design of a container, there are requirements the AppWizard simply cannot meet. Even so, AppWizard and MFC do supply a complete basic framework with only a few hints from you.

The first item required to create an OLE server appears in AppWizard's Step 3 (see Figure 18.10).

Figure 18.10. Creating an OLE server application: MFC AppWizard—Step 3.

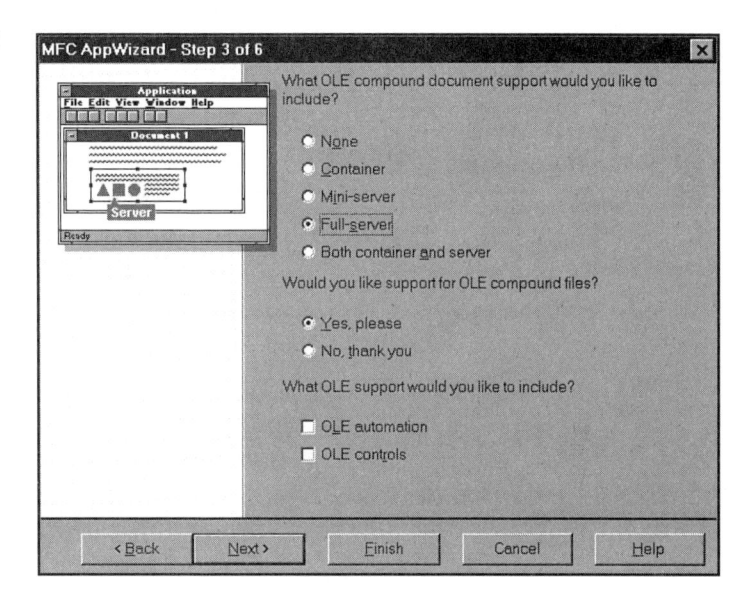

Figure 18.10 shows the options selected for a full server and for OLE automation support. A mini-server isn't a whole lot different to create but, for demonstration purposes, a full server is easier to develop (if only because a full server can operate in standalone fashion—which certainly makes it easier to test during development).

> Caution: Just because your server application works correctly as a standalone program does not mean that it will work as a server. At least one point of failure that occurs in server operation but that does not occur during standalone operation is discussed later in this chapter.

In addition to the usual application, mainframe, document, and view classes, AppWizard has also created an in-place frame class, CInPlaceFrame, and a server class, COle_srveSrvrItem. The principal source files are listed in Table 18.4.

Table 18.4. OLE server source files.

Source File(s)	Function
OLE_SRVR.CPP, OLE_SRVR.H	Source file for the COle_srvrApp application class.
MAINFRM.CPP, MAINFRM.H	Defines the CMainFrame class, derived from the CMDIFrameWnd class; controls all MDI frame features.
TOOLBAR.BMP	The standard bitmap file used to create the application toolbar.
ITOOLBAR.BMP	This bitmap file creates an alternative application toolbar constructed in the CInPlaceFrame class; it appears when the server application is activated in-place inside a container application. The principle difference from TOOLBAR.BMP is that nonserver commands have been removed.
OLE_SDOC.CPP OLE_SDOC.H	Document class files to create the COle_srvrDoc class. Edit these to add special document data and implement serialization features.
OLE_SVW.CPP OLE_SVW.H	View class files to create the COle_srvrView class; implements in-place editing capabilities.
OLE-Specific Classes	
SRVRITEM.CPP SRVRITEM.H	Connects the application's COle_srvrDoc class to the OLE system and optionally provides links to application documents.
IPFRAME.CPP IPFRAME.H	The in-place frame class is derived from the COleIPFrameWnd and controls all frame features during in-place activation.
Utility Files	
OLE_SRVR.REG	Registration script that can be used to register the application.
OLE_SRVR.ODL	Object Description Language (ODL) source code for the application Type library.

The two new, OLE-specific classes introduced in Table 18.4 are a good place to begin. The next section starts with the SrvrItem files, which create the COle_srvrSrvrItem class used to link the COle_srvrDoc documents to the OLE system.

The *COle_srvrSrvrItem* Class

The `COle_srvrSrvrItem` class is derived from the `COleServerItem` class, which provides the principle functionality linking application documents to the OLE system. However, even though the principle functionality is already provided by the parent class, there are opportunities in the derived class for customization.

For example, the derived constructor and destructor classes are implemented simply as shell functions. They can easily be modified to include specialized construction and clean-up code if required but are functional as provided by AppWizard (refer to the following code sample).

```
COle_srvrSrvrItem::COle_srvrSrvrItem(COle_srvrDoc* pContainerDoc)
   : COleServerItem(pContainerDoc, TRUE)
{
   // TODO: add one-time construction code here
   //  (eg, adding additional clipboard formats to the item's data source)
}

COle_srvrSrvrItem::~COle_srvrSrvrItem()
{
   // TODO: add cleanup code here
}
```

By default, the derived `Serialize` method calls on the document class's `Serialize` function for embedded items. Notice that the `IsLinkedItem` function is called and uses a negative (FALSE) result to determine whether the item is embedded:

```
void COle_srvrSrvrItem::Serialize(CArchive& ar)
{
   if (!IsLinkedItem())
   {
      COle_srvrDoc* pDoc = GetDocument();
      ASSERT_VALID(pDoc);
      pDoc->Serialize(ar);
   }
}
```

Alternatively, if the function returns TRUE, the item is linked; linking support requires additional implementation to serialize only a portion of the document.

The `OnGetExtent` method is intended to check the drawing aspect and return a `CSize` variable with the appropriate size information. The default version provided by AppWizard simply returns an arbitrary size of 3000×3000 HIMETRIC units:

```
BOOL COle_srvrSrvrItem::OnGetExtent(DVASPECT dwDrawAspect, CSize& rSize)
{
   if (dwDrawAspect != DVASPECT_CONTENT)
      return COleServerItem::OnGetExtent(dwDrawAspect, rSize);
   COle_srvrDoc* pDoc = GetDocument();
   ASSERT_VALID(pDoc);
   // TODO: replace this arbitrary size
   rSize = CSize(3000, 3000);    // 3000 x 3000 HIMETRIC units
   return TRUE;
}
```

Although the DVASPECT argument can be DVASPECT_CONTENT, DVASPECT_THUMBNAIL, DVASPECT_ICON, or DVASPECT_DOCPRINT, the default implementation handles only the drawing of an item's content aspect. Additional programming provisions are also needed in the OnDraw method to support other aspects.

> Note: Embedded or linked OLE items are always drawn using HIMETRIC units and a metafile device context. This topic is discussed further in the next section. Of course, if you are developing a full server application to be run in standalone fashion, you can use any drawing mode.

The server item's OnDraw method is also a stock default implementation that deserves customization. However, before you jump in and duplicate your entire application's drawing routines, be aware that this is not the purpose of the server item's OnDraw method.

Instead, the server item's OnDraw method is called only when the OLE item is inactive but still needs to be redrawn. If the OLE item is active, the view OnDraw method is called to refresh the item's image. Therefore, the server item's OnDraw method can be provided with a simplified set of drawing instructions (or instructions to draw an icon view, or whatever is necessary) to provide an inactive display.

The following code sample shows how AppWizard has provided a default implementation for the OnDraw method:

```
BOOL COle_srvrSrvrItem::OnDraw(CDC* pDC, CSize& rSize)
{
    COle_srvrDoc* pDoc = GetDocument();
    ASSERT_VALID(pDoc);

    // TODO: set mapping mode and extent
    //   (The extent is usually the same as the size returned from OnGetExtent)
    pDC->SetMapMode(MM_ANISOTROPIC);
    pDC->SetWindowOrg(0,0);
    pDC->SetWindowExt(3000, 3000);

    // TODO: add drawing code here.  Optionally, fill in the HIMETRIC extent.
    //   All drawing takes place in the metafile device context (pDC).

    return TRUE;
}
```

As provided by AppWizard, the server item's OnDraw method doesn't really do anything except set a mapping mode, origin, and window extent. It provides no default drawing operations for the inactive view because these operations are, of course, completely application dependent.

In addition to providing drawing instructions, one other item deserves attention: replace the hard-coded settings in SetWindowExt so that they use the CSize value returned by the OnGetExtent function. This change assumes that the OnGetExtent function has been modified to do more than return these same hard-coded values.

If you want the OLE server view to be drawn both when active and inactive, the simplest approach is to use shared drawing functions called by both OnDraw functions.

Drawing in a Metafile Context

Although both the view class's and server item class's OnDraw methods are called with a pointer to a device context, you should be aware that these are not the same device contexts. When the view's OnDraw method is called, the supplied device context is a normal screen device context. When the server item's OnDraw method is called (because the item is inactive), the supplied device context is a metafile context.

There are several differences between a *standard device context* and a *metafile context* but the important element to remember is that a metafile context does not supply information that relies on the context actually being of a window and being an active element in the window hierarchy. This difference means that functions like GetTextMetrics, GetDeviceCaps, or many of the other GetXxxxxx functions do not operate in a metafile context because there is no connection to the actual device context. Similarly, functions such as CreateCompatibleDC (to create a bitmap memory context) simply do nothing.

Because of these limitations, the server item's OnDraw function normally relies on the MM_ANISOTROPIC mode with an extent defined in MM_HIMETRIC units. Of course, to have your drawing operations compatible both with the active and inactive views, this means that MM_HIMETRIC units must be used in both views—which places an unfortunate restriction on your normal operations.

Unfortunately, this restriction to MM_HIMETRIC mode doesn't always work well—even for very well-designed applications—particularly when application fonts must be rendered in MM_HIMETRIC units. You may, however, consider using a conversion function such as CFont::CreateFont or CFont::CreateFontIndirect to force Windows to match the desired font based on relative size rather than using a font sized according to the metafile context.

Despite these restrictions, most of the output functions (MoveTo, LineTo, TextOut, and DrawText) remain valid.

> Tip: Use the CDC::HIMETRICtoDP and CDC::DPtoHIMETRIC functions to convert coordinates between your format context and device pixels.

The *CInPlaceFrame* Class

The CInPlaceFrame class is derived from the COleIPFrameWnd class, which creates and positions control bars within the OLE container application's document window. The COleIpFrameWnd class also handles notifications generated by embedded COleResizeBar objects when an in-place editing window is resized. Even though the principle functionality is provided by the parent class, there are a few opportunities in the derived class for customization.

In Table 18.4, the ITOOLBAR.BMP bitmap was identified as a toolbar image used for in-place editing; ITOOLBAR.BMP differs from TOOLBAR.BMP in that the nonserver command buttons found in TOOLBAR.BMP are removed.

Also, just as the MainFram.CPP file contains button assignments for the standard toolbar, the IPFrame.CPP (In-Place Frame) file contains button assignments for the ITOOLBAR.BMP toolbar buttons, as shown here:

```
static UINT BASED_CODE buttons[] =
{
   // same order as in the bitmap 'itoolbar.bmp'
   ID_EDIT_CUT,
   ID_EDIT_COPY,
   ID_EDIT_PASTE,
      ID_SEPARATOR,
   ID_APP_ABOUT,
};
```

Although the button assignments shown in this code fragment are the in-place equivalent of the more familiar button assignments made in the MainFrame class, if you are using a custom toolbar, you'll probably want to change both the TOOLBAR.BMP and the ITOOLBAR.BMP images and change the button assignments here as well as in the MainFram.CPP source file.

The CInPlaceFrame class has the usual constructor and destructor methods. Normally, neither requires any implementation:

```
CInPlaceFrame::CInPlaceFrame()
{
}

CInPlaceFrame::~CInPlaceFrame()
{
}
```

The heart of the CInPlaceFrame class is found in two create functions: the OnCreate and OnCreateControlBars methods.

The OnCreate method has two operations: creating a CResizeBar instance to implement in-place resizing and providing a default drop-target:

```
int CInPlaceFrame::OnCreate(LPCREATESTRUCT lpCreateStruct)
{
   if (COleIPFrameWnd::OnCreate(lpCreateStruct) == -1)
      return -1;
   if (!m_wndResizeBar.Create(this))
   {
      TRACE0("Failed to create resize bar\n");
      return -1;      // fail to create
   }
   m_dropTarget.Register(this);
   return 0;
}
```

Registering a drop-target has no effect on the frame window but does prevent drag-and-drop operations from "falling through" to some other container application that does support drag-and-drop.

The OnCreateControlBars method is called, when required, by the framework to create control bars on the container application's windows.

The pWndFrame member is a pointer to the container's top-level frame window—not the server's—and cannot be NULL. The pWndDoc member is the container's document frame window and is NULL if the container application has implemented a single-document interface.

Because the OLE server can place control bars in either the frame or document window, a better implementation of the OnCreateControlBars method begins by testing the pWndDoc parameter. If the parameter is valid, the OnCreateControlBars method creates the toolbar on the document window rather than simply defaulting to the application frame window. Depending on your application and the expected client applications, this is certainly an area for experimentation.

The following listing shows the OnCreateControlBars method implementation supplied by AppWizard.

```
BOOL CInPlaceFrame::OnCreateControlBars(CFrameWnd* pWndFrame,
                                        CFrameWnd* pWndDoc)
{
    // Create toolbar on client's frame window
    if (!m_wndToolBar.Create(pWndFrame) ||
        !m_wndToolBar.LoadBitmap(IDR_OLE_SRTYPE_SRVR_IP) ||
        !m_wndToolBar.SetButtons(buttons, sizeof(buttons)/sizeof(UINT)))
    {
        TRACE0("Failed to create toolbar\n");
        return FALSE;
    }
    // Set owner to this window, so messages are delivered to correct app
    m_wndToolBar.SetOwner(this);

    // TODO: Delete these three lines if you don't want the toolbar to
    //   be dockable
    m_wndToolBar.EnableDocking(CBRS_ALIGN_ANY);
    pWndFrame->EnableDocking(CBRS_ALIGN_ANY);
    pWndFrame->DockControlBar(&m_wndToolBar);

    // TODO: Remove this if you don't want tool tips
    m_wndToolBar.SetBarStyle(m_wndToolBar.GetBarStyle() |
        CBRS_TOOLTIPS | CBRS_FLYBY);

    return TRUE;
}
```

The toolbar docking and tool tips provisions, like the toolbar button assignments, provide operations only when the OLE item is active in-place. They do not otherwise affect the container application.

The *COle_srvrApp* Class

The `COle_srvrApp` class is derived from MFC's `CWinApp` class. Examples earlier in this chapter paid little, if any, attention to the application's `CWinApp` class; they simply assumed that the class was there and that, by default and inheritance, it provided the essentials for initializing and executing an application instance.

For the OLE server application, the derived `COle_srvrApp` class provides essentially the same functionality as in previous examples but also provides a few elements that conventional, non-OLE applications do not require.

For example, the CLSID (CLaSs ID) value used by the system registry is declared in the COle_srvrApp.CPP file as follows:

```
static const CLSID BASED_CODE clsid =
   { 0xf897f980, 0xde37, 0x11ce,
   { 0xbb, 0x7, 0x8e, 0x97, 0xe5, 0xbd, 0xd7, 0xdc } };
```

Although AppWizard has generated this identifier with the assumption that it will be statistically unique, you can change it to a custom identifier if desired.

> Note: Results are uncertain if duplicate identifiers are assigned to separate applications. If you are interested, the experiment is not difficult to perform—but use caution: experiment carefully.

The *InitInstance* Method

Perhaps the biggest difference between a non-OLE application and an OLE application is found in the `InitInstance` method. For the OLE application, the method is responsible for several new tasks including initializing the OLE libraries, registering the server and server templates and, not least, determining whether the application has been launched as an OLE object or if it is being executed conventionally (as a standalone application). For a mini-server, of course, the question of executing as a standalone application does not arise.

Because all these provisions are included by AppWizard as standard features, there is no need to add special code. However, it is still worthwhile to understand what these features are and how they are implemented.

The OLE libraries appear first and are handled quite simply by a call to the `AfxOleInit` function:

```
BOOL COle_srvrApp::InitInstance()
{
   // Initialize OLE libraries
   if (!AfxOleInit())
   {
      AfxMessageBox(IDP_OLE_INIT_FAILED);
      return FALSE;
   }
```

Next, the InitInstance method proceeds with initialization for the standard features. These features can be modified if your application requires special provisions; they can be removed if they are not needed to reduce the size of the finished executable.

```
Enable3dControls();
LoadStdProfileSettings();  // Load standard INI file options
// Register the application's document templates.  Document templates
//   serve as the connection between documents, frame windows and views.
CMultiDocTemplate* pDocTemplate;
pDocTemplate = new CMultiDocTemplate(
   IDR_OLE_SRTYPE,
   RUNTIME_CLASS(COle_srvrDoc),
   RUNTIME_CLASS(CMDIChildWnd),            // standard MDI child frame
   RUNTIME_CLASS(COle_srvrView));
```

Another provision that does not appear in conventional applications is the use of the SetServerInfo and AddDocTemplate operations. The SetServerInfo function is called to identify resources (including menus and accelerator tables) used by the server application when an embedded object is activated:

```
pDocTemplate->SetServerInfo(
   IDR_OLE_SRTYPE_SRVR_EMB, IDR_OLE_SRTYPE_SRVR_IP,
   RUNTIME_CLASS(CInPlaceFrame));
AddDocTemplate(pDocTemplate);
```

After setting the server information, the AddDocTemplate function adds the document template to the list of available templates maintained by the application. This action leads to the next task: connecting the template server to the document template. This is accomplished as shown here:

```
m_server.ConnectTemplate(clsid, pDocTemplate, FALSE);
```

After connecting the COleTemplateServer to the document template using the ConnectTemplate function, the COleTemplateServer class can use information in the document template to create new documents when requested by an OLE container.

> Note: For server applications that support two or more types of document (such as worksheets and charts), a separate COleTemplateServer object is required for each document.

The COleTemplateServer::RegisterAll function (or more accurately, the COleObjectFactory parent class method) is called to register the application's object factories with the OLE system DLLs, allowing the OLE libraries to create objects. The following code shows how this is accomplished:

```
COleTemplateServer::RegisterAll();
```

When the OLE Server is launched by a container application, a command-line parameter (/Embedding or /Automation) is included to indicate that the application is being launched as a server and in what capacity. Because this server has a multidocument interface, all server objects are registered without regard to the launch capacity.

InitInstance continues by creating the MDI frame window, as shown here:

```
// create main MDI Frame window
CMainFrame* pMainFrame = new CMainFrame;
if (!pMainFrame->LoadFrame(IDR_MAINFRAME))
    return FALSE;
m_pMainWnd = pMainFrame;
```

Next, the command-line parameter is checked using the RunEmbedded and RunAutomated functions to determine whether or not the server's main window should be shown:

```
if (RunEmbedded() || RunAutomated())
{
    return TRUE;
}
```

If the application has been launched as a server, the main window should not be shown. But if this application is being launched in its standalone capacity, the ShowWindow and UpdateWindow functions should be called.

Before doing so, however, the OLE server includes another provision: updating the system registry, as shown here:

```
m_server.UpdateRegistry(OAT_INPLACE_SERVER);
COleObjectFactory::UpdateRegistryAll();
```

The provision is included because this could be the first time the server application has been executed—or the system registry may have been damaged. In any case, updating the registry involves little overhead; not updating the registry can have serious consequences.

After updating the registry, the InitInstance method concludes by creating a new document, offering command-line processing, and creating the application window. These tasks are defined here:

```
// create a new (empty) document
OnFileNew();
if (m_lpCmdLine[0] != '\0')
{
    // TODO: add command line processing here
}
// The main window has been initialized, so show and update it.
pMainFrame->ShowWindow(m_nCmdShow);
pMainFrame->UpdateWindow();
return TRUE;
}
```

The *COle_srvrView* Class

The COle_srvrView class completes the server demo by providing the application view both in standalone mode and as an active OLE object. As in other applications, the COle_srvrView class is descended from the MFC CView class.

Beginning with the constructor and destructor methods, one item has been added to the default (empty) constructor: a call to the CreateMsg function:

```
COle_srvrView::COle_srvrView()
{
    CreateMsg();
}
COle_srvrView::~COle_srvrView()
{
}
```

The CreateMsg function is application specific and simply selects a random message from a block of string table entries. The following code shows how this is accomplished:

```
void COle_srvrView::CreateMsg()
{
    CString     csStr;
    SYSTEMTIME  sysTime;

    GetSystemTime( &sysTime );
    srand( sysTime.wMilliseconds );
    csStr.LoadString( IDS_STRING130 + ( rand() % 10 ) );
    m_csMsg = "The OLE Server advises: " + csStr;
}
```

There is one item of interest in this code. Even after a decade or more of development, Microsoft Visual C++ still does not provide comprehensive random primitives (features other compilers have offered as standard utilities almost from their inceptions). Instead, the old, original rand() pseudo-number generator is still the only randomizer available.

However, you can—and should—seed the pseudo-random generator; if you do not, it simply returns the same number sequence every time it is called. To seed the randomizer, use the srand function and supply some sort of random seed. In the preceding code, the srand function was seeded by querying the system clock (with a call to GetSystemTime) and then using the millisecond field as a seed.

> Note: The popular timeGetTime function, which supposedly retrieves the system time since Windows was started, is often used to seed random-generator functions. The function continues to be documented for both WinNT and Win95. There is a slight problem, however: the Visual C++ compiler no longer recognizes this particular API function.

For the demonstration server, the OnDraw method offers a choice of two display items. To offer the choice, OnDraw does not define separate document types—which would require a separate COleTemplateServer object for each. Instead, a simple menu entry is provided, under the heading *Objects*, which offers the choice between Advice and Graphic. These menu options toggle a pair of Boolean member variables which, in turn, determine whether the message (selected in the CreateMsg function) is drawn or whether the graphic display (a five-pointed and a seven-pointed star) is drawn. Aside from these, the OnDraw method offers no particular surprises because the actual drawing operations have all been demonstrated in previous chapters.

The `COle_srvrView` class includes one function, `OnCancelEditSrvr`, to support OLE operations::

```
void COle_srvrView::OnCancelEditSrvr()
{
    GetDocument()->OnDeactivateUI(FALSE);
}
```

This function simply provides a channel for the standard keyboard command to cancel an in-place editing session by passing the command to the document's `OnDeactivateUI` function.

An Example with an Error

Two methods have been created to respond to the Object, Advice and Object, Graphic menu options. Although these methods should be familiar in most respects, each includes three lines of commented-out code that serve to illustrate a very real problem.

```
void COle_srvrView::OnObjectAdvice()
{
//  CMenu * pMenu = AfxGetMainWnd()->GetMenu();
    COle_srvrDoc* pDoc = GetDocument();

    if( pDoc->m_Advice )
    {
        pDoc->m_Advice = FALSE;
//      pMenu->CheckMenuItem( ID_OBJECT_ADVICE, MF_UNCHECKED );
    }
    else
    {
        pDoc->m_Advice = TRUE;
//      pMenu->CheckMenuItem( ID_OBJECT_ADVICE, MF_CHECKED );
    }
    pDoc->UpdateAllViews(NULL);
    pDoc->UpdateAllItems(NULL);
    pDoc->NotifyChanged();
    pDoc->SetModifiedFlag();
    Invalidate();
}
```

When the Ole_Srvr application runs in standalone mode, the three disabled lines of code are perfectly normal provisions and are used to check or uncheck the menu option. However, if these lines are left in and the application is run as a server application, even though the `pMenu` variable is not NULL, the application will crash!

The point is simple: There are actions that are perfectly valid for a standalone application but that do not function as expected in a server capacity.

A Solution to the Error

Of course, it wouldn't be fair to simply say, "you can't do this" without offering an acceptable alternative. This menu error was pointed out to introduce the `OnUpdate` functions in a circumstance in which they are not merely a useful alternative but an essential one.

For the menu items in the Ole_Srvr demo program that cannot be checked or unchecked when the program is a server application, the solution is to use ClassWizard to create two new methods. These methods are created in the Ole_svw.CPP source file by selecting the UPDATE_COMMAND_UI messages for the ID_OBJECT_ADVICE and ID_OBJECT_GRAPHIC menu entries.

In the resulting OnUpdateObjectAdvice and OnUpdateObjectGraphic methods, the pCmdUI parameter (which points to the CCmdUI member for the menu item or other control) is given the SetCheck instruction to check or uncheck the menu item. The following code shows how this is accomplished:

```
void COle_srvrView::OnUpdateObjectAdvice(CCmdUI* pCmdUI)
{
    COle_srvrDoc* pDoc = GetDocument();

    pCmdUI->SetCheck( pDoc->m_Advice );
}
```

The CCmdUI class is used only within the ON_UPDATE_COMMAND_UI handler for a CCmdTarget-derived class, which includes the CView class. The CView class is derived from the CWnd class which, in turn, is derived from the CCmdTarget class.

With this ancestry, whenever an application menu is pulled down, the application framework (which may be the framework for the standalone application or the framework for the container application in which the server is embedded) searches for and calls each ON_UPDATE_COMMAND_UI handler found. When the OnUpdateObjectAdvice and OnUpdateObjectGraphic methods are polled, each of these responds with instructions *to the framework* to check or uncheck the menu items.

This functionality is not limited simply to menu items; it is also valid for control-bar buttons, status-bar displays, dialog-box controls, and CDialogBar controls. Tables 18.5 through 18.9 show how the various control types respond to the CCmdUI functions.

Table 18.5. ON_UPDATE commands for menu items.

Method	*Usage*
Enable	TRUE enables the menu item; FALSE disables (grays out) the menu item.
SetCheck	TRUE checks the menu item using a checkmark (✓); FALSE unchecks the item.
SetRadio	TRUE checks the menu item using a dot (•); FALSE unchecks the item.
SetText	Sets the menu item text to the string argument. *Note:* The menu item command remains unchanged.

Table 18.6. ON_UPDATE commands for toolbar buttons.

Method	Usage
Enable	TRUE enables the toolbar button; FALSE disables the button.
SetCheck	FALSE (0) deselects the toolbar button; TRUE (1) selects the toolbar button; 2 is indeterminate.
SetRadio	Same as SetCheck.
SetText	No effect.

Table 18.7. ON_UPDATE commands for status-bar panes.

Method	Result
Enable	TRUE makes text visible; FALSE renders text invisible.
SetCheck	TRUE sets a normal border, FALSE sets a pop-out border.
SetRadio	Same as SetCheck.
SetText	Sets pane text to string argument.

Table 18.8. ON_UPDATE commands for normal button in CDialogBar.

Method	Result
Enable	TRUE enables the button; FALSE disables the button.
SetCheck	TRUE (1) checks a checkbox, FALSE (0) clears the checkbox, 2 sets the checkbox to indeterminate (this is a three-state control).
SetRadio	Same as SetCheck.
SetText	Sets the button text to the string argument.

Table 18.9. ON_UPDATE commands for normal control in CDialogBar.

Method	Result
Enable	TRUE enables the control; FALSE disables the control.
SetCheck	No effect.
SetRadio	No effect.
SetText	Sets window (control) text to the string argument.

Server Application Menus

When AppWizard created the Ole_Srvr application, the resource script constructed includes four menus: IDR_MAINFRAME, IDR_OLE_SRTYPE, IDR_OLE_SRTYPE_SRVR_EMB, and IDR_OLE_SRTYPE_SRVR_IP.

The first menu, IDR_MAINFRAME, is shown in Figure 18.11. It appears to be a default menu created by AppWizard; it does not appear to be invoked by the application under any circumstances.

Figure 18.11. The IDR_MAINFRAME menu.

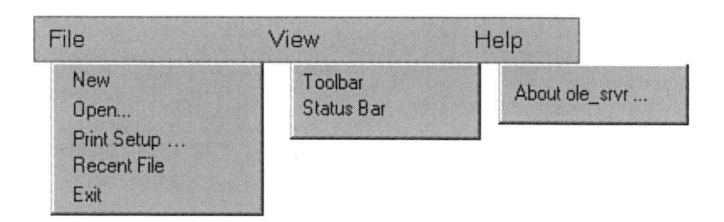

The second menu, IDR_OLE_SRTYPE, is shown in Figure 18.12. This menu appears when the application is run standalone; it is simply the standard menu created for all applications.

Figure 18.12. The IDR_OLE_SRTYPE menu.

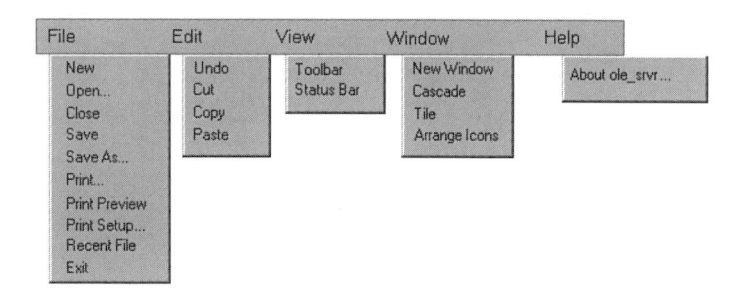

> Note: The IDR_OLE_SRTYPE menu uses the IDR_MAINFRAME accelerator table.

The third menu, IDR_OLE_SRTYPE_SRVR_EMB, is shown in Figure 18.13. This menu appears when an embedded object is edited. The menu does not appear in the container application, however; instead, it appears when the server is called to edit the embedded object. The IDR_OLE_SRTYPE_SRVR_EMB menu has two principle differences from the IDR_OLE_SRTYPE menu: the File, Save option is replaced by File, Update; and the File, Save As option becomes File, Save Copy As.

Figure 18.13. The IDR_OLE_SRTYPE_SRVR_EMB menu.

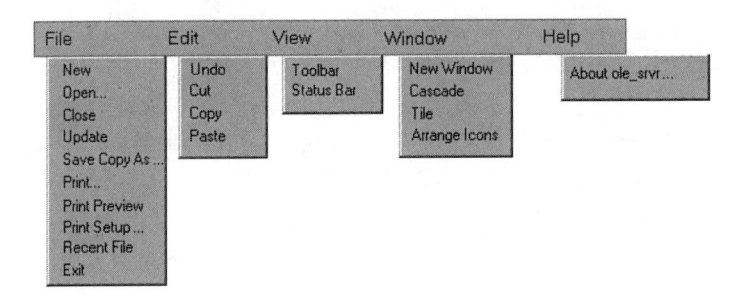

File	Edit	View	Window	Help
New	Undo	Toolbar	New Window	About ole_srvr...
Open...	Cut	Status Bar	Cascade	
Close	Copy		Tile	
Update	Paste		Arrange Icons	
Save Copy As...				
Print...				
Print Preview				
Print Setup...				
Recent File				
Exit				

Note: The IDR_OLE_SRTYPE_SRVR_EMB menu is served by an accelerator table with the same identifier.

The fourth menu, IDR_OLE_SRTYPE_SRVR_IP, is the one seen most frequently (see Figure 18.14). This menu appears when an object is edited in-place. This menu does not appear by itself; instead, it is added to or replaces the application's existing menu.

Figure 18.14. The IDR_OLE_SRTYPE_SRVR_IP menu.

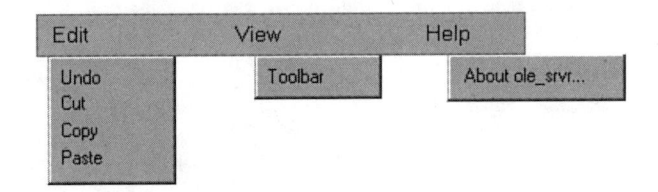

Edit	View	Help
Undo	Toolbar	About ole_srvr...
Cut		
Copy		
Paste		

When an OLE item is edited in-place, the Edit, View, and Help menus in the container application are replaced by the IDR_OLE_SRTYPE_IP menus.

Note: The IDR_OLE_SRTYPE_SRVR_IP menu is served by an accelerator table with the same identifier.

The OLE2View Utility

Visual C++ includes an application called OLE2View (look in the \MSDEV\Samples\MFC\OleView directory) that offers an alternative way to access the system registry and display information about OLE applications. The OLE2View application uses two tree structures (see Figure 18.15). The tree on the left has three root nodes for Objects, Type Libraries, and Interfaces. The tree on the right shows the individual item, selected from the tree on the left, as an expansion of the OLE Object, Library, or Interface's internal characteristics.

Figure 18.15. *The OLE2View utility.*

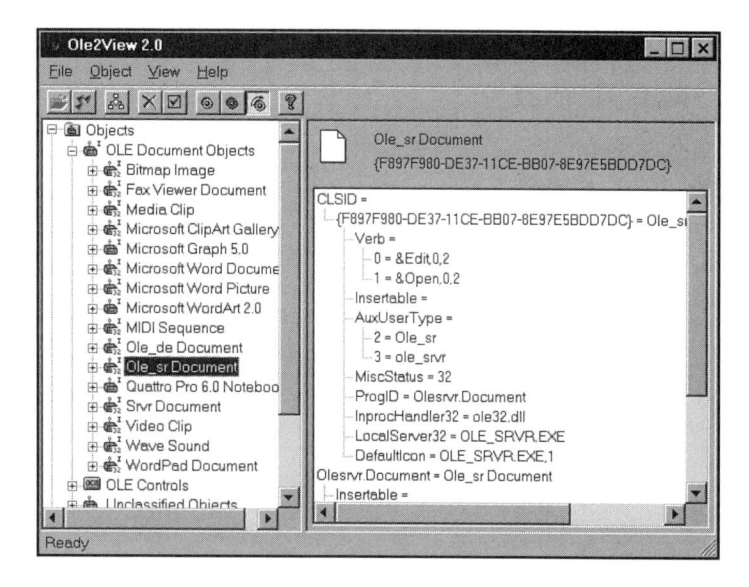

The OLE2View utility is undocumented (although there is a reference in the program to a HLP help file, the named file is not supplied). The utility also includes several functions that report only as Not yet implemented. Despite this, the OLE2View utility is interesting; more important, as source code, it provides a good view of a variety of OLE-support functions.

Summary

This chapter provided an overview of how to integrate separate applications. It began with a brief review of Clipboard and DDE operations and moved on to OLE applications, including examples of constructing both simple container and server programs. The chapter presented examples of embedded OLE objects and discussed compound documents, linked and embedded objects, and the Packager utility before it looked at the construction principles for both OLE containers and OLE servers.

Even with all this, the chapter barely scratched the surface of OLE operations. Unfortunately, scratching the surface is as far as this book goes. For more complete information on OLE, refer to other sources devoted to this complex and extensive subject.

Chapter 19, "More about MFC Classes," looks further at the MFC classes and checks on some of the tools available for application development.

CHAPTER 19

More about MFC Classes

The Microsoft Foundation Classes are commonly broken down into eight groups: General Purpose, Visual Object, Application Architecture, Collection, OLE2, Database, Windows Common Controls, and Windows Sockets.

The **General Purpose** classes include the CObject class with its descendent CFile classes providing file access functions, and its descendent CException classes providing exception error handling. The General Purpose classes also include such varied classes as CString, CTime, CRect, and CPoint as well as the CRunTime, CMemoryState, and CFileStatus classes, among others.

The **Visual Object** classes encompass virtually all application elements that may appear on-screen. These include drawing tools, windows, menus, and dialog control elements as well as the CRecordView class.

The **Application Architecture** classes provide the basic functionality for MFC's message-mapping and document classes used for file management, as well as the CWinApp class providing the application's main execution thread. Application architecture also provides the CCmdUI class for updating user-interface objects, and the CPrintInfo class used in Print and Print Preview operations.

The **Collection** classes offer an assortment of classes supporting collections of arrays, lists, and maps.

The **OLE2** classes provide the basis for object linking and embedding operations that allow independent applications to share operations and data.

The **Database** classes offer functional access and support for a variety of database sources.

The **Common Control** classes provide a new series of visual control objects.

The **Socket** classes allow MFC applications to use Window Sockets for network access.

Finally, the **DAO** (Data Access Object, new in version 4.0) classes provide a framework for database system access.

The following sections present the MFC class groups in hierarchies, along with a brief description of each class in the group. Further, each class appears with the class name at the left; on the right, the class ancestry appears, as in this example:

CComboBox [CObject→CCmdTarget→CWnd→]

In this example, the CComboBox class is derived from CWnd which, in turn, is derived from CCmdTarget, which is derived from CObject.

Where the class ancestry becomes unwieldy in presentation, some intermediate classes are omitted and replaced by an ellipsis, as in this example:

CRecordView [CObject→...→CScrollView→CFormView→]

If you are in doubt about ancestry, refer to the appropriate hierarchy chart to trace the class ancestry directly.

Because there are differences in how some classes are structured in Visual C++ version 2.x and in version 4.0, two class ancestries are shown to identify both paths of inheritance, as in this example:

CFileDialog (2.x) [CObject→CCmdTarget→CCWnd→CDialog→]
(4.0) [CObject→...→CDialog→CCommonDialog→]

Some classes are defined in Visual C++ version 4.0 only—that is, they do not exist in version 2.x. These classes are identified accordingly.

MFC General Purpose Classes

The MFC General Purpose classes begin with the CObject class, which is the base class for many of the MFC classes. But the General Purpose classes also include file and exception-handling classes; coordinate, string, and time classes; and debug utilities. The General Purpose class hierarchy appears in Figure 19.1 and is detailed following the figure.

Figure 19.1. *The General Purpose class hierarchy.*

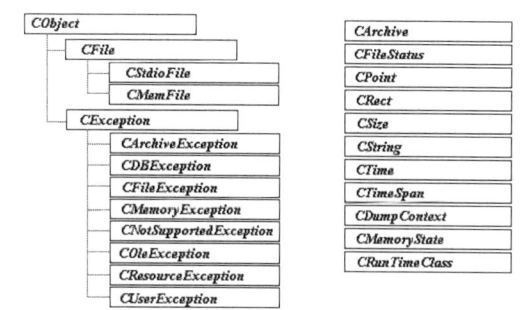

```
CObject
├── CFile
│   ├── CStdioFile
│   └── CMemFile
└── CException
    ├── CArchiveException
    ├── CDBException
    ├── CFileException
    ├── CMemoryException
    ├── CNotSupportedException
    ├── COleException
    ├── CResourceException
    └── CUserException

CArchive
CFileStatus
CPoint
CRect
CSize
CString
CTime
CTimeSpan
CDumpContext
CMemoryState
CRunTimeClass
```

CObject

The `CObject` class supports serializing data and obtaining runtime information about a class and provides the ultimate base class of almost all other classes.

CFile [CObject→]

The `CFile` class provides unbuffered, binary disk input/output services, and indirectly supports text files and memory files through derived classes. `CFile` also works in conjunction with the `CArchive` class to support serialization of Microsoft Foundation objects and provides facilities to maintain files including creating, opening, closing, and deleting files as well as setting file status.

CStdioFile [CObject→CFile→]

`CStdioFile` objects are used for buffered stream disk files which, by default, are accessed in text mode. `CStdioFile` objects may, however, be opened in binary mode. These operate in the same fashion as C runtime files opened using the `fopen` function.

CMemFile [CObject→CFile→]

`CMemFile` supports in-memory files that behave like binary disk files except that data is stored in RAM. These are useful for transferring raw bytes or serialized objects between independent processes.

CException [CObject→]

The `CException` class is the base for all the MFC exception classes described in the following eight sections. These exceptions are intended for use with the THROW, THROW_LAST, TRY, CATCH, AND_CATCH, and END_CATCH macros.

CArchiveException [CObject→CException→]
Handles archive-specific exceptions.

CDBException [CObject→CException→]
Handles database class exception conditions.

CFileException [CObject→CException→]
Handles file-specific exceptions.

CMemoryException [CObject→CException→]
Handles out-of-memory exceptions.

CNotSupportedException [CObject→CException→]
Handles requests for unsupported operations.

COleException [CObject→CException→]
Handles OLE operation exceptions.

CResourceException [CObject→CException→]
Handles Windows resources not found or not createable exceptions.

CUserException [CObject→CException→]
Handles application-specific exceptions thrown to stop end-user operations.

> Note: Additional General Purpose classes, which are not derived from the CObject class, are listed in the following sections as File classes, Coordinate classes, String classes, Date/Time classes, and Debug classes.

File Classes

The File classes, `CArchive` and `CFileStatus`, are used with the `CFile` class to extend file operations.

CArchive

The `CArchive` class, used with the `CFile` class, permits complex networks of objects to be written to or read from permanent storage through a process known as *serialization*. In effect, an archive object is a binary stream associated with a file to provide buffered storage in a nonredundant format. The overloaded extraction (>>) and insertion (<<) operators provide serialization interfaces to support primitive types as well as `CObject`-derived class objects.

> Note: Serializable object classes must have a `Serialize` member and must use the DECLARE_SERIAL and IMPLEMENT_SERIAL macros defined in the `CObject` class.

`CArchive` also supports the MFC Windows Sockets `CSocket` and `CSocketFile` classes through the `IsBufferEmpty` member function.

CFileStatus

The `CFileStatus` class is used with the `CFile::SetStatus` and `CFile::GetStatus` functions to set or retrieve file status information. The `CFileStatus` structure includes the dates and times that the file was created, last modified, and last accessed for read as well as the file size (in bytes), the file attribute byte, and the absolute path/filename for the file.

Coordinate Classes

The Coordinate classes, `CPoint`, `CRect`, and `CSize`, provide size and coordinate information for object windows.

CPoint

The `CPoint` class is similar to the Windows `POINT` structure and can be used wherever a `POINT` structure is used. The `CPoint` class, however, also provides member functions to manipulate both `CPoint` and `POINT` structures. Further, `CPoint` operators that use a size also accept either `CSize` objects or `SIZE` structures (see `CSize`).

CRect

The `CRect` class is similar to a Windows `RECT` structure and can be passed as a function parameter wherever an `LPRECT` or `RECT` structure is used. In addition, the `CRect` class includes member functions to manipulate both `CRect` objects and Windows `RECT` structures.

CSize

The `CSize` class is similar to the Windows `SIZE` structure and can be used wherever a `SIZE` structure is used. Further, the `CSize` class provides member functions to manipulate `SIZE` structures as well as provide public `cx` and `cy` data members.

CString

The `CString` class is used to replace the old C char arrays and offers powerful and flexible string operations.

The `CString` class provides variable-length character strings together with concatenation and comparison operators, and simplified memory management functions and operators similar to those defined in BASIC.

Because the `CString` class is based on the TCHAR data type, if the symbol _UNICODE is defined, TCHAR is defined as type wchar_t (a 16-bit character type); otherwise, TCHAR is defined as an 8-bit char. Likewise, under Unicode, `CString` objects are composed of 16-bit characters.

`CString` objects also have the following characteristics:

- Can grow as a result of concatenation operations.
- Follow "value semantics"; that is, you should treat a `CString` object as an actual string, not as a pointer to a string.
- Can be freely substituted for `const char*` and `LPCTSTR` function arguments.
- Provide a conversion operator for direct access to the string's characters, treating the `CString` as a read-only character array (that is, a C-style string).

Time Classes

The Time classes, `CTime` and `CTimeSpan`, provide convenient date/time information.

CTime

The `CTime` class objects represent absolute time and date, and incorporate the ANSI time_t data type and its associated runtime functions, including the capability to convert to and from Gregorian dates and 24-hour times. `CTime` values are based on UCT (Universal Coordinated Time or Greenwich Mean Time) with the local time zone identified by the TZ environment variable.

> Note: Because the `CTime` class uses the `strftime` function, which is not supported for Windows DLLs, the `CTime` class also cannot be used in a dynamic link library.

CTimeSpan

The `CTimeSpan` class represents a time interval as the difference between two `CTime` objects.

Debug and Utility Classes

A series of three debug and utility classes, `CDumpContext`, `CMemoryState`, and `CRunTime`, complete the MFC General Purpose classes.

CDumpContext

The `CDumpContext` class provides stream-oriented diagnostic output as a readable text format.

CMemoryState

The `CMemoryState` class offers a convenient method of detecting *memory leaks* (occurrences when memory for an object is allocated but not deallocated when no longer required) in an application. The `Checkpoint`, `Difference`, and `DumpStatistics` functions can be used to find differences in memory states (allocated objects) at different points during program execution. The `DumpAllObjectsSince` function provides a list, in order of allocation, of all objects allocated since the last call to `Checkpoint`.

> Note: To ensure that memory diagnostics are included only in debug builds, use the `#if defined(_DEBUG)...#endif` directives when declaring `CMemoryState` objects and while calling `CMemoryState` members.

CRunTimeClass

Each `CObject`-derived class is associated with a `CRunTimeClass` structure, which can be used to obtain information about an object or its base class at run time. This is useful when extra type-checking is required for function arguments or when special-purpose code is based on the class of an object.

> Note: To retrieve runtime information for a class, the IMPLEMENT_DYNAMIC, IMPLEMENT_DYNCREATE, or IMPLEMENT_SERIAL macros must be included in the class implementation.

MFC Visual Object Classes

The MFC Visual Object classes encompass virtually all the elements that may appear on-screen, including drawing tools, windows, and dialog control elements. The MFC Visual Object hierarchy appears in Figure 19.2 and is detailed in the following sections. Figure 19.3 shows the changes in this hierarchy based on MFC version 4.0.

Figure 19.2. *The MFC visual object hierarchy (version 2.x).*

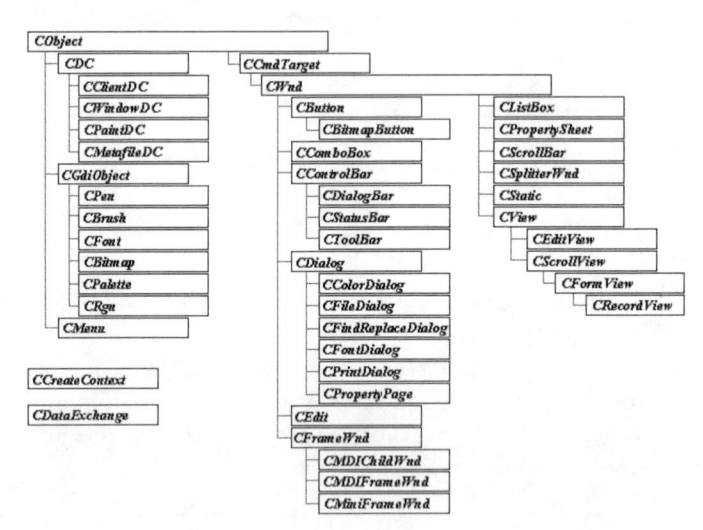

Figure 19.3. *The MFC visual object hierarchy (version 4.0 changes).*

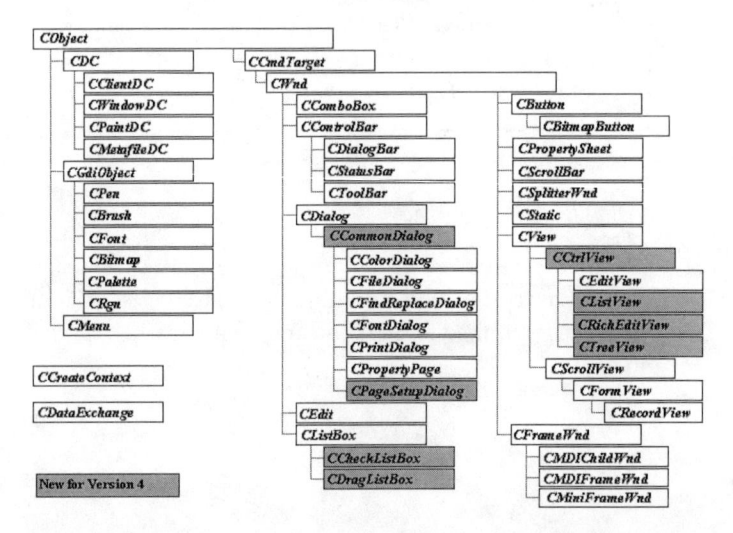

CCmdTarget [CObject→]

CCmdTarget is the base class for the MFC Library message-map architecture. The message map routes commands or messages from menu items, command buttons, or accelerator keys to the member functions written to respond to these instructions. In addition, several key framework classes are derived from the CCmdTarget class, including the CWnd class and its descendent CView and CFrameWnd classes as well as the CWinApp and CDocument classes.

> Note: New classes defined to handle messages would normally be derived from one of the CCmdTarget-derived classes rather than being derived directly from the CCmdTarget class.

CDC and CDC-Derived Classes

The CDC and CDC-derived classes are used to handle display and printer device context operations.

CDC [CObject→]

The CDC class defines a class of device-context objects providing member functions for working with a device context, such as displays or printers, and for working with the display context associated with a window's client area.

The CDC class provides member functions that parallel all Windows APIs that rely on device or display contexts and, therefore, are used for all drawing operations including working with drawing tools, GDI object selection, and working with colors and palettes. CDC member functions also provide text output, font handling, and printer escapes as well as drawing attributes, viewport, and window extents, converting coordinates, and working with regions and clipping rectangles. Additional functions handle drawing operations including lines, simple shapes, ellipses, and polygons.

MFC also provides several special classes derived from the CDC class.

CClientDC [CObject→CDC→]

This class manages a display context associated with a window's client area and is used, for example, to paint an immediate response to mouse events.

CWindowDC [CObject→CDC→]

This class manages a display context associated with an entire window, including its frame and controls.

CPaintDC   [CObject→CDC→]

This class is used in OnPaint member functions for windows and OnDraw member functions for views. The CPaintDC class automatically calls the BeginPaint function on construction and the EndPaint function on destruction.

CMetafileDC   [CObject→CDC→]

This class is a device context for Windows metafiles that contain a sequence of graphics device interface (GDI) commands, which create an image when replayed.

CGdiObject and CGdiObject-Derived Classes

The GDI (graphic device interface) classes provide a wide variety of graphics (drawing) operations.

CGdiObject   [CObject→]

The CGdiObject class is the base class for various Windows GDI objects including bitmaps, regions, brushes, pens, palettes, and fonts.

> Note: Custom GDI object classes are not derived directly from the CGdiObject class, but instead are derived from one of the CGdiObject descendants such as CPen or CBrush.

CPen   [CObject→CGdiObject→]

This class encapsulates a GDI pen that can be selected as the current pen in a device context.

CBrush   [CObject→CGdiObject→]

This class encapsulates a GDI brush that can be selected as the current brush in a device context.

CFont   [CObject→CGdiObject→]

This class encapsulates a GDI font and provides member functions for manipulating the font.

CBitmap   [CObject→CGdiObject→]

This class encapsulates a GDI bitmap and provides member functions to manipulate the bitmap.

CPalette [CObject→CGdiObject→]

This class encapsulates a Windows color palette, providing an interface between an application and a color output device. This interface allows an application to take full advantage of the color capabilities of the output device while minimizing interference with the colors displayed by other applications. Member functions are also provided for manipulating the palette.

CRgn [CObject→CGdiObject→]

This class encapsulates a GDI *region*, an elliptical or polygonal area within a window, and provides member functions that work together with the clipping functions in the CDC class to manipulate the region or to create, alter, or retrieve information about the region.

CMenu [CObject→]

The CMenu class is an encapsulation of the Windows HMENU handle and provides member functions for creating, tracking, updating, and destroying application menus. The LoadMenuIndirect member loads a menu from a memory template; resource menus are retrieved by calling the LoadMenu member.

CWnd and CWnd-Derived Classes

The CWnd class, derived from the CCmdTarget class, is itself the base class for a broad array of other GDI classes.

CWnd [CObject→CCmdTarget→]

Because the CWnd class is the base class for a large number of MFC classes, it provides the base functionality for all of the MFC window classes.

Although a CWnd object is not identical to a window, the two remain closely connected. Whereas a CWnd object is created and destroyed by the CWnd constructor and destructor methods, a window is a data structure internal to Windows and is created by the Create member and destroyed by the CWnd virtual destructor.

Also, MFC's CWnd class and message-map mechanism hide the API WndProc function and route messages through the message map to the appropriate OnMessage CWnd member functions or, of course, to the appropriate message function in the derived class. Further, instances of classes derived from CWnd use member variables to store data specific to aspects of an application.

> Note: The DestroyWindow function destroys a window without destroying the object instance and without destroying the member data for the instance.

MFC derives a variety of classes from `CWnd` to provide specific window types. These include `CFrameWnd`, `CMDIFrameWnd`, `CMDIChildWnd`, `CView`, and `CDialog`, which are designed to derive further child classes as well as control classes such as `CButton` or `CListBox`, which may be used directly or may also be parent classes for custom classes.

CButton [CObject→CCmdTarget→CWnd→]

The `CButton` class is the basis for the Windows button controls. Functionally, buttons are small, rectangular child windows that respond to either single or double mouse clicks. Typically, the response is indicated either by changing the button's appearance or by generating an event message that is sent to the parent application.

Standard `CButton` styles include these:

- **Pushbuttons:** Defined as `BS_PUSHBUTTON` or `BS_DEFPUSHBUTTON`
- **Checkboxes:** Defined as `BS_CHECKBOX`, `BS_AUTOCHECKBOX`, `BS_3STATE`, or `BS_AUTO3STATE`
- **Radio buttons:** Defined as `BS_RADIOBUTTON` or `BS_AUTORADIOBUTTON`

The `BS_GROUPBOX` style can also be assigned but, rather than create a button, it defines a rectangle used to surround and group other buttons.

The `BS_OWNERDRAW` style defines a button that notifies a `DrawItem` member (when the button is clicked) to change the visual aspect of the button image.

Button controls can be created either from a dialog template or directly in the application code. `CButton` objects created from dialog resources are destroyed automatically, however, when the dialog box closes.

Alternatively, if a `CButton` object is created directly in a window by allocation from the heap using the new function, the delete function must be used to destroy the object. If the button is allocated from the stack or embedded in a parent dialog object, deallocation is automatic.

CBitmapButton [CObject→CCmdTarget→CWnd→CButton→]

The `CBitmapButton` class creates button controls labeled with bitmaps rather than text. These may have separate bitmaps for the button's up, down, focused, and disabled states.

CComboBox [CObject→CCmdTarget→CWnd→]

The `CComboBox` class creates a combo box consisting of a list box combined with either a static or edit control. For simple combo boxes, the list box portion is visible at all times. For drop-down combo boxes and drop-down list combo boxes, the list box portion of the control appears only when the drop-down arrow is selected.

In a simple list box or a drop-down combo box, the edit box control can be used to enter an item. For drop-down list combo boxes, the static box does not accept direct entry, and selection can be made only from the items provided in the list box. Refer to "CListBox," later in this chapter.

CControlBar   [*CObject→CCmdTarget→CWnd→*]

The CControlBar class is the base for the CStatusBar, CToolBar, and CDialogBar classes and creates a control window that is normally aligned to the top or bottom of a frame window. CControlBar controls may contain both HWND-based child window controls and non-HWND-based controls managed by the application or framework code.

A *control bar* is a window that is usually aligned to the top or bottom of a frame window. It may contain child items that are either HWND-based controls (which are Windows windows that generate and respond to Windows messages) or non-HWND-based items (which are not windows and are managed by application code or framework code). List boxes and edit controls are examples of HWND-based controls; status-bar panes and bitmap buttons are examples of non-HWND-based controls.

Control-bar windows are usually child windows of a parent frame window and are usually "siblings" to the client view or MDI client of the frame window. A CControlBar object uses information about the parent window's client rectangle to position itself. It then informs the parent window as to how much space remains unallocated in the parent window's client area.

CDialogBar   [*CObject→CCmdTarget→CWnd→CControlBar→*]

The CDialogBar class acts like a modeless dialog box and contains standard Windows dialog controls that the user can tab between. Also like standard dialog, a dialog template can be used to represent the dialog bar.

CStatusBar   [*CObject→CCmdTarget→CWnd→CControlBar→*]

The CStatusBar class creates a control bar with a row of text output panes, or *indicators*, which are commonly used as message lines and status indicators.

The standard application status bar is an example of the CStatusBar class.

CToolBar   [*CObject→CCmdTarget→CWnd→CControlBar→*]

Objects of the class CToolBar are control bars that have a row of bitmapped buttons that may act like pushbuttons, checkbox buttons, or radio buttons. Toolbars are usually embedded members of frame window objects derived from the CFrameWnd or CMDIFrameWnd classes.

The standard application toolbar is an example of the CToolBar class.

CDialog [CObject→CCmdTarget→CWnd→]

The `CDialog` class provides the base for both modal and modeless dialogs. A modal dialog, of course, must be closed before the user can continue operations; a modeless dialog allows the user to switch tasks without closing the dialog.

The following common dialog classes are derived from the `CDialog` base class.

CCommonDialog (4.0 only) [CObject→...→CWnd→CDialog→]

New in Visual C++ version 4.0, the `CCommonDialog` class provides the base class for all classes that encapsulate the functionality of the Windows common dialog boxes.

CColorDialog (2.x) [CObject→CCmdTarget→CWnd→CDialog→]
(4.0) [CObject→...→CDialog→CCommonDialog→]

The `CColorDialog` class is used to incorporate a color selection dialog box in an application. The `CColorDialog` offers a selection of colors defined for the display system and reports the user's selection when the dialog box exits.

CFileDialog (2.x) [CObject→CCmdTarget→CWnd→CDialog→]
(4.0) [CObject→...→CDialog→CCommonDialog→]

The `CFileDialog` class is used to incorporate a File Open or File Save As, or other file selection dialog in an application.

CFindReplaceDialog
(2.x) [CObject→CCmdTarget→CWnd→CDialog→]
(4.0) [CObject→...→CDialog→CCommonDialog→]

The `CFindReplaceDialog` class is used to incorporate a standard string Find/Replace dialog box in an application. The `CFindReplaceDialog` class provides both a Find dialog and a Find/Replace dialog. Although the dialog boxes accept input search and search and replace strings, the actual search and/or replace operations must be implemented by the application itself.

Also, unlike other common dialog boxes, `CFindReplaceDialog` objects are modeless, allowing users to interact with other windows while the dialog remains on screen.

CFontDialog (2.x) [CObject→CCmdTarget→CWnd→CDialog→]
(4.0) [CObject→...→CDialog→CCommonDialog→]

The `CFontDialog` class is used to incorporate a standard font selection dialog box in an application. The supplied common dialog box offers a list of fonts that are currently installed in the system, and reports the user's selection to the application.

CPrintDialog (2.x) [CObject→CCmdTarget→CWnd→CDialog→]
(4.0) [CObject→...→CDialog→CCommonDialog→]

The `CPrintDialog` class is used to incorporate the standard Windows Print dialog box in an application. If the application framework is used to handle printing, the Print dialog box is called automatically. Alternatively, an application can call the Print dialog box directly and override the common Print dialog controls while still allowing the framework to handle printing, or an application may handle all aspects of printing by itself.

CPropertyPage (2.x) [CObject→CCmdTarget→CWnd→CDialog→]
(4.0) [CObject→...→CDialog→CCommonDialog→]

The `CPropertyPage` class is used to create individual pages of a property sheet (a.k.a. a tabbed dialog box). Each property sheet (tab) in a tabbed dialog box is represented by an object class derived from the `CPropertyPage` class.

CPageSetupDialog
(4.0 only) [CObject→...→CDialog→CCommonDialog→]

The `CPageSetupDialog` class is used to incorporate the standard Windows Page Setup dialog box services with additional support for setting and modifying print margins.

> Tip: This is an OLE Page Setup dialog box; after the dialog box is dismissed, any changes made by the user are not saved by the framework. The application must copy values set by this dialog box to a permanent location, such as to member variables in the application's document or application classes.

CEdit [CObject→CCmdTarget→CWnd→]

The `CEdit` class is used to create a Windows *edit control*, a rectangular child window in which the user may enter text.

CFrameWnd [CObject→CCmdTarget→CWnd→]

The CFrameWnd class is used to create SDI overlapped or popup frame windows together with member functions for managing the window. The CFrameWnd class is also the base class for the CMDIChildWnd, CMDIFrameWnd, and CMiniFrameWnd classes.

The CFrameWnd class provides default implementations to perform many of the functions customarily handled by an application's main window, including these functions:

- Tracking the currently active view independent of the Windows active window or the current input focus.
- Handling command messages and many common frame-notification messages, including those handled by the OnSetFocus, OnHScroll, and OnVScroll functions of CWnd.
- Positioning control bars, views, and other child windows inside the frame window's client area.
- Handling idle-time updating of toolbar and other control-bar buttons.
- Managing the main menu bar and using the UPDATE_COMMAND_UI mechanism to determine which menu items should be enabled, disabled, or checked.
- Providing an optional accelerator table to automatically translate keyboard accelerators.
- Acting as a drag-and-drop target to open files dragged from the File Manager and dropped on the frame window; and responding to DDE open requests from the File Manager or the ShellExecute function.
- Prompting the user to save any modified document belonging to the frame.
- Supporting context-sensitive help with an optional help ID and closing WinHelp.EXE on shutdown if help was opened through the frame.

CMDIChildWnd [CObject→CCmdTarget→CWnd→CFrameWnd→]

The CMDIChildWnd class creates an MDI child window. This looks like a typical frame window except that it appears inside an MDI frame window instead of on the desktop. The MDI child window does not have its own menu bar but shares the menu of the MDI frame window. The framework automatically changes the MDI frame menu to represent the currently active MDI child window.

CMDIFrameWnd [CObject→CCmdTarget→CWnd→CFrameWnd→]

The CMDIFrameWnd class creates an MDI frame window together with members for managing the window.

CMiniFrameWnd   [*CObject→CCmdTarget→CWnd→CFrameWnd→*]

The CMiniFrameWnd class creates a half-height frame window like those typically seen around floating toolbars. Mini-frame windows behave like normal frame windows except for the absence of minimize/maximize buttons and menus, and require only a single-click on the system menu for dismissal.

CListBox   [*CObject→CCmdTarget→CWnd→*]

The CListBox class creates a list box that displays a list of items that users can view and select. In a single-selection list box, only one item can be selected; a multiselection list box allows a range of items to be selected.

CCheckListBox   (4.0 only) [*CObject→...→CListBox→*]

The CCheckListBox class creates a Windows checklist box. A checklist box displays a list of items, such as filenames, that the user can view and select from. A checkbox appears next to each item in the list; the user can check or clear the selected item's checkbox.

CDragListBox   (4.0 only) [*CObject→...→CListBox→*]

The CDragListBox class creates a Windows list box with the added capability of allowing a user to move items within the list box. This arrangement allows items in the list—and associated data—to be reordered by the user.

CPropertySheet   [*CObject→CCmdTarget→CWnd→*]

The CPropertySheet class is used to create a property sheet (or tab dialog box) containing one or more CPropertyPage objects (that is, tabs).

> Tip: Property sheets may be executed modally using the DoModal function, or modelessly using the Create function.

CScrollBar   [*CObject→CCmdTarget→CWnd→*]

The CScrollBar class is used to create scrollbar controls for use in dialog boxes or windows. Scrollbar controls are used to specify a position within a range and can be initialized with a specific range and with an initial position.

CSplitterWnd   [CObject→CCmdTarget→CWnd→]

The `CSplitterWnd` class creates a *splitter window*; that is, a window that contains multiple panes. Individual panes are usually application-specific objects derived from the `CView` class, but may be any `CWnd` object with the appropriate child window ID.

CStatic   [CObject→CCmdTarget→CWnd→]

The `CStatic` class creates a static control. A static control consists of a simple text field, box, or rectangle used to label or separate other controls. Static controls accept no input and produce no output.

CView   [CObject→CCmdTarget→CWnd→]

The `CView` class provides the basic functionality for user-defined view classes. These are views attached to documents, and they act as a translator or intermediary between the document and the user by rendering an image of the document on the screen (or printer) and by interpreting user input as operations on the document.

Although a view may be attached to only one document, a document may have multiple views attached, and each view may provide a different look. Using multiple views of a word processing document, one view might display simple text, and another view might offer an outline or display section headings. Or, for a spreadsheet, one view might show a ledger sheet, and another view could offer a graphic display of the data.

Different types of views can appear in separate frame windows or, using a splitter window, in separate panes of a single frame window.

Different views may also be responsible for handling different types of input such as keyboard, mouse, or drag-and-drop operations. In like fashion, different views might respond to different commands from menus, toolbars, and scrollbars.

Although each view is responsible for displaying and, optionally, modifying the associated document's data, the view is not responsible for storing the data. Instead, it is the document's responsibility to provide the view with the necessary information. This may be handled by allowing the view to access the document's data members directly, or permitting access only through member functions.

When a view changes a document's data, the view is expected to call the document's `UpdateAllViews` function, which, in turn, notifies the other views by calling the `OnUpdate` member for each.

A `CView` object handles scrollbar events through its `OnHScroll` and `OnVScroll` member functions, either using the derived `CWnd` class to provide default handling, or by implementing custom scrollbar handling. Refer also to the `CScrollView` class.

CCtrlView   (4.0 only) [CObject→...CView→]

The CCtrlView class is new with MFC version 4.0 and provides the base class for the CEditView, CListView, CRichEditView, and CTreeView classes. These classes are used to adapt the document-view architecture to the new common controls supported by Windows 95, Windows NT versions 3.51 and later, and Win32 versions 1.3 and later.

CEditView   (2.x) [CObject→CCmdTarget→CWnd→CView→]
                                          (4.0) [CObject→...→CView→CtrlView→]

The CEditView class provides a view with a simple multiline text editor. This can be used as a control in a dialog box or as a document view.

CListView   (4.0 only) [CObject→...→CView→CCtrlView→]

The CListView class provides a simplified form of the CListCtrl class, encapsulating list-control functionality with MFC's document-view architecture.

CRichEditView   (4.0 only) [CObject→...→CView→CCtrlView→]

A *rich edit control* is a window in which a user can enter and edit text with character and paragraph formatting as well as embedded OLE objects. To make formatting operations available, however, the application must implement the necessary user interface components.

The CRichEditView class, together with the CRichEditDoc and CRichEditCntrItem classes (see MFC OLE2 classes in "User-Specified Base Classes," later in this chapter), provides rich edit control functionality within MFC's document view architecture. The CRichEditView class maintains text and formatting; the CRichEditDoc class maintains a list of OLE client items in the view; the CRichEditCntrItem class handles container-side access to the OLE client items.

> Note: See the WordPad sample application, distributed with Visual C++ 4.0, for an example of the CRichEditView class.

CTreeView   (4.0 only) [CObject→...→CView→CCtrlView→]

The CTreeView class provides a simplified form of the CTreeCtrl class; the CTreeView class provides tree-list control functionality.

CScrollView   [CObject→CCmdTarget→CWnd→CView→]

The `CScrollView` class adds additional scrolling capabilities to the base `CView` class by providing handling to do the following:

- Manage window and viewport sizes, and manage mapping modes.
- Scroll automatically in response to scrollbar messages.

CFormView   [CObject→CCmdTarget→CWnd→CView→CScrollView→]

The `CFormView` class provides a scrollable view that contains dialog-box controls and is based on a dialog template resource.

CRecordView   [CObject→...→CView→CScrollView→CFormView→]

The `CRecordView` class provides a form view that is linked directly to a recordset object with the DDX mechanism exchanging data between the recordset and the controls of the record view.

Like all form views, the record view is based on a dialog template resource.

Record views also support moving from record to record in the recordset, updating records, and closing the associated recordset when the record view closes.

Associated Object Classes

Last, there are two data structures associated with Visual Object classes: the `CCreateContext` structure used with window frameworks, and the `CDataExchange` structure used in data exchange and validation.

CCreateContext

The `CCreateContext` structure is used by the framework to create the frame windows and views associated with a document. It does this by providing information to connect the components making up the document and the view of the document's data.

> Note: When the framework defaults are used, the `CCreateContext` structure can be ignored.

CDataExchange

The `CDataExchange` class provides support for the dialog data exchange (DDX) and dialog data validation (DDV) routines. This class is used to write custom data exchange routines for custom controls, or data type or custom data validation routines.

MFC Application Architecture Classes

The MFC Application Architecture classes provide the basic functionality for MFC's message-map architecture, the document classes necessary for file management, and the `CWinApp` class, which provides the application's main execution thread. The MFC Application Architecture class hierarchy is shown in Figure 19.4, and is detailed in the following section.

Figure 19.4. *The MFC Application Architecture classes hierarchy.*

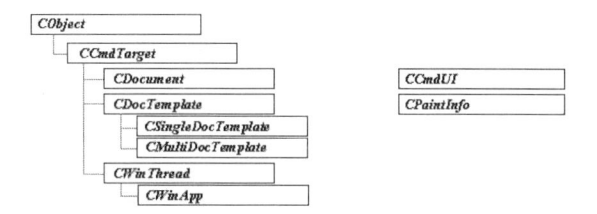

```
CObject
  └── CCmdTarget
        ├── CDocument              CCmdUI
        ├── CDocTemplate           CPaintInfo
        │     ├── CSingleDocTemplate
        │     └── CMultiDocTemplate
        └── CWinThread
              └── CWinApp
```

CCmdTarget [*CObject→*]

`CCmdTarget` is the base class for the MFC library message-map architecture. The message map routes commands or messages from menu items, command buttons, or accelerator keys to the member functions written to respond to these instructions. In addition, several key framework classes are derived from the `CCmdTarget` class, including the `CWnd` class and its descendent `CView` and `CFrameWnd` classes, as well as the `CWinApp` and `CDocument` classes.

> Note: New classes defined to handle messages would normally be derived from one of the `CCmdTarget`-derived classes rather than directly from the `CCmdTarget` class.

CDocument [*CObject→CCmdTarget→*]

The `CDocument` class provides the basis for all user-defined document classes.

> Note: A *document* is any unit of data (that is, a file) that the user can open with the File Open command or save with the File Save command.

The CDocument class supports standard operations such as creating, loading, and saving a document while the application framework manipulates documents using the interface defined by the CDocument class.

Applications may support multiple document types as, for example, both spreadsheets and text files, but each document type must have an associated template identified by a pointer to a CDocTemplate object.

User interactions with a document are handled through the associated CView object or objects (see the CView class under "MFC Visual Object Classes," earlier in this chapter).

Because a document is a part of the framework's standard command routing, documents receive commands from the standard user-interface components forwarded by the active view. If the document class does not have provisions for a specific command, the message is forwarded to the document template.

CDocTemplate [CObject→CCmdTarget→]

The CDocTemplate class is an abstract base class for the derived CSingleDocTemplate and CMultiDocTemplate classes.

A document template defines the relationships among three types of classes:

- The document class derived from the CDocument class
- A view class that displays data from the derived CDocument class. The view class may be derived from the CView, CScrollView, CFormView, or CEditView classes, or the CEditView class may be used directly.
- A frame window class that contains the view. For a single document interface, the frame window class would be derived from the CFrameWnd class. For a multidocument interface, the frame window class would be derived from the CMDIChildWnd class.

Alternatively, if there is no need to customize or modify the frame window behavior, the CFrameWnd or CMDIChildWnd classes can be used directly.

An application requires one document template for each document type supported. Each document template is responsible for creating and managing documents of its type.

The document template also stores pointers to the CRuntimeClass object for the document, view, and frame window classes specified while constructing the document template.

In addition, the document template contains the IDs for the resources used with the document type, including the menu, icon, and accelerator table resources as well as the name of the document type and the default file extension. Optionally, the template may also contain additional strings used by the application's user interface, the File Manager, or for OLE support.

For OLE container applications, the document template also contains the ID of the menu used during in-place activation or, for OLE servers, the document template contains the ID for the toolbar and menu used during in-place activation. These values can be set with the `SetContainerInfo` and `SetServerInfo` functions.

CSingleDocTemplate   [CObject→CCmdTarget→CDocTemplate→]

The `CSingleDocTemplate` class defines a document template for an SDI interface where only one document is displayed using the main frame window.

CMultiDocTemplate   [CObject→CCmdTarget→CDocTemplate→]

The `CMultiDocTemplate` class defines a document template for an MDI interface where multiple documents may be opened in separate document frame windows inside the main frame window.

Because an MDI application can support more than one document type and documents of different types can be opened at any time, the application must provide one document template for each supported document type. The document template is used each time a new document is created.

To support multiple document types, the framework retrieves the names of the supported types from the document templates, displaying these in a list in the File New dialog box. After a document type is selected, the application creates a document object, a frame window object, and a view object, attaching these to each other.

CWinThread   [CObject→CCmdTarget→]

The `CWinThread` class is the base class for the `CWinApp` class, which provides the main execution thread within an application. Additional `CWinThread` objects can provide multiple threads within an application, however.

`CWinThread` supports two types of threads: *worker threads* and *user-interface threads*. The distinguishing feature is that worker threads do not receive or process system messages and are used for background operations that do not require user input. The application's main thread must be a user-interface thread, obviously.

The real advantage of multiple threads, and of the `CWinThread` and derived classes, appears on multiprocessor systems where separate processes execute separate threads in parallel.

CWinApp   [CObject→CCmdTarget→CWinThread→]

The `CWinApp` class is the base class for a Windows application object that provides the member functions for initializing and running the application.

In addition to the `CWinApp` member functions, MFC provides several global functions to access the `CWinApp` object and other global information:

Function	Description
`AfxGetApp`	Returns a pointer to the `CWinApp` object
`AfxGetInstanceHandle`	Returns a handle to the current application instance
`AfxGetResourceHandle`	Returns a handle to the application's resources
`AfxGetAppName`	Returns a pointer to a string with the application's name

Associated Object Classes

In addition, there are two object classes associated with the application architecture classes: the `CCmdUI` class, used by the framework to set controls, and the `CPrintInfo` class, used during printing to transfer information between the framework and the view classes.

CCmdUI

The `CCmdUI` class provides an interface for enabling, disabling, checking, or unchecking user-interface objects; that is, menu items and control-bar buttons. It is used within the `ON_UPDATE_COMMAND_UI` handler in a `CCmdTarget`-derived class.

When an application menu is pulled down, the frame queries are available `ON_UPDATE_COMMAND_UI` handlers to determine whether menu entries should be enabled, disabled, checked, and so on.

In like fashion, `ON_UPDATE_COMMAND_UI` handlers can be used with control-bar buttons and other command user-interface objects. (See Chapter 18, "Using Simple OLE Operations," for examples.)

CPrintInfo

An instance of the `CPrintInfo` class is created each time the Print or Print Preview command is issued, and is used to store information about a print or print-preview task. When the command is completed, the `CPrintInfo` instance is destroyed.

Although the `CPrintInfo` object contains information both about the print job as a whole (including the range of pages to be printed) and the current print status (such as the current page being printed), some of this information is stored in the associated `CPrintDialog` object as the values entered by the user in the Print dialog box.

The `CPrintInfo` object is used to exchange information between the framework and view classes during the printing process.

MFC Collection Classes

The MFC Collection classes provide an assortment of classes supporting collections of arrays, lists, and maps. These Collection classes are alternatives to the standard C/C++ arrays and lists; the map classes have no direct C/C++ counterparts. The MFC Collection classes hierarchy is shown in Figure 19.5 and is detailed in the following sections.

Figure 19.5. *The MFC collection classes hierarchy.*

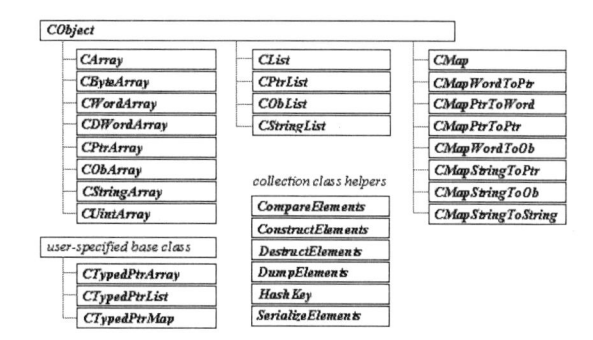

```
CObject
    ├── CArray
    │     ├── CByteArray
    │     ├── CWordArray
    │     ├── CDWordArray
    │     ├── CPtrArray
    │     ├── CObArray
    │     ├── CStringArray
    │     └── CUintArray
    ├── CList
    │     ├── CPtrList
    │     ├── CObList
    │     └── CStringList
    └── CMap
          ├── CMapWordToPtr
          ├── CMapPtrToWord
          ├── CMapPtrToPtr
          ├── CMapWordToOb
          ├── CMapStringToPtr
          ├── CMapStringToOb
          └── CMapStringToString

user-specified base class
    ├── CTypedPtrArray
    ├── CTypedPtrList
    └── CTypedPtrMap

collection class helpers
    ├── CompareElements
    ├── ConstructElements
    ├── DestructElements
    ├── DumpElements
    ├── HashKey
    └── SerializeElements
```

Array Collections

The array collection classes support arrays that, unlike C arrays, can shrink or grow dynamically. As with C arrays, indexes always start at 0, but the upper bounds may be fixed or may be allowed to expand as required. As arrays expand, memory is allocated contiguously from the upper bound.

The access time for an array collection object-indexed element is constant and is independent of the size of the array.

CArray   [CObject→]

The `CArray` class provides a template for user-defined array collection types.

> Note: Some member functions of the `CArray` class depend on global helper functions that must be customized for most uses. See the section, "Collection Class Helpers," later in this chapter.

CByteArray   [CObject→]

The `CByteArray` class stores an array of elements of type BYTE.

CWordArray [CObject→]

The `CWordArray` class stores an array of elements of type WORD.

CDWordArray [CObject→]

The `CDWordArray` class stores an array of elements of type DWORD.

CPtrArray [CObject→]

The `CPtrArray` class stores an array of void (generic) pointers.

CObArray [CObject→]

The `CObArray` class stores an array of pointers to objects of class `CObject` or pointers to class objects derived from `CObject`.

CStringArray [CObject→]

The `CStringArray` class stores an array of `CString` objects.

CUintArray [CObject→]

The `CUintArray` class stored an array of elements of type UINT.

List Collections

The list collection classes support ordered lists of nonunique objects accessible either sequentially or by value. Functionally, list collection lists act like doubly linked lists.

The key for each list is a variable of type POSITION that may be used iteratively to step though a list sequentially or as a temporary bookmark. The POSITION variable, however, is not an index to the list and is not publicly accessible.

New elements can be inserted in a list most efficiently at the head, tail, or the POSITION location. For other access, a sequential search is necessary to find elements by index or value; this search may be slow for long lists.

CList [CObject→]

The `CList` class provides a template for user-defined list collection types.

> Note: Some member functions of the CList class depend on global helper functions that must be customized for most uses. See the section, "Collection Class Helpers," later in this chapter.

CPtrList   [CObject→]

The CPtrList class stores a linked list of void (generic) pointers.

CObList   [CObject→]

The CObList class stores a linked list of pointers to objects of class CObject or pointers to class objects derived from CObject.

CStringList   [CObject→]

The CStringList class stores a linked list of CString objects.

Map Collections

The map collection classes are dictionary collection classes that map unique keys to values. After a key-value pair has been inserted into a map, the key offers efficient access to retrieve or delete the pair.

Map elements can also be iterated; as with the list collection classes, a POSITION variable is provided to offer alternative access and can be iterated through the map.

The map collection classes incorporate the IMPLEMENT_SERIAL macro, which supports serialization and dumping of map elements. If the map is stored to an archive, the elements are serialized sequentially.

Deleting a map collection element removes both the key and value for the element.

CMap   [CObject→]

The CMap class provides a template for user-defined map collection types.

> Note: Some member functions of the CMap class depend on global helper functions that must be customized for most uses. See the section, "Collection Class Helpers," later in this chapter.

CMapWordToPtr [CObject→]

The `CMapWordToPtr` class maps data elements of type WORD to void (generic) pointers; that is, it uses WORD data as keys to find void pointers.

CMapPtrToWord [CObject→]

The `CMapPtrToWord` class maps void pointers to data of type WORD; that is, it uses void pointers as keys for finding data of type WORD.

CMapPtrToPtr [CObject→]

The `CMapPtrToPtr` class maps void pointers to void (generic) pointers; that is, it uses void pointers as keys for finding other void pointers.

CMapWordToOb [CObject→]

The `CMapWordToOb` class maps data of type WORD to `CObject` pointers; that is, it uses WORD data as keys to find `CObject` pointers.

CMapStringToPtr [CObject→]

The `CMapStringToPtr` class maps `CString` objects to void (generic) pointers; that is, it uses `CString` objects as keys for finding void pointers.

CMapStringToOb [CObject→]

The `CMapStringToOb` class maps `CString` objects to pointers to `CObject` instances; that is, it uses `CString` objects as keys for finding pointers to `CObject`s.

CMapStringToString [CObject→]

The `CMapStringToString` class maps `CString` objects to `CString` objects; that is, it uses `CString`s as keys for finding other `CString`s.

Wrapper Classes

In addition, MFC supplies three wrapper classes that may be derived from either `CPtr...` or `COb...` array, list, or map base types.

User-Specified Base Classes

A user-specified base class can be CPtr... or COb... array, list, or map base types. Using CTypedPtr... rather than CPtr... or COb... allows the C++ type checking facility to help eliminate errors produced by mismatched pointer types. Also, the CTypedPtr... wrappers require less typecasting than COb... or CPtr... classes. The following sections list the types of classes you can specify.

CTypedPtrArray [CObject→user-specified→]

The CTypedPtrArray class is a type-safe wrapper for objects of the CPtrArray and CObArray classes.

CTypedPtrList [CObject→user-specified→]

The CTypedPtrList class is a type-safe wrapper for objects of the CPtrList and CObList classes.

> Note: CTypedPtrList lists derived from the CObList class may be serialized; those derived from CPtrList class may not.

CTypedPtrMap [CObject→user-specified→]

The CTypedPtrMap class is a type-safe wrapper for objects of the CMapPtrToPtr, CMapPtrToWord, CMapWordToPtr, and CMapStringToPtr classes.

Collection Class Helpers

The CArray, CList, and CMap collection classes use global helper functions to construct, destroy, or serialize elements. When implementing classes based on the CArray, CList, or CMap classes, these templated functions must be overridden with versions appropriate to the custom data types stored in the array, list, or map. MFC provides a series of global functions for use in customizing collection classes. These functions are described in the following sections.

CompareElements

The CompareElements function returns TRUE if the object pointed to by ptr1 is equal to the object pointed to by ptr2. This function should be overridden to compare elements as appropriate for the application. This may also require defining an overloaded comparison operator.

ConstructElements

The `ConstructElements` function is used to create a new array, list, or map element. The default implementation sets all bits of the new elements to zero.

DestructElements

The `DestructElements` function should be implemented to perform actions necessary to destroy an element. The default implementation, however, does nothing.

DumpElements

The `DumpElements` function is used for stream-oriented diagnostic output; the default implementation does nothing.

HashKey

The `HashKey` function calculates a hash key for a given key. The default implementation creates a hash key by right-shifting the key value four places.

SerializeElements

The `SerializeElements` function provides serialized access to and from an archive. The default implementation uses a bit-wise read and write.

MFC OLE2 Classes

The MFC OLE2 classes are the basis for the object linking and embedding processes, which make it possible for independent applications to share operations and data in various fashions. The OLE2 operations are described in Chapter 18, "Using Simple OLE Operations," and are shown in Figure 19.6. Figure 19.7 shows the hierarchy changes made by MFC version 4.0.

Figure 19.6. *The MFC OLE2 classes hierarchy (version 2.x).*

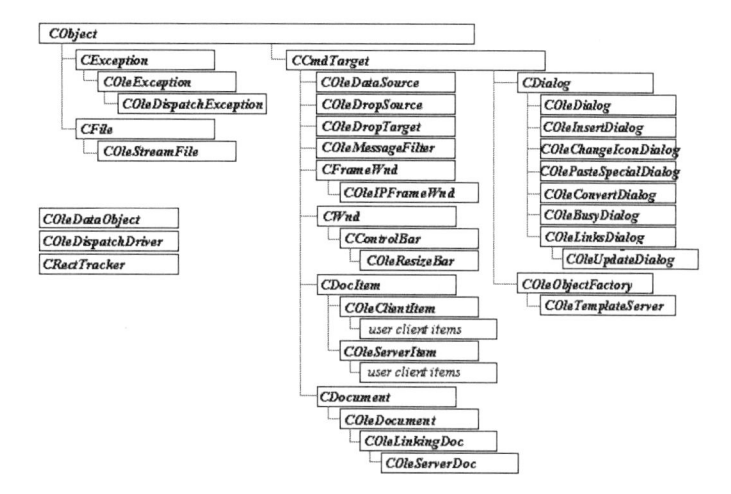

Figure 19.7. *The MFC OLE2 classes hierarchy (version 4.0).*

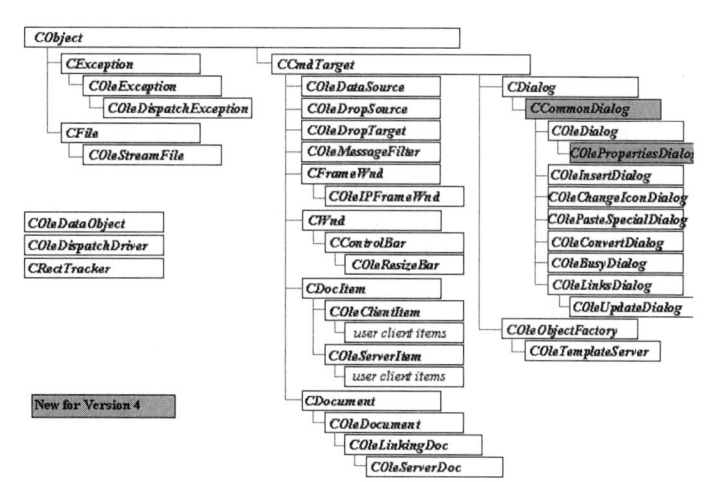

COleDataSource [CObject→CCmdTarget→]

The `COleDataSource` class is used for OLE data transfers, which is, in effect, an object-oriented Clipboard object. `COleDataSource` provides a cache to contain OLE application-supplied data for transfer with the Clipboard or a drag-and-drop operation.

COleDropSource [CObject→CCmdTarget→]

A `COleDropSource` class provides functions allowing data to be dragged to a drop target and is responsible for deciding when a drag operation begins, providing feedback during the drag operation, and ending the drag operation.

COleDropTarget [CObject→CCmdTarget→]

The `COleDropTarget` class provides the target for drag-and-drop operations. A `COleDropTarget` object corresponds to a window on-screen and determines whether dropped data will be accepted. It implements the actual drop operation.

COleMessageFilter [CObject→CCmdTarget→]

The `COleMessageFilter` class provides concurrency management for OLE application interactions.

> Note: The `COleMessageFilter` class is an advanced class and seldom requires custom implementation or direct access.

CFrameWnd [CObject→CCmdTarget→]

The `CFrameWnd` is the base class for an SDI application's main frame window and for the `COleIPFrameWnd` class.

COleIPFrameWnd [CObject→CCmdTarget→CFrameWnd→]

The `COleIPFrameWnd` class provides the view frame window when a server document is being edited in-place. `COleIPFrameWnd` creates and positions control bars within the container application's document window and handles notifications generated by an embedded `COleResizeBar` object when the user resizes the in-place editing window.

CDialog (2.x) [CObject→CCmdTarget→]

The `CDialog` class provides the base class for the OLE dialog classes in Visual C++ 2.x.

CCommonDialog (4.0 only) [CObject→CCmdTarget→CDialog→]

The `CCommonDialog` class provides the base class for the OLE dialog classes in Visual C++ 4.0.

COleDialog (2.x) [CObject→CCmdTarget→CDialog→]
(4.0) [CObject→...→CCommonDialog→]

The COleDialog class is used by the framework to contain common implementations for all OLE dialog boxes. All dialog box classes in the user-interface category are derived from COleDialog, but COleDialog is not used directly.

COlePropertiesDialog (4.0 only) [CObject→...→COleDialog→]

The COlePropertiesDialog class encapsulates the Windows OLE Object Properties common dialog box. The OLE Object Properties dialog box offers an easy way to display and modify OLE document item properties including information about the file represented by document item, icon display, image scaling options, and information on item links.

COleInsertDialog (2.x) [CObject→CCmdTarget→CDialog→]
(4.0) [CObject→...→CCommonDialog→]

The COleInsertDialog class displays the Insert Object dialog box, allowing the user to select an embedded or linked OLE item for insertion.

COleChangeIconDialog (2.x) [CObject→CCmdTarget→CDialog→]
(4.0) [CObject→...→CCommonDialog→]

The COleChangeIconDialog class displays the Change Icon dialog box, which is used to change the icon associated with an embedded or linked OLE item.

COlePasteSpecialDialog
(2.x) [CObject→CCmdTarget→CDialog→]
(4.0) [CObject→...→CCommonDialog→]

The COlePasteSpecialDialog class displays the Paste Special dialog box for the Edit Paste Special command.

COleConvertDialog (2.x) [CObject→CCmdTarget→CDialog→]
(4.0) [CObject→...→CCommonDialog→]

The COleConvertDialog class displays the Convert dialog box, which is used to convert OLE items from one type to another.

COleBusyDialog   (2.x) [CObject→CCmdTarget→CDialog→]
(4.0) [CObject→...→CCommonDialog→]

The COleBusyDialog class displays the Server Busy and Server Not Responding dialog boxes, which are used to handle calls to busy applications. These dialog boxes are normally displayed by the COleMessageFilter implementation.

COleLinksDialog   (2.x) [CObject→CCmdTarget→CDialog→]
(4.0) [CObject→...→CCommonDialog→]

The COleLinksDialog class displays the Edit Links dialog box, which is used to modify information about linked items.

COleUpdateDialog
(2.x) [CObject→...→CDialog→COleLinksDialog→]
(4.0) [CObject→...→CCommonDialog→COleLinksDialog→]

The COleUpdateDialog class displays the Update dialog box with an indicator showing the progress in updating all links in a document.

CControlBar   [CObject→CCmdTarget→CWnd→]

The CControlBar class is the base for the COleResizeBar class and creates a control window that is normally aligned to the top or bottom of a frame window. CControlBar controls can contain both HWND-based child window controls and non-HWND-based controls, which are managed by the application or framework code.

COleResizeBar   [CObject→CCmdTarget→CWnd→CControlBar→]

The COleResizeBar class provides the standard user interface for in-place resizing. COleResizeBar objects are used in conjunction with COleIPFrameWnd objects.

CDocument   [CObject→CCmdTarget→]

The CDocument class is the base class for application-specific documents including the COleDocument and descendent classes.

COleDocument [CObject→CCmdTarget→CDocument→]

The COleDocument class is the base class for OLE documents that support visual editing and uses the document and view architecture inherited from the CDocument class. Documents are treated as a collection of CDocItem objects.

The COleServerItem and COleClientItem classes, which are derived from CDocItem, manage the interactions between applications and OLE items.

COleLinkingDoc [CObject→...→COleDocument→]

The COleLinkingDoc class provides the infrastructure for linking OLE objects. To support links to embedded objects, container applications should derive their document classes from COleLinkingDoc rather than COleDocument.

COleServerDoc [CObject→...→COleDocument→COleLinkingDoc→]

The COleServerDoc class is used as the base class for server application document classes, and provides the bulk of the server support through interactions with COleServerItem objects. Visual editing capability is provided through the MFC document and view architecture.

COleObjectFactory [CObject→CCmdTarget→]

The COleObjectFactory class implements the OLE class factory to create OLE objects such as servers, automation objects, and documents. COleObjectFactory also handles object registration; it has member functions for updating the system registry and executing runtime registration to inform OLE which objects are running and available to receive messages.

COleTemplateServer [CObject→...→COleObjectFactory→]

The COleTemplateServer class is used to create documents using the framework's document and view architecture but delegates most of its work to an associated CDocTemplate object.

CDocItem [CObject→CCmdTarget→]

The CDocItem class is the abstract base class for the COleClientItem and COleServerItem classes. CDocItem-derived class objects represent parts of documents.

COleClientItem [CObject→CCmdTarget→CDocItem→]

The COleClientItem class is the base class for any user client items representing the client side of the connection to an embedded or linked OLE item.

CRichEditCntrItem   (4.0 only) [CObject→....→COleClientItem→]

A *rich edit control* is a window in which a user can enter and edit text with character and paragraph formatting as well as embedded OLE objects. To make formatting operations available, however, the application must implement the necessary user interface components.

The CRichEditCntrItem class, together with the CRichEditDoc and CRichEditView classes (see the MFC Visual Object hierarchy for version 4.0 in Figure 19.3, earlier in this chapter) provides rich edit control functionality within MFC's document view architecture. The CRichEditView class maintains text and formatting; the CRichEditDoc class maintains a list of OLE client items in the view; the CRichEditCntrItem handles container-side access to the OLE client items.

> Tip: See the WordPad sample application, distributed with Visual C++ 4.0, for an example of the CRichEditView class.

User Client Items

All client-side user item classes must be derived from the COleClientItem class.

COleServerItem   [CObject→CCmdTarget→CDocItem→]

The COleServerItem class represents the OLE interface to COleServerDoc objects. Normally, one COleServerItem object represents the embedded part of a document and many COleServerItem objects represent links to portions of the document.

> Note: A *linked item* represents some or all of a server document; an *embedded item* represents an entire server document.

CRichEditDoc   (4.0 only) [CObject→...→COleServerItem→]

A *rich edit control* is a window in which a user can enter and edit text with character and paragraph formatting as well as embedded OLE objects. To make formatting operations available, however, the application must implement the necessary user interface components.

The CRichEditDoc class, together with the CRichEditCntrItem and CRichEditView classes (see the MFC Visual Object hierarchy for version 4.0 in Figure 19.3, earlier in this chapter), provides rich edit control functionality within MFC's document view architecture. The CRichEditView class maintains text and formatting; the CRichEditDoc class maintains a list of OLE client items in the view; the CRichEditCntrItem handles container-side access to the OLE client items.

> Tip: See the WordPad sample application, distributed with Visual C++ 4.0, for an example of the CRichEditDoc class.

User Server Items

All server-side user item classes should be derived from the COleServerItem class.

CException [CObject→]

The CException class provides the base class for the OLE exception handler classes.

COleException [CObject→CException→]

The COleException class handles exceptions related to OLE operations and includes a public data member holding the status code indicating the reason for the exception.

> Note: Rather than use the COleException class directly, applications should call the AfxThrowOleException handler and use standard exception handling techniques.

COleDispatchException [CObject→CException→COleException→]

The COleDispatchException class handles exceptions specific to the OLE IDispatch interface used in OLE automation. COleDispatchException is intended to be used with the THROW, THROW_LAST, TRY, CATCH, AND_CATCH, and END_CATCH macros.

CFile [CObject→]

The CFile class provides the base class for the OLE stream class, COleStreamFile.

COleStreamFile [CObject→CFile→]

A COleStreamFile class treats a stream of data (IStream) in a compound file as part of OLE2 structured storage. Unless a memory stream is used, the IStorage object must exist before the stream can be opened or created. Other than this, COleStreamFile objects are manipulated exactly like CFile objects.

Associated OLE Classes

The three additional classes used with OLE operations are not derived from the CObject class. The COleDataObject is used for OLE data transfers, the COleDispatchDriver provides the client side for OLE automation, and CRectTracker is used to manipulate in-place editing for objects.

COleDataObject

The COleDataObject class is used to retrieve data in various formats from the Clipboard, through drag-and-drop operations, and from embedded OLE items. Each of these transfers involves both a source, implemented as a COleDataSource object, and a destination, implemented as a COleDataObject.

The COleDataObject class also allows determination of whether the data exists in a specified format, and allows enumerating the available data formats or checking whether a given format is available and then retrieving data in a preferred format.

Data object retrieval can be accomplished in several ways, including the use of a CFile, an HGLOBAL, or an STGMEDIUM structure.

COleDispatchDriver

The COleDispatchDriver class provides the OLE automation client side, providing access to an object's methods and properties. Member functions are used to attach, detach, create, or release an IDispatch connection and provide simplified methods for calling the IDispatch::Invoke function.

COleDispatchDriver can be used directly, but is normally used only by classes created by ClassWizard.

CRectTracker

The CRectTracker class allows in-place items to be displayed, moved, and resized in different fashions.

> Note: Although the CRectTracker class is designed to allow the user to interact with OLE items through a graphical interface, it is not restricted to OLE-enabled applications. You can use the CRectTracker class anywhere such a user interface is required.

MFC Database Classes

The MFC Database classes provide functional access to a variety of database sources with support for recordsets, blobs (Binary Large OBjectS), and record views. The MFC database classes hierarchy is shown in Figure 19.8 and is detailed in the following sections.

Figure 19.8. *The MFC Database classes hierarchy.*

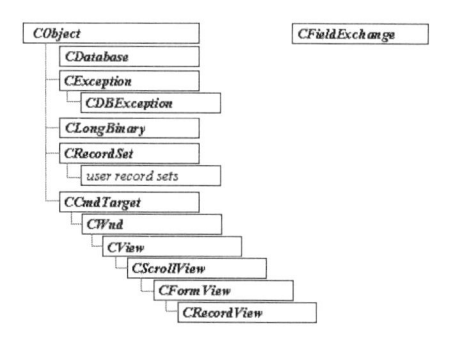

```
CObject              CFieldExchange
  CDatabase
  CException
    CDBException
  CLongBinary
  CRecordSet
    user record sets
  CCmdTarget
    CWnd
      CView
        CScrollView
          CFormView
            CRecordView
```

CDatabase   [CObject→]

The `CDatabase` class provides a connection to a database source such as SQL, Access, dBASE, or xBASE servers and provides methods for opening and accessing supported database systems. Multiple `CDatabase` objects can be active within an application.

CException   [CObject→]

The `CException` class provides the base class for a database exception handler: `CDBException`.

CDBException   [CObject→CException→]

The `CDBException` class handles exception conditions arising from the database classes and includes two public data members that can be used to determine the cause of the exception or to display a text message describing the exception. `CDBException` objects are constructed and thrown by member functions of the database classes.

Exceptions are cases of abnormal execution involving conditions outside the program's control, such as data source or network I/O errors. `CDBException` errors can be accessed in the scope of a `CATCH` expression or can be thrown using the `AfxThrowDBException` global function.

CLongBinary   [CObject→]

The `CLongBinary` class is used to work with very large binary data objects—blobs (Binary Large OBjectS)—in a database such as a record field in an SQL table containing a bitmap image. A `CLongBinary` object handles storage for blobs and tracks their size.

CRecordSet [CObject→]

The `CRecordSet` class encapsulates a set of records selected from a data source as a *recordset*. `CRecordSet` objects can be either dynasets or snapshots.

A *snapshot* recordset is a static recordset reflecting the state of the database at the time of the snapshot. A *dynaset* recordset is synchronized and updated to reflect changes made to the record, either by other users or by other recordsets in the application.

Recordsets permit the following activities:

- Scrolling through the records
- Updating records by adding, editing, or deleting records
- Specifying a locking mode
- Qualifying the selection with a filter to constrain which records are selected from those available on the data source
- Sorting the recordset
- Parameterizing the recordset to customize its selection with information obtained or calculated at run time

`CRecordSet` uses record field exchange (RFX) to support reading and updating of record fields through type-safe C++ members in the `CRecordSet`-derived class.

User Record Sets

User-defined record set classes are derived from the `CRecordSet` class to provide custom methods for reading and updating records.

CRecordView [CObject→...→CScrollView→CFormView→]

The `CRecordView` class provides a form view that is linked directly to a recordset object; the DDX mechanism exchanges data between the recordset and the controls of the record view.

Like all form views, the record view is based on a dialog template resource.

Record views also support moving from record to record in the recordset, updating records, and closing the associated recordset when the record view closes.

CFieldExchange

The `CFieldExchange` class supplies context information to support record field exchange (RFX), which exchanges data between the field and parameter data members of a recordset object and the corresponding table columns on the data source. `CFieldExchange` is similar to the `CDataExchange` class used for dialog data exchange (DDX).

MFC Windows Common Control Classes

The MFC Windows Common Control classes provide a new series of visual control objects for use in dialog boxes. The MFC Windows Common Control classes hierarchy is shown in Figure 19.9 and is detailed in the following sections.

Figure 19.9. *The MFC Windows Common Control classes hierarchy.*

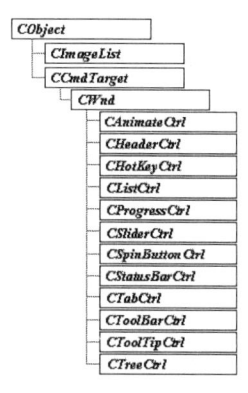

```
CObject
├─ CImageList
└─ CCmdTarget
   └─ CWnd
      ├─ CAnimateCtrl
      ├─ CHeaderCtrl
      ├─ CHotKeyCtrl
      ├─ CListCtrl
      ├─ CProgressCtrl
      ├─ CSliderCtrl
      ├─ CSpinButtonCtrl
      ├─ CStatusBarCtrl
      ├─ CTabCtrl
      ├─ CToolBarCtrl
      ├─ CToolTipCtrl
      └─ CTreeCtrl
```

> Note: All the Windows Common Controls described in the following sections are currently available only under Win95. All these controls are expected to be supported under future versions of WinNT and under Win32 version 1.3 or later.

CImageList [CObject→]

The `CImageList` class provides the Windows common image list control. An *image list* is a collection of same-sized images, each of which can be referred to by its zero-based index. Image lists are used to efficiently manage large sets of icons or bitmaps. All images in an image list are contained in a single, wide bitmap in screen-device format. An image list can also include a monochrome bitmap that contains masks used to draw images transparently (icon style). The Microsoft Win32 application programming interface (API) provides image list functions that enable you to draw images, create and destroy image lists, add and remove images, replace images, merge images, and drag images.

CAnimateCtrl [CObject→CCmdTarget→CWnd→]

The `CAnimateCtrl` class provides an animation control as a rectangular window displaying a simple AVI video clip. Video clips must have the following characteristics:

- ◆ Contain exactly one video stream and have at least one frame
- ◆ Not contain more than two streams; the second stream is normally an audio stream but is ignored by the animation control

- Be either uncompressed or compressed with RLE8 compression
- Not include any palette changes in the video stream
- AVI clips can be added to an application as an AVI resource or may accompany the application as a separate AVI file

CHeaderCtrl [CObject→CCmdTarget→CWnd→]

The CHeaderCtrl class creates a *header control*, a window commonly positioned above columns of text or numbers. Header controls contain a title for each column and can be divided into parts. The header section dividers can be dragged to set the width of each column.

CHotKeyCtrl [CObject→CCmdTarget→CWnd→]

The CHotKeyCtrl class provides a hotkey control dialog box, which is used to define hotkey combinations that can be used to perform actions quickly. The hotkey control displays the user's choices and ensures that only valid key combinations are selected.

CListCtrl [CObject→CCmdTarget→CWnd→]

The CListCtrl class provides a list view control displaying a collection of items, each consisting of an icon and a label with additional, optional information displayed in columns to the right of the icon and label.

CProgressCtrl [CObject→CCmdTarget→CWnd→]

The CProgressCtrl class creates a *progress bar control*, a window used to show the progress of a lengthy operation. The control consists of a rectangle that is filled from left to right, using the system's highlight color to show the progress of an operation.

CSliderCtrl [CObject→CCmdTarget→CWnd→]

The CSliderCtrl class creates a slider control, or trackbar. A *trackbar* is a window containing a slider and optional tick marks; it functions in the same fashion as conventional scrollbar control.

Slider controls are useful for selecting a discrete value or selecting a set of consecutive values within a range.

CSpinButtonCtrl [CObject→CCmdTarget→CWnd→]

The CSpinButtonCtrl class creates the Windows common *spin button control*, also called an *up-down control*. The control consists of a pair of arrow buttons that can be clicked to increment or decrement a value. Spin button operations may control a scroll position or a numerical value displayed in a companion edit box called a *buddy window*.

CStatusBarCtrl [CObject→CCmdTarget→CWnd→]

The CStatusBarCtrl class creates a *status bar control*, a horizontal window normally displayed at the bottom of a parent window to show various types of status information. The status bar control can be subdivided to display several types of information.

CTabCtrl [CObject→CCmdTarget→CWnd→]

The CTabCtrl class creates a tab control that defines multiple tabs, or pages, within a single window or dialog box. Each tab groups a set of controls or a set of information that is displayed when the corresponding tab is selected.

In an alternative form, the tabs are displayed as a series of buttons that perform commands rather than display a tabbed page.

CToolBarCtrl [CObject→CCmdTarget→CWnd→]

The CToolBarCtrl class creates a rectangular child window that contains one or more buttons displaying a bitmap image, a string, or both. When a button is selected, a command message is sent to the toolbar's owner window.

Toolbar buttons frequently correspond to items in the application menu, offering graphic controls for direct access to the application's principal commands.

CToolTipCtrl [CObject→CCmdTarget→CWnd→]

The CToolTipCtrl class creates *tool tip controls*, small popup windows displaying a single line of text to describe the function of an application tool. A *tool* can be a window, such as a child window or control, or any application-defined rectangular area within the client area.

Tool tips remain hidden and appear only when the cursor is positioned on a tool (or area) without moving for approximately 0.5 second. The tool tip appears near the cursor position and disappears as soon as the mouse button is clicked or the cursor is moved away from the tool.

A single tool tip control can provide information for more than one tool.

CTreeCtrl [CObject→CCmdTarget→CWnd→]

The CTreeCtrl class creates a tree view control that displays a hierarchical list of items such as a directory or file tree, an index list, or the outline of a document.

Each item in the tree view consists of a label together with an optional bitmapped image, and may include a list of associated subitems. By clicking on an item, the associated list of subitems—the branch—can be expanded or collapsed.

MFC Windows Socket Classes

The MFC Windows Socket classes allow MFC applications to use Windows Sockets for network communications. The MFC Windows Socket classes hierarchy is shown in Figure 19.10 and is detailed in the following sections.

Figure 19.10. *The MFC Windows Socket classes hierarchy.*

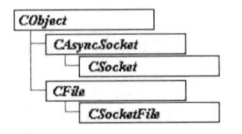

```
CObject
    CAsyncSocket
        CSocket
    CFile
        CSocketFile
```

CAsyncSocket [CObject→]

The CAsyncSocket class creates a Windows Socket object to serve as an endpoint for network communication. CAsyncSocket encapsulates the Windows Sockets version 1.1 API to provide an object-oriented abstraction, allowing programmers to use Windows Sockets in MFC applications.

The CAsyncSocket class is based on the assumption that the programmer understands network communication. Applications using CAsyncSocket objects are responsible for handling blocking, byte-order differences, and conversions between Unicode and multibyte character set (MBCS) strings.

> Note: For a more convenient interface, refer to the CSocket class described in the following section.

CSocket [CObject→CAsyncSocket→]

The CSocket class inherits CAsyncSocket's encapsulation of the Windows Sockets API, but offers a higher level of abstraction and uses the CSocketFile and CArchive classes to handle data transactions. Further, the CSocket class provides blocking, which is essential to CArchive synchronous operations, and avoids errors that could occur using inherited CSocket functions.

CSocketFile [CObject→CFile→]

The CSocketFile class is derived from the CFile class and provides capabilities for sending and receiving data across a network using Windows Sockets by attaching a CSocketFile object to a

CSocket object. CSocketFile objects can also be attached to a CArchive object to handle transactions using MFC serialization.

> Note: The CSocketFile class can also be used as a standalone file object or used with any archive-based serialization functions. Because the CSocketFile class does not support all of CFile's functionality, however, some of the default serialize functions are not compatible.

MFC DAO Classes

The MFC DAO classes work with the other application framework classes to provide convenient access to the DAO (Data Access Object) databases. The DAO databases use the same database engine as Microsoft Visual Basic and Microsoft Access but can also access a variety of databases through ODBC (Open DataBase Connectivity) drivers. The MFC DAO class hierarchy is shown in Figure 19.11 and detailed in the following sections.

> Note: Programs using DAO databases must have a minimum of a CDaoDatabase object and a CDaoRecordset object. The DAO database classes are distinct from the MFC ODBC database classes, even though ODBC data sources can be accessed through DAO classes. The DAO classes also support Data Definition Language (DDL) operations such as adding tables with the classes without calling DAO directly.

Figure 19.11. *The MFC DAO classes hierarchy (version 4.0 only).*

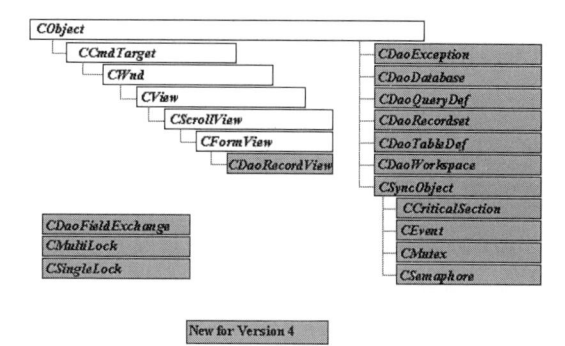

CDaoException (4.0 only) [CObject→]

CDaoException class objects are constructed and thrown by member functions of the DAO database classes and include public data members that can be used to determine the cause of the exception.

CDaoDatabase (4.0 only) [CObject→]

A `CDaoDatabase` class object provides a connection to a database that is used to access the database contents. Each `CDaoDatabase` object operates in a `CDaoWorkspace`, but a workspace can have more than one open database object. Refer to the `GetName` member function for information on the database formats supported.

CDaoQueryDef (4.0 only) [CObject→]

A `CDaoQueryDef` class object represents a query definition or querydef. A *querydef* is a data access object that contains an SQL statement defining the query and its properties and is commonly saved as a database entry. A `CDaoDatabase` object maintains a QueryDefs collection that contains saved querydefs.

CDaoRecordset (4.0 only) [CObject→]

A `CDaoRecordset` class object represents a set of records selected from a data source. Recordsets can take three forms: table-type recordsets, dynaset-type recordsets, and snapshot recordsets.

- **Table recordsets** represent a base table that can be used to examine, modify, or delete records from a single database table.
- **Dynaset recordsets** handle queries that have updatable records and can be used to examine, modify, or delete records from one or more tables in a database. Dynaset recordsets (unlike table or snapshot recordsets) reflect changes to the database after the recordset is opened.
- **Snapshot recordsets** provide a static copy of a set of records that can be examined to extract data or generate reports but not to modify or delete records. A snapshot recordset can contain fields from one or more tables in a database.

CDaoTableDef (4.0 only) [CObject→]

`CDaoTableDef` class objects represent stored definitions of a base table or an attached table. Each DAO database object maintains a TableDefs collection that contains all saved DAO TableDef object instances.

> Tip: To create saved tables, use Microsoft Access to create the tables and store them in the database. Then use the DAO classes to access the TableDef from the database.

CDaoWorkSpace   (4.0 only) [*CObject→*]

CDaoWorkspace class objects are used to manage a single-user, named, password-protected database session—beginning at logon and ending at logoff. In effect, a *workspace* is a transaction manager for a set of open databases in a single transaction space. Rather than opening multiple workspaces and creating explicit workspace objects while opening database and recordset objects, all database operations use the DAO's default workspace. To run multiple sessions, however, multiple workspace objects can be created.

CDaoRecordView   (4.0 only) [*CObject→…→CFormView→*]

The CDaoRecordView class provides a database version of the CRecordSet class, creating a view to display database records in controls. The provided view is a form view directly connected to a CDaoRecordView class instance. The view uses a dialog template resource to display the fields of a CDaoRecordset object. The dialog data exchange (DDX) and DAO record field exchange (DFX) mechanisms are used to automate the exchange of data between form controls and the recordset fields. Default provisions include implementation for selecting the first, next, previous, and last records and for updating the current record.

CSyncObject   (4.0 only) [*CObject→*]

The CSyncObject class is a pure virtual class used to provide common functionality for Win32 synchronization object classes including the CCriticalSection, CEvent, CMutex, and CSemaphore classes.

CCriticalSection   (4.0 only) [*CObject→CSyncObject→*]

CCriticalSection class objects provide synchronization objects to permit a single thread to access a resource or code section. Critical sections are used when only one thread should be permitted to modify data or access a controlled resource such as managing nodes in a linked list. Critical sections are used instead of mutexes in circumstances where speed is a critical factor and the resource will not be used across process boundaries (also refer to "CMutex," later in this chapter).

CEvent   (4.0 only) [*CObject→CSyncObject→*]

The CEvent class objects are used to represent *events*—synchronization objects passed as notifications from one thread to another to report the occurrence of an event. Event notification is necessary to tell a thread when a task should be performed; for example, when new data is available or when another thread has completed a blocking process.

CEvent objects can be manual or automatic. A manual CEvent object retains the state set by the SetEvent or ResetEvent functions until the opposite function is called to change the state. An automatic CEvent object returns to the nonsignaled state (unavailable) after at least one thread is released.

CMutex (4.0 only) [CObject→CSyncObject→]

The CMutex class represents a *mutex*, or a synchronization object permitting a single thread exclusive access to a resource or code section. Mutexes are used when only one thread should be permitted to modify data or access a controlled resource; for example, managing nodes in a linked list (also refer to "CCriticalSection," earlier in this chapter).

CSemaphore (4.0 only) [CObject→CSyncObject→]

The CSemaphore class objects provide a synchronization object to permit a limited number of threads—in one or more processes—to access a particular resource. It also maintains a count of the number of threads that are permitted access, decrementing the count for each thread using the resource and denying access when the count reaches zero.

CDaoFieldExchange (4.0 only)

The CDaoFieldExchange class provide DAO record field exchange (DFX) capabilities for the DAO database classes and is used when writing data exchange routines for custom data types. Otherwise, the CDaoFieldExchange class is not accessed directly.

CMultiLock (4.0 only)

The CMultiLock class provides the access-control mechanism called by the CCriticalSection, CEvent, CMutex, and CSemaphore classes to manage resource access in a multithreaded application. The CMultiLock class is used when multiple objects are involved; the CSingleLock class is used when only one object has limited access.

CSingleLock (4.0 only)

The CSingleLock class provides the access-control mechanism called by the CCriticalSection, CEvent, CMutex, and CSemaphore classes to manage resource access in a multithreaded application. The CMultiLock class is used when multiple objects are involved; the CSingleLock class is used when only one object has limited access.

Summary

In this chapter, you've been offered an overview of the Microsoft Foundation Classes (MFC) supported by both Visual C++ 2.*x* and 4.0. Although this coverage is not comprehensive, additional information and details are available through online documentation. What has been presented in this chapter is a quick reference to all the MFC classes, how the hierarchies are organized, and a few comments on the purpose of each. Hopefully, this will be enough to provide you with a guide to which classes can be used for your application and where to look for the appropriate functionality.

CHAPTER 20

Understanding DLLs and Derived Descendant Classes

In some ways, DLLs and derived descendant classes may sound like two different topics. In practice, however, the two are often very closely linked.

Granted, you create derived descendant classes regularly. Every time you create an application using MFC and AppWizard, several derived classes are created for the application's document and view classes and for other application-specific functional classes. But these are routine, one-time use classes, and are simply a part of programming an application.

But what about creating a derived class to fill some special function you intend to reuse repeatedly, and from which you can derive other application-specific classes?

There is ample reason to do this. It gives you functional code you don't have to keep recreating and, if done properly, doesn't require constant and repeated debugging. You don't have to reinvent the wheel every time you need a cart or a bicycle or a wheelbarrow.

More importantly, if you do it right, your wheel may become a marketable commodity in its own right. But then, how would you distribute it? As source code? (And give away all your trade secrets?) Or are you one step ahead already?

Dynamic Link Libraries

Dynamic link libraries (DLLs) offer a convenient package that serves several purposes. The most obvious is that DLLs allow you to distribute functional program code you can use for your own or other's applications. DLLs are much more than this, however.

A DLL is a library file containing functions that can be called externally by other applications. This, however, is only half the story.

A DLL can optionally contain much more than simple functions. DLLs can also contain application resources including dialog templates, icons, bitmaps, string tables, as well as complete object classes. In addition, object classes contained in DLLs can be used directly or as parents for derived classes, just as has been done in all previous application examples because all the APIs are implemented through dynamic link libraries.

Of course, in previous examples, the use of the DLL sources has been essentially a transparent feature provided by *load-time dynamic linking*, which is discussed in "Load-Time Dynamic Linking," later in this chapter.

The Dynamic Linking Process

Dynamic linking is a process that allows an executable module, which may be either a DLL or an EXE, to locate the executable code for an external DLL function at run time. In essence, the executable module contains information—the name of the dynamic link module and the names of external functions—that allows the external executable to be loaded on demand. Because the executable code is external to the application, multiple applications can share the same executable code, loading it into memory only when and as required, saving overhead both in persistent (disk) storage and in memory.

In contrast, the *static linking* process installs a copy of a library's executable code in the executable module (program) for every application using the library. (Although the original linkers simply incorporated entire libraries into an application, Borland's introduction of the smart linker ensured that only the relevant portions of a static library were incorporated, thus providing considerable space savings.)

Because dynamic link libraries are loaded separately from the executable applications, two load methods are provided for DLLs: load-time dynamic linking and runtime dynamic linking.

Load-Time Dynamic Linking

Load-time dynamic linking, the default process used by Windows applications to link MFC and Win32 DLLs, occurs whenever an application's code makes an explicit call to a function in the DLL. Load-time linking, however, requires the DLL's import library to be linked when the application is created, providing all the necessary information to locate DLL functions.

Using the import library, each DLL function call generates an external function reference in the object code, which is resolved by linking with the DLL's import library. During the link, when an external reference to a DLL function is found, the linker adds information telling the system where the function code is located within the DLL.

When an application containing dynamically linked references is loaded, the system uses the information in the executable program to locate the required DLLs. To do this, the system begins by searching for a set of preinstalled DLLs, including the KERNEL32.DLL performance library and the USER32.DLL security library.

After locating the preinstalled libraries, the system searches for DLLs in sequence, continuing with the following:

1. The directory in which the executable module for the current process is located.
2. The current directory.
3. The Windows system directory, commonly \WINDOWS\SYSTEM. (See the GetSystemDirectory function in online help.)
4. The Windows directory, commonly \WINDOWS. (See the GetWindowsDirectory function in online help.)
5. Other directories in the order listed in the PATH environment variable.

> Note: The LIBPATH environment variable is not searched.

After the DLL library is located, the system maps the DLL modules into the process's address space; if the system can't locate a required DLL, the load process is terminated and a dialog box reports the error.

After mapping the DLL into the process's address space, the system checks for a DllEntryPoint function, which returns a code reporting that the DLL is attaching to the process. Again, if the entry point function fails to return TRUE, the load process is terminated and a dialog box reports the error. (See the section, "The Entry-Point Function," later in this chapter.)

Last, the system modifies the process's executable code to provide addresses for the DLL functions.

> Note: The PRELOAD and LOADONCALL attributes used in DEF files under previous versions of Windows are now irrelevant and have no meaning. Instead, the DLL code is mapped to the process's address space when the process is started; it is loaded into memory when and as required.

Runtime Dynamic Linking

Unlike load-time dynamic linking, *runtime dynamic linking* requires the use of the LoadLibrary and GetProcAddress functions. These functions are used in the DLL_Test program (on the CD-ROM disc that accompanies this book) to retrieve DLL function addresses. The advantage of runtime dynamic linking is that the import library is not required during application linking.

With runtime dynamic linking, an application calls the LoadLibrary function with the name of the required DLL, instructing the system to locate the dynamic link library (see the previous section, "Load-Time Dynamic Linking").

When the DLL is located, the LoadLibrary function returns a handle to the DLL and increments the DLL module's reference count. If the DLL is not located or the DllEntryPoint function fails, the load process reports failure as described in "Load-Time Dynamic Linking."

After the DLL is located, the GetProcAddress function is used to retrieve the required DLL function addresses, linking these to application references.

> Note: When a DLL module has been loaded by one application thread, a second thread can retrieve a handle to the DLL using the GetModuleHandle function without requiring a second load. If separate threads attempt to use the DllEntryPoint function to perform initialization for each thread, however, only the first thread calling the DllEntryPoint function will succeed.

A runtime dynamically loaded module can be discarded when no longer needed by calling the FreeLibrary function, which decrements the module's reference count. If the reference count is zero, the FreeLibrary function unmaps the module from the process space.

Advantages and Disadvantages of Dynamic Linking

Dynamic linking offers a number of advantages over static linking but also has a few minor disadvantages and a couple of, well, idiosyncrasies.

Here are the principal advantages:

- Using DLLs saves memory space and reduces swapping because many different processes can use the same DLL simultaneously, sharing a single memory copy of the DLL.
- DLLs can be modified or updated without recompiling or relinking the calling applications as long as the functions' arguments and return values do not change. In contrast, with statistically linked libraries, the applications must be rebuilt to accommodate any changes in library functions.

- DLLs can be modified to provide after-market support such as modifying the DLL to support a display or other device that was not available when the original application was shipped.
- DLLs can be used by applications written in programming languages other than the language used to construct the DLL.

> Note: Compatibility does, of course, require calling applications to follow the DLL functions' programming conventions. These conventions include the order of arguments supplied (the stack order), whether the DLL function or the calling application is responsible for cleaning up the stack, and whether any arguments are passed in registers rather than as parameters.

Here are some of the disadvantages of using DLLs:

- Applications are not self-contained but depend on the locatable presence of a separate DLL module.
- Processes using load-time dynamic linking are terminated if the DLL is not available at startup.
- Processes using runtime dynamic linking are not terminated if the DLL is not available; the functions provided by the DLL are not available to the application, although they may be designed to use alternative methods in such cases.

Idiosyncrasies involved in DLLs are primarily associated with runtime dynamic linking:

- The capability to query the user for the location of a DLL that is not found in the normal search path. In such situations, the reported path can be stored in an INI file or in a system registry entry for future use.
- The capability to supply the names of the DLLs or the names of functions within a DLL at run time in the following ways: through a configuration file, with a registry entry, or directly by the user. This last avenue (requiring user entry) is not particularly recommended.

Creating a Dynamic Link Library

Creating a dynamic link library using AppWizard is every bit as simple as creating a conventional application. The process begins with Developer Studio's New Project Workspace dialog box, shown in Figure 20.1.

Figure 20.1. *Creating a DLL project.*

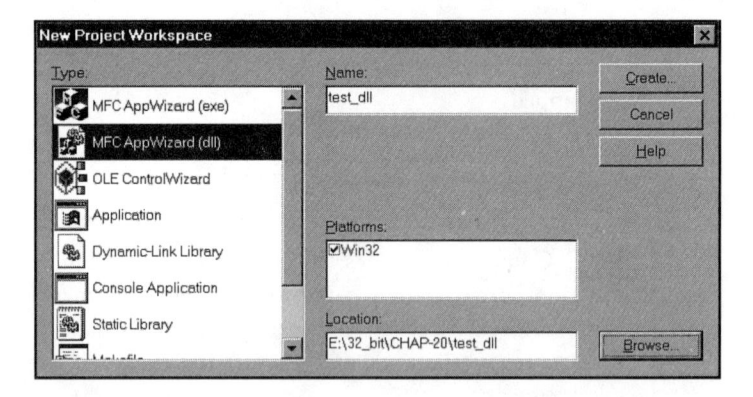

Note that the project Type list includes two DLL formats: MFC AppWizard (dll) or simply Dynamic-Link Library. Either one will do but, because you'll be using MFC classes, choose the MFC AppWizard option for DLLs.

After selecting the MFC AppWizard option, AppWizard has only one set of options to offer, as shown in Figure 20.2.

Figure 20.2. *Step 1 of 1: options for creating a DLL.*

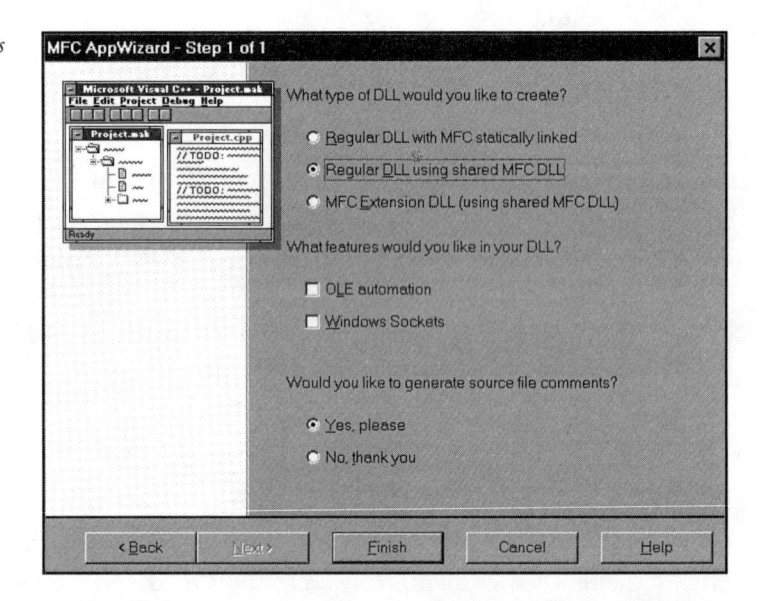

Note that you have the usual choice of using Regular DLL with MFC statically linked, Regular DLL using shared MFC DLL (the default), or MFC Extension DLL (using shared MFC DLL). Because you're creating a DLL anyway, there's no point in padding your DLL with code from the Microsoft Foundation Class library, so you'll certainly stick to using the shared DLL, the default.

Also, you'll ignore the OLE automation and Windows Sockets support because neither is relevant to your present design.

In response, AppWizard creates the files shown in Table 20.1.

Table 20.1. AppWizard-generated DLL source files.

Name	Description
STAR_DLL.MAK	Standard Visual C++ project file.
STAR_DLL.CPP	Main DLL source file includes DllMain() entry point.
STAR_DLL.RC	Resource file that, by default, includes only version resource information. Additional resources such as icons, bitmaps, cursors, dialog, string tables, and so on, can be added.
RES\STAR_DLL.RC2	Standard file for non-Visual C++ resources.
STAR_DLL.DEF	The definition file used to define exported functions as well as the name and description of the DLL.
STAR_DLL.CLW	Information used by ClassWizard to edit existing classes or add new classes.
STDAFX.H, STDAFX.CPP	These files are used to build a precompiled header (PCH) file named STAR_DLL.PCH and a precompiled types file named STDAFX.OBJ.
RESOURCE.H	Standard header file defining resource IDs.

Note that AppWizard does not generate a STAR_DLL.H header. Also note that the STDAFX.H header generated for the DLL is not as brief as those generated for most applications.

Also note the DEF definition file. Although this type of file was standard for Windows applications before MFC, this is the first time a DEF file has been generated for any of the applications in this book. For a dynamic link library, however, the DEF file is necessary.

The **LIBRARY** entry identifies the name of the DLL; the **DESCRIPTION** is optional. A sample DEF listing is shown here:

```
; star_dll.def : Declares the module parameters for the DLL.

LIBRARY        STAR_DLL
DESCRIPTION    'STAR_DLL Windows Dynamic Link Library'

EXPORTS
    ; Explicit exports can go here
    DrawStar
```

The **LIBRARY** identifier aside, the main item in the DEF file is under the **EXPORTS** entry, which is followed by a list of exported functions. Only the functions listed here as exports from the dynamic link library will be accessible to external applications. This list of exported functions must be supplied by the programmer—AppWizard does not have any way of providing these for you because it cannot predict which functions will be exportable.

At the same time, note that the export list (which has a single entry in this example) does not provide any information about calling parameters or arguments, nor does it identify the function's return value. Instead, you create a H header to provide this information:

```
/////////////////////////////////////////
// Start_DLL.h
//

// DLL function prototype(s)

int DrawStar( CDC *pDC, CRect cRect, int nPoints );
```

You use only one exportable function here, DrawStar, which is called with three arguments.

Place the remainder of the DLL in the Star_DLL.CPP source file. You can add include statements for the header you just created and also for the math.H library (because you'll need math functions).

```
// star_dll.cpp : Defines the initialization routines for the DLL.
//

#include "stdafx.h"
#include <afxdllx.h>
#include <math.h>
#include "star_dll.h"

#ifdef _DEBUG
#undef THIS_FILE
static char BASED_CODE THIS_FILE[] = __FILE__;
#endif

static AFX_EXTENSION_MODULE star_dllDLL = { NULL, NULL };
```

The Entry Point Function

The DllMain function, which is not listed in the header or in the EXPORTS list in the DEF file, is an entry point used to initialize or to shut down the dynamic link library. The provided DllMain function has provisions for two messages: DLL_PROCESS_ATTACH and DLL_PROCESS_DETACH.

The following code shows the DllMain function, as generated by AppWizard:

```
extern "C" int APIENTRY DllMain( HINSTANCE hInstance, DWORD dwReason,
                                 LPVOID lpReserved )
{
    if (dwReason == DLL_PROCESS_ATTACH)
    {
        TRACE0("STAR_DLL.DLL Initializing!\n");
        // Extension DLL one-time initialization
        AfxInitExtensionModule(star_dllDLL, hInstance);
        // Insert this DLL into the resource chain
        new CDynLinkLibrary(star_dllDLL);
    }
    else if (dwReason == DLL_PROCESS_DETACH)
```

```
    {
        TRACE0("STAR_DLL.DLL Terminating!\n");
    }
    return 1;    // ok
}
```

The DllMain function is an optional entry point called by the system when processes or threads are initialized or terminated. It is also called when calls are made to the LoadLibrary or FreeLibrary functions.

The hinstDLL parameter provides a handle to the DLL and may be used when calling GetModuleFileName or other module functions.

The fdwReason parameter is a flag specifying why the entry point function is called, and can be one of the four values detailed in Table 20.2.

Table 20.2. Entry point reasons.

Value	Description
DLL_PROCESS_ATTACH	Results from a call to the LoadLibrary function and indicates that the DLL is attaching to the address space of the current process. This provides an opportunity to initialize instance data or to use the TlsAlloc function to allocate a thread local storage index (TLS index).
DLL_THREAD_ATTACH	Indicates that the current process is creating a new thread, and offers an opportunity to initialize a TLS slot for the thread.
DLL_THREAD_DETACH	Indicates that a thread is exiting cleanly. If memory has been allocated for a TLS slot, this is the opportunity to free the memory.
DLL_PROCESS_DETACH	Results from a call to FreeLibrary or because the application is exiting and, therefore, the DLL is detaching from the address space of the calling process and offers an opportunity for the DLL to clean up if necessary.

The lpvReserved parameter specifies additional aspects of DLL initialization and cleanup. On a DLL_PROCESS_ATTACH, lpvReserved is NULL for dynamic loads, and non-NULL for static loads. On DLL_PROCESS_DETACH, lpvReseverd is NULL if the entry point function was called using FreeLibrary; it is non-NULL if the entry point function was called during process termination.

On return, the entry point function, when called with DLL_PROCESS_ATTACH, reports TRUE for success or FALSE on failure. If failure is reported when the entry point is called by the LoadLibrary function, the LoadLibrary function returns NULL. If the entry point reports failure during process initialization, the process terminates with an error (use GetLastError for extended error information).

When the entry point is called with any value except DLL_PROCESS_ATTACH, the return value is ignored.

> Note: The entry point function can simply be ignored by most DLL applications.

Adding a Function to a DLL

You can create one or more new source files to contain your functional code. If you were creating classes, this would be the approach to take, just as has been done in previous examples where multiple source and header files were each devoted to a single object class. In this example, however, because you have only one function and no class objects, you use the STAR_DLL.CPP source file for your code.

Adding a function to a DLL is similar to adding a function to any application. In the example in this chapter, however, you're creating a function for export, to be called by an external application. You've already seen the function name listed under EXPORTS in the DEF file and a function prototype placed in the H header. Now it's time for the body of the function.

The DrawStar function is similar to a routine used in previous examples. Because this is external to the application, the function has a couple of differences.

First, the DrawStar routine is called with a pointer to the calling application's device context, making it possible for the DLL to carry out drawing operations.

Second, although a previous example for the OLE server used the GetClientRect function to get the client rectangle, your exported function does not have the same capability. Therefore, pass the appropriate area in as a CRect argument.

The third and final argument is simply to provide a little versatility by specifying how many points the star should have—information that is specified by the calling application.

The source code for the DrawStar function is given in Listing 20.1.

Listing 20.1. The source code for the DrawStar function.

```
/////////////////////////////////////////////////
// DrawStar() — exported function
//

int DrawStar( CDC * pDC, CRect cRect, int nPoints )
{
    #define PI2 ( 2.0 * 3.1415 )   // radians in 360 degrees //

    int      i, j, k;
    CPoint   cPt[20];

    pDC->TextOut( 0, 0, "   Star_DLL reporting for duty!" );
```

```
    if( nPoints < 10 )  k = (int) nPoints / 2;
    else                k = (int) nPoints / 3;
    for( i=j=0; i<nPoints; i++, j=(j+k)%nPoints )
    {
       cPt[i].x = (int)( sin( j*PI2/nPoints ) * 100 )   - 110;
       cPt[i].y = (int)( cos( j*PI2/nPoints ) * 100 );
    }
    CPen cPen( PS_SOLID, 3, COLORREF(0L) );
    pDC->SelectObject( &cPen );
    pDC->SelectObject( GetStockObject( LTGRAY_BRUSH ) );
    pDC->SetMapMode( MM_ISOTROPIC );
    pDC->SetWindowExt( 440, -220 );
    pDC->SetViewportExt( cRect.Width(), cRect.Height() );
    pDC->SetWindowOrg( -220, 110 );
    pDC->SetPolyFillMode( ALTERNATE );
    pDC->Polygon( cPt, nPoints );
    return TRUE;
}
```

The body of the function is not particularly remarkable and serves only to demonstrate that the DLL is being called and is responding.

Of course, a DLL with a single function is pretty sketchy, but this is only to demonstrate *how*, not *what*.

Calling a DLL

Regardless of why you construct a DLL, you must also have a way to test the DLL. After all, a DLL is not capable of standalone execution; the only way to make sure that it works is to have another application load the DLL and call the exported functions. In this section, you create a simple application, DLL_Test, to load and test the Star_DLL library.

After creating DLL_Test, you'll see how the test application can be used to test the DLL in an interactive, debugging mode.

To create DLL_Test, begin by using AppWizard to create a single document application with no special features.

When AppWizard is finished, open the RC resource script and modify the application menu to add a Points pull-down menu with options for 5, 7, 9, 11, and 13 points.

Then use ClassWizard to provide COMMAND and UPDATE_COMMAND_UI functions for the new menu options.

After an m_nPoints member variable has been added to the CDll_testView class and the new functions have been implemented, add provisions for the DLL. Begin by declaring an instance handle as follows:

```
HINSTANCE  gLibStar_DLL = NULL;
```

Also, because you're using runtime dynamic linking, you need a definition for the DrawStar function, which isn't quite the same as the DrawStar function in the STAR_DLL.H header. Instead, use a typedef format as follows:

```
typedef int (*DRAWSTAR)( CDC*, CRect, int );
DRAWSTAR DrawStar;
```

Because you want the DLL to load when the test application starts, put the DLL load provisions in the view class constructor method, as follows:

```
/////////////////////////////////////////////////////////////////////
// CDll_testView construction/destruction

CDll_testView::CDll_testView()
{
   m_nPoints = 5;
   if( gLibStar_DLL == NULL )
   {
      gLibStar_DLL = LoadLibrary( "STAR_DLL.DLL" );
      if( gLibStar_DLL == NULL )
      {
         CString csMsg;

         csMsg = "Can't load STAR_DLL.DLL. The dynamic link library must ";
         csMsg += "be in your \\WINDOWS\\SYSTEM directory.";
         MessageBox( csMsg );
      }
   }
   DrawStar = (DRAWSTAR)GetProcAddress( gLibStar_DLL, "DrawStar" );
}
```

The gLibStar_DLL variable is defined as an instance handle and is initialized as NULL in the declaration, which makes the first test redundant in this circumstance. Under other circumstances, however, where there might be more than one avenue for calling the LoadLibrary function, this test is appropriate.

Calling the LoadLibrary function with the DLL specification returns a handle to the library instance that, assuming success, is used with the GetProcAddress function to link the DLL's DrawStar function address to your local declaration. This last step is repeated for as many additional DLL functions as necessary.

After the function or functions have been linked, the rest of the test is simply a matter of calling the imported DLL functions and ensuring that they execute correctly. For the purposes of this demonstration, this is simply a matter of calling the DrawStar function from the OnDraw method as follows:

```
/////////////////////////////////////////////////////////////////////
// CDll_testView drawing

void CDll_testView::OnDraw(CDC* pDC)
{
   CDll_testDoc* pDoc = GetDocument();
   ASSERT_VALID(pDoc);
   // TODO: add draw code for native data here
   CRect    cRect;
```

```
    GetClientRect( cRect );
    DrawStar( pDC, cRect, m_nPoints );
}
```

As you can see by experimentation, the DLL function can use the calling application's device context to draw a star with the specified points.

Testing a DLL During Development

Normally, when you develop an application, you rely on the interactive debugging capabilities that allow you to set break points and walk through the code and examine variables during execution. Further, you use this capability to switch back and forth between writing and testing your code, patching and adding features, testing the results, and then revising the code again.

Because the Star_DLL library can't be executed on a standalone basis, however, this development method isn't very useful if you have to exit and load a calling application before trying your development library.

The next best thing is to use the DLL_Test application to test and debug the DLL by specifying the test application in the interactive debugger. Do this by calling the **B**uild, **S**ettings option from the Developer Studio menu; then selecting the Debug tab from the Project Settings dialog box (see Figure 20.3).

> Note: In Visual C++ 2.*x*, select the Project, Settings options from the menu.

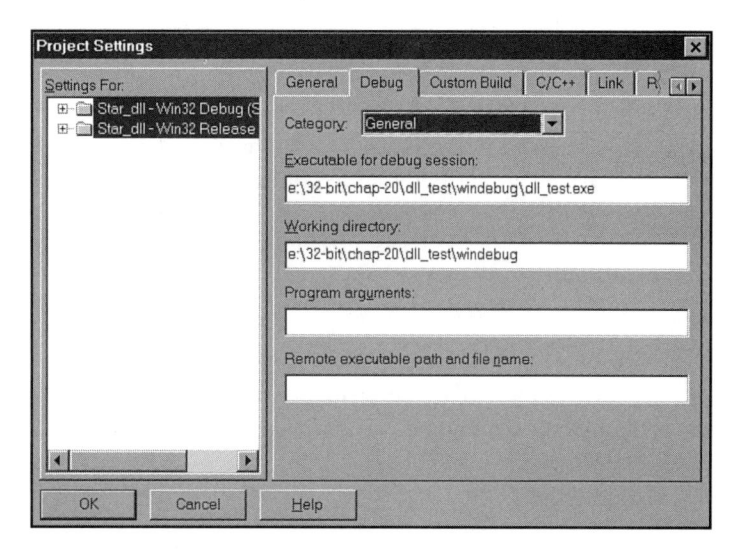

Figure 20.3. Specifying an executable for debugging.

In this dialog box, you enter two specifications: The **E**xecutable For Debug Session field specifies the name and path for the executable test application, DLL_Test.EXE. This is the application you use to test the DLL during development. And because this is the debug version of the executable, you can step into the test program as well as the DLL.

The second specification you enter is in the **W**orking Directory field, which tells the executable where the DLL is located. Without this information, DLL_Test checks its own directory, the system and Windows directories, and the directories in the PATH environment variable before concluding that the DLL can't be found. Alternatively, DLL_Test might find an older version of STAR_DLL in one of these directories and use the old version, instead of the version you're trying to debug.

Other options in the Project Settings dialog box include the Program Arg**u**ments entry, which provides command-line arguments passed to the executable program. The **A**dditional DLLs field allows specification of additional DLLs you might want to step into and test. The debugger loads symbolic information for any DLLs specified here. Finally, the Remote Executable Path and File **N**ame specification identifies the location of an application on a remote computer, which is useful for remote debugging.

With these provisions, debugging a DLL is not particularly different from debugging any other application. It is just a matter of care and patience.

Deriving Descendant Classes

Now that you have a place—that is, a dynamic link library—to create a class library, the next objective is to consider how you would create your own descendant class objects. In one sense, you've been creating descendant class objects in every application demonstrated in this book in the form of derived CDocument, CWinApp, CFrameWnd, CObject, CView, and CRecordset classes, but these have been routine descendant classes required by applications in general.

Now consider creating classes for your own custom purposes, not simply for standard MFC application elements. Of course, the key word here is *purposes*, because *what* the class is used for and *why* determines almost everything, from what base classes, if any, can be used as ancestors to what provisions or special capabilities are included in the class. Still, there are a few standard rules for almost all cases. (There are always exceptions if you look hard enough.)

Beginnings

The first step is to decide what your new class is intended to provide. Because this is theoretical, I begin by proposing a new class called CEncrypt. Briefly, the CEncrypt class will be used to encrypt or decrypt text material.

The CEncrypt class provides a good theoretical example because you can identify an obvious ancestor class, the CString class, to use as a basis for your custom class. One of the big advantages of object-oriented programming is being able to reuse existing code by inheritance from existing classes—and the CString class is an excellent container class for text data. It also offers a lot of functionality.

> Note: Technically, a container class is a `struct` with pretensions. The only real differences, under C++, between a `struct` and a class are quite arbitrary. The differences might be defined by saying that a class contains methods and a `struct` contains only data members. Still, as definitions go, this one is quite arbitrary and more honored in the breach than in the observance.

Because a `CString` instance can hold just under 2 gigabytes of data (assuming that the system has adequate RAM or swap space), this is certainly an adequately large container. Furthermore, because any kind of data can be assigned to a `CString` object, you're not limited to encrypting or decrypting text.

Of course, this is theoretical; for any structured data type, it might be advantageous to create a `CEncryptType` class as well, but this is not an immediate consideration.

Instead, begin by asking yourself what methodology the `CEncrypt` class inherits, what additional methods are needed, and what inherited methods should be overwritten in the new class.

As a base class, the `CString` class defines 40-odd methods and operators for constructing, testing, and manipulating strings—an imposing array of functionality (see Table 4.9 in Chapter 4, "Using Message Boxes").

A look through the list of `CString` methods reveals a variety of methods that do not have any direct application in the new `CEncrypt` class, but does not reveal any that are absolute anathema to the new class.

If used on an encrypted string or data set, several of these methods can quite easily trash the contents of your data. The most obvious potential offenders are the methods identified as Extractions and Other Conversions, but the Windows-Specific functions `AnsiToOem` and `OemToAnsi` can also disrupt your data if they are applied to an encrypted data block.

Still, you're under no obligation to make the new class completely bulletproof—or are you? Bulletproofing is a matter I'll come back to when I show you a second approach by creating an aggregate class (see "Other Methods of Creating a New Class," later in this chapter). For now, the next section looks at what must be added to make your new class operate.

Additions and Methods

Because you can load and extract the contents of the `CEncrypt` buffer using inherited methods, there isn't much need to provide this type of functionality. You need two methods, `Encrypt` and `Decrypt`, each of which can be called with a key to perform the requested task. At the same time, you should probably provide an `IsEncrypted` method to check the status and a `SetStatus` method to set a status member. And, of course, you should also have a Boolean member to store the status.

With these requirements, your Encrypt.H header might look something like this:

```
//========================
// encrypt.h

class CEncrypt : public CString
{
protected:
   BOOL      m_bStatus;
public:
   virtual ~CEncrypt();
   virtual BOOL Encrypt( CString csKeyword );
   virtual BOOL Decrypt( CString csKeyword );
   virtual BOOL IsEncrypted()    { return m_bStatus; };
   virtual BOOL SetStatus( BOOL Status ) { m_bStatus = Status; };
};
```

The result is a pretty simple header, except, of course, that you may find you need additional members as you proceed.

How you implement the two new class methods isn't important; you can use a variety of operations; this is only an example, not a complete implementation. Rather than worry about the details, you can move on to a second approach to creating a new object class.

Other Methods of Creating a New Class

I pointed out that creating the CEncrypt class using the CString class as a base means that you inherit a large number of member functions that are not only irrelevant to the new class but which, if invoked, can trash data.

One approach to preventing inappropriate parent methods from being invoked is to declare the parent private rather than public, as shown here:

```
class CEncrypt : private CString
```

This difference makes the parent class members inaccessible except where a child class member explicitly provides access. By declaring only child members for those functions you want the user to be able to access, the new class becomes pretty well bulletproofed. The down side, of course, is that you must explicitly declare member functions and operators for *all* inherited members that will be public.

Also, although it is possible (and not uncommon) for a descendant class to have two (or more) base classes so that you can inherit functions from all the parents, multiple inheritance has its own problems in sorting out conflicts between parent class methods.

A second, parallel approach is to create an *aggregate class*. In brief, this is simply a new class that does not inherit anything. Instead, it uses instances of another class within the class definition.

Continuing with the CEncrypt class as an example, instead of using CString as a base class at all, simply declare a CString data member, as shown here:

```
//=======================
// encrypt.h

class CEncrypt
{
protected:
   CString  m_csData;
   BOOL     m_bStatus;
public:
   virtual ~CEncrypt();
   virtual BOOL    LoadData( CString csDataIn, BOOL Status );
   virtual CString RetrieveData()    { return m_csData );
   virtual BOOL    Encrypt( CString csKeyword );
   virtual CString Encrypt( CString csDataIn, CString csKeyword );
   virtual BOOL    Decrypt( CString csKeyword );
   virtual BOOL    Decrypt( CString csDataIn, CString csKeyword );
   virtual BOOL    IsEncrypted()    { return m_bStatus; };
   virtual BOOL    SetStatus( BOOL Status ) { m_bStatus = Status; };
};
```

This code sample still uses the CString class as a storage member, but the only function members available from the CString class (or any other class you choose to use in this fashion) are those you provide access to explicitly. Because you're defining the access, you have complete control over how CString is used, leaving no chances for misuse.

Okay, it still isn't 100 percent bulletproof, but it's reasonably "idiot and English-major proof."

You can use as many "nonancestor" classes in your new aggregate class as you want without worrying about conflicts between duplicate methods because all calls to other class methods are explicit.

So, is there a down side to using "nonancestor" classes as well?

Obviously, yes. The biggest down side to this approach is that you sacrifice one of the strengths of object programming: you've aborted the open inheritance process. Any methods you haven't provided direct access to in the present class are not available in any descendant classes.

Reverting to Ancestral Methods

As you derive one object class from another and overwrite existing object methods with new methods to satisfy new circumstances, you sometimes find that you need a method that exists in one ancestor class but that has been replaced with a different method with the same name in a later class (which, nonetheless, is still an ancestor of the current class). This revised method could have been overwritten with new calling parameters, or might have been revised with new functional characteristics that don't exactly suit your present requirements—even though an earlier version of the same method matches your needs.

You could, of course, create another revised method to return to the original functionality, or you could take the easier route of simply invoking the ancestral method directly from the descendant object class instance.

Suppose that you have an object class, CNewClass, derived from COldClass. Both classes have member functions named MyMethod. In the CNewClass version, MyMethod is called with two parameters and performs both a screen and file operation. In this example, however, what you really want is the old MyMethod defined in COldClass, which performs only a screen operation and requires no parameters.

Invoking the earlier method is simple. All that is required is to explicitly reference the original object class by name in your function call, like this:

pNewClass->COldClass.MyMethod()

What could be simpler? This works for any class and any method as long as the ancestral class can be explicitly identified.

Further Considerations

The main consideration in creating any object class is a matter of design. When you're creating an object class, it's entirely too easy to carefully create exactly the methods you plan to use, but to forget to create a complete suite of methods to cover all the possible functions that might be needed at some future time.

Suppose that you've declared a private member variable m_Validation for an encoded date/time and validation stamp. Also suppose that you've defined a SetStamp method and insertion and extraction operators, as well as a validation function which checks a stamp against a record.

But have you also created both a GetStamp method and a set of comparison and assignment operators? You aren't planning to use these immediately, but m_Validation is private. If you later derive a descendant class that does have to perform comparisons or assignments, you won't have access unless these functions were defined in the parent class or, of course, unless you have the source code for the parent class and can modify it. That defeats the basic concept of inheritance and object class design.

The real point in creating any object class is that you provide complete access and functionality—not by making all your data members public, but by ensuring that you have created full access functions, whether you plan to use them now or not.

Although it's a little extra work, a little extra now can save a lot of work later. An old case of an ounce of prevention....

Summary

Object-oriented development aside, dynamic link libraries are probably the biggest single advance in programming in the past decade—and one of the simplest. Granted, static libraries have been around almost forever. Even though new hard drives and megabytes of addressable RAM have loosened the penalties on bloated code, the current move is toward shared functionality, with OLE2 and DLLs at the heart of the process.

In using DLLs, you have a choice between load-time and runtime dynamic linking, with the former the more popular choice. But both have advantages. Whichever load process you prefer, the DLLs themselves are the same both in design and in internal implementation.

As you develop a DLL, remember that Visual C++ offers excellent debugging capabilities using an executable to call the DLL, allowing you to step through exported functions as easily as you step through internal functions in a conventional application.

Last, DLLs give you an ideal container in which you can develop custom object classes, whether these are derived from existing classes or entirely from scratch. DLLs make them available to applications without the penalties of bloated code and bloated executables.

In Chapter 21, "Tracing and Debugging Classes," you look at tracing object classes and the various tools provided by Visual C++ and used within the Developer Studio for exploring object classes and applications during development.

CHAPTER 21

Tracing and Debugging Classes

One of the problems inherent in using the Microsoft Foundation Classes—or any other collections of object classes, including those you create or import from other sources—is simply that you're dealing with multiple layers of functional code. Too often, the layers in which your problems occur may be several layers back in the object ancestry.

Of course, this doesn't mean you have to dig back through the layers to patch ancestral source code (at least, I certainly hope not). But it often means you have to trace back through the inherited code to find out what has happened and why. You may have to make this trek to find out precisely what the ancestral code is expecting that you haven't supplied—or haven't supplied correctly.

Toward this end, this chapter looks at Developer Studio's debugging tools and how these tools can be used to uncover both features and idiosyncrasies of object classes.

The Developer Studio Tool Set

As an interactive debugger, both Visual C++ (version 2.*x*) and Developer Studio (version 4.0) offer a generous variety of tools that allow you not only to watch the execution of an application while stepping through the source code, but also to observe the values of individual variables (or even to change those values). You can also use the tools to trace the flow of execution across multiple source files.

Although it seems reasonable to assume that most readers are familiar with the Visual C++ environment, and particularly with the source code editor features, some mention of the less-familiar features and their uses is in order.

Figure 21.1 shows a typical Developer Studio debugging session with four of the eleven possible windows opened. Beginning at the top, the open windows are the Call Stack, Debug, Locals, and Watch windows.

> Note: Developer Studio offers a choice of four Watch windows (tab-selected); earlier versions of Visual C++ provided only one Watch window. The advantage, of course, is that different groups of watch variables can be assigned on different tabs so that you can switch to the appropriate tab while walking through the application.

Figure 21.1. The Visual C++ debugger.

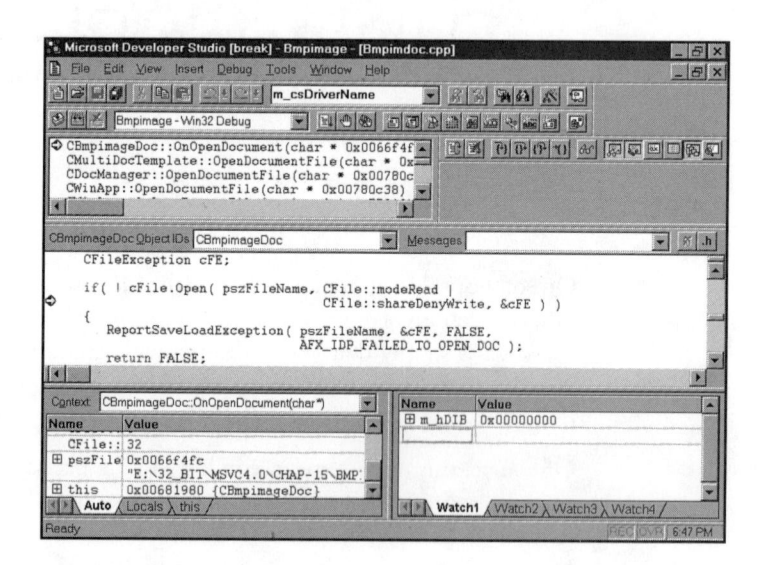

Of these windows, the Debug window (the middle window, showing the program source code) should be familiar because it is essentially the same as the conventional edit window. The only real difference is that, while you are debugging, this window always focuses on the current source file; as you step through execution, this window displays a small arrow (at the left margin) to indicate the program line to be executed next.

At the same time, a red dot in the left margin indicates a *breakpoint*, a point in the application source at which you have instructed the compiler to stop execution. Again, this should be a familiar practice with no particular surprises. These Debug toolbar action buttons should also be familiar to most programmers; from left to right, the buttons are the Restart and Stop Debugging buttons, and the Step Into, Step Over, Step Out, and Run To Cursor buttons.

What may not be as familiar are the uses of the various debug windows.

The Locals window (at the bottom left of Figure 21.1) should be relatively familiar because this window opens automatically any time you enter debugging mode. As you step through an application, the Locals window shows all variables local to the current function, including object class instances and conventional variables. More important, by double-clicking a variable in the Locals window, you can expand the variable listing to view additional layers of detail.

The Watch window (at the bottom right of Figure 21.1) is similar to the Locals window except that the Watch window displays only the variables you've requested. These variables are not, however, limited to variables local to the current subprocedure. Instead, if you set a watch on a variable that is now out of scope, you are advised `Error: expression cannot be evaluated`.

The Quick Watch Window

Alternatively, you can select an item in the Watch window or the Debug window and click the Quick Watch button in the Debug toolbar. The Quick Watch window appears (see Figure 21.2).

Figure 21.2. Examining a variable in the Quick Watch window.

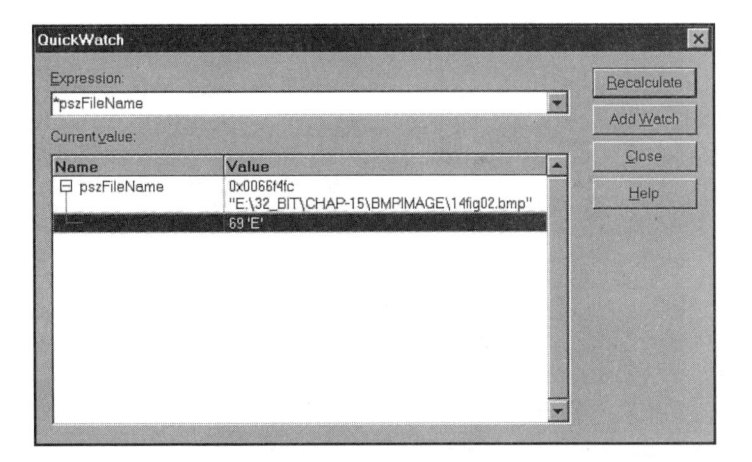

In this figure, the Quick Watch window is used to examine a variable: the `pszFileName` argument being passed to the `cFile.Open()` function.

> Note: In Visual C++ version 2.x, the Locals and Watch windows allow you only to examine variables; however, the Quick Watch window has the added advantage of allowing you to change the value of a variable.

> In Visual C++ version 4.0, this capability is retained but in a somewhat crippled form. For example, using version 2.x, the pszFileName string can be easily edited. In version 4.0, however, the edit feature both in the QuickWatch and the Watch windows allow you to edit the memory address of the variable—but not the contents of the array. (And, of course, it's the array contents we're more likely to want to edit. Changing the address of the array is pretty pointless, unless your point is to make the application crash.)

In addition to examining a variable, the Quick Watch window has a second powerful use, as shown in Figure 21.3. In this figure, an object class instance, cFile, is the target of the watch. Here, Quick Watch offers you a view of the cFile instance, which includes all member variables plus the base and exception (next) classes, both of which can be expanded further to see details of these classes.

Figure 21.3. *Examining a class using the Quick Watch window.*

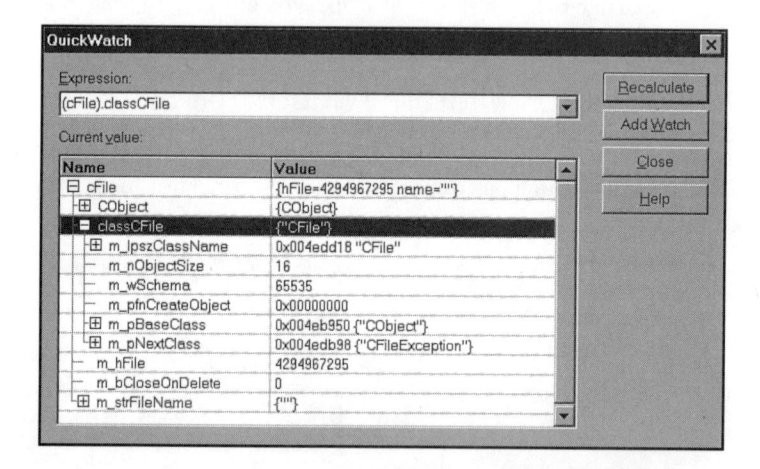

> Note: In Visual C++ version 2.x, the Quick Watch window allows you to select a class such as cFile—rather than being limited only to class instances. The advantage is that you cannot only see all aspects of the class—both functional members and data members—you can also see the class ancestry as, for example, the CObject and CRuntimeClass ancestors. By double-clicking either of these members (or any other member indicated as expandable by a + sign), you can view the details of the ancestor class. You can continue viewing details of ancestor classes as far back as you want—assuming, of course, that you have debug sources to supply the data.
>
> Unfortunately, this capability has been lost in version 4.0; attempting to watch a class rather than a class instance simply shows the constructor method for the class.

> Tip: Be careful what changes you make with the Quick Watch window. Although values can be altered with relative impunity, attempts to change addresses can adversely affect your operating system. If you are operating under WinNT, an invalid address normally terminates your application. Under Win95, however, an invalid address may terminate operations entirely and require a reboot.

The Call Stack Window

The Call Stack window (at the top of Figure 21.1) shows a list of the function calls leading up to the current statement. The *current statement* is the point in the program at which you have halted execution, by stepping through the application, by setting a break point, or because a TRY...CATCH exception has caused a break.

The Call Stack window lists functions in reverse order, with the currently executing statement at the top. The window shows each call with the arguments and argument types passed to each. The following example shows a call to the OpenDocumentFile member in the CMultiDocTemplate class as well as the values of the calling parameters:

`CMultiDocTemplate::OpenDocumentFile(char * 0x0060f400, int 1) line 146 + 15 bytes`

The first value is an address for a character array; you can use the memory window (refer to "The Memory Window," later in this chapter) to check the address or you can step back in the code and look at the argument directly using Quick Watch.

Instead of simply observing the stack, you can double-click any item in the stack to go to that point in the source code—whether that point is in your application source code, in an MFC library, or anywhere else—so that you can examine the events preceding the break.

When you use the stack to step back, you are not undoing execution, you are only viewing a snapshot of what has already happened. When you step back, the statement you step back to is highlighted in green in the stack list; a green arrowhead marks the position in the source code; and the Locals and Watch windows show the values of variable and arguments at that point.

By stepping back in the source code using the Call Stack list, you can also select an earlier point at which you want to assign a break so that you can trace forward. Remember that an exception break only tells you where the exception was discovered—the cause may lie somewhere further back in the application.

The Call Stack window offers a shortcut menu activated by right-clicking anywhere in the window. The shortcut menu offers the following options:

Option	Description
Copy	Copies the stack item at which the cursor is positioned to the Clipboard as text.
Go To Code	Jumps to the selected point in the source code, opening a source code file if necessary.
Insert/Remove Breakpoint	Toggles the breakpoint setting at the current location in the source code.
Parameter Values	If checked (default), parameter values are displayed in the Call Stack window.
Parameter Types	If checked (default), parameter types are displayed in the Call Stack window.
Docking View	If checked (default), the Call Stack window is displayed as a small, docked view. If deselected, the Call Stack window is expanded to a full window.
Hide	Closes (conceals) the Call Stack window. The Call Stack window can be reopened by right-clicking the Debug toolbar and selecting the Call Stack option from the View menu.

Other Debug Options

The Visual C++ debugger offers a number of options which, though useful, are not commonly selected. The Debug toolbar offers six buttons; from left to right, they are for the Watch, Locals, Registers, Memory, Call Stack, and Disassembly windows. Right-click anywhere on the Debug toolbar to display the shortcut menu, which duplicates these window options and offers additional choices.

The Output window with its Build, Debug, Find In Files, and Profile tabs isn't usually required during debug operations. It is normally displayed during edit, compile, and link operations.

The bottom half of the Debug toolbar's shortcut menu offers the Standard, Edit, Resource, Debug, and Browse options. Use these options to display or hide toolbars; the Standard and Debug toolbars are displayed by default. The remaining toolbars (in this context, at least) suggest more "creeping featurism" than any real utility.

The Registers and Memory windows, however, can be quite useful—even if they're needed only occasionally.

The Memory Window

The Memory window allows you to view the contents of a memory location in a mixed hex-and-ASCII format (see Figure 21.4). By default, memory locations begin at the base address 0x0001 0000; you can position the Memory window at a specific location by entering a reference (either a variable name or an address) in the **A**ddress field.

You can also use the Memory window to edit memory directly simply by positioning the cursor on the appropriate location in the Memory window and entering a new value. In the default (byte) display, you can edit the hex values at the left or the ASCII values at the right. Any key entries that do not fit the display format are ignored.

Figure 21.4. The Memory window.

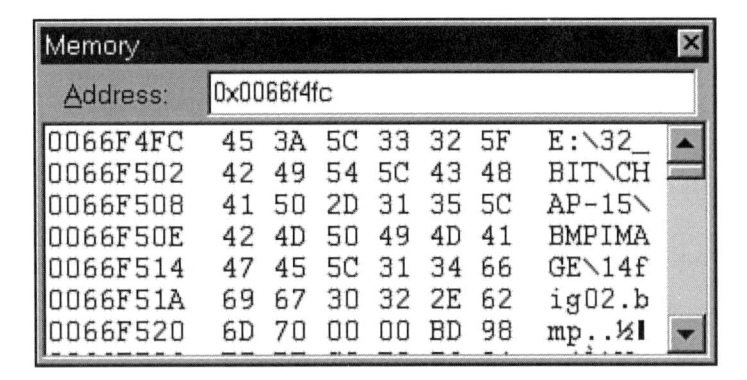

Address: 0x0066f4fc		
0066F4FC	45 3A 5C 33 32 5F E:\32_
0066F502	42 49 54 5C 43 48 BIT\CH
0066F508	41 50 2D 31 35 5C AP-15\
0066F50E	42 4D 50 49 4D 41 BMPIMA
0066F514	47 45 5C 31 34 66 GE\14f
0066F51A	69 67 30 32 2E 62 ig02.b
0066F520	6D 70 00 00 BD 98 mp..½¦

Right-click any where in the Memory window to display a shortcut menu with options for changing the display format, changing the window position or size, and concealing the Memory window.

The Registers Window

The Registers window, shown in Figure 21.5, displays both the contents of the native CPU registers and flags and the floating point stack. The value of any register or flag can be changed during debugging by selecting the register, flag, or floating point stack and entering a new value. Changed entries are highlighted in red.

> Tip: Press Ctrl+Z to undo changes in the Registers window.

Right-clicking any where in the Registers window to display a shortcut menu with options for concealing the floating point registers, changing the docking view to a standard window, and concealing the Registers window.

Figure 21.5. The Registers window.

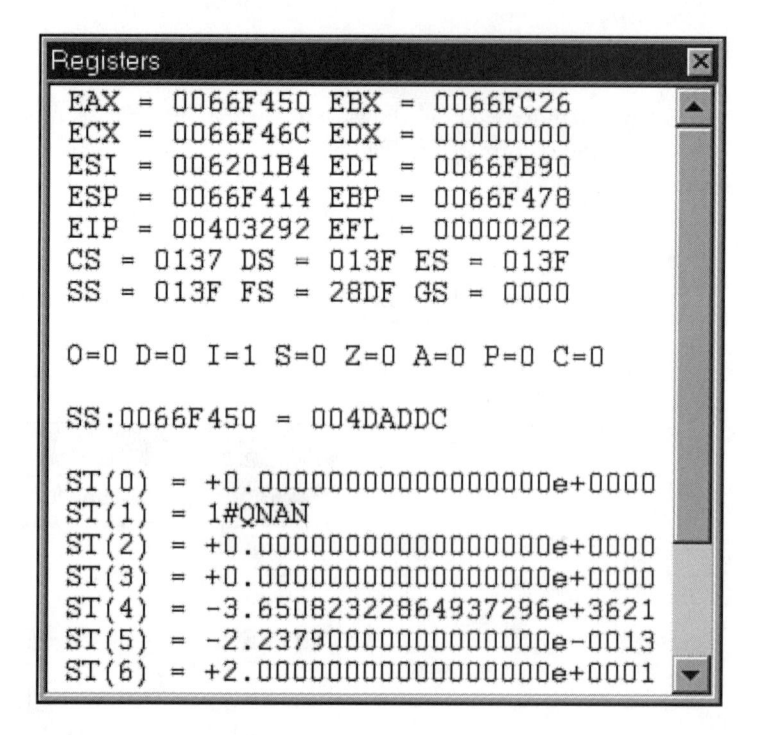

```
Registers
EAX = 0066F450   EBX = 0066FC26
ECX = 0066F46C   EDX = 00000000
ESI = 006201B4   EDI = 0066FB90
ESP = 0066F414   EBP = 0066F478
EIP = 00403292   EFL = 00000202
CS = 0137   DS = 013F   ES = 013F
SS = 013F   FS = 28DF   GS = 0000

O=0  D=0  I=1  S=0  Z=0  A=0  P=0  C=0

SS:0066F450 = 004DADDC

ST(0) = +0.000000000000000000e+0000
ST(1) = 1#QNAN
ST(2) = +0.000000000000000000e+0000
ST(3) = +0.000000000000000000e+0000
ST(4) = -3.65082322864937296e+3621
ST(5) = -2.23790000000000000e-0013
ST(6) = +2.00000000000000000e+0001
```

Summary

This chapter covered the tracing and debugging of classes. Sorry that there are no deep secrets to doing so. There are just a relatively easy-to-use set of tools to provide you, the programmer, with the insight to discover *what* is available and *where* something is wrong.

Why something is wrong is another matter entirely and depends on your insights. Perhaps you've passed a pointer where a value was expected (or passed a value where a pointer was needed). Perhaps you used a parameter that wasn't initialized properly, or you are trying to use something before it exists (such as trying to initialize a window before the window has been created). All these mistakes are easy to make and can be difficult to discover.

With the debugging tools introduced in this chapter, you can look inside the execution of your application to see what is actually happening. But be careful: it's also easy to see what you expect to see instead of what is actually there.

Index

SYMBOLS

& (ampersand), menu hotkeys, 124, 126
<< (insertion) operator, 385-386
>> (extraction) operator, 385-386
~ (tilde), 91
... (ellipses), popup menu entries, 126-127
16-bit operating systems
    compared to 32-bit, 9-10
    thunking, 62-65
32-bit application development, 17-24
    build process, 18-19
    Microsoft Developer Studio, 20-24
        AppStudio resource editor, 24
        AppWizard, 23
        ClassWizard, 23
        linker, 24
        Project Workspace dialog box, 21-23
        resource compiler, 24
        Source Browser, 24
        Visual C++ compiler, 23
32-bit disk access, 16
32-bit operating systems
    compared to 16-bit, 9-10
    thunking, 62-65

A

AARL_HAM example application (file I/O), 390-396
    GetEntry function, 394-396
    overloaded operators, 393-394
    reading/writing CArchive records, 392-393
    UpdateData function, 396
AARL3 example application (ODBC), 405-408
absolute RGB COLORREF, 307
accelerator keys, 109, 126
accessing files, 378-382
    AARL_HAM example application, 390-396
        GetEntry function, 394-396
        overloaded operators, 393-394

reading/writing CArchive records, 392-393
UpdateData function, 396
CArchive class, 383, 386-388, 451
CFile class, 378-380, 449, 483
    flags, 381-382
    opening files, 380-381
CStdioFile class, 389-390, 449
insertion/extraction operators, 385-386
random file access, 388-389
serialization, 382-386
    customizing, 383-385
Add Property dialog box (OCX controls), 212-214
adding
    functions to DLLs (dynamic link libraries), 506-507
    nodes to tree view control, 165-167
    properties to OCX controls, 211-214
addressable memory, 12
AFX (Windows Application Frameworks), naming convention prefixes, 53-54, 57
AfxMessageBox function, 85
aggregate classes, 512-513
Alternate fill mode, 340
ambient properties (OCX controls), 190
ampersand (&), menu hotkeys, 124, 126
ancestral class methods, invoking, 513-514
animation controls, 181-187
AVI files
    creating, 185-186
    requirements, 181-182
creating, 182-185
notification messages to parent windows, 185

APIs (application programming interfaces)
CopyBlock API, 370-371
CreateDIBPalette API, 370
GetColorCount API, 370
PaintDIB API, 367-370
ReadDIBFile API, 365-366
SaveDIBFile API, 366-367
Application Architecture classes (MFC), 447, 467-470
associated object classes, 470
message handling, 60
application development, 17-24
build process, 18-19
Microsoft Developer Studio, 20-24
    AppStudio resource editor, 24
    AppWizard, 23
    ClassWizard, 23
    linker, 24
    Project Workspace dialog box, 21-23
    resource compiler, 24
    Source Browser, 24
    Visual C++ compiler, 23
application files, 111-114
application frames, Windows 95 compared to Windows NT, 61
application menus (OLE servers), 443-444
Application Modal message boxes, 84
application resources, 107-108
accelerator keys, 109
AppStudio, 115
compiling/linking, 113
creating, 108-109, 116
dialog boxes, 109
editing as binary data, 117
fonts, 110
image resources, 110
importing/exporting, 117

menus, 110-111
Set Includes dialog box, 118
string resources, 111
Symbol Browser dialog box, 118
version information, 111
applications
creating, 27-50
    New Project dialog box, 30-32
    New Project Information dialog box, 42
    ODBC applications, 399-405
    project skeleton, 42-44
    ReadMe.TXT file, 45-46
    selecting file types, 28-29
    skeletal application, modifications, 47-50
    Step 1 (Architecture) dialog box, 32-33
    Step 2 (Database Options) dialog box, 33-34
    Step 3 (OLE Support) dialog box, 35-36
    Step 4 (Application Features) dialog box, 36-39
    Step 5 (Source Code Options) dialog box, 39-40
    Step 6 (Class Name Options) dialog box, 41
integrating
    Clipboard, 411-412
    DDE (Dynamic Data Exchange), 412
    metafiles, 412
migrating (MFC Migration Kit), 72
AppStudio, 24, 115
AppWizard, 23
creating
    ODBC applications, 399-405
    OLE servers, 429-430

file types, 111-114
generating DLL source files, 503
naming convention prefixes, 57
APS file extension, 112
Arc tool, 331, 335-337
architectures, Step 1 (Architecture) dialog box, creating applications, 32-33
archive methods, 97
ArcTo tool, 331
array collection classes, 471-472
Aspect dialog boxes, 282
ASPECTX flag, 265
ASPECTXY flag, 265
ASPECTY flag, 265
assigning member variables to dialog boxes, 146-147
assignment operators, CString class, 96
available addressable memory, 12
AVI (Audio Video Interleaved) files, 181-187
animation controls
creating dialog boxes, 182-185
requirements, 181-182
CAVICtrl class, 186-187
creating, 185-186

B

Bar (menu break setting), 126
Beacon Hill Software, Snapshot3, 352
Bézier curves, 343-344
BI_RLE4 image compression, 362-363
BI_RLE8 image compression, 364
binary data, editing application resources as, 117

Bitmap command (New menu), 128
bitmap images, 110
BmpImage demo program, 371-373
compression
BI_RLE4, 362-363
BI_RLE8, 364
creating toolbar bitmaps, 127-129
ImageAPI, 365
CopyBlock API, 370-371
CreateDIBPalette API, 370
GetColorCount API, 370
PaintDIB API, 367-370
ReadDIBFile API, 365-366
SaveDIBFile API, 366-367
writing to disk files, 358-362
see also BMP image format
BITMAPCOREINFO structure, 350-351
BITMAPINFO structure, 350-351
BITMAPINFOHEADER structure, 349-350
BITSPIXEL flag, 265
black brushes, 327
black pens, 324
BLTALIGNMENT flag, 266
BMP file extension, 113
BMP image format
BITMAPINFO structure, 350-351
compared to DIB, 348
BOOL data type, 54
break settings (menus), 126
breaks (menus), 127
brushes, 327-329
CBrush::CreateDIBPatternBrush method, 330
CBrush::CreateSolidBrush method, 331
creating, 330-331

deleting, 327
hatch patterns, 329-330
BSC file extension, 112
buffer access methods, CString class, 98
build process, application development, 18-19
bulletproofing classes, 512-513
buttons
dialog box toolbar buttons, 144-145
Dialog_1 (message box example), reporting selections, 92-95
message boxes, 81-82
BYTE data type, 54

C

C applications, migrating to Visual C++ (MFC Migration Kit), 72
CAboutDlg class, Dialog_1 (message box example), 87
Call Stack window (Developer Studio), 521-522
CALLBACK macro, 55
calling DLLs (dynamic link libraries), 507-509
CAnimateCtrl class, 181-187, 487-488
AVI files
creating, 185-186
requirements, 181-182
creating, 182-185
notification messages to parent windows, 185
Capture utility, 352-353
capturing screen images, 352
Capture utility, 352-353
CCaptureView::CaptureScreen procedure, 355-357
initialization, 353-374
OnImageDisplay procedure, 354-355

Snapshot3 (Beacon Hill Software), 352
viewing Clipboard contents, 357-358
WriteToFile procedure, 358-362
CArchive class, 383, 386-388, 451
   AARL_HAM example application, reading/writing records, 392-393
CArchiveException class, 450
CArray class, 471
CAsyncSocket class, 490
CAVICtrl class, 186-187
CBitmap class, 456
CBitmapButton class, 458
CBrush class, 456
   CreateDIBPatternBrush method, 330
   CreateSolidBrush method, 331
CButton class, 458
CByteArray class, 471
CCaptureView::CaptureScreen procedure, 355-357
CCheckListBox class, 463
CClientDC class, 455
CCmdTarget class, 455, 467
CCmdUI class, 470
CColorDialog class, 230-231, 460
CComboBox class, 458-459
CCommonDialog class, 460, 478
CControlBar class, 459, 480
CCreateContext class, 466
CCriticalSection class, 493
CCtrlView class, 465
CDaoDatabase class, 492
CDaoException class, 491
CDaoFieldExchange class, 494
CDaoQueryDef class, 492
CDaoRecordset class, 492
CDaoRecordView class, 493

CDaoTableDef class, 492
CDaoWorkspace class, 493
CDatabase class, 485
CDataExchange class, 467
CDBException class, 450, 485
CDC class, 455
CDialog class, 460, 478
CDialog_1App class, 87
CDialog_1Doc class, 87
CDialog_1View class, 87
CDialogBar class, 459
CDK (OLE Custom Development Kit), installing, 191-192
CDocItem class, 481
CDocTemplate class, 468-469
CDocument class, 467-468, 480
CDragListBox class, 463
CDumpContext class, 453
CDWordArray class, 472
CEdit class, 461
CEditView class, 465
CEncrypt class, deriving descendent classess, 510-513
CEvent class, 493-494
CException class, 449, 483, 485
CFieldExchange class, 486
CFile class, 378-380, 449, 483
   flags, 381-382
   opening files, 380-381
CFileDialog class, 244-250, 460
CFileException class, 450
CFileStatus class, 451
CFindReplaceDialog class, 252-256, 460
CFont class, 456
CFontDialog class, 230-231, 461
CFormView class, 466
CFrameWnd class, 462, 478
CGA display standard, 298
CGdiObject class, 456
CHeaderCtrl class, 488

Checked (menu item property checkbox), 125
child dialog boxes, connecting tab controls to, 176-179
CHOOSECOLOR structure, 241-244
CHOOSEFONT structure, 236-241
Chord tool, 331, 335-337
CHotKeyCtrl class, 488
CImageList class, 487
CInPlaceFrame class, creating OLE servers, 433-435
classes
   aggregate classes, 512-513
   bulletproofing, 512-513
   CAboutDlg, Dialog_1 (message box example), 87
   CAnimateCtrl, 181-187, 487-488
      AVI file requirements, 181-182
      AVI files, creating, 185-186
      creating, 182-185
      notification messages to parent windows, 185
   CArchive, 383, 386-388, 451
      AARL_HAM example application, 392-393
   CArchiveException, 450
   CArray, 471
   CAsyncSocket, 490
   CAVICtrl, 186-187
   CBitmap, 456
   CBitmapButton, 458
   CBrush, 456
   CButton, 458
   CByteArray, 471
   CCheckListBox, 463
   CClientDC, 455
   CCmdTarget, 455, 467
   CCmdUI, 470
   CColorDialog, 230-231, 460

classes

CComboBox, 458-459
CCommonDialog, 460, 478
CControlBar, 459, 480
CCreateContext, 466
CCriticalSection, 493
CCtrlView, 465
CDaoDatabase, 492
CDaoException, 491
CDaoFieldExchange, 494
CDaoQueryDef, 492
CDaoRecordset, 492
CDaoRecordView, 493
CDaoTableDef, 492
CDaoWorkspace, 493
CDatabase, 485
CDataExchange, 467
CDBException, 450, 485
CDC, 455
CDialog, 460, 478
CDialog_1App, 87
CDialog_1Doc, 87
CDialog_1View, 87
CDialogBar, 459
CDocItem, 481
CDocTemplate, 468-469
CDocument, 467-468, 480
CDragListBox, 463
CDumpContext, 453
CDWordArray, 472
CEdit, 461
CEditView, 465
CEncrypt, deriving descendent classess, 510-513
CEvent, 493-494
CException, 449, 483, 485
CFieldExchange, 486
CFile, 378-380, 449, 483
   flags, 381-382
   opening files, 380-381
CFileDialog, 244-250, 460
CFileException, 450
CFileStatus, 451
CFindReplaceDialog, 252-256, 460
CFont, 456
CFontDialog, 230-231, 461

CFormView, 466
CFrameWnd, 462, 478
CGdiObject, 456
CHeaderCtrl, 488
CHotKeyCtrl, 488
CImageList, 487
CInPlaceFrame, creating OLE servers, 433-435
CList, 472-473
CListBox, 463
CListCtrl, 488
CListView, 465
CLongBinary, 485
CMainFrame, Dialog_1 (message box example), 87
CMap, 473
CMapPtrToPtr, 474
CMapPtrToWord, 474
CMapStringToOb, 474
CMapStringToPtr, 474
CMapStringToString, 474
CMapWordToOb, 474
CMapWordToPtr, 474
CMDIChildWnd, 462
CMDIFrameWnd, 462
CMemFile, 449
CMemoryException, 450
CMemoryState, 453
CMenu, 457
CMetafileDC, 456
CMiniFrameWnd, 463
CMultiDocTemplate, 469
CMultiLock, 494
CMutex, 494
CNotSupportedException, 450
CObArray, 472
CObList, 473
COle_cntrCntrItem, 422-423
COle_cntrView, 420-422
COle_srvrApp, creating OLE servers, 436
COle_srvrSrvrItem, creating OLE servers, 431-433

COle_srvrView, creating OLE servers, 438-442
COleBusyDialog, 480
COleChangeIconDialog, 479
COleClientItem, 422-423, 481
COleControl, 191
COleConvertDialog, 479
COleDataObject, 484
COleDataSource, 477
COleDialog, 479
COleDispatchDriver, 484
COleDispatchException, 483
COleDocument, 481
COleDropSource, 477
COleDropTarget, 478
COleException, 450, 483
COleInsertDialog, 479
   selecting OLE servers, 425-426
COleIPFrameWnd, 478
COleLinkingDoc, 481
COleLinksDialog, 480
COleMessageFilter, 478
COleObjectFactory, 481
COlePasteSpecialDialog, 479
COlePropertiesDialog, 479
COleResizeBar, 480
COleServerDoc, 481
COleServerItem, 482
COleStreamFile, 483-484
COleTemplateServer, 481
COleUpdateDialog, 480
common dialog box class equivalents, 230
constructor methods, 91
CPageSetupDialog, 461
CPaintDC, 456
CPalette, 457
CPen, 456
CPoint, 451
CPrintDialog, 461

classes

CPrintInfo, 250-251, 470
CProgressCtrl, 488
CPropertyPage, 461
CPropertySheet, 463
CPtrArray, 472
CPtrList, 473
CRecordSet, 486
CRecordView, 466, 486
CRect, 452
CRectTracker, 484
CResourceException, 450
CRgn, 457
CRichEditCntrItem, 482
CRichEditDoc, 482-483
CRichEditView, 465
CRunTimeClass, 453-454
CScrollBar, 463
CScrollView, 466
CSemaphore, 494
CSingleDocTemplate, 469
CSingleLock, 494
CSize, 452
CSliderCtrl, 488
CSocket, 490
CSocketFile, 490-491
CSpinButtonCtrl, 488-489
CSplitterWnd, 464
CStatic, 464
CStatusBar, 459
CStatusBarCtrl, 489
CStdioFile, 389-390, 449
CString, 93, 95-98
CStringArray, 472
CStringList, 473
CSyncObject, 493
CTabCtrl, 171-180, 489
   child dialog boxes,
      connecting to, 176-179
   creating, 172-175
   member functions,
      179-180
CTime, 452-453
CTimeSpan, 453
CToolBar, 459
CToolBarCtrl, 489

CToolTipCtrl, 489
CTreeCtrl, 489-490
CTreeView, 465
CTypedPtrArray, 475
CTypedPtrList, 475
CTypedPtrMap, 475
CUintArray, 472
CUserException, 450
CView, 464
CWinApp, 469-470
CWindowDC, 455
CWinThread, 469
CWnd, 457-458
CWordArray, 472
descendant class objects,
   creating, 510-514
destructor methods, 91
invoking ancestral class
   methods, 513-514
linking menu items to class
   methods (Dialog_1
   message box example),
   86-89
MAPI support, 71
Step 6 (Class Name
   Options) dialog box,
   creating applications, 41
user interface classes
   (Windows 95), 71
Windows Sockets, 71-72
see also MFC (Microsoft
   Foundation Classes)
ClassWizard, 23
Message Maps tab, 88-89
trapping keyboard events,
   311-313
Clipboard, 65, 411-412
BmpImage demo program,
   372-373
retrieving images
   CopyBlock API, 370-371
   OnImageDisplay
      procedure, 354-355
viewing contents during
   screen captures, 357-358

ClipBook utility, screen captures, 352
CLIPCAPS * flag, 265
CList class, 472-473
CListBox class, 463
CListCtrl class, 488
CListView class, 465
CLongBinary class, 485
closing
   dialog boxes, 148-149
   Windows NT Special
      Controls dialog box, 155
CLW file extension, 112
CMainFrame class, Dialog_1 (message box example), 87
CMap class, 473
CMapPtrToPtr class, 474
CMapPtrToWord class, 474
CMapStringToOb class, 474
CMapStringToPtr class, 474
CMapStringToString class, 474
CMapWordToOb class, 474
CMapWordToPtr class, 474
CMDIChildWnd class, 462
CMDIFrameWnd class, 462
CMemFile class, 449
CMemoryException class, 450
CMemoryState class, 453
CMenu class, 457
CMetafileDC class, 456
CMiniFrameWnd class, 463
CMultiDocTemplate class, 469
CMultiLock class, 494
CMutex class, 494
CMYK color scheme, 305
CNotSupportedException class, 450
CObArray class, 472
CObject class, 449-450
CObList class, 473
COle_cntrCntrItem class, 422-423
COle_cntrView class, 420-422

COle_srvrApp class, creating OLE servers, 436
COle_srvrSrvrItem class, creating OLE servers, 431-433
COle_srvrView class, creating OLE servers, 438-442
COleBusyDialog class, 480
COleChangeIconDialog class, 479
COleClientItem class, 422-423, 481
COleControl class, 191
COleConvertDialog class, 479
COleDataObject class, 484
COleDataSource class, 477
COleDialog class, 479
COleDispatchDriver class, 484
COleDispatchException class, 483
COleDocument class, 481
COleDropSource class, 477
COleDropTarget class, 478
COleException class, 450, 483
COleInsertDialog class, 479
  selecting OLE servers, 425-426
COleIPFrameWnd class, 478
COleLinkingDoc class, 481
COleLinksDialog class, 480
COleMessageFilter class, 478
COleObjectFactory class, 481
COlePasteSpecialDialog class, 479
COlePropertiesDialog class, 479
COleResizeBar class, 480
COleServerDoc class, 481
COleServerItem class, 482
COleStreamFile class, 483-484
COleTemplateServer class, 481
COleUpdateDialog class, 480

Collection classes (MFC), 447, 471-476
  array collections, 471-472
  helper functions, 475-476
  list collections, 472-473
  map collections, 473-474
  user-specified base classes, 475
  wrapper classes, 474
color
  CColorDialog class, 230-231
  CHOOSECOLOR structure, 241-244
  CMYK color scheme, 305
  Color1 demo program, 305-306
  Color2 demo program, 309-311
    mouse messages, 316
  Color3 demo program, 320-321
  COLORREF values
    absolute RGB COLORREF, 307
    palette-index format, 307
    palette-relative format, 307-308
  composition, 303-305
  converting to gray scale, 316-318
  customizing, 309-311
  DIB image format, 351
  dithered colors, 308-309
  drawing modes, 318-320
    R2_NOT, 318
  half-toning, 305
  inverting screen color, 318
  RGB color scheme, 304
  values, 300-302
  Windows palettes, 298-300
    active windows, 303
    creating, 360
    reserved color entries, 302-303

COLORREF values
  absolute RGB COLORREF, 307
  palette-index format, 307
  palette-relative format, 307-308
COLORRES flag, 265
Column (menu break setting), 126
commands
  File menu (New), 28
  Insert menu (Resources), 123
  New menu (Bitmap), 128
  Resource menu
    Export, 117
    Import, 117
    New, 116, 142
    Open Binary Data, 117
    Set Includes, 118
    Symbols, 118
  shortcut menu (Call Stack window)
    Copy, 522
    Docking View, 522
    Go To Code, 522
    Hide, 522
    Insert/Remove Breakpoint, 522
    Parameter Types, 522
    Parameter Values, 522
Common Control classes (MFC), 448, 487-490
common dialog boxes, 229-257
  CColorDialog class, 230-231
  CFileDialog class, 244-250
  CFindReplaceDialog class, 252-256
  CFontDialog class, 230-231
  CHOOSECOLOR structure, 241-244
  CHOOSEFONT structure, 236-241
  CPrintInfo class, 250-251
  customizing, 241

data structures/class
  equivalents, 230
filter strings, 249
LOGFONT structure,
  232-235
  initializing, 235-236
OPENFILENAME
  structure, 245-249
  selecting multiple files, 250
**CompareElements
function, 475**
**comparison operators
(CString class), 97**
compilers
  resource compiler (Microsoft
    Developer Studio), 24
  Visual C++ compiler, 18, 23
  toolbar buttons, 48-50
**compiling application
resources, 113**
compound documents, 414
compressing bitmap images
  BI_RLE4, 362-363
  BI_RLE8, 364
**concatenation operators
(CString class), 96**
constants, *see* **flags**
**ConstructElements
function, 476**
constructor methods, 91
containers (OLE)
  compared to servers, 418
  creating, 418-423
    COle_cntrCntrItem
      class, 422-423
    COle_cntrView class,
      420-422
**Control Options dialog box,
creating OCX controls,
193-194**
controls
  animation controls, 181-187
    AVI file requirements,
      181-182
    AVI files, creating,
      185-186

creating, 182-185
notification messages to
  parent windows, 185
assigning member variables
  to dialog boxes, 146-147
creating for dialog
  boxes, 143
dialog box toolbar buttons,
  144-145
hotkey control, 156-157
initializing member variables
  in dialog boxes, 147
OCX (OLE Control
  eXtensions) controls,
  190-191
  adding properties to,
    211-214
  COleControl class, 191
  converting from version
    2.1 to 4.0, 202-203
  CreateFromBitmap
    function, 206-207
  creating via Visual C++
    version 2.x, 191-196
  creating via Visual C++
    version 4.0, 196-203
  events, 191
  events, testing, 221
  GetNScaleVal
    method, 216
  initializing, 203-204
  methods, 191
  mouse events, 208-210
  OCX_Demo example
    properties, 214-215
  OnDraw function,
    204-208
  painting, 204-208
  properties, 190, 210-211
  properties, testing,
    220-221
  Property Page dialog box,
    defining, 217-218
  PX_Bool function,
    215-216
  registering, 219

Render function,
  207-208
runtime files, 202
SetNScaleVal method,
  216-217
source code for demo
  example (listing 9.1),
  222-226
testing, 219-221
progress control, 157-159
retrieving values from dialog
  box controls, 148
selecting in dialog
  boxes, 143
slider control, 159-160
spin button control,
  160-162
tab controls, 171-180
  child dialog boxes,
    connecting to, 176-179
  creating, 172-175
  member functions,
    179-180
tree view control, 162-169
  adding nodes, 165-167
  selecting nodes, 167-168
VBX (Visual Basic
  eXtension), 189
see also dialog boxes
**Controls dialog box, creating
OCX controls, 194-195**
**ControlWizard project source
files, creating OCX controls,
199-203**
**conventions, menu format-
ting, 126-127**
**conversion methods (CString
class), 97**
converting
  color to gray scale, 316-318
  OCX controls from version
    2.1 to 4.0, 202-203
**Coordinate classes (MFC),
451-452**
**Copy command (Call Stack
shortcut menu), 522**

CopyBlock API, 370-371
CPageSetupDialog class, 461
CPaintDC class, 456
CPalette class, 457
CPen class, 456
   GetStockObject function, 324
CPoint class, 451
CPrintDialog class, 461
CPrintInfo class, 250-251, 470
CProgressCtrl class, 488
CPropertyPage class, 461
CPropertySheet class, 463
CPtrArray class, 472
CPtrList class, 473
CreateDIBPalette API, 370
CreateFromBitmap function (OCX controls), 206-207
CreateIC function, 262-263
CreateSolidBrush( ) method, 305
creating
   aggregate classes, 512-513
   animation controls, 182-185
   application resources, 108-109, 116
   AVI files, 185-186
   controls for dialog boxes, 143
   descendant class objects, 510-514
      CEncrypt class example, 510-513
   dialog boxes, 142-145
   DLLs (dynamic link libraries), 501-507
   exit messages, 98-100
   menus, 123-124
   MFC applications, 27-50
      New Project dialog box, 30-32
      New Project Information dialog box, 42
      project skeleton, 42-44

      ReadMe.TXT file, 45-46
      selecting file types, 28-29
      skeletal application, modifications, 47-50
      Step 1 (Architecture) dialog box, 32-33
      Step 2 (Database Options) dialog box, 33-34
      Step 3 (OLE Support) dialog box, 35-36
      Step 4 (Application Features) dialog box, 36-39
      Step 5 (Source Code Options) dialog box, 39-40
      Step 6 (Class Name Options) dialog box, 41
OCX controls
   via Visual C++ version 2.x, 191-196
   via Visual C++ version 4.0, 196-203
ODBC applications, 399-405
OLE containers, 418-423
   COle_cntrCntrItem class, 422-423
   COle_cntrView class, 420-422
OLE servers, 427-442
   via AppWizard, 429-430
   CInPlaceFrame class, 433-435
   COle_srvrApp class, 436
   COle_srvrSrvrItem class, 431-433
   COle_srvrView class, 438-442
   InitInstance method, 436-438
   MDI (Multiple Document Interface), 428
   metafile contexts, 433

   SDI (Single Document Interface), 428
   source files, 430
   tab controls, 172-175
   toolbar bitmaps, 127-129
CRecordSet class, 486
CRecordView class, 466, 486
CRect class, 452
CRectTracker class, 484
CResourceException class, 450
CRgn class, 457
CRichEditCntrItem class, 482
CRichEditDoc class, 482-483
CRichEditView class, 465
CRunTimeClass class, 453-454
CScrollBar class, 463
CScrollView class, 466
CSemaphore class, 494
CSingleDocTemplate class, 469
CSingleLock class, 494
CSize class, 452
CSliderCtrl class, 488
CSocket class, 490
CSocketFile class, 490-491
CSpinButtonCtrl class, 488-489
CSplitterWnd class, 464
CStatic class, 464
CStatusBar class, 459
CStatusBarCtrl class, 489
CStdioFile class, 389-390, 449
CString class, 93, 95-98, 452
CStringArray class, 472
CStringList class, 473
CSyncObject class, 493
CTabCtrl class, 171-180, 489
   child dialog boxes, connecting to, 176-179
   creating, 172-175
   member functions, 179-180
CTime class, 452-453

CTimeSpan class, 453
CToolBar class, 459
CToolBarCtrl class, 489
CToolTipCtrl class, 489
CTreeCtrl class, 489-490
CTreeView class, 465
CTypedPtrArray class, 475
CTypedPtrList class, 475
CTypedPtrMap class, 475
CUintArray class, 472
CUR file extension, 113
cursor images, 110
CURVECAPS query, 271-272
CUserException class, 450
custom data types, 54-55
custom properties (OCX controls), 190
customizing
   color, 309-311
   common dialog boxes, 241
   pens, 326
   serialization, 383-385
CView class, 464
CWinApp class, 469-470
CWindowDC class, 455
CWinmodesView::OnDraw function, 288
CWinThread class, 469
CWnd class, 457-458
   MessageBox method, 78
CWordArray class, 472

D

DAO (Data Access Object) classes, 448, 491-494
dark gray brushes, 327
DAT file extension, 113
data sources (ODBC), setting up, 397-399
data structures
   CHOOSECOLOR, 241-244
   CHOOSEFONT, 236-241
   common dialog boxes, 230
   FINDREPLACE, 254-256
   LOGFONT, 232-235
      initializing, 235-236
   OPENFILENAME, 245-249
   TV_INSERTSTRUCT, 165
   TV_ITEM, 163-164
data transfer (OLE2), 65-67
data types, 54-55
   custom data types, 54-55
   insertion/extraction operators, 385-386
   MFC class equivalents, 55-56
Database classes (MFC), 448, 485-486
   creating OLE data access controls, 68
databases, Step 2 (Database Options) dialog box, creating applications, 33-34
DDE (Dynamic Data Exchange), 65-66, 412
Debug toolbar (Developer Studio), 522
Debug window (Developer Studio), 518-519
debug/utility classes, 453-454
debugging tools (Microsoft Developer Studio), 517-522
   Call Stack window, 521-522
   Debug toolbar, 522
   Debug window, 518-519
   Locals window, 519
   Memory window, 523
   Quick Watch window, 519-521
   Registers window, 523
   Watch window, 519
DEF files, DLLs (dynamic link libraries), 503
default database (creating ODBC applications), 405
defining Property Page dialog box (OCX controls), 217-218
deleting
   brushes, 327
   pens, 327
deriving descendant class objects, 510-514
   CEncrypt class example, 510-513
descendant class objects
   deriving, 510-514
      CEncrypt class example, 510-513
   invoking ancestral class methods, 513-514
designing dialog boxes, 141-142
DESKTOPHORZRES flag, 266
DESKTOPVERTRES flag, 266
DestructElements function, 476
destructor methods, 91
Developer Studio, 20-24
   AppStudio resource editor, 24
   AppWizard, 23
   ClassWizard, 23
   debugging tools, 517-522
      Call Stack window, 521-522
      Debug toolbar, 522
      Debug window, 518-519
      Locals window, 519
      Memory window, 523
      Quick Watch window, 519-521
      Registers window, 523
      Watch window, 519
   linker, 24
   Project Workspace dialog box, 21-23
   resource compiler, 24
   Source Browser, 24
   Visual C++ compiler, 23

device contexts, compared to metafile contexts (creating OLE servers), 433
device drivers
    CreateIC function, 262-263
    CURVECAPS query, 271-272
    GetDeviceCaps function, 262
    LINECAPS query, 271
    POLYGONALCAPS query, 272-273
    printer resolution, 264-268
    RASTERCAPS query, 268-269
    TEXTCAPS query, 269-270
    version numbers, 264
    video resolution, 264-268
dialog boxes, 109
    Add Property (OCX controls), 212-214
    animation controls, 181-187
        AVI file requirements, 181-182
        AVI files, creating, 185-186
        creating, 182-185
        notification messages to parent windows, 185
    Aspect, 282
    common dialog boxes, 229-257
        CColorDialog class, 230-231
        CFileDialog class, 244-250
        CFindReplaceDialog class, 252-256
        CFontDialog class, 230-231
        CHOOSECOLOR structure, 241-244
        CHOOSEFONT structure, 236-241

        CPrintInfo class, 250-251
        customizing, 241
        data structures/class equivalents, 230
        filter strings, 249
        initializing LOGFONT structure, 235-236
        LOGFONT structure, 232-235
        OPENFILENAME structure, 245-249
        selecting multiple files, 250
    Control Options, creating OCX controls, 193-194
    Controls, creating OCX controls, 194-195
    creating, 142-145
    designing, 141-142
    Edit Colors, 308
    message boxes, 77-78
        AfxMessageBox function, 85
        buttons, 81-82
        Dialog_1 (message box example), 85-100
        exit messages, creating custom, 98-100
        icons, 80
        MessageBox function, 78-79
        modality, 83-84
        return values, 79, 83
    New Control Information, creating OCX controls, 195-196
    New Project, 30-32
    New Project Information, 42
    New Resource, 116
    Project Options, creating OCX controls, 192-193
    Property Page, defining, 217-218

    Set Includes, 118
    Standard Controls (example), 145-152
        assigning member variables, 146-147
        clearing local variables, 151-152
        closing, 148-149
        initializing dialog box elements, 150
        initializing member variables, 147
        retrieving results, 150-151
        retrieving values from controls, 148
    Step 1 (Architecture), creating MFC applications, 32-33
    Step 2 (Database Options), creating MFC applications, 33-34
    Step 3 (OLE Support), creating MFC applications, 35-36
    Step 4 (Application Features), creating MFC applications, 36-39
    Step 5 (Source Code Options), creating MFC applications, 39-40
    Step 6 (Class Name Options), creating MFC applications, 41
    Symbol Browser, 118
    tab controls, 171-180
        child dialog boxes, connecting to, 176-179
        creating, 172-175
        member functions, 179-180
    Toolbar Button Properties, 131
    toolbar buttons, 144-145

Windows 95 Special Controls, 155-169
  hotkey control, 156-157
  progress control, 157-159
  slider control, 159-160
  spin button control, 160-162
  tree view control, 162-169
Windows NT Special Controls, 152-155
  closing, 155
  initializing scrollbars, 153
  OnDlgCreate method, 152-153
  scrollbar event messages, 153-155

Dialog_1 (message box example), 85-100
  button selections, reporting, 92-95
  implementing member functions, 89-92
  menu items, 85-86
    linking to class methods, 86-89

DialoVW.CPP source code (listing 4.7), 101-104
DialoVW.H source code (listing 4.6), 100-101
DIB image format, 348-349
  BITMAPINFO structure, 350-351
  color table, 351
  compared to BMP, 348
  pixel data, 351
disk access, 32-bit, 16
disk compression, Windows 95/Windows NT comparisons, 11
displays
  mapping modes
    GetMapMode function, 286
    GetViewportExtEx function, 287

GetViewportOrg function, 288
GetWindowExtEx function, 287
GetWindowOrg function, 288
MM_ANISOTROPIC mode, 320-321
OffsetViewportOrg function, 288
OffsetWindowOrg function, 288
ScaleViewportExt function, 287
ScaleWindowExt function, 287
SetViewportExt function, 285-286
SetViewportOrg function, 288
SetWindowExt function, 285-286
SetWindowOrg function, 288
WinModes demo, 288-292
POLYGONALCAPS query, 272-273
RASTERCAPS query, 268-269
standards, 298-300
TEXTCAPS query, 269-270
video resolution, 264-268

dithered colors, 308-309
DLG file extension, 113
DLL file extension, 113
DllMain (entry point) function, 504-506
DLLs (dynamic link libraries), 114, 498-510
  adding functions to, 506-507
  advantages/disadvantages, 500-501
  calling, 507-509
  creating, 501-507

DllMain (entry point) function, 504-506
dynamic linking, 498-501
load-time dynamic linking, 498-499
runtime dynamic linking, 500
source files, generated by AppWizard, 503
testing during development, 509-510
Windows 95 32-bit DLLs, 62-64

docking toolbars, EnableDocking function, 133-134
Docking View command (Call Stack shortcut menu), 522
document classes (MFC), message handling, 59
Document Template Strings tab, creating MFC applications, 37-38
documents, compound (OLE), 414
DrawDotLine function, 333
drawing
  arcs, 335-337
  chords, 335-337
  Draw1 demo program, 337
  Draw2 demo program, 340
  Draw3 demo program, 342
  DrawDotLine function, 333
  Ellipse function, 334
  LineTo function, 332-333
  OCX controls, 204-208
  pie graphs, 338
  pie sections, 335-337
  PolyBezier function, 343-344
  PolyDraw function, 344-345
  Polygon function, 339-340
    fill modes, 340-341
  PolyPolygon function, 339-341
  PolyPolyline function, 342

Rectangle function, 333-334
ROP modes (R2_NOT), 318
ROP2 modes, 318-320
RoundRect function, 334-342
tools
   deleting, 327
   GetCurrentPosition method, 332
   logical brushes, 327-331
   logical pens, 324-327
   MoveTo method, 332
   shape tools, 331-342
drawing spaces, 283-285
drivers
   CreateIC function, 262-263
   CURVECAPS query, 271-272
   GetDeviceCaps function, 262
   POLYGONALCAPS query, 272-273
   printer resolution, 264-268
   RASTERCAPS query, 268-269
   TEXTCAPS query, 269-270
   version numbers, 264
   video resolution, 264-268
DRIVERVERSION flag, 264
DRV file extension, 113
dual booting,
   Windows 95/Windows NT comparisons, 12
dump methods, 97
DumpElements function, 476
DWORD data type, 54
Dynamic Data Exchange (DDE), 65-66, 412
dynamic link libraries (DLLs), 114, 498-510
   adding functions to, 506-507
   advantages/disadvantages, 500-501
   calling, 507-509
   creating, 501-507

   DllMain (entry point) function, 504-506
   dynamic linking, 498-501
   load-time dynamic linking, 498-499
   runtime dynamic linking, 500
   source files, generated by AppWizard, 503
   testing during development, 509-510
   Windows 95 32-bit DLLs, 62-64
dynamic linking, 498-501
   advantages/disadvantages, 500-501
   load-time, 498-499
   runtime, 500

E

Edit Colors dialog box, 308
editing
   application resources as binary data, 117
   indirect editing (ODBC), 408-410
   OCX controls, 194-195
EGA display standard, 299
Ellipse function, 334
Ellipse tool, 331
ellipses (...), popup menu entries, 126-127
embedding, 66
   compared to linking, 414-415
EnableDocking function, 133-134
Encoded mode of image compression, 362
entry point (DllMain) function, 504-506
events
   mouse events (OCX controls), 208-210
   OCX controls, 191
   testing, 221

EXE file extension, 113
exit messages, creating custom, 98-100
Export command (Resource menu), 117
exporting/importing application resources, 117
extended properties (OCX controls), 190
extraction (>>) operator, 385-386
extraction methods (CString class), 97

F

FALSE macro, 55
FAR macro, 55
file access, 378-382
   AARL_HAM example application, 390-396
      GetEntry function, 394-396
      overloaded operators, 393-394
      reading/writing CArchive records, 392-393
      UpdateData function, 396
   CArchive class, 383, 386-388, 451
   CFile class, 378-380, 449, 483
      flags, 381-382
      opening files, 380-381
   CStdioFile class, 389-390, 449
   insertion/extraction operators, 385-386
   random file access, 388-389
   serialization, 382-386
      customizing, 383-385
File classes (MFC), 451
File menu commands (New), 28

file systems
  Windows 95, 13-16
  Windows NT, 12-13
file types, selecting (creating applications), 28-29
filenames (Windows 95), 13-15
files, 111-114
  CFile class, 378-380, 449, 483
    flags, 381-382
    opening files, 380-381
  CFileDialog class, 244-250, 460
  CFileException class, 450
  CFileStatus class, 451
  creating OCX controls (ControlWizard), 199-203
  filter strings, 249
  header files, 114
  OCX control runtime files, 202
  OPENFILENAME structure, 245-249
  ReadMe.TXT file, creating MFC applications, 45-46
  resource files, 112-113
  selecting multiple files (File dialog box), 250
  work files, 112
fills (Polygon function), 340-341
filter strings (File dialog box), 249
Find/Replace dialog boxes (CFindReplaceDialog class), 252-256
FINDREPLACE structure, 254-256
flags
  ASPECTX, 265
  ASPECTXY, 265
  ASPECTY, 265
  BITSPIXEL, 265
  BLTALIGNMENT, 266

CFile class, 381-382
CHOOSEFONT structure, 239-240
CLIPCAPS *, 265
COLORRES, 265
DESKTOPHORZRES, 266
DESKTOPVERTRES, 266
DRIVERVERSION, 264
FINDREPLACE structure, 255-256
HORZRES, 265
HORZSIZE, 265
LOGPIXELSX, 265
LOGPIXELSY, 265
message boxes
  buttons, 81-82
  icons, 80
  modality, 83-84
NUMBRUSHES, 265
NUMCOLORS, 265
NUMFONTS, 265
NUMPENS, 265
NUMRESERVED, 265
OPENFILENAME structure, 247-249
PDEVICESIZE *, 265
PHYSICALHEIGHT *, 265
PHYSICALOFFSETX *, 265
PHYSICALOFFSETY *, 265
PHYSICALWIDTH *, 265
PLANES, 265
SCALINGFACTORX *, 265
SCALINGFACTORY *, 265
SIZEPALETTE, 265
TECHNOLOGY, 264
VERTRES, 265
VERTSIZE, 265
VREFRESH, 265
FNT file extension, 113
FON file extension, 113
font resources, 110

fonts
  CFontDialog class, 230-231
  CHOOSEFONT structure, 236-241
  LOGFONT structure, 232-235
    initializing, 235-236
formatting conventions (menus), 126-127
frame classes (MFC), message handling, 59
FreeLibrary function, 500
functions
  adding to DLLs (dynamic link libraries), 506-507
  AfxMessageBox, 85
  CompareElements, 475
  ConstructElements, 476
  CPen::GetStockObject, 324
  CreateFromBitmap (OCX controls), 206-207
  CreateIC, 262-263
  CTabCtrl class member functions, 179-180
  DestructElements, 476
  Dialog_1 (message box example) member functions, 89-92
  DllMain (entry point), 504-506
  DrawDotLine, 333
  DumpElements, 476
  Ellipse, 334
  EnableDocking, 133-134
  FreeLibrary, 500
  GetDeviceCaps, 262
  GetEntry, AARL_HAM example application (file I/O), 394-396
  GetMapMode, 286
  GetProcAddress, 500
  GetSystemPaletteEntries, 360
  GetViewportExtEx, 287
  GetViewportOrg, 288

GetWindowExtEx, 287
GetWindowOrg, 288
HashKey, 476
InsertMenu, 137-138
IsSelected, creating OLE
    containers, 420-421
LineTo, 332-333
linking to toolbars, 129-134
LoadLibrary, 500
MessageBox, 78-79
OffsetViewportOrg, 288
OffsetWindowOrg, 288
OnCancelEditCntr, creating
    OLE containers, 422
OnChangeCallsign, AARL3
    example application, 407
OnDraw
    creating OLE containers,
        420
    OCX controls, 204-208
OnInitialUpdate, creating
    OLE containers, 420
OnInsertObject, creating
    OLE containers, 421
OnNScaleChanged, 216
OnSetFocus, creating OLE
    containers, 422
OnSize, creating OLE
    containers, 422
OnSwitchMenu, 138
overloaded functions, 94-95
parameters, 79
PolyBezier, 343-344
PolyDraw, 344-345
Polygon, 339-340
    fills, 340-341
PolyPolygon, 339-341
PolyPolyline, 342
private, 91
protected, 91
public, 91
PX_Bool (OCX controls),
    215-216
Rectangle, 333-334
registry functions, 69-70

Render (OCX controls),
    207-208
RoundRect, 334-342
ScaleViewportExt, 287
ScaleWindowExt, 287
SerializeElements, 476
SetBarStyle, 134
SetMapMode, 277
SetViewportExt, 282, 285
SetViewportOrg, 288
SetWindowExt, 282, 285
SetWindowOrg, 288
UpdateData, AARL_HAM
    example application
    (file I/O), 396
see also methods; procedures

G

**General Purpose classes
    (MFC), 447-454**
    CObject class, 449-450
    Coordinate classes, 451-452
    CString class, 452
    debug/utility classes,
        453-454
    File classes, 451
    Time classes, 452-453
Generic Thunks, 64-65
GetColorCount API, 370
**GetCurrentPosition
    method, 332**
GetDeviceCaps function, 262
**GetEntry function,
    AARL_HAM example
    application (file I/O),
    394-396**
GetMapMode function, 286
GetNScaleVal method, 216
GetProcAddress function, 500
**GetSystemPaletteEntries
    function, 360**
**GetViewportExtEx
    function, 287**
**GetViewportOrg
    function, 288**

GetWindowExtEx
    function, 287
GetWindowOrg function, 288
Go To Code command (Call
    Stack shortcut menu), 522
graphics metafiles, 412
graphs, pie, 338
gray brushes, 327
Grayed (menu item property
    checkbox), 125
GUI (Graphical User Interface), 17

H

H file extension (header
    files), 113
half-toning, 305
HANDLE data type, 54
hardware requirements,
    Windows 95/Windows NT,
    10-11
HashKey function, 476
hatch patterns (brushes),
    329-330
header files, 113-114
Help (menu item property
    checkbox), 125
helper functions (MFC
    collection classes), 475-476
Hide command (Call Stack
    shortcut menu), 522
hierarchy limits (menus), 127
High Color display
    standard, 299
hollow brushes, 328
HORZRES flag, 265
HORZSIZE flag, 265
hotkey control, 156-157
hotkeys (menu), creating, 126
HPFS (Hewlett-Packard File
    System), 12
Hungarian notation, 52-53

I–J

I/O (input/output), 378-382
  AARL_HAM example application, 390-396
    GetEntry function, 394-396
    overloaded operators, 393-394
    reading/writing CArchive records, 392-393
    UpdateData function, 396
  CArchive class, 383, 386-388, 451
  CFile class, 378-380, 449, 483
    flags, 381-382
    opening files, 380-381
  CStdioFile class, 389-390, 449
  insertion/extraction operators, 385-386
  random file access, 388-389
  serialization, 382-386
    customizing, 383-385
ICO file extension, 113
icon images, 110
  message boxes, 80
IDE (integrated development environment), 18
IDs (resource identifiers), linking to toolbars, 129-134
ILK file extension, 112
image formats
  BITMAPINFOHEADER structure, 349-350
  BMP
    BITMAPINFO structure, 350-351
    compared to DIB, 348
    BmpImage demo program, 371-373
    compression
      BI_RLE4, 362-363
      BI_RLE8, 364
  DIB, 348-349
    BITMAPINFO structure, 350-351
    color table, 351
    compared to BMP, 348
    pixel data, 351
  ImageAPI, 365
    CopyBlock API, 370-371
    CreateDIBPalette API, 370
    GetColorCount API, 370
    PaintDIB API, 367-370
    ReadDIBFile API, 365-366
    SaveDIBFile API, 366-367
  OS/2 images, 351
    BITMAPCOREINFO structure, 350-351
  Windows images, 351
image resources, 110
ImageAPI, 365
  CopyBlock API, 370-371
  CreateDIBPalette API, 370
  GetColorCount API, 370
  PaintDIB API, 367-370
  ReadDIBFile API, 365-366
  SaveDIBFile API, 366-367
IMPLEMENT_SERIAL macro, 384-385
Import command (Resource menu), 117
importing/exporting application resources, 117
Inactive (menu item property checkbox), 125
indirect editing (ODBC), 408-410
INI files, compared to Windows registry, 68-70
initializing
  dialog box elements, 150
  LOGFONT structure, 235-236
  member variables in dialog boxes, 147
  OCX controls, 203-204
  screen captures, 353-374
  scrollbars (Windows NT Special Controls dialog box), 153
InitInstance method, creating OLE servers, 436-438
Insert menu commands (Resources), 123
Insert/Remove Breakpoint command (Call Stack shortcut menu), 522
insertion (<<) operator, 385-386
InsertMenu function, 137-138
installing OLE Custom Development Kit (CDK), 191-192
int data type, 54
integers, sized, 54
integrated development environment (IDE), 18
integrating applications
  Clipboard, 411-412
  DDE (Dynamic Data Exchange), 412
  metafiles, 412
Invalidate( ) method, 152
inverting screen color, 318
invoking ancestral class methods, 513-514
IsSelected function, creating OLE containers, 420-421

K–L

keyboard events, trapping, 311-313

Life demo, 292-295
light gray brushes, 328
limiting menu hierarchies, 127
LINECAPS query, 271
lines
  PolyDraw function, 344-345
  PolyPolyline function, 342

LineTo function, 332-333
LineTo tool, 331
linker (Microsoft Developer Studio), 24
linking, 67
   application resources, 113
   compared to embedding, 414-415
   dynamic linking, 498-501
      advantages/disadvantages, 500-501
   load-time dynamic linking, 498-499
   menu items to class methods (Dialog_1 message box example), 86-89
   messages/IDs to toolbars, 129-134
   runtime dynamic linking, 500
list collection classes (MFC), 472-473
listings
   1.1. Volume in drive C is NEWFORMAT, 14
   2.1. The ReadMe.TXT file generated by AppWizard for the HelloWin sample application, 45-46
   2.2. Changes made to the HelloVW.CPP file, 47
   20.1. The source code for the DrawStar function, 506-507
   3.1. The message map used by the HelloWin.CPP file in the HelloWin example, 58
   4.1. The skeletal function OnDlgExcl, generated by ClassWizard, 89
   4.2. The finished function OnDlgExcl, 90
   4.3. The OnDlgInfo, OnDlgQuestion, and OnDlgStop methods used in the Dialog_1 sample application, 92
   4.4. The completed OnDraw method, used to report which button was selected to close a message box, 93
   4.5. The completed OnAppExit method, used to call a message box to query the user before terminating the application, 99
   4.6. Source code for DialoVW.H, 100-101
   4.7. Source code for DialoVW.CPP, 101-104
   4.8. Source code for MainFram.CPP, 104-105
   9.1. Source code for the Ocx_DCtl.CPP demonstration program, 222-226
   14.1. The DrawDotLine function., 332
   14.2. The DrawOutline function., 333
   16.1. An excerpt from the Repeater.RPT data file, 388-389
load-time dynamic linking, 498-499
LoadLibrary function, 500
local variables, clearing in dialog boxes, 151-152
Locals window (Developer Studio), 519
LOGFONT structure, 232-235
   initializing, 235-236
logical brushes, 327-329
   CBrush::CreateDIBPatternBrush method, 330
   CBrush::CreateSolidBrush method, 331
   creating, 330-331
   deleting, 327
   hatch patterns, 329-330
logical pens, 324-327
   deleting, 327
   LineTo function, 332-333
   Rectangle function, 333-334
LOGPIXELSX flag, 265
LOGPIXELSY flag, 265
LPARAM data type, 54

M

macros
   CALLBACK, 55
   FALSE, 55
   FAR, 55
   IMPLEMENT_SERIAL, 384-385
   NEAR, 55
   PASCAL, 55
   VOID, 55
   WINAPI, 55
mail messages, MAPI (Messaging API), 71
Main Frame tab, creating MFC applications, 39
MainFram.CPP source code (listing 4.8), 104-105
map collection classes, 473-474
MAPI (Messaging API), 71
mapping modes, 275-277
   comparisons, 284
   GetMapMode function, 286
   GetViewportExtEx function, 287
   GetViewportOrg function, 288
   GetWindowExtEx function, 287
   GetWindowOrg function, 288
   Life demo, 292-295
   MM_ANISOTROPIC mode, 281-283, 290, 320-321

MM_HIENGLISH mode, 278-279
MM_HIMETRIC mode, 279-280
MM_ISOTROPIC mode, 281-283, 290
MM_LOENGLISH mode, 278-279
MM_LOMETRIC mode, 279-280
MM_TEXT mode, 277-278
MM_TWIPS mode, 281
OffsetViewportOrg function, 288
OffsetWindowOrg function, 288
ScaleViewportExt function, 287
ScaleWindowExt function, 287
selecting, 277
SetMapMode function, 277
SetViewportExt function, 285-286
SetViewportOrg function, 288
SetWindowExt function, 285-286
SetWindowOrg function, 288
WinModes demo, 288-292

MDI (Multiple Document Interface), OLE servers, 428
measurements, setting, 277-283
member functions, *see* **functions**
member variables
  assigning to dialog box controls, 146-147
  initializing dialog box controls, 147
memory, addressable, 12
Memory window (Developer Studio), 523

menu items, Dialog_1 (message box example), 85-86
  linking to class methods, 86-89
menus, 110-111, 121
  break settings, 126
  creating, 123-124
  formatting conventions, 126-127
  hierarchy limits, 127
  OLE server applications, 443-444
  overview, 122
  popup menus, 126-127
  property checkboxes, 125
  static menus, 122
  structure, 122, 124-126
  switching, 136-139
message boxes, 77-78
  AfxMessageBox function, 85
  buttons, 81-82
  Dialog_1 (message box example), 85-100
    button selections, reporting, 92-95
    implementing member functions, 89-92
    linking menu items to class methods, 86-89
    menu items, 85-86
  exit messages, creating custom, 98-100
  icons, 80
  MessageBox function, 78-79
  modality, 83-84
  return values, 79, 83
message mapping (MFC), 57-60
Message Maps tab (ClassWizard), 88-89
MessageBox function, 78-79
messages
  linking to toolbars, 129-134
  mouse events (OCX controls), 208-210

notification messages to parent windows (CAnimateCtrl class), 185
scrollbar events (Windows NT Special Controls dialog box), 153-155
Messaging API (MAPI), 71
metafile contexts, creating OLE servers, 433
metafiles, 412
methods
  ancestral class methods, invoking, 513-514
  CBrush class
    CreateDIBPatternBrush, 330
    CreateSolidBrush, 331
  constructor methods, 91
  CreateSolidBrush( ), 305
  CString class, 96-98
  CWnd::MessageBox, 78
  deriving descendent classes (CEncrypt class example), 511-512
  destructor methods, 91
  GetCurrentPosition, 332
  GetNScaleVal, 216
  InitInstance, creating OLE servers, 436-438
  Invalidate( ), 152
  linking menu items to (Dialog_1 message box example), 86-89
  MoveTo, 332
  OCX controls, 191
  OnChangeInput (AARL3 example application), 408
  OnChar, 312
  OnCreate, creating OLE servers, 434
  OnCreateControlBars, creating OLE servers, 435
  OnDlgCreate (Windows NT Special Controls dialog box), 152-153

OnDraw, creating OLE servers, 432-433
OnGetExtent, creating OLE servers, 431
OnHScroll (Windows NT Special Controls dialog box), 153-155
OnKeyDown, 312
OnLButtonDblClk, 316
OnLButtonDown, 316
progress bar methods, 158-159
ReadString, 389-390
SaveDC( ), 289
Seek methods, 388-389
Serialize, creating OLE servers, 431
SetNScaleVal, 216-217
SetScrollPos (Windows NT Special Controls dialog box), 154
slider control methods, 159-160
spin button methods, 162
tree view control methods, 168-169
WriteString, 390
see also functions; procedures

MFC (Microsoft Foundation Classes)
Application Architecture classes, 447, 467-470
  associated object classes, 470
  message handling, 60
Collection classes, 447, 471-476
  array collections, 471-472
  helper functions, 475-476
  list collections, 472-473
  map collections, 473-474
  user-specified base classes, 475
  wrapper classes, 474
Common Control classes, 448, 487-490
creating applications, 27-50
  New Project dialog box, 30-32
  New Project Information dialog box, 42
  project skeleton, 42-44
  ReadMe.TXT file, 45-46
  selecting file types, 28-29
  skeletal application, modifications, 47-50
  Step 1 (Architecture) dialog box, 32-33
  Step 2 (Database Options) dialog box, 33-34
  Step 3 (OLE Support) dialog box, 35-36
  Step 4 (Application Features) dialog box, 36-39
  Step 5 (Source Code Options) dialog box, 39-40
  Step 6 (Class Name Options) dialog box, 41
DAO (Data Access Object) classes, 448, 491-494
Database classes, 448, 485-486
  creating OLE data access controls, 68
General Purpose classes, 447-454
  CObject class, 449-450
  Coordinate classes, 451-452
  CString class, 452
  debug/utility classes, 453-454
  File classes, 451
  Time classes, 452-453
message mapping, 57-60
naming convention prefixes, 53-54
OLE2 classes, 448, 476-484
  associated OLE classes, 484
  user client items, 482-483
  user server items, 483
Socket classes, 448, 490-491
Visual Object classes, 447, 454-467
  associated object classes, 466-467
  CDC-derived classes, 455-456
  CGdiObject-derived classes, 456-457
  CWnd-derived classes, 457-466
Windows data type equivalents, 55-56
see also classes

MFC Migration Kit, 72
Microsoft Developer Studio, 20-24
AppStudio resource editor, 24
AppWizard, 23
ClassWizard, 23
debugging tools, 517-522
  Call Stack window, 521-522
  Debug toolbar, 522
  Debug window, 518-519
  Locals window, 519
  Memory window, 523
  Quick Watch window, 519-521
  Registers window, 523
  Watch window, 519
linker, 24
Project Workspace dialog box, 21-23
resource compiler, 24
Source Browser, 24
Visual C++ compiler, 23

Microsoft Foundation Classes, *see* **MFC**

migrating Windows applications (MFC Migration Kit), 72
MM_ANISOTROPIC mapping mode, 281-283, 290, 320-321
MM_HIENGLISH mapping mode, 278-279
MM_HIMETRIC mapping mode, 279-280
MM_ISOTROPIC mapping mode, 281-283, 290
MM_LOENGLISH mapping mode, 278-279
MM_LOMETRIC mapping mode, 279-280
MM_TEXT mapping mode, 277-278
MM_TWIPS mapping mode, 281
modality, message boxes, 83-84
mouse events
 OCX controls, 208-210
 trapping, 314-315
MoveTo method, 332
Multiple Document Interface (MDI), OLE servers, 428
multiple files, selecting (File dialog box), 250
multithreading, 17

N

naming conventions
 AFX prefixes, 57
 Hungarian notation, 52-53
 MFC prefixes, 53-54
NEAR macro, 55
networking
 peer-to-peer networking, 17
 Windows Sockets, 71-72
New command
 File menu, 28
 Resource menu, 116, 142

New Control Information dialog box, creating OCX controls, 195-196
New menu commands (Bitmap), 128
New Project dialog box, 30-32
New Project Information dialog box, 42
New Resource dialog box, 116
nodes
 adding to tree view control, 165-167
 selecting from tree view control, 167-168
None (menu break setting), 126
NTFS (NT File System), advantages/disadvantages, 12-13
null brushes, 328
null pens, 324
NUMBRUSHES flag, 265
NUMCOLORS flag, 265
NUMFONTS flag, 265
NUMPENS flag, 265
NUMRESERVED flag, 265

O

OBJ file extension, 112
Object Linking and Embedding (OLE), 17, 411-445
 compound documents, 414
 containers
  compared to servers, 418
  creating, 418-423
  creating controls via database classes (MFC), 68
  linked compared to embedded objects, 414-415
 object packager (Packager.EXE) utility, 417
 OLE2View utility, 444-445
 overview, 412-414

 packages, 415
 servers
  application menus, 443-444
  CInPlaceFrame class, 433-435
  COle_srvrApp class, 436
  COle_srvrSrvrItem class, 431-433
  COle_srvrView class, 438-442
  compared to containers, 418
  creating, 427-442
  creating via AppWizard, 429-430
  InitInstance method, 436-438
  MDI (Multiple Document Interface), 428
  metafile contexts, 433
  registering, 423-427
  SDI (Single Document Interface), 428
  selecting, 425-426
  source files, 430
  Step 3 (OLE Support) dialog box, creating applications, 35-36
  verbs, 416-417
  see also OCX controls
object packager (Packager.EXE) utility, 417
objects, 67
 linked compared to embedded, 414-415
 serialization, 382-386
  customizing, 383-385
OCX (OLE Control eXtensions) controls, 190-191
 adding properties to, 211-214
 COleControl class, 191

converting from version 2.1
    to 4.0, 202-203
CreateFromBitmap
    function, 206-207
creating via Visual C++
    version 2.x, 191-196
    Control Options dialog
        box, 193-194
    modifying controls,
        194-195
    New Control Informa-
        tion dialog box,
        195-196
    Project Options dialog
        box, 192-193
creating via Visual C++
    version 4.0, 196-203
    ControlWizard files,
        199-203
events, 191
    testing, 221
GetNScaleVal method, 216
initializing, 203-204
methods, 191
mouse events, 208-210
OnDraw function, 204-208
painting, 204-208
properties, 190, 210-211
    OCX_Demo example,
        214-215
    responding to value
        changes, 216
    testing, 220-221
Property Page dialog box,
    defining, 217-218
PX_Bool function, 215-216
registering, 219
Render function, 207-208
runtime files, 202
SetNScaleVal method,
    216-217
source code for demo
    example (listing 9.1),
    222-226

testing, 219-221
see also OLE (Object Linking
    and Embedding)
OCX_Demo example
    properties, 214-215
    source code (listing 9.1),
        222-226
**ODBC (Open DataBase
Connectivity), 68, 397-410**
    AARL3 example application,
        405-408
    creating applications,
        399-405
    data sources, setting up,
        397-399
    indirect editing, 408-410
**OffsetViewportOrg
function, 288**
**OffsetWindowOrg
function, 288**
**OLE (Object Linking and
Embedding), 17, 411-445**
    compound documents, 414
    containers
        compared to servers, 418
        creating, 418-423
    creating controls via database
        classes (MFC), 68
    linked compared to
        embedded objects,
        414-415
    object packager
        (Packager.EXE) utility, 417
    OLE2View utility, 444-445
    overview, 412-414
    packages, 415
    servers
        application menus,
            443-444
        CInPlaceFrame class,
            433-435
        COle_srvrApp class, 436
        COle_srvrSrvrItem class,
            431-433

COle_srvrView class,
    438-442
compared to
    containers, 418
creating, 427-442
creating via AppWizard,
    429-430
InitInstance method,
    436-438
MDI (Multiple Docu-
    ment Interface), 428
metafile contexts, 433
registering, 423-427
SDI (Single Document
    Interface), 428
selecting, 425-426
source files, 430
Step 3 (OLE Support) dialog
    box, creating applications,
    35-36
verbs, 416-417
see also OCX controls
**OLE Custom Development
Kit (CDK), installing,
191-192**
OLE2, 65-67
    classes, 448, 476-484
        associated OLE
            classes, 484
        user client items,
            482-483
        user server items, 483
    registry, 70
OLE2View utility, 444-445
**OnCancelEditCntr
function, creating OLE
containers, 422**
**OnChangeCallsign function
(AARL3 example applica-
tion), 407**
**OnChangeInput method
(AARL3 example applica-
tion), 408**
OnChar method, 312

OnCreate method, creating OLE servers, 434
OnCreateControlBars method, creating OLE servers, 435
OnDlgCreate method (Windows NT Special Controls dialog box), 152-153
OnDraw function
  creating
    OLE containers, 420
    OLE servers, 432-433
    OCX controls, 204-208
OnGetExtent method, creating OLE servers, 431
OnHScroll method (Windows NT Special Controls dialog box), 153-155
OnImageDisplay procedure, 354-355
OnInitialUpdate function, creating OLE containers, 420
OnInsertObject function, creating OLE containers, 421
OnKeyDown method, 312
OnLButtonDblClk method, 316
OnLButtonDown method, 316
OnNScaleChanged function, 216
OnSetFocus function, creating OLE containers, 422
OnSize function, creating OLE containers, 422
OnSwitchMenu function, 138
Open Binary Data command (Resource menu), 117
Open DataBase Connectivity (ODBC), 68, 397-410
  AARL3 example application, 405-408

creating applications, 399-405
data sources, setting up, 397-399
indirect editing, 408-410
OPENFILENAME structure, 245-249
opening files via CFile class, 380-381
operating systems, Windows 95 compared to Windows NT, 9-17
operators
  CString class, 96-98
  extraction (>>), 385-386
  insertion (<<), 385-386
  overloaded operators, 94-95
    AARL_HAM example application (file I/O), 393-394
OS/2 images, 351
  BITMAPCOREINFO structure, 350-351
overloaded functions, 94-95
overloaded operators, 94-95
  AARL_HAM example application (file I/O), 393-394

P

packages (OLE), 415
PaintDIB API, 367-370
painting OCX controls, 204-208
palette-index COLORREF format, 307
palette-relative COLORREF format, 307-308
palettes, 298-300
  active windows, 303
  converting to gray scale, 316-318
  creating, 360
  dithered colors, 308-309

reserved color entries, 302-303
values, 300-302
Parameter Types command (Call Stack shortcut menu), 522
Parameter Values command (Call Stack shortcut menu), 522
parameters (functions), 79
PASCAL macro, 55
PCH file extension, 112
PDB file extension, 112
PDEVICESIZE * flag, 265
peer-to-peer networking, 17
pens, 324-327
  deleting, 327
  LineTo function, 332-333
  Rectangle function, 333-334
PHYSICALHEIGHT * flag, 265
PHYSICALOFFSETX * flag, 265
PHYSICALOFFSETY * flag, 265
PHYSICALWIDTH * flag, 265
pie graphs, 338
pie sections, 335-337
Pie tool, 331
PLANES flag, 265
Plug-and-Play, 17
PolyBezier function, 343-344
PolyDraw function, 344-345
Polygon function, 339-340
  fill modes, 340-341
Polygon tool, 331
POLYGONALCAPS query, 272-273
PolyPolygon function, 339-341
PolyPolygon tool, 331
PolyPolyline function, 342
Pop-up (menu item property checkbox), 125

popup menus, 126-127
preemptive multitasking, 17
primary verbs (OLE), 417
Print dialog box (CPrintInfo class), 250-251
printer resolution
   device drivers, 264-268
   RASTERCAPS query, 268-269
private variables/functions, 91
procedures
   CCaptureView::CaptureScreen, 355-357
   OnImageDisplay, 354-355
   WriteToFile, 358-362
   see also functions; methods
progress control, 157-159
project files, 28
Project Options dialog box, creating OCX controls, 192-193
project skeleton, creating MFC applications, 42-44
project source files (ControlWizard), creating OCX controls, 199-203
Project Workspace dialog box, 21-23
properties
   menu item checkboxes, 125
   OCX controls, 190, 210-211
      adding properties to, 211-214
      ambient properties, 190
      custom properties, 190
      extended properties, 190
      OCX_Demo example, 214-215
      responding to value changes, 216
      stock properties, 190
      testing, 220-221
Property Page dialog box, defining (OCX controls), 217-218

protected variables/functions, 91
public variables/functions, 91
punchcards, 377
PX_Bool function (OCX controls), 215-216

Q-R

queries
   CURVECAPS, 271-272
   LINECAPS, 271
   POLYGONALCAPS, 272-273
   RASTERCAP, 268-269
   TEXTCAPS, 269-270
Quick Watch window (Developer Studio), 519-521
R2_NOT drawing mode, 318
random file access, 388-389
RASTERCAPS query, 268-269
RC file extension, 113
RC2 file extension, 113
ReadDIBFile API, 365-366
ReadMe.TXT file, creating MFC applications, 45-46
ReadString method, 389-390
Rectangle function, 333-334
Rectangle tool, 331
RegEdit utility, 423-425
registering
   OCX controls, 219
   OLE servers, 423, 426-427
      RegEdit utility, 423-425
Registers window (Developer Studio), 523
registry
   compared to INI files, 68-70
   OLE2, 70
RegSrv utility, registering OCX controls, 219
Render function (OCX controls), 207-208
RES file extension, 113

resource compiler (Microsoft Developer Studio), 24
resource files, 112-113
resource identifiers (IDs), linking to toolbars, 129-134
Resource menu commands
   Export, 117
   Import, 117
   New, 116, 142
   Open Binary Data, 117
   Set Includes, 118
   Symbols, 118
Resources command (Insert menu), 123
resources, 107-108
   accelerator keys, 109
   AppStudio, 115
   compiling/linking, 113
   creating, 108-109, 116
   dialog boxes, 109
   editing as binary data, 117
   fonts, 110
   image resources, 110
   importing/exporting, 117
   menus, 110-111
   Set Includes dialog box, 118
   string resources, 111
   Symbol Browser dialog box, 118
   version information, 111
return values
   message boxes, 79, 83
   retrieving from dialog box controls, 148
RGB color scheme, 304
   absolute RGB COLORREF, 307
ROP modes (R2_NOT), 318
ROP2 modes, 318-320
ROT (Running Object Table), 70
RoundRect function, 334-342
RoundRect tool, 331
runtime dynamic linking, 500
runtime files (OCX controls), 202

S

SaveDC( ) method, 289
SaveDIBFile API, 366-367
saving bitmap images, 366-367
SBR file extension, 112
ScaleViewportExt function, 287
ScaleWindowExt function, 287
SCALINGFACTORX * flag, 265
SCALINGFACTORY * flag, 265
screen captures, 352
　Capture utility, 352-353
　CCaptureView::CaptureScreen procedure, 355-357
　initialization, 353-374
　OnImageDisplay procedure, 354-355
　Snapshot3 (Beacon Hill Software), 352
　viewing, 357-358
　WriteToFile procedure, 358-362
scrollbars (Windows NT Special Controls dialog box)
　event messages, 153-155
　initializing, 153
SDI (Single Document Interface), OLE servers, 428
search methods (CString class), 97
secondary verbs (OLE), 417
Seek methods, 388-389
selecting
　colors (CHOOSECOLOR structure), 241-244
　controls for dialog boxes, 143
　file types (creating applications), 28-29
　fonts
　　CHOOSEFONT structure, 236-241
　　LOGFONT structure, 232-236
　multiple files (File dialog box), 250
　nodes from tree view control, 167-168
　OLE servers, 425-426
Separator (menu item property checkbox), 125
separators (menus), 127
serialization, 382-386
　customizing, 383-385
Serialize method, creating OLE servers, 431
SerializeElements function, 476
servers (OLE)
　application menus, 443-444
　compared to containers, 418
　creating, 427-442
　　via AppWizard, 429-430
　　CInPlaceFrame class, 433-435
　　COle_srvrApp class, 436
　　COle_srvrSrvrItem class, 431-433
　　COle_srvrView class, 438-442
　　InitInstance method, 436-438
　　metafile contexts, 433
　　source files, 430
　MDI (Multiple Document Interface), 428
　registering, 423, 426-427
　　RegEdit utility, 423-425
　SDI (Single Document Interface), 428
　selecting, 425-426
Set Includes command (Resource menu), 118
SetBarStyle function, 134
SetMapMode function, 277
SetNScaleVal method, 216-217
SetScrollPos method (Windows NT Special Controls dialog box), 154
SetViewportExt function, 282, 285
SetViewportOrg function, 288
SetWindowExt function, 282, 285
SetWindowOrg function, 288
shape tools, 331
　arcs, 335-337
　chords, 335-337
　Ellipse function, 334
　LineTool function, 332-333
　pie sections, 335-337
　Polygon function, 339-340
　　fill modes, 340-341
　PolyPolygon function, 339-341
　Rectangle function, 333-334
　RoundRect function, 334-342
shortcut menu commands (Call Stack window)
　Copy, 522
　Docking View, 522
　Go To Code, 522
　Hide, 522
　Insert/Remove Breakpoint, 522
　Parameter Types, 522
　Parameter Values, 522
Single Document Interface (SDI), OLE servers, 428
sized integers, 54
SIZEPALETTE flag, 265
skeletal applications, modifications to, 47-50
slider control, 159-160
Snapshot3 (Beacon Hill Software), 352
Socket classes, 448, 490-491

software environment,
  Windows 95/Windows NT
  comparisons, 11-16
Source Browser, 24
source code
  DialoVW.CPP (listing 4.7),
    101-104
  DialoVW.H (listing 4.6),
    100-101
  MainFram.CPP (listing 4.8),
    104-105
  OCX_Demo example
    (listing 9.1), 222-226
  Step 5 (Source Code
    Options) dialog box,
    creating applications,
    39-40
source files, 28
  creating OLE servers, 430
  DLLs (dynamic link
    libraries), generated by
    AppWizard, 503
Special Controls dialog box
  Windows 95 version,
    155-169
    hotkey control, 156-157
    progress control, 157-159
    slider control, 159-160
    spin button control,
      160-162
    tree view control,
      162-169
  Windows NT version,
    152-155
    closing, 155
    initializing scrollbars, 153
    OnDlgCreate method,
      152-153
    scrollbar event messages,
      153-155
spin button control, 160-162
Standard Controls dialog box
  (example), 145-152
  assigning member variables,
    146-147

  clearing local variables,
    151-152
  closing, 148-149
  initializing
    dialog box elements, 150
    member variables, 147
  retrieving
    results, 150-151
    values from controls, 148
static menus, 122
Step 1 (Architecture) dialog
  box, creating MFC applications, 32-33
Step 2 (Database Options)
  dialog box, creating MFC
  applications, 33-34
Step 3 (OLE Support) dialog
  box, creating MFC applications, 35-36
Step 4 (Application Features)
  dialog box, creating MFC
  applications, 36-39
Step 5 (Source Code Options)
  dialog box, creating MFC
  applications, 39-40
Step 6 (Class Name Options)
  dialog box, creating MFC
  applications, 41
stock properties (OCX
  controls), 190
string resources, 111
strings (CString class), 95-98
structure of menus, 122,
  124-126
structures
  CHOOSECOLOR,
    241-244
  CHOOSEFONT, 236-241
  common dialog boxes, 230
  FINDREPLACE, 254-256
  LOGFONT, 232-235
    initializing, 235-236
  OPENFILENAME,
    245-249
  TV_INSERTSTRUCT, 165
  TV_ITEM, 163-164

SVGA display standard, 299
switching
  menus, 136-139
  toolbars, 134-135
Symbol Browser dialog
  box, 118
Symbols command (Resource
  menu), 118
system menus,
  Windows 95 compared to
  Windows NT, 61
System Modal message
  boxes, 84

T

tab controls, 171-180
  child dialog boxes, connect-
    ing to, 176-179
  creating, 172-175
  member functions, 179-180
target options, creating
  project skeletons, 42-44
Task Modal message
  boxes, 84
TECHNOLOGY flag, 264
Test Container utility, testing
  OCX controls, 219-220
testing
  DLLs (dynamic link
    libraries) during develop-
    ment, 509-510
  events (OCX controls), 221
  OCX controls, 219-221
  properties (OCX controls),
    220-221
text
  input, ReadString method
    (CStdioFile class), 389-390
  output, WriteString method
    (CStdioFile class), 390
TEXTCAPS query, 269-270
thunking, 62-65
tilde (~), 91
Time classes, 452-453

title bars, Windows 95 compared to Windows NT, 61
tool tips, enabling, 134
Toolbar Button Properties dialog box, 131
toolbar buttons (Visual C++ compiler), 48-50
toolbars, 127-129
  creating toolbar bitmaps, 127-129
  EnableDocking function, 133-134
  images, 110
  linking messages/IDs to, 129-134
  overview, 122
  switching, 134-135
  tool tips, enabling, 134
tools
  application development, 17-24
    AppStudio resource editor, 24
    AppWizard, 23
    build process, 18-19
    ClassWizard, 23
    linker, 24
    Microsoft Developer Studio, 20-24
    Project Workspace dialog box, 21-23
    resource compiler, 24
    Source Browser, 24
    Visual C++ compiler, 23
  deleting, 327
  GetCurrentPosition method, 332
  logical brushes, 327-329
    CBrush::CreateDIBPatternBrush method, 330
    CBrush::CreateSolidBrush method, 331
    creating, 330-331
    hatch patterns, 329-330

  logical pens, 324-327
  MoveTo method, 332
  shape tools, 331
    arcs, 335-337
    chords, 335-337
    Ellipse function, 334
    LineTo function, 332-333
    pie sections, 335-337
    Polygon function, 339-340
    PolyPolygon function, 339-341
    Rectangle function, 333-334
    RoundRect function, 334-342
transferring data (OLE2), 65-67
trapping
  keyboard events, 311-313
  mouse events, 314-315
tree view control, 162-169
  adding nodes, 165-167
  selecting nodes, 167-168
True Color display standard, 299
TV_INSERTSTRUCT structure, 165
TV_ITEM structure, 163-164

U

UINT data type, 54
Universal Thunks, 64-65
UpdateData function, AARL_HAM example application (file I/O), 396
user interface classes (Windows 95), 71
user-defined record set classes, 486
user-specified base classes, 475

utilities
  Capture, 352-353
  ClipBook (screen captures), 352
  object packager (Packager.EXE), 417
  OLE2View, 444-445
  RegEdit, 423-425
  RegSrv, 219
  Test Container, 219-220
utility/debug classes, 453-454

V

variables
  member variables
    assigning to dialog box controls, 146-147
    initializing dialog box controls, 147
  naming conventions
    Hungarian notation, 52-53
    MFC prefixes, 53-54
  private, 91
  protected, 91
  public, 91
VBX (Visual Basic eXtension), 189
VCP file extension, 112
verbs (OLE), 416-417
version information (application resources), 111
VERTRES flag, 265
VERTSIZE flag, 265
VGA display standard, 299
video resolution
  device drivers, 264-268
  RASTERCAPS query, 268-269
view classes (MFC), message handling, 59
viewing Clipboard contents during screen captures, 357-358

viewports, 283-285
  origins, 288
views (Windows 95), 14
virtual window size, 285-286
Visual C++, migrating C applications to, 72
Visual C++ compiler, 18, 23
  toolbar buttons, 48-50
Visual C++ version 2.x, creating OCX controls, 191-196
  Control Options dialog box, 193-194
  modifying controls, 194-195
  New Control Information dialog box, 195-196
  Project Options dialog box, 192-193
Visual C++ version 4.0, creating OCX controls, 196-203
  ControlWizard files, 199-203
Visual Object classes (MFC), 447, 454-467
  associated object classes, 466-467
  CDC-derived classes, 455-456
  CGdiObject-derived classes, 456-457
  CWnd-derived classes, 457-466
Visual Workbench (Microsoft Developer Studio), 20-24
  AppStudio resource editor, 24
  AppWizard, 23
  ClassWizard, 23
  debugging tools, 517-522
    Call Stack window, 521-522
    Debug toolbar, 522
    Debug window, 518-519

  Locals window, 519
  Memory window, 523
  Quick Watch window, 519-521
  Registers window, 523
  Watch window, 519
linker, 24
Project Workspace dialog box, 21-23
resource compiler, 24
Source Browser, 24
Visual C++ compiler, 23
VOID macro, 55
VREFRESH flag, 265

W-Z

Watch window (Developer Studio), 519
white brushes, 328
white pens, 324
WINAPI macro, 55
Winding fill mode, 341
Windows
  data types, 54-55
    MFC class equivalents, 55-56
  images, 351
  macros, 55
  naming conventions
    Hungarian notation, 52-53
    MFC prefixes, 53-54
  thunking, 62-65
windows, 283-285
  origins, 288
Windows 95
  32-bit DLLs, 62-64
  compared to Windows NT, 9-17, 60-62
    disk compression, 11
    dual booting, 12
    hardware requirements, 10-11
    software environment, 11-16

    file system, 13-16
    Special Controls dialog box, 155-169
      hotkey control, 156-157
      progress control, 157-159
      slider control, 159-160
      spin button control, 160-162
      tree view control, 162-169
    user interface classes, 71
    views, 14
Windows Application Frameworks (AFX), naming convention prefixes, 53-54
Windows Common Control classes, 448, 487-490
Windows NT
  compared to Windows 95, 9-17, 60-62
    disk compression, 11
    dual booting, 12
    hardware requirements, 10-11
    software environment, 11-16
  file systems, 12-13
  Special Controls dialog box, 152-155
Windows On Windows (WOW) NT, thunking, 64-65
Windows palettes, 298-300
  active windows, 303
  converting to gray scale, 316-318
  creating, 360
  dithered colors, 308-309
  reserved color entries, 302-303
  values, 300-302
Windows registry
  compared to INI files, 68-70
  OLE2, 70
Windows Socket classes, 448, 490-491

Windows Sockets, 71-72
WinModes demo, 288-292
WORD data type, 54
work files, 112
WOW (Windows On Windows) NT, thunking, 64-65
WPARAM data type, 54
wrapper classes, 474
WriteString method, 390
WriteToFile procedure, 358-362
writing bitmap images to disk files, 358-362, 366-367

zero-based index (tab controls), 175

Add to Your Sams Library Today with the Best Books for Programming, Operating Systems, and New Technologies

The easiest way to order is to pick up the phone and call
1-800-428-5331
between 9:00 a.m. and 5:00 p.m. EST.
For faster service, please have your credit card available.

ISBN	Quantity	Description of Item	Unit Cost	Total Cost
0-672-30602-6		Programming Windows 95 Unleashed (Book/CD)	$49.99	
0-672-30474-0		Windows 95 Unleashed (Book/CD)	$39.99	
0-672-30611-5		Your Windows 95 Consultant	$19.99	
0-672-30685-9		Windows NT 3.5 Unleashed, 2nd Edition	$39.99	
0-672-30765-0		Navigating the Internet with Windows 95	$25.00	
0-672-30462-7		Teach Yourself MFC Library Programming in 21 Days	$29.99	
0-672-30568-2		Teach Yourself OLE Programming in 21 Days (Book/CD)	$39.99	
0-672-30594-1		Programming WinSock (Book/Disk)	$35.00	
0-672-30655-7		Developing Your Own 32-Bit Operating System (Book/CD)	$49.99	
0-672-30593-3		Develop a Professional Visual C++ Application in 21 Days (Book/CD)	$35.00	
0-672-30737-5		World Wide Web Unleashed	$39.99	

❏ 3 ½" Disk
❏ 5 ¼" Disk

Shipping and Handling: See information below.		
TOTAL		

Shipping and Handling: $4.00 for the first book, and $1.75 for each additional book. Floppy disk: add $1.75 for shipping and handling. If you need to have it NOW, we can ship product to you in 24 hours for an additional charge of approximately $18.00, and you will receive your item overnight or in two days. Overseas shipping and handling adds $2.00 per book and $8.00 for up to three disks. Prices subject to change. Call for availability and pricing information on latest editions.

201 W. 103rd Street, Indianapolis, Indiana 46290

1-800-428-5331 — Orders   1-800-835-3202 — FAX   1-800-858-7674 — Customer Service

Book ISBN 0-672-30762-6

GET CONNECTED
to the ultimate source of computer information!

The MCP Forum on CompuServe

Go online with the world's leading computer book publisher! Macmillan Computer Publishing offers everything you need for computer success!

Find the books that are right for you!
A complete online catalog, plus sample chapters and tables of contents give you an in-depth look at all our books. The best way to shop or browse!

➤ Get fast answers and technical support for MCP books and software

➤ Join discussion groups on major computer subjects

➤ Interact with our expert authors via e-mail and conferences

➤ Download software from our immense library:
  ▷ Source code from books
  ▷ Demos of hot software
  ▷ The best shareware and freeware
  ▷ Graphics files

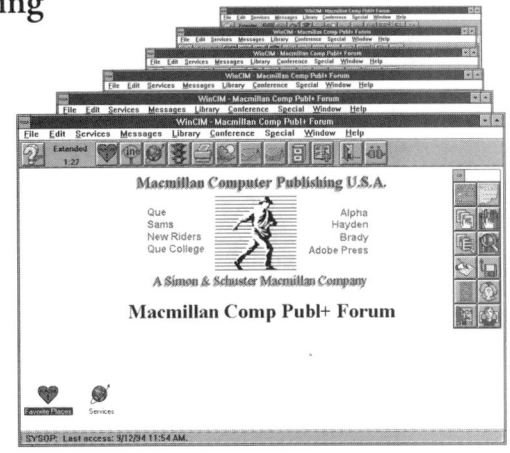

Join now and get a free CompuServe Starter Kit!

To receive your free CompuServe Introductory Membership, call **1-800-848-8199** and ask for representative #597.

The Starter Kit includes:
➤ Personal ID number and password
➤ $15 credit on the system
➤ Subscription to *CompuServe Magazine*

Once on the CompuServe System, type:

GO MACMILLAN

for the most computer information anywhere!

MACMILLAN COMPUTER PUBLISHING

CompuServe

PLUG YOURSELF INTO...

THE MACMILLAN INFORMATION SUPERLIBRARY™

Free information and vast computer resources from the world's leading computer book publisher—online!

FIND THE BOOKS THAT ARE RIGHT FOR YOU!
A complete online catalog, plus sample chapters and tables of contents give you an in-depth look at *all* of our books, including hard-to-find titles. It's the best way to find the books you need!

- **STAY INFORMED** with the latest computer industry news through our online newsletter, press releases, and customized Information SuperLibrary Reports.

- **GET FAST ANSWERS** to your questions about MCP books and software.

- **VISIT** our online bookstore for the latest information and editions!

- **COMMUNICATE** with our expert authors through e-mail and conferences.

- **DOWNLOAD SOFTWARE** from the immense MCP library:
    - Source code and files from MCP books
    - The best shareware, freeware, and demos

- **DISCOVER HOT SPOTS** on other parts of the Internet.

- **WIN BOOKS** in ongoing contests and giveaways!

TO PLUG INTO MCP: ➤ WORLD WIDE WEB: http://www.mcp.com

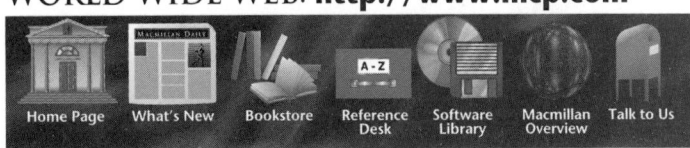

GOPHER: gopher.mcp.com
FTP: ftp.mcp.com

The Companion CD-ROM

The disc that accompanies this book contains new 32-bit Windows 95 applications, source code from the author, and much more. The CD-ROM is designed to be explored using a "Guide to the CD-ROM" program (\CDGUIDE\CDGUIDE.EXE).

Instructions for Windows 95 Users

If Windows 95 is installed on your computer and if you have the AutoPlay feature enabled, the Guide program starts automatically whenever you insert the disc into your CD-ROM drive.

Instructions for Windows 3.x Users

If you are running Windows 3.1 or if you have the Windows 95 AutoPlay feature disabled, you should run INSTALL.EXE from the root directory of the CD-ROM. INSTALL creates a Program Manager group named *32-Bit Windows Programming* and also creates a directory on your hard drive named \32prog. When INSTALL ends, the "Guide to the CD-ROM" program starts automatically. An icon in the 32-Bit Windows Programming group enables you to restart the Guide program without rerunning INSTALL.

The "Guide to the CD-ROM" program requires at least 256 colors. For best results, set your monitor to display between 256 and 64,000 colors. A screen resolution of 640×480 pixels is also recommended. If necessary, adjust your monitor settings before using the CD-ROM.